MW00441959

DATA ANALYSIS FOR THE SOCIAL SCIENCES

Sara Miller McCune founded SAGE Publishing in 1965 to support the dissemination of usable knowledge and educate a global community. SAGE publishes more than 1000 journals and over 800 new books each year, spanning a wide range of subject areas. Our growing selection of library products includes archives, data, case studies and video. SAGE remains majority owned by our founder and after her lifetime will become owned by a charitable trust that secures the company's continued independence.

Los Angeles | London | New Delhi | Singapore | Washington DC | Melbourne

DOUGLAS BORS

DATA ANALYSIS FOR THE SOCIAL SCIENCES

Integrating Theory and Practice

Los Angeles | London | New Delhi
Singapore | Washington DC | Melbourne

Los Angeles | London | New Delhi
Singapore | Washington DC | Melbourne

SAGE Publications Ltd
1 Oliver's Yard
55 City Road
London EC1Y 1SP

SAGE Publications Inc.
2455 Teller Road
Thousand Oaks, California 91320

SAGE Publications India Pvt Ltd
B 1/I 1 Mohan Cooperative Industrial Area
Mathura Road
New Delhi 110 044

SAGE Publications Asia-Pacific Pte Ltd
3 Church Street
#10-04 Samsung Hub
Singapore 049483

Editor: Jai Seaman
Assistant editor: Alysha Owen
Production editor: Ian Antcliff
Copyeditor: Richard Leigh
Proofreader: Neville Hankins
Indexer: Silvia Benvenuto
Marketing manager: Susheel Gokarakonda
Cover design: Shaun Mercier
Typeset by: C&M Digitals (P) Ltd, Chennai, India
Printed in the UK

© Douglas Bors 2018

First published 2018

Apart from any fair dealing for the purposes of research or private study, or criticism or review, as permitted under the Copyright, Designs and Patents Act, 1988, this publication may be reproduced, stored or transmitted in any form, or by any means, only with the prior permission in writing of the publishers, or in the case of reprographic reproduction, in accordance with the terms of licences issued by the Copyright Licensing Agency. Enquiries concerning reproduction outside those terms should be sent to the publishers.

IBM SPSS screen shot reprints courtesy of International Business Machines Corporation, © International Business Machines Corporation Foundation

Library of Congress Control Number: 2017939133

British Library Cataloguing in Publication data

A catalogue record for this book is available from the British Library

ISBN 978-1-4462-9847-3
ISBN 978-1-4462-9848-0 (pbk)

At SAGE we take sustainability seriously. Most of our products are printed in the UK using FSC papers and boards. When we print overseas we ensure sustainable papers are used as measured by the PREPS grading system. We undertake an annual audit to monitor our sustainability.

CONTENTS

ONLINE RESOURCES

Data Analysis for the Social Sciences: Integrating Theory and Practice is supported by a wealth of online resources for both students and lecturers to aid study and support teaching, which are available at https://study.sagepub.com/bors.

FOR STUDENTS

An introduction video from author Doug Bors gives you the chance to get to know your supporting statistics tutor and understand the fundamental principles of statistics.

A **maths diagnostic pre-test** helps you test or review your mathematical skills.

Interactive demonstrations and simulations offer hands-on experience in working with data and critical insight into evaluating numerical information.

SPSS datasets allow you to get to grips with the ins and outs of IBM SPSS software and practice the techniques you learn with real data.

Answers to the in-text review, challenge, and end of chapter questions give you the opportunity to check your work and identify areas in which you may need additional support.

FOR LECTURERS

PowerPoint slides featuring figures, tables, and key topics from the book can be downloaded and customized for use in your own presentations.

ABOUT THE AUTHOR

Dr Douglas Bors is currently an Associate Professor Emeritus at the University of Toronto, the institution from which he received his PhD. For over three decades he has taught courses in statistics at the undergraduate and graduate levels, ranging from the introductory level to multivariate statistics and structural equation modelling. He has served as a reviewer for several scholarly journals and has been a regular reviewer for *Personality and Individual Differences*. During his career his empirical research focused on problem-solving and abstract reasoning. The short form of the Advanced Raven's Progressive Matrices that he developed with Tonya Stokes is a widely used research instrument. Over the years he has acted as a consultant for major pharmaceutical firms as well as survey and marketing companies. Currently he is retained as a design and analysis consultant for a major marketing firm.

ACKNOWLEDGEMENTS

Acknowledgements are always difficult. There is never sufficient room to mention everyone who played a role in the development of your thoughts and in the production of a book. Should anyone feel overlooked, I apologize. I have been blessed with dedicated and thoughtful teaching assistants and graduate students. Many of their thoughts and comments about teaching and learning statistics have found their way into this book. There are far too many to name them all. A few deserve special mention, however. Dr. Blair Armstrong (now a professor and a valued colleague), Dr. Tim Cheng, Ron Chu, and Dwayne Pare have contributed in many ways. Ron Chu also programmed the interactive demonstrations found on the book's online resources page, at https://study.sagepub.com/bors. This book would have been further delayed if not for the insight and the eleventh-hour magical technical help of Adon Irani. He also produced and directed the book's introductory video. Adon's remarkable efforts were more than that of a colleague and friend; they reflect his truly kind-hearted nature. The support of the Department of Psychology at the University of Toronto at Scarborough and its Chair, Professor George Cree, must be recognized. Professor Gerald Cupchik deserves special mention for his constant encouragement which began long before Sage approached me. The Department provided monetary and personnel support at crucial times during the preparation of the manuscript. My friend and colleague Professor Gerald Cupchik deserves special mention for his encouragement, which began long before SAGE approached me. My wife Éva Székely must be acknowledged for her infinite patience and support throughout the long process, for her careful readings of the manuscript, and for helpful comments. Éva also kept our ship afloat during my mental secondment. My mother-in-law, Magda, must be thanked for brewing me several espressos every day. She seemed to sense when I was in need. I would be remiss if I did not acknowledge our beloved calico cat, Minou, for sitting on my desk day in and day out, keeping my blood pressure down. I need to thank Michael Carmichael at Sage for inviting me to write this book. Finally, I am grateful to Jai Seaman and Alysha Owen at Sage for their support and help in the process. Mr. Richard Leigh, must be thanked for his meticulous reading and editing of the text. Although those mentioned above were of immense help, any errors found in this book are the sole responsibility of the author.

PREFACE

This book is intended to provide students in the behavioural and social sciences with a comprehensive conceptual introduction to a full range of statistical techniques used to describe and analyse data generated by both experimental and observational research designs. By 'conceptual' I mean a way of understanding the logic and basic principles that generate statistical procedures and tests. Although the primary goal of the book is to give you a conceptual appreciation of statistics, this book does not avoid formulae and computations. The detailed presentation of formulae and the working through of computational examples, however, are always aimed at fostering your conceptual understanding of the material. To this end, computational examples are kept simple so that you can follow along. After these simple hand calculations, when larger data sets are analysed, SPSS (a statistical software package) will do the number crunching for you. Should you wish to test or review your mathematical skills, you can find a brief quiz on the textbook's web page; a link for it is at the end of this preface. The quiz is focused on those skills necessary for understanding the formulae and following the hand calculations.

Behavioural and social science students often enter their first statistics course with the notion that they are in a course much like mathematics. Two points need to be made about this myth. First, to the extent that statistics involves numbers and computations, it does involve mathematics. The level of mathematics required is usually exaggerated, however. The review quiz mentioned above will give you a good indication of the particular mathematical skills required. The review will also point you towards tutorials which will help you shore up your skills. Second, beyond those basic mathematical skills you need to have an open mind and a willingness to spend time playing with the material. The material may not come easily to everyone, but the challenge is at the conceptual level, not at the computational.

The subtitle of this book (*Integrating Theory and Practice*) is reflective of the approach at several levels. First and foremost, the approach is integrative because of the contextual reiteration of key ideas and principles. Each chapter is presented as a synthesis and extension of material previously covered. Chapter 1 sets the stage conceptually for all that follows. Therefore, it is crucial that you grasp the basic framework and orientation described in Chapter 1. (A link to a short video summary of the framework and orientation is given at the end of this preface.) All subsequent chapters point back to and develop from that chapter. This means that you will need to read the book iteratively, returning to reread previously covered material. As you loop back you will see the earlier material in a new light, often making more sense. Do not view each chapter as a stand-alone unit. Second, the approach is integrative in that what may appear at first to be separate statistical procedures are shown to be variations of others, and often interchangeable. The approach is also integrative in that SPSS is introduced not only as a technical skill to be acquired but also as a pedagogical tool which will allow you to play with data in ways that will foster your understanding of the relations underlying the procedures and basic concepts. Once you have a feel for SPSS you may wish to create your own data sets and explore further the material being presented in each chapter.

Although there are the usual end-of-chapter review questions, interspersed throughout each chapter you will find *review* and *challenge* questions which are designed to test your understanding of the material before proceeding further. Some of these questions require you to refer back to material covered in previous chapters. Some of these questions only require you to recall particular information; others, as the name implies, require you to do some integration and application. Additionally, you will find in the chapters links to interactive demonstrations on the textbook's web page. These demonstrations were created to provide you with the means to visually as well as quantitatively explore key concepts and statistical tests. The end-of-chapter review questions are of three types: multiple-choice, short-answer, and data set analysis. The short-answer questions are not intended to be a memory or look-up 'test'. These questions ask you to frame and express your understanding of the chapter's material in your own words. If you are inventive, many of these questions will allow you to make link after link with much of the material previously covered. The data set questions are there for you to apply your conceptual understanding to actual data. The answers to all questions and data sets are given on the book's web page. By the end of each chapter in Parts II and III of the book you should be able to conduct, from beginning to end, an analysis of the data types described in the chapter.

Although many of you will not go on to be researchers and actively analyse data, it is my hope that this book will give you the critical skills necessary to evaluate the mountain of numerical information with which we are bombarded daily.

🐭 Web Link 0.1 for the math quiz.

🐭 Web Link 0.2 to the introductory video.

PART I

THE FOUNDATIONS

The materials covered in the chapters that comprise this first part of this book provide the general framework for the specific statistical tests presented in Parts II and III. Part I reveals the plot and the main characters who are encountered throughout the book in the evolving episodes, each a surprising sequel. Despite the increasing twists and turns of each instalment, in Parts II and III, the most general plot and character types remain the same.

In Chapter 1 the logic which applies to all forms of data analysis covered in this book is described. The basic form of the logic revolves around four interrelated questions: What is *expected*? What is *observed*? What is the difference between the expected and the observed? How much of a difference between the expected and the observed can be *expected due to chance alone*? In this first chapter the concept of *randomness* is introduced along with other key concepts and the most common forms of research design.

In Chapter 2 the pictorial and numerical techniques researchers use to summarize their data are described. An informative summary is the first and, arguably, the most important stage in all forms of data analysis. Most statistical tests can be viewed as estimates of the reliability of the picture painted by the summary.

The coverage of probability theory and its laws in Chapter 3 is the basis for estimating the *reliability* or *replicability* of the picture portrayed in the summary. Parts II and III are built upon the foundation constructed in Part I. Each chapter in Parts II and III represents an application of probability theory (Chapter 3) to the summary of specific data (Chapter 2) to be analysed within a variation and adaptation of the general framework (Chapter 1).

1

Chapter contents

OVERVIEW

KEY CONCEPTS: randomness, experiment, quasi-experiment, observational designs, question of difference, question of association, categorical data, measurement data, null hypothesis, Simpson's paradox, Type I error, Type II error, variables, population, sample, random sample, independent variable, dependent variable.

PURPOSE

The first purpose of this chapter is to introduce you to a few concepts and themes that will be present, directly or indirectly, throughout this book. If there is one concept that is omnipresent, if not explicitly then at least implicitly, it is *randomness*. As will be seen, the concept underlies other phrases used either to refer to the presence of randomness or to its absence. To claim that two groups of people differ in some respect is to say that group membership is not completely random; for example, height is not random with respect to basketball players versus non-basketball players. To say that two groups do not differ in some regard is to say that group membership is random; for example, the maximum speed at which a car can travel is probably unrelated to the car's colour. To assert that two events are related is to say that they do not occur randomly with respect to each other; for example, tsunamis are associated with earthquakes. To state that two events are unrelated is to say that they occur randomly with respect to each other. Related to our use of randomness are four key questions: What is *expected*? What is *observed*? What is the *difference between the expected and the observed*? How much of a difference can be *expected due to chance alone*?

The second purpose of this chapter is to review some basic strategies and principles of empirical research. We differentiate the basic forms of research (experimental, quasi-experimental, and observational designs) and review the main characteristics of each.

THE GENERAL FRAMEWORK

Statistics, which are the numbers researchers use to describe their data and to test the trustworthiness or *replicability* of their findings, can feel convoluted and mysterious both for students and for researchers. In this section I offer you a three-part framework; if you use it, it will make the material in this book, and the statistics you encounter in everyday life, more easily understood.

> The great comedian George Burns said at his 100th birthday party, 'once you reach 100 you have it made. Very few people die after the age of 100.'

Part 1. As a researcher, you begin with a question (or questions) about the nature of the world, or at least that aspect of the world which interests you. Let us start with the simplest type of research, where there is only one question. Regardless of your topic, your question will take one of two basic forms.

The first form is one of *difference*. For example, imagine yourself as a political science professor who wishes to know if your students prefer term papers or essay examinations as a means of evaluation. Or think of yourself as a clinical psychologist wishing to know if cognitive behavioural therapy (CBT) reduces your patients' anxiety symptoms more than does the most commonly prescribed anxiolytic (a medication to reduce anxiety). In both of these examples you suspect that one set of scores will be different from the other: more students will prefer one form of assessment over the other; the CBT group on average will show fewer symptoms than the anxiolytic drug patients.

The second form a research question may take is one of *relation* or *association*. For example, you may manage a coffee shop and are interested in customer behaviour. Is the choice of beverage (coffee versus tea) associated with gender (men versus women)? Or if you are an educational psychologist you may suspect that there is an association between the number of hours per week a student works off-campus and his or her grades at the end of term. In both of these examples you suspect that one set of scores will be related (or will predict) the other set of scores. Perhaps a greater proportion of women will prefer tea than will men. Perhaps the more hours a student works off-campus the lower his or her grade point average will tend to be. The type of question – difference versus association – orients you towards appropriate statistical procedures. Questions of differences are linked with one family of statistical tests, and questions of association are linked with another family of tests.

Questions of differences and questions of association are not as dissimilar as they may appear. They are usually two sides of a single coin, with one question implying the other. Furthermore, a research project in psychology and in the social sciences often entails more than one question, and it may involve both questions of differences and questions of associations. For example, you may be a 'sportologist' wishing to know why some baseball players hit more home runs than others. You suspect that the taller the player, the more home runs he will hit (this is a question of a possible association between height and the number of home runs). You may also suspect that players who use aluminium bats will hit more home runs than will players who use the old-fashioned wooden bats (this is a question of a possible difference between types of bats).

Part 2. As an empirical researcher you collect data. Regardless of your area of interest, the observations usually take one of two general forms.

The first form your observations can take is that of *frequency data* or *categorical data*. Remember, as a political science professor you wished to know if among your students term papers are more popular than essay examinations as a form of evaluation. You are keeping count of the number of students in the two categories: those who prefer a term paper versus those who prefer an essay examination. As a manager of a coffee shop you were keeping track of the frequencies in four categories: the number of women who prefer coffee, the number of women who prefer tea, the number of men who prefer coffee, and the number of men who prefer tea.

The second form your observations can take is that of *measurement data*. As a clinical psychologist you wished to know if two groups of patients (CBT versus anxiolytic) differ in terms of their average number of anxiety symptoms. You are recording the number of symptoms each patient exhibits. It is possible that no two patients will exhibit the same number of symptoms. As an educational psychologist interested in hours worked and academic performance, you are recording the actual number of hours per week each student works off-campus and his or her grade. It is possible that no two students in your study will have worked the same number of hours or have exactly the same grade.

I need to warn you: the two types of data are not as different as they may at first appear, nor do they encompass all possible types of data. And often one type of data can be transformed or treated as if it were the other type. Examples of this transformation will appear at the end of Chapter 3.

• • • • •

As we will see in Chapter 2, frequency/categorical data and measurement data can be further divided into four types of number scales: nominal, ordinal, interval, and ratio. Where nominal and ordinal number scales are described as being frequency/categorical data, interval and ratio scales are considered as measurement data. As will become apparent in Part II of this book, for purposes of analysis ordinal data (such as percentile scores on an examination) often form an intermediate form of data or are transformed into a type of measurement data called z-scores, which are discussed in detail in Chapter 3.

We now have two basic research questions and two types of data. Earlier we said that each research question is linked with its own family of statistical tests. The same may be said with respect to the two types of data. Frequency data are linked with one family of statistical tests and measurement data are associated with another family of tests.

There are four families of statistical test:

Tests for a question of difference with frequency data

Tests for a question of relation with frequency data

Tests for a question of difference with measurement data

Tests for a question of relation with measurement data.

Keep in mind that this framework is not carved in stone, nor are the boundaries between the four categories impermeable. Rather, the framework is a guideline for following the flow of this book. It will help you to cut through what appear to be so many unrelated procedures and formulae and to see the general storyline and character types.

Part 3. We have seen that there are different families of statistical tests which reflect an intersection of the type of question the researcher asks and the type of data he or she has collected. Surprisingly, almost all statistical tests – at least those covered in this book – have the same underlying logic based on a few simple questions.

Question 1: What do you as a researcher *expect* to find?

You may have taken a course that introduces you to research methodology and know that what the researcher expects to find is often defined in two ways. One, as a researcher you have an educated guess as to what you will find. For example, from past experience you expect that students prefer term papers over essay examinations. The *expectation* with which we usually begin a data analysis is a negation of what we actually expect. That is, we expect that our observations are only random; for example, students have no clear preference.

For the past hundred years there have been serious debates about the value of the null hypothesis test as developed by Neyman and Pearson (1933) and Fisher (1935). Several alternatives to testing the null hypotheses have been proposed, and all have their supporters as well as their critics. There will be more details concerning this debate in Chapter 4.

This is the famous *null hypothesis* which is considered in detail in Chapter 4. For now, the null hypothesis assumes that whatever your research idea (alternative hypothesis) may be, it is wrong, meaning that the data do not confirm it. This depiction of the null hypothesis is another over-generalization (and there are also important alternatives to null hypothesis testing), but this model helps us to get started.

• • • • •

The primary reason for the null hypothesis, and for assuming randomness, is that it allows us to know exactly what to expect. To claim that where a student sits during an examination (front versus back of the room) affects his or her mark is rather vague. How will it affect his or her mark and by how much? There could be an infinite number of predictions to be made. It is easier to say that nothing is going on other than randomness. With this position there is only one prediction: the averages of the two groups (front and back of room) will be identical. If there is sufficient evidence to reject this position, then there is indirect evidence that seating location is related to examination marks.

Question 2: What do you *observe?*

You will always find some difference between what you expect and what you observe. It is almost impossible to find exactly no difference or exactly no association. Remember, the expectation (null hypothesis) is randomness. For example, the frequency with which women prefer coffee will be no different than the frequency with which men prefer coffee, and the examination marks of those seated at the front of the room will not differ from those who are seated at the back of the room. But the frequencies will not be exactly the same, nor will the examination marks. Things are almost never as expected.

Question 3: Is this difference *trustworthy?*

The question statistical tests are designed to answer relates to the issue of the likelihood that the difference between the expected and the observed is real. 'Real' is a slippery concept. Here it means that if we repeated the observations we would observe a similar difference between the expected and the observed. If tomorrow we again recorded the choice of beverage of women and men, would the difference in relative frequencies be roughly the same? If next semester we compared the examination marks of those who are seated at the front and those seated at the back of the room, would the difference in the averages be about the same? Or were the differences all a tempest in a teapot (pun intended)? We call the reliability of findings the *replicability* of the findings.

Question 4: How much of a difference can we expect *due to chance alone?*

How great a difference between 'what is expected' and 'what is observed' is required for you to conclude that the difference between the two is trustworthy and not a random accident? We typically wish to be 95% confident of our conclusion. Determining the necessary size of the difference between the expected and the observed is the heart of the issue. This is the tricky part of statistics. If the required

> Keep this framework in mind; it will help you learn the material. Good luck in your statistics course, and I hope you enjoy the remainder of this book.

size of a difference between the expected and the observed were a fixed amount, the problem would be simple, but it is not. The necessary difference, however, is contingent upon how much of a difference is expected due to chance alone. And what is expected due to chance alone is contingent upon several factors, depending upon the nature of the research and the type of data.

To summarize, you have a research question. You collect data. You have an expectation, negative in nature. You have an observation. You find a difference between the two. And you need to determine if that difference is reliable.

1 ● 3 RECOGNIZING RANDOMNESS

Can you tell which of the following 10 strings of 10 digits were produced randomly by blindly picking numbers out of a hat; that is, picked without any aim, purpose, plan, criteria, or design? (There are large and equal numbers of the digits 0, 1, 2, …, 9 in the hat.)

String 1:   9,7,4,3,7,2,2,8,0,2

String 2:   3,3,6,8,9,9,8,0,2,7

String 3:   6,6,6,0,3,9,8,9,9,5

String 4:   1,3,5,4,5,0,2,9,1,1

String 5:   1,1,9,6,7,4,1,2,8,4

String 6:   3,1,5,4,6,8,1,6,0,7

String 7:   0,9,9,3,0,5,0,4,6,0

String 8:   7,3,6,9,8,2,7,3,5,2

String 9:   0,7,7,3,0,6,4,1,2,8

String 10:   6,8,6,9,5,8,9,6,1,0

See https://study.sagepub.com/bors for the answer and to judge your ability to identify when things are not random.

Web Link 1.1 for the answer and to judge your ability to identify when things are not random.

Are you able to differentiate those occasions when your favourite sports team is on a *real* winning streak and shows promise from those occasions when the team is having a lucky string of wins and will soon sink back into mediocrity? Clearly it is difficult to describe ahead of time what to expect if the events are not random. There are so many different criteria one might use. For example, too many of the same number or too many of the same number in a row. On the other hand, we will see that expectations are easier to describe when the events or observations are assumed to be random.

1●4 LIES, DAMNED LIES, AND STATISTICS

In today's world numerical information and statistics are everywhere. It often appears that we live in a world where everything is reduced to numbers, even when it seems absurd to do so: 'Our ice cream is twice as tasty as is our leading competitor's.' Truly there can be misuses and abuses of numbers and statistics. As Mark Twain (Figure 1.1) lamented, there are 'lies, damned lies, and statistics'. One way in which abuse occurs on a daily basis is through the technique of 'cherry picking'. Cherry picking is a process where politicians, advertisers, and even researchers report only some of the evidence and ignore or suppress the rest. This biased reporting and analysis of data can occur both intentionally or unintentionally. For the purposes of this book, we must ignore the scientific crime of intentional cherry picking.

If you are a baseball fan, imagine you are told that a particular batter (batter A) has a higher *overall* batting average than batter B, but batter B has a higher batting than batter A against both left-handed pitchers and right-handed pitchers. (Overall batting average is derived by combining data from the batters' performances against both right-handed and left-handed pitchers.) Is this a lie? Is it a damned lie? Or can it possibly be true?

The statistical description and testing of empirical data, however, can play a legitimate and central role in answering most research questions in the psychological, social, and biological sciences. This does not mean that the findings and conclusions from all research studies are 'true' and can be accepted uncritically. A sound appreciation of the fundamentals of the various statistical procedures used by researchers is crucial for understanding the appropriateness, the value, and the limitations of research findings and conclusions, as well as for avoiding the statistical lies and damned lies we encounter on a daily basis. This applies just as much, if not more, to those of us who are only consumers of statistics as it does to those who are engaged in research. As you will see in this book, there are a few basic notions that underpin nearly everything we use to describe and analyse our data.

Implicit in all difficult-to-comprehend stories is a simple – though not necessarily simplistic – plotline. Statistics is such a story. If we could ask Shakespeare about writing a play, he would tell us that there are only a few good plots, but that they can be told with many twists and turns and in many social, familial, and historical settings. Each variation requires the dramatist to adapt the plot to the particulars, even though the underlying theme and moral remain the same. English literature students often find it difficult to understand Shakespeare's plays. Without discerning the underlying plot, the dialogue and details make little sense. Furthermore, the difficulty often is exacerbated by the language: although Shakespeare's plays are written in English, it is not the vernacular of today.

Figure 1.1   Photo of Mark Twain. His name means 'Take note! the water is two fathoms (12 feet or 3.66 meters) deep, on average'.

Many students experience introductory statistics textbooks in an analogous manner. They often are so perplexed by the language and details that they lose the plot: the purpose of a particular analysis. Browse through any textbook and you will find strange symbols, elaborate formulae, and common words with unexpected usages (e.g., *power*). Most students approach their statistics course as they approach a Shakespearean play, with trepidation, and they find much of the material initially incomprehensible. But when we carefully examine each play, act, and scene of statistics we find beneath the plethora of terms, tests, and formulae a small set of common themes and characters, as described earlier. Understanding these common themes is vital for understanding the particulars of any given statistical test. This first chapter presents the core plotline of the epic story of statistics as it is commonly employed in psychology, sociology, education, political science, and areas of biology. Let us begin; to quote *Henry V*, 'The game's afoot.'

1.5 TESTING FOR RANDOMNESS

Here we have 10 scores on a quiz in macroeconomics: 1, 7, 4, 5, 3, 4, 5, 2, 6, and 3. Inexplicably – as with most events in economics – we find the scores sorted into two groups. Group A comprises 1, 4, 2, 5, and 3. Group B comprises 7, 5, 3, 4, and 6. Do you think that those scores have been sorted 'randomly' into those two groups? This can be viewed as the rudimentary version of the 'to be or not to be' question of statistics.

The notion of randomness is one element of the plot that underlies much of this book. The idea of randomness – to reference Shakespeare one more time, 'like the sun; it shines everywhere' – is present explicitly or implicitly in all: collecting the data, analysing the data, and drawing conclusions. We all have a sense of what we mean when we say that something is random, but it might be difficult to clearly articulate that sense. In fact, humans have difficulty creating or recognizing randomness. According to the *Oxford English Dictionary* online, 'random' refers to something that was made or happened without method or conscious decision. For example, we speak of acts of random violence, horrendous acts that cannot be explained. But we usually discover that these acts were not random, but planned, albeit that the plan often appears crazy.

As mentioned above, sometimes we assume that we know the meaning of a word that is used by an author, when in fact the author's meaning is considerably different. For example, in a Shakespearean play the word 'abuse' usually means to deceive, as when King Lear says to his daughter Cordelia in Act IV 'do not abuse me'. In the domain of statistics, one important meaning of the word *random* is that all members of a set have the same chance or probability of appearing or of being selected as a member of a subset. The key words here are *set, chance, probability, appearing*, and *selected*. Let us begin by looking at some examples.

We may wish to randomly *select* 10 students (subset) from a class of 100 (set). What does 'random' mean in terms of selection? In brief, it means that all 100 students in the class have the same *chance* or *probability* of being *selected* for our subset of 10. What would an equal chance look like? It means that no member or subset of members of the set is more likely than any other to be selected. In our example, tall students in the class of 100 are no more likely to be selected than short students; those who sit at the front of the class are no more likely to be selected than those who sit at the back; those who are eager to be selected are no more likely to be chosen than are those who wish to avoid selection; etc. It is as if the selection daemon or mechanism is blind to all characteristics of the members of the set.

Let us jump ahead and anticipate material to be covered in greater detail in Chapter 3 and state that all members of the class of 100 have a one-in-a-hundred chance of being selected: 1/100. Said another way, they all have a 1% chance of being selected; or as we will express it later, they have a *probability* of 0.01. If there were only 50 students in the class, then each student would have a 1/50 chance of being selected, or a probability of 0.02.

Random with respect to …

As mentioned earlier, randomness in the domain of statistics also means that observing one outcome or event does not change the likelihood of observing another outcome or event. That is, there is no systematic relationship between two possible observations. For example, with respect to the heights and the weights of our 100 students, we might ask if the heights of the students are random with respect to their weights. That is, do all of the weights have an equal chance of *appearing* or being associated with all heights? This would mean that regardless of a student's height, all weights would have the same chance of being associated with that student. In looking at the exam grades of the 100 students, we might ask if the students' grades are random with respect to where they sat during the final exam: front versus back of the room. As we will see, we can render this into the question of 'did one section of the room have a higher average grade than the other?' or 'are grades related to section of the room?' – a question of *difference* versus a question of *association*. We may have good reason to think or *hypothesize* that weight is not random with respect to height, and we may have good reason to think that grades are not random with respect to seating location. It is useful to know what to expect if randomness existed in both cases.

Expected value versus observed value

Although we have focused on randomness, underlying all of these examples is an issue of *expectation*. For purposes of statistical testing there are two types of expectations. What would we expect to see if things were random? What would we expect to see if they were not? Recall that at the outset of the chapter we said that it was not easy to describe what a string of digits would look like if they were *not* random. We also asked if 10 quiz scores were randomly sorted into two groups. As we will discover, it is far easier to state what is expected if things are random than it is to state what we would expect if they were not random.

In most forms of data analysis the expectation, or *expected value*, commonly takes the form of a magnitude or a frequency. The expected value is normally, but not always, what reasoning tells us we should observe, if things are random. If we flip a coin a number of times, then half of the time it should come up heads. Or if seating section is unrelated to exam score, then the average exam scores of the two sections should be the same. The *observed value* is simply the magnitude or the frequency that we actually find. The most common magnitude is a type of average. A frequency is the number of times something is observed. This could be the number of heads observed after 10 tosses of a coin. What is usually of interest to researchers is the discrepancy between the *expected value* and the *observed value* and the size of any discrepancy.

Rarely will the *observed value* correspond exactly to the *expected value*. If we knew that there were an equal number of men and women enrolled in our university and if introductory statistics were a required course, then introductory statistics students might be a random subset of the university's student population. Therefore, we might expect to find an equal number of men and women in our statistics class: 50% men and 50% women (*expected value*). In the terminology used above, we would expect our selection or subset of students (the class) to reflect the university student body (set). If we found that only 49% of the students (*observed value*) in the class were men, should we question our knowledge that there were equal numbers of men and women enrolled in our university? What if we observed only 40% men in the class, or 25% men, or even 1% men? There are good reasons why we might not observe exactly a 50%–50% split in every statistics class. Due to chance alone, we would expect to see some variation in the percentages of men and women. While in some semesters we might see more men than women, in other semesters there would be more women than men. While in some semesters we might see relatively small differences in the percentages of men and women, in other semesters we might see somewhat larger differences. In everyday life we usually refer to all of these purely chance disparities as accidental.

Although we *expect* to find a 50%–50% split in the number of men and women in the class, we also recognize that it is highly unlikely that we will *observe* an equal number of men and women. Thus, a 49%–51% split is probably not too large a discrepancy for us to continue assuming that there are an equal number of men and women at the university, whereas a 1%–99% split might cause us to question our assumption. What about intermediate discrepancies such as 40%–60%? We recognize that there will be class-to-class fluctuations in the percentages, but how much fluctuation is reasonable? Where do we draw the line when it comes to maintaining or rejecting our assumption of equal percentages of men and women? As we will find, there is no single, absolute threshold upon which we can make our decision. Furthermore, any conclusion that we draw may be wrong, no matter at what level we set the threshold. Consequently, it is being able to describe reasonable fluctuation and how to determine the threshold that is key.

For purposes of making decisions, we usually begin by retaining our expectation – or the assumption it is based upon – unless the chance of obtaining the *observed value* is less than 5%. Thus, if we could determine the threshold where the difference between the *expected value* (e.g., 50% men and 50% women) and the *observed value* is 5% then we could draw a tentative conclusion about whether or not to retain our assumption.

Randomization testing

In this section we introduce the notion of *randomization testing*. This most basic form of statistical testing will be discussed in more detail beginning in Chapter 5. To describe the randomization test we return to our earlier example of scores on a quiz in macroeconomics: 1, 7, 4, 5, 3, 4, 5, 2, 6, and 3. Remember, we inexplicably found the scores sorted into two groups. Let us assume that the two groups represent left-handed students and right-handed students. The right-handed group's scores were 1, 4, 2, 5, and 3. The left-handed group's scores were 7, 5, 3, 4, and 6. Do we think that those scores have been sorted 'randomly' into those two groups? That is, do we think that, with respect to quiz scores, there is no difference between left-handed students and right-handed students?

How might we determine where the threshold is for our 95% confidence? If we assume (expect) that the scores are randomly sorted into the two groups and that handedness is not a factor, then the scores as currently grouped are just one of a large number of other possible random sorts. We might then compare the present grouping with other random sorts. The question is: how? If the current grouping is random, then we *expect* the averages of the scores of the two groups to be equivalent. This is our null hypothesis. But the observed means are not equivalent. The average of the right-handed students is 3 and the average of the left-handed students is 5. The difference between the two groups is 2, not 0. The question now is: does this difference have less than a 5% chance of being due to chance alone?

How can we determine what are the chances of randomly sorting the quiz scores and observing a difference of 2? The procedure is simple, although tedious. We write those 10 quiz scores on slips of paper and put them in a hat. Then we pull them out and place the first score drawn in group A, the second score drawn in group B, the third in group A, the fourth in group B, and so on, until we have a new sort of the 10 scores. We then record the difference in the averages of the new sort. Then we put back the scores that had been drawn into the hat and start over again. We obtain another sort, another two averages, and we record the difference. We do this a very large number of times. Ideally, we repeat the process for every possible sort.

· · · · ·

After one random sort, group A could contain the scores of 1, 2, 3, 3, and 4; group B would then contain the scores 4, 5, 5, 6, and 7. The difference in the averages would be 2.6 − 5.4 = −2.8. After another random sort, group A could contain the scores 1, 2, 4, 6, and 7; group B would contain the scores 3, 3, 4, 5, and 5. The difference in the averages would be 4 − 4 = 0.0. There are far too many possible sorts for us to enumerate them here.

Once we complete recording all those differences in the averages we have the basis for determining the differences we might expect to see due to chance alone. First, we order the differences from the smallest to the largest. Next, we count the number of differences in the ordering which are greater than 2. If we divide this number by the total number of sortings, we have the proportion of differences that are greater than 2. If we went through this process we would find that about 4% of the differences are larger than 2.

Before we reach any conclusion about handedness and quiz scores, there is one more twist in the process. Although in the case of the original quiz scores the left-handed students did better than the right-handed students, it could actually be the other way around. The right-handed students may have accidentally done better than the left-handed students by an average score of 2. Thus, the chances of a difference of 2, regardless of the direction, are about 8%. Earlier we said that the chances would need to be less than 5% before we would no longer assume randomness. Stated more formally, the chances need to be less than 5% before we reject the null hypothesis.

Because the chances of our observed difference between what is expected and what is observed are greater than 5%, we conclude that there is insufficient evidence to support the idea that handedness influences quiz scores. Of course, we could be wrong. When we incorrectly fail to reject the assumption of the null hypothesis, we call this a *Type II* error. When the chances of the difference between the expected and the observed are less than 5%, we reject the null hypothesis. We may be correct. On the other hand, we may be wrong. Remember, all the outcomes that were ordered from smallest to largest were randomly created. Thus, 5% of the time when nothing is affecting the sort, we will incorrectly think that something is affecting the sort, in our example the handedness of the students. This mistake is called a *Type I* error.

The problem with the randomization testing of the null hypothesis is more than tediousness. Even with the use of computers, it becomes unviable when the research design is more complex and the number of scores increases. Try producing all the possible sorts for the 10 scores in our example. In large part, this book is about the shortcuts taken to make the analyses possible. These shortcuts require making certain assumptions. The testing of the assumptions and the 'correcting' for any violations become an important part of statistical analyses. We will cross those bridges when we come to them.

Finally, this was only an example using the question of *difference* and *measurement* data. There are other variations of the randomization test for other combinations of research questions and data types. The example of handedness and quiz scores illustrates the basic framework, however.

 RESEARCH DESIGN AND KEY CONCEPTS

In this part of this chapter we review the basic empirical research designs and key concepts. Here we cover only those designs and details which are needed to provide the necessary background in research methodology for understanding the statistical procedures presented in this book. For more detailed coverage of empirical research methodologies see Nestor and Schutt (2015) and Privitera (2016).

There is an important distinction to be made between generalizing across people and generalizing across situations (Aronson et al., 2007). In the first case you are making a prediction about how people in the same population (your university students) will respond. In the second case you are making a prediction about how others elsewhere in the same circumstance may respond. This second type of generalization is made clear in our discussion of the experiment.

All researchers collect data from sources or subjects. Because most of our research in psychology, the social, and biological sciences is directed at human or animal activity, we shall refer to *subjects*.

Central to all research designs are the key elements of variables, population, sample selection, and sample assignment.

All empirical research asks about either a possible difference or a possible association between two or more variables. *Variables* are anything that can take more than one value or form. They can be *differences in amount*, such as quiz scores or the number of anxiety symptoms reported by patients. These are called quantitative or *measurement* variables. Variables can reflect *differences in form*, such as choice of beverage or the type of treatment used to treat severe anxiety. These are called qualitative or *categorical* variables.

The meaning of the term *population* in statistics is different from the everyday or geographical usage of the term. In statistics 'population' refers to the entire set of events to which the researcher wishes to generalize his or her findings. Imagine that you are a clinical psychologist working in a university counselling centre and you wish to know whether cognitive behavioural therapy or the new anxiolytic is more effective for the students who visit the counselling centre. What is the population to which you wish to generalize? It is not every young adult on the planet. It is not even all university students, or even all students at your university. The population of interest to you is all the students who walk into your counselling centre and report symptoms of anxiety. For a detailed discussion of the issue of generalization see Cook and Campbell's (1979) groundbreaking work on the topic.

Researchers do not test or observe all members of the population to which they wish to generalize. Furthermore, it is usually impossible to observe all members of a population. Instead, researchers observe a subset of the population. This subset drawn from the population is called a *sample*. Samples are used to make inferences about populations. In order to make such inferences the sample must be representative of the population. The best way to ensure that is to randomly sample from the population. A *random sample* means that all members of the population have an equal chance of being drawn for the sample. Ideally, the sample is a mini version of the population. It is almost impossible to adhere to this ideal. Most random samples are really *quasi-random* samples. A quasi-random sample usually uses some systematic device to select subjects, such as every third person who walks through the counselling centre door who reports anxiety symptoms. There are other sampling methods that are beyond the scope of this chapter, such as the matching strategy (Rubin, 1973). Much of the academic research carried out at universities, particularly in psychology, uses the *convenience sampling* technique. This method samples from the population members who are conveniently available to participate in the research (e.g., university students). To the extent that undergraduate university students represent the young adult population, there is little bias in the sample. This is likely the case when the researcher is studying colour perception. If the researcher is investigating political attitudes, university students may not be an unbiased sample of young adults. For most purposes in this book we will assume that the selected samples are either random or at least representative of the population to which the researcher wishes to generalize.

In some research designs, once a sample has been selected the members must be assigned to different treatment conditions. It is important that members of the sample are randomly assigned to conditions. Random assignment requires that all members of the sample have an equal chance of being assigned to a given condition. Just as the overall sample should be a mini version of the population, so each condition should initially be a mini version of the overall sample. As in the case of sample selection, it is almost impossible to adhere to this ideal of equal chances with assignment. Most condition assignments are in practice *quasi-random* in nature. A quasi-random assignment uses a simple technique for the assignment of subjects. For example, the odd-numbered subjects in your anxiety treatment study will be assigned to the cognitive behavioural therapy group, and the even-numbered subjects will be in the anxiolytic group.

Figure 1.2 summarizes three basic research designs, the names of the variables associated with them, and the type of possible conclusions associated with each design.

Design type	Variable types	Possible conclusions
True experiment	Independent Dependent Nuisance Confounding	Causal/influence
Quasi-experiment	Pseudo-independent Dependent Nuisance Confounding	Marker/association
Observational	Predictor Criterion Nuisance Third-variable	Association

Figure 1.2

Experiment

Although experiments can be run inside or outside of a laboratory, we shall focus on experiments conducted inside a laboratory. Many argue that the laboratory experiment is the ideal form of research. Others argue that it has serious limitations. The reason why it is deemed by many to be ideal is that the experiment is designed to allow the researcher to evaluate whether the changes in the dependent variable are related to the manipulation of the independent variable or are due to chance alone (Privitera, 2016). Stated differently, it offers the researcher an opportunity to determine if one variable is the 'cause' of another.

• • • • •

Random selection of subjects is the best way of ensuring the *external validity* of the research. That is, random selection allows the researcher to generalize to the population of interest. The random assignment of subjects to conditions is a way to ensure the *internal validity* of the experiment. An internally valid experiment is one where only the independent variable could be responsible for changes in the dependent variable, all else being a constant across the treatment conditions.

There are two forms of an experiment: the *between-subjects design* and the *within-subjects design*. In the between-subjects design, subjects in the selected sample are (quasi-)randomly assigned to different treatment conditions. For example, the odd-numbered subjects in your anxiety treatment study are assigned to the cognitive behavioural therapy (CBT) group, and the even-numbered subjects assigned to the anxiolytic group. The two types of variables of importance in an experiment are the *independent variable* (IV) and the *dependent variable* (DV). The IV is called independent because it is theoretically independent or random with respect to all other variables in the population of interest. The type of treatment your patients receive is your IV: CBT or the anxiolytic. Because the IV levels are a difference in kind or type of treatment, your IV is qualitative or categorical. The DV is the variable whose values are dependent (not random) on the values or levels of the IV. Your DV is the anxiety level of your patients after treatment. The logic is as follows:

1 if the two groups of patients are equivalent prior to treatment,
2 and if the only difference in the two groups is the difference in treatment,
3 then any observed difference in the anxiety levels in the two groups post treatment can be attributed to the differences in the treatment.

For example, if the CBT treatment group manifests fewer symptoms than the anxiolytic treatment group, you might conclude that the 'cause' of (reason for) the difference is that CBT is a superior treatment.

At this point we need to introduce the key notion of *operational definition* (Bridgman, 1927). Thus far we have used general descriptions for our variables. Someone might ask, 'What form of CBT and how many sessions?' They are asking you to operationally define your treatment. An operational definition describes a variable either in quantitative terms, or how it was measured,

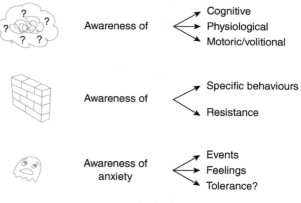

Awareness of → Cognitive, Physiological, Motoric/volitional

Awareness of → Specific behaviours, Resistance

Awareness of anxiety → Events, Feelings, Tolerance?

Figure 1.3

or in terms of its composition. For example, you may operationally define CBT as 1 hour per week for 12 weeks of standard CBT (Figure 1.3) where the patient is asked to be aware of one or more aspects of anxiety.

You may operationally define the anxiolytic treatment as 1 mg of Oxazepam per day for 12 weeks (Figure 1.4).

Finally, you may operationally define your DV (anxiety level) as the number of symptoms subjects check off on a standard symptom checklist.

Of course there are innumerable variables that will influence the number of symptoms a patient checks off on the list: how long the patient has been anxious, how severely he or she experiences some of those symptoms, how many hours he or she slept last night, just to name a few. We assume, however, that because the subjects were randomly assigned to the two treatment conditions, the two groups are roughly equivalent on these other variables. These additional variables which can influence an

Figure 1.4

individual's score are often referred to as *nuisance* or *extraneous variables*. A *confounding variable* is a special type of nuisance variable. It is an extraneous variable that is associated with both the IV and the DV. As a consequence, it is impossible to determine if the changes in the DV are due to changes in the IV or to changes in the confounding third variable. Interpretation of the findings is rendered hopeless. Such variables are undesirable. Despite the researcher's best intentions of randomly assigning subjects to conditions, confounding variables will occur from time to time. For example, due to chance alone your CBT condition may be composed primarily of men, and your anxiolytic group may be composed primarily of women. Thus, any difference between the two treatment groups in terms of the DV (reported number of symptoms) will also be found between men and women. Interpreting your results will be a hopeless task. For example, is CBT a more effective treatment than the anxiolytic, or is it that men (who were the majority in the CBT group) are less anxious in general?

There are two important reasons for using operational definitions. First, they allow the reader to know what exactly the researcher studied. Second, they allow other researchers to try to replicate the original findings, which is a crucial part of establishing and confirming knowledge.

In the within-subjects design all subjects are tested in all conditions. Having the same subject in all conditions provides a statistical problem, but it is easily solved. Other than that, the logic of the within-subjects design is no different than that of the between-subjects design.

• • • • •

Experiments are usually considered a research strategy designed to answer questions of differences. For example, your anxiety treatment experiment can be viewed as asking a question about the difference in the effectiveness of the two treatments, CBT and anxiolytic. The question guiding your experiment can be turned into one of association: is outcome (reported number of symptoms) related to the type of treatment?

While many researchers maintain that the experiment is the ideal for conducting empirical research, there are others who have serious reservations. The reservations centre on a specific aspect of what was described above as external validity: *ecological validity*. Critics of the laboratory experiment, particularly when it is the only strategy some researchers are willing to use, argue that what is found in the laboratory is not necessary what will be found in the natural or social world (Schmuckler, 2001). An obvious example is often described. Drugs are usually tested on young male rats that have one disorder, but usually they are prescribed for elderly female humans who have several disorders and are receiving multiple treatments. Can we be sure that the effect of the drug (and side effects) observed in the lab will also be the effect when they are prescribed to humans?

Quasi-experiment

The *quasi-experiment* is often confused with the true experiment described above. A quasi-experiment can have the appearance of an experiment and can be run under controlled laboratory conditions. The key difference is that in a quasi-experiment the IV is not an IV, far from it. Examples of quasi-experiments include research exploring the difference between men and women on a spatial abilities test; native English speakers and native French speakers on a short-term memory test; and tall people and short people on a personality test. The key is that no one can walk into your lab and be assigned to a gender, or to a first language, or to a height, or any other characteristic of someone. These are called *subject variables*.

Furthermore, any difference that you find with respect to some DV comes with an infinite number of confounding variables. The IV is best called here a *marker variable*. It indicates that there are differences between the groups, but it does not imply causality. The simple way to know if you are faced with a true experiment or a quasi-experiment is to ask the following question: Could the subjects be randomly assigned to the conditions? If the answer is no, then the research is quasi-experimental in nature.

Observational or descriptive studies

Unlike in an experiment, subjects in a *descriptive or observational study* are not assigned, randomly or otherwise, to a limited set of conditions. These studies use samples to describe populations, particularly the associations among two or more variables. In its simplest form, one variable (called a *predictor*) is used to try to predict changes in another variable (called a *criterion* or outcome variable). For example, a sociologist may be interested in knowing if the average income level (predictor) of a city is predictive of its crime rate (criterion). Of course, cities cannot randomly be assigned to average income levels. The goal of such research is to describe the nature and the strength of the possible associations.

At a more complex level, a number of predictor variables are used to improve the researcher's ability to predict events or an *outcome*. Imagine yourself as the dean of a medical school, and you wish to know how you can predict which applicants will do well in your programme. In addition to their average marks in medical school (criterion) you have a number of pieces of information (predictors) on students accepted into the programme in previous years: average university marks, marks on a standardized entrance examination, number of volunteer placements, among others. To some degree, all of the predictors will be associated with one another. Despite the problem of confounding, you wish to know which of the variables are the important predictors of performance in your medical school.

There are other forms of empirical research as well as variations and combinations of the three we have briefly described. Elaborations on these designs will be described as we move through the book and the relevant forms of data analysis are introduced.

1 ⬤ 7 PARADOXES

As we said, it is always possible to conclude that things are random when they are not, and it is always possible to conclude that things are not random when they are. In addition to these problems there are strange, almost magical occurrences that can happen when we begin analysing data. In this section

	Treatment A	Treatment B
Small stones	(81/87) 93%	(234/270) 87%
Large stones	(192/263) 73%	(55/80) 69%
Overall	(273/350) 78%	(289/350) 83%

Figure 1.5

we will focus on only one of those occurrences, sometimes called the amalgamation paradox or Simpson's paradox (Simpson, 1951). The most general form this paradox takes is where a difference or association appears in different groups but disappears when the groups are combined. A real-life example found in Julious and Mullee (1994) will help make the point.

Julious and Mullee compared the rates of success with two common treatments for kidney stones. Overall, treatment A was effective in 273 of 350 (78%) of the cases in which it was used. Overall, treatment B was effective in 289 of 350 (83%) of the cases in which it was used. Thus, treatment B appears to be the slightly more effective of the two treatments. The magic happens when we take into account that there are large and small kidney stones, and physicians tend to prescribe treatment B to those patients with small stones and treatment A to those patients with large stones. Figure 1.5 illustrates the relative effectiveness of the two treatments with respect to the two stone types separately.

The bottom row of the figure repeats what we already know, that overall treatment B appears to be more effective. But when we take into account small versus large stones and different rates of treatment, we find that treatment A is more effective than treatment B for the treatment of small stones (93% versus 87%), and treatment A is also more effective than treatment B for the treatment of large stones (73% versus 69%). From Chapter 4 onwards we will be discussing this phenomenon as the third-variable problem.

═══════════ CHALLENGE QUESTION ═══════════

The manager of the local baseball team had completed choosing eight of his starting nine players. He decided to choose the last player on the basis of the highest batting average. Player A was delighted because he had the highest batting average of the remaining players. The manager told him, however, that the opposing team had a right-handed pitcher and that although he (player A) had the highest batting average overall, player B had a higher batting average against right-handed pitchers. Player A was devastated but he understood. It rained and they never played the game. The next day the manager again decided to choose the ninth player on the basis of the highest batting average. Player A was delighted because he had the highest batting average of the remaining players. The manager told him, however, that the opposing team now had a left-handed pitcher and that although he (player A) had the highest batting average overall, player B had a higher batting average against left-handed pitchers. Player A was devastated and could not understand how he had the highest overall batting average but player B had a higher average against both right-handed and left-handed pitchers. (There are only left-handed and right-handed pitchers.) How is this possible? Can you make up a set of batting averages illustrating your answer?

Web Link 1.2 for an answer to the challenge question.

---

1 8 CHAPTER SUMMARY

In this chapter we have presented a general framework to organize the remainder of the book. Statistical tests can be described as falling into one of four categories defined by type of research question and type of data.

1 Tests for a question of difference with frequency data
2 Tests for a question of relation with frequency data
3 Tests for a question of difference with measurement data
4 Tests for a question of relation with measurement data.

We also summarized basic research terminology (e.g., types of variables) and the three basic designs to be analysed in this book: experiments, quasi-experiments, and observational studies. Finally, we looked at an example of Simpson's paradox, an issue with which we will need to be concerned before rushing to any conclusion, regardless of the form of analysis.

1 9 RECOMMENDED READINGS

Mlodinow, L. (2008). *The drunkard's walk: How randomness rules our lives*. New York: Random House. This very popular book discusses how randomness plays more of a role in the everyday events of our lives than we are usually willing to admit or even suspect. The author also points out our propensity to over-interpret and attribute causes to these random events.

Nestor, P. G., & Schutt, R. K. (2015). *Research methods in psychology: Investigating human behavior.* Los Angeles: Sage.
This book provides a comprehensive overview of the methods used by psychologists to collect and analyse data concerning human behaviour. Of note is Chapter 5 on survey research, a topic we will not be able to cover in any detail.
Privitera, G. J. (2016). *Research methods for the behavioral sciences* (2nd ed.). Los Angeles: Sage.
This book offers a very comprehensive treatment of the research process from beginning to end. Of particular relevance are Chapters 4–6. The entire book should be required reading for any student in psychology or the social sciences. It is worthwhile to keep on your shelf as a handy reference book.

Don't forget to use the online resources! Meet your supporting stats tutor through an **introductory video**, review your maths skills with a **diagnostic pre-test**, explore statistical principles through **interactive simulations**, practice analysis techniques with **SPSS datasets**, and check your work with **answers to all in-text questions**.

https://study.sagepub.com/bors

2

Chapter contents

DESCRIPTIVE STATISTICS

KEY CONCEPTS: scales of measurement, measurement and frequency data, frequency histograms, measures of central tendency, measures of spread, outliers.

2●1 PURPOSE

Once researchers have collected their data, the first step in the analysis process is to summarize the observations, both pictorially and numerically. The purpose of this chapter is to examine the most commonly employed graphs and statistics for summarizing different types of data. The focus is on graphs and statistics used to describe individual variables: *univariate* graphs and statistics. We begin by examining the types of numbers researchers use to record their data. As will be seen, a 2 is not necessarily 1 plus 1. Then we introduce the notation system used throughout this book. Following that is a presentation of the most common pictorial forms researchers use to summarize their data, focusing on the histogram. Next is an examination of the numerical descriptions used for summarizing different types of data: mean, median, mode, variance, and index of qualitative variation. Throughout the chapter the instructions for the relevant SPSS procedures are illustrated.

2●2 INTRODUCTION

Below are the hypothetical quiz scores from two sections of a statistics course. Are you able to scan them and summarize the performances of the two sections?

Section 1: 7, 8, 5, 5, 9, 10, 2, 7, 6, 4, 8, 7, 8, 7, 3, 9, 6, 8, 6, 9, 8, 9, 5, 7, 6, 7, 6, 7, 9, 5, 5, 9, 7, 11, 7, 6, 4, 7, 8, 10

Section 2: 6, 3, 6, 8, 5, 7, 6, 7, 8, 7, 8, 5, 5, 8, 7, 2, 7, 6, 4, 7, 7, 8, 5, 5, 8, 10, 1, 7, 6, 4, 8, 7, 2, 7, 3, 4, 6, 8, 10, 8

If someone began reading aloud the litany of individual scores, would you have a sense of how well the two sections performed or how they performed comparatively? Even with this relatively small data set it is virtually impossible. Therefore, the first step in any analysis is to describe and summarize the data. A description needs to be more than a listing of all of the observations, however. A listing of the quiz scores tells us how each student performed on the quiz, but it tells us little of a section's overall performance or of how the two sections compare. Researchers need ways of summarizing the individual observations without distorting the data's overall structure, such as average, and without losing too much information, such as the important details. Some descriptive statistics form the basis for testing important assumptions necessary for answering *inferential* questions, such as whether there are any reliable differences between the two sections. *Reliable* in this case means that any observed difference between the two sections is likely *not* due to chance alone.

Any summary comes at a cost. Think of the last time you tried to summarize a novel or a film for a friend. While you were attempting to capture the plot you needed to decide which details to ignore and which to include. A statistical summary faces the same challenge. With the appropriate use of graphs and descriptive statistics the overall quantitative and qualitative character of the observations can be captured, with minimal distortion and loss of vital information.

2 ● 3 NUMERICAL SCALES

Statistics is all about numbers: the manipulation of numbers and their comparison. A single number, such as an interest rate, by itself means very little. Furthermore, not all numerical calculations are appropriate in all circumstances. Appropriateness depends upon the nature of the numbers used to record the observations. The differences in the nature of numbers are often related to four different scales of measurement. These scales were first articulated by Stevens (1946) when he defined measurement as the assignment of numbers to objects according to rules. Today we describe these scales in terms of four properties.

● ● ● ● ●

1   Numbers on a *nominal scale* merely name categories of observations and have no intrinsic value.
2   In addition to providing a name, numbers on an *ordinal scale* have the property of ordering categories in terms of 'more or less'.
3   In addition to the property of ordering, numbers on an *interval scale* have the property of equal size intervals between the adjacent categories or numbers.
4   Numbers on a *ratio scale* have all three of the previous properties – naming, ordering, and equal intervals – plus the additional property of a true zero.

Nominal scales

The word *nominal*, which comes from the Latin word *nominalis*, refers to the property of naming. Numbers on a nominal scale name categories of observations that are *mutually exclusive*. For categories to be mutually exclusive no single observation can be a member of more than one of the categories. The simplest example of mutually exclusive categories is that of heads versus tails. A coin toss will either come up heads or tails. The principle is simple. If it is heads, it cannot be tails. Mutual exclusiveness means that if the observation is a member of one category in a set of categories, it necessarily *excludes* that observation from being a member of any other category in that set. Mutual exclusiveness does not recognize dual citizenship or fusion cuisine. We will discuss the notion of mutually exclusive categories in more detail in Chapter 3.

All four scales contain the property of naming. The key is that all the observations will fall into one and only one of a scale's categories. Numbers on a nominal scale are only names and are completely arbitrary. If we were researching music preferences, we might assign a '1' to those who prefer jazz, a '2' to those who prefer rock, and a '3' to those who prefer classical music. Or we could capriciously change our mind and assign a '1' to those who prefer classical music, a '2' to those who prefer jazz, and a '3' to those who prefer rock. The 1, 2, and 3 do not refer to amounts or rankings. They are only names. Thus, for most purposes, the actual numbers are irrelevant. A '–0.0000017' could be assigned to those who prefer jazz, a '1.000001' to those who prefer rock, and a '9' to those who prefer classical music. In fact, numbers (names) can be randomly assigned to each category.

The number used for your car's licence plate and the number on a baseball jersey are everyday examples of numbers used only as names. We do not produce player '13' by adding players '8' and '5'.

Because the numbers on a nominal scale are arbitrary, when analysing such data we are not interested in the values assigned to the categories; rather, we are interested in the *number of instances* or *relative frequencies* we observe in each category. It would make no sense to add, subtract, multiply, or divide such arbitrarily assigned names any more than it would be to subtract Douglas from Alexander. Some exceptions to this limitation can be made, as we will see later in the book.

Ordinal scales

The word *ordinal*, which comes from the Latin word *ordinalis*, indicates that in addition to the number providing a name, there is an underlying *order* to the numbers. The property of order relates to the comparative relationship of 'more or less'. 'More' and 'less' are only qualitative comparisons, the quantitative extent of the comparison is unknown and likely changeable. One example of an ordinal scale with which many students are familiar is the assigning of numerical grades: 1, 2, 3, 4, and 5. These numerical grades often indicate failure, barely passing, average, above average, and excellent, respectively. The numbers are names, but they also indicate a relation of 'more or less' in terms of a student's performance: the larger the number, the better the performance. We know that a 5 is greater than a 4 and a 4 is greater than a 3, but we do not know if the difference between a 5 and 4 is the same as the difference between a 4 and 3. Nominally (in name) – pun intended – both differences are 1, but are the two 1s quantitatively equal? The values assigned to each category are in part arbitrary. We could have just as easily used –2, –1, 0, 1, and 2 for our grading scale, as long as the transformation maintains the order of performance, so that the –2 represents failure, the –1 represents barely passing, and so on.

Furthermore, because there is no assurance that the difference between failure and barely passing is equal to the difference between barely passing and average performance, the values chosen do not need to be numerically adjacent, as long as they reflect an underlying rank ordering. For example, the numbers could be –1, 2, 10, 45, and 100, as long as that order indicates failure, barely passing, average, above average, and excellent performance, respectively.

Ordinal number scales allow comparisons of 'more and less' to be made. Because the *apparent equal differences* in the numbers are likely *quantitatively unequal*, however, the numbers on an ordinal scale cannot be added, subtracted, multiplied, or divided. We have only a qualitative grasp of the relations between the named categories. Similarly to when analysing nominal data, when analysing ordinal data the researcher is not particularly interested in the values assigned to the categories, but rather in the number of instances observed in each category.

• • • • •

Rankings, such as league tables or standings, are examples of ordinal scales. Is the difference between the top team and the second-placed team the same as the difference between the second-placed team and the third-placed team? Perhaps it is, but not necessarily. How could we know? If there were 20 teams in the league, would the team at the top be 5% better than the second-placed team, or be 95% better than the team at the bottom? We may manipulate the numbers, but any such conclusions would have little validity. What about the rankings of hockey, tennis, or soccer players? Are the differences between adjacently ranked players all equal?

Interval scales

The word *interval* comes from the Latin word *intervallum*. During the Middle Ages this referred to the spaces between the ramparts on castle walls (Figure 2.1), which tended to be of equal width.

In terms of measurement scales, the term 'interval' refers to the distance between numbers. Like the nominal and ordinal scales, interval scales name mutually exclusive categories. And like ordinal scales, numbers on interval scales indicate comparative relations of 'more or less' – the larger the number, the more of something. The additional property associated with interval scales is that of *equal intervals* between numbers such that one difference of 3 (6 – 3) is the same as any other difference of 3 (99 – 96). In this case, a rose is always a rose.

The property of equal intervals allows for addition and subtraction as well as

Figure 2.1

relevant comparisons, but it allows for only some forms of multiplication. A common example of an interval scale with which we are all familiar is temperature. The difference between –30° and 0° Celsius is equal to the difference between 0° and +30° Celsius. We need to be careful, however. If the temperature yesterday was 10°C and today it is 20°C, it does not mean that today it is twice as warm as it was yesterday: 20/10 = 2. To illustrate this, convert the temperatures from Celsius to Fahrenheit: $F = C(9/5) + 32$. The two temperatures become 50°F yesterday and 68°F today. It no longer appears to be twice as warm today as it was yesterday: 68/50 = 1.36.

PERSONALITY AND IQ

Some say that true interval scales in the behavioural and biological sciences are rare. Consequently, care must be taken. Researchers typically treat scores on personality and IQ tests as if they were interval in nature. Such scores are not the number of items answered correctly or answered in a particular manner. Performance on such tests is reported as *standardized scores*,

(Continued)

and it is unlikely that the intervals are equal. For example, the difference between an IQ of 95 and an IQ of 100 is unlikely to represent the same difference in intellectual ability as the difference between an IQ of 120 and 125. Many would argue that scores on personality and IQ tests are best considered ordinal in nature. Treating ordinal scores as interval in nature will result in distortions when inappropriate manipulations are performed.

How much distortion will result? It depends. If the intervals between consecutive scores vary greatly, there will be considerable distortion. If the intervals vary only slightly, then the distortion will be minimal. It is common, particularly in educational research, to convert percentile scores, which are ordinal in nature, into something called *normal curve equivalent* scores, which will be presented in Chapter 3.

Ratio scales

Although intervals may be equal within a scale, they may not be equal across scales. Also notice that the zero on the Celsius scale (Figure 2.2) is not a zero on the Fahrenheit scale.

Figure 2.2

The word *ratio* comes from the Latin verb *reri*, referring to think, reckon, or calculate. A ratio scale has all three of the previously mentioned properties – naming, ordering, and equal intervals – plus the additional property of a true zero. It is the presence of a true zero that allows meaningful ratios to be *calculated*. Unlike the case with interval scales, when there is a true zero, the units of measurement can be converted, but any computed ratios will be equivalent. Time is a good example. The ratio of 2 minutes to 1 minute is 2/1 = 2. If we convert the minutes into seconds the ratio is unchanged: 120/60 = 2. In experimental areas of psychology, because they are ratio in nature, *reaction time* (RT) or latency and *accuracy* have been the two most common *dependent variables*. RT is the time it takes someone to complete a task, be it simple or complex. Accuracy is the number of correct responses observed over a period of time. Both have true zeros.

Some researchers have treated personality, IQ, and social surveys as if they represented ratio scales. Treating these measures as such will result in distortions and possible erroneous conclusions when some statistical analyses are performed. How much distortion? Again, it

The time it takes runners to complete the 100 metre dash is one obvious example of a ratio scale. Scores (times) can be converted into ratios. Someone can be twice as fast as someone else.

depends. If the data have little resemblance to a ratio scale, there will be considerable distortion in any calculation. The closer the data approximate a ratio scale, the less the distortion.

━━━━━━━━━━━━━━━ REVIEW QUESTION ━━━━━━━━━━━━━━━

With which of the four scales of measurement do you associate the following measures? Using the four properties, explain why.

1   Your year of birth.
2   Your marks in secondary school.
3   Your shoe size and width.
4   The number of the row in which you sat during the last lecture (from front to back).
5   Your income last month.

🔖 Web Link 2.1 for a discussion of possible responses.

As stated at the outset, this chapter surveys the graphs and statistics that researchers use to summarize and describe individual variables: *univariate* statistics and graphs. The term 'data' usually refers to the set of individual observations the researcher collects with respect to the *dependent* or *criterion* variable. (For a review of the distinction between dependent and criterion variables, see p. 19 in the previous chapter.)

━━━━━━━━━━━━━━━ REVIEW QUESTION ━━━━━━━━━━━━━━━

What is the difference between an experiment and a quasi-experiment?

🔖 Web Link 2.2 for an answer to the review question.

Other ways of categorizing data

As mentioned in the previous chapter, although there are four scales of measurement, researchers discuss data as being one of two types: measurement or categorical. Measurement data are sometimes called *quantitative* data, and categorical data are sometimes called *qualitative* or frequency data. With respect to measurement data, each of a researcher's observations can result in a unique value. Measurement data are associated with interval and ratio scales and they can be either *continuous* or *discrete*. Reaction time (RT) is a continuous variable. It is continuous in the sense that there are an infinite number of values between any two RTs. There are an infinite number of units of time between 1 and 2 seconds just as there are an infinite number of units between 1 and 2 milliseconds. The number of items correctly answered on a multiple-choice examination is an example of a discrete variable. It is discrete because there are adjacent values which have no values between them. On a true-or-false test, a student answers either 21 or 22 items correctly. There are no scores of 21.5.

Continuous variables, like sliding boards, are smooth from top to bottom. Discrete variables have a fixed number of steps, like staircases.

Categorical data, usually associated with nominal and ordinal scales, by their nature are discrete. When examining frequency data the focus is not on the particular values (names) assigned to the categories of the observations, but rather on the number of observations (frequencies) observed in each category. As we will see, there are different descriptive statistics associated with these different types of data.

Notation

At this point it is necessary to begin introducing the notation system used throughout this book. When computing statistics we often carry out simple computations iteratively. That is, we repeat a procedural step or computation. Often a computation is performed on all observations. Rather than write out each instance, we have a system for notating the process. The Greek symbol Σ (Sigma) is used for this purpose. Assume we have a data set (y) of five observations: 2, 1, 4, 5, and 3. If we wish to obtain the total of the y-values, it could be written out 'add up all of the observations': $2 + 1 + 4 + 5 + 3 = 15$. Or we can simply express this as $\Sigma y = 15$. Latin letters, usually y, are used to indicate a variable. Σy indicates the sum of the y-values. $\Sigma(y - C)$ instructs us to subtract a constant from each of the y-values and sum the differences: $(2 - C) + (1 - C) + (4 - C) + (5 - C) + (3 - C)$. These forms of summation notation, as well as elaborations on them, will be used throughout this book. It should be noted that

$$\sum_{i=1}^{n} y_i$$

is the more formal expression of Σy, where i indicates where to begin the summing. Unless stated otherwise, begin with the first observation. n is the total number of observations and, thus, the last observation in the set. With each iteration, i is incremented by one. Because summations almost always involve all observations in a data set or in a subset, the notation is simplified by dropping the i and the n. Notational variations will be introduced as necessary.

Web Link 2.3 for a more comprehensive review of summation notation and related rules.

In addition to summation notation, there is a need to clarify how letters will be used to symbolize variables and statistics. Figure 2.3 summarizes how some of the Latin and Greek letters are used in the text.

For example, Latin letters are used to indicate variables. The letter y usually is used for dependent or criterion variables and the letter x for independent or predictor variables. Most of the letters in Figure 2.3 are introduced in this chapter, the others appear in subsequent chapters. Statistics are said to be *descriptive* when they are used to merely describe a set of observations. Statistics are said to be *inferential* when they are used to make inferences about populations and their parameters or to test hypotheses. The reporting of all research results begins with the presentation of descriptive statistics.

Type of letter		Function	Data type
Roman			
	y	Dependent variable or criterion	Measurement
	x	Independent variable or predictor	Measurement
	$\bar{y}, S, S^2, r$	Sample descriptive statistics	Measurement
	VR, IQV	Sample descriptive statistics	Categorical
	t, F	Inferential test statistic	Measurement
Greek			
	$\mu, \sigma, \sigma^2, \rho$	Population parameters	Measurement
	ϕ	Sample descriptive statistic	Categorical
	χ^2, λ, τ	Inferential test statistics	Categorical

Figure 2.3   Some letters used as symbols

2 ● 4   HISTOGRAMS

Entering data

Although there are many ways to pictorially summarize data, the histogram is the most common univariate graph. One reason for its wide use is that it provides a visual summary of a variable with a minimal loss of information. Furthermore, the histogram allows for easy identification of any anomalies that may need to be addressed. As we will see, anomalies include such things as a problematic shape of the distribution of the observations or an observation that is considerably greater or smaller than all others. Problematic shapes and extreme scores will restrict the type of statistical analysis that may appropriately be applied. Some of the ways to correct these anomalies are discussed at points throughout the book.

Histograms can be appropriately applied to most forms of data, including measurement, categorical, discrete, and continuous data. Histograms are often employed to summarize the dependent variable in experimental studies and to depict both criterion and predictor variables in observational research. Let us examine the data given in Section 2.2 above.

Begin by entering the data into the SPSS *Data Editor*. Go to this *SPSS* link at https://study.sagepub.com/bors. **Once SPSS opens you will see a window labelled *IBM SPSS STATISTICS* (Figure 2.4). In the small white box below the label you will see an option called *New Dataset*. Select that option and then click the *OK* button at the bottom right of the window.**

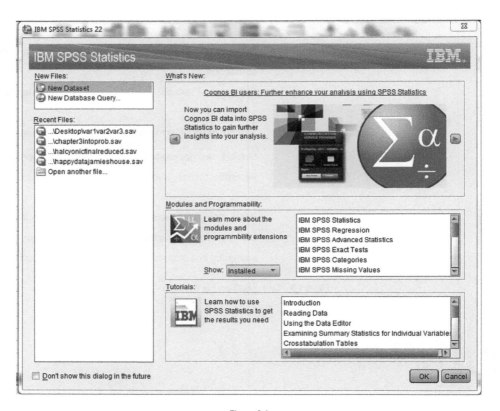

Figure 2.4

A new window labelled *IBM SPSS Statistics Data Editor* appears with a row of menu tabs and a matrix of empty boxes (Figure 2.5). The columns are labelled *var* for 'variable'. The rows are labelled 1–39 to begin with. The rows usually represent subjects and the numbers in the first column often serve as subject numbers.

At the bottom left of the screen there are two tabs: *Data View* and *Variable View*. We are currently in the *Data View* window. By clicking the *Variable View* tab we can switch to the *Variable View* window and name our variable and define our *variable type*. When the window opens, move the cursor to the *Name* cell in the first row and type our variable's name. Let us use *section1* as the name (Figure 2.6). Notice that when you hit return other cells in the row

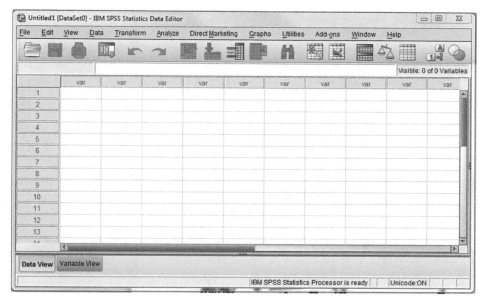

Figure 2.5

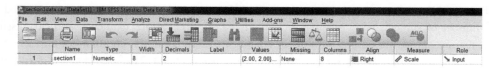

Figure 2.6

are automatically filled in. Ensure that the variable is listed as *Numeric* under the *Type* heading and as *Scale* under *Measure* heading. Although the number of items correct on the quiz is an example of a ratio scale, SPSS does not differentiate ratio and interval scales. The term *Scale* under the heading *Type* is used for either ratio or interval data. For now we will use the other default settings.

Because we are only exploring one variable, click the *Data View* tab and return to the *Data Editor* window (Figure 2.7). Move the cursor to the cell immediately under the variable labelled *section1* and enter the first score. After entering a 7 in the first row either arrow down or hit the enter key to move to the second row. Continue doing so until all 40 observations for *section1* are entered in the first column of the matrix.

Once the data are entered, we can construct a *frequency table*. From the menu row in the *Data Editor* click *Analyze*, scroll down to the *Descriptive Statistics* option and then over to *Frequencies*. When the *Frequencies* window appears, highlight and move (using the arrow between the boxes) *section1* over to the *Variable(s)* box (Figure 2.8). Ensure the *Display frequency table* box in the bottom left corner is checked. Then click *OK*. The *Statistics Viewer* or output window will appear (Figure 2.9).

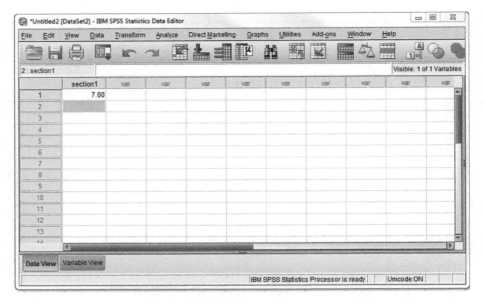

Figure 2.7

The small box at the top of the window reports the number of observations analysed (N) and the number of subjects with missing data. We have 40 observations (subjects) and no missing data. Below that in the output window is a table with five columns. The first column lists the categories of the observations; we had scores ranging from 2 to 11. The second column indicates

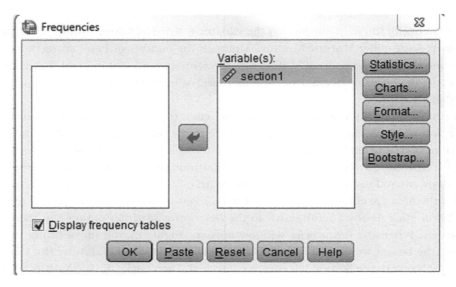

Figure 2.8

Statistics

section1

N	Valid	40
	Missing	0

section1

		Frequency	Percent	Valid Percent	Cumulative Percent
Valid	2.00	1	2.5	2.5	2.5
	3.00	1	2.5	2.5	5.0
	4.00	2	5.0	5.0	10.0
	5.00	5	12.5	12.5	22.5
	6.00	6	15.0	15.0	37.5
	7.00	10	25.0	25.0	62.5
	8.00	6	15.0	15.0	77.5
	9.00	6	15.0	15.0	92.5
	10.00	2	5.0	5.0	97.5
	11.00	1	2.5	2.5	100.0
	Total	40	100.0	100.0	

Figure 2.9

the frequency or the number of observations found in each category. The third column reports the percentage of the observations associated with each score or category. We will ignore the fourth column for now. The fifth column provides the percentage as it accumulates from the lowest score to the highest score.

Although a frequency table provides important summary information, such as the lowest and highest scores as well as the frequencies for each of the scores, researchers in many areas often prefer to view frequencies in pictorial form: a histogram.

To produce a *frequency histogram*, return to the *Frequencies* window and select the *Charts* tab. Click the *Histogram* button (Figure 2.10)

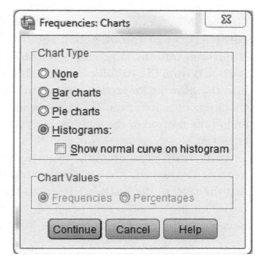

Figure 2.10

Histogram

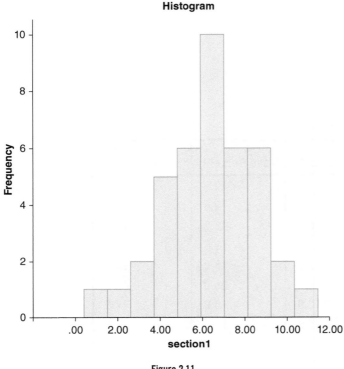

Figure 2.11

and then *Continue.* **When you return to the *Frequencies* window, click *OK.***

In addition to the previous output, you now will find a frequency histogram (Figure 2.11). On the horizontal axis, or *x*-axis, the observed scores or categories are listed in ascending order. The vertical or *y*-axis represents the frequency or number of observations. For example, we can see from the histogram that there were two scores of 4 and five scores of 5. Summing the frequency of all of the categories gives us the total number of observations. Most of the information from the frequency table is contained in the frequency histogram. The percentages and cumulative percentages would need to be calculated, however. SPSS does provide histograms with that information. As an example, we will construct a *relative frequency histogram.* For that we need to switch to a different option in the *Data Editor* window.

In the *Data Editor* window we move over from *Analyze* to the *Graphs* option and scroll down and select *Chart Builder.* For our purposes, when the *Chart Builder* window appears (Figure 2.12) click *OK.*

Two windows will simultaneously appear: a second *Chart Builder* window and an *Element Properties* window (Figure 2.13). From the bottom left of the *Chart Builder* window select the *Histogram* option and then drag the leftmost of the four examples (*Simple Histogram*) into the large empty rectangular box. Next select and drag the variable name (*section1*) from the *Variables* box into the *X-Axis* field in the box to the right. Next go back into the *Element Properties* window in the *Chart Builder* and click the little down arrow that appears across from *Histogram* under *Statistic.* Choose the *Histogram Percent* option and at the bottom of the window click *Apply.* Move over to the *Chart Builder* window and click *OK.*

An alternative version of the frequency histogram appears in the output window: a relative frequency histogram. These two histograms look identical. There is only one difference. Notice that the label of the *y*-axis has been changed from *Frequency* to *Frequency Percent.* The current histogram provides the percentage of the total number of observations represented by each category on the *x*-axis. With a relative frequency histogram, an important piece of information

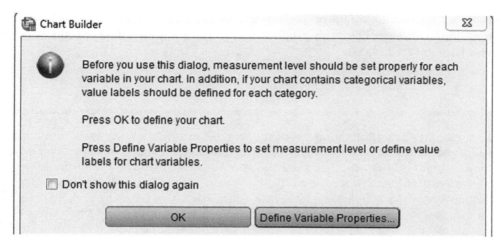

Figure 2.12

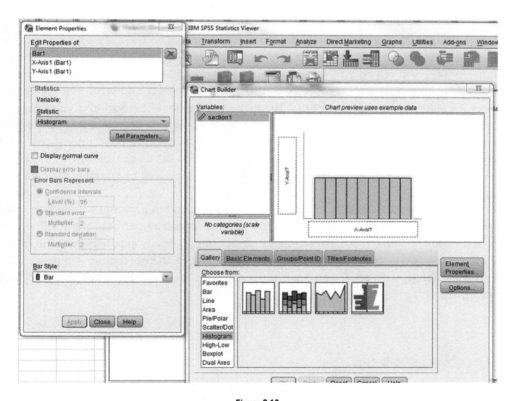

Figure 2.13

is lost. If I tell you that 20% of the people surveyed preferred coffee over tea, you have no way of knowing, unless I tell you, how many people were surveyed. I may have surveyed only 10 people or I may have surveyed 10,000.

Remember that an important factor when we evaluate the reliability of numerical information is *sample size*, or the number of observations upon which a summary is based. My data may indicate that 50% of Americans surveyed earned over $5 million a year. My summary, however, may have been based on only two observations: a professional football player and myself. Thus, when evaluating percentages, be they in a relative frequency histogram or merely reported in a news article, it is important to know the total number of observations upon which the percentages were calculated. Of course factors other than sample size are important. For example, an income survey may be conducted in the New York Yankees locker room or it may be conducted by randomly selecting income tax statements.

The above procedures for constructing a histogram work well when there are a limited number of observed values or categories on the *x*-axis. In the current set of discrete data there are only ten different observed values: 2 to 11. Thus there are 10 categories on the *x*-axis with a number of observations in several of the categories. But what if there were considerably more categories (e.g., exam scores ranging from 23 to 99), with rarely more than one observation in any category? A glance at the hypothetical data in the frequency table in Figure 2.14 illustrates that a histogram with all observed values represented on the *x*-axis is only marginally more informative than merely listing the individual scores. Moreover, when the dependent variable is continuous in nature, such a limitation is always the case. This limitation is resolved by grouping the data into categories or *bins*.

When the data in the frequency table are categorized into ten bins and the bins are used to construct the histogram in Figure 2.15, the data are found to be more than a litany of random individual values. A pattern emerges that was not originally apparent. Like the earlier histogram when the values ranged from 2 to 11, the bulk of the observations cluster in the middle of the range, with fewer and fewer observations as we move towards the highest and the lowest scores.

Rules for constructing bins

It is clear that binning data can be quite helpful when pictorially summarizing data where there are either a large number of discrete scores or the scores are continuous in nature. Binning must follow certain rules or the resulting histogram can be misleading, however.

1   The bins should be of equal width. In the current example there are 10 bins each with a width of eight. If the bins were of unequal width, the relative frequency of certain categories on the x-axis may be exaggerated and misinterpreted. There are justifiable exceptions. There may be instances where the bins are unequal because of the nature of the scale of interest. For example, marks in a course may be based on a final examination with scores ranging from 23 to 99. For the purpose of examining the students' performance, bins should be kept equal. If we are assigning grades 1, 2, 3, 4, and 5 to represent failure, barely passing, average performance, above average, and excellent, with scores 0–49, 50–59, 60–69, 70–79, and 80–99, respectively, then the bins for depicting the data will appear unequal: the first and last categories are wider than the others. In this second case, for analytical purposes, we are changing the measurement scale from ratio to ordinal.

2   The number of bins a researcher chooses can make a big difference to how the data appear. When the bulk of the observations is clustered in the middle of the observed values, with fewer and fewer observations further towards the highest and lowest scores, the number of bins makes little difference to the nature of the histogram. When, however, the distribution of scores diverges from that pattern, as will be seen, a change in the number of bins can make a great difference to the shape of the histogram.

3   Additionally, the appropriate number of bins is also related to sample size. The more observations upon which the histogram is based, the more categories a researcher is free to employ. If you have relatively too few observations for the number of bins, the observed shape of the histogram will be less reliable. If there are 20 observations and 10 bins are used to visually summarize the data, a change in one or two

section1

		Frequency	Percent	Valid Percent	Cumulative Percent
Valid	23.00	1	2.5	2.5	2.5
	33.00	1	2.5	2.5	5.0
	36.00	1	2.5	2.5	7.5
	39.00	1	2.5	2.5	10.0
	41.00	1	2.5	2.5	12.5
	44.00	2	5.0	5.0	17.5
	48.00	1	2.5	2.5	20.0
	50.00	1	2.5	2.5	22.5
	53	1	2.5	2.5	25.0
	54.00	1	2.5	2.5	27.5
	57	1	2.5	2.5	30.0
	58	1	2.5	2.5	32.5
	59.00	2	5.0	5.0	37.5
	60.00	1	2.5	2.5	40.0
	61.00	2	5.0	5.0	45.0
	64.00	1	2.5	2.5	47.5
	67.00	3	7.5	7.5	55.0
	68.00	2	5.0	5.0	60.0
	71.00	2	5.0	5.0	65.0
	72.00	1	2.5	2.5	67.5
	73.00	2	5.0	5.0	72.5
	74.00	1	2.5	2.5	75.0
	75.00	2	5.0	5.0	80.0
	80.00	1	2.5	2.5	82.5
	81	2	5.0	5.0	87.5
	84.00	1	2.5	2.5	90.0
	85	2	5.0	5.0	95.0
	86	1	2.5	2.5	97.5
	99.00	1	2.5	2.5	100.0
	Total	40	100.0	100.0	

Figure 2.14

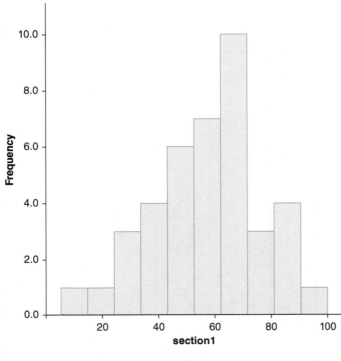

Figure 2.15

of the observations or a change in the number of bins may drastically change the shape of the histogram.

Web Link 2.4 for SPSS instruction and practice with binning.

Other forms of graphing and pictorially displaying data are described later on in this book, as needed.

Descriptive statistics

Descriptive statistics are another way to summarize the researcher's observations or data. Where graphs pictorially display the data, descriptive statistics provide numerical summaries. These numerical summaries are often utilized in further analyses of the data. We first examine the descriptive statistics used with measurement data; these are summarized in Figure 2.16.

Descriptive statistics	Measurement	Data
Measures of central tendency		
	Mean	The arithmetic average of the observations
	Median	The value that divides the rank-ordered observations in half
	Mode	The most common value of the observations among the data
Measures of spread		
	Range	The difference between the largest and the smallest value in the data
	IQR	The range of the middle 50% of the rank-ordered observations
	Variance	The average squared difference between each observation and the mean of the observations
	Standard deviation	The square root of the variance

Figure 2.16

2 ● 5 MEASURES OF CENTRAL TENDENCY: MEASUREMENT DATA

Mean

The most basic statistics are those of central tendency or the values that represent the centre of the distribution of the observed scores. These statistics are commonly referred to as averages. These statistics can represent a variable's *expected values*. The most common measure of central tendency is the *mean*. The mean is what most people think of when they hear the word *average*. The mean is calculated by summing all of the observations and dividing this sum by the number of observations. We can write this as

$$\bar{y} = \frac{\Sigma y}{n},$$

where $\bar{y}$ is the mean of y, Σy is the sum of the observations, and n is the number of observations. For example, assume the following 19 scores are from a 10-item multiple-choice quiz:

4, 8, 5, 7, 1, 6, 2, 5, 3, 7, 5, 5, 4, 9, 4, 5, 3, 6, 6.

To obtain the mean the quiz scores are summed and divided by the number of scores:

$$\bar{y} = \frac{\Sigma y}{n} = \frac{95}{19} = 5.$$

Thus, the mean of the 19 scores is 5. The mean cuts the *total value* in half. Half of the *value* will be below the mean score of 5 and half will be above it. This does not necessarily mean that half of the observations will be below the mean and half will be above it. That is the function of our next measure of central tendency.

Return to the **Data Editor** window with the variable **section1** and select **Analyze** from the menu bar. From the drop-down menu, select **Descriptive Statistics**, move to the next drop-down menu and click **Frequencies**. Highlight the variable **section1** and click the arrow moving **section1** to the **Variable(s)** box (Figure 2.17). Select the button on the right labelled **Statistics**. In the menu that pops up (Figure 2.18) click on the **Mean, Median,** and **Mode** boxes and then on the **Continue** button at the bottom. When you return to the previous menu, click **OK**.

In the output window labelled *Statistics Viewer* the small upper box (Figue 2.19) lists several things: *N Valid* (40, which is the number of observations), *N Missing* (0, how many subjects are missing a score), mean, median, and mode. We see that the mean ($\bar{y}$) is 6.9250, the median is 7.0000, and the mode is 7.00.

Means are often referred to as descriptive statistics. Once the mean is used for any purpose other than describing the particular observations on which it is based, it becomes an *inferential statistic*. That is, the mean is being used to infer something beyond the sample, even if it is simply considered an estimate of the population mean from which the sample was drawn. Although first and foremost descriptive, means and other 'descriptive' statistics are also used *inferentially* for comparative or predictive purposes.

The related population parameter, the mean of the population, is expressed as

$$\mu = \frac{\Sigma Y}{N},$$

where μ (pronounced 'myu') is the true mean of the population from which samples may be drawn. ΣY is the sum of all the observations in the population, and N is the total number of observations in the population. μ indicates the true mean of the population, regardless of whether the population is finite or infinite.

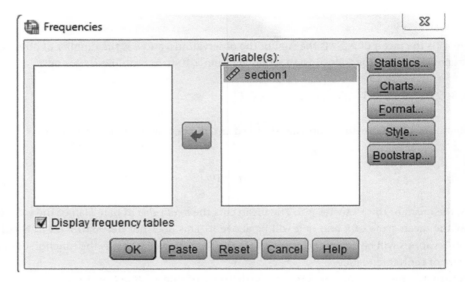

Figure 2.17

Median

The median is the value which divides the observations in half after they have been arranged in order from the smallest to the largest: 50% of the scores – not 50% of the value – will be below the median and 50% of the scores will be above the median. To find the median of the scores from the 10-item multiple-choice quiz we looked at earlier, let us begin by arranging the scores in ascending order:

1, 2, 3, 3, 4, 4, 4, 5, 5, 5, 5, 5, 6, 6, 6, 7, 7, 8, 9.

Which value divides these scores in half? Suppose there are n scores. The median score is the one in the $\frac{1}{2}(n+1)$ th position.

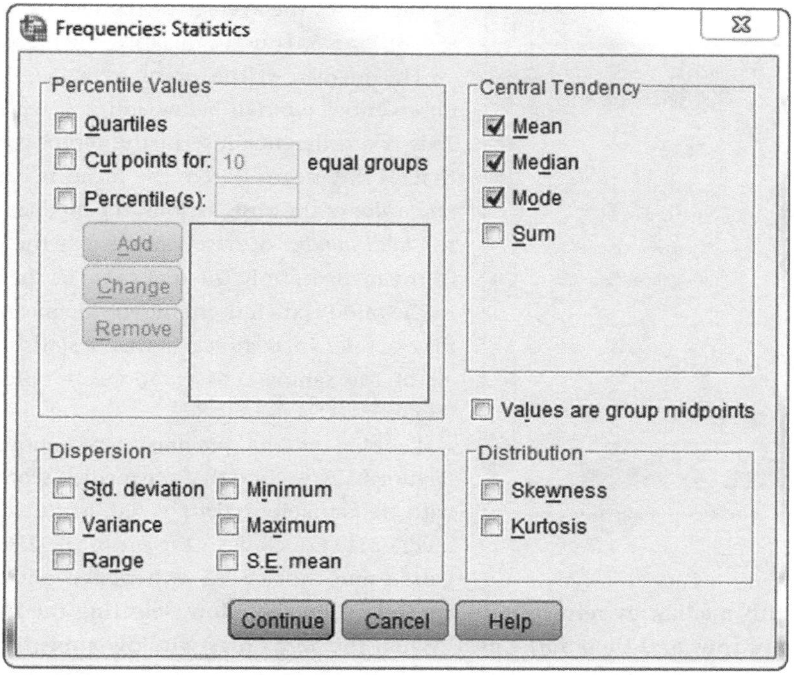

Figure 2.18

For a data set with an odd number of observations, like the one above where $n = 19$, the position of the median is $\frac{1}{2}(n+1) = \frac{1}{2}(19+1) = 10$. The answer, 10, represents the 10th position, *not* the value of the median. As can be seen in the above rank ordering, the value associated with the 10th position is 5. Thus, the median is 5.

For a data set with an even number of observations, such as

1, 2, 3, 3, 4, 4, 4, 5, 5, 5, 6, 6, 6, 6, 7, 7, 8, 8, 9, 10,

Statistics

section1

N	Valid	40
	Missing	0
Mean		6.9250
Median		7.0000
Mode		7.00

Figure 2.19

there is one additional step. We now have $n = 20$, so $\frac{1}{2}(n+1) = 10.5$. Again, the answer, 10.5, represents the 10.5th position, *not* the value of the median. But the 10.5th position falls between the 10th and the 11th scores, between a 5 and a 6.

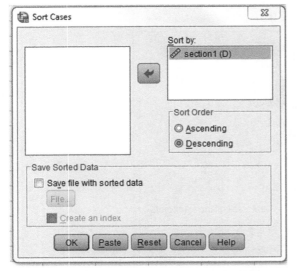

Figure 2.20

In such cases the average of the two values is taken: $(5 + 6)/2 = 5.5$. Thus, in this case, the median is 5.5.

The median is the point at which half of the observations will fall below and half will fall above. This is a different sense of the term 'average' from that of the mean. Where the mean is based on the *total value* of the observations, the median is based on the *total number* of observations. For the calculation of the median, only the one value or the two values in the middle are important. For the mean, all values play a role. In technical terms a statistic that uses all of the sample's observations is called *sufficient* (Howell, 2002).

Looking at the previous SPSS output window (Figure 2.19), we find that the median score associated with the variable *section1* is 7.0. In this data set the median is very close to the mean (6.9250). **You can gain some more SPSS experience and check the accuracy of this median by returning to the *Data Editor* window, selecting the *Data* option from the menu row, and then *Sort Cases*. When the *Sort Cases* window appears, select and move the variable *section1* from the left-hand box over to the *Sort by* box (Figure 2.20). Select the descending *Sort Order* option and then click *OK*.**

Notice that the data in the *Data Editor* have been quickly sorted, beginning with 11 and ending with 2. A question remains, however. Which of the 7s in the data set is the median?

Remember, the median of a data set will be in position $\frac{1}{2}(n+1)$. In the case of the variable *section1* this will be position $\frac{41}{2} = 20.5$. The 20.5th position, however, falls between the 20th and the 21st scores, between a 7 and a 7. When we take the average of the two values, we get $(7 + 7)/2 = 7$. In effect, the median value of 7 is not one of the actually observed 7s found in the variable *section1*, but an invisible value found between two of the observed 7s. When we count the number of observations above and below that invisible 7, we find 20 observations below it and 20 above it.

Mode

The mode provides yet another sense of the term 'average'. When the numbers are discrete, the simplest definition of the mode is that it is the most frequent value in the data set. Let us again use the above rank-ordered data from the hypothetical quiz ($n = 19$):

1, 2, 3, 3, 4, 4, 4, 5, 5, 5, 5, 5, 6, 6, 6, 7, 7, 8, 9.

We find one 1, one 2, two 3s, three 4s, five 5s, three 6s, two 7s, one 8, and one 9. The most frequent value in the data is 5. Thus, the mode is 5.

Returning to the SPSS output window for variable *section1*, the *Statistics* box indicates that the mode of those 40 observations is 7.0. This is identical to the

Section 1: 7, 8, 5, 5, 9, 10, 2, 7, 6, 4, 8, 7, 8, 7, 3, 9, 6, 8, 6, 9, 8, 9, 5, 7, 6, 7, 6, 7, 9, 5, 5, 9, 7, 11, 7, 6, 4, 7, 8, 10.

median and very close to the mean for this data set. To the chagrin of researchers, this is not always the case.

The computation of the mode is not always straightforward. When there are a great many different values and perhaps only one or two observations with the same value it makes little sense to speak of the mode. An obvious example of this could be the marks on the final examination in a biochemistry course (let us give statistics a rest). There may be 50 students in the class and no two with the same mark on the examination. In such cases, as when constructing a frequency histogram, it is common to cluster or *bin* the marks before calculating a mode. We may wish to use bins with a width of 20, for example, where we look at the number of students who scored between 81 and 100, between 61 and 80, between 41 and 60, between 21 and 40, and between 0 and 20. If we found 7 students scoring between 81 and 100, 17 students between 61 and 80, 14 students between 41 and 60, 10 students between 21 and 40, and 2 students scoring between 0 and 20, then 61–80 could be identified as the *modal category*. Notice the mode is a bin and not an individual score. The rules and limitations regarding binning that presented earlier also apply here.

Whereas a sample can have only one mean and one median, a sample may have two or more modes. Not all variables are unimodal. Look at the following two samples of data that have been rank-ordered to make examination easier:

Sample I: 1, 2, 2, 3, 3, 3, 3, 4, 5, 6, 7, 7, 8, 8, 8, 8, 9, 9, 10.

Sample II: 1, 2, 2, 3, 3, 3, 3, 4, 5, 6, 7, 7, 8, 8, 8, 8, 8, 9, 10.

If you calculate the mean for each of the two samples, you find them to be 5.58 and 5.53, respectively. The two corresponding medians are 6.00 and 6.00. When Sample I is examined, two values or scores that are equally the most common are found: 3 and 8. Such a distribution of observations is deemed *bimodal*. When Sample II is inspected, 8 is found to be the most common value, but just by one observation. For most purposes, even though 8 is the most common score in Sample II, this distribution of observations also is deemed bimodal. The reason for the designation is that the frequencies of the two scores (3 and 8) stand out from the others. Of course there can be more than two modes. For most purposes researchers are concerned with knowing that the distribution of their data is unimodal.

After examining the two sets of observations again you may begin to understand why researchers are often hoping that the data are unimodal. Are the means of these two samples (5.58 and 5.53) as meaningful (pun intended) as the mean of the *section1* data (7), which was unimodal? In the case of bimodal data, do means and medians reflect *average* or *expected* scores? Clearly they do not. Should we randomly select an observation from Sample I or II, we *expect* it to be either above or below the centre. Excuse this coarse but instructive example: after calculating the mean of a large sample of young adults we find that the average human being has one testicle.

The mean and the median are the measures of central tendency most often employed to describe the *average* or the *centre* of a set of observations. As seen above, all three (mean, median, and mode) can be the same value. This occurs only in one particular circumstance: when the observations are *unimodal* and they are distributed symmetrically around the mode. In terms of measurement data, the mode is the least applied measure of central tendency. The mode is most useful when denoting the most frequent observation among a small set of options, particularly when summarizing nominal data. For example, when describing voter preferences, political scientists may wish to identify the most *popular* party. The *expected* choice of political party is not some sort of *middle* choice. Remember, numbers that are assigned to the political parties are nominal in nature and thus not amenable to calculating a mean or median.

Mean versus median

The mean and the median both describe data and form the basis for further inferential analyses. As will be seen later, the mean is typically employed when researchers analyse their data with *parametric* statistics, whereas the median is often employed when *nonparametric* statistics are used. At this point let us simply say that nonparametric statistical procedures do not use sample statistics, such as the mean ($\bar{y}$), to estimate corresponding population parameters (μ). This is an important distinction to which we will return in Parts II and III of the book. Here the groundwork is laid, however, through an exploration of how the mean and the median are differentially affected by small modifications to a data set.

To examine how the mean and the median react differently to small modifications in a data set, open a new SPSS *Data Editor* window and enter the set of 19 scores from the hypothetical 10-item multiple-choice quiz which we first encountered earlier:

1, 2, 3, 3, 4, 4, 4, 5, 5, 5, 5, 5, 6, 6, 6, 7, 7, 8, 9.

Run the *Descriptive Statistics* (mean, median, and mode) on these 19 observations four times. Begin by running the program with the above data as given, then three more times: first, after changing the highest score, the 9, to a 10; next, after changing the 9 to a 20; and finally, after changing the 9 to 100. Notice that across the four analyses the median is constant. The value in the middle, 5, remains the value in the middle, regardless of the increases to the highest value. Rounding to the nearest two decimal places, however, the mean increases from 5.00 to 5.05, then to 5.58, and finally to 9.80. In the last case, the mean of the 19 observations is now greater than the second highest value in the data set. Note that there are also no changes in the mode. A statistic insensitive to outliers is said to be *resistant*. While the median and mode are resistant, the mean is not.

━━━━━━━━━━━ CHALLENGE QUESTION ━━━━━━━━━━━

As you have seen, the mean of a data set may change simply by changing a single value in the set. Here are several challenge questions:

1   What is the minimum number of values you would need to change the median?
2   How many values can you change without changing the median?
3   How many values can you change without changing the mean?
4   Can you change the value of only one score without changing the mean?

You might wish to return to the SPSS data set and play around with changing some of the values.

🖰 Web Link 2.5 for an answer to the challenge questions.

There are other differences between the mean and the median. An important one mentioned here involves minimizing the *total distance* the individual observations are from a single value (the absolute deviations) versus minimizing the *total squared distance* the individual observations are from a single value (the squared deviations). The value that minimizes the *absolute value* of the deviations is the median. For example, if a data set is composed of 1, 2, and 9, the median will be 2. If we subtract 2 from our three scores – which we will call *deviations* or *errors* – we get the absolute values of $|1|$, $|0|$, and $|7|$. We have $\Sigma(|y - \text{median}|) = 8$. If any value other than the median is used, the *total absolute distance* will be greater than 8. This includes using the mean of our three scores:

$$\bar{y} = \frac{\Sigma y}{n} = \frac{12}{3} = 4.$$

If the mean of 4 is subtracted from the three scores the absolute distances are $|3|$, $|2|$, and $|5|$, and $\Sigma(y - \bar{y}) = 10$. If you were allowed to use only one value to guess all of the values hidden in a hat, and you wished to minimize the total absolute value of your error (total absolute distance), then you should choose the median of the values. If, however, you wish to minimize the *squared deviations* or squared total errors using a single value, then you will want to know the mean of the values in the hat. Analysing the three scores of 1, 2, and 9, we find the following. Recall the mean is 4. Then

$$\Sigma(y - \bar{y})^2 = (1 - 4)^2 + (2 - 4)^2 + (9 - 4)^2 = 38.$$

When any value other than their mean is used, the total of the squared errors will be greater than 38. This includes using the median of the three scores:

$$\Sigma(y - \text{median})^2 = (1 - 2)^2 + (2 - 2)^2 + (9 - 2)^2 = 50.$$

These differences between the mean and median are important to note. They will become important for tests of statistical significance and the problem of assumptions.

════════════ REVIEW QUESTION ════════════════════════════════

When will it make no difference whether we use the mean or the median for calculating the total absolute difference and the total squared difference?

➘ Web Link 2.6 for an answer to the review question.

════════════ • • • • • ════════════════════════════════

Note that the mean and the median may be defined as being the *expected values*, and the three scores (1, 2, and 9) described as the *observed values*. This is the simplest use of these terms (expected and observed) introduced in Chapter 1.

Composite mean: mean of means

To extend the application of the notation and symbol systems found throughout this book, the concept of *composite mean* is explored. A composite mean is defined as the overall mean or grand mean of all observations across several groups or samples. For example, there may be three sections of students in your statistics course. Imagine you are told each section's mean score on a quiz and you wish to know the overall or grand mean (*GM*) of all students across all three sections. There are two circumstances in which the solution is simple. First, if we have the marks from all of the individual students, we can simply sum them – ignoring sections – and divide by the total number of students. This can be written as

$$GM = \frac{\Sigma y_{ij}}{N},$$

where *GM* represents the grand mean across all sections or samples, and y_{ij} represents the *i*th subject in the *j*th section or sample. In simple terms, Σy_{ij} is the sum of the marks of all students across all sections of the course. *N* represents the total number of students across all sections, and lower-case n_j represents the number of students in a given section. Thus, $N = \Sigma n_j$. The notation denotes summing all n_j scores across all sections or subsamples.

Second, if there is an equal number of students in each section of the course, we can sum the section means and divide them by the number of sections. This is the simple mean of the means, written

$$GM = \frac{\Sigma \bar{y}_j}{K},$$

where K is the number of sections, and $\bar{y}_j$ represents the mean of the jth section. We can write $\Sigma \bar{y}_j$ more formally as $\Sigma_{j=1}^k \bar{y}_j$.

A problem arises when the individual observations are not available and the section sizes are unequal. When the n are unequal, it is highly unlikely that the GM is a simple mean of the means. For example, sample sizes in Figure 2.21 vary greatly.

The first three columns are the scores in three samples. The fourth column is all scores from the three samples: Σy_{ij}. The means for the three samples are 2, 4, and 3, respectively. The simple mean of the means is $GM = \left(\Sigma \bar{y}_j \right)/k = 3$. But notice that the simple mean of the means is not the true mean of all 13 scores. The mean of all scores across the three samples is actually 3.3077. The problem is not insurmountable, however. Remember what a mean is: the total value divided by the number of observations.

With the sample means and the number of observations for each sample, it is possible to reconstruct $GM = \left(\Sigma y_{ij} \right)/N$. The numerator, $\Sigma y_{ik} \left(\Sigma y_{i1} + \Sigma y_{i2} + \ldots + \Sigma y_{ij} + \ldots + \Sigma y_{ik} \right)$, represents the total value of the observations

> Enter the data from Figure 2.21 into SPSS using the four columns as variables and obtain the means for the four variables for practice and for comparison with the subsequent calculations in the text. Note: there may be small differences due to rounding.

Sample 1	Sample 2	Sample 3	All scores
1	1	2	1
2	2	3	2
3	3	4	3
	4		1
	5		2
	6		3
	7		4
			5
			6
			7
			2
			3
			4

Figure 2.21

in the last groups. Because K is the total number of groups, it is also the number associated with the last group. Next, recall that $\bar{y} = (\Sigma y)/n$. Thus, with a little algebra, $\Sigma y = n\bar{y}$. That is, the total of the marks of the students in any section can be recovered by multiplying the number of students in the section by the mean of the section. The result of completing this for all sections and summing the products is the total of all of the individual marks across all sections: $\Sigma n_j \bar{y}_j = \Sigma y_{ij}$. The individual marks are not recoverable, but the total is. Summing the number of observations across all sections provides the total number of observations: $N = \Sigma n_j$. Thus,

$$GM = \frac{\Sigma n_j \bar{y}_j}{\Sigma n_j} = \frac{\Sigma y_{ij}}{N}.$$

For our example,

$$\frac{(2 \times 3) + (4 \times 7) + (3 \times 3)}{3 + 7 + 3} = \frac{43}{13} = 3.3077.$$

━━━━━━━━━━━━ CHALLENGE QUESTION ━━━━━━━━━━━━

When the sample *n* are unequal, is it ever possible to calculate the grand mean by summing the means of the subgroups and dividing by the number of groups? If it is never possible for this to happen, then why not? If it is possible, when is it?

 Web Link 2.7 for an answer to the challenge question.

2 ● 6 MEASURES OF SPREAD: MEASUREMENT DATA

This section covers another crucial dimension of descriptive statistics: measures of spread. Locating the centre of a set of observations is important when summarizing data, but the centre alone is insufficient. How much of a description can the mean alone provide? For example, if an instructor informs the class that the mean score on an examination was 75, this provides some information about how well the class performed. But knowing the centre says nothing of the spread of the scores. If the instructor informs the class that the marks range from 70 to 80, this gives a very different impression than if the instructor says the marks range from 30 to 90. In this section various measures of spread (range, inter-quartile range, variance, and standard deviation) along with their uses and limitations are surveyed.

Either calculate or enter into a new SPSS *Data Editor* window the following two variables:

Var1: 0, 2, 4, 4, 5, 5, 5, 6, 6, 8, 10.

Var2: 4, 4, 4, 5, 5, 5, 5, 6, 6, 6.

They can be labelled *var1* and *var2*.

As earlier, select *Analyze* from the *Data Editor* menu in SPSS. Then select *Descriptive Statistics* and then *Frequencies*. From the *Statistics* menu calculate the mean, median, and mode of both *var1* and *var2*.

Notice that both groups have a mean of 5.0, a median of 5.0, and a mode of 5.0. A visual examination of *Var1* and *Var2* reveals a clear difference in the two sets of observations. The two groups of scores are considerably different in terms of their *spread*.

Range and inter-quartile range

In *Var1* the observations range from 0 to 10. In *Var2* the observations range from 4 to 6. The *range* is defined as the difference between the highest and the lowest values in a set of observations. For *Var1*, range = 10 – 0 = 10. For *Var2*, range = 6 – 4 = 2. Thus, although the two groups of observations have the same means, medians, and modes, they differ considerably in their range. Combining the mean and the range offers a more informative summary description of the two variables than either alone does. The measure of range has its utility, but it also has limitations. Consider the following three groups of data:

var1: 2, 4, 5, 5, 6, 6, 6, 7, 7, 7, 7, 7, 7, 8, 8, 8, 9, 9, 10, 12.

var2: 2, 2, 2, 2, 2, 3, 3, 3, 3, 4, 10, 10, 11, 11, 12, 12, 12, 12, 12, 12.

var3: 6, 6, 6, 6, 6, 6, 6, 6, 6, 7, 7, 7, 7, 7, 7, 7, 7, 7, 7, 16.

The observations are rank-ordered for ease of visual examination. If you enter the 20 observations of these three variables into SPSS and examine the descriptive statistics, you will discover that all three variables have a mean and median of 7.0 and a range of 10. But the shapes of the distributions of the observations about their means and across their range differ greatly. This is one reason why pictorial summaries, particularly histograms, of data are always valuable. Look at the difference in these three variables, all with the same mean, median, and range.

The observations in *var1* (Figure 2.22) are clustered near the mean, median, and mode, and are symmetrically spread out around the central value. There are no observations near the mean or median in *var2* (Figure 2.23), nor is there a clear single mode, although 12 is slightly more frequent than 2. Where the observations in *var1* are clustered near the centre, the observations in *var2* are clustered at the extremes. When a variable's scores have two or more clusters as we see in *var2*, the mean and the median have little value as measures of central tendency. The *expected value* is certainly not the centre. In effect, there are two expected values, one at either extreme. The observations in *var3* (Figure 2.24), like those in *var1*, have a mean, 1 median, and mode all of 7.0. And like those observations in *var1*, those of *var3* also have a range of 10. The observations

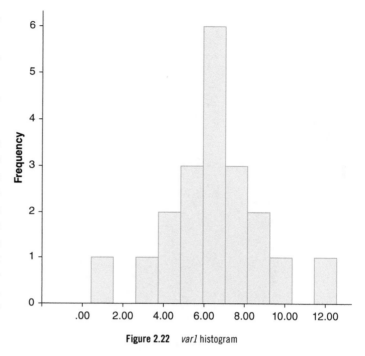

Figure 2.22 *var1* histogram

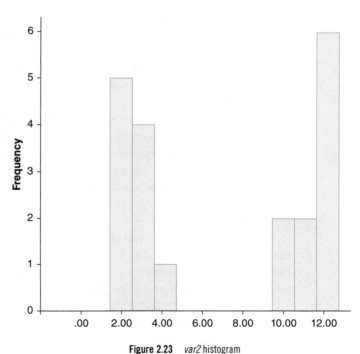

Figure 2.23 *var2* histogram

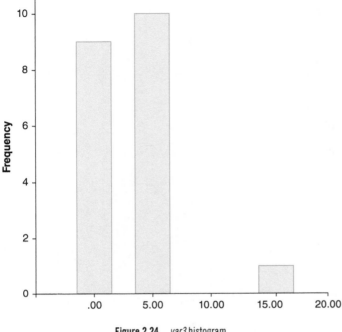

Figure 2.24 *var3* histogram

in *var3*, however, are clustered at the low end of the range, with the single exception at the highest value.

Although the centre and spread of *var1* is what we typically assume to be the case, *var2* and *var3* illustrate that it is important to examine how the observations are clustered in order to avoid misinterpretation. *var3* illustrates the effect of a single extreme value. Remember, all three variables have a mean of 7.0 and a range of 10. Despite this equivalence in these measures of central tendency, the distribution of the observed values in these three variables differs greatly. In this case, using only the mean and range to describe the data fails to adequately summarize the three variables and leads to erroneous comparative conclusions. For example, if these were quiz marks from three sections of a class, using only the

mean and the range to describe the performance of the three sections leads to the conclusion that the three sections performed similarly. Clearly, this is not the case. Is it this sort of dilemma which drove Mark Twain and Benjamin Disraeli to say that there were 'lies, damned lies, and statistics'?

To avoid some of the problems associated with clustering differences and extreme scores, some researchers report the *inter-quartile range* (IQR) when describing their data. The IQR range can be computed by segmenting the rank-ordered values into quartiles. This is done by determining the median of the scores and then determining a median for the upper and lower halves of the rank-ordered scores. This divides the scores into four equal segments or *quartiles*. (Note: SPSS uses a different procedure for determining the quartile cut-offs. This can result in slightly different values at times.) Once this is done, the median of the lower half is subtracted from the median of the upper half to produce the inter-quartile range: $IQR = Q_3 - Q_1$. Half of the observations will fall between the median of the lower half and the median of the upper half. Returning to our three variables used for examining the overall range, it is clear how the IQR helps to differentiate the three sets of observations.

If you entered the data into SPSS, you can return to the *Data Editor* window, select *Analyze*, then *Descriptive Statistics*, and finally *Frequencies*. From the *Statistics* menu click the box in the upper left-hand corner next to *Quartiles* (Figure 2.25). This will add the values associated with the 25th, 50th, and 75th percentiles for each variable to the output (Figure 2.26). The value associated with the 50th percentile is the median; the value associated with the 25th percentile (Q_1) is the median of the lower half; and the value associated with the 75th percentile (Q_3) is the median of the upper half.

For *var1*, the values associated with the 75th and 25th percentiles are 8.0 and 6.0, respectively, and the IQR is 8.0 – 6.0 = 2.0. For *var2*, the values associated with the 75th and 25th percentiles are 12.0 and 2.25, respectively, and the IQR is 9.75. For *var3*, the values associated with the 75th and the 25th percentiles are 7.0 and 6.0, respectively, and the IQR is 1.0. Remember, 50% of the scores will always fall within the IQR. With respect to the three variables, the IQRs indicate that the observations in *var2* have the greatest spread of the three and those of *var3* are spread out the least. Looking at the histograms again, the IQRs correspond better with the data than do the three overall ranges. Of course, the IQR does not indicate the spread of the observations beyond the middle two quartiles. Nor does it specify how the observations are spread out within the middle two quartiles.

In addition to being a descriptive statistic of spread, the IQR is used to construct another pictorial representation of data: the box-and-whisker plot (Tukey, 1977). Box-and-whisker plots are graphic representations of a variable's centre, IQR, and range. Box-and-whisker plots are often used to graphically compare the distributions of two or more variables. Figure 2.27 depicts the box-and-whisker plots for *var1*, *var2*, and *var3*.

The *y*-axis is scaled in the units of measurement used to record the variables depicted in the graph. If multiple variables

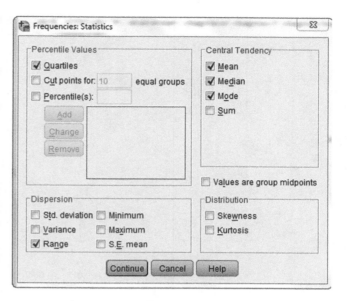

Figure 2.25

Statistics

		var1	var2	var3
N	Valid	20	20	20
	Missing	0	0	0
Mean		7.0000	7.0000	7.0000
Median		7.0000	7.0000	7.0000
Mode		7.00	12.00	7.00
Range		10.00	10.00	10.00
Percentiles	25	6.0000	2.2500	6.0000
	50	7.0000	7.0000	7.0000
	75	8.0000	12.0000	7.0000

Figure 2.26

are depicted in a single graph, they must be recorded using the same scale of measurement (e.g., the number of correct items on a quiz). The bottom of each rectangular box represents the 25th percentile. The top of each box represents the 75th percentile. The horizontal line inside a box denotes the median. The whiskers extend as far above and as far below the box to the highest and lowest score within 1.5 IQRs from the median.

Any scores beyond the 1.5 IQRs above or below the median are represented by dots or special characters. The dot above the whisker in *var1* represents the score of 12. The '20' next to it identifies it as case (row) 20 for *var1* in the *Data Editor*. The star above the whisker in *var3* represents the score of 16. The '20' next to it again identifies it as case (row) 20 for *var3* in the

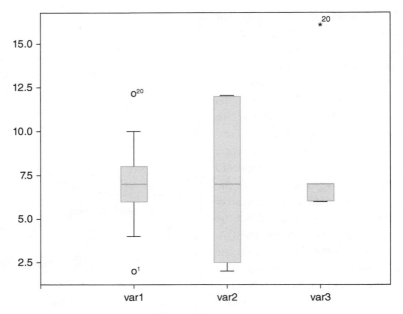

Figure 2.27   Box-and-whisker plots for *var1*, *var2*, and *var3*

Data Editor. The nearly complete (virtually invisible) lack of whiskers for *var2* and *var3* reflects the constricted clustering of the observations.

To create the box-and-whisker plots for *var1*, *var2*, and *var3* select the *Graphs* category in the *Data Editor*, cursor down to the *Legacy Dialogs* and then move over and down to the *Boxplot* option. Because we are summarizing more than one variable, select the *Summaries of separate variables* button when the *Boxplot* window appears (Figure 2.28) and click *Define*. In the *Define Simple Boxplot* window highlight and move the three variables over to the *Boxes Represent* area (Figure 2.29) and click *OK*. The box-and-whisker plots will appear in the output window.

━━━━━━━━━━ REVIEW QUESTION ━━━━━━━━━━

In *var2* there are no scores above the IQR. The whisker is equal to the top of the box. Why? Why are there no whiskers on the box for *var3*?

Web Link 2.8 for an answer to the review question.

Variance and standard deviation

For measurement data, the most common measure of central tendency is the mean. When the mean is used, the most common measure of spread reported by researchers is the *variance*. Like the range and IQR, the variance is a single value that indicates something about how the observations are spread out. It is not directly based on the span of the observations, which only involves two values. Rather, it is based on each observation's relation to the mean. It is the *average squared distance* or deviation of a set of scores from their mean. Remember, a mean is the value that minimizes those squared distances, so using those squared distances as a measure of spread should not be a surprise. The formula for the sample variance is

$$s^2 = \frac{\sum(y - \bar{y})^2}{n-1} = \frac{\text{sum of squared deviations}}{\text{degree of freedom}}.$$

When $n - 1$ is in the denominator, rather than n, variance is being used as an inferential statistic. That is, it is employed as an estimate of the population variance, σ^2. When variance is an inferential statistic, because $\bar{y}$ is only an estimate of μ, we need to subtract 1 from the number of observations.

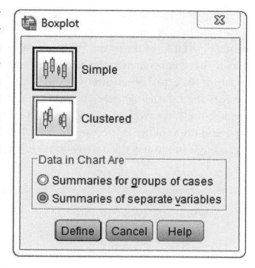

Figure 2.28

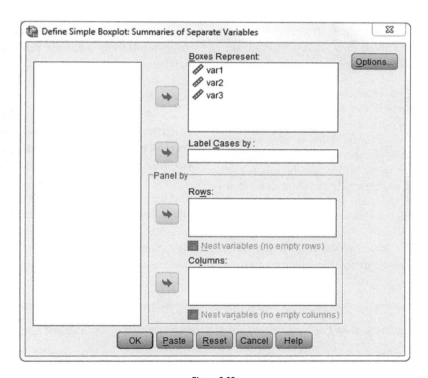

Figure 2.29

Using the mean and variance to summarize a set of observations results in the following understanding. If an observation (observed score) is randomly selected from a given sample, we would *expect* it to be the mean. We intuitively know, however, that the chance of randomly selecting a score that is equivalent to the mean is extremely small. In fact, a sample's mean may not correspond to any of the actual observations in the sample. How wrong will our expectation be? In other words, what is the *expected difference* between the mean and any randomly observed score? In terms of squared units, on average, we will *expect* to err by the value of the variance. The mean is the *expected score* and the variance is the *expected error*. This is most applicable for those cases where the variable has a single mode and the observations are roughly symmetrically distributed about the mean.

REVIEW QUESTIONS

1   Why are the variances of the following two sets of scores the same?

Set A: 1, 2, 3.
Set B: 101,102,103.

2   Can you create a data set of five observations that has a mean of 3 and a variance of 4?

Web Link 2.9 for the answers to the two review questions.

The greater the variance, the greater the spread in the scores about their mean. It is this last element – *about their mean* – that makes the variance different from the range and IQR. Variance creates a link between the measure of central tendency and spread. If you entered *var1*, *var2*, and *var3* into SPSS, return to the *Data Editor* window.

> Note that the variances in *var1* and *var3* are identical, despite the fact that the spread of the scores is very different. This points to the limitations of variance. That is, the variances are most safely comparable when the variables have a single mode and when the observations are roughly symmetrically distributed about the means. Despite such limitations, variance is a crucial element in most forms of statistical analysis.

Select *Analyze*, then *Descriptive Statistics*, and then *Frequencies*. From the *Statistics* menu select *Std. deviation* and *Variance* in the *Dispersion* box.

In the output for *var1*, *var2*, and *var3*, we find that the variances are 4.737, 20.947, and 4.737, respectively (Figure 2.30). Why is the variance of *var2* so much greater than the variance of the other two variables? Look back at the histograms. It is because most of the scores in *var2* are clustered further from their mean than are the scores in the other two variables.

REVIEW QUESTION

How is it possible that *var1* and *var3* can look so different in terms of their spread and have the same variance?

Web Link 2.10 for an answer to the review question.

The formula for the true population variance is

$$\sigma^2 = \frac{\Sigma(y - \mu)^2}{N},$$

where N is the number of observations that comprise the population of interest. Because variance is computed in squared units, it is difficult to picture it as a measure of spread. Variance does have important advantages, but transparency is not one of them. For this reason, particularly for descriptive purposes, variance is often converted into *standard deviation*.

By taking the square root of variance we return to the initial units of measurement. Thus the sample standard deviation is given by

Statistics

		var1	var2	var3
N	Valid	20	20	20
	Missing	0	0	0
Mean		7.0000	7.0000	7.0000
Median		7.0000	7.0000	7.0000
Mode		7.00	12.00	7.00
Std. Deviation		2.17643	4.57683	2.17643
Variance		4.737	20.947	4.737
Skewness		.000	.015	4.084
Std. Error of Skewness		.512	.512	.512
Kurtosis		1.232	-2.114	17.613
Std. Error of Kurtosis		.992	.992	.992

Figure 2.30

$$\sqrt{s^2} = s = \sqrt{\frac{\Sigma(y - \bar{y})^2}{n-1}}.$$

The corresponding formula for true population standard deviation is

$$\sqrt{\sigma^2} = \sigma = \sqrt{\frac{\Sigma(y - \mu)^2}{N}},$$

where N is the number of observations that comprise the population of interest.

The standard deviations of *var1*, *var2*, and *var3* are 2.18, 4.58, and 2.18, respectively. These values inform us that if we randomly select observations from *var1* and use their mean (7.0) to blindly guess the observations' values, on average we would be wrong by approximately 2.18 quiz items. The same is true for *var3*. With respect to *var2*, we would be wrong on average by 4.58 items.

It is not easy to understand what a variance of 143.36 means with respect to the height of the nine characters shown in Figure 2.31 (1 inch equals 2.54 cm). Variance is in squared units of measurement: squared seconds, squared dollars, the squared number of correct answers on an exam, etc.

| 77 | 67 | 54 | 46 | 68 | 64 | 62 | 38 | 56 | **Height (inches)** |

Figure 2.31

It may be asked why we square the difference between the mean and the scores in the first place, if subsequently the results will be unsquared. First, because the mean cuts the total value of the sample in half, half of the total value will be positive and half will be negative. Thus, the total difference between the mean and the individual observations will always be zero. This can be rectified, of course, by calculating the absolute value of the differences. Will this result in the same value as first squaring the deviations and then taking the square root? No, it will almost always be different. Furthermore, as we will see, by first squaring the deviations, our measure of spread gains an important quality.

Web Link 2.11 for a discussion regarding the difference between the squared and the absolute deviations.

The effect of a single score on variance

Like the mean, variance is not a *resistant* statistic and is sensitive to extreme scores. To examine this sensitivity we will explore the set of 19 scores from the hypothetical 10-item multiple-choice quiz which we first encountered in Section 2.5:

1, 2, 3, 3, 4, 4, 4, 5, 5, 5, 5, 5, 6, 6, 6, 7, 7, 8, 9.

If you wish, open the SPSS *Data Editor* window and enter the scores. First calculate the mean, median, standard deviation, and variance with the data as given. Then calculate those statistics three more times: after changing the 9 first to a 10; after changing it to a 20; and finally, after changing it to 100. Notice that there are no changes in the median. Note also the dramatic increase in variance (from 4.00, to 4.50, to 15.26, to 480.29). Because the mean and the variance are sensitive to extreme scores, vigilance is required to ensure that such scores do not unduly influence our analyses and conclusions. Regarding the fourth data set, do you think that stating that it has a mean of 9.79 and a variance of 480.29 is a fair description? Are the scores in the fourth version of the data set really that different from those in the first? Your answer in both cases should be *no*.

Besides being extreme, researchers worry that such scores may be erroneous. Perhaps there was a mistake recording the score or some special circumstance existed that produced the score, a special circumstance with which the researcher is unconcerned. Stated differently, perhaps the observation does not arise from the same population as do the other scores. Researchers certainly do not want recording errors or special circumstances to unduly influence the outcome of their research. When scores are found to be too extreme it is standard practice either to eliminate them or to transform them.

• • • • •

Imagine you are recording the speed with which a sample of 10 university students can name primary colours that flash onto a computer screen. We would normally expect that students will be able to do so in less than half a second. Now imagine that unbeknown to you one of the students is not a native English speaker. Having to name the colours in English rather than in his or her mother tongue may slow that person down substantially. As a consequence, the mean and variance of your sample of 10 students will be greater than it would be without the non-native English speaker. This is a simple example where one observation originates from a different population and reflects a circumstance that we were not interested in exploring (e.g., differences in mother tongue). The term 'different population' does not refer to a geographical location. A *different population* refers to observations that have a *different μ* from the population from which you believe you are sampling. In this case, you assume that you are sampling native English speakers.

The first question that needs answering is: when is a score too extreme? This question needs to be answered before data are collected. It is *not* appropriate to establish the criterion after viewing the data. Typically, researchers use a distance of either three or four standard deviations from the mean as the criterion. Unless stated otherwise, throughout this book we use four standard deviations as the cut-off. That is, if an observation is more than four standard deviations above or below its mean, it will be considered too extreme, an *outlier*. This can be tested by subtracting the mean from any questionable score and then dividing the difference by the sample's standard deviation. If we examine the four versions of the above data set,

1, 2, 3, 3, 4, 4, 4, 5, 5, 5, 5, 5, 6, 6, 6, 7, 7, 8, 9,(10, 20, 100),

we find that only in the final version, where the highest score is 100, do we find an outlier:

$$\frac{100 - 9.79}{21.92} = 4.23.$$

Because 4.23 is greater than 4.0, we conclude that a score of 100 is an outlier in this sample and it must be either deleted or transformed. If we test the largest value (20) in the third version of the data set, we find that the 20 is not an outlier,

$$\frac{20 - 5.58}{3.88} = 3.70.$$

Remember, scores in themselves are not outliers. They are only outliers – too large or too small – for a given sample with a particular mean and standard deviation.

The second question which needs to be answered is: what should be done with an outlier? The first, and perhaps the most common, strategy is to simply delete the outlier from the sample. After doing so, the descriptive statistics must be recalculated. In the example above, once we have removed the 100 from the fourth version of the sample, the new mean, variance, and standard deviation are 4.78, 3.24, and 1.80, respectively. This is a great change from the mean and standard deviation of 9.79 and 480.29 when the 100 was included in the sample. Note that the median and mode continue to remain unchanged: 5.00 and 5.00. The outlier's effect is on the mean and variance. This strategy of removing an observation is not always the most desirable, especially with small sample sizes.

Another common strategy is to 'winsorize' the observation. Winsorizing (a process named after the biostatistician C. P. Winsor) recodes the outlier to the nearest acceptable higher or lower value (Hastings et al., 1947). In our current working example, we calculate the winsorized score using the original mean and standard deviation. The highest acceptable score is four standard deviations ($21.92 \times 4 = 87.68$) above the mean (9.79). The new winsorized score (9.79 + 87.68) is 97.47 (rounded to 97), which is not that different from the original score of 100. Again a new mean, variance, and standard deviation must be calculated. In this case they become 9.63, 450.69, and 21.23, respectively.

━━━━━━━━━━━ REVIEW QUESTION ━━━━━━━━━━━

What would be the new mean and variance had we winsorized the score of 100 to three standard deviations above the mean rather than to four?

🐭 Web Link 2.12 for the answer to the review question.

The choice of strategy for addressing outliers can make a big difference to the findings. In our example, when we chose the strategy of deleting the outlier, the descriptive statistics were much closer to the original statistics when the highest score was 9 than they were when the highest score was 100. On the other hand, after winsorizing, the statistics were not greatly different from those produced when the outlier was included. The choice of criterion for identifying outliers also makes a difference in the results of analyses discussed in Parts II and III of this book.

Sampling distribution of the mean

Not only is there variance in observations or scores, there is also variance in statistics that summarize observations. Recall that statistics, such as the mean, are used as estimates of population parameters. As a consequence, there will be sample-to-sample differences in those estimates. Imagine randomly sampling the accumulated debt of 100 students graduating from your university this year. Now imagine taking another random sample of 100 students, again from this year. It is extremely unlikely that the means of the two samples will be the same. Therefore a mean, variance, and standard deviation of the means can be computed. Conceptually, with a very large number of sample means all drawn from the same population, the formulae for the mean of the means, the variance of the means, and the standard deviation of the means are straightforward. These formulae assume that sample size is held constant. The mean of the means is

$$u_{\bar{y}} = \frac{\Sigma \bar{y}}{k},$$

where k is the number of samples, which theoretically could be infinite. The variance of the means is

$$\sigma_{\bar{y}}^2 = \frac{\Sigma(\bar{y} - \mu)^2}{k}$$

and the standard deviation of the means is

$$\sigma_{\bar{y}} = \sqrt{\frac{\Sigma(\bar{y}-\mu)^2}{k}} \ .$$

It can be demonstrated that with only one sample mean the variance of the mean, referred to as the sampling distribution of the mean, and the standard deviation of the mean, referred to as the standard error of the mean, can easily be estimated. The sampling distribution of the mean is

$$\sigma_{\bar{y}}^2 = \frac{s^2}{n},$$

where s^2 is the variance of the sample's observations and n is the sample size; the standard error of the mean is

$$\sigma_{\bar{y}} = \frac{s}{\sqrt{n}},$$

where s is the standard deviation of the sample's observations.

These 'statistics of statistics' are central to almost all inferential tests which will be presented in Parts II and III of this book. The reason for the change in terminology is context. While *variance* and *standard deviation* indicate that the statistics refer to observations, *sampling distribution* and *standard error* indicate that the statistics refer to statistics.

 ## WHAT CREATES VARIANCE?

The answer to this question is one key to understanding research design and statistical testing. Why is there variance? There is variance because people, animals, plants – all members of any class of things – differ. No two people are exactly the same. But that simply begs the question, why do they differ? From the perspective of research and statistical analysis the answer requires a bit of a digression.

Anything you wish to study is a variable, either a dependent or a criterion variable. Memory is an example. If you test the memories of a group of people, you will find that they vary. There will be a mean and a variance in the memory scores. Like any activity, memory performance will be influenced by an unknown number of other variables. Some of these will have a positive effect on a person's memory and some will have a negative effect. Those with more positive effects than negative effects will be above the average performance and those with more negative effects will be below the average performance. The greater the preponderance of positive effects, the further above average the subject's memory performance. The greater the preponderance of negative effects, the further below average the subject's memory performance. Memory for a list of words may be influenced by such factors as the person's familiarity with the words, the time spent studying the words, as well as a host of other factors such as how much sleep they had the night before, their memorization strategy, and how much coffee they have consumed. There is a host of influences of which you are unaware.

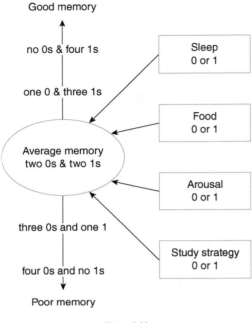

Figure 2.32

Let us assume that variable y (memory test score) is influenced by four factors: x_1 (sleep), x_2 (food), x_3 (arousal), and x_4 (study strategy). Insufficient sleep and nutrition negatively affect memory performance. Being unmotivated or being overly anxious (arousal level) also negatively affect memory performance. Finally, having a strategy other than simply using rote memory to study improves memory performance. Assume that each of the four factors can only take the value of either 0 or 1. The 0 represents the negative effect of the factor and the 1 the positive effect. This hypothetical model of memory performance is depicted in Figure 2.32.

Someone may have the following pattern of 0s and 1s: $x_1 = 0$, $x_2 = 1$, $x_3 = 1$, and $x_4 = 1$. The total of the person's 1s and 0s is 3. Another person may have two 1s and two 0s and thus a total of 2. Yet another person, albeit someone very unlucky, may have no 1s and four 0s (assume that it is the 1 that improves memory).

This person would have a total of 0. The individual totals are the memory scores that we observe. Our group's observed scores will range from 0 to 4. Of course there are many more factors than four which affect performance on a memory test, and not all are either a 0 or a 1. The more factors that are affecting the memories, the greater the range of scores and the greater the variance. If in the current four-factor model you hold one of those four factors constant at 0, however, then the scores will only range from 0 to 3, and the resulting variance will be reduced.

One important goal of experimental control mentioned in the previous chapter is to hold constant as many of the sources of variance as possible, and to reduce the variance in the observed scores. Reducing the variance is important when researchers are evaluating the reliability of the observed differences or the associations. In this regard, variance is a key factor for answering a key question posed in Chapter 1: what is expected due to chance alone?

Web Link 2.13 for an interactive demonstration concerning the source of variance based on the logic of Figure 2.32.

Skewness and kurtosis

Two other descriptive statistics associated with spread are *skewness* and *kurtosis*.

Skewness indicates how symmetrical the observations are about their mean. A value of 0 indicates that the spread of the observations is perfectly symmetrical about their mean. Negative values indicate that the observations below the mean stretch out further than do the observations above the mean. Positive skewness values indicate the opposite. One easy estimate of skewness allows for some conceptual understanding of the measure:

$$\text{skewness} = 3\,\frac{\text{sample mean} - \text{sample median}}{\text{sample standard deviation}}.$$

Remember that when the distribution is symmetrical, the mean and median will be the same value. Looking at the above formula, it can be seen that if the sample standard deviation is held constant, then the greater the difference between the sample mean and the sample median, the greater the skewness. It can also be seen that if the difference between the sample mean and the sample median is held constant, then the smaller the sample standard deviation, the greater the skewness.

It is misleading to speak of the 'average' or 'per capita' income or wealth in most societies today. As this fictional distribution in Figure 2.33 illustrates, income is markedly skewed. A few people have much of the wealth and many people have little of the wealth. Such skewness is disclosed by many economic, social, political, and cultural indices. When describing such indices, it is important to be specific about which 'average' is being reported. When data are substantially skewed, it is always best to report all three measures of central tendency.

Kurtosis   tells us how clustered or how flat is a set of scores. A kurtosis value of 0 indicates that the observations are mesokurtic, neither overly clustered nor overly flat. Negative values indicate that the spread of the observations is relatively flat. Positive kurtosis values mean that the spread of the observations is clustered and very pointy. The larger the absolute values of skewness and kurtosis, the greater the degree of skewness and kurtosis.

Skewness and kurtosis are related to the famous *normal distribution* (skewness = 0 and kurtosis = 0), a topic dealt with in more detail in the next chapter. At this point, let us simply say that a *normal distribution* is one that is unimodal (the mean, median, and mode are all the same value), it is symmetrical, and it is neither overly flat (platykurtic) nor overly clustered (leptokurtic). It is the normal distribution that is often assumed for using parametric statistics. Nonparametric statistics make no such assumptions about the distribution of the scores.

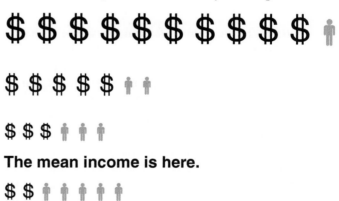

The mean income is here.

The median income is here.

The model income is here.

Figure 2.33

Kurtosis as defined originally by Karl Pearson is a measure of the frequency of extreme deviations from the mean and the standard normal distribution would have a kurtosis of 3. It is common practice now to subtract 3 from Pearson's measure, giving the standard normal distribution a kurtosis of 0.

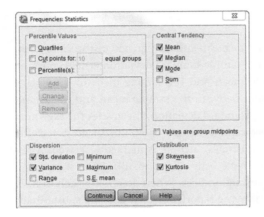

Figure 2.34

Statistics

		var1	var2	var3
N	Valid	20	20	20
	Missing	0	0	0
Mean		7.0000	7.0000	7.0000
Median		7.0000	7.0000	7.0000
Mode		7.00	12.00	7.00
Std. Deviation		2.17643	4.57683	2.17643
Variance		4.737	20.947	4.737
Skewness		.000	.015	4.084
Std. Error of Skewness		.512	.512	.512
Kurtosis		1.232	-2.114	17.613
Std. Error of Kurtosis		.992	.992	.992

Figure 2.35

Return to the *Data Editor* window where we have entered the data for *var1*, *var2*, and *var3*. Again select *Analyze*, then *Descriptive Statistics*, and then *Frequencies*. In addition to the previous choices, from the *Statistics* menu, select *Skewness* and *Kurtosis* (Figure 2.34).

The output window (Figure 2.35) reveals that *var1* has a skewness of 0.0. Inspecting the observations in *var1*, we see that they are symmetrical about the mean. *var2* has a slight positive skewness: 0.015. Finally, *var3* is considerably skewed: 4.084. The positive kurtosis for *var1* (1.232) indicates that the observations in *var1* are somewhat flat. *var2* (−2.114) is somewhat clustered. Finally, *var3* is substantially clustered (17.613). How important are the deviations from 0 and when are they important? We will address these questions in a later chapter. There are rules of thumb for the severity of skewness and kurtosis. Notice in the SPSS output that along with *Skewness* and *Kurtosis* there are their *standard errors*: *Std. Error of Skewness* and *Kurtosis*. These standard errors are a type of variance, the *expected variances* in the statistics themselves. More pertinent is the fact that these standard errors represent the variability in these statistics that is *expected due to chance alone*. According to one rule of thumb, if you divide the statistic (skewness or kurtosis) by its standard error you can evaluate the severity. A rule of thumb is that if the quotient is greater than ±1.96, then the key assumption for *parametric* tests is called into question. Figure 2.36 presents the results of the evaluations of skewness and kurtosis for the three variables. The skewness in *var3* and the kurtosis in *var2* and *var3* are problematic.

As will be seen in the last few sections of Chapter 3, 1.96 is an important and almost magical number. Many other numbers used for evaluating statistics are derived from it.

	Variable	Statistic	Std. Error	Quotient
Skewness				
	Var1	0.000	0.512	0.00
	Var2	0.015	0.512	0.03
	Var3	4.084	0.512	7.98
Kurtosis				
	Var1	1.232	0.992	1.24
	Var2	−2.114	0.992	−2.13
	Var3	17.613	0.992	17.76

Figure 2.36

An outlier can be, at least in part, responsible for a variable's skewness by creating a tail at one end of the distribution. Addressing the outlier often reduces any problem regarding skewness. Earlier in the chapter we saw how a single score can greatly influence a sample's mean and variance. Returning to the data depicted in the histogram (Figure 2.37) and calculating the mean, variance, skewness, and kurtosis with and without the highest observation (16) makes clear the potential impact of a single observation on skewness and kurtosis.

Simply removing the single observation changes the mean from 7.00 to 6.53; it changes the variance from 4.74 to 0.26; it changes the skewness from 4.08 to –0.12; and it changes the kurtosis from 17.61 to –2.24. Not only are there quantitative changes in the skewness and the kurtosis,

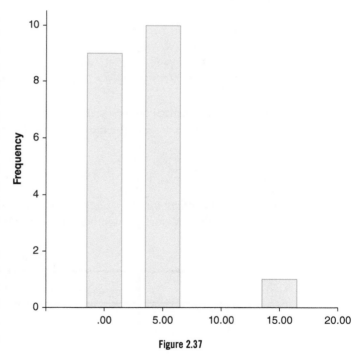

Figure 2.37

but in some cases changes in kind. The skewness went from being positive to negative and the kurtosis went from being clustered to being nearly flat.

MEASURES OF CENTRAL TENDENCY: CATEGORICAL DATA

Nominal data

For nominal data, where numbers are merely names, the calculation of means and medians makes little sense. If we can change all of the 3s to 1s, change the 1s to 2s, and change the 2s to 3s, what sense does it make to sum all of the 1s, 2s, and 3s and calculate a mean or median? For example, imagine that you are examining the students' choices of beverage in your class. You assign all of those students choosing coffee a score of 1; you assign all of those choosing tea a 2; and you assign all of those choosing juice a 3. Then you find that 10 students chose coffee, 15 chose tea, and 5 chose juice. You might wish to enter these 30 observations into the SPSS *Data Editor* window and run the descriptive statistics of mean and median. If we calculate the mean and median, we find that they are 1.83 and 2.00, respectively. If, however, you recoded the 5 juices as 1, the 10 coffees as 2, and the 15 teas as 3, you find a mean of 2.33 and a median of 2.5. The median goes from being in the tea range to being between tea and coffee.

Furthermore, because both the numbers (names) and their rank ordering are arbitrary, it makes no sense to calculate the usual measures of spread such as range and variance. Imagine what would happen not only to the mean and median but also to the range and variance if we decided to name the choice of juice '100'. Would the spread in the choice of beverage really change?

> Will the real mean and median choice of beverage please stand up? Do we really wish to say that the mean choice of beverage is either 1.83 or 2.33 and that the median choice is either 2.00 or 2.50?

The mode, as an indicator of the most common category of response, does have a role to play in summarizing nominal observations. In this context, however, the mode is not a measure of central tendency; it is simply an indicator of the most common observation. In the beverage example, tea was the most frequently chosen beverage.

Ordinal data

For ordinal data, where numbers represent a rank ordering of categories, both the mode and the median are useful measures. The mode again reveals the most common category. The numbers

VAR00001

		Frequency	Percent	Valid Percent	Cumulative Percent
Valid	1.00	5	10.0	10.0	10.0
	2.00	17	34.0	34.0	44.0
	3.00	10	20.0	20.0	64.0
	4.00	13	26.0	26.0	90.0
	5.00	5	10.0	10.0	100.0
	Total	50	100.0	100.0	

Figure 2.38

as names of categories are still arbitrary, but because in an ordinal scale their ordering from smallest to largest is not arbitrary, the median can be useful. The median indicates where in the rank ordering of the observations the middle is to be found. For example, an employer records the level of education of his or her employees and finds that 10% have not completed high school, 34% have completed high school, 20% spent some time at university, 26% have completed university, and 10% have completed at least one postgraduate programme. The most common category of level of education, or the mode, of the employees is 'completed high school'. Because the median divides the observations in half (the 50th percentile), the median would be the category 'spent some time at university'.

Let us enter the following 50 observations into the SPSS *Data Editor* reflecting the above information, where the coding for not completing high school, completing high school, some university, completed university, and completed postgraduate programme is 1, 2, 3, 4, and 5, respectively (the data are rank-ordered for ease of entry and analysis):

1, 1, 1, 1, 1, 2, 2, 2, 2, 2, 2, 2, 2, 2, 2, 2, 2, 2, 2, 2,
2, 2, 3, 3, 3, 3, 3, 3, 3, 3, 3, 4, 4, 4, 4, 4, 4, 4, 4,
4, 4, 4, 4, 4, 5, 5, 5, 5, 5.

Statistics

VAR00001

N	Valid	50
	Missing	0
Median		3.0000
Mode		2.00

Figure 2.39

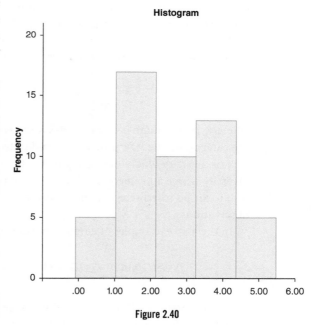

Figure 2.40

Be sure that the *Display Frequency Tables* option is selected along with the statistical options of median and mode. The results in Figures 2.38–2.40 confirm that the mode is category 2 (completed high school) and that the median is category 3 (some university). That is, although the most common level of education is *completed high school*, at least half of the employees had at least some university education.

2.9 MEASURES OF SPREAD: CATEGORICAL DATA

Because both nominal and categorical data have neither equal intervals between categories nor a true zero, the usual measures of spread have little relevance. There have been, however, many attempts to develop single-number indices of *spread* for categorical data. Many of these indices involve the relative predominance of the mode. Also, rather than being indices of distance or squared distance from a measure of central tendency, they are indices of the proportion of observations that differ from the mode, relative to the number of categories observed.

Perhaps the simplest measure of spread for nominal data is Freeman's (1965) *variation ratio* (VR). It is most frequently used when there are only two nominal categories, such as men and women. The variation ratio is

$$VR = 1 - \frac{fm}{N},$$

where *fm* is the frequency of the modal category and N is the total number of observations. Thus, if the modal category is 60 out of 100 observations, then $fm/N = 60/100 = 0.6$. The resulting $VR = 1 - 0.6 = 0.4$. The greater the VR, the more equally distributed are the observations. If the modal category in the previous example was 75 out of 100, then $VR = 1 - \frac{75}{100} = 1 - 0.75 = 0.25$, less equally distributed than the previous example.

Another useful index of spread for categorical data that is applicable for both nominal and ordinal scales is the *index of qualitative variation* (IQV):

$$IQV = K(100^2 - \Sigma pct^2)/\left\{100^2(K-1)\right\},$$

where K is the number of categories and Σpct^2 is the sum of the squared frequencies of all of the categories. The IQV provides a standardized value between 0 and 1: a 0 indicates a complete lack of diversity where one category totally dominates; a 1 indicates the maximum amount of diversity where all categories have the same frequency. When the IQV is multiplied by 100, the result can be interpreted as the percentage of the maximum possible diversity present in the observations.

In the above examples of employees' education level the researcher finds the following IQV:

$$IQV = 5\left((10,000) - \Sigma(10^2 + 34^2 + 20^2 + 26^2 + 10^2)\right)/(10,000 \times 4) = 0.946 = 94.6\%.$$

This means that 94.6% of the diversity possible in the observations is present. An examination of the data's histogram illustrates that although there is a clear mode, it certainly does not dominate the distribution of the observations.

━━━━━━━━━ CHALLENGE QUESTION ━━━━━━━━━

Would changing the numbers that label the categories in the above education-level example to 1, 3, 5, 7, and 9 change the median and IQV? If you think the change will alter the median and IQV, why and how? If you think the change will make no difference, why not?

🖰 Web Link 2.14 for an answer to the challenge question.

2 ● 10 UNBIASED ESTIMATORS

■■■■■■ • • • • • ■■■■■■

μ is the value to *expect* (best guess) when an observation is randomly selected from a population, and $\bar{y}$ is an estimation of μ. s^2, often called *error*, describes the *observed* unpredictability of the observations which are, at least initially, *due to chance alone*. The word 'initially' in the previous sentence captures the starting point for all forms of data analysis. Although it is unexplained, what is *due to chance alone* is not *unexplainable*. One way to understand empirical research is to frame it as an effort to explain some of the as yet unexplained: an attempt to reduce the *error* in our predictions. The reason for s^2 is not supernatural. s^2 has its sources, and the goal of research is to identify those sources.

In the above section on variance and standard deviation, $n - 1$ rather than n was used in the denominator to calculate the average sum of squared deviations or variance. Also, the mean and the standard deviation were both found to be sensitive to extreme scores or outliers. Although the mean and the variance are not *resistant* statistics, they are important when conducting a parametric analysis. The reason for their importance is that, unlike other measures of central tendency and spread, the sample mean ($\bar{y}$) and variance (s^2) – with $n - 1$ in the denominator – are unbiased estimators of their corresponding population parameters, μ and σ^2.

An unbiased estimator is a statistic whose expected value (E) is the true population parameter. An E is a type of mean. It is a mean of a statistic rather than a mean of individual observations. Furthermore, it is the mean of an infinite number of instances of a statistic or of all possible instances of a statistic. The sample size for these instances must be held constant.

Without going through the algebraic proof here, it may be worthwhile to illustrate in other ways the unbiased nature of the sample mean and variance. First, let us examine a very small population of three observations: 101, 102, and 103. Other authors, such as Howell (2002), have found this type of empirical example to be effective for illustrating the point. The μ of the population is (101 + 102 + 103)/3 = 102. The σ^2 of the population is $[(101 - 102)^2 + (102 - 102)^2 + (103 - 102)^2]/3 = (1 + 0 + 1)/3 = 0.67$. These are the true μ and true σ^2 of the small population. The first column of Figure 2.41 shows all possible randomly selected samples of two observations from the population in question. The second column reports the mean of each of those samples. The third column reports the variance as calculated with n in the denominator. The fourth column reports the sample variance with $n - 1$

Sample	$\bar{y}$	$s^2(n)$	$s^2(n-1)$
101,101	101.00	0.00	0.00
101,102	101.50	0.25	0.50
101,103	102.00	1.00	2.00
102,101	101.50	0.25	0.50
102,102	102.00	0.00	0.00
102,103	102.50	0.25	0.50
103,101	102.00	1.00	2.00
103,102	102.50	0.25	0.50
103,103	103.0	0.00	0.0
E =	102.0	0.33	0.67

Figure 2.41

in the denominator. The bottom row of the figure reports the expected values (E) for the sample mean and variance from both forms of calculation. In this case the expected value is the mean of all possible two-observation samples as reported in the table.

Note that the $E(\bar{y}) = \mu$: 102.0. Also note that the average s^2 with $n - 1$ in the denominator equals σ^2 (0.67), whereas the average s^2 with n in the denominator underestimates σ^2 (0.33). This does not mean that a sample variance with $n - 1$ in the denominator will always be closer to the population's true value. This systematic underestimate when n is used in the denominator is related to the fact that each sample mean minimizes the sum of squared deviations for each individual sample.

Any value (including μ) other than $\bar{y}$ results in a greater total of the squared deviations. If μ is known, why use a different estimate for each sample? In fact, we should not. Look at Figure 2.42. The first column of Figure 2.42 again enumerates all possible randomly selected two-observation samples from the population in question. The second column reports μ, which here is used to calculate all of the sample variances. The third column reports the variance for each sample as calculated with n in the denominator. The fourth column reports the sample variance with $n - 1$ in the denominator. Again, the bottom row of the figure reports the expected values (E) for the sample mean and variance from both forms of calculation. Not surprisingly, again $E(\bar{y}) = \mu$: 102.0. Now, however, the s^2 version with $n - 1$ in the denominator on average overestimates σ^2(1.33), whereas the s^2 version with n in the denominator now equals σ^2(0.67). These two figures illustrate that $n - 1$ in the denominator of sample variance is there to correct for the fact that we are estimating μ with $\bar{y}$. Should μ be known, there would be no need to make the correction.

Sample	μ	$s^2(n)$	$s^2(n-1)$
101,101	102.00	1.00	2.00
101,102	102.00	0.50	1.00
101,103	102.00	1.00	2.00
102,101	102.00	0.50	1.00
102,102	102.00	0.00	0.00
102,103	102.00	0.50	1.00
103,101	102.00	1.00	2.00
103,102	102.00	0.50	1.00
103,103	102.00	1.00	2.00
E =	102.00	0.67	1.33

Figure 2.42

====== CHALLENGE QUESTION ======

How does sample size affect the extent of bias when n rather than $n - 1$ is used in the denominator of the variance formula?

✎ Web link 2.15 for the answer to and discussion of the challenge question.

---

2 ● 11 PRACTICAL SPSS SUMMARY

We now return to the problems that were posed at the outset of this chapter. You were given hypothetical quiz scores from two sections of a statistics course. You were asked, if the scores were read to you, would you have a sense of how each section performed and how their performances compared?

Section 1: 7, 8, 5, 5, 9, 10, 2, 7, 6, 4, 8, 7, 8, 7, 3, 9, 6, 8, 6, 9, 8, 9, 5, 7, 6, 7, 6, 7, 9, 5, 5, 9, 7, 11, 7, 6, 4, 7, 8, 10.

Section 2: 6, 3, 6, 8, 5, 7, 6, 7, 8, 7, 8, 5, 5, 8, 7, 2, 7, 6, 4, 7, 7, 8, 5, 5, 8, 10, 1, 7, 6, 4, 8, 7, 2, 7, 3, 4, 6, 8, 10, 8.

You begin by summarizing and exploring each section's 40 scores separately. In many cases it is best to begin with frequency histograms.

Enter the data from the two variables into the SPSS *Data Editor* window, if you have not done so already. Temporarily switch to the *Variable View* (tab at lower left of screen) and ensure that the variables are listed as *Numeric* under *Type* and as *Scale* under *Measure* (Figure 2.43). The number of items correct on the quiz is an example of a ratio scale. SPSS does not differentiate ratio and interval scales. The term *Scale* under the heading *Type* is used for either ratio or interval data.

	Name	Type	Width	Decimals	Label	Values	Missing	Columns	Align	Measure	Role
1	section1	Numeric	8	2		None	None	8	Right	Scale	Input
2	section2	Numeric	8	2		None	None	8	Right	Scale	Input

Figure 2.43

After returning to the *Data Editor* window, select the *Frequencies* option from *Descriptive Statistics* under the *Analyze* menu. Highlight and move both variables over to the *Variable(s)* field (Figure 2.44). After opening the *Statistics* window, select the *Mean*, *Median*, and *Mode*

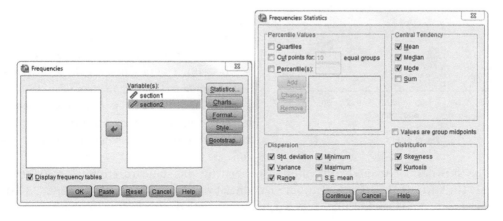

Figure 2.44

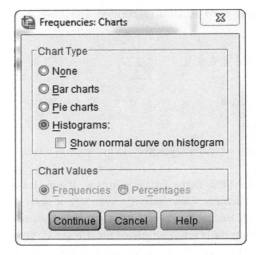

Figure 2.45

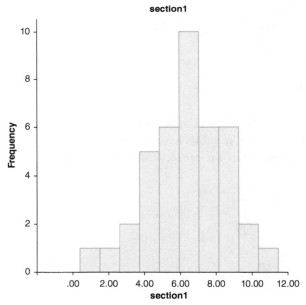

Figure 2.46

central tendency options. Also select the *Std. deviation*, *Variance*, *Range*, *Minimum*, and *Maximum* from the dispersion options. Finally, from the distribution area, select the *Skewness* and *Kurtosis* options.

Press *Continue* and return to the *Frequencies* window and open the *Charts* window. Select the *Histograms* chart type (Figure 2.45) and then *Continue*. When you return to the *Frequencies* window click *OK*.

Scroll down the output window and find the histograms. The histogram for *section1* clearly is unimodal (Figure 2.46) with most scores being clustered in the middle. It appears to be quite symmetrical. The histogram does not suggest the presence of any unusually low or high scores well beyond the others (possible outliers). The histogram for *section2* also is unimodal (Figure 2.47). Its distribution is less symmetrical than that of *section1*, however, and it appears to be negatively skewed. Like the *section1* histogram, the *section2* histogram does not suggest the presence of extreme scores or outliers.

This type of histogram is appropriate for the type of data in these two variables. When there are many possible scores (*x*-axis categories) and very few observations in any one score, binning is necessary. Frequency histograms are not very suitable when there are very few observations (e.g., less than 20). In such cases researchers rely solely on the descriptive statistics.

Next the descriptive statistics are examined (Figure 2.48). The fact that all three measures of central tendency (mean, median, and mode) are so similar indicates that *section1* is symmetrically distributed. Using four standard deviations as the criterion, the scores can be examined for outliers. None are found.

The skewness of *section1*'s distribution divided by the standard error is −0.303/0.374 = −0.81. The kurtosis of *section1*'s distribution divided by the standard error is 0.082/0.733 = 0.11. Because both values are less than 1.96, you may conclude that there is no problem with either of these measures.

The scores for *section2* had a mean of 6.15, a median of 7.00, and a mode of 7.00. The fact that the mean is somewhat lower that the median and the mode indicates that *section2*'s scores may be somewhat asymmetrically distributed. The skewness of *section2*'s distribution divided by the standard error is $-0.605/0.374 = -1.62$. The kurtosis of *section2*'s distribution divided by the standard error is $0.122/0.733 = 0.17$. The skewness for *section2* is greater than the corresponding values for *section1*, as initially suggested by the histograms. Because both values again are less than 1.96, you may conclude that there is no problem with either of these measures.

At the outset of Chapter 1 it was asked if 10 digits had been randomly sorted into two columns or groups. Here we are faced with a more concrete incarnation of that problem: has one group's performance been statistically different from the other? Imagine the two sections were given different textbooks from which to study. Did the difference in the textbook make a difference in performance? Some of the descriptive statistics suggest that there was no difference in performance: the medians, modes, and ranges are identical, and the variances and standard deviations are quite similar. The difference in the means (6.93 versus 6.15) and the fact that the minimum and maximum scores are higher in *section1* than in *section2* suggest a difference in performance. But of course, as we know from Chapter 1, these differences could be due to chance alone. The question is: how reliable are those differences? Can we conclude that textbook makes a difference?

To answer these inferential questions, we need procedures for determining the likelihood of observing such a difference (e.g., $6.93 - 6.15 = 0.78$). To answer such inferential questions, it is necessary to combine descriptive statistics with procedures for calculating probabilities, which is the focus of the next chapter.

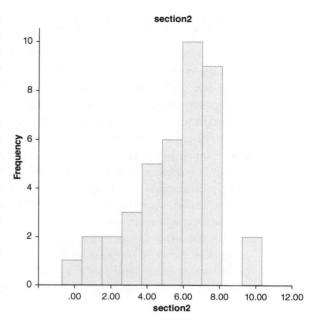

section2

Figure 2.47

Statistics

		section1	section2
N	Valid	40	40
	Missing	0	0
Mean		6.9250	6.1500
Median		7.0000	7.0000
Mode		7.00	7.00
Std. Deviation		1.95314	2.08228
Variance		3.815	4.336
Skewness		-.303	-.605
Std. Error of Skewness		.374	.374
Kurtosis		.082	.122
Std. Error of Kurtosis		.733	.733
Range		9.00	9.00
Minimum		2.00	1.00
Maximum		11.00	10.00

Figure 2.48

2 ● 12 CHAPTER SUMMARY

In this chapter the most common *univariate* graphs and statistics used to summarize both *measurement* and *categorical* data were examined. Measurement data include *interval* and *ratio* number scales; categorical data include *nominal* and *ordinal* scales. This chapter focused on the importance of descriptively examining data as a first step in the process of analysis. Various versions of the most important univariate graphic display, the *histogram*, were explored. The most common *descriptive statistics* were defined and compared. For measurement data, the *mean* and the *median* are two important *measures of central tendency*. For categorical data, the *mode* is the most common measure of central tendency. In terms of *measures of spread*, while *variance*, being an unbiased estimator, is central for measurement data, the *variation ratio* is the typical measure of spread for categorical data.

The importance of the shape of a variable's distribution was discussed and the need to examine the data for *outliers* was examined. The notions of *skewness* and *kurtosis*, indices of the symmetry and the flatness of a distribution respectively, were considered. Of particular note was the distorting effect of outliers and skewness on the mean and the variance. The material covered in this chapter provides half of the fundamentals for what is needed to understand the *inferential statistical* tests presented in Parts II and III of this book. The other half of the fundamentals is the topic of the next chapter: probability.

2 ● 13 RECOMMENDED READINGS

Phillips, J. L. (1999). *How to think about statistics* (6th ed.). New York: W. H. Freeman.
Chapters 1–4 provide a simple summary of the core material covered in this chapter.
Weisberg, H. F. (1992). *Central tendency and variability*. London: Sage.
Weisberg's book provides more detail about some of the descriptive statistics discussed in this
    chapter. He also covers some descriptive measures not presented in this chapter.
Wheelan, C. (2013). *Naked statistics: Stripping the dread from the data*. New York: W.W. Norton.
Wheelan provides a light-hearted approach to the material covered in this and subsequent
    chapters, along with examples from popular culture.
Holcomb, Z. C. (1998). *Fundamentals of descriptive statistics*. New York: Pyrczak Publishing.
This book is almost entirely dedicated to a detailed exposition of the graphs and statistics presented
    in this chapter. It elaborates on everything from graphs to *z*-scores, from means to outliers.

2 ● 14 CHAPTER REVIEW QUESTIONS

Multiple-choice questions

1   A researcher is interested in examining the voting behaviour of individuals in a small town. He
    contacted those eligible to vote to set up interviews with them. Of the people living in the town 7000 are
    eligible to vote. The researcher contacted 5000 of them; 5% of those contacted agreed to an interview
    with the researcher. What is the population?

a   Everyone in the small town
b   The 7000 eligible voters
c   The 5000 individuals contacted
d   The 250 individuals who were interviewed
e   None of the above

2   A researcher is interested in examining the voting behaviour of individuals in a small town. He contacted those eligible to vote to set up interviews with them. Of the people living in the town 7000 are eligible to vote. The researcher contacted 5000 of them; 5% of those contacted agreed to an interview with the researcher. What is the sample?

a   Everyone in the small town
b   The 7000 eligible voters
c   The 5000 individuals contacted
d   The 250 individuals who were interviewed
e   None of the above

3   During the interviews the researcher questions the interviewees about their income and how many times they had voted previously. Income is what type of variable?

a   Ratio and discrete
b   Nominal and discrete
c   Nominal and continuous
d   Interval and continuous
e   Categorical and discrete

4   During the interviews the researcher questions the interviewees about their income and how many times they had voted previously. Previous voting behaviour is what type of variable?

a   Ratio and discrete
b   Nominal and discrete
c   Nominal and continuous
d   Interval and continuous
e   Categorical and discrete

5   Counting the number of patients who are categorized into one of several diagnostic categories for the sake of comparison is an example of _____.

a   a continuous variable
b   a categorical data
c   measurement data
d   an ordinal scale
e   a leptokurtic scale

6   If we attached numbers to the labels for the disorders used in Question 2, those numbers would be an example of _____.

a   an ordinal scale
b   frequency data
c   a nominal scale
d   a ratio scale
e   a continuous variable

7 The _____ is more sensitive to outliers than is the _____.

   a   median; mean

   b   mode; median

   c   mode; mean

   d   a continuous variable; a discrete variable

   e   standard deviation; mode

8 The most common measure of central tendency for nominal data is the _____.

   a   median

   b   mean

   c   variance

   d   variation ratio

   e   mode

9 A common measure of spread for nominal and ordinal data is the _____.

   a   median

   b   standard error of the mean

   c   variance

   d   variation ratio

   e   mode

10 When a distribution is overly flat it is said to be _____.

   a   positively skewed

   b   negatively skewed

   c   leptokurtic

   d   platykurtic

   e   bimodal

11 When a distribution is positively skewed, the _____ will be greater than the _____.

   a   mean, median

   b   mode, median

   c   mean, variance

   d   mode, median

   e   None of the above

12 The sampling distribution of the mean indicates _____.

   a   how much variance there is in your data due to chance alone

   b   how much variance in your observed mean is due to chance alone

   c   how much variance you expect due to chance alone in means sampled from the same population

   d   how much variance you expect due to chance alone in observations sampled from the same population

   e   how much variance you expect due to chance alone in variances sampled from the same population

Short-answer questions

1 When could we use n rather than $n - 1$ in the denominator for sample variance? Why?

2 What is the difference between a frequency histogram and a relative frequency histogram?

3 When binning data is required for a histogram, what determines the number of bins?

4 What is the difference between a variance and a sampling distribution?
5 What causes variance?
6 What does it mean to say a statistic is resistant?
7 What does it mean to say a statistic is unbiased?
8 When will a single new observation added to a data set leave the mean unchanged?
9 What is the primary difference between parametric and nonparametric statistics?
10 Why is the mean not very informative when a distribution is bimodal?

Data set questions

1 With the following data, construct a frequency distribution table and a frequency histogram with bin widths of 10. Observations: 44, 46, 47, 49, 63, 64, 66, 68, 72, 72, 75, 76, 81, 84, 88.
2 With the data below, create a frequency histogram with five categories (bins) on the x-axis. Data: 24, 21, 2, 5, 8, 11, 13, 18, 17, 21, 20, 20, 12, 12, 10, 3, 6, 15, 11, 15, 25, 11, 14, 1, 6, 3, 10, 7, 19, 17, 18, 9, 18, 12, 15.
3 What are the mean, the variance, sampling distribution of the mean, and the standard error of the mean for the data in Question 2?
4 For the data in Question 2, are the skewness and kurtosis values a concern for the researcher who is assuming a normal distribution? (You will need SPSS to answer this question.)
5 Create a population of three numbers (e.g., 10, 11, 12). Then analyse *all* possible samples of two, including samples such as 10 and 10. For all samples calculate the variance using both n and $n-1$. Then repeat this analysis using the population mean for each calculation, rather than the individual sample means. In the two series of analyses, which formula (using n or $n-1$) produces an unbiased estimator and why?
6 Students are often asked to rate their professor, typically on a 1–5 scale, 1 being the lowest ranking and 5 being the highest. In an educational psychology class of 25 students, 3 gave their instructor a rating of 1, 4 students gave a rating of 2, 8 students gave a rating of 3, 7 students gave a rating of 4, and 3 students gave a rating of 5.
   (a) What are the mean and median ratings?
   (b) What are the variance and standard deviation of the ratings?
   (c) What might be a problem with computing the statistics in (a) and (b)?
   (d) What are alternative descriptive statistics for those in (a) and (b)?
7 A charity hired three groups of clowns (balloon-twisters, magicians, and jugglers) to perform at a fund-raising event. Figure 2.49 shows the number of clowns and the average amount of donations (per clown) raised by the three groups. The jugglers raised a total of $800.

Clown type	No. of clowns	Average $/clown
Balloon-twister	20	75
Magician	20	70
Juggler		80

Figure 2.49

   (a) How many clowns were there in total?
   (b) What was the total amount of donations raised by the three groups?
   (c) How much did the average clown raise?

8   Create two distributions with identical means, medians, and ranges. One distribution should be platykurtic and the other leptokuric.

9   There are three sections of quiz scores in your class. One has 10 students and a mean of 7. The second has 5 students and a mean of 9. The third has only 5 students and a mean of 5. What is the composite or grand mean of the 20 students?

10 If you took the three means in Question 9 (7, 9, and 5) and simply divided by 3 (the number of sections), how would that compare with the composite mean computed in Question 9. Why?

Don't forget to use the online resources! Meet your supporting stats tutor through an **introductory video**, review your maths skills with a **diagnostic pre-test**, explore statistical principles through **interactive simulations**, practice analysis techniques with **SPSS datasets**, and check your work with **answers to all in-text questions**.

https://study.sagepub.com/bors

3

Chapter contents

PROBABILITY

KEY CONCEPTS: rational and empirical approaches to probability, independence, mutually exclusive, the laws of probability, standard normal distribution, *z*-scores.

3 ● 1 PURPOSE

As stated at the end of the previous chapter, inferential statistics are based on combining descriptive statistics and probability theory. In this chapter the second part of that combination is explored. We begin with a description of the basic terminology and the two traditional approaches to probability: the *rational* and the *empirical*. To appreciate how probability is used inferentially it is necessary to understand the *laws* of probability. We discuss how the laws pertain to categorical data. *Bayes' rule* provides a way to apply these laws to everyday questions and problems. Next, the laws are transferred to continuous data through an examination of the *standard normal distribution*, *z-scores*, and *confidence intervals*. Finally, we apply our first inferential test by asking what the likelihood is that a particular observation is a member of a given population.

3 ● 2 INTRODUCTION

Which is the image of Chevalier de Méré and which is that of Blaise Pascal in Figure 3.1? What is the probability of guessing correctly?

Figure 3.1

Source: Blaise Pascal (1623–1672), artist unknown. Permission is granted to copy, distribute and/or modify this document under the terms of the GNU Free Documentation License, Version 1.2 or any later version published by the Free Software Foundation

Probability theory provides a description of the hidden structure that exists within an infinite or very large population of observations or *outcomes*. Stated another way, probability theory gives us a way of uncovering *order* within what appears to be the *chaos* of mere chance events. Actually, nothing is more ordered than mere chance. Probability is also a way of defining the boundaries between what *probably* is the result of mere chance and what *probably* is not. Thus, probability theory assists us in tentatively answering the question of whether or not the 10 digits at the outset of Chapter 1 were randomly sorted. It will also assist us in assessing the *reliability* of the difference in the quiz means we saw at the end of the previous chapter.

In the seventeenth century the well-known French gambler Chevalier de Méré inadvertently initiated an inquiry that produced what are today the basic laws of probability. De Méré made a living from rolling dice (Figure 3.2) and wagering on the outcome. It worked for a while, but after losing his shirt he sought help from Blaise Pascal – the famous mathematician, physicist, and theologian – and the rest is history.

Figure 3.2

Specifically, de Méré thought that the chance of rolling at least one 1 in four rolls of a single die was slightly better than 50%, and he was correct. When he bet on that outcome he won the wager more often than not. Thus, in the long run he made money. Once no one was willing to bet against that outcome any longer, he devised another game. He wagered that he could roll at least one pair of 1s (double 1s) within 24 rolls of a pair of dice. His analysis led him to conclude that the chance of this outcome was also slightly better than 50%. To his chagrin, he was wrong. He lost more often than not. Later in this chapter we will see why.

3 ● 3 APPROACHES TO PROBABILITY

Figure 3.3 summarizes key characteristics of the two main approaches to probability.

Approaches to probability

Approach	Source	Priority	Starting point
Rational	Logic	Reason trumps experience	Expected outcome
Empirical	Observation	Experience trumps reason	Observed outcome

Figure 3.3

The *a priori* or rational approach

The Latin phrase *a priori* (literally 'from the earlier') refers to knowledge that is rational or logical in nature, rather than empirical (based on experience). For example, the idea that 'no bachelor is married' does not require data collection. This approach states what is *expected* in terms of an outcome. If the person is a bachelor, he is not expected to be married. The rational approach raises reasoning and logic to the level of mathematical precision. This was Chevalier de Méré's approach to gambling. Let us examine a simple example.

Assume that a box contains one red ball and three black balls. If you reach into the box and draw out one ball, which colour ball would Chevalier de Méré wager that you have drawn? Logically the chances are one in four (there are four balls in the box) that you have drawn a red ball, and three in four that you have drawn a black ball. This assumes that all balls have the same chance (one in four) of being drawn and that the balls are drawn *randomly*: this is the way a lottery is intended to function. Once we have determined the individual chances, probability becomes the ratio $A/(A+B)$, where A represents the chance of the desired outcome and B represents the chances of all other possible outcomes. In our example, if we desire to draw a red ball, the probability (P) is

$$P(\text{red ball}) = \frac{\text{chance of a red ball}}{\text{chance of a red ball} + \text{chances of a black balls}} = \frac{\frac{1}{4}}{\frac{1}{4} + \frac{3}{4}} = \frac{1}{4} = 0.25.$$

The probability of drawing a black ball is

$$P(\text{black ball}) = \frac{\text{chance of a black ball}}{\text{chances of a black ball} + \text{chance of a red ball}} = \frac{\frac{3}{4}}{\frac{3}{4} + \frac{1}{4}} = \frac{3}{4} = 0.75.$$

Consequently, if we continue to draw balls out of the box, record their colour, and place them back into the box, we would *expect* that 25% of the drawn balls will be red and 75% will be black. These percentages are determined prior (*a priori*) to drawing a single ball from the box. This is what makes this approach analytical or rational. Note that this approach will always make an assumption about the probability of the individual outcomes. In our example, it is assumed that all four balls have the same chance of being drawn: 1/4. The assumption of equal probability is not essential for the approach. It might be assumed that the chance of drawing the red ball is 4/10 and the chance of drawing a black ball is 6/10. These changed odds could be assumed even if there continues to be one red and three black balls in the box. It should be noted that probability is expressed as a decimal. Odds and chances are given as ratios.

Another way to discuss the ratio of A to $A + B$ is to define A as the number of ways a given outcome can occur and B as the number of ways the outcome can fail to occur. We may be interested in knowing the probability of rolling an even number on a six-sided die. The outcomes can be enumerated: there are three ways to roll an even number (2, 4, and 6); there are three ways *not* to roll an even number (1, 3, and 5). The resulting formula and computation for the probability of rolling an even number on a single roll of a die are

$$P(\text{roll an even number}) = \frac{\text{number of ways to roll an even number}}{\text{number of ways to roll an even number} + \text{number of ways} \atop \text{not to roll an even number}}$$

$$= \frac{3}{3+3} = \frac{3}{6} = \frac{1}{2}.$$

Although the formula is simple, it is not always easy to enumerate A and B.

The *a posteriori* or empirical approach

The Latin phrase *a posteriori* (literally 'from the later') refers to knowledge based on experience or observation, rather than on logic or reason alone. Where the analytical approach produces probabilities based on what is *expected*, the empirical approach produces probabilities based on what is *observed*. In terms of relative frequency, a probability based on the analytic approach reflects the *expected relative frequency* of an outcome, whereas a probability based on the empirical approach reflects the *observed relative frequency* of an outcome.

Let us re-examine our example of a box that contains red and black balls. This time we assume nothing other than there are red and black balls in the box. Rather than assuming the chances of the different colours, we begin sampling. We draw balls one by one from the box. We record the ball's colour and place it back into the box.

There are two forms of sampling: sampling *with* replacement and sampling *without* replacement. Sampling with replacement means that after each observation the sample is returned to the set of possible observations. Sampling with replacement is used with the current example of red and black balls and it is the form of sampling used throughout this book. Sampling without replacement means that after recording an observation the sample is *not* returned to the set of possible observations.

After 40 such draws we find that we have drawn 12 red balls and 28 black balls. The basic formula for probability remains the same, $A/(A + B)$, with the expected odds being replaced by the observed frequencies. If we are interested in the probability of a red ball being drawn, the formula is

$$P(\text{red ball}) = \frac{\text{number of red balls drawn}}{\text{number of red balls drawn} + \text{number of black balls drawn}} = \frac{12}{12 + 28} = \frac{12}{40} = 0.30.$$

The probability of drawing a black ball is

$$P(\text{black ball}) = \frac{\text{number of black balls drawn}}{\text{number of black balls drawn} + \text{number of red balls drawn}} = \frac{28}{28 + 12} = \frac{28}{40} = 0.70.$$

If we continue to draw balls from the box, we would *expect* that 30% of them will be red and 70% will be black. Note: as we continue to draw more balls from the box we may continue to update the probabilities and our *expectations*. This is what makes this approach to probability empirical.

There are a few additional points to be made. Look at the denominator in the formula for both the analytic and empirical approaches. In the first case the denominator represents the assumed odds related to all possible outcomes. In the second case it represents the total number of observations. In both cases the denominator represents 100% of the *possible* or *observed* outcomes. In the case of the analytic approach this is seen by the fact that the odds in the denominator must always add up to 1, of which the numerator is a fraction. In the case of the empirical approach, the denominator must include all of the observations of all of the observed outcomes. Probability is the ratio of (*A*) the outcome of interest divided by the sum of *A* and not-*A* (or *B*). *B* represents all other possible or observed outcomes.

This formula can be used even to determine the probability of my horse winning the Kentucky Derby or Grand National. It is simply the chance of my horse winning divided by the chance of my horse winning plus the chance of my horse not winning. This holds regardless of which approach to probability is used to set the odds for the horses.

• • • • •

The odds posted for a horse race are determined by factors other than previous outcomes or logic. The owners of the race track or the betting agency want to make money. The odds for the horses in a race are largely produced by taking into account the total amount of money wagered on the race, the amount wagered on each of the horses in the race, and how much profit the owners of the track or the betting agency wish to make. Furthermore, you will find that the odds in a horse race never add up to 1.0. And like Chevalier de Méré, in the long run, the owners of the track wish to be the winners.

From our $A/(A + B)$ formula for probability, we see that probabilities can range from 0 to 1. When there are no *A* outcomes, possible or observed, the probability is 0. When there are no *B* outcomes, possible or observed, the probability is 1. Thus, the percentage of the total observations falling into the A category can range from 0 to 100%.

FREQUENCY HISTOGRAMS AND PROBABILITY

section1

		Frequency	Percent	Valid Percent	Cumulative Percent
Valid	2.00	1	2.5	2.5	2.5
	3.00	1	2.5	2.5	5.0
	4.00	2	5.0	5.0	10.0
	5.00	5	12.5	12.5	22.5
	6.00	6	15.0	15.0	37.5
	7.00	10	25.0	25.0	62.5
	8.00	6	15.0	15.0	77.5
	9.00	6	15.0	15.0	92.5
	10.00	2	5.0	5.0	97.5
	11.00	1	2.5	2.5	100.0
	Total	40	100.0	100.0	

Figure 3.4

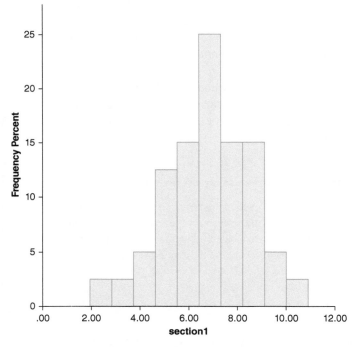

Figure 3.5

In this section we connect the frequency histogram discussed in Chapter 2 with probability. You may have thought of a connection while reading the description of the empirical approach to probability. It may be asked, what is the probability of a student in *section1* of the class receiving a mark of 4 on the quiz? Let us re-examine the frequency table (Figure 3.4) and the relative frequency histogram (Figure 3.5) for data from the variable *section1* in the previous chapter.

The scale on the y-axis of the relative frequency histogram is the percentage of students. The scale of the x-axis represents the various marks received by the students. The bar for the score of 4 on the x-axis reaches 5 on the y-axis. This indicates that 5% of the students in *section1* received a mark of 4 on the quiz. Stated another way, if we placed all 40 students' names in a box and randomly pulled one out, the probability of that student having received a mark of 4 is 0.05. Probability as *observed relative frequency* simply is the *observed* percentage divided by 100.

The frequencies for the scores for *section1* and their percentages are also found in the frequency table (Figure 3.4). Using the second column (Frequency), we can apply our $p = A/(A + B)$ formula to calculate the probability of a student receiving a mark of 4. There are two ways to select a student with a mark of 4 (the frequency of the score of 4 is 2), thus $A = 2$. If we add up the frequencies of all other scores, we find that $B = 38$. Thus the probability of randomly selecting a student from *section1* who has a mark of 4 is

$$P(\text{mark of } 4) = \frac{\text{number of students with a mark of } 4}{\text{number of students with a mark of } 4 + \text{number of students with a mark other than } 4}$$

$$= \frac{2}{2 + 38}$$

$$= 40$$

$$= 0.05.$$

Thus, from the perspective of the empirical approach to probability, there is a straightforward path from observed relative frequency to percentage, and then from percentage to probability.

> The phrase 'per cent' comes from the Latin *per centum*, meaning 'for every hundred'. This is why 100 is always in the denominator when the percentage is calculated. If we used 50 instead, we might talk about *perquinquages*.

THE ASYMPTOTIC TREND

In this section it is shown how the two approaches to probability can operate in tandem. Earlier it was said that probability is a way of finding order within the apparent chaos of chance events. One form of order found in random or chance events is the *asymptotic trend*. The asymptotic trend states that as you increase the number of *observed outcomes* the difference between the *expected frequencies* (rational in nature) and the *observed frequencies* (empirical in nature) of the outcomes becomes progressively smaller. This assumes that the expected frequencies reflect reality. With a finite number of observed outcomes, however, the disparity between the *expected* and the *observed* never reaches zero.

We begin tossing a coin and assume that the probability of heads is 0.5 (rational approach). The probability of tails then must be 0.5. This implies 50% of your tosses should come up heads and 50% should come up tails. Obviously, if you toss a coin four times, you will not always find that two of the tosses come up heads. The more you flip the coin, however, and examine the relative frequencies (empirical approach), the closer the proportions approach 50–50. (In the end, whether or not you believe the 'real' proportions are 50–50 will depend on which approach to probability you adopt.)

Figure 3.6 illustrate this general trend. The categories on the *x*-axes represent the number of possible heads. The *y*-axes represents the *observed* frequency for each category. The left histogram in Figure 3.6 illustrates the outcome after a colleague of mine tossed a coin 9 times, recorded the number of heads, and repeated the process 20 times. If the probability of heads was 0.5, we expect the total number of outcomes in categories 0–4 to be 10 (50%) and the total number of outcomes in categories 5–9 to be 10 (50%). Half of the time we expect more heads than tails and half of the time we expect more tails than heads. However, the number of outcomes in categories 0–4 is 7/20 (35%). Thus, 35% of the 20 trials resulted in more tails than heads and 65% of the trials resulted in more heads than tails. When my colleague repeated the nine tosses 40 times, however, the results were different. As illustrated in the histogram on the right in Figure 3.6, the number of outcomes in categories 0–4 was 22/40 (55%), closer to the expected 50–50 split. This outcome is consistent with an asymptotic trend.

↖ Web Link 3.1 for an interactive demonstration of the asymptotic trend.

If you explore the interactive asymptotic demonstration, you will find that the asymptotic trend is a 'general' or an 'average' trend. There are occasions when the number of trials is increasing, but the percentage change is temporarily in the *unexpected* direction. This is an inevitable product of random events. Simultaneously there is a counter-intuitive, yet predictable, second trend. The greatest chance of finding 50% of the tosses coming up heads is after the minimum number of tosses, which is two. The least chance of having 50% of the tosses coming up heads is after a very, very large number of tosses. The key is to keep in mind that these are average trends. Who knows what apparent chaos you will observe on any one particular series of tosses? What is ordered, predictable, and reliable are the average results after you repeat your series of coin tosses many, many times. The more the coin is flipped, the closer the *observed proportion* of heads is to the *expected or true proportion* (50% or otherwise). Simultaneously, the more the coin is flipped, the less likely it is that 50% of the tosses will come up heads.

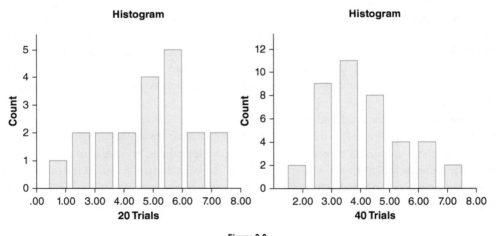

Figure 3.6

━━━━━━━━━ CHALLENGE QUESTION ━━━━━━━━━

Will these trends be found if the probability of heads is 0.1? If so, how will the trends be different from the trends found when the probability of heads is 0.5?

↖ Web Link 3.2 for an interactive demonstration and answer to the challenge question.

3 ● 6 THE TERMINOLOGY OF PROBABILITY

Sometimes two different terms refer to the same thing. The use of synonyms in statistical textbooks is often the consequence of a need to differentiate contexts, rather than a wish to confuse.

Event

In terms of probability, an *event* is something which is observed or may be observed (Brown, 1997). It is often synonymous with

> Chevalier, before we wager, is that a two-headed coin?

outcome. When flipping a coin, there are two possible events or outcomes: heads and tails. When rolling a die, there are six possible events or outcomes: a 1, a 2, a 3, a 4, a 5, or a 6. On a 50-question multiple-choice examination, there are 51 possible outcomes (scores); this includes the possible score of 0. Events may be pairs or groups of outcomes, however. For example, an event may be a pair of 6s on a roll of two dice. In this case, the event is made up of two outcomes: a 6 on the first die and a 6 on the second die. Of course, not all possible outcomes will necessarily be observed.

Figure 3.7 summarizes three important characteristics of events that we will cover in this section.

Characteristic	Brief definition
Mutually exclusive	The occurrence of one event precludes another's occurrence.
Independence	The occurrence of one event does not alter the chance of another occurring.
Exhaustive	A set of events that include all possible outcomes of a given type.

Figure 3.7

Events almost always come in sets, otherwise we would not be able to calculate probabilities, or else all probabilities would be either 0 or 1. There must be *A* and not-*A*. Where heads is possible, so is tails. Where the roll of the die may be a 2, there must be the possibility of a 1, a 3, a 4, a 5, or a 6. From the empirical approach, particularly, it is possible of course for there to be only one member of a set. If flipping a coin 1000 times results in 1000 heads, then the probability of heads is 1000/1000 or 1, and we suspect it is a two-headed coin from Chevalier de Méré's pocket.

Mutually exclusive events

Two events are mutually exclusive if the occurrence of one event *precludes the occurrence* of the other. Students often confuse *mutual exclusiveness* with the concept of *independence*. Being mutually exclusive pertains to the notion that one event cannot have simultaneously more than one of its possible outcomes. For example, if a coin is tossed and it comes up heads, then it cannot on the same toss also come up tails. Thus, heads and tails are mutually exclusive *on any given toss*, just as rolling an even number on any given roll is mutually exclusive with rolling an odd number. The coin coming up heads and being worth £1 are not mutually exclusive events. Coming up heads does not preclude the coin from being worth £1, nor does its being a £1 coin preclude it from coming up heads.

Independent events

Two events are *independent* if the occurrence of one event does not influence the likelihood of the other event. Where being mutually exclusive pertains to a single event having only one of its possible outcomes, independence pertains to the occurrence of two events. For example, if the first toss of a coin comes up heads, the outcome of the second toss is independent of the first, if the probability of heads is unchanged. From the analytic approach, we assume that the probability of heads on any toss is 0.5. The probability of heads is fixed across all tosses. If the probability of heads on the second toss is also 0.5 – which we assume is the case – then the two tosses are independent. If drawing a red ball out of the box in the earlier example does not change the probability of a coin toss coming up heads, then these two events are independent. It might also be said that the occurrence of one event is *random* with respect to the other. If two events are *not* independent, they are said to be dependent: the outcome of one event changes the probability of the possible outcomes of the other event. For example, if drawing a red ball somehow increased the chances of a coin toss coming up heads, then ball colour and coin toss are not independent.

	Independence				Non-independence	
	Eye colour				Eye colour	
	Blue	Brown			Blue	Brown
Men	30	30		Men	30	30
Women	20	20		Women	10	20

| Figure 3.8 | Figure 3.9 |

Let us examine a somewhat more complicated example of independence. In Figure 3.8 we see an example of eye colour being independent of gender. In Figure 3.9 eye colour and gender are not independent.

Why is Figure 3.8 an example of independence? Notice that if you are a man in Figure 3.8, the probability of having blue eyes is 0.5. There are 30 ways for man to have blue eyes and 30 ways for a man not to have blue eyes (brown eyes): $A = 30$ and $B = 30$, so

$$\text{P(blue eyes for men)} = \frac{30}{30+30} = 0.5.$$

Notice that the probability of having blue eyes, if you are a woman, is also 0.5: $A = 20$ and $B = 20$, so

$$P(\text{blue eyes for women}) = \frac{20}{20+20} = 0.5.$$

Because knowing the gender of the person in Figure 3.8 does not alter the probability of that person having blue eyes, eye colour and gender are in this case independent. The actual number of men and women is irrelevant. The question can be posed the other way around: is gender independent of eye colour? It is now being asked if the probability of being a man changes depending on eye colour. Of those who have blue eyes, 30 are men (A) and 20 are not men (B):

$$P(\text{man who has blue eyes}) = \frac{30}{30+20} = 0.6.$$

Of those with brown eyes, again, 30 are men (A) and 20 are not men (B):

$$P(\text{man who has brown eyes}) = \frac{30}{30+20} = 0.6.$$

Because knowing the eye colour of a person in Figure 3.8 does not change the probability of that person being a man, gender and eye colour are independent. If A is independent of B, then B must be independent of A.

Why is Figure 3.9 an example of non-independence? Notice that if you are a man in Figure 3.9, the probability of having blue eyes is 0.5. There are 30 ways for men to have blue eyes and 30 ways for them not to have blue eyes: $A = 30$ and $B = 30$, so

$$P(\text{blue eyes for men}) = \frac{30}{30+30} = 0.5.$$

In Figure 3.9, however, the probability of having blue eyes if you are a woman is not 0.5. In this case, $A = 10$ and $B = 30$, so

$$P(\text{blue eyes for women}) = \frac{10}{10+30} = 0.25.$$

Because knowing the gender of the person in Figure 3.9 alters the probability of that person having blue eyes, gender and eye colour are deemed *non-independent*. In Figure 3.9 eye colour is not random with respect to gender; the two variables are related.

Statistically speaking, the term *independence* is synonymous with the term *unrelated*. It is also synonymous with the term *uncorrelated*, which will be discussed in detail in later chapters. When events are independent, they are unrelated and uncorrelated. This implies that knowing the outcome of one event does not help to predict the outcome of the other, just as knowing someone's gender in Figure 3.8 does not help predict their eye colour. When two events are deemed non-independent, this is synonymous with the terms *related* and *correlated*. These terms imply that knowing the outcome of one event helps to predict the outcome of the second: women in Figure 3.9 have a far greater chance of having brown eyes than do men. Stated differently, eye colour is *not* random with respect to gender. Why have these synonymous terms? As stated earlier, the different terms have come to be associated with specific contexts: type of research question and type of data.

Sometimes due to chance alone, events that are actually unrelated appear to be related. For example, a survey of 165 people found that only 19% of those who could vocally roll their Rs use cologne, whereas 40% of those who were unable to roll their Rs use cologne. Should it be concluded that cologne use is related to the ability to vocally roll Rs? Probably not. This raises a question that may have been in the back of your mind. As we saw with the asymptotic trend, the fewer the number of observations, the greater the discrepancy between the expected and the observed outcomes. Analogously, when we examine samples and not populations, it is *unlikely* that two events will be found to be perfectly independent, even when they *are* independent. Thus, how big a difference is required between what is *observed* and perfect independence (*expected*) to conclude that the events are related? Of course, as already mentioned in several places in the first few chapters, the difference must have a probability of less than 0.05. How this is established is presented in the coming chapters.

The question of independence is fundamental for much of research and statistics. Recall the example of 10 digits (e.g., quiz scores) sorted into two groups in Chapter 1. There are 10 digits: 1, 7, 4, 5, 3, 4, 5, 2, 6, and 3. The scores are sorted into two groups. Group I comprises 1, 4, 2, 5, and 3. Group II comprises 7, 5, 3, 4, and 6. Do you think those scores have been sorted 'randomly' into those two groups? The question can be posed in terms of independence. Are the scores independent of group? Or recall the Chapter 2 example of the quiz grades for two sections of a statistics class. Are the grades independent of section? Does knowing the group help you predict the score? Does knowing the section help you predict the quiz score?

===== CHALLENGE QUESTION =====

Return to the 10 digits sorted into two groups at the beginning of Chapter 1. Is being an above-average digit independent of group? You might wish to use the median as your measure of central tendency.

Web Link 3.3 for an answer to the challenge question.

Exhaustive events

A set of possible events is *exhaustive* if the set includes *all* possible outcomes. You cannot calculate the probability of any one outcome without knowing all possible outcomes relevant to the situation. This is true for both the analytic and the empirical approach to probability. Imagine what happens if only five of the six sides of a die are recognized. From the analytic perspective, the probability of rolling a 4 would be based incorrectly on $A = 1/5$ and $B = 4/5$. Thus P(rolling a 4) would evaluate to $\frac{1}{5} / (\frac{1}{5} + \frac{4}{5}) = 0.2$, rather than the correct value $\frac{1}{6} / (\frac{1}{6} + \frac{5}{6}) = 0.17$.

From the empirical perspective, let us assume a die is rolled 60 times, but for some reasons the number of times a 6 was the outcome (11 times) was not recorded. All that was recorded were ten

1s, nine 2s, eleven 3s, nine 4s, and ten 5s. The probability of rolling a 4 would be based incorrectly on $A = 9$ and $B = 49$. Thus P(rolling a 4) would evaluate to $9 / (9 + 40) = 0.18$, rather than the correct value $9 / (9 + 51) = 0.15$.

For the probability of any outcome to be correctly calculated, we need the set of outcomes to be both exhaustive and mutually exclusive – although sometimes it can be exhausting to ensure that the set we have is the complete set of outcomes.

Conditional probabilities

Conditional probability refers to the probability of an event occurring IF another event has occurred. This discussion of conditional probabilities was implicitly initiated with the earlier examples regarding the independence and non-independence of eye colour and gender. Examine Figure 3.10. What is the probability of having blue eyes IF the person is a man? We are not concerned with eve-

	Eye colour	
Gender	**Blue**	**Brown**
Men	40	60
Women	60	40

Figure 3.10

ryone in Figure 3.10, only the men. We are asking about a probability on the *condition* we only consider the men. In this case, the 100 observations regarding the women are not included in either A or B of the probability formula. The word IF or the | symbol is used to indicate a conditional probability. The formula for the probability of a man having blue eyes is thus written as P(blue eyes IF man) or as P(blue eyes | man). There are 40 men with blue eyes (A) and 60 men with brown eyes (B). In reality, there are more eye colours than blue and brown. But for the sake of demonstration, we assume that those two colours represent an exhaustive set of mutually exclusive outcomes. The result is

$$\text{P(blue eyes IF man)} = \frac{40}{40 + 60} = 0.40.$$

The formula for the probability of a woman with blue eyes is written as P(blue eyes IF woman) or as P(blue eyes | woman). There are 60 women with blue eyes (A) and 40 women with brown eyes (B). So

$$\text{P(blue eyes IF woman)} = \frac{60}{60 + 40} = 0.60.$$

The probability of being a man in Figure 3.10 if the person has blue eyes is 0.4, while the probability of being a woman if the person has blue eyes is 0.6. Knowing how the IF delimits A and B is the key to understanding and to calculating conditional probabilities. If we want to know the probability of being a man if the person in Figure 3.10 has blue eyes, we are only interested in those men and women who have blue eyes. B will be all of the observations in the blue eyes column that are not men (60), while A will be the observations in the blue eyes column that are men (40).

Joint probabilities

A joint probability is the probability of the co-occurrence of two or more events. In Figure 3.10, what is the probability of being a man AND having blue eyes? The key word is AND. Sometimes this can be phrased as the probability of being a man who has blue eyes. Because there is no IF, there is no restriction on what is to be considered in Figure 3.10. The A is defined by the *cell* in the upper left-hand corner of Figure 3.10, the intersection of the men row and blue eyes column: $A = 40$. This is the cell that meets the observational requirements of both being a man and having blue eyes. B is defined by the other three cells in the table: men who have brown eyes, women who have blue eyes, and women who have brown eyes. Two of the cells meet one of the observational requirements. Men who have brown eyes meet the gender requirement but fail to meet the eye colour requirement. Women who have blue eyes meet the eye colour requirement but fail to meet the gender requirement. Both requirements must be met for an observation to be included in A. In our current example, $B = 60$ (men who have brown eyes) + 60 (women who have blue eyes) + 40 (women who have brown eyes). So

$$P(\text{man AND blue eyes}) = \frac{40}{40 + (60 + 60 + 40)} = 0.20.$$

There is one more common situation to address: OR. In Figure 3.10, what is the probability of being either a man OR having blue eyes? Again we have two observational requirements, but in this case only one of the two must be met. The A in the formula will now include men with blue eyes (40), men with brown eyes (60), and women with blue eyes (60). Only the cell that represents women with brown eyes fails to meet one of the requirements: $B = 40$. Thus

$$P(\text{man OR blue eyes}) = \frac{(40 + 60 + 60)}{(40 + 60 + 60) + 40} = 0.80.$$

A common mistake is to confuse the AND situation with the OR situation. They are very different. For example, there is a considerable difference between the situation where you order pancakes with (AND) maple syrup and the curious situation where you might order pancakes OR maple syrup.

3.7 THE LAWS OF PROBABILITY

In this section we examine the basic ways in which probabilities can be combined: additively and multiplicatively. The basic laws of probability are what Pascal uncovered while aiding de Méré in avoiding further gambling debts. These laws are connected to the event characteristics we discussed in the previous section: mutually exclusive and independent events.

The additive law of probability

The *additive law* of probability states that if two events are *mutually exclusive* then the probability of either one of the two events occurring is the sum of their individual probabilities. The additive law pertains to the situations where OR is the conjunction. Looking back at Figure 3.10, what is the probability of being either a man with blue eyes or being a woman with blue eyes? Because these two conditions are mutually exclusive, we can sum the probability of the two individual conditions or cells:

$$P(\text{man and blue eyes}) = \frac{40}{200} = 0.20 \text{ plus } P(\text{woman with blue eyes}) = \frac{60}{200} = 0.30.$$

Thus, the probability of being either a man with blue eyes or a woman with blue eyes is 0.50.

This summing of the individual probabilities is only possible when the two events are mutually exclusive. Here is an example where the events are not mutually exclusive. Given two tosses of a coin, what is the probability of obtaining heads on either the first or the second toss? Or, to put it another way, what is the probability of obtaining heads at least once from two tosses of a coin? The probability of heads is 0.5 on any given toss of the coin. If we sum the two probabilities associated with heads on the two tosses we end up with a probability of 1. From this it would be concluded that every time a coin is tossed twice, it will come up heads at least once. We had better be careful or we could end up like de Méré.

Let us enumerate the possible outcomes from two tosses of a coin. The first toss may come up heads and the second toss heads. Or the first toss may come up heads and the second toss tails. Or the first toss may come up tails and the second toss heads. Or, finally, the first toss may come up tails and the second toss tails. This is the exhaustive set of mutually exclusive outcomes from two tosses of a coin. The possibilities are shown in Figure 3.11.

	First toss	**Second toss**
Outcome 1	Heads	Heads
Outcome 2	Heads	Tails
Outcome 3	Tails	Heads
Outcome 4	Tails	Tails

Figure 3.11

There are four possible outcomes. In three of the four outcomes the coin comes up heads at least once. So P(at least one head in two tosses) = 3/(3 + 1) = 0.75, not 1.0. The reason for the inconsistency with our first calculation (summing the two probabilities) is that heads on the first toss and heads on the second toss are *not mutually exclusive*, as seen in outcome 1. When we sum the two individual probabilities – which are based on the columns – we count outcome 1 twice (because there is heads in both columns in that row) as a member of A in the $A - B$ formula.

When the events are not mutually exclusive and we wish to sum the probabilities, we need to subtract the overlap from the sum. In this case, the overlap is one outcome (outcome 1) and one outcome out of four has a probability of 0.25. The resulting probability is then

P(heads at least once from two tosses) = P(heads on the 1st toss) + P(heads on the 2nd toss) – P(heads on both the 1st and the 2nd toss)

$$= 0.5 + 0.5 - 0.25 = 0.75.$$

This agrees with the corresponding proportion of the enumerated outcomes in Figure 3.11.

━━━━━━━━━━━ CHALLENGE QUESTION ━━━━━━━━━━━━━━━━━━━━━━━━━━━

What is the probability of obtaining heads at least once from three tosses of a coin?

🖰 Web Link 3.4 for an answer to the challenge question.

The multiplicative law of probability

The multiplicative law of probability states that if events are *independent*, then the probability of the events both occurring is the product of their individual probabilities. The multiplicative law pertains to those situations where AND is the conjunction. Using the above example of tossing a coin twice, we might ask, what is the probability of obtaining two heads from two tosses? Look at Figure 3.11 again. Of the four possible outcomes only one meets the requirement of two heads. Thus, the probability is 0.25. What if the multiplicative law was applied to the problem? The probability of heads on the first toss is 0.50 and the probability of heads on the second toss is 0.50. Because the probability of heads on the second toss is unchanged by the outcome of the first toss (look at the two columns), the events are independent and the probabilities can be multiplied: $0.50 \times 0.50 = 0.25$.

In Figure 3.10 what was the probability of being a woman and having blue eyes? Because the probability of having brown eyes is different for men (0.40) than it is for women (0.60), gender and eye colour are not independent. Consequently, the probability of being a woman and the probability of having brown eyes cannot simply be multiplied. To do so, we would find that P(woman) = $100/(100 + 100) = 0.50$ and P(brown eyes) = $100/(100 + 100) = 0.50$. We incorrectly would conclude the P(woman AND brown eyes) = $0.50 \times 0.50 = 0.25$.

Looking at Figure 3.10, we find that $A = 40$ (women with brown eyes) and $B = 60$ (women with blue eyes) + 60 (men with brown eyes) + 40 (men with blue eyes) = 160. Thus, the actual probability of women with brown eyes is $40/(40 + 160) = 0.20$. When events are not independent there is a need to correct for the degree of their relatedness. To make the correction, the probability of being a woman (0.50) is multiplied by the probability of being a woman IF the person has brown eyes $(40/(40 + 60) = 0.40)$. Thus, $0.50 \times 0.40 = 0.20$.

This correction works even when the events are independent. Look again at the four outcomes for the two coin tosses in Figure 3.11 where the two events are independent. The probability of heads on the first toss (column 1) is $2/4 = 0.50$ and the probability of heads on the second toss IF the first toss was heads is $1/2 = 0.50$. Thus, the computed probability of two heads after two tosses is 0.25, the same value found by simply multiplying the two independent probabilities.

What if there are more than two events? For example, what is the probability of obtaining heads on each of three tosses? Assuming that the tosses are all independent of each other, as they should be unless the coin is unbalanced, then the probability is the product of the three individual probabilities:

$$P(\text{three heads after three tosses}) = 0.50 \times 0.50 \times 0.50 = 0.125.$$

Notice that it is becoming tedious if we need to enumerate all mutually exclusive outcomes to identify those associated with *A* and *B*. The tree diagram in Figure 3.12 illustrates how all possible outcomes can be systematically enumerated, but this is unnecessary.

Subtraction strategy

What if we wished to know the probability of heads on the first toss OR heads on the second toss OR heads on the third toss? In other words, heads on any of the tosses would satisfy us. We could enumerate the outcomes as in Figure 3.12 and derive the probability. Consider the problem for a minute. There is only one outcome that would *not* provide at least one head after three tosses: when all three tosses resulted in tails. The probability of all three tosses resulting in tails is, of course, the same as of all three tosses resulting in heads: $0.50 \times 0.50 \times 0.50 = 0.125$. Bear in mind that the total probability of all possible outcomes is 1. Thus, the probability of observing heads at least once from three tosses is 1.0 minus the probability of all three tosses coming up tails: $1.000 - 0.125 = 0.875$.

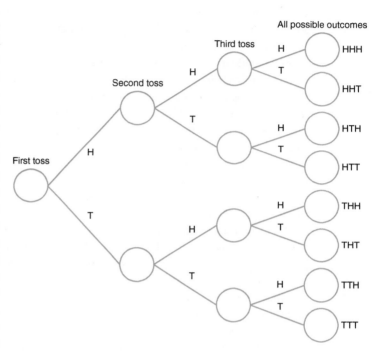

Figure 3.12

Chevalier de Méré revisited

Early in this chapter we saw that Chevalier de Méré was correct when thinking that the chance of rolling at least one 1 after four rolls of a single die was slightly better than 50–50. But what is the exact probability of rolling at least one 1 after four rolls of a die? This is easier to calculate if we first turn it around. After doing so, we find that there is only one way *not* roll at least one 1, that is to roll a 2, or a 3, or a 4, or a 5, or a 6 on all four rolls. Because those five outcomes are mutually exclusive we can sum their probabilities (additive law) and obtain the probability of *not* rolling a 1 on any given roll: $\frac{1}{6} + \frac{1}{6} + \frac{1}{6} + \frac{1}{6} + \frac{1}{6} = \frac{5}{6}$. Assuming the outcome of one roll is independent of the outcome of any other roll, we can multiply the probabilities (multiplicative law) to determine the probability of *not* rolling at least one 1 after four rolls: $\frac{5}{6} \times \frac{5}{6} \times \frac{5}{6} \times \frac{5}{6}$. This can be written as $\left(\frac{5}{6}\right)^4$. Thus the probability of *not* rolling at least one 1 after four rolls is $625 / 1296 = 0.482$. We are interested, however, in the probability of rolling at least one 1 after four rolls. The problem needs to be turned back around. Using the subtraction strategy, the probability of *not* rolling at least one 1 can be subtracted from 1.000. Thus, the probability of rolling at least one 1 after four rolls of a die is $1.000 - 0.482 = 0.518$. It is thus slightly greater than a 50% chance and it allowed de Méré to win this bet more often than not, giving him a modest return.

Never forget: probabilities predict a *population* of events, not what will be observed in a small sample. Probability will not allow us to *know* what will happen on any particular occasion. It only advises us what to *expect* in the long run, sometimes over the very long run. This means that over the course of days, weeks, and months de Méré won slightly more often than he lost. The more often he made the wager, the more money he won.

Next we examine the situation where de Méré wagered that he could obtain at least one pair of 1s from rolling a pair of dice 24 times. Recall that his analysis led him to conclude that the odds of this wager were also slightly better than 50–50. In this case, however, the more frequent his wagering, the more money he lost. What is the exact probability of obtaining at least one pair of 1s from 24 rolls? The same analytic strategy used to analyse the previous wager is employed here. First the problem is turned around. There is only one way *not* to roll a pair of 1s: rolling combinations other than a pair of 1s on all 24 rolls.

The key is to know how many possible outcomes there are on one roll of a pair of dice. It was easier to enumerate all possible outcomes for the previous wager than it is here. Try to enumerate them all for a single roll of a pair of dice. You might start with rolling a 1 on the first die and a 1 on the second die (1,1), then (1,2), then (1,3), on through to (6,6). Be sure not miss any possible outcomes or the final calculation of the probability will be distorted. Constructing the tree diagram is becoming a chore. Besides requiring close attention to detail, constructing the tree may take some time. There is an easier method for determining the number of such combinations: the formula n^r. The method will not enumerate the outcomes, but it does convey the number of possible outcomes. In this case, n is the number of possible outcomes on one die (6) and r is the number of rolls or dice (2). Thus, when you try to enumerate all possible outcomes for one roll of two dice, you will find 36 possible outcomes. Thus, the probability of any one of the outcomes is $\frac{1}{36} = 0.0278$. The probability of rolling one of the outcomes other than a pair of 1s is $\frac{1}{36} \times 35 = \frac{35}{36} = 0.972$. (Because there is one way to roll two 1s, $\frac{1}{36}$ is multiplied by 35 rather than 36.)

Assuming one roll of the dice is independent of the others, the 24 probabilities can be multiplied to determine the probability of *not* rolling at least one pair of 1s after 24 rolls of the dice. This can be transformed into exponent form, $\left(\frac{35}{36}\right)^{24}$. Thus the probability of *not* rolling at least one pair of 1s after 24 rolls is 0.509. To answer our question the problem needs to be turned back around. The probability of *not* rolling at least one pair of 1s is subtracted from 1.000. Thus, the probability of rolling at least one pair of 1s after 24 rolls of the dice is $1.000 - 0.509 = 0.491$. Contrary to de Méré's prediction, the chances are less than 50%, which is why he lost his shirt.

━━━━━━━━━━━ REVIEW QUESTION ━━━━━━━━━━━

What is the probability of rolling at least one pair of 6s after three rolls of a pair of dice?

Web Link 3.5 for an answer to the review question.

3 ● 8 BAYES' RULE

In this section we leave the domain of gambling and look at a more serious aspect of life and a more complicated application of the laws of probability. Imagine that a patient's physician has informed him that he has tested positive for the dreaded disease skewed leptokurtosis. Assume it is known that this rare disease is found in only 0.4% of the population.

> Do not worry. Skewed leptokurtosis does not strike individual human beings. It infects only distributions. Granted, some of the distributions that are susceptible to this debilitating disease, such as income, are related to human activity.

The physician further informs her patient that a person known to be infected with skewed leptokurtosis will test positively for the disease 75% of the time. This probability (0.75) is called the *sensitivity* of the test. There appears to be more bad news, however. Only 1.8% of those who do not have the disease test positive. This probability (0.018) is called the *specificity* of the test.

━━━━━━━━━━━ ● ● ● ● ● ━━━━━━━━━━━

Related to the statistics of *sensitivity* and *specificity* are the notions of *false positive* and *false negative*. A false positive occurs when someone who does *not* have the disease tests positive. A false negative occurs when someone who does have the disease tests negative. There are very, very few tests that are perfect in the sense of never producing false positives or false negatives. If our test for skewed leptokurtosis were perfect, there would be no need to use Bayes' theorem to answer the question concerning our hypothetical patient: if he tests positive, there is no question, he has the disease.

As the patient has tested positive for this dreaded disease, what is the probability he actually is infected? Many people will immediately answer 75%. If that were the correct answer, there would be no need for this section in the chapter. The 75% speaks to an attribute of the test. It says nothing about the patient. It does not specify the probability of the patient having the disease. To explore this problem, we begin by constructing Figure 3.13 with an imaginary population of 1000 patients.

First, recall that only 0.4% of the population is infected with this disease. That is represented in Figure 3.13 by the total in the Yes column: 4 out of 1000 people in this imaginary population

	Infected with skewed leptokurtosis?		
	Yes	No	Total
Test +	3	18	21
Test −	1	978	979
Total	4	996	1000

Figure 3.13

have the disease. Next, recall that 75% of the time IF (notice this IF) you have the disease you will test positive. This percentage is reflected in the three people who are in the Test + row of the Yes column. Finally, remember that 1.8% of those who do *not* have the disease will test positive. This percentage is represented by the 18 people in the Test + row under the No column.

The conjunction IF is related to conditional probabilities. There is a 75% chance a patient will test positive IF he or she has the disease. But this is not the conditional probability for which we are looking. We wish to know the probability of having the disease IF the patient tests positive. In terms of our $A/(A + B)$ formula, A is the number of people who have the disease AND test positive. B is the number of people who do *not* have the disease AND test positive. A and B are represented in Figure 3.13 by the columns Yes and No in the Test + row: 3 and 18, respectively. Remember, what follows the IF identifies the denominator in the probability formula. In this case it is the total of those testing positive (21). We are not interested in those members of the population who test negative. Thus, the probability of a patient having skewed leptokurtosis IF he or she tests positive is

$$P(\text{having skewed leptokurtosis IF Test +}) = \frac{3}{3+18} = 0.143.$$

Therefore, only 14.3% of patients who test positive will actually be infected with skewed leptokurtosis. This is a far lower rate than likely expected at first. The next step is to be able to solve this type of problem without frequencies but with probabilities alone.

To solve the problem with probabilities alone requires making good use of the laws of probability. In doing so, we will reproduce Bayes' rule. Rev. Thomas Bayes was an eighteenth-century English philosopher, Presbyterian minister, and statistician. One of his important contributions was what we now refer to as *Bayes' rule* or *law*. This states that

$$P(x \text{ IF } y) = \frac{P(x)P(y \text{ IF } x)}{P(y)}.$$

In our example this translates into

$$P(\text{having the disease IF testing positive}) = \frac{P(\text{having the disease}) \, P(\text{testing positive IF having the disease})}{P(\text{testing positive})}.$$

We begin by converting the percentages from our example into probabilities: 0.4% becomes a probability of 0.004; 75% becomes a probability of 0.75; and 1.8% becomes a probability of 0.018. We can begin by filling in Figure 3.14. The total probabilities of both the rows and columns must be 1. Therefore, P(having the disease) plus P(not having the disease) must sum to 1, and P(testing positive) plus P(testing negative) must sum to 1.0. Having the disease and not having the disease represent an exhaustive set of mutually exclusive outcomes, as do testing positive and testing negative. Thus, the missing cell (the probability of not having the disease) in the bottom row of Figure 3.14 can be obtained by subtraction: 1 – 0.004 = 0.996.

	Infected with skewed leptokurtosis?		
	Yes	No	Total
Test +			
Test –			
Total	0.004	0.996	1.000

Figure 3.14

To determine the patient's probability of having the disease after testing positive, the Test + row of the table must be completed. Because we cannot assume that *testing outcome* and *disease status* are independent, the probability of having the disease cannot be multiplied by the probability of testing positive, if we knew it. We must multiply the probability of having the disease (0.004) by the probability of testing positive IF the patient has the disease (0.75). Thus, the probability of having the disease AND testing positive is 0.003. This fills in the Yes column in the Test + row, but this is not the probability for which we are looking. (For a discussion of the multiplicative law of probability, see p. 96 earlier in this chapter.)

Next we need to fill in the No column in that row, which will provide us with the A and B we need. Again, using the multiplicative law, the probability of not having the disease and testing positive is the product of not having the disease (0.996) and the probability of testing positive IF the patient does not have the disease (0.018). Thus, the probability of not having the disease AND testing positive is 0.0179 (rounded to 0.018).

We now have A and B. A is the probability of testing positive AND having the disease. B is the probability of testing positive AND not having the disease. We now can calculate the probability of having the disease IF the patient tests positive. Do not be concerned that the values are now probabilities rather than frequencies. Again, we are only interested in those patients who test positive. The probability is

$$P(\text{having the disease IF test positive}) = \frac{0.003}{0.003 + 0.018} = 0.143.$$

The patient can be told that, despite earlier dire conjectures, the probability that he has skewed leptokurtosis is only 0.143. This is the same result as we found above by working through the example frequencies.

Using the additive law of probability, we can also fill in the remainder of Figure 3.14 (see Figure 3.15). The total probability of the Test + row is 0.021. If the total probability of the Yes column is 0.004, then the Yes cell of the Test – row must be 0.004 – 0.003 = 0.001. If the total probability of the No column is 0.996, then the No cell of the Test – row must be 0.996 – 0.018 = 0.978. Finally, if the total of the Totals is 1.000, then the Total cell of the Test – row must be 1.000 – 0.021 = 0.979.

The A/(A + B) formula and the laws of probability work the same regardless of the nature of

	Infected with skewed leptokurtosis?		
	Yes	No	Total
Test +	0.003	0.018	0.021
Test –	0.001	0.978	0.979
Total	0.004	0.996	1.000

Figure 3.15

A and *B*. As we have seen, *A* and *B* can be expected frequencies, observed frequencies, percentages, or probabilities.

━━━━━━━━━━ ■ REVIEW QUESTIONS ■ ━━━━━━━━━━

What is the probability of being infected with skewed leptokurtosis if 10% of the population have the dreaded disease, if 75% of those with the disease will test positive, and if 1.8% of those who do not have the disease will test positive?

What is the probability of being infected with skewed leptokurtosis if 4% of the population have the dreaded disease, if 90% of those with the disease will test positive, and if 1.8% of those who do not have the disease will test positive?

 Web Link 3.6 for an interactive demonstration and answers to the review questions.

3●9 CONTINUOUS VARIABLES AND PROBABILITY

So far this chapter has largely focused on instances of probability where the outcomes are categorical, such as tossing a coin or disease status. In Chapter 2 the topic of continuous distributions was discussed. This section examines computing probabilities when the data are measurement in nature: both discrete and continuous.

In Sections 3.4 and 3.5 the role that frequency tables and histograms can play in determining the probability of an event was introduced. For example, the probabilities associated with quiz marks in *section1* of an imaginary class. Such data are ratio in nature; someone may receive a mark of 0, and that 0 represents a true 0 with respect to the number of items correct. Two students out of 40, or 5%, received a mark of 4. When the percentage is divided by 100, we obtain a probability of 0.05. We were not limited to single-outcome events. We asked more complex questions of the frequency table and histogram (Figure 3.16).

What is the probability of a score of 4 or a score of 5 on the quiz? (Yes, the additive law is appropriate, because the scores are mutually exclusive.) From the frequency table (Figure 3.16) we see that a score of 5 represents 12.5% of the scores, or a probability of 0.125. Summing the two probabilities, the probability of a score of 4 or 5 is 0.175. You might ask, what is the probability of a score of 4 or a score of 9? A score of 9 represents 15% of the scores and has a probability of 0.15.

section1

		Frequency	Percent	Valid Percent	Cumulative Percent
Valid	2.00	1	2.5	2.5	2.5
	3.00	1	2.5	2.5	5.0
	4.00	2	5.0	5.0	10.0
	5.00	5	12.5	12.5	22.5
	6.00	6	15.0	15.0	37.5
	7.00	10	25.0	25.0	62.5
	8.00	6	15.0	15.0	77.5
	9.00	6	15.0	15.0	92.5
	10.00	2	5.0	5.0	97.5
	11.00	1	2.5	2.5	100.0
	Total	40	100.0	100.0	

Figure 3.16

Thus, the probability of a score of 4 or 9 is 0.05 + 0.15 = 0.20. You might also ask, what is the probability of a score of 9 or greater? To put it another way, what percentage of the 40 scores are 9 or greater? We know that 15% of the 40 scores are 9: the corresponding probability is 0.15. A score of 10 represents 5% of the scores: the corresponding probability is 0.05. A score of 11 represents 2.5% of the scores: the corresponding probability is 0.025. Summing the probabilities, we find the probability of a score of 9 or greater on the quiz is 0.225.

This relative frequency approach works well when the observations are discrete and we have a set of outcomes from which to produce the relative frequency table and histogram. What happens when the data are continuous, rather than discrete? You may recall from your calculus class that the probability of any particular x-value (its area under the curve) for a continuous variable is 0. Thus, all of the probabilities calculated

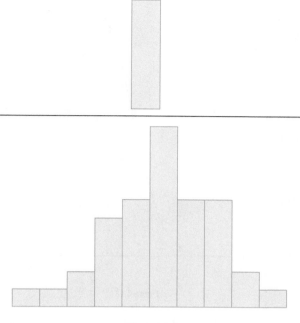

Figure 3.17

in the previous paragraph would be 0, if the scores on the quiz were deemed to be continuous. The one exception is the last calculation: the probability of a 9 or greater.

The percentage of the total represented by a score of 4 can be translated from frequencies into a percentage of an area in the histogram. Figure 3.17 is a graphical depiction of the area-based probability formula. The numerator of the fraction is that area of the histogram represented by a score of 4 (this is A in the $A/(A + B)$ probability formula). The denominator is the total area of the histogram and it represents $A + B$. The presentation of Bayes' rule illustrated how A and B could be either frequencies or probabilities. The formula for probability works the same, regardless. Furthermore, the A and the B components of the ratio or fraction also can be defined in terms of area. Literally, the proportion of the total area (denominator) represented by the area in the numerator is the probability.

The issues we face with a continuous variable are that (1) the values on the x-axis represent points on a line, and (2) a point has no length, no width, and takes up no space. It only denotes a location which divides one segment of the line from the other. Consequently, there is no area associated with a point, nothing to place in the numerator of the formula. Recall that the one exception to this impediment was the question of the probability of a score of 9 or greater. This represents a range of x-axis values (9 to 11, inclusive) and the range has an

This solution of constructing a range of values will require a process similar to the technique of *binning* that was discussed in Chapter 2.

For a discussion of binning, see p. 38 in Chapter 2.

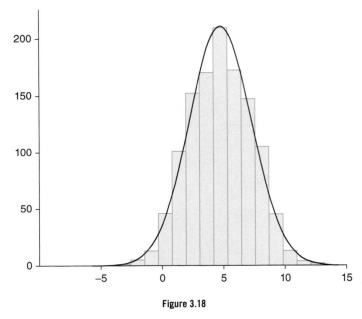

Figure 3.18

area associated with it, even if the variable is continuous. The solution to finding the probabilities associated with a continuous variable is based on computing the probability of a range of scores.

Before examining a solution to the problem of continuous variables, further exploration of the frequency histogram variable is based on computing the probability of a range of scores.

Before examining a solution to the problem of continuous variables, further exploration of the frequency histogram approach for a approach for a discrete variable will be informative. Imagine flipping a coin 14 times and recording the number of heads, which can range from 0 to 14. This represents a ratio scale that is discrete in nature. Assume that we observed 4 heads after the 14 tosses. There are ways to compute the probabilities from the *rational approach* to probability, but we will address those later. For now we approach the problem empirically. To create a stable frequency histogram, it is necessary to repeat this procedure a great number of times. This has been done for us 1185 times by my computer. The frequency histogram for those 1185 events is depicted in Figure 3.18. The x-axis represents the observed number of heads after 14 tosses. The y-axis represents the frequencies of the observed outcomes.

As we have seen, probabilities for the 15 possible outcomes can be derived by taking their frequencies and dividing them by the total (1185). The histogram in Figure 3.18 has an interesting property. The shape of the distribution of the number of heads observed after 14 tosses greatly resembles a *normal distribution*. In Chapter 2 we described various shapes a distribution may exhibit. The smooth curve superimposed on the frequency histogram represents the perfect normal distribution for a continuous variable. The mean, median, and mode are the same value and the skewness and kurtosis are both 0.

================= REVIEW QUESTION =================

How many sets of 10 tosses are required for the shape of the frequency histogram to stabilize? How many sets of 100 tosses are required for the shape of the frequency histogram to stabilize? You might contemplate how what you discover from answering these questions relates to the *asymptotic trend* that was discussed in Section 3.5.

⌕ Web Link 3.7 for an interactive demonstration and discussion of the review question.

Figure 3.19 shows a distribution produced by repeatedly flipping a coin and recording the number of observed heads after each set of 100 tosses. The discrete steps which characterize this frequency histogram almost appear to be the smooth curve of the normal distribution of a continuous variable. The questions of when and how a discrete variable may be treated as a continuous variable will be addressed in a later chapter.

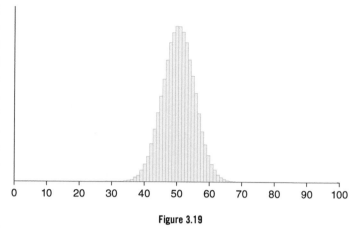

Figure 3.19

Distributions come in many shapes. In addition to the normal distribution, there are bimodal, positively skewed, negatively skewed, leptokurtic, and platykurtic distributions, and many more. Why is the normal distribution considered to be important? First, the normal distribution is important because it is surprising how many phenomena are *approximately* normally distributed, such as height, memory test scores, blood pressure, and errors in measurement. The key word here is *approximately*. No empirical sample of observations, regardless of the sample size, is perfectly normal, even if the underlying population is perfectly normal. If the underlying distribution is normal, however, we will observe a parallel of the *asymptotic trend* mentioned in Section 3.5. As the sample size increases, the shape of a *random sample's* distribution will, on average, more closely approximate normality.

The second reason why the normal distribution is considered important relates to the possible inferences that can be made about the variable's population and about individual observations. These inferences are the topic of much of the remainder of this chapter. The third reason why the normal distribution is important concerns assumptions that are necessary for many inferential statistical tests discussed later in Parts II and III of this book.

• • • • •

Many inferential tests are *parametric* in nature. They are based on estimating population parameters with sample statistics. There are alternatives to parametric tests, most of which are called *nonparametric* and avoid some of the assumptions required by parametric tests. In most circumstances, the results and conclusions drawn from parametric and nonparametric tests differ very little. One of the earliest and strongest advocates of nonparametric alternatives was Bradley (1968). Others have argued vociferously that parametric tests are usually superior to their nonparametric alternatives, even when the parametric assumptions are moderately violated (Rasmussen, 1987). The debate continues today as the number and the types of alternative tests are developed. Both parametric tests and their alternatives will be discussed, beginning in Chapter 4.

What causes a distribution to be non-normal? Many distributions by their nature are non-normal. For example, income distributions are some of the most (positively) skewed distributions (see Figure 3.20).

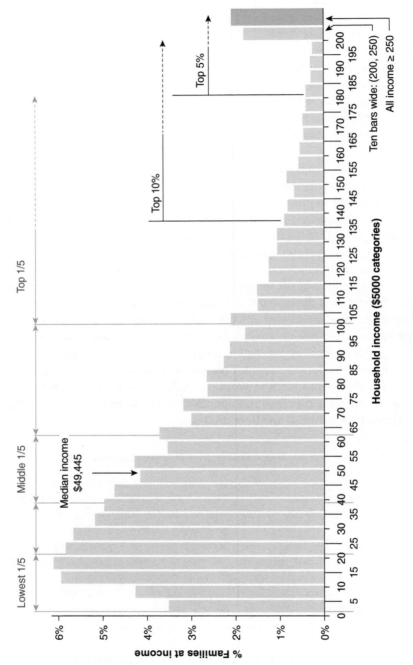

Figure 3.20

In many developed countries the modal income is below the poverty line, while the mean is far above it. Such distributions are not distributed like the 100 coin flips. A further problem with such non-normal distributions is that the shape of many of them is constantly changing. For example, just in the last eight years the skewness of the distribution of incomes has increased dramatically.

There are other reasons for a distribution to be non-normal, some of which are related to research procedures, and not necessarily inherent to the shape of the underlying population's distribution. First, as we have noted in Chapter 2, outliers can create skewness. Outliers can be recording errors or they can represent true scores. Second, the overlap of two or more conditions may produce a non-normal distribution. Imagine you are testing subjects' hand–eye coordination and you test some subjects in the morning and others in the afternoon, not realizing that time of day may influence hand–eye coordination. If you inspect the distribution of scores recorded in the morning and those recorded in the afternoon separately, you might find them both to be relatively normal.

Figure 3.21 illustrates the distribution of your imaginary morning scores; Figure 3.22 illustrates your afternoon scores; Figure 3.23 depicts the distribution of all scores from both morning and afternoon. If you examine only the combined distribution (Figure 3.23), you may have serious doubts about the normality of the distribution of hand–eye coordination.

──────────── CHALLENGE QUESTION ────────────

Can you create two skewed distributions which will give the appearance of normality when they are combined? Use SPSS to create the data and to view the histograms. Use the *Skewed to normal* link on the book's web page to see a possible solution and discussion.

 Web Link 3.8 for a discussion of the challenge question.

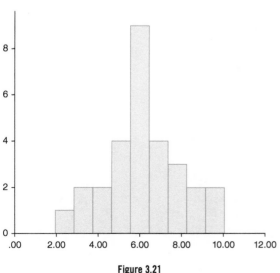

Figure 3.21

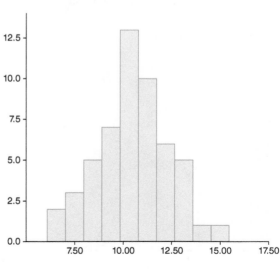

Figure 3.22

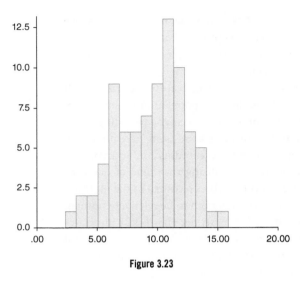

Figure 3.23

A third cause of a non-normal distribution is the overlapping scores sampled from two populations. Sometimes researchers are unaware of an uncontrolled variable having an effect on their dependent variable. As pointed out, sometimes that variable is related to the research design. Sometimes, however, that variable is related to differences among the subjects, often called a *subject variable*. Think of Figures 3.21, 3.22, and 3.23 as representing subjects in a hand–eye coordination experiment, some with 20/20 vision (Figure 3.21) and some whose vision is in need of correction (Figure 3.22). Again, the scores of the two groups viewed separately are normal, but when combined the distribution looks markedly skewed (Figure 3.23).

REVIEW QUESTION

Is the distribution in Figure 3.23 unimodal? Explain.

Web Link 3.9 for an answer to the review question.

Although there are many reasons for distributions to appear non-normal, only one further reason will be mentioned here: the *truncation* of one end of the distribution. Truncation has two sources: natural and methodological. Natural limits can truncate either the upper or the lower bound of

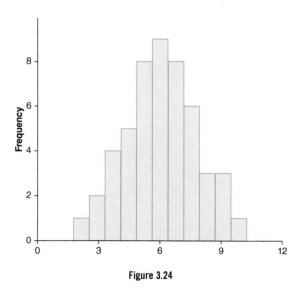

Figure 3.24

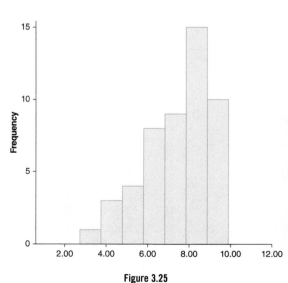

Figure 3.25

scores. When researching reaction time (RT) there is a physical limitation to the speed with which a subject can respond. There is no such limitation on how long a subject takes to respond. Consequently, a distribution of RTs often is similar to a distribution of incomes, positively skewed. Methodological causes of truncation are often the result of a task being either too easy or too difficult for the subjects. For example, a quiz designed for the first week of a first course in statistics is likely to be too easy for those in the final week of a second course in statistics.

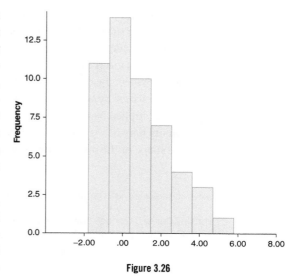

Figure 3.26

Figure 3.24 illustrates imaginary data from a 10-item matrix algebra quiz. The scores range from 0 to 10 and the distribution is normal. Figure 3.25 depicts a situation where the quiz is too easy for those being tested and is negatively skewed. The scores range from 4 to 10 and are clustered at the top of the range. This is often called a *ceiling effect*. The quiz is missing items that are difficult enough to differentiate those who are above average. Figure 3.26 depicts the converse, where the quiz is too difficult. The scores range from 0 to 6 and are clustered at the bottom and are positively skewed. This is often called a *basement effect* or *floor effect*. The quiz is lacking items that would differentiate those who are below average.

Students often think they know why a test which is 'too difficult' is unfair: because it is too difficult! It is unfair, but not for the reason students usually think. Furthermore, a test that is 'too easy' is also unfair. This is something students do not wish to admit.

Web Link 3.10 for an explanation of how a test which is either too easy or too difficult is unfair.

Although there are statistical tests to assess the normality of a distribution, a visual examination of a frequency histogram is often the easiest and a reasonable test. When there are few subjects in a sample and no two subjects have the same score, it is impossible to assess the data's normality or to detect outliers. In such cases there is little to do other than assume normality, unless previous research or other sources of information indicate the variable may be non-normal. This situation often occurs in experimental research with a continuous dependent variable and a small sample size.

Linear transformations

It is possible to change the mean and variance of any set of observations to any other mean and variance without changing the shape of the distribution or the relative differences among the scores. Consider the formula for a straight line: y-value = slope (x-value) + y-intercept. If all of the original scores are multiplied by a constant or a constant is added to them, the shape of the new distribution is identical to the original. Only the units of measurement change – and not even that, if all we do is add a constant to all of the scores.

If you add or subtract a constant from all of the scores in a sample, the new mean is simply the old mean plus or minus the constant. You need not sum all of the new scores to obtain the new mean. If you multiply (or divide) all of the scores by a constant, you can obtain the new mean by multiplying (or dividing) the old mean by that constant. Adding or subtracting a constant from all scores does not change their variance; the distribution is merely moved to the left or right on the *x*-axis. Multiplying or dividing the scores by a constant, however, does change the variance. The new variance is the old variance multiplied by the square of the constant. Not all transformations leave the shape of the distribution unchanged. An exponential transformation of the scores, for example, is nonlinear, and changes the shape of the distribution as well as the relative differences among the scores.

REVIEW QUESTION

The link below describes how you can use the *Transform* menu on the SPSS *Data Editor* screen. After you are comfortable with the *transform* function, create a variable that has a mean of 30 and a variance of approximately 36. This may take a bit of trial and error on your part. Then transform the variable so that the new mean is 50 and the new variance is approximately 9. *Hint*: Use a sample size no more than 10 and do not worry about the initial variance, it can always be transformed to 36.

⌕ Web Link 3.11 for how to use the SPSS *Transform* menu.

---

3 ● 10 THE STANDARD NORMAL DISTRIBUTION

The most common linear transformation subtracts the sample mean from all of the scores and divides the resulting differences by the standard deviation. The resulting values are called *z-scores*:

$$z\text{-score} = \frac{\text{score} - \text{mean of the scores}}{\text{standard deviation of the scores}}.$$

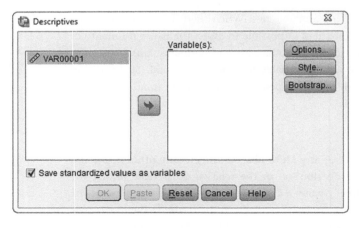

Figure 3.27

Assuming normality, *z*-scores reflect what is called the standard normal distribution, which is known to many as the *bell curve*. Any set of scores transformed into *z*-scores has a mean of 0 and a variance (and standard deviation) of 1. A *z*-score indicates how many standard deviations the corresponding original score is from the original mean. For example, a *z*-score of −2.5 indicates that the original score was 2.5 standard deviations below the original mean; a *z*-score of +1.0 indicates that the original score was 1.0 standard deviations above the mean. Creating

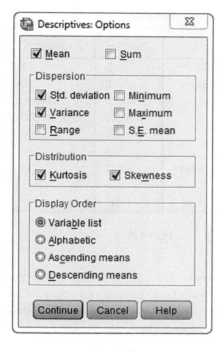

Figure 3.28

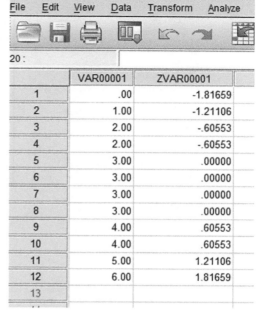

Figure 3.29

z-scores is the first step towards computing the probabilities of possible outcomes from a continuous variable.

There is a simple procedure in SPSS for obtaining the descriptive statistics and simultaneously transforming original scores into z-scores. Open a new file with the SPSS *Data Editor* and enter the following scores into the first variable (column): 0, 1, 2, 2, 3, 3, 3, 3, 4, 4, 5, 6.

Scroll down the *Analyze* menu to *Descriptive Statistics* and then choose the *Descriptives* option. Once the Descriptives window opens (Figure 3.27), move the variable over to the *Variable(s)* box. Be sure to click the *Save standardized values as variables* box in the lower left of the screen. Next, click the *Options* button. When the *Descriptives: Options* window opens (Figure 3.28), select *Mean* and *Std. deviation* and then *Continue*. Once you return to the *Descriptives* window, click *OK*.

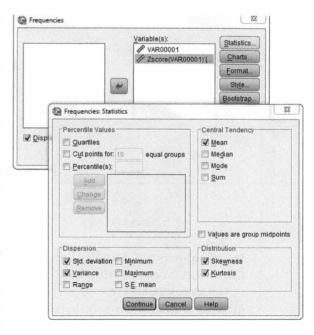

Figure 3.30

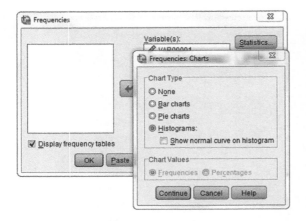

Figure 3.31

Statistics

		VAR00001	Zscore (VAR00001)
N	Valid	12	12
	Missing	0	0
Mean		3.0000	.0000000
Std. Deviation		1.65145	1.00000000
Variance		2.727	1.000
Skewness		.000	.000
Std. Error of Skewness		.637	.637
Kurtosis		.161	.161
Std. Error of Kurtosis		1.232	1.232

Figure 3.32

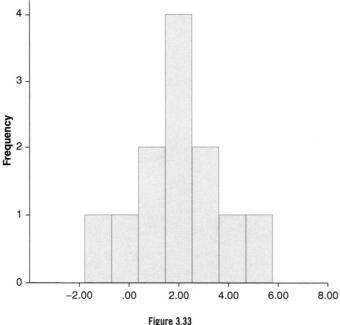

Figure 3.33

Ignore the output window for the moment. Look back at the *Data Editor* screen (Figure 3.29). A new variable has been created. These scores in the new variable are the original scores transformed into *z*-scores, based on the original variable's mean and standard deviation. For example, an original score of 2 has a corresponding *z*-score of –0.60553. Look at the mean and standard deviation in the output window. After subtracting the mean (3.0) from 2 and dividing the difference by the standard deviation (1.65145) the result is –0.60553, the corresponding *z*-score seen in the *Data Editor*.

Again scroll down the *Analyze* menu to *Descriptive Statistics* and this time choose the *Frequencies* option. In the Frequencies window (Figure 3.30), move both variables over to the *Variable(s)* box. From the *Statistics* options, choose the mean, standard deviation, variance, skewness, and kurtosis (Figure 3.30), and from the *Charts* options choose *Histograms* (Figure 3.31). Click *Continue* and then *OK*.

The statistics table in the output window (Figure 3.32) illustrates the expected changes in mean (from 3.0 to 0), in the variance (from 2.727 to 1), and in the standard deviation (from 1.65145 to 1). Because the standard deviation is the square root of the variance, if the variance is 1, the standard deviation is 1. Notice that those statistics that describe the shape of the distribution also are unchanged. The skewness remains 0 and the kurtosis remain 0.161.

The histograms of the original scores (Figure 3.33) and of the corresponding z-scores (Figure 3.34) illustrate how the linear transformation did nothing to change the shape of the distribution. A close examination reveals that nothing has changed, save the units of measurement on the x-axis.

An easy way to test for outliers is to create z-scores while obtaining the descriptive statistics. In Chapter 2 it was stated that any score more than 4 standard deviations above or below the mean will be declared an outlier; z-scores specify how many standard deviations a score is from the mean. Examining the z-scores in the SPSS *Data Editor* in our above example, none have an absolute value of 4 or greater. Thus, there are no outliers.

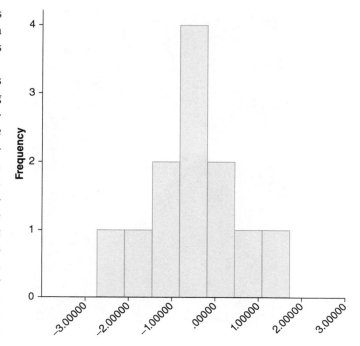

Figure 3.34

• • • • •

In Chapters 1 and 2 the technique of transforming percentile scores (which are ordinal in nature) into measurement data was mentioned. The procedure is simple. First z-scores are computed for the percentile scores. Then the z-scores are multiplied by 21.063. Finally, 50 is added to each product. The resulting distribution of scores has a mean of 50 and a standard deviation of 21.063. Using a standard deviation of 21.063 gives the resulting scores – now called normal curve equivalent (NCE) scores – a range from 1 to 99. The primary advantage of NCE scores is that, if the distribution of percentile scores is roughly normal, then the NCE scores can be assumed to be on an (equal) interval scale and they can be averaged. Finally, the NCE scores can be analysed using parametric tests described in Part II of this book.

 ## THE STANDARD NORMAL DISTRIBUTION AND PROBABILITY

The standard normal distribution, along with the calculation of z-scores, provides a basis for determining the probabilities of possible observations for a continuous variable. Two qualifications must be made, however. First, using the standard normal distribution to determine probabilities requires that μ (population mean) and σ (population standard deviation) are known. These two values are

Figure 3.35 Johann Carl Friedrich Gauss

rarely known, however. There are two practical exceptions made to this qualification. First, in some situations there are reasons to assume that we know these values. For example, it is assumed that μ and σ for a common IQ test are 100 and 15, respectively. Second, there are situations where sample sizes are large. As the size of a random sample increases (and randomness is of paramount importance) beyond 100, the efficiency of μ increases and approaches asymptote. That is, the sample statistics are likely to be very good estimates of their population counterparts. When sample sizes are smaller or the potential error in the estimates is unacceptable, there are other statistics, such as t-scores, which can compensate for the fact that $\bar{y}$ and s are only estimates of μ and σ. These statistics are covered in Part II.

The second qualification which must be made regards the nature of a continuous variable. As mentioned earlier in the chapter, with continuous variables, the probability of any individual value (score) is 0. Because of this, a *binning-like* tactic is required. For example, when scores on a continuous variable range from 0 to 100, the probability of any given score (e.g., 70) cannot be determined: P(70) = 0. Assuming μ and σ are known and the distribution is approximately normal, however, we can determine the probability of having a score between 70 and 71 or between 69.5 and 70.5. We can also determine the following probabilities: the probability of a score between 35 and 60; the probability of a score greater than 80; and the probability of a score less than 20 or greater than 80.

The nature of the standard normal distribution

The bell-like shape of the standard normal distribution is given by the formula which describes the curve:

$$f\left(x,\mu,\sigma\right) = \frac{1}{\sigma\sqrt{2\pi}}e^{-\frac{(x-\mu)^2}{2\sigma^2}}.$$

The formula's more formal name is the *Gaussian function*, named after the early nineteenth-century German mathematician (Figure 3.35).

In the above function, $\pi = 3.1416$ and $e = 2.7183$. μ and σ can be any values, but for a *standard normal distribution* they are always 0 and 1, respectively. Thus by integrating the function ranging from one value of x (x_1) to another (x_2), the probability of randomly selecting a value within that range of the population can be derived. Do not worry about the calculus, it has been completed and is contained in the z-tables found in Appendix A.

• • • • •

The nineteenth-century Russian mathematician Pafnuty Chebyshev provided a rule regarding the minimum proportion of a distribution that will be found between μ and K standard deviations from the mean: $1 - 1/K^2$. K must be greater than 1, however.

Thus, for example, regardless of the shape of the distribution, the minimum proportion of the distribution that will be between the mean and 2 standard deviations is $1 - 1/2^2 = 0.75$ or 75%. If normality cannot be assumed, the proportions will be greater than these.

When normality is assumed, *one size fits all*. That is, any population of scores, regardless of the original μ and σ, can be converted to the standard normal distribution. Figure 3.36 depicts the standard normal distribution and the approximate proportions of the observations falling between 1, 2, and 3 standard deviations of the mean. For example, 34% of the observations fall between the mean and +1 standard deviation above the mean. And because of the distribution's symmetry, 68% of the observations fall

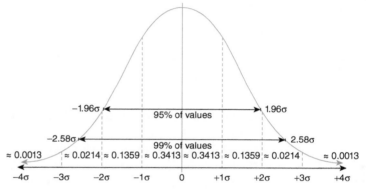

Figure 3.36

within 1 standard deviation of the mean, that is between the −1 and +1 standard deviations' boundaries. Summing the percentages, virtually 100% of the observations are found to fall within 3 standard deviations of the mean.

While the rules of thumb regarding the proportions of observations and standard deviations mentioned here are of practical use, mathematically the distribution extends out to infinity in both the positive and the negative directions. Beyond 3 standard deviations from the mean, however, the expected proportion of observations rapidly approaches 0, but never actually reaches it.

The rule of thumb provides justification for considering any score more than 4 standard deviations below or above the mean as an outlier. Although the distribution is often spoken of in terms of proportions, because the distribution is considered to be continuous, it is more appropriate to speak in terms of probabilities. Thus 68% becomes 0.68 and 100% becomes 1.00.

3 ● 12 USING THE Z-TABLES

As stated above, if we assume a population is approximately normal, we can use the z-tables to derive the probabilities associated with various outcomes related to a continuous variable.

Although there are many versions of the z-tables, they differ only in the way in which probabilities are recorded, not in the probabilities themselves. In this book, we use two z-tables, one for negative z-scores and one for positive z-scores. The probabilities in the two tables pertain to the shaded areas found in Figure 3.37.

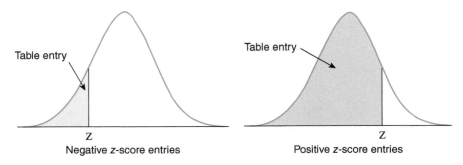

Figure 3.37

The z-tables

To use the z-tables in Appendix A first requires computing a z-score. Assume a population with $\mu = 60.0$ and $\sigma = 4.0$ and a randomly selected score of 53.0. The resulting z-score is $(53 - 60)/4 = -1.75$. Because this z-score is negative, we go to the z-table with the negative z-score entries. The first column in this table lists the z-scores from –3.4 to 0.0. (Recall that the mean of a standard normal distribution is always 0.0.) The additional columns to the right provide z-scores to the second decimal place. For example, the value associated with –1.75 is the intersection of the –1.7 row and the 0.05 column: 0.0401. This 0.0401 pertains to the shaded area in the negative z-score distribution in Figure 3.37 and indicates that the probability of a score to the left of (less than) –1.75. In terms of proportions, 4.01% of the population's scores are below the observed score of 53.0.

Remember that with a continuous variable any individual score – original observed score or z-score – has a probability of 0. A score is only a point on the x-axis that divides the distribution. Our z-score of –1.75 divides the distribution into two parts. Thus, it follows that the probability of a z-score *greater* than –1.75 (an observed score greater than 53.0) is $1 - 0.0401 = 0.9599$, and 95.99% of the scores in the population are greater than 53.0. Finally, because, by definition, the probability of a score less than μ (original mean of 60 and z-score of 0) is 0.50, the probability of a score falling between –1.75 (53.0) and 0.0 (60) is $0.50 - 0.0401 = 0.4599$.

What if the randomly selected score is 67 rather than 53? The resulting z-score is $(67 - 60)/4 = +1.75$. Because this z-score is positive, the z-table with the positive z-score entries is used. The first column in this table lists the z-scores from 0.0 to 3.4. Again, the additional columns to the right provide z-scores to the second decimal place; 1.75 is the intersection of the 1.7 row and the 0.05 column. The value of 0.9599 in that cell pertains to the shaded area in the positive z-score distribution in Figure 3.37. The probability of a z-score to the left of (less than) 1.75 is 0.9599; that is, 95.99% of the population's scores fall below the observed score of 67.0. Thus, using the subtraction strategy, the probability of a z-score greater than 1.75 (observed score greater than 67) is 1 − 0.9599 = 0.0401. Thus, 4.01% of the scores in the population are greater than 67.0. Because the probability of a score greater than 60 (z-score = 0.0) is 0.50, the probability of a score falling between 1.75 (67.0) and 0.0 (60) is 0.50 − 0.0401 = 0.4599. Note the symmetry in the probabilities of the two z-scores −1.75 and +1.75.

Let us return to the questions we posed at the beginning of the previous section:

1   What is the probability of a score falling between 70 and 71?
2   What is the probability of a score falling between 35 and 60?
3   What is the probability of a score being greater than 80?
4   What is the probability of a score being less than 20 or greater than 80?

Before answering these questions, it is necessary to know the mean and standard deviation of the population. For these examples, assume that $\mu = 50$ and $\sigma = 15$.

It is always helpful to begin by drawing a normal distribution and locating the relevant scores ($x_1 = 70$ and $x_2 = 71$) with respect to the mean. Figure 3.38 illustrates the area for which we wish to derive the probability: the area above the mean between 70 and 71.

First derive the probability of a score being less than x_2 (71). The z-score for an observed score of 71 is (71 − 50)/15 = +1.4. We find in the z-table (positive z-scores) that the probability of a z-score less than +1.4 is 0.9192. (Remember to use the table for positive z-scores.) Next, derive the probability of a score being less than x_1 (70). The z-score for 70 is (71 − 50)/15 = +1.33. We find in our z-table that the probability of a z-score less than +1.33 (observed score of 71) is 0.9082. Because the area of interest is the area to the left of 71 but not to the left of 70, we subtract the latter probability from the former. Thus, the probability of a score falling between 70 and 71 is 0.9192 − 0.9082 = 0.011. Only 1.1% of the scores in the population fall between 70 and 71.

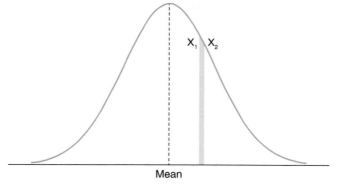

Figure 3.38 $\mu = 50, x_1 = 70, x_2 = 71$

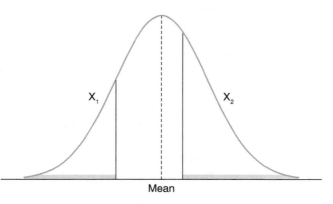

Figure 3.39 $x_1 = 35, \mu = 50, x_2 = 60$

To answer the second question, again begin by drawing a normal distribution and locating where the two scores ($x_1 = 35$ and $x_2 = 60$) are with respect to the mean. Figure 3.39 helps us to visualize the area in question.

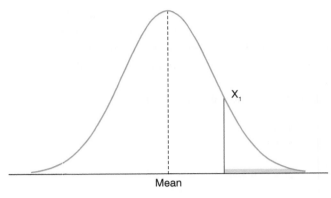

Figure 3.40 $\mu = 50$, $x_1 = 80$

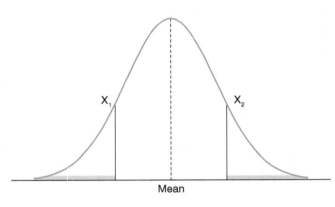

Figure 3.41 $x_1 = 20$, $\mu = 50$, $x_2 = 80$

Again a subtraction strategy will be used. First derive the probability of a score being less than our x_2 (60). The z-score for 60 is $(60 - 50)/15 = +0.67$. In our z-table for positive z-scores we find the probability of a z-score less than +0.67 is 0.7486. Next, derive the probability of a score being less than our x_1 (35). The z-score for 35 is $(35 - 50)/15 = -1.00$. We find in our z-table for negative z-scores that the probability of a z-score less than -1.00 is 0.1587. Again we subtract to remove the overlap. Thus, the probability of randomly selecting a score between 35 and 60 is $0.7486 - 0.1587 = 0.5899$. In terms of percentages, 58.99% of the scores in the population will fall between 35 and 60.

To answer the third question, once more draw a normal distribution and locate the score of 80 (x_1) in the distribution.

The black line in Figure 3.40 locates the score of 80 in relation to the mean and the blue highlighted line on the x axis indicates that the area of interest is to the right, rather than to the left, of the z-score. The z-score for the observed score of 80 is +2.00. In the table of positive z-scores we find the probability of a score *less* than 80 (z-score of +2.00) is 0.9772. But our interest is in the probability of a score *greater* than 80. Again a subtraction strategy is useful. Because the total probability is 1 and the probability of a score less than 80 is 0.9772, the probability of a score greater than 80 is $1 - 0.9772 = 0.0228$. Only 2.28% of the population's scores are greater than 80.

To answer the fourth question it is necessary to employ both a subtraction and an addition strategy. As always, begin by drawing a normal distribution and locating where the two scores ($x_1 = 20$ and $x_2 = 80$) are in relation to the mean in the distribution. Figure 3.41 helps us to identify the areas of interest and which areas need to be combined. The black lines identify x_1 (20) and x_2 (80) and locate them in relation to the mean. The blue highlighted lines on the x axis indicate the areas of interest.

The z-score for an observed score of 20 is -2.00. In the z-table for negative z-scores we find the probability of a z-score less than -2.00 is 0.0228. As already discovered, for this population, the z-score for a score of 80 is +2.00. The probability of a score less than 80 is 0.9772. But we are interested in the probability of a score greater than 80. Using the subtraction strategy, the probability of a score being greater than 80 is $1 - 0.9772 = 0.0228$. Next, the probability of a score being less than 20 needs to be combined with the probability of a score being greater than 80. Because the two events ($x_1 < 20$ and $x_2 > 80$) are mutually exclusive (they do not overlap), the two probabilities can simply be summed (additive law of probability). Thus, the probability of a score being either less than 20 or greater than 80 is $0.0228 + 0.0228 = 0.0456$.

Even though with a continuous variable a table is used to derive probabilities, the basic formula of $A/(A + B)$ remains. As discussed earlier, areas rather than frequencies can be used to define A and B. Using z-scores and the standard normal distribution means that the denominator $(A + B)$ is always 1.

For a discussion using frequency and area to derive the A and B components of the probability formula, see p. 103.

The four questions just answered can be viewed as the area of interest under the curve divided by the total area under the curve, which is 1.0.

Setting probable limits: 95%

There is another type of question that may be posed: *setting probable limits*. Assume we know that a population has a μ of 50 and σ of 15. Being symmetrical, within what two scores will 95% of the observations fall? Here the probability (0.95) is known and it is necessary to work back to the two scores that bracket 95% of the possible observations. Because of the need to be symmetrical, the two corresponding z-scores will differ only in sign. Again, because of the need to be symmetrical, half of the 0.95 (or 0.475) must be

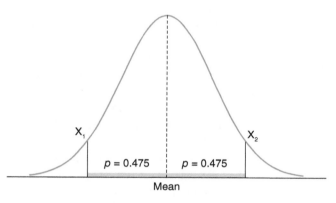

Figure 3.42 $x_1 = ?, \mu = 50, x_2 = ?$

above the mean and half must be below the mean. To answer this question, again begin by drawing a normal distribution and roughly locating the as yet unknown x_1 and x_2 with respect to the mean: one above and the other below the mean. Figure 3.42 defines the probabilities associated with the area enclosed by the two as yet unknown scores.

Again a subtraction strategy is useful. If the probability of a score being below the mean is 0.5, then the negative z-score for which we search corresponds to a tabled probability of $0.5 - 0.475 = 0.025$. Examining the table for negative z-scores, we find the probability of 0.025 is associated with a z-score of -1.96. That is, the probability of a score falling below a z-score of -1.96 is 0.025. Working backwards with the z-score formula, we have

$$z = \frac{\text{observed score} - \mu}{\sigma}.$$

Substituting the known values into the formula,

$$-1.96 = \frac{\text{observed score} - 50}{15}.$$

With a little algebra we can solve for the *observed score*:

$$-1.96 \times 15 = \text{observed score} - 50$$

$$-1.96 \times 15 + 50 = \text{observed score},$$

or, flipping the formula around,

$$\text{observed score} = -1.96 \times 15 + 50 = 20.6.$$

Thus the probability of a score in the population falling below 20.6 is 0.025.

Because of the required symmetry, the x_2 must be 1.96 standard deviations above the mean. When −1.96 is replaced by +1.96 in the computation we find the observed score above the mean of 50 is $1.96 \times 15 + 50 = 79.4$. We conclude that 95% of the scores in the original population fall between 20.6 and 79.4. This is referred to as an example of 95% confidence limits or interval.

Confidence intervals are a simple inferential test. As stated in Chapter 1 of this book, usually researchers wish to have 95% confidence in the conclusions drawn from their observations. For example, it may be asked if a score of 20 is likely a member of a given population ($\mu = 50$ and $\sigma = 15$). What should we conclude? Because a score of 20 is less than 20.6 and falls outside of the confidence interval, we may conclude the score is not a member of that population. What about a score of 30? Because a score of 30 falls within the 95% confidence interval, we may conclude that the score is a member of the population.

The basic logic of the test revolves around μ (50) as the *expected* value. Then there is the *observed* score, for example 20. The hypothesis is that the observed score is a member of the population ($\mu = 50$ and $\sigma = 15$). Due to chance alone, with 95% confidence, a score may be anywhere between 20.6 and 79.4 and still be a member of the population. It is the variance ($\sigma = 15$) that determines the range in values *expected to be due to chance alone*. Because the observed score of 20 is below the lower limit of the 95% confidence interval, we reject the hypothesis that it is a member of the population, but we accept that 30 is. Of course, nothing is proven. One or both of the conclusions may be wrong. That is, we may be making a Type I or a Type II error.

3 ● 13 CHAPTER SUMMARY

The chapter began with a presentation of the rational and empirical approaches to probability. We discovered that, regardless of approach, the basic formula for P(any outcome) is $A/(A + B)$. The formula works when A and B are expected frequencies or when they are observed frequencies. The formula works when A and B are frequencies, when they are areas, and when they are probabilities. It works when the observations are categorical in nature and when they are measurement in nature. It works when the observations are discrete and when they are continuous. The same can be said of the additive and multiplicative laws of probability. We saw how a seventeenth-century gambler's conundrum initiated the development of these laws. An application of these laws, Bayes' rule, provided an example of how these laws can aid in the solving of real-life problems. Finally, through the use of confidence intervals, we had a first look at how probability theory and descriptive statistics combine to form an inferential statistical test.

3 ● 14 RECOMMENDED READINGS

Lowry, R. (1989). *The architecture of chance: An introduction to the logic and arithmetic of probability*. New York: Oxford University Press.

This book is for those who wish to delve deeper into probability theory. The rewards are great, if you take your time and reread sections that are difficult.

Mlodinow, L. (2008). *The drunkards walk: How randomness rules our lives*. New York: Random House.

This book illustrates how randomness and our view of probability are so much a part of our daily lives. Mlodinow demonstrates how we attribute specific causes to our successes (I am clever) and failures (others ruin it), when so much of what happens is the product of many small (what can be called random) events. Although the book is a bit challenging at times for students on an introductory statistics course, it is one of the most entertaining books addressing the topic or randomness.

Tijms, H. (2007). *Understanding probability: Chance rules in everyday life*. New York: Cambridge University Press.

The first part of Tijms' book helps to demystify probability through the use of many interesting examples from everyday life.

3 ● 15 CHAPTER REVIEW QUESTIONS

1   In a 'name the can' campaign brand X randomly prints an equal number of 100 common names on their cans of cherry cola. What is the probability of your picking a can with the name 'Tim' on it, assuming that 'Tim' is one of the names?

   a   0.010
   b   0.001
   c   0.100
   d   1.00
   e   None of the above

2   In the above question, which approach to probability does the solution represent?

   a   Empirical
   b   Rational
   c   Multiplicative
   d   Additive
   e   Conditional

3   During one afternoon a barista at Csillag's coffee shop records how many customers order whipped cream on their espresso coffee. He finds that 150 out of the 200 customers order whipped cream. He concludes that the probability of a customer ordering whipped cream is 0.75. Which approach to probability does his conclusion represent?

   a   Empirical
   b   Rational

c   Multiplicative

d   Additive

e   Conditional

4   You roll a pair of dice, but one rolls off of the table. The one on top of the table that you see is a 6. You are unable to see the other die. What is the probability of its being a 6?

a   0.500

b   0.167

c   0.027

d   0.333

e   0.050

5   You roll a pair of dice, but one rolls off of the table. The one on top of the table you see came up a 6. You are unable to see the other die. What is the probability that both dice came up 6?

a   0.500

b   0.167

c   0.027

d   0.333

e   0.050

6   Which of the following two sets of playing cards are mutually exclusive?

a   Red cards and black cards

b   Red cards and kings

c   Black cards are kings

d   The four of hearts and red cards

e   All of the above sets are mutually exclusive

7   Which of the following pairs of variables are independent?

a   The flip of a coin and the roll of a die

b   Drawing a playing card from a deck and rolling a die

c   Two flips of a coin

d   Two rolls of a pair of dice

e   All of the above pairs of variables are independent

8   At a soccer penalty shootout the probability of a goal keeper saving a goal is 0.02. What is the probability of the goal keeper saving three out of three penalty shots, if all of the shots are independent? (Round to two decimal places.)

a   0.02

b   0.04

c   0.01

d   0.13

e   0.02

9   The probability of studying sociology and owning a car is an example of _____.

a   Bayes' law

b   continuous probability

c   conditional probability

d   joint probability

e   asymptotic trend

10   What are the new population mean and the new standard deviation when a population of scores with a mean of 50 and a standard deviation of 12 has been transformed to a standard normal distribution?

a   50 and 12

b   100 and 15

c   0 and 0

d   1 and 1

e   0 and 1

11   What is the probability of randomly selecting an observation with a z-score of 1 from a population?

a   0.00

b   0.84

c   0.50

d   0.16

e   0.01

12   What is the probability of randomly selecting an observation with a score less than 29 when the population has a mean of 50 and a standard deviation of 12?

a   0.96

b   0.84

c   0.04

d   0.48

e   0.23

Short-answer questions

1   How do the rational and empirical approaches to probability differ?

2   What is the 'asymptotic trend'?

3   How is the *ceiling effect* related to skewness?

4   Why is it important to identify outliers?

5   In a deck of playing cards, are *hearts* and *queens* mutually exclusive? Why?

6   What is the additive law of probability? How is it related to the assumption of mutual exclusivity?

7   How do a medical test's *sensitivity* and *specificity* influence the likelihood that a patient will have the disorder for which he or she was tested, if he or she tests positive?

8   Imagine creating a frequency histogram from a very large set of observations. Now imagine transforming those observations into z-scores and creating another frequency histogram. How will the two histograms compare with each other?

Data set questions

1   In the table in Figure 3.43, are height (tall or short) and choice of beverage (coffee or tea) independent? Why?

2   Using the table found in Question 1, what is the probability of being tall and preferring tea?

3 In the table in Figure 3.44, are height (tall or short) and choice of beverage (coffee or tea) independent? Why?

	Height	
	Tall	**Short**
Coffee	312	312
Tea	298	298

Figure 3.43

	Height	
	Tall	**Short**
Coffee	121	312
Tea	121	198

Figure 3.44

4 If the probability of a basketball player making a free throw is 0.5, what is the probability of the player making 9 out of 10 free throws?

5 If the probability of a basketball player making a free throw is 0.8, what is the probability of the player making 9 out of 10 free throws?

6 Your car dealer has informed you that her computer assessment of your car indicates that your emission control device is about to fail. Assume this device only fails in about 5% of all cars. The dealer further informs you that in those cases where the emission control device fails the computer would correctly identify the problem 80% of the time. Furthermore, her computer indicates a problem in only 2% of the cars when there is no problem with the emission device. What is the probability that your car's emission control device will shortly fail?

7 If we assume the emission control device in Question 6 fails in about 10% of all cars, what is the probability that your car's device will shortly fail?

8 If a population has a mean of 60 and a variance of 81, within what two scores will 95% of the observations fall?

9 An instructor who teaches introductory-level Italian has found over the years that students in her classes spend on average 28 minutes a week practising in the language lab. She also knows that the standard deviation is 5 minutes per week. She looks at the log book for the lab and finds a student who spent 38 minutes in the lab this week. Does she have evidence that this student comes from a different 'population' than the other students who are in her course? On what basis can she draw the conclusion? What limitation should she place on her conclusion?

Don't forget to use the online resources! Meet your supporting stats tutor through an **introductory video**, review your maths skills with a **diagnostic pre-test**, explore statistical principles through **interactive simulations**, practice analysis techniques with **SPSS datasets**, and check your work with **answers to all in-text questions**.

https://study.sagepub.com/bors

PART II
BASIC RESEARCH DESIGNS

The discussion of z-scores in the previous chapter represented an initial use of *inferential statistics* and *hypothesis testing*. That is, we began integrating the core material necessary for all data analyses which was presented in the first three chapters: the logic, descriptive statistics, and probability theory. In the chapters that comprise Part II of this book the material covered in Part I is further applied and expanded to allow for the analysis of basic research designs. The application involves various combinations of (1) the type of research question (difference versus association), (2) the type of data (measurement versus categorical), and (3) probability theory. The forms of analysis to be considered include the binomial test, the χ^2 tests, the *t*-test, the correlation and regression coefficients, and the one-way analysis of variance.

Regardless of the type of question or the type of data, the form of analysis always centres on what is to be *expected*, in terms of both the researcher's hypothesis and the *null hypothesis*. As mentioned in Chapter 1, what is *expected* in terms of the hypothesis tested usually is *not* what the researcher is expecting. For purposes of hypothesis testing, usually it is the *null hypothesis* that is formally *expected* and used to assess what is *observed*. When the data are categorical in nature, the null hypothesis is stated in terms of frequencies. When the data are measurement in nature, the null hypothesis is often stated in terms of means. Probability theory provides the foundation for estimating how much variability in the frequencies or means can be reasonably anticipated (expected) due to chance alone. Probability theory also provides the basis for estimating the *reliability* of the difference or association observed.

4

Chapter contents

CATEGORICAL DATA AND HYPOTHESIS TESTING

KEY CONCEPTS: Bernoulli trial, binomial distribution, permutation, combinations, normal approximation, null hypothesis, Type I errors, Type II errors, power, chi-square goodness-of-fit test, expected frequency, observed frequency, Fisher's exact test, *P*-rep, Bayesian approach, *G*-test.

4 1 PURPOSE

The purpose of this chapter is to extend the introduction to hypothesis testing initiated in the previous chapter in which the standard normal distribution and z-scores were used to introduce testing a hypothesis concerning a single observation. Similarly, in this chapter the *binomial* distribution is presented and used as a bridge to a discussion of hypothesis testing. This requires a detailed presentation of the tradition of *null hypothesis* (H_0) testing. Criticisms of H_0 testing are reviewed and alternative approaches are briefly described. Finally, our first analysis of group data within the context of H_0 testing is presented through a detailed introduction to Pearson's chi-square goodness-of-fit test and common alternatives. With respect to our orienting framework, in this chapter we focus on a family of tests based on the intersection of (1) a research question of difference and (2) categorical data.

4 2 INTRODUCTION

Let us momentarily return to the classic probability paradigm of flipping a coin. In the previous chapter we used the laws of probability to determine the likelihood of observing various outcomes. Using the multiplicative law, we were able to calculate the probability of two heads resulting from two tosses, or even ten heads (or ten tails) after ten tosses. Furthermore, by combining the multiplicative law with a subtraction strategy we were able to calculate the probability of obtaining nine heads after ten tosses. Other questions may be posed, however. What is the probability of obtaining six heads after ten tosses? Moreover, what is the probability of *six or more* heads after ten tosses? Such questions can be placed within the context of testing an *hypothesis*. For example, I suspect (hypothesize) that the probability of obtaining heads and the probability of obtaining tails with this particular coin are unequal. To test my suspicion I conduct a little experiment. I toss the coin ten times and observe eight heads. Is there sufficient evidence to support my suspicion concerning the coin?

4 3 THE BINOMIAL DISTRIBUTION

In this section an elementary distribution related to categorical data and the logic for its associated inferential test are presented. The *binomial* distribution is to a categorical binary variable what the standard normal distribution is to a continuous measurement variable. We now extend the Chapter 3 discussion of the laws of probability and combine that extension with a further discussion of hypothesis testing. As will be found throughout this book, two procedures or tests at first appearing to be disparate may suddenly be seen to be alike. For example, as the number of observations increases, the binominal distribution can be treated as a continuous measurement variable, allowing for the conversion to the standard normal distribution and the inferential use of z-scores.

The components of the binomial distribution

1   *Bernoulli trial.* A Bernoulli trial is an event that results in one of only two mutually exclusive outcomes (e.g., a coin flip). See the discussion of mutually exclusive events in Section 3.6.

2   *A series of independent trials.* The Bernoulli trial is repeated a given number of times. For example, the coin may be flipped 10, 100, or 1000 times and the number of observed heads (or tails) is recorded. See the discussion of independent events also in Section 3.6.

3   *Combinations.* The law of combinations (combinatorials) is a procedure for determining the number of ways a given number of items (subsets) can be drawn from a larger set (or population) of the items. For example, how many ways can 8 heads be obtained after 10 tosses of a coin?

4   *Multiplicative law of probability.* The multiplicative law is combined with the formula for determining the number of combinations in order to produce an *expected* frequency distribution or histogram for the possible outcomes. For example, if you are flipping a coin 10 times, there are 11 possible outcomes in terms of the number of observed heads: 0, 1, 2, 3, 4, 5, 6, 7, 8, 9, 10. What are the *expected* relative frequencies for these possible outcomes?

==== REVIEW QUESTION ====

What does the multiplicative law of probability state? What does it assume? What is the probability of all 10 tosses of a coin coming up heads?

Web Link 4.1 for an answer to the review question.

Let us construct a binomial distribution for a set of 10 Bernoulli trials. If you are bored with flipping coins, you might imagine a classrooms of students, none of whom have studied, making *random* guesses on a 10-item true/false quiz. (Who knows, perhaps they are flipping a coin to determine the answers to the 10 questions.) The operative word is *random*. Accordingly, the distribution we are constructing reflects the distribution of grades on the 10-item true/false quiz, assuming the students are only guessing and that guessing true and guessing false are equally probable (probability 0.5).

Permutations and combinations

We begin by defining the concepts of permutations and combinations. The *permutations* associated with an event are all of the possible ways of arranging a given number of items being selected from a larger set, where the order of selection is important. Imagine you have a set of four letters: A, B, C, and D. You write each letter on a slip of paper and place the slips in a hat. You select the slips in subsets of two. On your first draw you may select an A and then on the second draw you select a B. You now have one permutation: AB. You return the two slips to the hat and repeat the process. Because the order of selection is important, selecting B on the first draw and selecting an A on the second (BA) is considered a different permutation from AB. It is possible to enumerate and determine how many permutations there are for a set of four letters taken two at a time. Figure 4.1 lists all 12 possible permutations.

First draw	Second draw
A	B
A	C
A	D
B	A
B	C
B	D
C	A
C	B
C	D
D	A
D	B
D	C

Figure 4.1

••••••

The term 'permutation' comes from the Latin noun *permutatio*: *per* meaning 'thoroughly' and *mutatio* meaning 'an alteration or an exchange'. The term is also related to the Latin verb *mutare*, which means to change. The English verb 'to mutate' also is derived from *mutare*.

As the set of letters becomes larger and larger – imagine doing this for the entire alphabet – it becomes an onerous a task to enumerate all possible permutations of two. Although it is not always necessary to identify each particular permutation, what is vital is knowing exactly how many possible permutations exist.

••••••

Figure 4.2

Source: Rubik's Cube. Permission is granted to copy, distribute and/or modify this document under the terms of the GNU Free Documentation License, Version 1.2 or any later version published by the Free Software Foundation

In 1974 the Hungarian architect Ernő Rubik developed the puzzle that is known as Rubik's cube (Figure 4.2). In the Standard 3 × 3 × 3 configuration with six colours, how many possible positions (permutations) are there?

See http://b.chrishunt.co/how-many-positions-on-a-rubiks-cube. This link provides a step-by-step solution to this challenging question.

Thanks to the twelfth-century Indian mathematician Bhaskara II and others, there is a mathematical shortcut for deriving the number of possible permutations (Bigg, 1979). Some authors credit our old friend from Chapter 3, Blaise Pascal, with the formalization of the procedure.

The mathematical shortcut is straightforward, and is expressed as

$$P_k^N = \frac{N!}{(N-k)!},$$

where P is the number of possible permutations, N is the number of items in the entire set, k is the number of items to be selected, and '!' is not an indication of excitement, but a factorial sign. Applying this formula to the above example of four letters selected two at a time, we find the following:

$$P_k^N = \frac{N!}{(N-k)!} = \frac{4!}{(4-2)!} = \frac{4 \times 3 \times 2}{2} = 12,$$

which is the number of permutations found when enumerated in Figure 4.1.

When computing permutations the order of selection is considered, and selecting AB is different from selecting BA. For the binomial distribution, however, order is unimportant. On your 10-item true/false quiz, you will need a subset of the permutations called *combinations* that eliminates the irrelevant redundancy. If you examine the 12 permutations enumerated in Figure 4.1 and eliminate the redundancy, you arrive at the six possible combinations of the four letters listed in Figure 4.3.

A	B
A	C
A	D
B	C
B	D
C	D

Figure 4.3

Again, thanks to our friendly mathematicians, we have a shortcut:

$$C_k^N = \frac{N!}{k!(N-k)!},$$

where C is the number of possible combinations, N is the number of items in the set, and k is the number of items to be selected. Applying this to the four letters selected two at a time, we find the following:

$$C_k^N = \frac{N!}{k!(N-k)!} = \frac{4!}{2!(4-2)!} = \frac{4 \times 3 \times 2}{2 \times 2} = 6,$$

which is the number of combinations enumerated in Figure 4.3.

To begin constructing the distribution for students guessing on a 10-item true/false quiz, let us return to the basic building block. If there is only one item on the quiz and the students were merely guessing, the expected frequency distribution would be 50% incorrect (a score of 0) and 50% correct (a score of 1). The histogram representing these relative frequencies is found in Figure 4.4.

What if there were two questions on the false/true quiz? Figure 4.5 enumerates the possible outcomes. As seen in the figure, 25% (1/4) of the possible combinations are expected to have two incorrect answers (score = 0), 50% (2/4) of the combinations are expected to have one correct and one incorrect answer (score = 1), and 25% of the combinations are expected to have two correct answers (score = 2).

The expected binomial distribution is represented by the relative frequency histo-

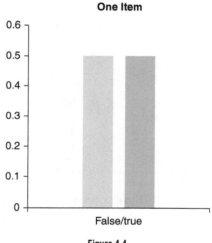

One Item

Figure 4.4

Item 1	Item 2
Correct	Correct
Correct	Incorrect
Incorrect	Correct
Incorrect	Incorrect

Figure 4.5

Unless stated otherwise, we are assuming that both possible outcomes of the binomial have a probability of 0.5.

gram in Figure 4.6. Another way to express the expected distribution is in terms of probability. For example, if students are merely guessing on a two-item false/true quiz, the probability of a student having a score of 0 is 0.25.

━━━━━━━━━━ REVIEW QUESTION ━━━━━━━━━━

What is the probability of a student having a score greater than 0 on the two-item false/true quiz? Does this question remind you of another question in Chapter 3?

Web Link 4.2 for an answer to the review question.

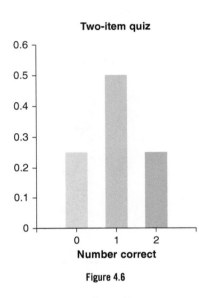

Two-item quiz

Number correct

Figure 4.6

There is also a shortcut for deriving the probabilities associated with each of the possible combinations. If we start with the binomial (correct/incorrect) and assume that the probability of each outcome is 0.5, we can easily compute the probabilities associated with the three possible outcomes. Because there are two quiz items, we simply square the binomial to derive the probabilities:

$$(0.5 + 0.5)^2 = (0.5 + 0.5)(0.5 + 0.5)$$
$$= 0.5^2 + 2 \times 0.5 \times 0.5 + 0.5^2$$
$$= 0.25 \ (\text{score} = 0) + 0.50 \ (\text{score} = 1)$$
$$+ 0.25 \ (\text{score} = 2).$$

The same strategy can be applied to a true/false quiz with three items by cubing the binomial, and arriving at the following set of probabilities associated with the four possible combinations: 0 correct, 1 correct, 2 correct, and 3 correct. The expected binomial distribution is represented by the relative frequency histogram in Figure 4.7.

$$(0.5 + 0.5)^3 = 0.5^3 + 3 \times 0.5^2 \times 0.5 + 3 \times 0.5 \times 0.5^2 + 0.5^3$$
$$= 0.125 \ (0 \text{ correct}) + 0.375 \ (1 \text{ correct}) + 0.375 \ (2 \text{ correct}) + 0.125 \ (3 \text{ correct}).$$

It is clear that this method for constructing the binomial distribution will quickly become tedious, to say the least. One of the redeeming features of mathematics is that it always provides another route, or shortcut. We now return to constructing a distribution that reflects the *expected distribution* of grades on your 10-item true/false quiz, based on the assumption the students are only randomly guessing. We further assume the probability of guessing true on any given item is 0.5. This is the point where the combinatorials and the multiplicative law of probability are put together. The following formula reflects the amalgamation:

Note that, as discussed in Chapter 3, the sum of the probabilities of all possible outcomes (combinations) must sum to 1.

Remember, any number raised to the zero power is 1; for example, $0.5^0 = 1.0$.

$$P(k) = C_k^N p^k q^{(N-k)}.$$

In our example, P(k) is the probability of answering k number of items correctly; N is the number of trial or items on the quiz; C_k^N is the number of ways (combinations) of answering k number of items correctly on a quiz consisting of $N = 10$ items,

$$C_K^N = \frac{N!}{K!(N-K)!};$$

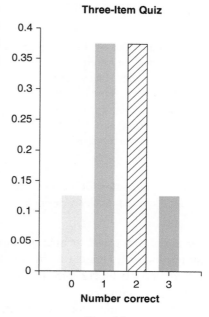

Three-Item Quiz

Number correct

Figure 4.7

p is the probability of the desired outcome (correct answer); and q is the probability of the undesired outcome (incorrect answer), $1 - p$.

To construct the binomial distribution for your 10-item quiz you need to solve the above formula 11 times, once for each possible number of items answered correctly. Begin with your luckiest students, those who answered all 10 items correctly, simply by guessing:

$$P(10) = C_{10}^{10} \times 0.5^{10} \times 0.5^0.$$

Note that

$$C_{10}^{10} = \frac{10!}{10!10!} = 1,$$

meaning there is only one way (combination) for a student to answer 10 out of 10 correctly. Thus,

$$P(10) = 1 \times 0.5^{10} \times 0.5^0 = 0.001,$$

so 0.1% of your students who are guessing on the 10-item quiz are expected to answer all 10 items correctly.

Repeating the process for those students correctly guessing 9 out of the 10 items correctly, we find

$$P(9) = C_9^{10} \times 0.5^9 \times 0.5^1.$$

Now

$$C_9^{10} = \frac{10!}{9!1!} = \frac{10}{1} = 10,$$

so there are 10 ways (combinations) for a student to answer 9 out of 10 items correctly. Thus,

$$P(9) = 10 \times 0.5^9 \times 0.5^1 = 0.01$$

The reason why the qualifying word 'expected' is placed in front of the words 'probabilities' and 'frequencies' is that these probabilities and frequencies are based on the rational approach to probabilities discussed in Chapter 3. Consequently, they represent the probabilities and frequencies theoretically found after the 10-item true/false quiz was administered to an infinite number of students, all of whom were merely guessing.

For the discussion of rational versus empirical approaches to probability, see p. 83 in Chapter 3.

or 1% of your students are expected to guess 9 of the 10 items correctly. Figure 4.8 reports the *expected probabilities* associated with all 11 possible outcomes. Figure 4.9 is a relative frequency histogram of the expected probabilities.

Notice that, even with as few as 10 items on your true/false quiz, the *expected distribution* of the scores is an 'edgy' approximation of normality centred on the score of 5. You may suspect this to be the case because the probability of both correct and incorrect guesses is 0.5. Your suspicion is both correct and incorrect. Returning to the two-item version of your true/false quiz and assuming the probability of guessing correctly to be only 0.25, rather than 0.5, Figure 4.10 then reflects the *expected distribution* of scores: P(0 correct) = 0.56; P(1 correct) = 0.38; P(2 correct) = 0.06. The distribution is severely, positively skewed. Your suspicion seems confirmed.

When the number of true/false items on your quiz is increased to 100, however, the picture changes dramatically. The upper right-hand histogram in Figure 4.11 depicts the *expected distribution* of the scores when the probability of guessing correctly is only 0.25, but in this case there are 100 items. Although the distribution looks very normal, it is not perfect. As with all four distributions in Figure 4.11, the tails of the distributions extend to both the minimum and maximum possible values. Therefore, in the upper right-hand histogram there is more of a tail to the right than to the left of the modal score. Thus, the distribution is slightly, positively skewed. After exploring all four histograms in Figure 4.11, it is evident that when there are 100 or more binomial trials (e.g., true/false questions), all *expected* binomial distributions approximate normality. This is even the case in the upper left-hand histogram in Figure 4.11 where the probability of guessing correctly is only 0.1. It is the location of the modal score and not the basic shape of the distribution that changes as the probability of guessing correctly changes. Remember, this is based on the rational approach to probability where an infinite number of observations are assumed.

No. correct	Probability
0	0.001
1	0.010
2	0.044
3	0.117
4	0.205
5	0.246
6	0.205
7	0.117
8	0.044
9	0.010
10	0.001

Figure 4.8

The normal approximation

It is this characteristic of normality which allows the standard normal distribution and *z*-scores to be used to estimate probabilities related to a binomial variable. This is another shortcut. If you

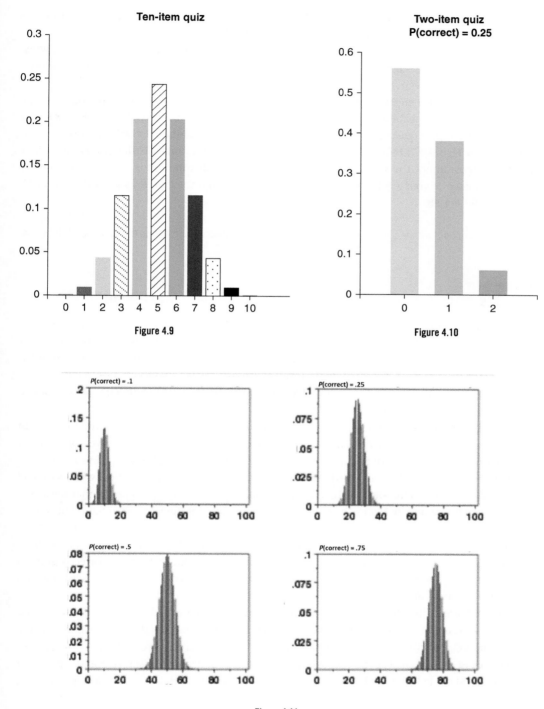

Figure 4.9

Figure 4.10

Figure 4.11

re-examine the four histograms in Figure 4.11, you will notice that the centre of all of the distributions is $100 \times$ P(guessing correctly), 100 being the value of N. When P(guessing correctly) is 0.1 the centre of the distribution is near 10; when P is 0.25 the centre of the distribution is near 25; when P is 0.5 the centre of the distribution is near 50; and when P is 0.75 the centre of the distribution is near 75.

In fact, the *expected* mean of a binomial distribution can be estimated by multiplying the number of trials by the probability of the desired outcome (e.g., guessing correctly): Np. For example, when $N = 10$ and $p =$ P(guessing correctly) is 0.5 the mean of the binomial distribution is 5. This is confirmed by Figure 4.7. Moreover, the expected variance of a binomial distribution is Npq, where q is $1 - p$. Accordingly, the standard deviation of a binomial distribution is $\sqrt{Npq}$. Therefore, the *expected* variance of your 10-iten quiz is $10 \times 0.5 \times 0.5 = 2.5$ and the *expected* standard deviation is $\sqrt{10 \times 0.5 \times 0.5} = 1.58$.

 Web Link 4.3 for the interactive demonstration for an empirical approach to the binomial distribution.

4 ● 4 HYPOTHESIS TESTING WITH THE BINOMIAL DISTRIBUTION

Earlier in the chapter the binomial was deemed a distribution that provided a framework for hypothesis testing. The *binomial* distribution is a discrete probability distribution, unlike the standard normal distribution, which is continuous in nature. In the previous chapter during the discussion of the z-table, a 95% confidence interval was established to fashion a simple inferential test. As mentioned in Chapter 1, typically researchers wish to have 95% confidence in the conclusions they draw regarding their observations.

We begin our discussion of using the binomial distribution for inferential purposes with the simplest of examples and a 95% confidence interval. Is a single observation a member of a given population? (For a discussion of the 95% confidence interval and the z-table, see pp. 120 and 115) in Chapter 3.

Again return to your 10-item true/false quiz where all of the students are merely guessing and the probability of guessing correctly is 0.5. In such cases, the rational expectation is that the scores on the quiz will be distributed as they are in Figures 4.8 and 4.9. Imagine a student comes to us and claims he studied and was not guessing. Subsequently we find that he answered eight items correctly. Do we have evidence that he was not simply guessing? (Note that the question is about evidence with respect to guessing, not studying.) Is answering 8 out of 10 items correctly enough to persuade us? To answer the question, we apply a strategy analogous to that used with the 95% confidence intervals and the z-table in Appendix A.

Unless there are compelling reasons to do otherwise we will always conduct a two-tailed test. This is one of those occasions where it might make sense to consider a one-tailed test. Certainly it makes little sense to suppose studying is detrimental to performance. Let us begin, however, with the two-tailed test to keep the discussion parallel to that of the z-table and 95% confidence intervals. To evaluate the claim that a score did not belong to a given population it is necessary to determine the two scores bracketing 95% of the population, 2.5% on the lower end of the distribution and 2.5% on the upper end.

The simplest way to evaluate your student's claim is to determine if guessing 8 or more items correctly has a probability less than 0.025. A probability less than 0.025 would put the score outside of the 95% confidence interval for the 'guessing' population. There is no single binomial table of probabilities for discrete variables, but we have already constructed a table that is appropriate for your purpose. Figure 4.8 provides the basis for the evaluation. We simply need to sum the probabilities of guessing 8, 9, or all 10 items correctly. If the sum of the probabilities is greater than 0.025, we must conclude that there is insufficient evidence to support the student's claim that he was not guessing. To be specific, there is insufficient evidence to reject the assumption that he is a member of the guessing population. The sum of the relevant probabilities is shown in Figure 4.12.

Bear in mind that his claim is not what was directly evaluated. What was tested was his possible membership in the guessing population. This will be further discussed later in the section on null hypothesis testing.

No. of items correct	probability
P(8)	0.044
P(9)	0.010
P(10)	0.001
Total probability	0.055

Figure 4.12

Unfortunately for your student, the total probability (0.055) is greater than 0.025. Had the sum of the probabilities been less than 0.025, we would have rejected the notion that the student was a member of the population of students who were merely guessing. This would indirectly support his claim to have studied.

================ REVIEW QUESTION ================

Had we decided to use a one-tailed test, how would the test be conducted and what conclusion would you draw?

Web Link 4.4 for an answer to the review question.

Returning to the normal approximation, we find another shortcut useful for testing the student's claim. As we saw, the *expected value* or mean number of items correctly guessed on a 10-item test is 5, and the standard deviation is 1.58. The binomial problem can be converted into a z-score problem. The question is how to calculate the probability of a score of 8 or greater. Recall that we have a discrete, not a continuous, variable. Consequently, the score of 8 has a probability associated with it (0.044), unlike a score of 8 on a continuous variable, which has a probability of 0. Consequently, the first task is to determine the value to be converted into a z-score. If the score of 8 is converted, we will obtain a probability for a score greater than 8, but it will not include the score of 8. As an adjustment, we might transform the question into what the probability is of a score greater than 7, which would include the probability associated with a score of 8:

$$z = \frac{y - \mu}{\sigma} = \frac{7 - 5}{1.58} = 1.27;$$

Turning to Appendix A and the table of probabilities we find that the probability of a z-score less than 1.27 is 0.8980. Thus, the probability of a z-score greater than 1.27 is $1 - 0.8980 = 0.102$. It might be thought that the probability of correctly guessing 8 or more items correctly is 0.102. Because this probability is greater than 0.025, we continue to fail to find sufficient evidence that the student is not a member of the guessing population. Notice that the probability associated with the conversion to a z-score problem (0.102) is substantially different from the probability associated with the binomial approach (0.055). The source of the difference resides in the disparity between the smooth distribution of a continuous variable and the staircase-like distribution of a discrete variable.

We might attempt to minimize the disparity and smooth out the steps of the discrete variable by basing the z-score on a quiz score of 7.5. When we do so we find

$$z = \frac{(y - \mu)}{\sigma} = \frac{7.5 - 5}{1.58} = 1.58.$$

Turning to Appendix A, we find that the probability of a z-score less than 1.58 is 0.9429. Therefore, the probability of a z-score greater than 1.58 is $1 - 0.9429 = 0.057$, which is similar to the original binomial probability of 0.055. As the number of trials (e.g., quiz questions) increases and approaches 100, the disparity between the two approaches becomes negligible.

======== REVIEW QUESTION ========

If the probability of guessing the correct answer on a 10-item true/false quiz were 0.25, what would be the mean score of a population of guessers? What would be the probability of guessing 8 or more of the 10 items correctly? What would you conclude?

Web Link 4.5 for the answers to the review question.

In the next chapter we will see how the binomial distribution forms the basis for another elementary inferential statistic: the sign test. Later in this chapter we will see how the χ^2 goodness-of-fit test is an extension of the logic that underpins the binomial test.

======== CHALLENGE QUESTION ========

Dr. Rongeur has discovered there is a particular type of cheese that is toxic for mice and affects their locomotion. Normally, when placed on a treadmill mice walk almost exclusively forwards, rarely backwards. Mice that have ingested the toxic cheese have a probability of 0.6 of walking forwards. To test a particular mouse for the toxin, Dr. Rongeur placed the mouse on a treadmill and observed 10 steps. If after the 10 steps the mouse is 8 steps forward of where it was placed, does Dr. Rongeur have evidence that the mouse has ingested the toxic cheese?

Web Link 4.6 for an answer to the challenge question.

---

4 ● 5 CONDUCTING THE BINOMIAL TEST WITH SPSS

On the book's web page click on and open the data file *drama10.sav*.

From within the **Data Editor**, select **Analyze** from the menu along the top and drop down to **Nonparametric Tests**, slide over to **Legacy Dialogs**, and finally slide over to and select **Binomial**.

When the **Binomial Test** window opens, highlight and move the variable *drama* over to the **Test Variable List** (Figure 4.13). Leave the **Test Proportion** option set at 0.50. This sets the probabilities of the two possible outcomes (1 and 0) for the test. When the option is set at 0.50, H_0 is that the two possible outcomes are equally probable. Finally, click **OK** to run the test.

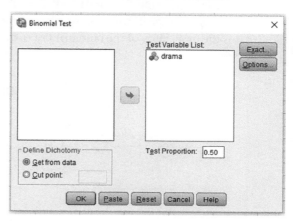

Figure 4.13

The SPSS output window displays the results of the test (Figure 4.14). The **Binomial Test** table lists the conditions (*Category*) 1.00 and 0.00, which correspond to the items answered correctly and incorrectly. *N* states the number of observations in each category. The next column reports the *observed* probability (*Observed Prop.*) associated with the number of observations in each category. The column labelled *Test Prop.* reports the probability assigned to the first category according to H_0. The last column reports the probability (*Exact Sig. (2-tailed)*) for the observed distribution: 0.109. Because the probability is greater than 0.05, we fail to reject H_0.

●●●●●

You may wonder why the probability of the binomial test is reported as the *exact* probability of a two-tailed test (*Exact Sig. (2-tailed)*). The easiest way to explain the word 'exact' is that there is no intermediate step of computing a *test statistic*. The intermediate test statistic is then used to obtain a probability, assuming H_0. The X^2 goodness-of-fit test we will discuss later in this chapter involves the computation of a test statistic. Rather than deriving an intermediate test statistic, an exact test directly calculates the probability. When extended beyond the binomial test, the procedure for calculating an exact probability is referred to as Fisher's (1922) exact test, or simply the *exact test*. In some cases, for measurement data, SPSS makes available an analogous procedure called 'bootstrapping', which will be introduced in the next chapter. These procedures for directly calculating the probability associated with a set of observations are related to the randomization test, which was briefly described in Section 1.5. You may ask, why use the intermediate step of test statistics when exact probabilities can be calculated? There are two reasons. The first is historical. When exact tests or randomization testing was theoretically developed, for all but small samples, the calculations were prohibitively time-consuming. There were no computers! The second reason is availability. As data sets become larger and research designs more complicated, the procedures needed for calculating exact probabilities become more complicated and software packages with appropriate procedures are not readily available. Fortunately, under most circumstances test statistics provide reasonably accurate estimates of the probabilities.

Looking back at the analysis of the quiz data, we arrived at a probability of 0.055 for 8 or more correct guesses. Recall that we were testing the probability of 8 or more correct guesses against 0.025 in order to conduct a two-tailed test. We only examined one end of the distribution. To fully complete the two-tailed test at $\alpha = 0.05$ we also need to compute the probability of guessing 2 or fewer items correctly. Looking back at Figure 4.8, we discover that the combined probability of correctly guessing, 2, 1, or 0 items correctly is also 0.055. When we combine the probabilities of the two ends of the distribution we have a probability of 0.11. Allowing for rounding differences, this is the probability of the binomial test (two-tailed) reported in the SPSS output (0.109).

Binomial Test

		Category	N	Observed Prop.	Test Prop.	Exact Sig. (2-tailed)
drama	Group 1	1.00	8	.80	.50	.109
	Group 2	.00	2	.20		
	Total		10	1.00		

Figure 4.14

On the book's web page open the data file **drama100.sav. When the Binomial Test window opens again, highlight and move the variable drama over to the Test Variable List. Leave the Test Proportion option set at 0.50. Then click OK to run the test.**

Binomial Test

		Category	N	Observed Prop.	Test Prop.	Exact Sig. (2-tailed)
drama	Group 1	.00	20	.20	.50	.000
	Group 2	1.00	80	.80		
	Total		100	1.00		

Figure 4.15

The SPSS output window displays the results of the test (Figure 4.15). The *Binomial Test* table lists the conditions (*Category*) 0.00 and 1.00, the number of observations in each category (20 and 80), the observed probability, and the probability assigned to the first category according to H_0. Because the test probability (approaching 0.000) is less than 0.05, we reject H_0. Although the binomial test for 8 of 10 and the test for 80 of 100 are proportionately the same, in the case of the former we fail to reject, but in the case of the latter we reject the null hypothesis. This illustrates the crucial role sample size plays in statistical analysis.

Rerun the pervious analysis on the *drama100.sav* file but change the *Test Proportion* option to 0.3 (Figure 4.16). What are the results and what do you conclude?

Web Link 4.7 for an answer to the review question.

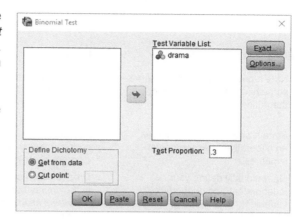

Figure 4.16

4 ● 6 NULL HYPOTHESIS TESTING

● ● ● ● ●

The term 'null hypothesis' can be traced back to the Latin phrase *null hypothesin*. Null is short for *nullus* and is made up of the negation *ne* and *ullus* meaning 'any'. Together they mean 'none'. The word 'hypothesis' goes back to the Greek words ὑπο (hypo) meaning 'under' and θεσις (thesis) meaning 'placing' or 'proposition'. Therefore, null hypothesis denotes 'no proposition'; that is, the researcher begins with the assumption that nothing is happening.

In Chapter 1 the traditional model of null hypothesis testing was briefly introduced. In practice today the model is an amalgamation of the approaches of Fisher (1935) and Neyman and Pearson (1933). The traditional null hypothesis (H_0) provides researchers with an evaluation framework, regardless of the type of research question, the type of data collected, or the statistical test. It is the framework, though not without its critics, that is often used to determine if there is sufficient evidence to support (albeit *indirectly*) the researcher's actual hypothesis, often called the *experimental hypothesis* or *alternative hypothesis* (H_1). The operative word in the previous sentence is 'indirectly'. Evidence supporting H_1 is said to be indirect because the support is based on testing and rejecting H_0, which typically states that randomness alone is responsible for what is observed. There are exceptions to this characterization of H_0, one of which will be encountered later in this chapter. This section further elaborates the pivotal notions of Type I error, Type II error, and statistical *power*.

Figure 4.17 summarizes the iterative process of empirical research in which H_0 plays a crucial role.

Activity	Examples
1 Note a practical problem, observe something intriguing, confront a theoretical problem.	An increase in the dropout rate in my statistics course; Many sports fans hate winning teams: Manchester United, New York Yankees, Collingwood Magpies; Is intelligence one thing or many things?
2 State a proposition or your idea, an alternative or experimental hypothesis: H_1.	The amount of individual attention students receive in a statistics course influences the dropout rate: comparing two classes with different levels of individual attention.
3 Operationally define your independent and dependent variables.	*Dropout rate* equals the proportion of those who were registered in the course but who did not write the final examination. *Individual attention level* equals the number of students per teaching assistant (TA) in the course.
4 Construct the null hypothesis: H_0.	The number of students per TA in a course is unrelated to the dropout rate.
5 Construct a sampling distribution, a baseline for evaluating the observation relative to H_0.	How much class-to-class variability would be expected in the dropout rate due to chance alone?
6 Evaluate H_0: reject or fail to reject.	Rejection is based on the strength of the association between the student per TA ratio and the dropout rate.
7 Draw conclusion.	Consistent with the evaluation of H_0, conclude that there *is* or there *is not* sufficient evidence to support the idea that the level of individual attention influences the dropout rate in my statistics course.
8 Critique and evaluate the research; redesign or abandon the project and return to step 2.	Perhaps having fewer students per TA did not actually produce increased individual attention; perhaps there was too small of a difference in the student/TA ratio to produce an effect; insufficient statistical power.

Figure 4.17

To illustrate the null hypothesis, and the general research paradigm (Figure 4.17) within which it is imbedded, picture the following scenario. Imagine that you and I investigate various personality dimensions of rabbits. To supply our needs, for the past 10 years we have bred a colony of Jersey Wooly rabbits. Yesterday in the faculty club we were accosted by several of our colleagues from the visual arts department. They accused us of running a sloppy laboratory and of allowing our rabbits to escape and run amok. One colleague reported finding a brazen bunny on her desk munching the remains of her salad.

We know we operate a secure lab. We must establish empirical evidence that these rogue rabbits are not ours, however. Fortunately, we have population data describing several personality traits of our rabbits. One way to establish if the rogue rabbits are not from our lab is to compare an aspect of their personalities with what we know of our rabbits. For example, imagine we have data on the willingness of our rabbits to explore. In terms of

this personality dimension, we suspect the rogue rabbits behave differently from ours. Specifically, we expect the rogues

> Here we see point 1 from Figure 4.17: *a problem is encountered.*

are more willing to explore. H_1 makes an empirical prediction. Sometimes the prediction is strong and directional (e.g., the rogue rabbits will be more willing to explore than will ours), and sometimes it is weak and non-directional (e.g., the rogue rabbits will behave differently from our rabbits).

How do we empirically measure a rabbit's willingness to explore? In our lab we operationally define 'willingness to explore' as the number of squares in an *open field* a rabbit enters during a five-minute testing session. There may be many operational definitions of 'willingness to explore', and some researchers may take exception to ours and question its *ecological validity*. Furthermore, different choices of operational definition may yield different results. Although divergent results may be frustrating, they also provoke and aid in the development of the

> Here we see point 2 from Figure 4.17: *an experimental hypothesis.*

researcher's theory. A good operational definition has two important qualities: reliability and validity. As described in Chapter 1, a *reliable* operational definition results in stable scores. A broken thermometer is not likely to provide me with consistent estimates of my temperature over a brief time period, assuming that my body temperature remains unchanged. Instruments need not be 'broken' to be unreliable. For example, if our subjects do not understand instructions, their responses may reflect circumstances other than those described by our operational definition. To the degree our measures – as shaped by our operation definitions – are unreliable, unnecessary variance will be added to our data, we will lose statistical power, and our results will be difficult to replicate. Furthermore, without adequate reliability, our dependent variable's *validity* is compromised. An operational definition is valid only to the extent that it leads to observations which actually measure the concept being investigated. Does open-field behaviour truly represent a rabbit's willingness to explore? Does it estimate the rabbit's willingness to explore? How many other factors may influence open-field behaviour? These are all important questions. Finally, it must be kept in mind that an operational definition may be reasonably reliable and valid for one population, but not for another.

■■■■■ • • • • • ■■■■■

The open-field apparatus has been found to be quite reliable; whether or not it is a valid measure of our breed of rabbits' 'willingness to explore' is less certain. It has been used to measure anxiety-like behaviours in rabbits (Seibenhener & Wooten, 2015). The apparatus's ecological validity for our rabbits, however, is still another question. That is, will performance in the open-field apparatus predict how our jersey wool rabbits will behave in the overgrown wilds of my garden?

For the discussion of ecological validity, see p. 18 in Chapter 1.

An open-field apparatus is neither open nor is it in a field. It is a box in a lab (see Figure 4.18). The rabbit is placed in the box and its movements across grid lines on the floor are recorded.

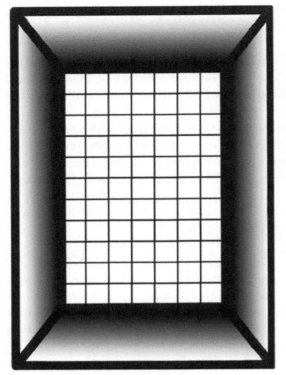

Figure 4.18

Here we see point 3 from Figure 4.17: *operational definitions.*

Here we see point 4 from Figure 4.17: *stating the null hypothesis.*

Here we see point 5 from Figure 4.17: *constructing a sampling distribution.*

A difference of 0.5 minutes may appear small. A difference of 30 seconds may sound larger. A difference of 3000 milliseconds may sound huge. The three differences are, of course, identical. Furthermore, whether that difference is small or large is unknown without further information.

We know the population mean and standard deviation of our colony. To test our suspicion that the rogue rabbits are not from our lab, we capture ten of the rouges and test them in our open-field apparatus.

We are not directly testing the hypothesis that the rogue rabbits are more willing to explore the open field than are our rabbits. We are testing the hypothesis that any difference between the open-field activity of the rogue rabbits and the open-field activity of our rabbits is not large enough for us to conclude that they do not originate from our colony: H_0. The null hypothesis can be expressed in different ways. It might be stated in terms of the two means:

$$\bar{y}_{\text{rogue rabbits}} = \bar{y}_{\text{our rabbits}}, \quad \text{or}$$
$$\mu_{\text{rogue rabbits}} = \mu_{\text{our rabbits}}, \quad \text{or}$$
$$\mu_{\text{rogue rabbits}} - \mu_{\text{our rabbits}} = 0.$$

(Of course, we are hoping that any observed difference is large enough for us to conclude that there is sufficient evidence to reject the notion that the rogue rabbits are members of our colony.)

Not all empirical research has a fully developed H_1 and H_0. Particularly in the early stages of researching a topic, alternative hypotheses are often not expressed at all. Furthermore, as will be evident in the last two chapters of this book, some very important forms of empirical research will make few if any specific predictions.

Simply comparing the mean of the rogue rabbits' open-field behaviour with our rabbits' population mean will not be an adequate assessment of their similarity or dissimilarity. Differences between means that seem large may in fact be trivial; differences that appear slight may prove to be immense.

As seen in the previous chapters, the probability of the two means being exactly the same is virtually 0, even if the rogue rabbits are escapees from our lab. Because we are comparing means, we need to know how much sample-to-sample variance we might expect in the means of a samples drawn from our lab's population. This sample-to-sample variance (sampling distribution) forms the basis for evaluating the difference between the rogue rabbits' open-field activity and that of our population. The sampling distribution allows for a probability to be assigned to the assessment of H_0. The details regarding the comparison of two means will be presented in the next chapter. (For the sampling distribution of the mean, see p. 60) in Chapter 2.)

Sampling distributions are sensitive to sample size. In our current case, the sampling distribution of the mean is the standard deviation of the population divided by the sample size,

$$\sigma_{\bar{y}}^2 = \frac{\sigma^2}{n},$$

and the standard error of the mean is

$$\sigma_{\bar{y}} = \frac{\sigma}{\sqrt{n}} .$$

When the population variance is unknown, the sample variance is substituted into the formula.

We now are in the position to assess H_0. If the probability of a difference of the observed

> Here we see point 6 from Figure 4.17: *evaluate H_0.*

magnitude or greater is less than 0.05 we *reject H_0*. If the probability is greater than 0.05, we *fail to reject*. We never 'prove' H_0 or H_1. When we fail to reject, we are merely stating that there is insufficient evidence to reject H_0.

Any conclusion drawn must be consistent with the evaluation of H_0. If we reject H_0, we may conclude that there *is* evidence supporting our hypothesis (H_1) that the rogue rabbits are not from our lab. If our H_1 was strong and directional, we need to examine the means again. If we had hypothesized that the rogue rabbits are more willing to explore the open field than are our rabbits, then the mean of the rogue rabbits must be greater than that of our population's mean. Otherwise, even though we may reject H_0, the results do not

> Unless otherwise stated, in this book we will always use a two-tailed test to evaluate H_0.

> Here we see point 7 from Figure 4.17: *draw a conclusion.*

> Here we see point 8 from Figure 4.17: *critique and evaluate.*

support our specific hypothesis. There is still some evidence, however, that the rogue rabbits did not originate in our lab. If we fail to reject H_0, we must conclude that there *is* insufficient evidence to support our H_1.

If we reject H_0 and conclude there is evidence supporting our H_1, the argument with our colleagues is not over. One experiment never resolves a debate nor answers a practical question.

• • • • •

There are those who have argued that no amount of empirical research will settle theoretical debates. This does not mean that empirical research is irrelevant, only that empirical evidence alone is insufficient to unseat the dominant theoretical position. For those interested in this topic, the seminal work of Thomas Kuhn (1996) on the distinction between periods of 'normal science' and periods of 'revolutionary science' and on the role of 'anomalies' in 'paradigm shifts' in science is recommended.

As mentioned in Chapter 1, it is possible to incorrectly reject H_0: a Type I error. Besides, we certainly wish to design further research comparing the rogue rabbits with our population on this and other personality dimensions, in hopes of further supporting our suspicion. If we fail to reject H_0 and conclude there is insufficient evidence to support our H_0, all may not be lost. As also mentioned in Chapter 1, it is possible to incorrectly fail to reject H_0: a Type II error. In such cases, we need to examine our research design, particularly in terms of the operational definitions and the reliability of our measures. The issue of *statistical power* always looms whenever we fail to reject H_0. Regardless of the outcome of our experiment with the rogue rabbits, we need to evaluate and design further research and then loop back to point 2 in the research process.

How sure are we of our conclusions?

Because they are present throughout the rest of this book, the problems of *Type I errors*, *Type II errors*, and *statistical power* deserve further attention. When a null hypothesis is tested it is because the researcher is unsure of its veracity: is it true or false? Certainly, when research involves the replication of previous findings, the researcher often has an informed idea about its veracity. Yet, even then, he or she cannot be absolutely certain what will emerge from his or her data. Whenever a researcher statistically tests H_0 there are four possible outcomes. These outcomes are depicted in Figure 4.19.

	State of the null hypothesis	
	True	**False**
Reject	Type I error α	Correct rejection power $= (1 - \beta)$
Fail to reject	Correct failure to reject $(1 - \alpha)$	Type II error β

Figure 4.19

The four outcomes are embedded in a two-dimensional matrix. The state of H_0 is either true or false (but unknown) and the researcher either rejects or fails to reject H_0. Glancing down the 'True' column of Figure 4.19, we see that when H_0 is true, there are only two possible outcomes. The researcher either incorrectly rejects H_0 and commits a Type I error, or he or she correctly fails to reject H_0.

The probability of incorrectly rejecting a true H_0 is symbolized by the Greek letter α (alpha). The α level is set by the researcher prior to testing H_0. Typically, for the sort of simple designs discussed in this part of the book, α is set at 0.05. Thus, IF H_0 is true, the researcher has a 5% chance of finding 'hens teeth': that is, something that does not exist.

> The only way for researchers to be 100% certain of not making a Type I error is for them to never reject H_0, which means they will never have evidence to support their H_1.
>
> For the discussion of conditional probability, see p. 93 in Chapter 3.

Stated in terms of expected frequencies, IF H_0 is true and 100 researchers ran the same experiment, we expect 5 of them to reject H_0 and conclude they have evidence supporting H_1. Because it is impossible to be 100% certain that a Type I error is avoided, 95% is the commonly agreed-upon level. As discussed in detail in Chapter 11, there are circumstances in which it is necessary to reduce α to 0.01 or even smaller.

The probability of correctly failing to reject a true H_0 is $1 - \alpha$, usually $1 - 0.05 = 0.95$. There are only two outcomes when H_0 is true. From what was presented in Chapter 3, we know the total probability of an exhaustive set of mutually exclusive outcomes must be 1. Consequently, IF H_0 is true and $\alpha = 0.05$, the probability of correctly failing to reject a true H_0 is 0.95. This corresponds to the 95% confidence intervals. If $\alpha = 0.01$, then the probability of correctly failing to reject a true H_0 is 0.99.

• • • • •

Note that the probabilities of *correctly* failing to reject H_0 or *incorrectly* rejecting H_0 are both 0 when H_0 is false. The word IF in the previous two paragraphs conditionalizes the probabilities to only those circumstances when H_0 is true.

Scanning down the 'False' column of Figure 4.19, we see that IF H_0 is false, there are only two possible outcomes. The researcher either correctly rejects H_0 because it is false, or incorrectly fails to reject.

Let us first examine the bottom row of the 'False' column. IF H_0 is false and the researcher fails to reject it, he or she is committing a Type II error. The probability of incorrectly failing to reject a false H_0 is symbolized by the Greek letter β (beta). Unlike in the case with α, the researcher cannot directly determine the β level. Instead, he or she attempts to minimize β by increasing the probability of correctly rejecting a false H_0.

The probability of correctly rejecting a false H_0 is called *power*, the researcher's chances of finding an existing effect. Power is $1 - \beta$. Turning it around, the probability of β is 1 minus power. Power is affected by a researcher's knowledge of the topic and by the appropriateness of the research design. In psychology, the social sciences, and the biological sciences researchers aim for a minimum power of 0.80. That is, IF H_0 is false, the researcher hopes to have at least an 80% chance of rejecting H_0. Why settle for 80% when we desire a 95% chance of being correct when H_0 is true? The reason is that the data in these disciplines tend to be very 'noisy'. The dependent variables (DVs) are influenced by many uncontrollable incidental variables; consequently, the DVs have relatively large variances, an important factor in determining power. (For the discussion of incidental variables, see p. 16 in Chapter 1.)

• • • • •

Imagine I wish to wear my new cardigan today. I ask my mother if she has seen my new cardigan. She replies (hypothesizes) that she believes it is in my closet. I open the closet door and quickly glance inside. I do not see it. My mother tells me to look closer, because my closet is always a mess. This time I quickly scan most of the contents. Still I do not find my missing cardigan. My mother is certain that the cardigan is in my closet and implores me to take my time and systematically look through each item. I may or may not locate my cardigan, but that is not the moral of the story. The point is that should I wish to be certain that the cardigan is not in my closet, I need to give myself a good chance of finding it. The parable of my missing cardigan teaches us about the need for statistical power. The three examinations of the contents of my closet parallel what can be called weak, moderate, and strong *power*. When we spend significant amounts of time and money planning our research, regardless of whether it is experimental or observational in nature, IF H_0 is false, we want to have a strong chance of rejecting it and finding evidence for our predicted *difference* or association. All too often researchers fail to ensure adequate levels of power. Why spend the time and money when the chances of rejecting a false H_1 are weak, no better than flipping a coin: heads I reject and tails I fail to reject.

Assuming we set α at 0.05, power is determined by three factors:

1   The size of difference between the *expected* and the *observed*
2   The amount of the variance in the DV
3   The number of observations or sample size.

The first factor is the size of the difference between what was *expected* (H_0) and what was *observed*. In the case of the above rogue rabbit experiment, what was *expected* was no difference between the two means. What was observed was something other than a difference of 0. This first factor may also be described in terms of associations. For example, according to H_0 we may *expect* no association between (1) the price of a pair of shoes and (2) how quickly they wear out. In itself, the size of the difference between what is *expected* and what is *observed* is not very informative. But the larger the difference between the *expected* and the *observed*, the greater the power. As a consequence, it is important to maximize the range in the levels of the independent variable (IV) in order to allow any influence it has on the DV to be uncovered. Of course, the range of the levels of the IV needs to be consistent with theoretical or practical concerns.

This second and the third factors together determine the variability in the differences or in the associations *expected due to chance alone*. The amount of the variance in the DV influences power. The smaller the variance, the greater the power. Variance in the DV is often referred to as *noise*. You walk into a party listening for the voice of a friend who may be there: your H_1.

The more people there are in the room speaking (the greater the noise), the more difficult it will be to hear her voice. In research, looking for your predicted difference or association (H_1) is analogous to listening for that voice. The variance in your DV is analogous to the noise level at the party. As a consequence, researchers try as much as possible to exert control over their data collection procedures. By holding constant as many sources of variance (incidental variables) as possible, the variance in the DV is reduced and the power is increased. In many ways statistical analysis is all about variance. The existence of variance is the primary, if not the only, reason for this book as well as the entire field of statistics.

Turning to the third factor, once the levels of the IV have been determined and the researcher has done what he or she can do to reduce the noise in the DV, the size of the sample is decisive. Where an increase in variance will reduce power, an increase in the number of observations (sample size) increases statistical power.

Usually the most difficult of the three factors to manipulate is the first, the size of the difference or the strength of the association. The next most difficult is usually variance. Even in experimental research, there is only so much that can be done to reduce variance in the DV. Researchers at times appear to be obsessed with reducing 'noise'. There have been occasions when I resorted to administering a visual acuity examination to ensure that my subjects in a reaction time experiment had 20/20 vision (Bors et al., 1993). All of the individual differences found among humans and animals contribute to the variance in our DVs. Typically it is sample size that the researcher has the most freedom to control. There are exceptions, however, particularly in clinical areas and other forms of applied research.

— — — ● ● ● ● ● — — —

When the sample size is small and it is impossible to substantially increase it over a reasonable time frame, power of 0.80 is difficult to attain. This is often common in clinical studies where the rate of encountering a particular diagnosis is low. In such cases it is crucial that the researcher attempts to improve design elements to increase effect size and to reduce noise, which is easier said than done. There are cases when it is best to admit that the study should not be conducted, as currently designed.

Sample size is so often the key to power that Jacob Cohen (1992), who 'wrote the book' (Cohen, 1988) on power, created tables for researchers to consult to ensure a power of 0.80 (see Appendix B, Tables B.1 and B.2 (Cohen, 1992)). Our first inspection of the range of required sample sizes found in the table should illustrate convincingly the role of sample size (n) in determining the probability of rejecting a false H_0. If we examine row 1 of Table B.2 (Mean Dif) and inspect the three central columns ($\alpha = 0.05$), we find the required n per condition ranges from 393 to 64 down to 26, depending upon whether the researcher is interested in a small (Sm), medium (Med) or large (Lg) effect. There will be numerous occasions throughout this book to consult Appendix B.

Several authors have pointed out some practical limitations inherent in the use of Cohen's tables. For example, the first step in using Cohen's tables (Appendix B) is to identify the desired effect size. This is not always obvious or easy (Lenth, 2001). There are circumstances when small effects are theoretically or practically valuable. Similarly, it is often difficult to have an accurate estimate of the expected variance in a DV (as operationally defined). Furthermore, effect size estimates are highly sensitive to a DV's reliability for the particular population from which the sample was drawn. These issues underline the usefulness of pilot studies to aid the researcher in refining his or her design (Hulley et al., 2007).

• • • • •

The purpose of conducting a pilot study is to examine the feasibility of the researcher's approach. It is a small-scale trial run of the instruments, DVs, methods, and testing procedures to be used in the full-scale study. While the sample size can be relatively small, it should be large enough to provide the researcher with an evaluation of the procedures, and with estimates of the effect size and variance. Thus, a pilot study helps the researcher in gauging the number of subjects required for adequate power.

Criticism of traditional H_0 testing

We begin with three criticisms that are often true, but are easily addressed:

1   H_0 is never true.
2   H_0 testing confuses statistical significance with theoretical or practical significance.
3   H_0 testing leads to a 'lost and found' approach to interpreting results.

The effect size for our rogue rabbit example would be the difference between two means divided by the population standard deviation, or its sample estimate.

The claim that H_0 is never true rests on a particular understanding of the concept of population. The discussion concerning finite and infinite populations and their relationship to this criticism is beyond the scope of this book. For a defence of H_0 against this and other criticisms see Hagen (1997).

One of the standard, almost uncontested, criticisms is that H_0 is never true. Cohen (1990, p. 1308) himself states: 'The null hypothesis, taken literally (and that's the only way you can take it in formal hypothesis testing), is always false in the real world.'

Although there is much merit to this criticism, the case is often overstated (Abelson, 1997). No one is claiming to attempt to *prove* H_0, or at least they should not be. Furthermore, it is better to understand H_0 in relation to the effect size being tested rather than to an absolute zero effect. Assume that for practical or theoretical reasons a researcher is interested in a moderate effect and, using Table B.2 in Appendix B, collects data from a sample designed to test a moderate effect. A failure to reject H_0 connotes that there is insufficient evidence to reject the assumption (H_0) of a moderate or larger effect. Failure to reject does not imply that there is absolutely no effect. On the other hand, a researcher who is interested only in a large effect size may collect data sufficient for testing for a small effect size. In such cases rejecting H_0 is of less importance than establishing the size of the effect. To report only the *p*-value and the rejection of H_0 and no further information is poor practice and deserves strong criticism.

A second criticism of H_0 testing is that the practice leads to confusion between *statistical significance* and *theoretical* or *practical significance*. Sometimes this criticism is framed in terms of *p*-value versus effect size. If a researcher has a very large sample, it is possible to obtain a *statistically significant difference* or association, although the actual size of the difference or the observed strength of the association is negligible and of little consequence either theoretically or practically. As seen earlier with regard to the binomial test, holding constant the proportional difference between the frequencies in two categories while increasing the number of observations from 10 to 100 will change the outcome's probability from 0.055 to near 0.000.

A third and parallel criticism is that H_0 testing leads to a 'lost and found' approach to interpreting results. Unfortunately, researchers all too often believe that if their results have $p > 0.05$, they have *lost* (i.e., found nothing), even when the *p*-value is as small as 0.051. Likewise, researchers too often are absolutely certain they have found something if $p < 0.05$, even when the *p*-value is as large as 0.049. When researchers act in this simplistic manner they are illustrating a disregard for the issues of Type I errors, Type II error, and power, and should be censured. The flaws portrayed by these first three criticisms, however, are not inherent in H_0 testing and can be addressed through proper practice.

For those interested in reading what amounts to a roundtable discussion of the pros and cons of H_0 testing, Vol. 8 of *Psychological Science* (1997) is a special issue of the journal devoted to this debate.

Other criticisms of H_0 testing will be examined within the context of alternative approaches.

The *P*-rep alternative

Some critics point out that H_0 testing results in a probability regarding the *absence* of any effect, not the *presence* of an effect. Killeen (2005) and others argue for an alternative that would report the probability of *replicating* the *observed* effect. P-rep (the probability of replication) is approximated by the following formula:

$$P\text{-rep} = \left\{ 1 + \left(\frac{p}{1-p} \right)^{2/3} \right\}^{-1}$$

where p is the observed *p*-value from the statistical test of H_0.

For example, imagine you decide to test H_1 that customers in your coffee shop prefer *Helen's Home Made* donuts to *Frank's Factory Made* donuts and found the results yielded a *p*-value of 0.04. You reject H_0 and conclude there is sufficient evidence to reject the notion of equal preference, and thus you find *indirect* support for your H_1. (This assumes that Helen's donuts were the preferred brand.) Appling the *p*-value resulting from the test, you would arrive at

$$P\text{-}rep = \left\{ 1 + \left(\frac{0.04}{1-0.004} \right)^{2/3} \right\}^{-1} = 0.89.$$

From this you would conclude there is an 89% chance of replicating the preference for Helen's Home Made donuts over Frank's Factory Made product. *P*-rep values of 0.85 or greater are considered large.

P-rep initially found support and was accepted as an alternative to the reporting of *p*-values. It has since lost some support due to several criticisms. Iverson et al. (2009) examined *P*-rep under various conditions and found it was (1) commonly miscalculated, (2) misapplied outside of a narrow scope, and (3) frequently resulted in values leading to the misinterpretation of data. Furthermore, because *P*-rep estimates are derived directly from the observed *p*-value, no new information is gained. If you examine the formula, you will discover that a *P*-rep value of 0.85 roughly corresponds to a *p*-value of 0.06. In other words, the *P*-rep cut-off roughly corresponds to the *p*-value it is intended to replace.

The randomization testing alternative

The logic of the randomization test was briefly introduced in Chapter 1. Proponents of the *randomization* or the *permutation test* are not necessarily opposed to testing H_0, but rather the manner in which it is tested. They highlight the potential distortions associated with the assumption of normality necessary for *indirectly* obtaining a probability from a *hypothetical* sampling distribution. Their point is that it is unlikely that the assumption is ever met. (For the discussion of a normal distribution, see p. 110 in Chapter 3.)

As an alternative, the randomization test derives the probability of an observed test statistic *directly* by calculating all possible values of the test statistic by iteratively rearranging the collected data. Thus, an *empirical* sampling distribution is produced from the researcher's data.

Recall from Chapter 1 the sorting of ten scores into two groups of five. Imagine two waiters working in a restaurant in Budapest, Hungary. Waiter 2 tells waiter 1 that because he smiles more than waiter 1 he receives larger tips. To test the waiter's belief (H_1) each waiter serves five customers. For the sake of the example, assume that all ten customers order a bowl of *gulyás* and their bills are identical. Once the customers have left, the two waiters examine their tips. The results are in Figure 4.20. Because the restaurant is in Hungary, the currency is the forint. We find in Figure 4.20 that waiter 1 received a total of 1500 forints and waiter 2 a total of 2500 forints, a difference of 1000 forints. There is a test statistic (the *t*-test) used to estimate the probability of such a difference being due to chance alone. We will discuss this test in detail in the next chapter. That test requires the assumption of normality, however. The randomization test avoids this assumption and directly computes the probability of a difference of 1000 forints. The H_0 is that there is *no reliable difference* in the tips received by the two waiters and any *observed difference* is due to chance alone. Stated another way, the tips have been randomly received by the waiters.

Waiter 1	Waiter 2
Tips	Tips
100	700
400	500
200	300
500	400
300	600

Figure 4.20

The first step in the randomization test is to take those ten tips (values) and randomly reassign them to the two waiters, recalculate the two new totals, and record the difference. For example, Figure 4.21 is one possible reassignment. Waiter 1 now has a total of 1700 forints and waiter 2 a total of 2300 forints, a difference of 600 forints. We then repeat the random reassignment, totalling, and recording of the difference. Figure 4.22 depicts the results of this iteration, where the difference is only 100 forints, and this time in waiter 1's favour.

Waiter 1	Waiter 2
Tips	Tips
500	100
400	700
200	500
300	400
300	600

Figure 4.21

This process of randomization, computing the totals, and recording the differences is repeated a very large number of times. Ideally all possible *combinations* are used. Employing the combinatorial formula we used in the section on the binomial test, we find that there are 252 possible combinations. (See p. 129 for the section on combinations.)

Once the calculations are completed, the 252 differences are rank-ordered. This becomes the *sampling distribution* against which the original difference is assessed. The original, observed difference can be located in the rank ordering of the 252 differences. The number of differences greater than 1000 forints is divided by the total number of combinations examined (252). For example, if 21 of the differences are greater than 1000 for-

Waiter 1	Waiter 2
Tips	Tips
300	300
400	500
500	100
200	600
700	400

Figure 4.22

ints, the empirically derived probability of a difference of 1000 forints or greater would be 0.083 (21/252). Because the probability (0.083) is greater than 0.05, the waiter fails to reject H_0 and concludes that there is insufficient evidence to support his hypothesis. If there are only 5 differences greater than 1000 forints, the probability would be 0.02. Because 0.02 is less than 0.05, the waiter would reject H_0, and conclude that there is evidence supporting his hypothesis.

The randomization approach to testing hypotheses is not new. The idea goes back at least as far as Fisher's (1922) early work. Computational limitations restricted its use, however. There were no computers! Even now when samples are large and research designs are complex, as they are in Part III of this book, constructing empirical sampling distributions becomes an arduous task, to say the least. Fisher's major contribution was to demonstrate that by making a small number of assumptions about the underlying distribution of the observations, a reasonable estimate of the randomization test could be calculated. Although software is becoming more available which allows for the randomization testing of more complicated designs, it continues to have limited application, particularly for those researchers without advanced programming skills.

The Bayesian alternative

Over the last two decades the Bayesian approach has become the most established alternative to null hypothesis testing. The central criticism of proponents of the Bayesian approach is that traditional H_0 testing does *not* test the researcher's H_0. Rather, it tests the probability of H_0. Consequently, support for the researcher's is H_0 *indirect*. The Bayesian approach to hypothesis testing is unique in that it does not involve H_0. Instead, alternative hypotheses, often referred to as *models*, are compared. Following the collection of data, the model that 'best fits', in terms of probability, is deemed to be the one supported (Burnham & Anderson, 2002). The foundational framework for this approach was already presented in Section 3.8 on Bayes' theorem (see p. 99).

Another way to describe the difference between H_0 testing (often referred to by the Bayesians as the *frequentist* approach) and the Bayesian approach is to compare their assumptions at the outset of an experiment. The frequentist approach to testing uses only the data generated by the current experiment, and the typical H_0 of no effect is tested. The Bayesian approach incorporates previous results and what might be called a *subjective* appraisal of previous research. This is manifested in what is called the 'priors' or the prior probabilities, which replace the null hypothesis. Most beneficially, the *priors* can be updated following each round of data collection.

> It may help to think of the priors as *informed estimates* of the size of the differences or of the strength of the associations.

> For those interested in a full description of the Bayesian alternative, *A Student's Guide to Bayesian Statistics* (2018) offers a readable and comprehensive resource. Like other alternatives, the Bayesian critique and alternative is most understandable after you have completed the first two parts of this book.
>
> The following web link provides a good discussion of the pros and cons of Bayesian hypothesis testing: http://andrewgelman.com/2011/04/02/so-called_bayes/

It is the *priors* which represent both the purported strength and the alleged weakness of this approach. The strength is reflected in the fact that researchers know more than 'nothing' when they undertake a research project. On the other hand, it is not always easy to assign prior probabilities, and therein lies the weakness. Small adjustments to the estimates of the priors can make substantial differences in the relative probabilities of the competing models. As user-friendly software is being developed, Bayesian alternatives are becoming more popular in many areas of research, and many proponents of the approach recognize the crucial issue of how best to determine the priors. For example, Punt and Hilborn (1997), researching fish stocks, point out how crucial it is to fully document the basis for the choice of priors.

4 ● 7 THE X^2 GOODNESS-OF-FIT TEST

When discussing the binomial test we imagined a classroom of students, none of whom had studied, randomly guessing at the answers on a true/false quiz. Assuming that guessing true and guessing false were equally probable (0.5), we constructed expected frequency distributions, which served as sampling distributions, for quizzes with 1, 2, 3, and 10 items. (See Figures 4.4–4.10 on pp. 131–135.)

We also used the distribution of the ten-item quiz to assess the likelihood of someone guessing eight or more items correctly. In the above section on null hypothesis testing we elaborated more formally the process of empirical research and statistical testing, including the necessity of evaluating all possible outcomes.

In this section we extend the logic of binomial testing. Rather than comparing one observation against the expected distribution, we will compare an *observed distribution* against an *expected distribution*. This will be our first example of an inferential statistic often found in published research papers. For this section, imagine that you are the artistic director for your university's drama department. For purposes of future programme planning, you wish to know if students, staff, and faculty prefer comedies or tragedies. To answer your question you send out a survey to the members of the university community. If their choices are unconsidered and random, the probabilities of the two theatrical forms would be equal (0.5). The probabilities would be the same if half of the university community thoughtfully preferred comedies and the other half tragedies: a 50–50 split. However, you have the suspicion (H_1) that more members of the university community prefer comedies over tragedies.

REVIEW QUESTION

If you had 10 respondents to your drama survey, what would be the probability of 8 or more respondents choosing comedies, if the community were equally divided in their preferences?

Web Link 4.8 for an answer to the review question.

CHALLENGE QUESTION

If you had 100 respondents to your survey, what would be the probability of 80 or more of your respondents choosing comedies, if the community in fact were equally divided in their preferences?

Web Link 4.9 for an answer to the challenge question.

To answer the above review question you could use the binomial test as we did earlier when examining performance on the true/false quiz. Or, you might use the z-score transformation as we also did earlier in this chapter and use either 7 or 7.5 rather than 8 for computing the z-score (see Section 4.4).

To answer the above challenge question, for practical reasons, you may wish to forgo constructing a binomial distribution and immediately utilize the z-score transformation. There is a lesson to be learned from a comparison of the answers to the review and challenge questions. The

> Always beware when percentages are reported without specifying the total number of observations. Unfortunately, you will frequently find this ploy used in advertisements. Those writing in the business and sports pages and on blogs often also are guilty of this, intentionally or unintentionally.

percentage difference between the *expected* and the *observed* is *not* indicative of the probabilities associated with the binomial test. When eight out of ten respondents (80%) prefer comedies the probability is greater than 0.05 (two-tailed test). When 80 out of 100 (again 80%) respondents prefer comedies the probability approaches 0 (a z-score of 6 is off of the table). This also demonstrates the importance of sample size, as discussed in relation to power. (See the above discussion of sample size and power on p. 149.)

In this section we will discuss a third approach to analysing your survey data regarding theatre preferences. In doing so, we meet Karl Pearson (1900) for the first time. He developed what is now called the Pearson χ^2 test to evaluate the probability that an observed set of categorical frequencies differs from the set of expected frequencies. The test takes two forms, although the computations are identical. The first form, the χ^2 goodness-of-fit test, is described here. The second form, the χ^2 test of independence, will be addressed in a later chapter.

The assumptions of the χ^2 test are as follows:

1   Both forms of the test assume that the observations have been randomly sampled from a population.
2   Both forms also assume independence of observations. Practically speaking, this means that there is only one observation per subject and that a subject's response fits into one and only one of the mutually exclusive categories.
3   Finally, both forms assume that all *expected frequencies* are 5 or greater.

For a discussion of mutual exclusiveness, see p. 89 in Chapter 3.

● ● ● ● ●

The χ^2 test is a *nonparametric* test developed for assessing differences between observed and expected frequencies when the dependent variable is nominal in nature. *Nonparametric* tests do *not* rely on estimating population parameters, such as those described in Chapter 2 (e.g., means and variances). Nor do nonparametric tests require some assumptions about the underlying distribution of the data. *Parametric tests*, which we will begin to discuss in the next chapter, rely upon estimating population parameters, and require certain assumptions about the underlying distributions. As you will discover in subsequent chapters, researchers often have a choice between using a parametric test and using a nonparametric test to analyse their data. That choice will often revolve around the researcher's willingness to make certain assumptions.

The χ^2 goodness-of-fit test formula is straightforward, and reflects our basic framework of *observed versus expected*:

$$\chi^2 = \Sigma \left(\frac{(\text{the category's observed frequency} - \text{the category's expected frequency})^2}{\text{the category's expected frequency}} \right)$$

or in symbolic terms,

$$\chi^2 = \Sigma\left(\frac{(O - E)^2}{E}\right),$$

where the calculation is repeated for each category and summed.

· · · · ·

The reason for dividing the difference between the observed and the expected frequencies (squared) by the expected frequencies is to 'standardize' the difference. A difference of 3 is large if the observed frequency is 8 and the expected frequency is 5. A difference of 3 is relatively smaller, however, if the observed frequency is 80 and the expected frequency is 77. In the former instance, the observed frequency is 1.6 times greater than the expected frequency. In the latter case the observed frequency is only 1.04 times greater than the expected frequency.

· · · · ·

The χ^2 formula can be understood and written in terms of probabilities:

$$\chi^2 = N\Sigma\left(\frac{(p_{Oi} - p_{Ei})^2}{p_{Ei}}\right)$$

where p_{Oi} is the probability of the observed frequencies in a given category, p_{Ei} is the probability of the expected frequencies in a given category, and N is the total number of observations. The probability of an observed frequency is calculated by dividing the observed frequency by the total number of observations. This version of the formula makes clear the relationship between the number of observations and the resulting χ^2 value. Holding the two probabilities constant (probabilities can also be understood in terms of percentages), as N increases so does the χ^2 value and, as a result, the likelihood of rejecting H_0.

We know the *observed* frequencies for your two categories: 8 (comedy) and 2 (tragedy). The corresponding *expected* frequencies need to be determined. These are obvious when you have only two categories and you assume that they are equally probable. With your 10 respondents, the expected frequency is 5 in each category. We need, however, a more systematic way of determining the expected frequencies for circumstances when the probabilities are unequal and when there are more than two categories. The general formula for computing the expected frequencies is to multiply the total number of observations by the *expected probability* for each category: Np_i, where N is the total number of

If you assumed that the probabilities for comedy and tragedy were 0.6 and 0.4, respectively, then E(comedy) = 10 × 0.6 = 6 and E(tragedy) = 10 × 0.4 = 4.

observations and p_i is the probability for the particular category. In terms of your survey data, the two expected frequencies are

$$E(comedy) = 10 \times 0.5 = 5 \quad \text{and} \quad E(tragedy) = 10 \times 0.5 = 5.$$

Now that we have determined the expected frequencies we can calculate the χ^2 value:

$$\chi^2 = \Sigma \left(\frac{(O-E)^2}{E} \right) = \frac{(8-5)^2}{5} + \frac{(2-5)^2}{5} = 1.8 + 1.8 = 3.6.$$

Is 3.6 a large enough χ^2 value to reject H_0? That is, is the probability of the observed χ^2 value less than 0.05? As will be the case with most tests discussed in this book, the degrees of freedom (*df*) are crucial. The *df* for a χ^2 goodness-of-fit test is the number of categories minus one, or ($k - 1$). You have two categories in your survey (comedy and tragedy): 1 *df*. The next step is to consult the table of *critical values* in Appendix C.

A *critical value* is a value or criterion used for determining whether or not an observed statistic is significant at a given α level, usually 0.05, 0.025, or 0.01. Generally the *observed* value must be greater than the critical value for H_0 to be rejected, but there are tests where the observed value must be smaller than the critical value.

The table of critical values found in Appendix C is organized by α and *df*. Looking across the *df* = 1 row to the α = 0.05 column we find a critical value of 3.841. To reject H_0 an *observed* χ^2 with 1 *df* must be great than 3.841. Because your observed χ^2 (3.6) is less than the critical value (3.841), you fail to reject H_0 and conclude that you have insufficient evidence to reject the assumption that your university community are equally divided with regard to theatrical preferences. As a consequence, in terms of your suspicion (H_1), you conclude that there is insufficient evidence to support the idea that a majority of the university community prefer comedies.

 Web Link 4.10 for a χ^2 interactive demonstration of the interrelationships among the elements of the formula.

4●8 THE χ^2 GOODNESS-OF-FIT TEST WITH MORE THAN TWO CATEGORIES

In the previous section we used the χ^2 goodness-of-fit test to analyse your survey where respondents had a choice between two categories. Again let us imagine that you are the artistic director, and for purposes of future programme planning you wish to know if the university community prefer comedies, tragedies, or musicals. Because we are now dealing with a multinomial variable (more than two categories of responses), you cannot resort to the binomial test, nor can you transform the data into a *z*-score problem. If the university community are equally divided among the three theatrical forms, all three probabilities would be 1/3. Should you find that the university community is not equally divided in their preferences, you are willing to reconsider an earlier decision to stage an equal number of performances of the three forms. After receiving 15 responses to your survey you find that 9 respondents prefer comedies, 2 respondents prefer tragedies, and 4 respondents prefer musicals.

Recall from Chapter 2 the *variation ratio*, a measure of a categorical variable's variability: $VR = 1 - fm/N$, where fm is the frequency of the modal category and N is the total number of observations. Not many, but some disciplines routinely report the VR. The frequency of your modal category (comedy) is 9. The resulting $VR = 1 - \frac{9}{15} = 0.4$. The greater the

VR, the more equally distributed are the observations. If your modal category contained only 7 out of the 15 respondents, then $VR = 1 - \frac{7}{15} = 0.53$. In general, the less dominant the modal category, the more variable (spread out across the categories) the observations.

For the discussion of variance and categorical data, see p. 66 in Chapter 2.

We know the *observed* frequencies for the three categories, but the corresponding *expected* frequencies need to be determined. The formula for computing the expected frequencies is to multiply the total number of observations by the *expected probability* of each category: Np_i, where N is the total number of observation and p_i is the probability for the particular category. In terms of your new survey data, the three expected frequencies are $E(comedy) = 15 \times \frac{1}{3} = 5$, $E(tragedy) = 15 \times \frac{1}{3} = 5$, and $E(musical) = 15 \times \frac{1}{3} = 5$. Now that we have determined the expected frequencies we can calculate the χ^2 value:

$$\chi^2 = \Sigma \left(\frac{(O-E)^2}{E} \right) = \frac{(9-5)^2}{5} + \frac{(2-5)^2}{5} + \frac{(4-5)^2}{5} = 3.2 + 1.8 + 0.2 = 5.2.$$

Is 5.2 a large enough χ^2 value to reject H_0? The *df* for a χ^2 goodness-of-fit test is the number of categories minus one, or $k - 1$. With three categories there are 2 *df*. The next step is to consult the table of *critical values* in Appendix C. Looking across the $df = 2$ row over to the $\alpha = 0.05$ column we find a critical value of 5.991. Because your observed χ^2 (5.2) is less than the critical value (5.991), you fail to reject H_0 and must conclude that you have insufficient evidence to reject the assumption that your university community are equally divided with regard to the three theatrical preferences.

CONDUCTING THE χ^2 GOODNESS-OF-FIT TEST WITH SPSS

On the book's web page click on and open the **data file *drama3categories.sav*. From within the Data Editor,** select **Analyze** from the menu along the top and drop down to **Nonparametric Tests,** slide over to **Legacy Dialogs,** and finally slide over to and select **Chi-square.** When the

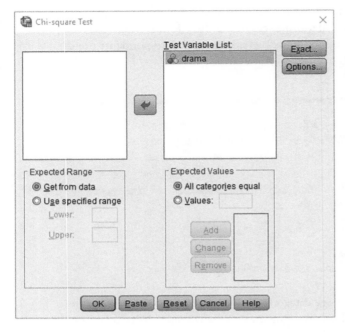

Figure 4.23

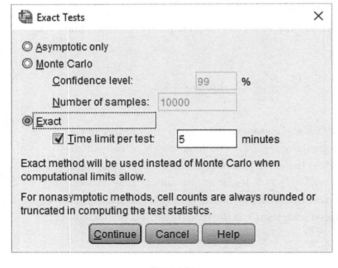

Figure 4.24

Chi-square Test window opens, highlight and move the variable drama over to the *Test Variable List* (Figure 4.23). *Leave the Expected Values* option set at *All* categories equal. Next click the *Exact* button on the right. When the *Exact Tests* window opens (Figure 4.24) click the *Exact* button and then *Continue*. Finally, click *OK* to run the test.

The SPSS output window displays the results of the test. The *Frequencies Test* table (Figure 4.25) lists the categories for the variable *drama* (*Category*): 0.00 (comedy), 1.00 (tragedy), and 2.00 (musical), along with their observed frequencies (*Observed N*) and expected frequencies (*Expected N*). The final column in the table (Residual) reflects the difference between the observed and expected frequencies.

The second table (*Test Statistics*, Figure 4.26) provides the analysis. The first row reports the Pearson X^2 value (5.200). Not surprisingly, it is identical to the one we computed for these data in the previous section. The second row reports the degrees of freedom: $df = 2$. The third row provides the p-value (0.074) based on the X^2 value (*Asymp. Sig.*). The next row (*Exact Sig.*) reports the probability derived using Fisher's (1922) exact test (0.093) as discussed earlier in the chapter. Rather than using Pearson's estimate, the exact test directly calculates the probability from the observations, assuming H_0. There is a slight difference in the two reported probabilities. In both cases, however, you fail to reject H_0. Nonetheless, you can see that it is possible for there to be borderline results where one probability may result in rejection of H_0 and the other probability results in a failure to reject.

The exact probability (*Exact Sig.*) always takes precedence over the probability based on the X^2 value (*Asymp. Sig.*). As the number of observations increases, the difference between the two

Frequencies

drama

	Observed N	Expected N	Residual
.00	9	5.0	4.0
1.00	2	5.0	-3.0
2.00	4	5.0	-1.0
Total	15		

Figure 4.25

Test Statistics

	drama
Chi-Square	5.200[a]
df	2
Asymp. Sig.	.074
Exact Sig.	.093
Point Probability	.050

a. 0 cells (0.0%) have expected frequencies less than 5. The minimum expected cell frequency is 5.0.

Figure 4.26

probabilities diminishes. When there are expected frequencies of 50 in all categories, the difference between the two estimates of the probability is virtually zero. The final row of the table (*Point Probability*) is irrelevant to your analysis. Note 'a' is of relevance, however. As stated earlier, the χ^2 goodness-of-fit test requires that all expected frequencies be 5 or greater. Moreover, it is prudent to require a minimum of 10. In an analysis where any of the expected frequencies is less than 10, it is absolutely imperative that the exact probability (*Exact Sig.*) be reported. Even then, additional data should be collected, if it is at all possible.

 10 POWER AND THE χ^2 GOODNESS-OF-FIT TEST

As discussed in the section on H_0, researchers should attempt to have at least an 80% chance of rejecting a false H_0. That is, they should strive for statistical *power* of 0.8 or greater. In a text box in Section 4.7 (see p. 154), an algebraic alternative formula for χ^2 was presented:

$$\chi^2 = N\Sigma\left(\frac{(p_{Oi} - p_{Ei})^2}{p_{Ei}}\right).$$

This formula can be used to calculate the minimum number of observations required to obtain a given χ^2 value. For example, turning to Appendix C, the critical value for a χ^2 with 1 *df* is 3.841. Substituting 3.841 for the χ^2 in the formula and solving for N using your data from the comedy versus tragedy survey (see p. 157) we find the following:

$$\chi^2 = N\Sigma\left(\frac{(p_{Oi} - p_{Ei})^2}{p_{Ei}}\right)$$

$$3.841 = N\left(\frac{(0.8-0.5)^2}{0.5} + \frac{(0.2-0.5)^2}{0.5}\right)$$

$$N = \frac{3.841}{\dfrac{(0.8-0.5)^2}{0.5} + \dfrac{(0.2-0.5)^2}{0.5}} = 10.7.$$

Thus, a minimum of 10.7 or 11 respondents would be required for the observed proportions to be statistically significant. Should you try, you will find that it is impossible to add one observation and maintain the same proportions for the observed frequencies: 80% versus 20%. This is a minor issue, however. More importantly, do not think that the calculation provides the number of observations (sample size) required for a minimum power of 0.8.

The above calculation provides the minimum sample size that would *make possible* a rejection of H_0. It does *not* indicate the *probability* of correctly rejecting a false H_0 with a sample of that size. Remember, the *expected* frequencies may remain fixed, but it is improbable that your *observed* frequencies will remain constant from sample to sample, regardless of the veracity of H_0. That is, there will be chance variability in your observed frequencies, regardless of the veracity of H_0. Cohen (1992) combined the above formula, without the N, with the fact that there would be variability in the observed frequencies to develop estimates of the required sample sizes for the researcher's test to have a minimum power of 0.8. Determining the required sample size for small, medium, and large effect sizes can be accomplished by the following steps:

1   The researcher determines the proportional difference among the categories that would be either theoretically or practically significant.
2   The proportions are translated into probabilities.
3   The probabilities are used to calculate W. For this we make use of our alternative χ^2 formula:

$$W = \sum\left(\frac{(p_{Oi} - p_{Ei})^2}{p_{Ei}}\right).$$

4   The obtained W is compared with the values found in Table B.1 in Appendix B.
5   The researcher establishes which standardized effect size is being tested.
6   The researcher uses Table B.2 to ascertain the required sample size to ensure a minimum power of 0.8.

Return to your comedy versus tragedy survey example and assume that you were only interested in changing your theatrical programming if there was at least a substantial (80%–20%) split in preference. These percentages translate into the probabilities of 0.8 and 0.2. Assuming an H_0 of equal probabilities (0.5 and 0.5) and substituting the values into the formula, you arrive at $W = 0.36$. Turning to row 6 for the χ^2 test in Table B.1, we find that 0.36 most closely matches the value for a medium effect size (0.30). Turning to Table B.2, you find that the required sample size for a χ^2 with 1 *df* and an α of 0.05 is 87. That is, you will need at least 87 respondents to ensure a power of 0.80.

If the researcher simply decides on a *standardized effect size* of interest rather than on a specific set of differences, then the procedure has fewer steps. For example, assume that for practical purposes a researcher considers only a large standardized effect size to be of interest. He or she then may go immediately to step 5. If we assume that the researcher has three categories in his or her data set ($df = 2$), then by turning to Table B.2 we find that the researcher will require at least 39 subjects.

The question often arises as to what to do about findings that 'approach significance'. What if the resulting probability of your test statistic (in this case, x^2) is somewhat greater than 0.05 (e.g., 0.061). Assume that the recommended sample size was used. There is nothing magical about 0.05. Reviewers, editors, and thesis supervisors usually require authors to address this 'shortcoming', however. Where possible, the best solution is to collect more data, perhaps 25% to 50% more. This usually will resolve the question, one way or another. Two issues must be kept in mind. First, you may think that when your *p*-value is 0.061 you are making a Type II error, if you fail to reject. But it is also possible that you are barely avoiding a Type I error. Second, you are allowed only one chance to add observations. To add subjects and retest repetitively until your x^2 has a *p*-value less than 0.05 is forbidden. To do so opens you up to an inevitable Type I error, if H_0 is true. You may staunchly believe your H_1, but the appropriate path is to redesign your research and start over.

4●11 THE *G*-TEST

The *G*-test, sometimes called the likelihood ratio test or log-likelihood ratio test, is presented here because it has become common in several disciplines. The term 'likelihood' is another way of expressing probability. The *G*-test is what Pearson would have proposed, but limitations on calculating *natural logs* at the time led him to develop a fairly accurate alternative with the x^2 test. Rather than using the observed and expected frequencies, the *G*-test uses the log of the ratio of two likelihoods as the basis of calculating a x^2 test statistic. The formula is straightforward, except for the need to be sure that you use the 'natural log' of the likelihood ratios. The coefficient of '2' outside of the summation sign in the formula transforms the resulting value into one that conforms to the x^2 distribution. Consequently, the x^2 table of critical values may be used to evaluate the results. As with the standard (Pearson) x^2, the *df* are the number of categories minus one, ($k - 1$). The formula is

$$G = 2\Sigma\left[O \ln\left(\frac{O}{E}\right)\right],$$

where ln is the natural log, *O* is the observed frequency for the given category, and *E* is the expected frequency for the given category.

Assume we randomly select 10 students from a symbolic logic course (everyone's favourite). They are asked if they prefer an essay or a multiple-choice examination. Eight of the sample of ten students preferred the essay examination. Is there evidence that the class is not equally divided in their preferences? We substitute the observed (8 and 2) and expected (5 and 5) frequencies into the formula:

$$G = 2\Sigma\left[O \ln\left(\frac{O}{E}\right)\right] = 2\left[8 \ln\left(\frac{8}{5}\right) + 2 \ln\left(\frac{2}{5}\right)\right] = 2\{[8 \times 0.47] + [2 \times (-0.916)]\} = 3.85.$$

In Appendix C we find that the critical value at $\alpha = 0.05$ with 1 df is 3.841. Because our observed G (X^2) of 3.85 is greater than the critical value of 3.841, we reject H_0 and conclude that we have evidence that the students are not equally divided in their preferences. If we enter the data into an SPSS data file and run a binomial test, as we found earlier with these data (80% versus 20%, 10 observations), the resulting probability (0.109) is greater than 0.05 and we would fail to reject H_0. If we then run in SPSS a X^2 goodness-of-fit test, again as earlier, we find the X^2 of 3.6 has a probability of 0.058, and we fail to reject H_0. As you recall from the earlier discussion of the X^2 goodness-of-fit test, when any of the expected frequencies are less than 5, the results are unreliable. With both expected frequencies being 5, the results are somewhat suspect. Although the G-test is considered more accurate in terms of the resulting p-values, when the sample size is small the reliability of the G-test suffers at least as much as the X^2 goodness-of-fit test. As a consequence, when sample sizes are less than 10, if there are only two categories, the binomial test is preferred. When there are more than two categories, the exact test is preferred. Having said that, regardless of the test, when the results are borderline it is best to collect more data prior to drawing any conclusions.

============ REVIEW QUESTION ============

Open the *threetestsdata.sav* data set on the book's web page. Compute a G-test, a X^2 goodness-of-fit test, and a binomial test. How do the results compare? You will need to calculate the G-test yourself. There are many natural log calculators on line (e.g., http://calculator.tutorvista.com/natural-log-calculator.html). But this will not be onerous. What can you conclude about the three tests' sample sizes?

Web Link 4.11 for an answer to the review question.

4 ● 12 CAN A FAILURE TO REJECT INDICATE SUPPORT FOR A MODEL?

It is not obligatory to test the hypothesis that your university community are equally divided in terms of theatrical preference (comedy versus tragedy). You might have the suspicion of a 70%–30% split in favour of comedy; this could be used as H_0 to derive your expected frequencies. Assume that you have 20 respondents to your survey and 16 prefer comedy while 4 prefer tragedy. Your H_0 (0.7 versus 0.3) produces expected frequencies of $20 \times 0.7 = 14$ and $20 \times 0.3 = 6$. The resulting X^2 of 1.111 is less than the critical value of 3.841 and you fail to reject H_0, which in this case corresponds to your H_1. There are several problems with using the failure to reject as evidence supporting H_0. First, logically, no support for one position can be claimed if you are not simultaneously contradicting another position. You need two to tango. Practically, it means that your H_0 and your H_1 cannot be one and the same. A further serious problem, however, is that other reasonable hypotheses may also result in a failure to reject when assessed with your data. For example, your colleague, Juliet Capulet, may have a different suspicion (H_1), a 90%–10% difference in preference. Juliet tests her suspicion against your data. Her expected frequencies are $20 \times 0.9 = 18$ and $20 \times 0.1 = 2$. Her resulting χ^2 (0.476) also is less than the critical value of 3.841 and she fails to reject her H_0, and claims support for her hypothesis. In fact there are a large number of possible sets of expected frequencies which will result in failures to reject when applied to your 20 observations. All of the hypotheses cannot be correct. Which is most likely to be correct?

This is where the proponents of the Bayesian approach wish to enter the discussion. For example, the Bayesians will point out that it may be more productive to simultaneously apply both models, yours and Juliet's, to your data. When two hypotheses (or *models* as they were called earlier in the discussion of the Bayesian approach) are applied to the data, the Bayesian analysis will identify the hypothesis which has the stronger possibility of being correct, at least for the present. The outcome will not end the debate between you and your colleague, however. Just because Juliet's hypothesis appears dead, the death may be only temporary. Nor will this analysis settle the Bayesian–frequentist debate. It is in such instances, however, that the Bayesian approach has some clear advantages.

CHAPTER SUMMARY

In this chapter we began to inferentially apply the material covered in Part I of the book. We combined combinatorial calculations with the multiplicative law of probability to construct a binomial distribution table. This table, now a sampling distribution, was used to test a hypothesis regarding the likelihood of an observation's membership in a specific population. This was followed by a detailed presentation of the role of null hypothesis testing within the larger context of empirical research. The key concepts of Type I error, Type II error, and power were discussed, particularly in terms of their probabilities. A number of criticisms of null hypothesis testing were reviewed. Some, such as the confusion between statistical significance and theoretical or practical significance, could be addressed by abandoning the null hypothesis paradigm. Other criticisms, such as those raised by proponents of the Bayesian approach, are more difficult to resolve. The Bayesian approach, grounded in Bayes' theorem which was covered in Chapter 3, was identified as a viable alternative to null hypothesis testing, particularly in certain circumstance.

Pearson's χ^2 goodness-of-fit test was introduced. Its formula and the resulting values and the use of critical values in Appendix C reflect our basic framework of (1) what is expected, (2) what is observed, and (3) what is expected due to chance alone. The χ^2 test allows for an extension of the logic of the binomial test. First, the extension allows for the comparison of two distributions of frequencies, one expected and one observed. Second, the extension allows for the analysis of the frequency distribution of more than two categories.

The assumptions and the limitations associated with Pearson's χ^2 goodness-of-fit test were discussed. Particularly with small sample sizes, Fisher's exact test was identified as the preferred test. The importance of sample size with respect to power, *p*-values, and methods for calculating *p*-values was highlighted throughout the chapter. In this chapter we focused on *nonparametric* tests of categorical data (nominal scales) and research questions stated in terms of differences. The next chapter also is concerned with research questions stated in terms of differences, but the tests will be *parametric* and the data will be measurement in nature.

4  14   RECOMMENDED READINGS

Kuhn, T. (1996). *The structure of scientific revolutions* (3rd ed.). Chicago: University of Chicago Press.
The book offers an alternative description of the practice of *normal science*, the role of empirical
    research, and how theoretical or *paradigm* shifts occur. Where this chapter in part located
    hypothesis testing in the larger context of the research loop, Kuhn places that loop within the
    context of normal science.
Hagen, R. L. (1997). In praise of the null hypothesis statistical test. *American Psychologist, 52*, 15–24.
This represents an unapologetic defence of testing the null hypothesis. It is clearly written and at
    times fun, regardless of where one stands on the Bayesian–frequentist debate.
Volume 8 of *Psychological Science* (1997) is a special issue of the journal devoted to this debate. It
    is a must-read. This issue of an important journal contains a number of perspectives on testing
    the null hypothesis. It covers several viewpoints, from the extremes to everything in between,
    and more.

4   15   CHAPTER REVIEW QUESTIONS

Multiple-choice questions

1   A Bernoulli trial is an event that results in _____.

   a   one of only two independent outcomes

   b   one of several mutually exclusive outcomes

   c   one of only two mutually exclusive outcomes

   d   one of several independent outcomes

   e   None of the above

2   How many ways can 9 heads be obtained from 10 tosses of a coin?

   a   45

   b   9

   c   90

   d   10

   e   None of the above

3   A pharmaceutical company claims to have developed a drug that improves personality. When testing
their drug, what was the null hypothesis?

   a   The drug improves personality

   b   The drug worsens personality

   c   The drug will in some way change personality

   d   The drug does not change personality

   e   None of the above

4   What is the probability of a Type I error when the null hypothesis is false?

   a   0.05

   b   0.95

   c β

d $1 - \beta$

e   None of the above

5   What is the probability of a Type II error when the null hypothesis is false?

a   0.05

b   0.95

c β

d $1 - \beta$

e   None of the above

6   As variance in the dependent variable increases, _____.

a   effect size increases

b   power increases

c β increases

d   sample size increases

e   None of the above

7   What type of data is analysed with a χ^2 goodness-of-fit test?

a   Categorical

b   Continuous

c   Interval

d   Measurement

e   None of the above

8   With 4 degrees of freedom, how many subjects are required to ensure that a χ^2 test for a small effect size has a minimum power of 0.8? (Assume $\alpha = 0.05$.)

a   785

b   100

c   133

d   1194

e   None of the above

9   If 121 subjects are required to ensure that a χ^2 test for a moderate effect size has a minimum power of 0.8, how many categories were used by the researcher? (Assume $\alpha = 0.05$.)

a   4

b   3

c   2

d   1

e   None of the above

10   A failure to reject a false null hypothesis is a _____ and has a probability _____.

a   correct rejection; 0.05

b   Type I error; 0.05

c   Type II error; unknown from what is given

d   Type I error; 0.95

e   a correct rejection; unknown from what is given

Short-answer questions

1 How can a binomial test be transformed into a z-score question?
2 What are the limitations to keep in mind when transforming a binomial test into a z-score question?
3 What are the three factors that influence power? How do they each influence power?
4 How does the traditional null hypothesis testing approach differ from the randomization approach?
5 How does the traditional null hypothesis testing (frequentist) approach differ from the Bayesian approach?
6 What are two problems with using a failure to reject as evidence supporting the null hypothesis?

Data set questions

1 Construct a frequency distribution and histogram for 12 tosses of a coin. Assume the probability of a head is 0.5.
2 A drinkologist is interested in consumers' abilities to differentiate between two brands of a lemon-and-lime drink. When blindfolded, subjects were asked to taste 14 samples. There were seven samples from each brand randomly presented. A subject correctly identified 11 of the 14 samples.

   (a) What was the drinkologist's null hypothesis?
   (b) If the subject is merely guessing, what is the probability of correctly identifying 11 of the 14 samples correctly?
   (c) Does the drinkologist have sufficient evidence to conclude that the subject was doing anything other than guessing at the brand of the 14 samples?

3 Linda was organizing a holiday party for her marketing survey company. In previous years, 40% ate the chicken dish, 40% ate beef, and the remainder ate the vegetarian entrée. She suspects that with all of the new employees, the distribution of preferences will be changed. Of the 100 employees who showed up for the party, 44 ate the chicken, 44 ate the beef, and only 12 ate the vegetarian entrée.

   (a) What was Linda's null hypothesis?
   (b) What was Linda's alternative hypothesis?
   (c) What are the expected frequencies for chicken, beef, and vegetarian dishes?
   (d) What is the observed x^2 value?
   (e) What is the critical x^2 value?
   (f) Is there sufficient evidence to support Linda's suspicion?

4 A telecommunications researcher does not believe that two internet providers are equally popular among the local residents. If the researcher determines that the proportional differences between the two providers needs to be at least 70%–30% to be of consequence, how many subjects must the researcher survey to ensure a power of 0.8, if the null hypothesis is false? (Assume $\alpha = 0.05$.)
5 In an infant experiment, a target stimulus and a control are presented randomly on one of two screens (left and right). The baby's eye movements are tracked. If the infant turns his or her eyes towards the target screen on 18 or more of 20 trials, is there sufficient evidence that the infant can differentiate the target? Use the G-test to answer this question.

Don't forget to use the online resources! Meet your supporting stats tutor through an **introductory video**, review your maths skills with a **diagnostic pre-test**, explore statistical principles through **interactive simulations**, practice analysis techniques with **SPSS datasets**, and check your work with **answers to all in-text questions**.

https://study.sagepub.com/bors

5

Chapter contents

TESTING FOR A DIFFERENCE: TWO CONDITIONS

KEY CONCEPTS: one-sample *t*-test, independent-samples *t*-test, paired-samples *t*-test, sampling distribution of the mean, sampling distribution of the difference between means, additive sum law, *d*-scores, confidence intervals, randomization test, bootstrapping, Cohen's *d*, sign test, Mann–Whitney test, Wilcoxon signed-rank test.

 PURPOSE

The purpose of this chapter is to examine statistical tests used to determine if two sets of scores arise from identical populations. Can it be assumed that the scores are random across two groups (between-subjects design) or across two conditions (within-subjects design)? Connections to previously covered material will be encountered: hypothesis testing, the normal distributions, the binomial distribution, and χ^2. We begin by extending the z-score test into a consideration of the most common *parametric* tests used to analyse *measurement* data: *t*-tests. To address those circumstances where the assumptions necessary for a *t*-test are violated or where the data are ordinal in nature, we explore alternative *nonparametric* procedures. Statistical tests can be segregated into four families that are based on one of two types of research questions and one of two types of data. In the previous chapter we focused on a family of tests based on the intersection of (1) a research question of difference and (2) categorical data. In this chapter we focus primarily on a family of tests based on the intersection of (1) a research question of *difference* and (2) *measurement* data.

5 2 INTRODUCTION

Imagine you are a psychologist who wants to examine the effects of shading the figures on a test of three-dimensional spatial reasoning. Each trial begins with a subject being shown a line-drawing

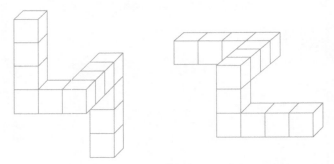

like in Figure 5.1 (left). Then a second figure appears to its right. The subject's task is to determine whether or not the second figure is simply a rotated version of the first figure. You hypothesized that shading the figure would make the line-drawings easier to visualize and improve performance. This is the experimental or alternative hypothesis (H_1). Five subjects in the standard condition saw standard line-drawings and five subjects in the shaded condition saw the same line-drawings, but with shading to enhance the 3-D effect. After collecting the data,

Figure 5.1   Based on Shepard and Metzler's mental rotation task

you inspected the 10 scores (the number of correct responses after 20 trials) to determine if there was sufficient evidence to reject the assumption that the scores were *random* with respect to condition: the null hypothesis (H_0). This takes us back to problems posed at the outset of Chapter 1. The data you collected are listed below. What do you think: are the scores random with respect to condition?

Standard condition: 3, 12, 5, 10, 12.

Shaded condition: 17, 4, 4, 11, 14.

Web Link 5.1 for an interactive demonstration where the student attempts to guess if two groups of scores (5 each) were both randomly drawn from a set of scores between 0 and 20.

Regardless of how complicated our research designs may be, the crucial questions often come down to examining two conditions. In the simplest terms, were the scores in one condition influenced by something that did not influence the scores in the other condition: shading? Recall the paradigmatic problem posed in Chapter 1: were the digits randomly sorted into the two groups? Parallel to our discussion of the χ^2 test in Chapter 3, the answer to this question involves determining what to *expect* if the numbers were randomly sorted, comparing the *expected* with what is *observed*, and determining if the difference between *the expected* and *the observed* is too great for us to continue assuming that the numbers were randomly sorted. We continue to use the probability of 0.05 as a decision-making criterion. That is, if a difference between the *expected* and the *observed* has a probability less than 0.05, we will reject H_0.

In Chapter 3 we used a z-score and the *standard normal distribution* to determine whether or not a single *observed score* was likely to be a member of a given population. To make that determination the *expected score* (the population mean, μ) is subtracted from the *observed score* (y), and the resulting difference is standardized on (divided by) the population standard deviation (σ): $z = (y - \mu) / \sigma$. We begin by assuming that y is a member of the given population. If the z-score is greater than ± 1.96 ($p < 0.05$, two-tailed), we conclude that y likely is *not* a member of the given population. If the z-score is less than or equal to ± 1.96 ($p > 0.05$, two-tailed), we continue to assume that y is a member of the given population. In the present chapter, we extend this model and pose somewhat different questions, questions that require changes and additions to the formula used with the z-score test. To begin, we ask whether a sample of scores likely was selected from a given population. Next, we ask whether the scores from two groups are representative of the same population. Finally, we ask whether subjects' scores in a second condition reflect any change from their scores in a first condition, what we described in Chapter 1 as a within-subjects or repeated-measures design (see p. 16).

BUILDING ON THE Z-SCORE

As we saw, when we know both a population's mean (μ) and its standard deviation (σ), we can determine the probability of an observed score being a member of that population. To do so we standardize the difference between the *observed score* and μ (*expected score*) using the standard deviation of the population of scores: $z = (y - \mu) / \sigma_y$. Using the z-table, we can determine the probability of a difference of that magnitude or greater. Of course, regardless of the outcome, our conclusion may be wrong.

Using the z-score as a model, when we know both μ and σ^2, we can determine the probability that a sample of scores was drawn from the population by examining the difference between the *expected mean* (μ) and the *observed sample mean* ($\bar{y}$). Remember, if we randomly sample from a population, $\bar{y}$ is an unbiased estimator of μ: $E(\bar{y}) = \mu$. Because we are examining a sample mean and not an individual score, rather than standardizing the difference between the *observed* and the *expected* on the standard deviation in the scores, we use the standard deviation in sample means: $\sigma_{\bar{y}}$.

Assuming a two-tailed test, the critical *z*-score value is ±1.96. If we continuously select individual scores randomly from a single population and calculate their *z*-scores, 5% of the time we will *incorrectly* conclude that the score was not a member of the population. That is, even though all of the selected scores are members of the same population, 2.5% of the scores will appear to be too big to be members of the population, and 2.5% will appear to be too small.

In Chapter 2 we discussed how to derive *unbiased* estimates of the sampling distribution and the standard errors of the mean. Recall the importance of *n* regarding the *efficiency* of statistics such as means and variances. Similarly, the estimates of the sampling distribution and the standard error of the mean will vary with sample size: the smaller the value of *n*, the greater the variability in the sample means.

The estimate of the variance in sample means is called the *sampling distribution of the mean* ($\sigma_{\bar{y}}^2$) and its square root is called the *standard error of the mean* ($\sigma_{\bar{y}}$). According to the *central limit theorem* the mean of the sampling distribution of the means (μ_y) is equal to the mean of the population from which the scores were sampled (μ). Furthermore, the theorem states that $\sigma_{\bar{y}}^2$ is equal to the variance in the population divided by the sample size (σ^2/n) and the standard error of the mean is thus ($\sigma/\sqrt{n}$). $\sigma_{\bar{y}}$ describes the fluctuation *expected* in the means for samples of a given *n due to chance alone*. Regardless of the shape of the distribution of scores, as sample size increases, the shape of $\sigma_{\bar{y}}$ more closely approximates a normal distribution. With this information we can begin to determine if the *observed* differences in means are likely to be due to something other than mere chance.

TESTING A SINGLE SAMPLE

Rarely do we know a population's mean and standard deviation, but such instances do exist. Examining such cases provides us with a conceptual bridge from *z*-scores to more common forms of comparing means: *t*-tests. We begin with a simple case.

Imagine you are a teacher curious to know if the IQs of the students who elect to study contemporary film are representative of the general population. Because of the nature of the IQ test, you know that the population mean and standard deviation are 100 and 15, respectively. Furthermore, the distribution of the IQ scores is deemed to be normal. After testing a sample of nine of your students, you *observe* that their mean IQ is 109. The null hypothesis (H_0) is that the nine students are a sample drawn from the general population and their *expected* mean IQ is 100. Because you have no *a priori* reason to predict how these students might differ from the general population, you use a two-tailed test. They may be above-average students looking for a challenge, or they may be weak students thinking that this will be an easy course. Using our extended *z*-score model, we arrive at the formula

$$z = \frac{\bar{y} - \mu}{\sigma/\sqrt{n}},$$

and using your data,

$$z = \frac{109 - 100}{15/\sqrt{9}} = 1.80.$$

Because you know μ and σ, and because the population is normally distributed, you can treat the resulting z-score like any other z-score. Using the table of positive z-scores in Appendix A, you find that the probability of obtaining a $\bar{y}$ of that magnitude (109) or less is 0.9641. Thus, the probability of obtaining a $\bar{y}$ of that magnitude (109) or greater is $1 - 0.9641 = 0.0359$. Because you are conducting a two-tailed test, you also need to include the probability of a z-score of -1.80 or smaller. The combined probability is 0.072. Because 0.072 is greater than 0.05, you fail to reject H_0 and continue to assume the nine students are representative of the normal population. Because we know that the magic z-score for a two-tailed test at $\alpha = 0.05$ is ± 1.96, these calculations are primarily intended to refresh your understanding of the logic of the test and z-tables.

Let us inspect the calculations a bit closer. Examining the formula, we see that if $\bar{y}$, μ, and σ remain the same and we increase n to 11, the results and conclusion would be very different:

$$z = \frac{109 - 100}{15/\sqrt{11}} = 1.99.$$

With an n of 11 the probability of the two-tailed test is 0.046 and you would reject H_0 and conclude there is evidence that those who elect to study contemporary film do not represent the general population. You might argue that if you initially had sampled the IQ scores from 11 or more students, then you surely would have rejected the null hypothesis. This is not necessarily the case, however.

If we increase the sample size, there are several potential outcomes. To begin with, if H_0 is true, you are correctly failing to reject it. If H_0 is true, increasing the sample size can result in one of two outcomes. First, recall from Chapter 3 the notion of *efficiency*: as n increases, a statistic's *efficiency* improves. Regarding sample means, as n increases, $\sigma_{\bar{y}}$ will shrink.

🐭 Web Link 5.2 for an interactive demonstration of the relation between sample size and the standard error of the mean.

That is, on average, our observed sample mean will be closer to the true population mean (100). Remember, this is what we *expect on average in the long run*. Due to chance alone, there are occasions when, as n increases, the sample mean may move further away from μ, even though H_0 is true. Second, for any given n it is possible incorrectly to reject a true H_0: make a Type I error. This of course will happen 5% of the time, when H_0 is true.

If H_0 is false, increasing n will not result in the sample means converging to μ (100), but rather to the true μ of those who elect to study contemporary film. In such cases, as n increases, the efficiency of the estimate increases, $\sigma_{\bar{y}}$ shrinks, and *power* – the probability of correctly rejecting the false H_0 – increases. For a review of Type I error, Type II error, and power, see p. 141 in Chapter 4.

🐭 Web Link 5.3 for an interactive demonstration of the effect that both sample size and variance have on the standard error of the mean.

━━━━━━━━━━━ REVIEW QUESTION ━━━━━━━━━━━

Assuming that the mean IQ of the population is 100 and that the standard deviations is 15, and that you as the teacher are able to sample only 9 students, how large or how small would the mean IQ of the sample need to be for you to reject H_0 (two-tailed test, $\alpha = 0.05$)?

👉 Web Link 5.4 for an answer and discussion of the review question.

Although also rare, there are occasions when μ is known, but σ^2 and σ are unknown. In such cases we must replace σ with an unbiased estimate: the sample standard deviation (s). Because the shape of the sampling distribution of s^2 is skewed, our ratio of the difference over the standard error $((\bar{y} - \mu) / (s/\sqrt{n}))$ no longer is normally distributed. Recall from Chapter 3 that although s^2 is an unbiased estimate of σ^2, the distribution of s^2 over repeated samples is positively skewed; the smaller the n, the greater the skewness. Therefore, s^2 is more likely to be an underestimate of σ^2 than an overestimate. As a consequence, the ratio of the difference between μ and $\bar{y}$ over the standard error of the mean will frequently produce an inflated z-score. Thus, if H_0 is true, the probability of a Type I error will be greater than 0.05, if ± 1.96 is used as the critical value. It is the matrix of critical values found in Appendix D that corrects for the skewness in the sampling distribution of s^2.

The computational change required to make the correction is simple. When s^2 is used as an estimate for σ^2 the formula changes from

$$z = \frac{\bar{y} - \mu}{\sigma/\sqrt{n}}$$

to

$$t = \frac{\bar{y} - \mu}{s/\sqrt{n}} \, ,$$

and we use a t-table rather than a z-table. A t-table is a modified z-table turned inside out. Rather than being a table of probabilities related to standardized differences, the t-table is composed of a set of critical values. They represent the values that the observed t must exceed, specific to a sample size and a desired level of α, to reject H_0. The columns represent the desired α level and the rows represent the degrees of freedom (df). The degrees of freedom for a t-test are those associated with s^2, our estimate of σ^2 see p. 55.

Recall that if we conduct a two-tailed z-score test ($\alpha = 0.05$) the critical value our observed z-score must exceed is ± 1.96. If you examine the t-table and view the entry for $\alpha = 0.05$ (column) and ∞ (infinite) df (row), you find the critical value is 1.96. With $df = 100$ the critical t-value is 1.98. When n is large the sampling distribution of s^2 approximates normality and the t-distribution approximates the standard normal distribution. The values in the $\alpha = 0.05$

column represent the necessary adjustments to 1.96 required as the *df* are reduced from ∞ and the resulting skewness in the sampling distribution of s^2 increases: the fewer the *df*, the greater the adjustment required to hold the Type I error rate at 0.05. Appendix D also illustrates the relationship between α and the critical value. As you decrease your desired α level to 0.025 (decrease the probability of a Type I error), the critical value increases; and as α is allowed to increase to 0.100, the critical value decreases. For example, with *df* = 10, when α = 0.100 the critical *t* is 1.812; when α = 0.05 the critical *t* is 2.228; when α = 0.025 the critical *t* is 2.634. Although cases where we know μ and estimate σ^2 with s^2 are rare, it is the basic model for the two common forms of the *t*-test:

$$t = \frac{\text{what is observed} - \text{what is expected difference if } H_0 \text{ is true}}{\text{standard error of the observed if } H_0 \text{ is true}}$$

$$= \frac{\text{observed mean} - \text{expected mean}}{\text{standard error of the observed mean}}.$$

As we will see, when we assume that H_0 is true, suddenly we know what to expect.

5 ● 5 INDEPENDENT-SAMPLES *T*-TEST

In the simplest experimental design researchers randomly assign subjects to two conditions. Because there are different subjects in the two conditions, it is called a between-subjects design. (For a review of random *selection* and *assignment* see p. 15.)

Typically, the conditions represent either two *levels* of a treatment variable (e.g., 50 mg versus 100 mg of caffeine) or two *types* of treatment (e.g., caffeine versus a placebo). As discussed in Chapter 1, the former case represents a *quantitative independent variable* (IV) and the latter case a *qualitative* IV. The implications for analysis and interpretation with respect to these two forms are discussed in detail in Chapter 10.

Once more we face the problem posed in Chapter 1: were the scores *randomly* sorted into the two groups? The questions remain the same. What would be *expected* if the numbers were randomly sorted? We saw in Chapter 4 that we normally expect nothing (H_0). In this case, 'nothing' implies we expect the two means to be the same. What is the *observed* difference in the means? How much variability in the difference is to be *expected due to chance alone*? Finally, is the difference between the *expected* and the *observed* too great ($p < 0.05$) for us to continue assuming that the numbers were sorted randomly?

Corresponding to a between-subjects design is the most common forms of the *t*-test: SPSS refers to this as the *independent-samples t-test*. Rather than estimating the probability that a single sample mean ($\bar{y}$) was not drawn from a given population, the question becomes: what is the probability that the two condition means ($\bar{y}_1$ and $\bar{y}_2$) do not estimate the same population? Is the difference between $\bar{y}_1$ and $\bar{y}_2$ too great to continue assuming that the subjects in the two conditions are members of the same population: the null hypothesis (H_0)?

Care needs to be taken with the nature of the question. We are not asking if, *when selected*, the subjects in the two conditions were members of the same population; we assume they were. That is, we assume that subjects were *selected* from a single population and then were *randomly* assigned to conditions. Random assignment, remember, is an attempt to ensure the *internal validity* of the experiment, that the independent variable (IV) is actually independent, and thus unconfounded. Without differential treatment, the two conditions are assumed to be two *random samples* from a single population. Experimentally, we hypothesize that differential treatment (e.g., caffeine versus placebo) will produce condition means that are no longer two unbiased estimates of a single μ. The condition means, subsequent to differential treatment, are *expected* to estimate two different population means. This is the *experimental* or *alternative* hypothesis (H_1).

Despite the description of the design in the previous two paragraphs, the logic of a single-sample t-test with a known μ and an unknown σ^2 is retained. We are still asking if an observation is significantly different from a population mean. What has changed is the nature of the 'sample' and the 'population'. We now consider the difference between the two condition means to be a 'sample': a sample drawn from a population of differences in means. If we were to repeat, ideally an infinite number of times, the process of selecting n subjects, randomly assign them to two conditions (but without any differential treatment), calculate the two means, and obtain a difference, eventually we would have a distribution of *differences in means* that has a population mean approaching 0. We could also calculate the variance in differences in the means. This variance is called a *sampling distribution of the difference between the means*. The spread of the distribution would be contingent upon n, that is the efficiency of estimate. The question becomes: is the *observed* difference in the means too great for us to continue assuming H_0?

The experimental hypothesis (H_1) proposes that the constant (i.e., treatment effect) that is added to all of the scores in one condition is different from that added to the scores in the other condition. Recall from Chapter 2 that, at its simplest, the model of a subject's score comprises two components: μ and error (e). The error represents the sum of all factors, other than the independent variable, which influence a subject's score and are not controlled by the researcher. The assumption is that these influences are *random*. We are now adding another element to the model, the IV.

If H_1 is correct, the effect of the IV differs across the two conditions and the two condition means now are estimating two different population means. The model for a score in the standard condition is $y = \mu + \tau_1 + e_1$, where y represents a given score, μ the population mean, τ_1 (tau) the constant added to all scores in the standard condition, and e_1 the sum of all of the other factors randomly influencing an individual score. The model for a subject's score in the shaded condition is $y = \mu + \tau_2 + e_2$, where μ represents the same population mean as in the standard condition, τ_2 the constant that is added to all scores in the shaded condition, and e_2 the sum of all of the other factors randomly influencing a score. The result is that the two sample means estimate two distinct populations with different means, the difference being the true value of τ, plus any difference in error. Remember, error is the variability that is due to chance alone.

If H_0 is true, and $\tau_1 = \tau_2$, the *expected* value of $\bar{y}_1 - \bar{y}_2$ is 0. Stated more completely, *observed difference* $(\bar{y}_1 - \bar{y}_2)$ – *expected difference* (0) = 0. Because we are dealing with a sample, the probability of the *observed* difference being 0 is itself close to 0, regardless of the veracity of H_0. That is, the probability that $e_1 - e_2 = 0$ approaches 0. It is the difference in errors that is responsible for the *observed* difference in the means, when there is no treatment effect ($\tau_1 = \tau_2$).

Previously when we used a *t*-test to evaluate the difference between a sample mean and a known μ and an unknown σ^2 we used the standard error of the mean ($\sigma_{\bar{y}} = s/\sqrt{n}$) as the distribution to standardize the *observed* difference. When we evaluate the difference between two condition means we need an unbiased estimate of the *standard error of the difference between two means* ($\sigma_{(\bar{y}_1 - \bar{y}_2)}$), for a given sample size. We need to estimate how much sample-to-sample variation in the difference we can *expect to observe due to chance alone*. Our estimate of the standard error of the difference between two means is made simple by the *variance sum law*.

To understand this law and its role in the *t*-test, let us examine the nature of the data associated with the present between-subjects design. We select *n* subjects from a population that is normally distributed and we randomly assign each of them to one of two conditions. At this point there is no difference in the treatment of the two groups. Without differential treatment, we could calculate a mean and a variance for each condition: $\bar{y}_1$, s_1^2 and $\bar{y}_2$, s_2^2, respectively. Because the subjects were randomly assigned to the two conditions, these two conditions represent two independent samples drawn from a single population. Thus, both $\bar{y}_1$ and $\bar{y}_2$ are unbiased estimates of a single μ. Also, both s_1^2 and s_2^2 are unbiased estimates of a single σ^2. We then subtract $\bar{y}_1$ from $\bar{y}_2$ and record the difference. Because we are dealing with samples, the probability of this difference being 0 is itself close to 0. Theoretically, we could repeat this procedure an infinite or a very large number of times. We could then calculate the mean of all of the differences. Recall that, when H_0 is true, the expected value of this difference is 0. But because the difference between any pair of means will not be 0, we need a standard error on which to base the probability of observing a given difference or greater.

The variance sum law states that the variance in the difference between (or in a sum of) two independent variables is estimated by the sum of the variances of the two variables. To keep the terminology clear, when we are addressing means and not scores, such variances are called sampling distributions. In this between-subjects design, the two sample means represent two independent variables. Because s_1^2 and s_2^2 are unbiased estimates of their respective population parameters σ_1^2 and σ_2^2, the estimates of the sampling distribution of each sample mean are thus given by

$$\sigma_{\bar{y}_1}^2 = \frac{s_1^2}{n_1} \text{ and } \sigma_{\bar{y}_2}^2 = \frac{s_2^2}{n_1}.$$

Given the variance sum law, the estimate of the standard deviation or standard error of the difference in the means is as follows:

$$\sigma_{(\bar{y}_1 - \bar{y}_2)} = \sqrt{\frac{s_1^2}{n_1} + \frac{s_2^2}{n_2}}.$$

We can write the formula for our between-subjects *t*-test as

$$t = \frac{\text{observed differences in means} - \text{expected differences if } H_0 \text{ is true}}{\text{standard error of the differences in means}},$$

and we can reformulate our *t* statistic as follows:

$$t = \frac{(\bar{y}_1 - \bar{y}_2) - (\mu_1 - \mu_2)}{\sqrt{\frac{s_1^2}{n_1} + \frac{s_2^2}{n_2}}} = \frac{(\bar{y}_1 - \bar{y}_2) - 0}{\sqrt{\frac{s_1^2}{n_1} + \frac{s_2^2}{n_2}}} = \frac{\bar{y}_1 - \bar{y}_2}{\sqrt{\frac{s_1^2}{n_1} + \frac{s_2^2}{n_2}}}.$$

If n_1 and n_2 are the same, then the above formula is appropriate. If they are unequal, then the variance must be pooled (see p. 56) and the formula is again slightly modified as follows:

⌦ Web Link 5.5 for a demonstration of how treatment effect does not influence the sampling distribution of the difference between two means.

$$t = \frac{\bar{y}_1 - \bar{y}_2}{\sqrt{\dfrac{s^2_{\text{pooled}}}{n_1} + \dfrac{s^2_{\text{pooled}}}{n_2}}}.$$

The final question concerning the independent-samples t-test regards the degrees of freedom used to determine the critical value of t. In the one-sample t-test (unknown σ^2) the df were equal to the df associated with the calculation of the sample variance ($n - 1$). In the current case, two sample variances are used in the estimation of $\sigma_{(\bar{y}_1 - \bar{y}_2)}$. As $\sigma_{(\bar{y}_1 - \bar{y}_2)}$ is the square root of the sum of the two sampling distributions, the df associated with $\sigma_{(\bar{y}_1 - \bar{y}_2)}$. is the sum of the individual dfs associated with the two variances: $(n_1 - 1) + (n_2 - 1)$.

T-TEST ASSUMPTIONS

In addition to the assumptions that (1) the data are measurement in nature, (2) the sample was selected from a normally distributed population, and (3) subjects were randomly assigned to the two conditions, there are other important assumptions which should be evaluated prior to conducting a t-test.

First, recall from Chapter 3 that although the sample mean and variance are unbiased estimators of their respective population parameters, they are sensitive to outliers. An outlier can lead to an overestimate or an underestimate of the mean and an overestimate of the variance. Furthermore, outliers create skewness. As skewness increases, the extent to which the sampling distribution of the mean will approach normality is undermined. (For a review of the nature and the effect of outliers, see p. 59.)

Second, because subjects are randomly assigned to conditions, we assume that the two condition variances are estimating a single population variance. Due to *sampling error* alone, the difference in the two condition variances can be so great that we cannot trust that assumption. To sum the two sampling distributions to obtain the standard error of the difference in means would be like summing apples and lemons. Violations of these assumptions can result in increased Type I or Type II error rates, depending upon the veracity of H_0. Therefore, it is incumbent upon the researcher to examine the data for possible violations and make corrections prior to conducting the t-test. Because treatment is a constant within a condition, even subsequent to differential treatment the variances should remain unchanged and homogeneous.

---

5 ● 6 INDEPENDENT-SAMPLES T-TEST EXAMPLE

Let us complete an example of an analysis from beginning to end. Figures 5.2 and 5.3 contains data from your fictitious study described at the outset of the chapter: the effects of shading the figures on a test of 3-D spatial reasoning. The subjects in the *standard condition* saw standard simple line-drawings of the 3-D figures. The subjects in the *shaded condition* also saw 3-D line-drawings, but with shading to enhance the 3-D effect. Each trial begins with a subject being shown a line-drawing. Then a second figure appears to its right. Your subjects' task is to determine whether or not the second figure is simply a rotated version of the first figure. The alternative hypothesis is that the shading improves performance on the test. The independent variable is the type of drawing (standard versus shaded) and the dependent variable is the number of items a subject answers correctly.

As discussed in Chapter 4 (see Section 4.4), an important step in empirical research is to determine the number of subjects needed so as to have at least an 80% chance (power = 0.80) of rejecting H_0, should it be false.

Assume that for theoretical reasons, you are only interested in testing for the presence of a *large effect*. The first row of the effect size table (Table B.1) in Appendix B defines a large effect for a difference between two means as $d = 0.80$. The first row of the sample size table (Table B.2) corresponds to a test of a difference between two means. As we see in the first row under the column for a large effect size and $\alpha = 0.05$, 26 subjects per condition are required. In Figure 5.3 we find 52 scores that represent 26 subjects in each of the two conditions. We assume you have selected a sample that is representative of the population to which you wish to generalize, and you have randomly assigned the subjects to the two conditions.

Once the data are collected, you compute descriptive statistics. Go to the data set on the web page and produce the descriptive statistics using SPSS. Be sure to select *Options* and then click on *variance* and *skewness*.

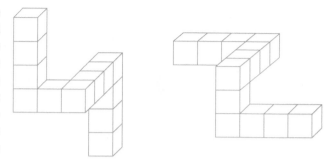

Figure 5.2

Standard condition	Shaded condition
1	2
3	6
3	4
4	5
4	7
4	5
5	6
5	4
5	6
5	6
5	6
6	7
6	10
6	5
6	7
6	7
7	8
7	8
7	8
7	12
8	9
8	9
8	7
9	10
10	11
11	8

Figure 5.3 Data from 3-D spatial reasoning experiment

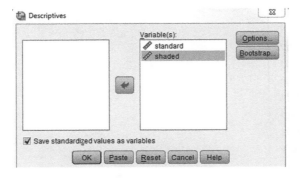

Figure 5.4

Web Link 5.6 for SPSS data set *independsampledescriptives.sav*.

The two conditions are initially examined separately. You begin by looking for outliers. As discussed in Chapter 3, throughout this book 4 standard deviations will be used as the cut-off for the identification of an outlier. A score more than 4 standard deviations either above or below its condition mean is deemed an outlier. Four times the standard deviation in standard condition $(s_1 = 2.24)$ equals 8.98. Adding and subtracting this from the mean ($\bar{y}_1 = 6.00$), we see that a score must be less -2.96 or greater than 14.96 for it to be considered an outlier; clearly there are no outliers in the standard condition. For the shaded condition, a score must be less than -2.12 or greater than 16.20 for it to be considered an outlier, and again you find no outliers. **An alternative method of checking for outliers is to tick the *Save standardized values as variables* box in the bottom left of the SPSS *Descriptives* dialog box when selecting the variables (Figure 5.4).**

Once the *Descriptives* procedure is run (Figure 5.5), return to the SPSS *Data Editor* and view the z-scores for each variable (Figure 5.6). These new variables are identified by a 'Z' preceding the name of the original variable name (e.g., *Zstandard*). An outlier will be identified by a z-score greater than ±4.00.

If you identify an outlier, there are three common strategies for correcting the problem. The first strategy is to complete the *t*-test twice, first with the outlier and then after removing it. Should the results of the two analyses result in the same conclusion, you merely need to report the initial analysis and state that the removal of the outlier did not change the outcome. If the two *t*-tests result in different outcomes, then another strategy must be used. The second strategy is to remove that outlier from the data set and report only the subsequent analysis. Removing the outlier requires a recalculation of the descriptive statistics for that condition. The third strategy for addressing an outlier is to *winsorize* the outlier: to replace the extreme score with a less extreme score. The outlier is moved inwards so it is 4 standard deviations from the mean. Again, the descriptive statistics for that condition are recalculated.

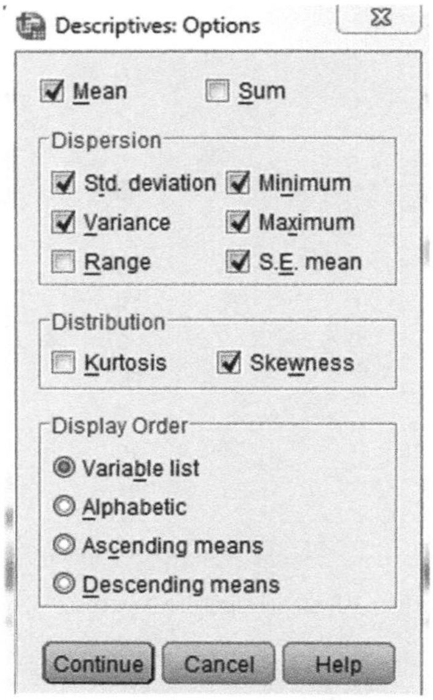

You can inspect the shape of the two distributions by examining the skewness of the data as reported in the *Descriptive Statistics* table (Figure 5.7). The extent of skewness can be evaluated by dividing the skewness *statistic* by its *standard error*. The skewnesses and their standard errors are given in the

Figure 5.5

	standard	shaded	Zstandard	Zshaded
1	1.00	2.00	-2.22718	-2.20139
2	3.00	6.00	-1.33631	-.45372
3	3.00	4.00	-1.33631	-1.32755
4	4.00	5.00	-.89087	-.89064
5	4.00	7.00	-.89087	-.01680
6	4.00	5.00	-.89087	-.89064
7	5.00	6.00	-.44544	-.45372
8	5.00	4.00	-.44544	-1.32755
9	5.00	6.00	-.44544	-.45372
10	5.00	6.00	-.44544	-.45372
11	5.00	6.00	-.44544	-.45372
12	6.00	7.00	.00000	-.01680
13	6.00	10.00	.00000	1.29394
14	6.00	5.00	.00000	-.89064
15	6.00	7.00	.00000	-.01680
16	6.00	7.00	.00000	-.01680
17	7.00	8.00	.44544	.42011
18	7.00	8.00	.44544	.42011
19	7.00	8.00	.44544	.42011
20	7.00	12.00	.44544	2.16778
21	8.00	9.00	.89087	.85703
22	8.00	9.00	.89087	.85703
23	8.00	7.00	.89087	-.01680
24	9.00	10.00	1.33631	1.29394
25	10.00	11.00	1.78174	1.73086
26	11.00	8.00	2.22718	.42011

Figure 5.6

Descriptive Statistics

	N	Minimum	Maximum	Mean		Std. Deviation	Variance	Skewness	
	Statistic	Statistic	Statistic	Statistic	Std. Error	Statistic	Statistic	Statistic	Std. Error
standard	26	1.00	11.00	6.0000	.44028	2.24499	5.040	.138	.456
shaded	26	2.00	12.00	7.0385	.44886	2.28877	5.238	.144	.456
Valid N (listwise)	26								

Figure 5.7

Descriptive Statistics table in Figure 5.7. The resulting values are 0.30 (standard condition) and 0.32 (shaded condition). These values can be tested against a critical value of z ($\alpha = 0.05$): ±1.96 (Tabachnick & Fidell, 1996). The H_0 is that skewness equals 0. Because both values are less than 1.96, you fail to reject both H_0s and may assume there are no serious skewness problems. Typically, removing any outliers usually eliminates any problems related to skewness.

Your next step is to test the assumption of homogeneity of variance using Hartley's F_{max} test (Hartley, 1950). We simply divide the larger of the two variances (shaded condition, $s_1^2 = 5.24$) by the smaller of the two (standard condition, $s_2^2 = 5.04$). The resulting *observed* F_{max} value is 1.04. The H_0 regarding homogeneity of variance is that the two sample variances are estimating the same population variance: the *expected* F_{max} is $s_{larger}^2 / s_{smaller}^2 = 1$. Because we pool the two variances when computing our *t*-value, if you cannot assume homogeneity of variance, then you must transform your data or use an alternative statistical test. We will postpone a detailed discussion of this problem and data transformation until Chapter 8.

The chance that two sample variances will be exactly the same approaches 0. The question is how much greater than 1 the observed F_{max} value needs to be before we reject H_0. The table in Appendix E contains the critical values that the observed F_{max} must exceed before we reject H_0. The columns in the F_{max} table represent the number of treatments or conditions (k) and the rows represent the *df* associated with a single condition. Additionally, the table assumes that the degrees of freedom are constant across conditions. In the present case $k = 2$ and with 26 subjects in each condition $df = 25$. There is no cell in the table for $k = 2$ and $df = 25$; there are critical F_{max} values for $k = 2$ and $df = 20$ (2.46) and for $k = 2$ and $df = 30$ (2.07). The critical value for $k = 2$ and $df = 25$ would be between those two values. Because your observed F_{max} value of 1.39 is less than the smaller of the two critical values (2.07), you fail to reject H_0 and continue to assume homogeneity of variance. When conducting the *t*-test, SPSS will provide you with an exact probability for the test of homogeneity of variance using an alternative test, Levene's test. There are a number of tests

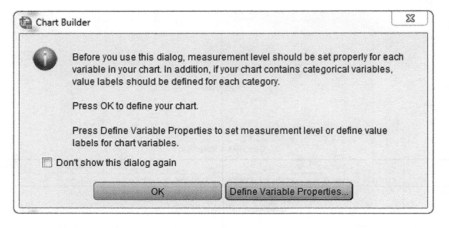

Figure 5.8

of homogeneity of variance. All have their advantages and disadvantages (Lee et al., 2010). When dealing with typical sample sizes, removing any outliers usually eliminates any problem related to homogeneity of variance. The next step is to create a pictorial display that summarizes your data and compares the two conditions. For this purpose, open the SPSS file *independsampledescriptives. sav* where your data are reformatted for the next two procedures.

Web Link 5.7 for SPSS data set *independsamplettest.sav.*

Creating a bar graph using SPSS

Before constructing the graph, switch from *Data View to Variable View* in the *Data Editor*. Ensure that the *Measure* column for the *Condition* variable has been changed from *Scale* to *Nominal*. From within the *Data Editor* window, select *Graphs* from the menu along the top. Then select *Chart Builder* from the drop-down menu and click *Define Variable Properties* from the lower right of the small window that pops up (Figure 5.8). Click on the independent variable *Score* from the *Variables* list on the left (Figure 5.10) and move it to the *Variables to Scan* box on the right and click *Continue*. Select *Automatic Labels* from the lower right of the window that pops up (Figure 5.9) and then *OK* from the menu at the bottom. An SPSS output screen will appear. Return to the SPSS *Data Editor* window. Reselect the *Graphs* then *Chart Builder* options. We have already defined the variable properties so select *OK* at the bottom left of the window. A new *Chart Builder* window will appear. Drag the *simple bar* graph picture from the upper left of the choices at the bottom up into the window in the

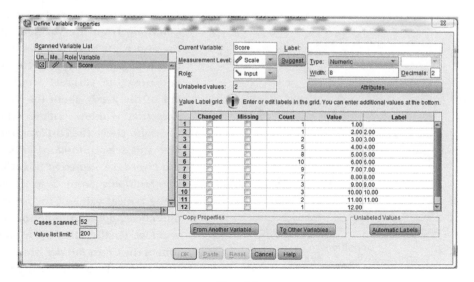

Figure 5.9

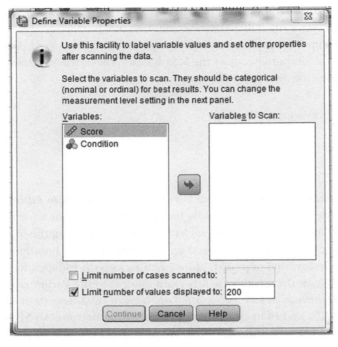

Figure 5.10

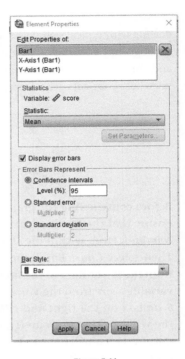

Figure 5.11

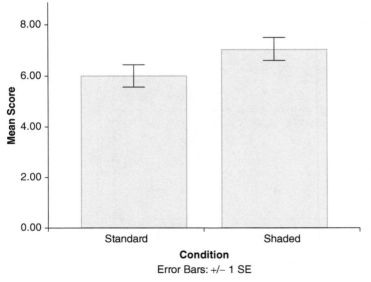

Figure 5.12

upper right to the *chart preview* box. Then drag the dependent variable *Condition* from the *Variables* list in the upper left into the *chart preview* box and place it below the *x-axis* and drag the variable *Score* to the left of the *y-axis*. From the *Elements Properties* window (Figure 5.11) on the right, check the *Display error bars* box and select *Standard error* from the *Error Bars Represent* box. Change the *Multiplier* from 2 to 1, which is the typical value of the error bars, and click *Apply* at the bottom of the window. Finally, click *OK* at the bottom of the *Chart Builder* window. The bar graph will appear in the SPSS output window.

With a between-subjects design, data are usually displayed with a bar graph. Figure 5.12 displays the bar graph created by the SPSS *Graphs* procedures. The *x*-axis represents our two conditions: standard and shaded. The *y*-axis is calibrated in the units of the dependent variable: the subjects' scores. The tops of the two bars reflect the mean scores for each condition. The little Ts – called *error bars* – extending above and below the wider bars represent the standard error of the mean for each condition. The fact that the mean of the shaded condition is greater than that of the standard condition is consistent with your experimental hypothesis.

The next step is to calculate the probability of a difference of the observed magnitude or greater being due to chance alone. To do so we substitute the condition means, variances, and sample sizes into the independent-samples *t*-test formula:

$$t = \frac{\bar{y}_1 - \bar{y}_2}{\sqrt{\dfrac{s_1^2}{n_1} + \dfrac{s_2^2}{n_2}}} = \frac{6.00 - 7.04}{\sqrt{\dfrac{5.04}{26} + \dfrac{5.24}{26}}} = -1.65 \,.$$

The *df* associated with the observed *t* is the sum of the *df* associated with each estimate of variance in the denominator: $(n_1-1) + (n_2-1)$. When the entry for $\alpha = 0.05$ (column) and 50 *df* (row) in the *t*-table in Appendix D is examined, you find the critical value to be 2.01. Because your observed *t* is less than the critical value, you fail to reject the null hypothesis and find insufficient evidence that the shaded condition has a large positive effect on students' performance. The result is usually reported as $t_a = 0.05(50) = -1.65$, n.s. The 50 in the bracket refers to the *df*, the −1.65 to the observed *t*, and the 'n.s.' to the fact that the result is non-significant, $p > 0.05$. The sign of the observed *t* is irrelevant, as long as you keep in mind which condition had the larger mean.

Running an independent-samples *t*-test (between-subjects) using SPSS

From within the *Data Editor*, select *Analyze* from the menu along the top, and drop down and select *Compare Means*. Next select the *Independent-Samples* T-test option that appears in the new window. In the *Independent-Samples T Test* window (Figure 5.13) highlight and move the dependent variable (*Score*) to the *Test Variable(s)* box. Then move the independent variable (*Condition*) to the *Grouping Variable* box. When the *Define Groups* window opens, enter how the conditions are identified: 1 and 2. Click *define groups* and enter the values in the *Define Groups* window (Figure 5.14) and then click *Continue*. When returned to the *Independent-Samples T Test* window, click *OK*.

The results appear in the SPSS output window (Figure 5.15). The first box (*Group Statistics*) reports a summary of the descriptive statistics. The second box (*Independent Samples Test*) reports the test results. The first row provides the results for when homogeneity can be assumed. We see the *F*-value (0.014) for Levene's test of homogeneity of variance. The *Sig.* value ($p = 0.906$) indicates that homogeneity of variance can be assumed. When the *Sig.* value is less than 0.05, the bottom row of the table is reported and used for drawing conclusions. In this case, you can

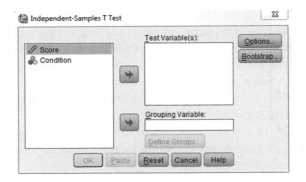

Figure 5.13

Figure 5.14

Group Statistics

	Condition	N	Mean	Std. Deviation	Std. Error Mean
Score	Standard	26	6.0000	2.24499	.44028
	Shaded	26	7.0385	2.28877	.44886

Independent Samples Test

		Levene's Test for Equality of Variances		t-test for Equality of Means						95% Confidence Interval of the Difference	
		F	Sig.	t	df	Sig. (2-tailed)	Mean Difference	Std. Error Difference	Lower	Upper
Score	Equal variances assumed	.014	.906	-1.652	50	.105	-1.03846	.62875	-2.30134	.22442
	Equal variances not assumed			-1.652	49.981	.105	-1.03846	.62875	-2.30135	.22443

Figure 5.15

assume homogeneity of variance and use the *Equal variance assumed* row. The next three columns provide the *t*-value, the *df*, and the probability of a *t* of that magnitude or greater. Because the probability is greater than 0.05 (0.105, two-tailed), you fail to reject your H_0.

You failed to find a *large* effect; you did not fail to find *any* effect. The fact that you failed to find sufficient evidence for a *large effect* does not mean that a medium, a smaller, or even a large effect does not exist. Remember, failure to find something does not mean it does not exist; a failure to catch fish does not prove that there are no fish in the lake.

As discussed in Chapter 4, when we fail to reject a null hypothesis we may be making a Type II error. The shaded condition may actually improve performance but you may not have enough power for the effect (τ) to be significant. If we are making a Type II error, several factors may be responsible. The observed difference in the means may be an underestimate of the true difference, or the observed estimates of variance may be accidentally large; both circumstances reduce power. Both can occur due to sampling error, or chance alone. Furthermore, keep in mind that we were testing for a large effect. Had you been interested in a medium effect size ($d = 0.50$) and tested the corresponding required number of subjects, the outcome might have been different. In the sample size table (Table B.2) in Appendix B , we find that to have an 80% chance of rejecting a false null hypothesis a minimum of 64 subjects per condition is required.

As a consequence of your findings, you might view the above experiment as a pilot study and use the current descriptive statistics to estimate an effect size. The estimate of an effect size for a difference between two independent means is $d = (\bar{y}_1 - \bar{y}_2) / \sigma$, where σ is estimated by the average of the two condition standard deviations, $(s_1 + s_2) / 2$:

$$d = \frac{6.50 - 7.73}{(2.92 + 2.39) / 2} = -0.46.$$

Thus, your data indicate that, if the null hypothesis is false, the effect size is in the medium range. Thus, you need to increase the current sample size to at least 64 subjects per condition. If you decide that a medium effect is of either theoretical or practical importance, there is nothing wrong with now increasing the sample size to the necessary level and reanalysing the data. What is *not* permissible is to repeat the process of adding subjects and testing, adding more subjects and testing, over and over again in the hope of eventually rejecting the null hypothesis. Such illegitimate procedures have been called '*p*-hacking' by Simonsohn (2013) and may result in Type I error rates increasing up to 0.60.

As discussed in Section 5.4, if we increase the sample size, depending on the status of the null hypothesis, there are several potential outcomes. If the null hypothesis is false, increasing the sample size, on average, increases power. If the null hypothesis is true, as *n* increases, on average, the difference in the condition means will approach 0. Remember, these outcomes are what we expect on average. For any given *n* it is possible incorrectly to reject a true null hypothesis (a Type I error) or incorrectly fail to reject a false null hypothesis (a Type II error). It is not a matter of *whether* these could happen, it is a question of *when*. The Type I error will happen randomly 5% of the time, when the null hypothesis is true. As we have seen in Chapter 4, the Type II error is more difficult to predict.

Web Link 5.8 for an interactive demonstration of the relations among *n*, effect size, and Type I and Type II error rates.

===== REVIEW QUESTION =====

Using SPSS, create a series of data sets (eight subjects in each of two conditions). In the first data set the presence of an outlier is responsible for a significant *t*-test ($p < 0.05$). When the outlier is removed the results are found to be non-significant ($p > 0.05$). What is the simplest way to create a data set with an outlier whose presence or absence does not change the outcome of the *t*-test? In this second phase, use an outlier of the same magnitude as the one you used in the first phase of the question (same *z*-score > 4.0).

Web Link 5.9 for a discussion and a solution to the review question.

5●7 PAIRED-SAMPLES *T*-TEST

Imagine, after analysing the data in the previous section, you are told that the data do not represent a *between-subjects* design, but rather two sets of scores for one group of 26 subjects (a *within-subjects* or a *repeated-measures* design). SPSS refers to the corresponding analysis as a *paired-samples t-test*. In this case the first column of Figure 5.16 is for the subject number. The second and third columns

Subject	Standard condition	Shaded condition	d- score
1	1	2	−1
2	3	6	−3
3	3	4	−1
4	4	5	−1
5	4	7	−3
6	4	5	−1
7	5	6	−1
8	5	4	1
9	5	6	−1
10	5	6	−1
11	5	6	−1
12	6	7	−1
13	6	10	−4
14	6	5	1
15	6	7	−1
16	6	7	−1
17	7	8	−1
18	7	8	−1
19	7	8	−1
20	7	12	−5
21	8	9	−1
22	8	9	−1
23	8	7	1
24	9	10	−1
25	10	11	−1
26	11	8	3

Figure 5.16

of the table represent the subjects' two scores, one for each of the two conditions. The fourth column will be addressed below. The data found in Figure 5.16 are available on the book's web page. (For a review of a within-subjects design in Chapter 1, see p. 16.)

Web Link 5.10 to data file *pairedsamplesttest.sav.*

To ensure internal validity, assume that half of your 26 subjects had the 20 simple line-drawings first and then the 20 shaded figures. The other half of the subjects had the line-drawings in the reverse order. This counterbalancing minimizes any *practice* or other *order effects*. Usually there are advantages to using a within-subjects design (e.g., increased power). There is a serious problem associated with a within-subjects design, however: it violates the assumption of *independence of observations*. There is always a relation between the observations in the two conditions. If we look at the scores in Figure 5.16 row by row, we can see a general trend. High scores in the standard condition are often paired with high scores in the shaded condition, and low scores in the standard condition tend to be paired with low scores in the shaded condition. For example, see rows 3 and 25. Scores in the standard condition are not random (not independent) with respect to scores in the shaded condition. This is typically the case with *repeated measures, matched samples*, and *randomized block designs*. The cause of the violation is simple: subjects who are fast in one condition usually are fast in other conditions, and subjects who are accurate in one condition usually are accurate in other conditions. Or, to pick more everyday examples, people who are adept in one sport usually are adept in other sports, and students who do well in one course – such as statistics – tend to do well in other courses.

● ● ● ● ●

This violation actually lurks in places not normally considered problematic. For example, if you as a researcher were interested in examining the possible differences in the happiness of teenage boys and girls and used brothers and sisters as your source of data, the independence of observations could *not* be assumed. Many of the factors that influence the happiness of a boy obviously would influence the happiness of his sisters. The violation of the assumption of independence of observations must be corrected or the results will be biased.

Fortunately, the procedure used for correcting this violation also reduces the variance in the DV, which usually produces an increase in *power*. In Figure 5.16 the fourth column (difference scores or *d*-scores) represents the difference between each subject's scores in the two experimental conditions. A positive *d*-score means that a subject scored higher in the standard condition than in the shaded condition. A negative *d*-score indicates that the subject scored higher in the shaded condition. If the scores are random with respect to the two conditions (e.g., there is no treatment effect), you would *expect* roughly an equal number of positive and negative *d*-scores. More accurately, you would expect the total values of the negative and positive *d*-scores to be equal. If there is no treatment effect, the expected value of the mean *d*-score is 0. Thus, our H_0 is that the average *d*-score will be 0.

If H_1 is correct, as discussed above with respect to the between-subjects design, a constant has been added to the scores in the shaded condition. The result is that the two condition means are estimating two different population means and the *expected value* of the mean *d*-score will be non-zero. The model for a score in a within-subjects design has an additional element from the model described in the previous section. For a within-subjects design, a model for the standard condition is

$$y_1 = \mu + sub_i + \tau_1 + e_1,$$

where y represents a given score, μ the population mean, sub_i is the effect of being that particular subject, τ_1 represents the constant that is added to scores in the standard condition, and e_1 the sum of all of the other factors randomly influencing a score in that condition. The model for the subject's score in the shaded condition is

$$y_2 = \mu + sub_i + \tau_2 + e_2,$$

where sub_i is the effect of being that particular subject, τ_2 represents the constant that is added to scores in the shaded condition, and e_2 the sum of all of the other factors randomly influencing a score in that condition. Remember, it is the same subject in both conditions.

When a subject's score in one condition is subtracted from his or her score in the second condition, μ is removed from the resulting *d*-score. Additionally, the subtraction removes all of the factors associated with the individual subject which are responsible for making his or her performance different from that of other subjects. All of these individual differences are sources of variance, and in a between-subjects design are components of e. Each *d*-score now can be viewed as an estimate of τ, plus random error. The H_0 can be understood as predicting that $\tau = 0$. If H_0 is true and $\tau = 0$, then any difference in the condition means is due solely to error. To derive the model for the resulting *d*-scores, we add a subject component to our previous between-subject model.

$$y_1 - y_2 = (\mu - \mu) + (sub_i - sub_i) + (\tau_1 - \tau_2) + (e_1 - e_2)$$
$$= e_1 - e_2.$$

If H_0 is false, then the two condition means estimate two different populations, the true difference being the value of τ, which is itself estimated by the observed mean *d*-score. The model for the resulting *d*-scores is

$$y_1 - y_2 = (\mu - \mu) + (sub_i - sub_i) + (\tau_1 - \tau_2) + (e_1 - e_2)$$
$$= (\tau_1 - \tau_2) + (e_1 - e_2).$$

Focusing on the d-scores and their sign allows us to see that we have not travelled far from the hypothesis testing discussed in Chapter 4. The pattern of positive and negative d-scores can be related back to the binomial test. To make a clear connection, let us concern ourselves only with the sign of the d-scores: whether it is negative or positive, as if we were back in Chapter 4 evaluating students guessing on a true/false quiz. In Figure 5.16 there are 22 negative values and 4 positive values. If H_0 is true and the probability of a negative d-score is 0.5, we would *expect* – over a very large number of samples of 26 d-scores – to find an average of 13 negative values. We can construct a binomial distribution and examine the probability of finding 22 or more negative values out of 26 observations. Used in this manner, the binomial is referred to as the *sign test*. (For the details of the binomial calculations, see Section 4.2.)

Using the binomial model, we find that the probability of 22 or more negative observations out of 26 is very small, less than 0.001. When we take into account the other end of the distribution and the probability of 3 or fewer negative observations and double 0.001 ($p = 0.002$, for a two-tailed test), we find that the probability of 22 or more negative d-scores is less than 0.05. Consequently, we reject H_0 and conclude that there is evidence supporting H_1 regarding the effect of shading the line-drawings.

A review of running a binomial test of the d-score signs using SPSS

From the histogram of a binomial distribution (Figure 5.19), here acting as a sampling distribution, we can see that there are relatively few instances of 22 negative d-scores due to chance alone with an n of 26 and $p = 0.5$. After 10,000 trials the mean was 13.00 and the standard deviation was 2.57.

First, a new binomial variable must be created in the *Data Editor* window for the *pairedsamplesttest.sav* file. In the column next to the variable *dscore* enter a 1 if *dscore* is negative, or a 0 if *dscore* is positive (Figure 5.17). Next select *Analyze* from the menu along the top and drop down to *Nonparametric Tests*. Next select the *One Sample* option that appears in the window. In the *One-Sample Nonparametric Tests* window move the new binomial variable from the *Fields* box to the *Test Fields* box and click *OK*. The results appear in the SPSS output window (Figure 5.18).

We might view this binomial test as a z-score problem with a known μ and σ, as provided by the binomial distribution by 10,000 trials. We appear to have come full circle. We have

$$z = \frac{y - \mu}{\sigma_y} - \frac{22 - 13}{2.57} = 3.5.$$

Because the z-score is greater than ±1.96, you reject H_0.

Such an analysis, however, reduces the d-scores to one of two states (+ or −) and ignores their magnitude. As we will see, there may be times when the sign test and other alternative analyses are appropriate. But in the present case of your 3-D line-drawing experiment, we return to the t-test analysis, which is the typical analytic strategy employed with measurement data and when the requisite assumptions are met.

Return to SPSS and run the descriptive statistics for the *d*-scores (Figure 5.20). Note that the mean of the *d*-scores is equal to the difference between the means of the standard and shaded conditions.

The numerator in this *t*-test will be no different from that in the independent-samples *t*-test: –1.04. Then why calculate *d*-scores? The reason for computing *d*-scores is related to the fact that 3 – 5 and 113 – 115 both equal –2. When analysing a within-subjects design we are only concerned with the sign and magnitude of the *change* from one condition to another, and not with the magnitude of the subject's individual scores. This transformation has consequences for the variance used in the denominator of the *t*-test.

To all intents and purposes, after the calculation of *d*-scores, you have only one score per subject. We are back to a single-sample *t*-test. You can forget the scores in the two original conditions for the moment. You no longer need to worry about the two original conditions being independent or not, because you now have only one condition: the *d*-scores. The design is now one that we already have used: a known population mean and an unknown variance. This is the underlying model for testing the difference between two means, regardless of design. The question here is framed as follows: is the difference between the *observed* mean of

standard	shaded	dscore	VAR00002
1.00	2.00	-1.00	1.00
3.00	6.00	-3.00	1.00
3.00	4.00	-1.00	1.00
4.00	5.00	-1.00	1.00
4.00	7.00	-3.00	1.00
4.00	5.00	-1.00	1.00
5.00	6.00	-1.00	1.00
5.00	4.00	1.00	.00
5.00	6.00	-1.00	1.00
5.00	6.00	-1.00	1.00
5.00	6.00	-1.00	1.00
6.00	7.00	-1.00	1.00
6.00	10.00	-4.00	1.00
6.00	5.00	1.00	.00
6.00	7.00	-1.00	1.00
6.00	7.00	-1.00	1.00
7.00	8.00	-1.00	1.00
7.00	8.00	-1.00	1.00
7.00	8.00	-1.00	1.00
7.00	12.00	-5.00	1.00
8.00	9.00	-1.00	1.00
8.00	9.00	-1.00	1.00
8.00	7.00	1.00	.00
9.00	10.00	-1.00	1.00
10.00	11.00	-1.00	1.00
11.00	8.00	3.00	.00

Figure 5.17

the *d*-scores and the *expected* mean of the *d*-scores (0) greater than what we would *expect due to chance alone*? Analogous to the single-sample *t*-test in Section 5.4 where we estimated the population variance with the sample variance, we use the variance in the *d*-scores to estimate the variance in the population of *d*-scores. After substituting in the *d*-score descriptive statistics we calculate the following *t*:

$$t = \frac{\bar{d} - \mu}{s_d / \sqrt{n}} = \frac{-1.04 - 0}{1.56 / \sqrt{26}} = -3.39.$$

Hypothesis Test Summary

	Null Hypothesis	Test	Sig.	Decision
1	The categories defined by dscore = 1.00 and 0.00 occur with probabilities 0.5 and 0.5.	One-Sample Binomial Test	.001	Reject the null hypothesis.

Asymptotic significances are displayed. The significance level is .05.

Figure 5.18

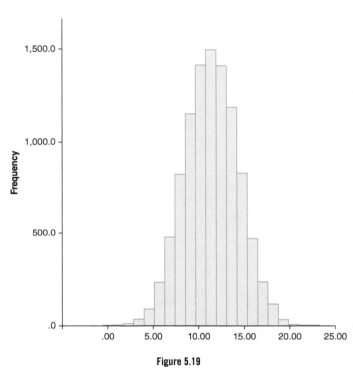

Figure 5.19

Before consulting the *t*-table in Appendix D, the associated degrees of freedom must be determined. For testing purposes, you have only one set of scores, the *d*-scores. The mean, the variance, the standard deviation, and the degrees of freedom are those associated with the *d*-scores. Thus, the *df* are now 25, rather than the 50 that were associated with this data set when it was considered to be a between-subjects design. A careful examination of the above *t*-test formula reveals that a reduction in the *df* alone leads to a reduction in power. At the same time, the standard deviation in the *d*-scores is less than the standard deviations of the two original conditions, and this alone leads to an increase in power. This reduction in variance is produced by removing the variance associated with the individual differences in the subjects. The typical increase in power associated with a within-subjects design is the result of a proportionately greater reduction in the variance than the reduction in the *df*. In the case of your 3-D line-drawing experiment, despite the reduced *df* there is an increase in the *t* ratio. The critical value found in Appendix D for $\alpha = 0.05$ and $df = 25$ is 2.06. Because your observed t (−3.39) is greater than the critical value, you reject

H_0. Furthermore, because the difference in the condition means is in the direction you predicted, you have evidence supporting your H_1.

Running a paired-samples *t*-test (within-subjects) using SPSS

From within the data window, select *Analyze* from the menu along the top and drop down and select *Compare Means*. Next select the *Paired-Samples T Test* option that appears in the

Descriptive Statistics

	N	Minimum	Maximum	Mean		Std. Deviation	Variance	Skewness	
	Statistic	Statistic	Statistic	Statistic	Std. Error	Statistic	Statistic	Statistic	Std. Error
dscore	26	-5.00	3.00	-1.0385	.30625	1.56156	2.438	-.136	.456
Valid N (listwise)	26								

Figure 5.20

window to the right. In the *Paired-Samples T Test* window (Figure 5.21) highlight and move the variable *standard* to the *Paired Variables* box and into the cell next to *Pair 1* and under *Variable 1*. Then highlight and move the variable *shaded* to the *Pair 1–Variable 2* cell and click *OK*. The results appear in the SPSS output window. The first box (*Paired-Samples Statistics*) produces descriptive statistics. The second box (*Paired Samples Correlations*) reports that the 26 pairs of scores were highly correlated (0.76). The third box (*Paired Samples Test*) provides the results (Figure 5.22). We see the mean *d*-score (–1.04), the standard deviation of the *d*-scores (1.56), the standard error of the mean *d*-score (0.31); the *t*-value is –3.391 with *df* = 25. Finally, the probability associated with that *t* at those *df* is 0.002.

> The fact that the mean of the *d*-scores is equal to the difference in the condition mean should not be a surprise. You can sum the two columns and then subtract the mean of one column from the mean of the other, or you can subtract one column from the other one row at a time and then take the average of the individual differences. The order of those operations is inconsequential.

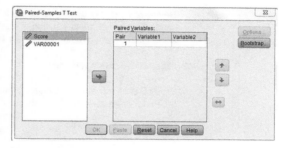

Figure 5.21

Paired Samples Test

| | | | | | 95% Confidence Interval of the Difference | | | | |
	Mean	Std. Deviation	Std. Error Mean		Lower	Upper	t	df	Sig. (2-tailed)
				Paired Differences					
Pair 1 standard - shaded	-1.03846	1.56156	.30625		-1.66919	-.40773	-3.391	25	.002

Figure 5.22

When H_0 is rejected it is standard practice to report an estimate of the standardized effect. Cohen's *d*, also used in Appendix B, is the most common estimate. The difference in the means is standardized using the estimate of the population standard deviation – in the case of your 3-D line-drawing data, the *d*-scores. (Do not confuse Cohen's estimate of effect size (*d*) with a difference score (*d*-score).) Because Cohen's *d* is reported in terms of its absolute value, the sign from the $\bar{d}$ used in the numerator is removed. We have

$$d = \frac{\bar{d} - \mu}{\sigma_d} = \frac{1.23 - 0}{1.48} = 0.83.$$

When the data are a product of a within-subjects design, we still begin by describing and examining the two conditions separately: computing and tabling descriptive statistics, looking for outliers, testing the assumptions of normality and homogeneity of variance, and then constructing a figure. The figure used to depict within-subjects data is often different from the one used to depict a between-subjects design.

Creating a line graph using SPSS

From within the data window, select *Graphs* from the menu and then *Chart Builder* from the drop-down menu (Figure 5.23). Click on *Define Variable Properties* and highlight the two conditions from the *Variables* box on the left (*standard* and *shaded*; Figure 5.24) and move them to the *Variables to Scan* box on the right and click on *Continue*. Select *Automatic Labels* from

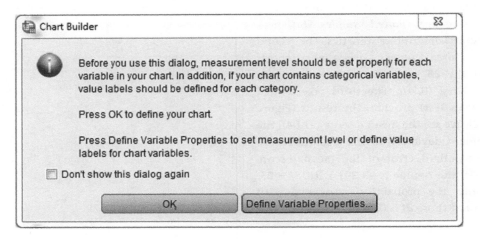

Figure 5.23

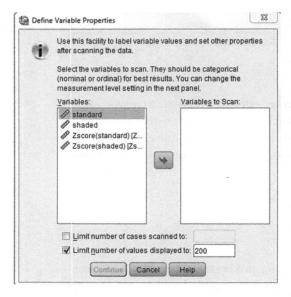

Figure 5.24

the lower right of the window that appears (Figure 5.25) and then *OK*. An SPSS output screen will appear displaying the values of the variables. Return to the *Data Editor* window and again select *Graphs* then the *Chart Builder* options. We have already defined the variable properties, so select *OK*. A new *Chart Builder* window appears (Figure 5.26). From the *Choose from* box at the bottom left highlight the *Line* option. Drag the single line graph image up into the *Chart preview* box. Then drag the two condition variables into the *Chart preview* box and place them in the box along the *y*-axis. You will need to hold down the Ctrl key to highlight the two variables. From the *Elements Properties* window to the side (Figure 5.27), check the *Display error bars* box and select the *Standard error* option from the *Error Bars Represent* box. Change the multiplier from 2 to 1 and click *Apply* at the bottom of the window. Titles

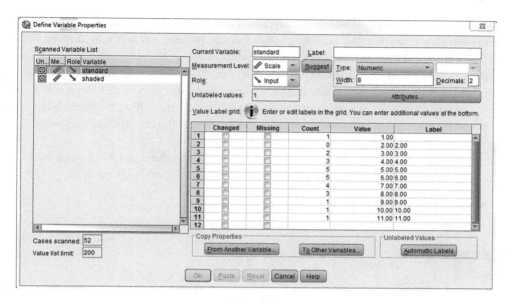

Figure 5.25

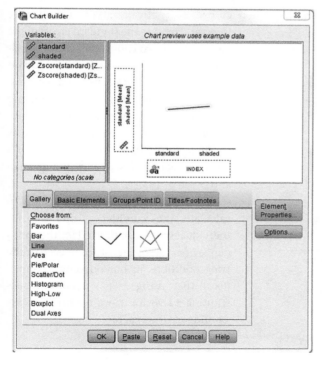

Figure 5.26

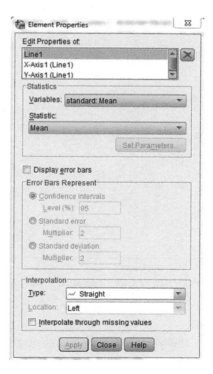

Figure 5.27

and notes may be added by selecting the *Titles/Footnotes* option in the middle of the *Chart Builder* window (Figure 5.26). Finally, click *OK* at the bottom of the *Chart Builder* window. The line graph will appear in the SPSS output window.

Figure 5.28 depicts a line for a within-subjects design. The line connecting the two means indicates that the same subjects are tested in the two conditions. Again the *x*-axis represents your two conditions (standard and shaded) and the *y*-axis is calibrated in the units of the dependent variable. The points on the line where the error bars are placed represent the condition means, which are no different from those depicted in Figure 5.12.

It is often thought that a within-subjects design *always* gives the researcher more power than a between-subjects design, and hence is always preferable. This is not always the case.

🖰 Web Link 5.11 for an exploration of power and a within-subjects design.

5 ● 8 CONFIDENCE LIMITS AND INTERVALS

As discussed in Chapter 4, not all researchers use the H_0 testing approach to data analysis. Some researchers prefer to report results in terms of confidence intervals, effect sizes, or confidence limits, whether or not the *t*-test and its *p*-value are also presented. In some publications and journals graphs accompanied by effect sizes or confidence limits are preferred to *t*- and *p*-values. The error bars used in the graph of your 3-D line-drawing data (Figure 5.28) are already a type of confidence interval. They are the standard errors of the means of the two conditions. These standard errors form the basis for the standard error of the difference between the means, which is a key element in calculating the confidence limits of the difference between the means. (For a review of how to calculate the 95% confidence intervals for a population of scores with a given μ and σ, see p. 147.)

A variant of the formula we used to calculate the confidence intervals for individual scores can be used for the confidence intervals of the means in each of the two conditions in our ongoing example. Recall that, using $z = (y - \mu)/\sigma$ and substituting ±1.96 for z, we obtained a 95% confidence interval of

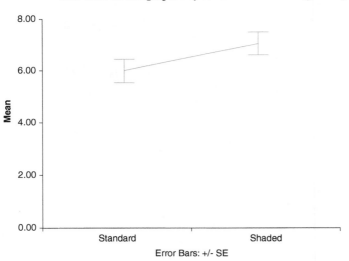

Error Bars: +/- SE

Figure 5.28

The '*y*' in the formula represents the two raw scores corresponding to the upper and lower limits.

$$\text{CI}_{(95\%)} = y = \mu \pm 1.96\sigma.$$

We solve the equation once using +1.96 and once using –1.96, giving us the upper and lower bounds of the $CI_{(95\%)}$ in raw scores working from the standard normal distribution.

When converting the z formula to its t equivalent, $\bar{y}$ replaces y and $\sigma_{\bar{y}}$ replaces σ, and the critical value of t is based on the df. Using the t-table in Appendix D, we find the critical value of t for $df = 25$ and $\alpha = 0.025$ is 2.06. The mean and standard deviation of the standard condition were 6.00 and 2.24, respectively. We solve for two values of μ, an upper and a lower limit. For our researcher's data, using $t = (y - \mu)/(\sigma / \sqrt{n})$, we find the following $CI_{(95\%)}$ for the standard condition:

$$CI_{(95\%)} = y = \mu \pm 2.06(\sigma / \sqrt{n}),$$

so that

$$\mu = 6.00 \pm 2.06 \frac{2.44}{\sqrt{26}} = 6.00 \pm 2.06 \times 0.44.$$

The upper bound is thus 6.91 and the lower bound is 5.09. We might say that there is a 95% chance that our confidence interval (from 5.09 to 6.91) captures the true population mean.

Repeating the computations for the shaded condition, we find

$$\mu = 7.04 \pm 2.009 \times 0.4,$$

so that the upper bound is 7.84 and the lower bound is 6.24. Notice that the $CI_{(95\%)}$s for the two conditions overlap; the upper bound of the standard condition (6.91) is greater than the lower bound for the shaded condition (6.11). This illustrates that the values in the overlapping area could be the true μ of either condition.

After analysing a between-subjects design we are also interested in presenting the confidence limits of the 'difference between the two means'. We substitute the difference between the means in the place of an individual mean, and we substitute the standard error of the difference in the mean in place of the standard error of a single mean. Using the t-table we find the critical value of t for $df = 50$ and $\sigma = 0.025$ is 2.009. The difference between the two means is –1.04 and the variances of the two conditions are 5.04 and 5.24. As before, we are solving for two values, an upper and a lower value. For between-subjects data you find the following $CI_{(95\%)}$:

$$t_{(df=50,\alpha=0.025)} = \frac{-1.04 - \mu}{\sqrt{5.04/26 + 5.24/26}}$$

thus,

$$\mu = -1.04 \pm 2.009 \times 0.6287.$$

If H_0 is true, the true *mean of the difference* between the two population μ_s has a 95% chance of falling between –2.301 and 0.224. Zero, which represents the situation where there is no difference, falls within these confidence limits. As we know, if you test the difference between the two means, as you have in Section 5.7, with an independent-samples t-test you will fail to reject H_0. The 95% confidence limits of the difference are reported in the SPSS output window (Figure 5.29).

Independent Samples Test

		Levene's Test for Equality of Variances		t-test for Equality of Means						
		F	Sig.	t	df	Sig. (2-tailed)	Mean Difference	Std. Error Difference	95% Confidence Interval of the Difference	
									Lower	Upper
score	Equal variances assumed	.014	.906	-1.652	50	.105	-1.03846	.62875	-2.30134	.22442
	Equal variances not assumed			-1.652	49.981	.105	-1.03846	.62875	-2.30135	.22443

Figure 5.29

The situation with a within-subjects design is somewhat different. Although, as in the case of the between-subjects design, it is standard practice to present the descriptive data of the two conditions separately and create a figure that includes the error bars, the nature of the confidence limits for a within-subjects design is different. Rather than the confidence limits of the difference between two means, we are now interested in the confidence limits of the mean and the standard error of the d-scores. Because there are only 26 d-scores in our example, there are now only 25 df:

$$t_{(df=25,\alpha=0.025)} = \frac{-1.04 - \mu}{2.24/\sqrt{26}},$$

so that

$$\mu = -1.04 \pm 2.06 \times 0.6287.$$

If H_0 is true, with 95% certainty, the true μ of the d-scores falls somewhere between -1.67 and -0.41. Zero, which represents the situation where there is no difference between the two conditions, does *not* fall within these limits. As we already know, if you were to test the data with a paired-samples t-test, you would reject H_0. The 95% confidence limits of the d-scores are reported in the SPSS output (Figure 5.30).

Paired Samples Test

		Paired Differences							
		Mean	Std. Deviation	Std. Error Mean	95% Confidence Interval of the Difference		t	df	Sig. (2-tailed)
					Lower	Upper			
Pair 1	standard - shaded	-1.03846	1.56156	.30625	-1.66919	-.40773	-3.391	25	.002

Figure 5.30

We conclude this section with a t-test summary:

1 If μ and σ are known, then treat $\bar{y}$ as y in a z-score formula:

$$z = \frac{\bar{y} - \mu}{\sigma/\sqrt{n}}.$$

2 If μ is known and σ is unknown, then s replaces σ:

$$t = \frac{\bar{y} - \mu}{s/\sqrt{n}} \; .$$

3 If there are two independent samples, then the sampling distribution of the mean is replaced by the sampling distribution of the difference between two means:

$$t = \frac{\bar{y}_1 - \bar{y}_2}{\sqrt{s_1^2/n + s_2^2/n}} \; .$$

4 If there are two related samples, then $\bar{d}$ replaces $\bar{y}_1 - \bar{y}_2$, and $s_d/\sqrt{n}$ (where n is the number of d-scores) replaces $\sqrt{s_1^2/n + s_2^2/n}$:

$$t = \frac{\bar{d}}{s_d/\sqrt{n}} \; .$$

Reviewing the above formulae, we see the common plot,

$$\frac{\text{what is observed} - \text{what is expected}}{\text{what variability is expected in the observed due to chance alone}} \, ,$$

that is played out in different settings.

RANDOMIZATION TEST AND BOOTSTRAPPING

As discussed in Chapter 4, *parametric* statistics, such as the *t*-test, are based on estimates of population parameters, such as means and variances. The likelihood that all necessary assumptions for such tests will be met is close to nil. Various alternatives to parametric testing of the null hypothesis have been offered. In this section we focus once more on the randomization test as an alternative to traditional H_0 testing. (For the discussion of alternatives to traditional H_0 testing, see p. 141 in Chapter 4.)

The effects that typical violations have on Type I and Type II error rates have been found by some authors to be minor, particularly when the number of subjects is equal across conditions (Box, 1953; Boneau, 1960). Boneau (1960) examined the effects of different distributions, different sample sizes, and different sample variances on Type I errors and concluded that only multiple violations had a discernible effect on Type I error rates, but the effect was considered to be relatively minor. Furthermore, he found the effects shrink as a function of increased sample size such that they are negligible when both conditions had at least 10–15 subjects. Mewhort (2005), more interested in Type II errors, reported that when sample sizes were relatively small (4–10 per condition) and there was substantial skewness, then the randomization test had substantially more power in comparison to its traditional parametric counterpart.

The randomization test (sometimes called *resampling* or the *permutations* test) was first outlined by Fisher (1935). The test was designed to calculate the probability of randomness. The initial example explored in Chapter 1 (10 scores sorted into two groups of five) is a version of the classic problem that Fisher addressed and it is the basis for most statistical tests.

The randomization test for a between-subjects design is a direct application of the problem we posed in the first chapter: have these 10 numbers been randomly sorted into these two groups? Assuming that there are equal numbers of scores in each group or condition, we begin with the initially observed difference in the two means, medians, or modes. Or, as we will see here, we can calculate *t*, although it will not be compared to a critical value. Because population parameters are not estimated, the randomization test is free from any assumptions concerning the shape of the underlying distribution. There is no need to test for outliers, for homogeneity of variance, or for skewness. In conducting a randomization test we employ the general strategy discussed in Chapter 1. After computing the original *t*-value we follow these steps:

Step 1: We randomly reassign the observations to the two conditions.

Step 2: We compute the *t* for the difference between the two new condition means based on the new variances.

Step 3: We record the new *t*.

Step 4: We repeat steps 1–3 a large number of times (*N*), say, 1000 or 5000.

Step 5: We rank-order the absolute values of the *N* *t*s. This becomes the specific sampling distribution necessary for testing our initially observed *t*.

Step 6: We observe that many of these *t*s are greater than the absolute value of our initially observed *t*, which we call *g*.

Step 7: We calculate the probability of our initially observed *t* occurring due to chance alone by dividing *g* by *N*.

The randomization test for a within-subjects design, like the analogous *t*-test, is concerned only with *d*-scores and assumes that if H_0 is true, then the average *d*-score will be 0. We begin by calculating the mean and variance for the *d*-scores for the collected data and calculating the *t*. Next we follow the steps used for a between-subjects design, with one important modification:

Step 1: We randomly re-pair the observations in the second condition to the scores in the first condition. That is, the scores do *not* change their condition location. What is randomized is the order of the scores in the second condition.

Step 2: We compute the *t* for the new set of *d*-scores using the new mean and new variance of the *d*-scores.

Step 3: We record the new *t*.

Step 4: We repeat steps 1–3 a large number of times (*N*), say, 1000 or 5000.

Step 5: We rank-order the absolute values of the *t*s. This becomes the specific sampling distribution necessary for testing our initially observed *t*.

Step 6: We observe how many of these *t*s are greater than the absolute value of our initially observed *t*, which we call *g*.

Step 7: We calculate the probability of our initially observed *t* occurring due to chance alone by dividing *g* by *N*.

We use $\alpha = 0.05$ as the cut-off for decision-making purposes concerning H_0. At times a randomization test may be more effective than a parametric *t*-test at holding the Type I error rate at the desired level, or reducing the chances of a Type II error. What often is overlooked is the problem of generalization. To accurately compute the probability of the observed results we may not need a random sample from a population, but we need a representative sample if we wish to generalize beyond the collected data.

In Fisher's time, a means of effectuating the large number of combinations required to execute the test was not available. It is primarily for this reason that we have the strong tradition of parametric procedures that Fisher (1935) and Pitman (1937) developed as shortcuts to the randomization tests. Because of today's immense computing power, randomization and other similar tests, such as bootstrapping, are becoming more widely used alternatives to their parametric counterparts.

SPSS contains bootstrapping alternatives for a number of standard parametric tests, including *t*-tests. Some of these alternatives will be incorporated into the text at appropriate points. Bootstrapping differs from the randomization test in terms of the procedure used to reassign the observations for each new sample it creates. Bootstrapping treats the originally observed data as a population from which it samples for each iteration. It takes the original data set of *n* scores – in our example there are 52 of them – and samples from it to create a new sample (usually called a 'resample' or 'bootstrap sample') the same size as the original sample. The bootstrap resample is taken from the original 52 scores. But unlike in the case of randomization testing where all of the original 52 scores appear in all resampled data sets, in the case of bootstrapping, scores are sampled from the original sample *with replacement*. A score is randomly selected from the original data set and assigned to a condition, but is then returned to the data set which is serving as the population. There are important consequences accompanying sampling with replacement. First, any score may be selected multiple times. Second, sampling with replacement also means that rarely will all of the original scores be members of a resampled data set. Despite this difference, where randomization tests would be the choice of technique, the bootstrapping approach yields nearly identical results.

Running the bootstrapping option in the independent-samples *t*-test using SPSS

From within the *Analyze* option through the *Define Groups* window and clicking on *Continue* to return to the *Independent-Samples T Test* window, nothing changes from the previous independent-samples *t*-test instructions. The one *important* addition is to select the blue *Bootstrap*

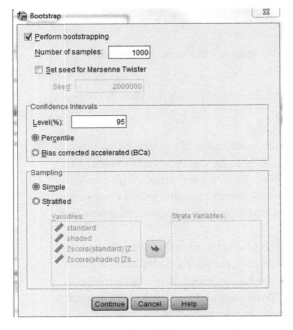

Figure 5.31

option in the upper right corner of the *Independent-Samples T Test* window. Then click on the *Perform bootstrapping* option and *Continue* (Figure 5.31). The results appear in the SPSS output window.

Note that the results in the *Independent Samples Test* table (Figure 5.32) are identical to what you found earlier. These results are merely a repetition of the results for the earlier parametric *t*-test of your 3-D line-drawing data. What is new in the output window is the bottom table: the *Bootstrap for Independent Samples Test* box (Figure 5.33). These results are an alternative analysis in which the 52 scores are analysed in a manner described in the seven steps above. The first box lists the dependent variable's name: *Score*. The second box provides the mean difference averaged over all 1000 resamples. The shape of the distributions produced by the 1000 resamples will often systematically differ, if only slightly, from the original distributions; this difference is referred to as *bias* in the third column of the output window. A bias of 0.00609 is very small. SPSS will automatically make the correction necessary for the bias and ensure that the reported 95% confidence intervals (last two columns) are unbiased.

Independent Samples Test

		Levene's Test for Equality of Variances		t-test for Equality of Means						
									95% Confidence Interval of the Difference	
		F	Sig.	t	df	Sig. (2-tailed)	Mean Difference	Std. Error Difference	Lower	Upper
score	Equal variances assumed	.014	.906	-1.652	50	.105	-1.03846	.62875	-2.30134	.22442
	Equal variances not assumed			-1.652	49.981	.105	-1.03846	.62875	-2.30135	.22443

Figure 5.32

Bootstrap for Independent Samples Test

		Mean Difference	Bootstrap[a]				
			Bias	Std. Error	95% Confidence Interval	
					Lower	Upper
Score	Equal variances assumed	-1.03846	.00609	.62963	-2.21224	.19630
	Equal variances not assumed	-1.03846	.00609	.62963	-2.21224	.19630

a. Unless otherwise noted, bootstrap results are based on 1000 bootstrap samples

Figure 5.33

There are a few points to note when comparing the results in the *Independent Samples Test* box (parametric *t*-test) and the *Bootstrap for Independent Samples Test* box. The mean difference is identical across the two analyses. The standard error of the mean (*Std. Error*) is slightly larger in the case of the bootstrapping analysis: 0.62963 versus 0.62875. Because the *expected* value that corresponds to H_0 (0) falls within the confidence limits, we fail to reject H_0 with the bootstrapping version of the *t*-test as you had with the parametric version of the test.

Running the bootstrapping option in the paired-samples *t*-test using SPSS

From within the *Analyze* option through to the moving of the variables into the *Paired Variables* box, nothing changes from the above independent-samples *t*-test instructions. The one *important* addition is to select the blue *Bootstrap* option in the upper right corner of the window (Figure 5.34). Then chick on the *Perform boot-strapping* option and *Continue* (Figure 5.35). The results appear in the SPSS output window.

Note that the results in the parametric paired-samples test are identical with those of your initial test (Figure 5.36). What is new in the output window this time is the bottom window: the *Bootstrap for Paired Samples Test* (Figure 5.37). The first box lists the condition variables names: standard and shaded. The second box provides the mean *d*-score averaged over all 1000 resamples. A bias of 0.01823 is very small and SPSS will automatically make the required correction. There are a few points to note when comparing the results in the *Paired Samples Test* box (the parametric *t*-test) and the *Bootstrap for Paired Samples Test* box. The mean *d*-scores are identical across the two analyses. The standard error of the mean (*Std. Error*) is slightly smaller in the case of the bootstrapping analysis. Remember, less error results in greater power, all else being held equal. It is this reduced standard error that is responsible for the slightly smaller *p*-value in the case of the bootstrapping. The fact that the *p*-value is less than 0.05 is also reflected in the fact that the *expected* value of the *d*-scores (0) is outside the 95% confidence limits: −1.61538 to −0.42045.

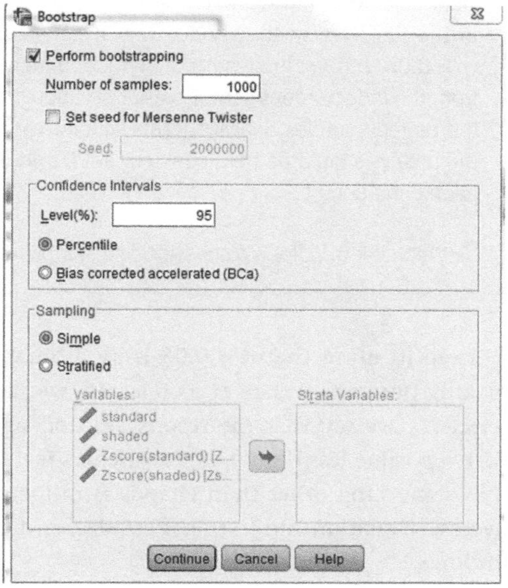

Let us summarize what we have seen so far. When 52 scores were examined as if they were the

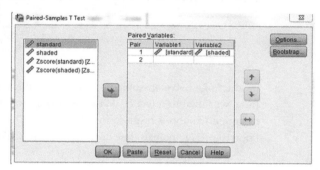

Figure 5.34

Figure 5.35

Paired Samples Test

		Paired Differences							
				Std. Error Mean	95% Confidence Interval of the Difference		t	df	Sig. (2-tailed)
		Mean	Std. Deviation		Lower	Upper			
Pair 1	standard - shaded	-1.03846	1.56156	.30625	-1.66919	-.40773	-3.391	25	.002

Figure 5.36

Bootstrap for Paired Samples Test

		Bootstrap[a]					
						95% Confidence Interval	
		Mean	Bias	Std. Error	Sig. (2-tailed)	Lower	Upper
Pair 1	standard - shaded	-1.03846	.01823	.29109	.001	-1.61538	-.42405

a. Unless otherwise noted, bootstrap results are based on 1000 bootstrap samples

Figure 5.37

product of a between-subjects design, regardless of which procedure we used, including bootstrapping, we failed to reject H_0. When we examined the same scores as the product of a within-subjects design, all analyses resulted in rejecting H_0. There may have been a slight power advantage to the bootstrapping analysis, but nothing close to making a difference with respect to the outcome.

========= CHALLENGE QUESTION =========

Hold constant the difference between two condition means. Construct two versions of a data set. In the first version the results from a paired-samples analysis should be found to be significant ($p < 0.05$) but *not* the results of an independent-samples analysis. In the second version the results from the independent-samples analysis should be found to be significant ($p < 0.05$) but *not* those of the paired-samples analysis. (This second version is a super-challenge question.) In both versions the means should be held constant at 20 and 30, respectively. There should be 12 observations in each condition.

Web Link 5.12 for a discussion and sample answer to the challenge question.

Keep in mind that $\alpha = 0.05$ is an arbitrary value agreed upon by researchers for decision-making purposes. When H_0 is rejected, we say that the results are significant. When we fail to reject H_0, we say that the results are non-significant. The word 'significant' only means that with a p-value less than 0.05, researchers feel confident enough to conclude, at least tentatively, that something other than chance is influencing the data. Furthermore, the p-value bears no necessary relationship to the effect size, and certainly does not indicate the 'importance' of the findings.

Web Link 5.13 for a discussion of the relation between effect size, sample size, and p-value.

- - - - -

The importance of distinguishing between p-value, effect size, and theoretical or practical importance cannot be overstated. The American Statistical Association has released a statement of principles regarding p-values. The statement is summarized here.

1   p-values *may* indicate that the data are incompatible with the null hypothesis or another model.
2   p-values do *not* indicate the probability either that the data were produced by random chance alone or that the alternative hypothesis is true.
3   p-values should *not* be the sole basis for drawing scientific conclusions.
4   A p-value (or statistical significance level) is *not* an indicator of effect size or of the importance of the results.
5   p-values alone do not provide evidence for or against any given model or hypothesis.

When we reject H_0 we may be making a Type I error; when we fail to reject we may be making a Type II error. Regardless of the procedure used for analysing the data, when we reject H_0 we are asserting that there is evidence to justify this line of investigation. We are *not* claiming proof of anything. The only way to increase our confidence in the results is through actual replication: repeating the experiment with other subjects and having other researchers repeat the experiment.

- - - - -

The parametric versus randomization (bootstrapping) debate is something of a tempest in a teacup. If we had randomization alternatives for all of our parametric statistical procedures and software to easily run them, it would be worthwhile to switch our standard practices to such procedures. But change occurs slowly. The use of parametric statistics is not about to disappear. If researchers examine their data for outliers, normality, and heterogeneity of variance, and if prior to collecting data they estimate the number of subjects they require to have appropriate power, then the outcomes from parametric tests will differ little from their randomization counterparts. When running t-tests in SPSS it is always worthwhile to simultaneously run the bootstrapping option.

NONPARAMETRIC TESTS

The randomization and the bootstrapping tests discussed in Section 5.9 use the numerical values of the scores, making the assumption that the scores were either interval or ratio in nature. In this section we examine several traditional nonparametric tests, beginning with one that makes no assumptions other than that we can reliably say that one number is greater than another: 4 is greater than 2 and 6 is greater than 4, even if we are unsure that the difference in amount between 2 and 4 is the same as the difference between 4 and 6. We have referred to data of this type as ordinal in nature. For example, subjects are asked to rank 20 pop stars from least favourite (1) to most favourite (20). We know that the higher the ranking, the more positive the respondent's attitude, but it is doubtful that the differences between adjacent rankings are constant.

Between-subjects design

The most common nonparametric alternative to the *t*-test for a between-subjects design is the Mann–Whitney *U*-test (Mann & Whitney, 1947), sometimes called the Wilcoxon rank-sum test. Like the *t*-test, the Mann–Whitney test assumes that the observations are independent. Practically, this means that subjects have been randomly assigned to conditions. Unlike its parametric counterpart, the *t*-test, the Mann–Whitney test does not assume normality. Where the *t*-test assumes at least *interval* data, the Mann–Whitney test assumes only ordinality. The H_0 for the Mann–Whitney does not concern any particular parameter of the population, such as the mean. Rather, H_0 is simply that the two underlying distributions are *expected* to be identical. If this is true, then we *expect* both high and low rankings to be distributed equally across the two conditions. The test is based on the rankings or the ordinal positions of the observations.

If the population distributions of both groups are normal, then the Mann–Whitney becomes a test for a difference in central tendency: means, medians, or modes.

With small samples the following hand calculations are typically used:

1   Rank all scores (disregarding condition membership) from lowest to highest, with 1 being the lowest rank.
2   Sum the ranks assigned to scores in condition 1 (Ranks1). The sum of the ranks for condition 2 (Ranks2) is then the total of the rankings ($\frac{1}{2}N(N + 1)$) minus the sum of Ranks1.
3   Rankslarge = the larger of the two rankings sums.
4   Identify n_1, n_2, and n_{large}, where n_1 is the number of observations in condition 1, n_2 is the number of observations in condition 2, and n_{large} is the number of observations in the condition which has the largest sum of the rankings.
5   $U = n_1 \times n_2 + (n_{large}(n_{large} + 1) / 2) - \text{Rankslarge}$.
6   *U* is evaluated against a critical value from the table in Appendix F. The rows in the table represent the number of subjects or observations in one condition and the columns represent the number of subjects or observations in the other condition. Because the table is symmetrical, it is inconsequential which condition is designated as the row and which is designated as the column.
7   The value of *U* must be equal to or *less* than the critical value to reject H_0.

For example, if there are 10 observations, the rankings would be 1, 2, 3, 4, 5, 6, 7, 8, 9, 10.

1   The sum of the rankings is $\frac{1}{2}N(N + 1) = 55$.
2   If the sum of the rankings in condition 1 is 14, then condition 2 must have a sum of 55 − 14 = 41.
3   Rankslarge is the sum of the ranks in condition 2 (41).
4   $n_1 = 4$, $n_2 = 6$, and $n_{large} = 6$.
5   $U = 4 \times 6 + (6(6 + 1) / 2) - 41 = 4$.
6   In the table in Appendix F, the intersection of $n_1 = 4$ and $n_2 = 6$ is 2 (critical value).
7   Because the observed *U* of 4 is greater than the critical *U* of 2, we fail to reject H_0.

We conclude that there is insufficient evidence to reject the assumption that the observations come from one distribution.

When two (or more) scores are the same and the rankings thus tied, both scores are given their mean ranking. For example, Figure 5.38 shows a hypothetical set of scores with tied scores and rankings (there are two 12s and two 18s).

Control group						Treatment group				
Raw scores	27	15	18	25	12	21	9	12	16	18	24
Rankings	11	4	6.5	10	2.5	8	1	2.5	5	6.5	9
Sum of rankings = 42						Sum of rankings = 24				

Figure 5.38

═══════════ CHALLENGE QUESTION ═══════════

On the book's web page there is a data set (*mwreveiwsdata.sav*) with one independent variable (condition) and three dependent variables: *score1*, *score2*, and *score3*. Analyse all three dependent measures using the SPSS independent-samples nonparametric test used above. How do the three results compare? Given the differences in the range of the scores in the three dependent measures, how do you explain the results?

🔖 Web Link 5.14 for the data set and a discussion or the results.

As we saw in Chapter 4, a binominal problem can be converted into a *z*-score problem. When there are at least 20 observations in each condition, the distribution of U approaches normality and a *z*-score is computed:

$$z = \frac{U - (\text{mean of } U)}{\text{standard deviation of } U},$$

where the mean of U is $n_1 n_2 / 2$, and the standard deviation of U is $\sqrt{n_1 n_2 (n_1 + n_2 + 1)/12}$. As usual, 1.96 is the critical absolute value for a two-tailed test at $\alpha = 0.05$.

For the above example with 10 observations and the rankings of 1, 2, 3, 4, 5, 6, 7, 8, 9, 10 we find that the mean of U is $n_1 n_2 / 2 = 4 \times 6/2 = 12$ and the standard deviation of U is $\sqrt{n_1 n_2 (n_1 + n_2 + 1)/12} = \sqrt{24 \times 11/12} = 4.69$, so

$$z = \frac{4 - 12}{4.69} = -1.71.$$

Again, we fail to reject H_0.

Running an independent-samples nonparametric test using SPSS

We again analyse our data from the 3-D line-drawings experiment. From within the *Data Editor* window in the *independentsamplesttest.sav** file select *Analyze* and then drop down and select *Nonparametric Tests*. Next select the *Independent Samples* option. In the

---

*Be sure that *Score* is identified as a measurement variable and that *Condition* is identified as a nominal variable in *Variable View in the Data Editor.*

Nonparametric Tests: Two or More Independent Samples window (Figure 5.39) select the *Fields* tab at the top. In the next window (Figure 5.40) move the variable *Score* to the *Test Fields* box and move the variable *Condition* to the *Groups* box. Finally, click *Run* at the bottom left of the window.

The results appear in the SPSS output window (Figure 5.41). The first column shows H_0. The second column identifies the test. The third column reports the *p*-value of the test statistic, $p = 0.102$. Finally, the fourth column offers a decision based on $\alpha = 0.05$.

There has been considerable discussion about effect size indices for nonparametric tests. One of the easiest to understand is what McGraw and Wong (1992) called the *common language effect size statistic*. Remember, we are dealing with a between-subjects design, and the first score in the standard condition in theory is unrelated to the first score in the shaded condition. They are like two people who have accidentally bumped into each other on the street. As we did with the paired-samples *t*-test, we again compute *d*-scores. As with the sign test, we are only interested in the sign of the *d*-score. The *common language effect size* is the percentage of negative (or positive, depending upon which you wish to report) *d*-scores. In the case of your 3-D line-drawing experiments 22 of the 26 differences are negative: 22/26 = 0.85. Thus, the effect size is 85%.

A common variant on this index is the *rank-biserial correlation* which can be easily calculated by subtracting the percentage of positive differences from the percentage of negative differences (Kerby, 2014). In the 3-D line-drawings example, the rank-biserial correlation is 85 − 15 = 70%. The value can vary from 0% (a 50–50 split) to 100%.

Within-subjects design

The test with the fewest assumptions for a within-subjects design is the sign test (Dixon & Mood, 1946). We have already completed one version of the sign test when we examined the *d*-scores in Figure 5.16 using the binomial test in Section 5.7. The sign test is concerned only with the number of positive and negative *d*-scores. The H_0 assumes an equal number of negative and positive *d*-scores. The *observed difference* is then compared with this *expected difference* (zero). When the binomial test was used to analyse the *d*-scores, we found that the probability of 22 out of 26 scores being negative was approximately 0.002 and we rejected H_0.

After our discussion in Chapter 4, it should not be surprising that one alternative approach for testing the difference between the *expected* and *observed* number of negative *d*-scores is to convert the number of negative scores into a *z*-score as we did earlier. As you recall, the mean of a binomial distribution is *np* (the number of observations multiplied by the probability of a negative *d*-score, assumed to be 0.5); the variance of the distribution is *npq* (*q* being the probability of a positive *d*-score, assumed to be 0.5); and the standard deviation of the distribution is $\sqrt{npq}$. Thus, where $n = 26$, $p = 0.05$, and $q = 0.05$,

$$z = \frac{\text{observed number of negative } d\text{-scores} - np}{\sqrt{npq}} = \frac{22 - 13}{2.55} = 4.53.$$

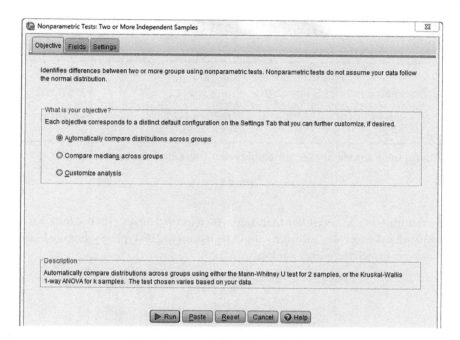

Figure 5.39

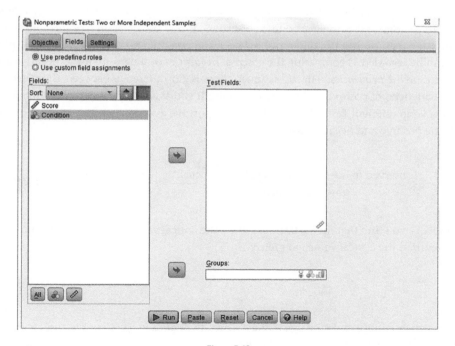

Figure 5.40

Hypothesis Test Summary

	Null Hypothesis	Test	Sig.	Decision
1	The distribution of Score is the same across categories of Condition.	Independent-Samples Mann-Whitney U Test	.102	Retain the null hypothesis.

Asymptotic significances are displayed. The significance level is .05.

Figure 5.41

Because the resulting z (3.53) is greater than 1.96, you reject H_0. Again, when significant results are found a standardized effect size measure should be reported. The typically reported standardized effect size measure associated with a z-test is r, given by

$$r = \frac{z}{\sqrt{n}} = \frac{3.53}{5.099} = 0.69.$$

Regarding r, small effects range from 0.10 to 0.30; medium effects range from 0.30 to 0.50; and values greater than 0.50 are considered large. Your r of 0.69 indicates a large effect.

Looking back yet again to Chapter 4, it should not be surprising that another alternative approach to the sign test is the χ^2 goodness-of-fit test. When the data are binomial and there are only two categories, testing the difference between the *expected* and *observed* number of negative d-scores can be regarded as comparing the *observed frequencies* of the positive and negative z-scores with their *expected frequencies*. The H_0 assumes there is no difference between the *observed* and *expected* frequencies of positive and negative d-scores. If you assume that the probability of a negative d-score is no different from the probability of a positive d-score, then the expected frequency for both the positive and negative d-scores is 13. Then

$$\chi^2 = \sum \frac{(\text{observed frequencies} - \text{expected frequencies})^2}{\text{observed frequencies}} = \frac{(22-13)^2}{13} + \frac{(4-13)^2}{13} = 12.46.$$

In Appendix C, you find that for $\alpha = 0.05$ and $df = 1$ the critical value is 3.84. Because your observed χ^2 is greater than the critical value, you reject H_0.

Signed-rank test

Where the sign test utilizes only the sign of the d-scores, the *Wilcoxon signed-rank test* uses both the sign and the magnitude. The signed-rank test has been a common choice when analysing measurement data where the distributional assumptions are obviously violated and the *n*s are small (less than 10). Both the sign test and the Wilcoxon signed-rank test are easily computed using SPSS.

Running a two-related-samples nonparametric test using SPSS

Return to the data from the 3-D line-drawings experiment found in the *pairedsamplettest. sav* file. From within the *Data Editor* window, select *Analyze* and drop down and select *Nonparametric Tests*. Next select the *Related Samples* option that appears in the new window. In the *Nonparametric Tests: Two or More Related Samples* window (Figure 5.42) select the *Fields* tab at the top. In the next window (Figure 5.43) move the *standard* and the *shaded* variables to the *Test Fields* box and select the *Settings* tab at the top of the window. Click the *Customize tests* button on the screen that appears (Figure 5.44). In the box on the right (*Compare Median Differences to Hypothesized*) check the *Sign test* and the *Wilcoxon matched-pair signed-rank (2 samples)* options. Finally, click *Run* at the bottom left of the window.

The results appear in the SPSS output window (Figure 5.45). The first column shows H_0. The second column identifies the test statistic. The third column reports the *p*-value of the test statistic. Finally, the fourth column offers a decision based on $\alpha = 0.05$.

Both the *sign test* and *signed-rank test* provide evidence that shading aids performance on the 3-D line-drawing task. As Dixon and Mood (1946) point out, *d*-scores can be zero. When this is the case, they argued that half of the zeros be treated as negative differences and half be treated as positive differences.

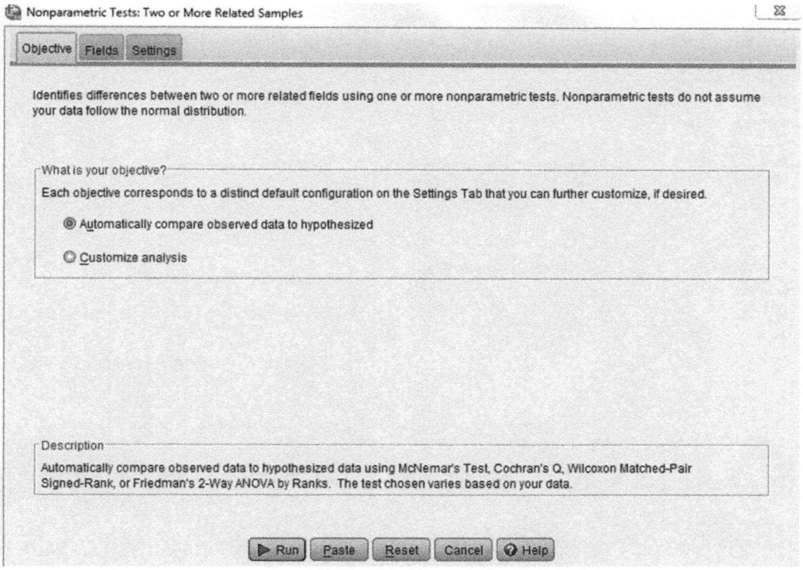

Figure 5.42

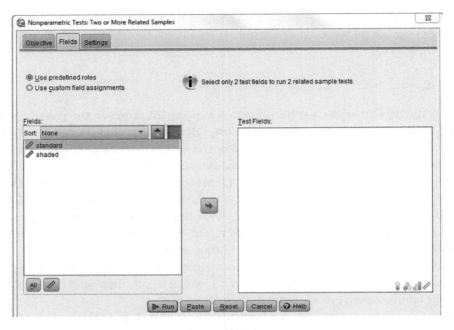

Figure 5.43

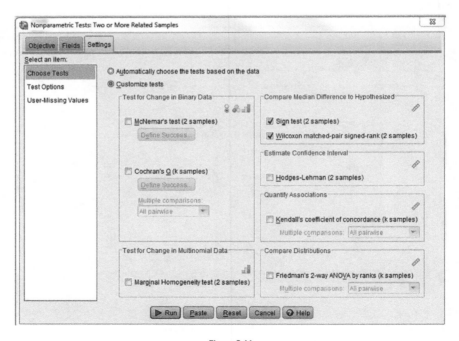

Figure 5.44

Hypothesis Test Summary

	Null Hypothesis	Test	Sig.	Decision
1	The median of differences between shaded and standard equals 0.	Related-Samples Sign Test	.001	Reject the null hypothesis.
2	The median of differences between standard and shaded equals 0.	Related-Samples Wilcoxon Signed Rank Test	.001	Reject the null hypothesis.

Asymptotic significances are displayed. The significance level is .05.

Figure 5.45

5 ● 11 CHAPTER SUMMARY

The underlying plot has remained the same throughout the chapter: the difference between what is *expected* and what is *observed* is evaluated against what can be expected due to chance alone. What changed were assumptions about the data, and whether there were differences between groups or differences within a group across two conditions.

Data from a fictitious experiment were used as an example. We found that regardless of statistical test, when the experiment was viewed as a between-subjects design, all tests yielded non-significant results, with only small differences in the estimated p-values. We also found that regardless of statistical test, when the experiment was viewed as a within-subjects design, all tests yielded significant results. The differences between the within-subjects and between-subjects results illustrate the power that can be gained from a within-subjects design. Although such consistency between the parametric and the nonparametric results is not always the case, it is typical when prior to parametric tests a little care is taken: outliers are identified and addressed; homogeneity of variance can be assumed; and sample size is adequate for the desired effect size.

Nonparametric alternatives are required, however, when there are major and multiple violations of parametric assumptions or when the data cannot be regarded as interval. Remember, regardless of the type of test used and the sample size, Type I and Type II errors are always possible. There is no substitute for independent replication of results to demonstrate their reliability.

A last word of caution concerning p-values. What is meant when it is said that a result is statistically significant? The simple answer, although not entirely true, is that the probability of the *observed results* being due to chance alone is less than 0.05. Remember, a p-value is related to (1) the size of the difference in the two conditions, (2) the variance involved, and (3) the number of observations. The p-value tells us nothing about the absolute size of the difference between the two conditions or even the standard effect size (d). The same difference or the same Cohen's d can have an infinite number of possible p-values, some significant and some non-significant. This is why statistics such as confidence intervals and Cohen's d must be reported. Furthermore, this is why data collection begins *after* determining the number of subjects required for the desired effect size. Cut-offs for *p*-values, such as 0.05, are benchmarks for deciding whether or not to consider findings reliable enough to be further pursued. Depending on the effect sizes and the samples sizes, there are occasions when a *p*-value of 0.06 suggests something of great importance, and there are occasions when an effect associated with a *p*-value of 0.001 is trivial.

5.12 RECOMMENDED READINGS

Boneau, C. A. (1960). The effects of violations of assumptions underlying the t test. *Psychological Bulletin, 57*, 49–64.

This is a classic paper that demonstrates the robustness of the standard parametric *t*-test.

Fay, M. P., & Proschan, M. A. (2010). Wilcoxon–Mann–Whitney or *t*-test? On assumptions for hypothesis tests and multiple interpretations of decision rules. *Statistics Surveys, 4*, 1–39.

This paper summarizes the different null hypotheses associated with the parametric *t*-test and the non-parametric alternatives. The paper also compares the assumptions underlying each test.

Mewhort, D. J. K. (2005). A comparison of the randomization test with the F test when error is skewed. *Behavioral Research Methods, 37*, 426–435.

This paper describes the conditions under which the randomization test has more statistical power than its parametric alternative. Of particular interest is the importance of sample size.

5.13 CHAPTER REVIEW QUESTIONS

Multiple-choice questions

1   The standard error of the mean _____ as the _____ increases.

    a   decreases; *n*

    b   decreases; variance

    c   decrease; mean

    d   increases; *n*

    e   increases; mean

2   When testing for the difference between two conditions resulting from a between-subjects design, we statistically need to take into account_____.

    a   the two means

    b   the two variances

    c   the number of subjects in each condition

    d   All of the above

    e   Both A and C

3   We are more likely to find a significant difference ($\alpha < 0.05$) between two means if_____.

    a   the variance is relatively large

    b   the subjects are randomly assigned to conditions

c   the null hypothesis is true

d   All of the above

e   None of the above.

4   The results of a *t*-test can be compromised by which of the following?

a   Outliers

b   Heterogeneous variance

c   Skewness

d   All of the above

e   None of the above

5   As a *p*-value decreases,_____.

a   effect size necessarily increases

b   sample size necessarily increases

c   effect size necessarily decreases

d   the importance of the findings increases

e   None of the above

6   If a researcher wishes to test for a large difference between two means ($d = 0.80$), how many subjects would he or she require per condition with $\alpha = 0.05$?

a   Cannot be determined from the information provided

b   10

c   26

d   64

e   100

7   The critical value for a *t*-test ($\alpha = 0.05$) with 29 degrees of freedom is _____.

a   Cannot be determined from the information provided

b   2.045

c   12.706

d   1.96

e   29

8   In a within-subjects design, if the mean of condition 1 is 5.5 and the mean of condition 2 is 3.2, the mean of the *d*-scores is _____.

a   Cannot be determined from the information provided

b   8.8

c   0.0

d   3.2

e   2.3

9   The assumptions for the Mann–Whitney *U*-test include _____.

a   independent observations

b   at least ordinal data

c   interval data

d   normal distributions

e   Both a and b

10 Assume there are 5 observations in condition 1, 7 observations in condition 2, and the total of the ranking in condition 1 is 20. Using the Mann–Whitney U-test, what is the value of the U to be evaluated?

a   5

b   4

c   20

d   58

e   None of the above

Short-answer questions

1   In a paragraph, describe the logic of a repeated-measures t-test (related samples). For the purpose of constructing the 'sampling distribution of the difference between means', which variance is used? What is the null hypothesis?

2   How does the randomization test differ from the traditional parametric t-test?

3   Imagine you have analysed your data, thinking that they were collected using a within-subjects (repeated-measures) design. The t-value was non-significant ($p > 0.05$). Subsequently you are told the data were collected using a between-subjects (independent-samples) design. Is there any chance that the findings will be significant after you reanalyse the data with an independent-samples t-test? If no, why not? If yes, under what circumstances?

4   What is the difference between the sign test and signed-rank test?

5   How do we calculate the standard error for a 'difference between two means'? What is its use?

6   Why is a mean d-score the expected value used in the null hypothesis for a repeated-measures t-test?

Data set questions

1   You want to know whether people are able to identify emotions correctly when they are extremely tired. We know that in the general population (who are not tired), accuracy ratings are on average 82% with a variance of 20. In the present study, however, you test 50 people after they participate in strenuous cardiovascular exercise for 45 minutes. You find a mean of 78%. What is the most appropriate test? What can you conclude?

2   What simple change can you make to the scores in the shaded condition in Figure 5.3 so that the resulting t-value will have a p-value less than 0.05? (The variance in the condition should not be changed.)

3   Professor Pigeon hypothesized that Long–Evans rats are smarter than the common Norway brown rats. To test out his idea he randomly selected 10 rats from each of the two populations. He tested the rats on the standard rat intelligence test: a maze. His data are depicted in Figure 5.46. The scores indicate the number of days it took a rat to learn the maze. Did Professor Pigeon find sufficient evidence to support his idea? Include descriptive statistics, tests of assumptions and outliers, an appropriate graph, 95% confidence intervals, and standard effect size estimate, if necessary.

4   A clinical psychologist wanted to know if a new form of relaxation therapy would reduce the symptoms of her anxious patients. She had her patients report the number of daily symptoms both before and after four weeks of the new therapy. Do the data in Figure 5.47 provide evidence for the effectiveness of the new form of relaxation therapy?

Because she believed anxiety symptoms are not normally distributed, she used a nonparametric test. Do the data in Figure 5.47 still provide evidence for the effectiveness of the new form of relaxation therapy? What do you think about the normality of the distribution of the symptoms?

Long–Evans	Norway brown
3	6
6	7
5	8
2	6
4	9
7	4
4	7
8	8
2	5
3	3

Figure 5.46

Patient	Symptoms before	Symptoms after
1	13	8
2	16	5
3	12	7
4	9	9
5	24	25
6	15	12
7	22	12
8	6	5
9	22	18
10	6	4

Figure 5.47

Don't forget to use the online resources! Meet your supporting stats tutor through an **introductory video**, review your maths skills with a **diagnostic pre-test**, explore statistical principles through **interactive simulations**, practice analysis techniques with **SPSS datasets**, and check your work with **answers to all in-text questions**.

https://study.sagepub.com/bors

6

Chapter contents

OBSERVATIONAL STUDIES: TWO CATEGORICAL VARIABLES

KEY CONCEPTS: x^2 test of independence, Cramér's V, phi (ϕ), Yates's continuity correction, the likelihood ratio, Fisher's exact test, lambda (λ).

PURPOSE

The purpose of this chapter is to introduce the statistical tests used to determine whether two nominal or ordinal variables are related and, if so, to what degree. We focus primarily on the χ^2 *test of independence* and accompanying indices of effect size. Specifically, these tests are designed to answer the question: are the observed *frequencies* random with respect to two variables? Connections are made to the inescapable laws of probability, which are crucial for understanding how to derive the *expected frequencies* necessary for the χ^2 *test of independence*. Although the chapter is a direct extension of the χ^2 *goodness-of-fit test* covered earlier, links also are made to inferential tests covered in the previous chapter, both parametric and nonparametric. We open with a surprise. We discover that the *t*-test that was covered in the previous chapter is conceptually not so different from some of the material covered in this chapter. As we begin, recall our orienting framework. Statistical tests can be loosely segregated into four families that are based on one of two types of research questions and one of two types of data. In Chapter 5, we had a rather large family of tests based on (1) a research question of *difference* and (2) *measurement* data. In this chapter we have a family of tests based on the intersection of (1) a question of *relation* (or association) and (2) categorical data.

INTRODUCTION

In the previous chapter we focused on a possible *difference* between groups of scores. The core concern of the current chapter is centred on a possible *association* between two variables. As we will see, the question of a possible *difference* and the question of a possible *association* are often simply two ways of posing the same question. Answering the question of a difference and answering the question of an association both involve, first and foremost, determining what is *expected*:

1 What is expected if the scores in the two conditions are *not* different?
2 What is expected if the scores in the two variables are *not* associated?

Questions of difference and questions of association both require examining the difference between what is *expected* and what is *observed*. Both questions involve determining the *probability* of the difference between the two. Furthermore, conclusions that there is a *difference* or that there is an *association* can be translated into statements about the reduction of error when making predictions. Knowing that there is a difference between the scores in two conditions implies that there is an *association* between the scores and the conditions.

In addition to the change of question from one of difference to one of association, where the previous chapter focused on measurement data, the present chapter involves the analysis of categorical or frequency data.

This chapter begins with a modification of a fictional study previously used. In the current version, your subjects are shown a line-drawing like the one in Figure 6.1 (left). Then a second figure appears to its right. The subject's task is to determine whether or not the second figure is simply a rotated version of the first figure. Some subjects are shown the standard figures and some are shown a shaded version of the figures. All subjects ($n = 60$) are shown only one pair of figures. You as the researcher hypothesized that those subjects shown the shaded figure would more frequently be correct than those shown the standard figures. Subjects had a score of either 0 (incorrect) or 1 (correct). The SPSS data file is available on this chapter's web page.

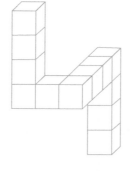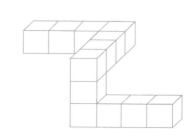

Web Link 6.1 for the SPSS data file: mentalrotation1.sav.

Figure 6.1

As mentioned in the previous chapter, regardless of the research design, crucial theoretical and practical questions often come down to examining pairs of conditions. Were the observations in one condition possibly influenced by something that did not influence the observations in the other condition: in this case, shading? Recall the paradigmatic problem posed in the opening chapter: were the 10 scores randomly sorted into the two groups? Answering the question involved (1) determining what to *expect* if the numbers were randomly sorted, (2) comparing the *expected* with what was *observed*, and (3) determining whether the difference between *the expected* and *the observed* was too great for us to continue assuming that the numbers were randomly sorted. We will continue to use the probability of 0.05 as the decision threshold. In the current example, you hypothesized that those subjects shown the shaded figures would be more likely to be correct than those subjects shown the standard figures. This is the experimental or alternative hypothesis (H_1). The null hypothesis (H_0) is that the 0s (incorrect) and the 1s (correct) would be random with respect to condition.

We might frame the current research question in terms similar to those used to address the version of three-dimensional line-drawing study introduced in the previous chapter: an independent-samples *t*-test. We have a variable, *condition*, which could be considered the independent variable. We have another variable, *score*, which could be considered the dependent variable. We answered the question of the possible randomness of the scores (H_0) in the previous chapter by comparing the mean scores of the two conditions. In the current example, however, the dependent variable has only two possible outcomes, 0 or 1 (incorrect or correct). Let us not concern ourselves with that for the moment. If we run an independent-samples *t*-test on the current data set, we find the following results (if necessary, review the instructions in the previous chapter for running an independent-samples *t*-test).

REVIEW QUESTION

What is the difference between an independent-samples *t*-test and a paired-samples *t*-test?

Web Link 6.2 for an answer to the review question.

The mean ($\bar{y}$) for the *standard condition* (1) is 0.62 with a standard deviation (S) of 0.496. Because the variance (S^2) is the square of the standard deviation, $S^2 = 0.246$. For the *shaded condition* (2), $\bar{y} = 0.85$, $S = 0.359$, and $S^2 = 0.129$ (Figure 6.2).

Group Statistics					
	condition	N	Mean	Std. Deviation	Std. Error Mean
response	1	26	.62	.496	.097
	2	34	.85	.359	.062

Figure 6.2

From the *Independent Samples Test* table (Figure 6.3) we find that the *t*-value (assuming homogeneity of variance) of –2.151 is significant ($p = 0.036$). Levene's test ($F = 17.249$, $p < 0.001$) in the table is significant, however, and indicates that we should *not* assume homogeneity of variance. The alternative *t*-value (–2.062) is also significant, even when we compensated for the difference in the two variances ($p = 0.045$). Because the *t*-value is significant and the mean of the *shaded condition* is greater than the mean of the *standard condition*, we may conclude that there is evidence that shading the figure results in improved performance.

Independent Samples Test

		Levene's Test for Equality of Variances		t-test for Equality of Means					95% Confidence Interval of the Difference	
		F	Sig.	t	df	Sig. (2-tailed)	Mean Difference	Std. Error Difference	Lower	Upper
response	Equal variances assumed	17.249	.000	-2.151	58	.036	-.238	.110	-.459	-.017
	Equal variances not assumed			-2.062	43.760	.045	-.238	.115	-.470	-.005

Figure 6.3

You might wonder if this result is an artefact of the values that were chosen for incorrect and correct responses: 0 and 1. If you are following along in SPSS, notice that in the data file there is a third variable: *newscore*. The *newscore* values represent the original *score* values multiplied by 100. Replacing *score* with *newscore* and rerunning the independent-samples *t*-test, we find that some things change and some things remain the same. The *Group Statistics* window (Figure 6.4) reveals that the means, standard deviations, and variance have all increased, as has the difference between the two means. In the *Independent Samples Test* table (Figure 6.5), however, we find that the test statistic information is unchanged. Levene's test for homogeneity of variance remains the same, as do the two *t*-values and their respective *p*-values (0.036 and 0.045). Again we would reject H_0 and conclude that there is enough evidence to suggest that shading the figure improves performance. It is worthwhile to keep the *p*-values in mind.

Group Statistics

	condition	N	Mean	Std. Deviation	Std. Error Mean
newresponse	1	26	61.5385	49.61389	9.73009
	2	34	85.2941	35.94906	6.16521

Figure 6.4

Independent Samples Test

		Levene's Test for Equality of Variances		t-test for Equality of Means						95% Confidence Interval of the Difference	
		F	Sig.	t	df	Sig. (2-tailed)	Mean Difference	Std. Error Difference		Lower	Upper
newresponse	Equal variances assumed	17.249	.000	-2.151	58	.036	-23.75566	11.04178		-45.85818	-1.65313
	Equal variances not assumed			-2.062	43.760	.045	-23.75566	11.51887		-46.97401	-.53730

Figure 6.5

===== CHALLENGE QUESTION =====

Why do the *t*-values and *p*-values remain unchanged in the two analyses, despite the dramatic increase in the difference between the two means? Reflect on the notion of a linear transformation and *z*-scores as you formulate your answer.

Web Link 6.3 for an answer to the challenge question.

Although an independent-samples *t*-test might be used to analyse these data, it would not be considered the first choice by most researchers. Nor is it the most appropriate test. When faced with frequency data, possible randomness would not be expressed in terms of the difference between two means. Rather, researchers will hypothesize (H_1) that there will be proportionately more 1s in the group of subjects shown the shaded figure (condition 2) than in the group shown the standard figure (condition 1). The corresponding null hypothesis (H_0) is that 0s and 1s will be random with respect to the two groups. The hypotheses are thus framed in terms of frequencies. Notice that we have transformed a study from one based on measurement data to one that is based on categorical or frequency data. Conceptually, we are also changing the question from whether we *observe* a *difference* in the condition means to whether we *observe* an *association* between *score* and *condition*. This illustrates how questions of *difference* and questions of *association* are two sides of the same coin. If we find a difference, we find an association.

• • • • •

If there is a difference between the mean height of men and the mean height of women, then there is an association between height and gender. The choice of how to express the hypothesis and how to present the results is a question of suitability in terms of the research design and the theoretical or practical issues being examined. Sometimes the translation of the question from one form to the other is difficult, but it is always possible.

6 3 χ^2 GOODNESS-OF-FIT TEST REVIEWED

In this section we review the logic of Pearson's χ^2 *goodness-of-fit* test and discover one of its limitations. Recall from Chapter 4 that Pearson's χ^2 goodness-of-fit test is a procedure for determining the extent to which an *observed* pattern of observations (frequencies) conforms to an *expected* pattern. The first pattern that was tested was that of complete randomness. That is, we tested whether or not a sample of observations was random with respect to a set of categories. The formula for the χ^2 test of independence used later in this chapter is identical to the one used for the χ^2 goodness-of-fit test. The key is the small addition to the logic behind deriving the expected frequencies,

$$\chi^2 = \Sigma \frac{(O-E)^2}{E},$$

where O is the observed frequency of a cell and E is its expected frequency.

With respect to the current 3-D line-drawing data, we might ask if *scores* are random, similar to flipping a coin. There are two categories, 0 and 1: incorrect and correct. If subjects were simply guessing, we would expect to observe an equal number of subjects in the correct and incorrect categories. That is what we would expect due to chance alone, if we were to repeat the experiment with 60 different subjects over and over again a large number of times. With any given sample, the observed is rarely, if ever, equal to the expected, even when H_0 is true.

If we run a χ^2 goodness-of-fit test on the variable *score* in the *meantalrotation1.sav* file using the *All Categories Equal* as the *Expect Values* option, we find the following results. The *Score* table (Figure 6.6) reveals that 15 subjects were incorrect in judging the figure and 45 subjects were correct. The *Test Statistics* table (Figure 6.7) indicates that the χ^2 value ($df = 1$) of 15.00 is significant ($p < 0.001$). Thus, there is evidence that subjects were doing more than merely guessing.

This variability in the difference between the *expected* and the *observed*, due to chance alone, can be seen as one way to answer the question: why do we need statistical analysis?

━━━ REVIEW QUESTION ━━━

Could a binomial test be used as an alternative to the χ^2? Why or why not?

Web Link 6.4 for an answer to the review question.

score

	Observed N	Expected N	Residual
0	15	30.0	-15.0
1	45	30.0	15.0
Total	60		

Figure 6.6

Test Statistics

	score
Chi-Square	15.000[a]
df	1
Asymp. Sig.	.000

Figure 6.7

═══ CHALLENGE QUESTION ═══

If in the general population the success rate in determining whether a line-drawing is a rotated version of an original is 75%, how might we test whether a new sample of 50 subjects was a random sample drawn from the general population? What is the null hypothesis? How is the notion of randomness then a part of the null hypothesis?

Web Link 6.5 for the answer to the challenge question.

This analysis does not answer your research question, however. It is possible that subjects in the *standard condition* may be guessing, whereas those subjects in the *shaded condition* use the shading information to solve the problem. It is also possible, however, that some subjects in both conditions are able to solve the problem and that there is no difference in success rate across the two conditions.

These are only two of the possibilities. To address the first possibility you might consider running χ^2 goodness-of-fit tests on the two conditions separately. If you run a χ^2 goodness-of-fit test on *score* on those subjects in the *standard condition* (1), again using the *All Categories Equal* as the *Expect Values* option, you find the following results. The *Score* table (Figure 6.8) reveals that 10 subjects were incorrect in their responses and 16 subjects were correct. The *Test Statistics* table (Figure 6.9), however, indicates that the χ^2 value of 1.385 ($df = 1$) is non-significant ($p = 0.239$). Thus, you have insufficient evidence that subjects in the *standard condition* were doing anything other than guessing, even though 16 out of 26 subjects' responses were correct.

score

	Observed N	Expected N	Residual
0	10	13.0	-3.0
1	16	13.0	3.0
Total	26		

Figure 6.8

Test Statistics

	score
Chi-Square	1.385[a]
df	1
Asymp. Sig.	.239

Figure 6.9

If you run a χ^2 goodness-of-fit test on *score* on those in the *shaded condition* (2), again using the *All Categories Equal* as the *Expect Values* option, you find the following results. The *Score* table (Figure 6.10) reveals that 5 subjects were incorrect in their responses and 29 subjects were correct. The *Test Statistics* table (Figure 6.11) indicates that the χ^2 value of 16.941 ($df = 1$) is significant ($p < 0.001$). Thus, you have evidence indicating that subjects in the *shaded condition* were doing something more than guessing. It may well be that the subjects were using the information provided by shading to solve the problem. Some may consider that by comparing these two results your research question concerning the effect of shading is answered. Such an approach is inadequate and cannot answer your question. The strategy of dividing the data set and conducting separate analyses and then comparing the result is found in χ^2 and many other forms of analyses, and it often leads to misleading results.

score

	Observed N	Expected N	Residual
0	5	17.0	-12.0
1	29	17.0	12.0
Total	34		

Figure 6.10

Test Statistics

	score
Chi-Square	16.941[a]
df	1
Asymp. Sig.	.000

Figure 6.11

There were more correct responses than there were incorrect response by subjects in both the *standard* and the *shaded* conditions. It may well be that there was simply not enough statistical *power* in the standard condition for the difference to be significant.

> The issues of Type I errors, Type II errors, and *power* are never far from us.

Testing your subjects in each condition separately is not a direct test of your research question, which asks about the possible association between *condition* and *score*. Stated differently, is the rate of being correct *independent* of condition? Such a question requires that you begin by creating the kind of tables (contingency tables) that were used in Chapter 3 when we discussed the multiplicative law of probability.

6 ● 4 χ^2 TEST OF INDEPENDENCE

In this section the nature of the χ^2 *test of independence* is developed by introducing the notion of the *contingency table*. We then describe how the *expected frequencies* are derived by applying the *multiplicative law* of probability along with the assumption of *independence*. Next we revisit the notion of the *degrees of freedom* as it pertains to tests of independence and determining the probability of the observed χ^2 value. Finally, we address the issue of bias associated with the χ^2 value, particularly as it relates to a 2×2 contingency table, and describe the conventional approach to addressing the problem, *Yates's continuity correction.*

In Chapter 3 while describing the laws of probability we examined a 2×2 table (Figure 6.12) and the issue of the *independence* of eye colour (brown versus blue) and gender (men versus women). Such two-dimensional tables are now called *contingency tables.* These tables and the frequency information contained within them are also referred to as *crosstabulations* or *crosstabs.* The formula for the x^2 test of independence is offered for the purpose of fostering an appreciation of the factors that influence the outcome.

	Eye colour	
Gender	**Blue**	**Brown**
Men	40	60
Women	60	40

Figure 6.12

Remember that testing for a difference or testing for an association means that we are hoping to reduce the amount of error in our predictions. The goal of much research is to reduce as much as possible the amount of error in our predictions.

The question of the independence of two variables is the inverse of the question of whether or not two variables are associated or related. To be independent is to be unassociated. To be *associated* means that knowing the value of one variable (e.g., eye colour) assists you in predicting the value of the other variable (e.g., gender). Your research question concerning a possible association between *condition* and *score* can be phrased as 'is *score* independent of *condition?'*

We saw above that overall 75% (45/60) of the responses were correct, regardless of condition. If *score* is independent of *condition* (unrelated), then we *expect* the proportion of correct responses to be 75% in both conditions. Stated differently, if *score* is independent of *condition*, then guessing that an observation is 'correct' will result in a 25% error rate, regardless of condition. Any *observed* deviation from this expectation would be due to chance alone, if *score* and *condition* are independent. We can begin by constructing a *contingency* table. Figure 6.13 shows the observed frequencies in the four *categories* or *cells* of a 2×2 contingency table.

In Chapter 3 we simply compared the percentages repeated in Figure 6.12 to determine whether or not the columns (eye colour) were independent of the rows (gender). In that chapter any difference in the percentages, regardless of how slight, was considered to denote non-independence. As we know, when examining samples, the probability of an *observed* value being exactly equal to the *expected* value is virtually zero. If we randomly select 60 students in a classroom, then we *randomly*

		score	
		0	1
		Count	Count
condition	1	10	16
	2	5	29

Figure 6.13

assign them to two groups by flipping a coin, what is the probability that we will have the same proportion of men to women in each of the two groups? Extremely small. Analogously, we might randomly select 60 students from the class and randomly assign them to two groups, one called *standard* and the other called *shaded.* Then, to simulate the *score* variable, we *randomly* assign a 0 or a 1 to each student. What is the probability that we will have exactly the same proportion of 0s to 1s in each of the two conditions? The probability is virtually zero, despite the entire process being random. There is always 'noise' or error in a 'sample'.

The question is how much of a deviation from the *expected* is required before we reject H_0 and conclude that the variables (*score* and *condition*) likely are not independent? The most common answer, as you should know by now, is that the observed deviation of that magnitude or greater must have a probability of less than 0.05. The probability will depend in part upon how much deviation is *expected* due to chance alone, which itself is contingent upon several factors, one of which is the total number of observations.

The calculation of the χ^2 value for a χ^2 *test of independence* is no different from the calculation of the χ^2 value for a χ^2 *goodness-of-fit* test. The squared differences between the *observed* (O) and *expected* (E) frequencies are standardized on the *expected* (E) frequencies. The structure of the formula is not dissimilar from that of z-score or the *t*-test. At the most general level, we have a difference between the *observed* and the *expected* that is standardized on what would be *expected due to chance*:

$$\chi^2 = \Sigma \frac{(O-E)^2}{E},$$

where O is the observed frequency of a cell and E is its expected frequency.

When calculating the Es for a χ^2 goodness-of-fit test there were two basic approaches. The first approach was to assume that the observations were completely random with respect to the categories. In that approach the total number of observations is divided by the number of categories and that provides the Es for all categories. Such an approach is not applicable here, except in one particular situation: when the row and column totals are all equal. If it were assumed that the 60 observations in the current data set were completely random with respect to cells (categories), the E for all four cells would be 15 (60/4). That would imply that there would be 30 observations in each of the two conditions, but there are not. There are 34 observations in condition 2 and only 26 observations in condition 1. It would be impossible to have 15 zeros and 15 ones (total of 30) in condition 1, even if *condition* and *score* were perfectly independent.

The second approach to calculating the Es was to create a customized model. For the χ^2 goodness-of-fit test we could distribute the Es across the categories as we wished, as long as they summed to the total number of Os. Ordinarily the customized approach is based on a theory or on previous findings. In the case of the χ^2 test of independence, however, we need to customize the Es based on the *assumption of independence*. It is the assumption of independence and the multiplicative law of probability that produce the Es for each cell of the contingency table.

■■■■■ • • • • • ■■■■

Recall from Chapter 3 that probability based on the empirical approach reflects the *observed relative frequency* of an outcome. In our current data, the probability of being correct is the number of correct responses divided by the total number of responses. Also recall from Chapter 3 that the multiplicative law of probability states that if two events are *independent* then the probability of both events occurring is the product of the individual probabilities. The multiplicative law pertains to the situations where AND is the conjunction. For example, in our current data, the probability of being correct and simultaneously being in the standard condition is the probability of being correct times the probability of being in the standard condition.

Using what we have learned about the laws of probability we can derive the following:

1   P(condition 1) = (no. of observations in condition 1)/(total no. of observations)

$$= 26/60 = 0.43$$

2   P(condition 2) = (no. of observations in condition 2)/(total no. of observations)

$$= 34/60 = 0.57$$

3   P(score 0) = (no. of observations in score 0)/(total no. of observations)

$$= 15/60 = 0.25$$

4   P(score 1) = (no. of observations in score 1)/(total no. of observations)

$$= 45/60 = 0.75.$$

Then, assuming independence and using the multiplicative law of probability, we can derive the following:

1   P(condition 1 and score 0) = P(condition 1) × P(score 0) = 0.43 × 0.25 = 0.11
2   P(condition 1 and score 1) = P(condition 1) × P(score 1) = 0.43 × 0.75 = 0.32
3   P(condition 2 and score 0) = P(condition 2) × P(score 0) = 0.57 × 0.25 = 0.14
4   P(condition 2 and score 1) = P(condition 2) × P(score 1) = 0.57 × 0.75 = 0.43.

Once these probabilities are derived, the *Es* for the four cells can be obtained by multiplying the probabilities of the four cells by the total number of observations:

> Remember that the probabilities of an exhaustive set of mutually exclusive events must sum to 1.

1   *E*(condition 1 and score 0) = 0.11 × 60 = 6.6
2   *E*(condition 1 and score 1) = 0.32 × 60 = 19.2
3   *E*(condition 2 and score 0) = 0.14 × 60 = 8.4
4   *E*(condition 2 and score 1) = 0.43 × 60 = 25.8.

> The expected frequencies (*Es*) represent a redistribution of the observed frequencies (*Os*) based on the assumption of independence. As such, the total of the *Es* must equal that of the *Os*.

The observed and expected frequencies are summarized in Figure 6.14. The χ^2 test of independence for our data now can be computed:

$$\chi^2 = \Sigma \frac{(O-E)^2}{E}$$

	Incorrect (0)	Correct (1)
Condition 1	O = 10 E = 6.6	O = 16 E = 19.2
Condition 2	O = 5 E = 8.4	O = 29 E = 25.8

Figure 6.14

$$= \frac{(10-6.6)^2}{6.6} + \frac{(16-19.2)^2}{19.2} + \frac{(5-8.4)^2}{8.4} + \frac{(29-25.8)^2}{25.8} = 4.30.$$

To calculate the critical x^2 value the degrees of freedom (*df*) must be determined. When there were four categories for a x^2 *goodness-of-fit* test, the *df* were the number of categories (*k*) minus one, (*k* − 1). In such cases the categories were all on a single dimension or row. In the case of a x^2 *test of independence* there are variables on two dimensions: columns and rows. In our example we have a 2 × 2 design. There are four categories in total, thus 3 *df* overall. There are two rows, thus 1 row *df*. There are two columns, thus 1 column *df*. That leaves 1 *df* for the test of the row by column independence. The *df* for a x^2 *test of independence* can be easily computed by multiplying the row *df* by the column *df*: (2 − 1)(2 − 1) = 1.

Web Link 6.6 for a detailed discussion of the rationale and computation of degrees of freedom for the χ^2 test of independence.

We now turn to Appendix C and the table of x^2 critical values. The rows of the table are the *df*. Looking across row 1 (1 *df*) until we are under the $\alpha = 0.05$ column, we find the critical value to be 3.841. Because your observed x^2 (4.30) is greater than the critical value, you reject H_0 and deem that there is sufficient evidence to suggest that there is an association between the two variables (*condition* and *score*). Specifically, there is evidence that the rate of answering correctly is associated with condition, with those in the shaded condition outperforming those in the standard condition.

Yates's correction of χ^2

Pearson's x^2 test statistic is evaluated against the x^2 distribution, the critical values for which are provided in the x^2 table. The evaluation of a x^2 value assumes that the *discrete* probability of the observed binomial frequencies in the table can be estimated by the *continuous* x^2 distribution. The estimations are not perfect and can result in underestimates of the probabilities. If H_0 is true, an underestimate increases the likelihood of a Type I error. Yates (1934), an English statistician, developed a modification to the x^2 formula for use with 2 × 2 contingency tables to compensate for such errors in the estimates of the probabilities. The modification simply subtracts 0.5 from the differences between the *observed* frequencies and the corresponding *expected* frequencies:

$$\chi^2_{\text{Yates}} = \Sigma \frac{\{(O-E)-0.5\}^2}{E}.$$

This reduces the squared differences between observed and expected frequencies, which reduces the overall x^2, increases the probability of the x^2, and in turn decreases the chance of rejecting H_0.

If Yates's correction (also called the *continuity correction*) is applied to our current data set, we get

$$\chi^2_{\text{Yates}} = \Sigma \frac{\{(O-E)-0.5\}^2}{E}.$$
$$= \frac{\{(10-6.6)-0.5\}^2}{6.6} + \frac{\{(16-19.2)-0.5\}^2}{19.2} + \frac{\{(5-8.4)-0.5\}^2}{8.4} + \frac{\{(29-25.8)-0.5\}^2}{25.8}$$
$$= 3.23.$$

Recall that the critical x^2 ($\alpha = 0.05$) value with 1 *df* is 3.841. Thus our new observed x^2 (3.23) is not significant. You no longer have sufficient evidence to conclude that there is an association between *score* and *condition*. There are two possible conclusions to draw from this. First, if H_0 is true, the continuity correction has prevented us from making a Type I error. If, however, H_0 is false, the correction has resulted in a Type II error. A further complication is the fact that Yates's continuity correction tends to produce overcorrections, which consequently leads to an increase in the Type II error rate when H_0 is false. In light of this, it is recommended that Yates's continuity correction be used only when sample sizes are small and the expected frequency of at least one cell is 5 or less (Sokal & Rohlf, 2012).

· · · · · ·

Remember, should we fail to reject the null hypothesis, we cannot conclude that we have proven that there is no effect, in this case no association between the two variables. We can conclude only that we have insufficient evidence that there is an association of a given strength. The question of power and the corresponding possibility of a Type II error must always be addressed.

6 ● 5 THE ϕ COEFFICIENT

As discussed in Chapter 5, when H_0 is rejected it is standard practice to report a standardized estimate of the effect size. When *differences* were tested and reported in the previous chapter, Cohen's *d* was the most common estimate of the standardized effect size. In this section we examine effect size measures commonly used when reporting associations between two categorical variables.

When reporting the strength of associations, the measure used depends on the type of data analysed and the specific question that was asked. In this chapter categorical data are analysed: nominal and ordinal data. To begin with, we are focusing on nominal data. The most common measure reported with nominal data is the ϕ coefficient. The ϕ coefficient provides a numerical value for describing the extent of the association between the two nominal variables. It is simply the square root of the obtained χ^2 value divided by the total number of observations:

$$\phi = \sqrt{\frac{\chi^2}{N}} \; .$$

· · · · · ·

The standardized effect for a significant χ^2 can be reported in terms of Cohen's *d*, if so desired:

$$d = 2\sqrt{\frac{\chi^2}{N - \chi^2}}.$$

This is usually only done when the researcher is reporting the results of both *t*-tests and χ^2 analysis. The reason for doing so is to have a single, comparable measure of effect size.

When analysing a 2 × 2 contingency table the value can range from 0.0 to 1. A ϕ coefficient of 0.0 indicates no association or complete independence, and is rarely reported when the χ^2 is non-significant.

A ϕ coefficient of 1 indicates a prefect association between the two variables. In our example, $x^2 = 4.3$ and $N = 60$, thus

$$\phi = \sqrt{\frac{4.3}{60}} = 0.27.$$

Looking at another method for calculating ϕ affords insight into what the statistic reflects in terms of frequencies. The ϕ coefficient can be computed and understood as the average percentage difference in rows and columns. We can calculate the average percentage difference as follows. First, we examine the difference in *condition* percentages:

Condition 1: (frequency of condition 1, score 0) divided by (total frequency of condition 1) = 10/26 = 38%

Condition 2: (frequency of condition 2, score 0) divided by (total frequency of condition 2) = 5/34 = 15%

The difference in percentages for condition is (38% − 15%) = 23%.

Next, we examine the difference in score percentages:

Score 0: (frequency of score 0, condition 1) divided by (total frequency of score 0) = 10/15 = 67%

Score 1: (frequency of score 1, condition 1) divided by (total frequency of score 1) = 16/45 = 36%

The difference in percentages for score is (67% − 36%) = 31%

Therefore, the average difference in percentages is (31% + 23%)/2 = 27% or $\phi = 0.27$.

========== REVIEW QUESTION ==========

In our example, if the row totals remain fixed, what must the cell frequencies be for there to be a ϕ coefficient of 0? What must the cell frequencies be to produce a ϕ coefficient of 1?

Web Link 6.7 for an answer to the review question.

There are several rules of thumb regarding the interpretation of the ϕ coefficient. We offer here one of the more common rules. A ϕ value greater than 0 but less than 0.2 indicates a weak or no association. If the corresponding x^2 is non-significant, then the usual interpretation is that there is insufficient evidence of an association. If the x^2 is significant, then the association is deemed to be weak. When the value is 0.3 or greater but less than 0.5, the ϕ is said to indicate a moderate association. When the ϕ value is 0.5 or greater, the association is said to be strong.

When ϕ is 1.0 it implies that when you know to which row the observation belongs you know the column, without error. It was stated above that the ϕ coefficient was the average percentage difference in row and columns. In the case of a 2×2 contingency table, the ϕ coefficient can also be understood as a measure of the *percentage of concentration* along a diagonal. For example, if all 26 subjects in condition 1 were incorrect in their response (*score = 0*) and all 34 subjects in condition 2 were correct in their response (*score = 1*), we would have the contingency table shown in Figure 6.15, which would yield:

	Incorrect (0)	**Correct (1)**
Condition 1	$O = 26$ $E = 11.3$	$O = 0$ $E = 14.7$
Condition 2	$O = 0$ $E = 14.7$	$O = 34$ $E = 19.3$

Figure 6.15

$$\chi^2 = \Sigma \frac{(O-E)^2}{E}$$

$$= \frac{(26-11.3)^2}{11.3} + \frac{(0-14.7)^2}{14.7} + \frac{(0-14.7)^2}{14.7} + \frac{(34-19.3)^2}{19.3} = 60$$

$$\phi = \sqrt{\frac{60}{60}} = 1.0.$$

When the concentration along the diagonal is less than perfect, ϕ is attenuated. For example, if 1 of the 26 subjects in condition 1 were correct in his or her response and 1 of the 34 subjects in condition 2 were incorrect in his or her response, we would find the following changes in the contingency table (Figure 6.16), χ^2, and ϕ:

	Incorrect (0)	**Correct (1)**
Condition 1	$O = 25$ $E = 11.3$	$O = 1$ $E = 14.7$
Condition 2	$O = 1$ $E = 14.7$	$O = 33$ $E = 19.3$

Figure 6.16

$$\chi^2 = \Sigma \frac{(O-E)^2}{E}$$

$$= \frac{(25-11.3)^2}{11.3} + \frac{(1-14.7)^2}{14.7} + \frac{(1-14.7)^2}{14.7} + \frac{(33-19.3)^2}{19.3} = 52.132$$

$$\phi = \sqrt{\frac{52.132}{60}} = 0.932.$$

● ● ● ● ●

Note that as long as the row and column totals remain unchanged, the corresponding probabilities for the row and columns remain unchanged, and the expected frequencies remain unchanged. As the observed frequencies deviate less and less from the expected frequencies, the χ^2 value and the ϕ coefficient approach 0. As the observed frequencies deviate more and more from the expected frequencies, the χ^2 value approaches the total number of observations and the ϕ coefficient approaches 1.

 NECESSARY ASSUMPTIONS

In this section we address the important assumptions which must be met for the results of a χ^2 test of independence to be reliable and unbiased:

1   The independence of observations.
2   A minimum expected frequency of 5 in all cells.
3   The inclusion of cases of non-occurrence.

The first assumption is that the observations are independent. The assumption that the observations are independent is *not* the same as the assumption that the variables are independent. In our example, the assumption of the independence of observations requires that one subject's response – either incorrect or correct – has no effect on another subject's response. That is, one subject responding correctly does not increase or decrease the probability of another subject responding correctly. Furthermore, this assumption requires that there be only one observation per subject.

The typical way in which this assumption of the independence of observations is violated is by recording more than one observation for one or more subjects. If a subject responds correctly once, it likely increases the probability of his or her subsequent response being correct. On the other hand, if a subject responds incorrectly once, it is likely that he or she will subsequently respond incorrectly. Thus, one observation becomes predictive of another.

───────────── CHALLENGE QUESTION ─────────────

Imagine another researcher is also interested in the effect of shading of figures on the 3-D line-drawing test. He decides to use the students in his perception and cognition course as subjects. Because there are only 40 students in his class, he decides to test the students during two consecutive class meetings. Create a data set where the x^2 test of independence is non-significant on both day 1 and day 2 of testing but significant when the data from the two days are combined. We will add one further question. Because the same students are tested on both days, assume that all the students perform the same on both days. How is this related to the assumption of the independence of observations?

Web Link 6.8 for an answer to the challenge question.

A second assumption is that none of the expected frequencies are less than 5. This arises because the x^2 distribution, upon which the observed x^2 is evaluated, is continuous. As we have seen, when there are a large number of observations of a discrete variable its distribution will approximate a continuous variable. This, for example, allowed us to transform the binomial test into a *z*-score problem. When one of the expected frequencies in a x^2 test is less than 5, the discrete distribution will poorly fit the continuous x^2 distribution which underlies the x^2 table of critical values. When conducting a x^2 test of goodness of fit we might combine, under certain circumstances, adjacent categories to rectify the violation of this assumption. When conducting a x^2 test of independence it is much more difficult to employ this strategy, and it is impossible when analysing a 2 × 2 contingency table.

The third assumption is more of an error to be avoided than an assumption. Lewis and Burke (1949) pointed out an error that often occurs when analysing frequency data. They referred to it as a violation of the need to include cases of non-occurrence. We might call this the assumption that all independent observations the researcher collects are included in the analysis. The violation of this assumption most often takes the form of incorrectly reducing a x^2 test of independence to a x^2 test of goodness of fit.

Imagine that you are a lecturer and wish to know if the men and women in your course differed in terms of their choice of examination form: oral or written. You observed that 15 men and 10 women preferred the written examination (Figure 6.17). You analyse these data by a x^2 goodness-of-fit test on those men and women who preferred the written examination. As seen in the *Test Statistics* table (Figure 6.18), the observed x^2 of 1.0 was non-significant, $p = 0.317$. You concluded that because there appears to be no difference in the number of men and women who preferred a written examination, gender was unrelated to examination-type preference. The problem is that the original question was not about the number of men and women who preferred a written examination. The question concerned the possible association between gender and examination-type preference. To answer that question we need to include in the analysis the men and women who preferred an oral examination.

gender

	Observed N	Expected N	Residual
1.00	15	12.5	2.5
2.00	10	12.5	-2.5
Total	25		

Figure 6.17

Test Statistics

	gender
Chi-Square	1.000[a]
df	1
Asymp. Sig.	.317

Figure 6.18

You then ran a x^2 test of independence using all 30 observations: 15 men and 10 women who preferred written examinations, and 2 men and 12 women who preferred oral examinations. If you calculate the x^2 test of independence you find the resulting x^2 of 7.627 to be significant ($p = 0.006$), even with the continuity correction. When all of the relevant observations are included in the analysis, you find that in your course there is enough evidence to suggest an association between gender and examination-type preference. A greater proportion of men than women preferred the written examination.

=== REVIEW QUESTION ===

Create a 2 × 2 data set where the x^2 test of independence is non-significant but the individual x^2 goodness-of-fit tests are significant. How is this possible?

Web Link 6.9 for a discussion of and answer to the review question.

6.7 χ^2 TEST OF INDEPENDENCE: SPSS EXAMPLE

Let us analyse the 3-D line-drawing data example using SPSS. This will give us an opportunity to explore related statistics. Open the *mentalrotation1.sav* file on the book's web page.

From the menu at the top of *Data Editor,* click *Analyze* and then *Descriptive Statistics* on the drop-down menu. Slide over and select *Crosstabs,* and when the *Crosstabs* window opens,

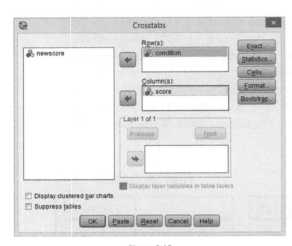

Figure 6.19

highlight and move the *condition* variable to the *Row(s)* area and the *score* variable to the *Column(s)* area (Figure 6.19). Then click on the *Statistics* button. When the *Crosstabs: Statistics* window opens, check *Chi-square, Contingency coefficient,* and *Phi and Cramer's V* (Figure 6.20), and then click *Continue.* When you return to the *Crosstabs* window, click on the *Cells* button. When the *Crosstabs: Cell Display* window opens, check *Observed and Expected* in the *Counts* area, and then click *Continue.* When you return to the *Crosstabs* window, select the *Bootstrap* button. When the *Bootstrap* window opens, check *Perform bootstrapping* and *Set seed for Mersenne Twister* and then *Continue.* When you return to the *Crosstabs* window, click *OK.*

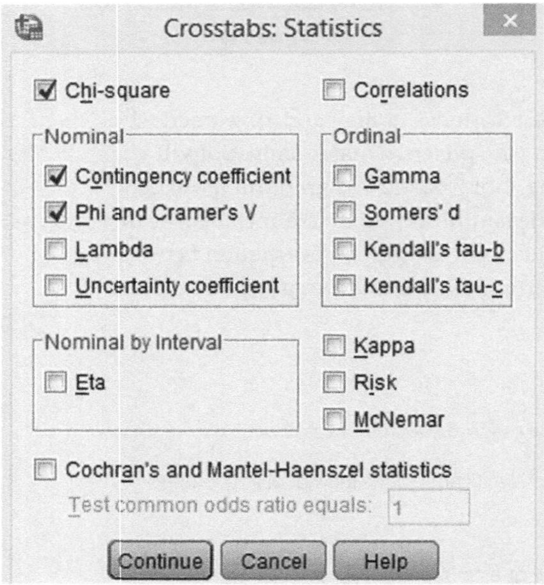

Below the review of the *default specifications* for the bootstrapping procedure in the output window is the *Case Processing Summary* table (Figure 6.21). This table summarizes the number of valid cases, the number of missing cases, and the total number of cases in the data file, as well as their related percentages. Your line-drawing data set contains 60 valid cases with no missing data. The *condition * score Crosstabulation* (Figure 6.22) table breaks down the observations into the *observed* cell frequencies (*Count*) along with their corresponding *expected* frequencies (*Expected Count*).

The *Chi-Square Tests* table (Figure 6.23) reports the values for various test statistics along with their degrees of freedom and corresponding *p*-values: *Asymp. Sig. (2-sided).* Reported first is the χ^2 value (*Pearson Chi-Square*) we discussed earlier in the chapter. Consistent with our earlier calculation, there is a significant $\chi^2 = 4.434$ (*df* = 1) with $p = 0.035 < 0.05$. Also consistent with our earlier calculations is a non-significant $\chi^2 = 3.258$ (*df* = 1) with Yates's *continuity correction* that has $p = 0.071 > 0.05$.

Figure 6.20

Case Processing Summary

	Cases					
	Valid		Missing		Total	
	N	Percent	N	Percent	N	Percent
condition * score	60	100.0%	0	0.0%	60	100.0%

Figure 6.21

condition * score Crosstabulation

			score		Total
			0	1	
condition	1	Count	10	16	26
		Expected Count	6.5	19.5	26.0
	2	Count	5	29	34
		Expected Count	8.5	25.5	34.0
Total		Count	15	45	60
		Expected Count	15.0	45.0	60.0

Figure 6.22

Chi-Square Tests

	Value	df	Asymp. Sig. (2-sided)	Exact Sig. (2-sided)	Exact Sig. (1-sided)
Pearson Chi-Square	4.434[a]	1	.035		
Continuity Correction[b]	3.258	1	.071		
Likelihood Ratio	4.439	1	.035		
Fisher's Exact Test				.069	.036
Linear-by-Linear Association	4.360	1	.037		
N of Valid Cases	60				

a. 0 cells (0.0%) have expected count less than 5. The minimum expected count is 6.50.

Figure 6.23

• • • • •

If we compare the p-values of the χ^2 (0.035) and χ^2 with Yates's continuity correction (0.071) with those of the independent-samples t-tests (0.036 and 0.045) conducted on these data at the outset of the chapter, we find them to be quite similar. The χ^2 test of independence is the more appropriate test, however, when the data are nominal. When analysing a 2 × 2 contingency table, under most circumstance with large samples the two types of tests will produce very similar results. The logic behind the analysis remains the same; it is the type of data that dictates the appropriate test.

In the next line in the *Chi-Square Tests* table, we see the *Likelihood Ratio*. As mentioned above, the smaller the expected frequencies, the less well the discrete Pearson x^2 test fits the continuous x^2 distribution. This results in potential errors in the reported *p*-values. The likelihood ratio is designed to address this problem. Like the Pearson x^2, at its heart it is the ratio of observed frequencies over expected frequencies:

$$\text{likelihood ratio} = 2\Sigma\left(O\ln\frac{O}{E}\right),$$

where O is the observed frequency of a cell, ln denotes the log function, and E is the expected frequency of a cell. Inserting our data, we find a likelihood ratio of

$$2\left(10\ln\frac{10}{6.5} + 16\ln\frac{16}{9.5} + 5\ln\frac{5}{8.5} + 29\ln\frac{29}{25.5}\right) = 4.439.$$

As sample sizes become large, the difference between the Pearson x^2 test and the *likelihood ratio*, along with their *p*-values, becomes negligible. Despite avoiding the problem of fitting a discrete measure onto a continuous distribution to arrive at a *p*-value, the likelihood ratio is not the choice of tests for small sample sizes or cases where there are cells with small expected frequencies. Under those circumstances, the usual choice is the final test statistic we will mention here, *Fisher's exact test*, found on the line below the likelihood ratio in the *Chi-Square Tests* table.

Like Yates's continuity correction, Fisher's exact test is used specifically with 2 × 2 contingency tables. Looking at the *Chi-Square Tests* table, we find the probability of Fisher's exact test to be 0.069 (*Exact Sig. (2-sided)*), which is non-significant at $\alpha = 0.05$. Fisher's exact test is deemed by many to be the best choice when the sample size is small because it does not have the problem of overestimating the *p*-value, a problem associated with Yates's continuity correction. Some authors have argued, however, that Fisher's exact test is itself too conservative (Liddell, 1976). In order to avoid the problem of computing *p*-values when fitting discrete data to a continuous distribution many authors advise avoiding fixed significance levels, such as 0.05. Yates (1984) argued for this approach 50 years after his paper putting forward the continuity correction.

●●●●●

This controversy helps to highlight the need *not* to become fixated on *p*-values. Remember, the *p*-value is only one method we have for estimating the reliability or *replicability* of the results, and it is the replicability and *not* the *p*-value that is our concern. How much more faith do you have in a result which has a *p*-value of 0.049 than you do in a result which has a *p*-value of 0.051? When we deem results to be *significant*, it means that we believe there is sufficient evidence to conclude that the results can be replicated. Nothing more.

As discussed in Section 6.5, if we deem the test statistic to be *significant*, it is important to report one or more standardized measures of effect: measures indicating the strength of the association

Symmetric Measures

		Value	Approx. Sig.
Nominal by Nominal	Phi	.272	.035
	Cramer's V	.272	.035
	Contingency Coefficient	.262	.035
N of Valid Cases		60	

Figure 6.24

between the two variables. Here we review the ϕ *coefficient* and examine frequent alternatives: *Cramér's V* and the *contingency coefficient*.

As seen in the *Symmetric Measures* table (Figure 6.24), the p-values of all three measures are significant ($\alpha = 0.05$) and all have exactly the same value. This complete agreement will only be the case when analysing a 2 × 2 contingency table. When the numbers of columns and rows increase, the measures will begin to diverge.

You may have noticed a contradiction between the *Chi-Square Tests* table and the *Symmetric Measures* table. If the researcher chooses to use either the *continuity-corrected χ^2* or *Fisher's exact test*, he or she likely will fail to reject H_0 and may conclude that there is insufficient evidence of an association between *condition* and *score*. But the *Symmetric Measures* table reports significant p-values (0.035) for all three measures of the strength of association. In such contradictory cases, preference often is given to the test statistic: the continuity corrected χ^2 or Fisher's exact test.

Unfortunately, ambiguous results are not rare. In such cases researchers will likely consider the issue of *power* and will increase their sample size, if possible, and reanalyse the data prior to drawing conclusions. If that is not possible, researchers usually report the ambiguous nature of the results and include the measures of the strength of the association along with their corresponding p-values.

It is not uncommon for researchers to report ϕ, *Cramér's V*, or the *contingency coefficient* even when the test statistic is determined to be non-significant. This is often the case when the researcher is reporting multiple tests.

Figure 6.25 summarizes the indices of strength of association used with the analysis of nominal data.

Nominal indices of strength of association

Index name	Index type	Usage
Phi coefficient	Symmetrical	2 × 2 tables only
Cramer's V	Symmetrical	No. of rows ≠ no. of columns
Contingency coefficient	Symmetrical	No. of rows = no. of columns
Lambda	Directional	Limited by modal categories (see text)
Goodman and Kruskal tau	Directional	Unlimited by modal categories

Figure 6.25

As described above, the formula for the ϕ coefficient is $\phi = \sqrt{\chi^2 / n}$. ϕ, however, is only appropriate for estimating the association between two binary variables: a 2×2 contingency table. Once the contingency table contains more than two rows or columns, ϕ can exceed 1. The maximum value of ϕ is $\sqrt{k-1}$, where k is the number of rows or columns. Thus, when there are 10 rows, the maximum value of ϕ is 3. Another way to state the problem is to say that ϕ is only a standardized measure of association for 2×2 contingency tables. Cramér's V corrects the ϕ for the overestimate related to the number of rows and columns:

$$V = \sqrt{\frac{\chi^2}{n(k-1)}},$$

where n is the number of observations and k is either the number or rows or the number of columns, whichever is smaller. Looking at Cramér's V, it is clear that when $k = 2$, the formula reduces to the standard ϕ formula.

The contingency coefficient also corrects for increases in the number of rows and columns. It is given by $\sqrt{\chi^2 / (n + \chi^2)}$, where n is the number of observations. Like Cramér's V, the contingency coefficient compensates for the fact that s_1^2 is sensitive to the number of cells being analysed. As the number of cells increases so does the value of $\Sigma(O - E)^2 / E$, even if the difference between O and E is a small constant. As a consequence, when the number of rows and columns is greater than two, the χ^2 value can exceed the total number of observations. When χ^2 exceeds the number of observations, the ϕ coefficient will exceed 1. As can be seen from the formula for the contingency coefficient, the amendment to the denominator prevents this from ever occurring. This also means that the absolute value of the contingency coefficient will always be less than that of the ϕ coefficient. Although, when the contingency table is 2×2, the p-values of the two coefficients will be identical.

• • • • •

Which measure of association should I report? When you have analysed a 2×2 contingency table there is no reason to report anything other than the ϕ coefficient. When you have analysed a table with three or more rows and columns, the contingency coefficient is the best choice. The proviso is that there must be an equal number of rows and columns in the contingency table. When the contingency table has more than two rows and columns but the numbers of rows and columns are unequal, then Cramér's V is the best estimate of the strength of the association between the two variables.

Examining the bootstrapping results, we find the same *Phi*, *Cramer's V*, and *Contingency Coefficient* values we saw earlier, 0.272, 0.272, and 0.262, respectively (Figure 6.26). When the lower limit of the 95% confidence intervals approaches 0, this suggests the two variables may be independent. The upper limit indicates the estimate of the maximum strength of the association. In the current example, all three measures of strength of association range from near independence (e.g., 0.017) to nearly a moderate association (e.g., 0.504).

Bootstrap for Symmetric Measures

			Bootstrap[a]			
					95% Confidence Interval	
		Value	Bias	Std. Error	Lower	Upper
Nominal by Nominal	Phi	.272	-.003	.128	.017	.504
	Cramer's V	.272	-.002	.124	.031	.504
	Contingency Coefficient	.262	-.006	.110	.031	.450
N of Valid Cases		60	0	0	60	60

a. Unless otherwise noted, bootstrap results are based on 1000 bootstrap samples

Figure 6.26

Lambda

The measures of the strength of association described above along with their *p*-values were reported in the *Symmetrical Measures* table. There is a reason for the table's name: ϕ, *Cramér's V*, and the *contingency coefficient* all are said to be characterized by *symmetry*; for all three measures it makes no difference which variable is viewed as the *independent* or predictor variable and which is viewed as the *dependent* or criterion variable. There is no supposition about which variable is doing the influencing and which variable is being influenced. In your 3-D line-drawing experiment, however, there is reason to suspect that *condition* – whether the subject saw an unshaded or a shaded figure – was the influencing variable and *score* – whether a subject's response was correct or incorrect – was the variable being influenced. Stated differently, there is reason to view the association as asymmetrical or directional. Furthermore, ϕ, Cramér's V, and the contingency coefficient all tend to give biased estimates of the strength of an asymmetrical association.

Lambda (λ) is the most common measure of asymmetrical or directional association for use with nominal variables, such as your data. Like other measures of association, λ can vary from 0 to 1. More specifically, λ indicates the percentage increase in the ability to predict one variable (dependent variable or criterion) using another variable (independent or predictor) given the baseline of dependent variable alone. λ is referred to as a *proportion reduction in error* (PRE) measure. For example, if $\lambda = 0.25$, we increase our ability to predict the value of the criterion variable by 25%. Lambda can be calculated by examining the change in the relative frequencies:

$$\lambda = \frac{E_1 - E_2}{E_1},$$

where E_1 is the error in prediction made when the predictor variable is ignored, and E_2 is the error in prediction when it is based on the predictor. E_1 is obtained by identifying the frequency of the modal category of the criterion (dependent) variable and subtracting it from the total number of observations (n). The difference is considered the error in prediction when ignoring the predictor variable. E_2 is obtained by repeating the process for each level of the predictor variable separately and then summing the error related to each level. Conceptually, λ is the amount of reduction in the error of prediction afforded by the predictor variable standardized on the total error in the criterion. The formula is similar to that of χ^2, the *z*-score, and the *t*-test, where the difference between the means is standardized on the variance (error) in the dependent variable. As usual, we have the difference between the *observed* and the *expected*, standardized on what would be expected due to chance alone.

Using our 3-D line-drawing data and with *score* as the criterion variable we have

$$E_1 = 60 - 45 = 15$$
$$E_2 = (26 - 16) + (34 - 29) = 15$$
$$\lambda = \frac{15 - 15}{15} = ?$$

There is clearly a problem or limitation. When the contingency table is examined it appears that knowing if a subject is in the standard or shaded condition reduces the error in your prediction, but the λ indicates that *condition* and *score* are unrelated. Let us recompute λ using *condition* as the criterion variable. Knowing if the subject's response is correct or incorrect reduces the error in your prediction and λ is non-zero:

$$E_1 = 60 - 34 = 26$$
$$E_2 = (15 - 10) + (45 - 29) = 21$$
$$\lambda = \frac{26 - 21}{26} = 0.192.$$

In this second case we do not encounter the problem we had when using *score* as the criterion variable. This example illustrates one of the limitations of λ. When the modal categories of the criterion variable are all at the same level of the predictor, E_1 and E_2 will be identical, thus calculating λ is meaningless. This is the case when using *condition* as the predictor variable. At both levels of condition, *score* 1 is the modal category. But when *score* is used as the predictor, at one level of *score*, *condition* 1 is the modal category. And at the other level of *score*, *condition* 2 is the modal category.

For this and other reasons, the Goodman and Kruskal tau (τ) is considered to be the best measure of asymmetrical or directional association for use with nominal variables. Similarly to λ, τ is a PRE measure that indicates the percentage increase in the ability to predict a criterion variable using a predictor variable, given the baseline error rate of the criterion. The computations are somewhat more complex than those of λ. The difference in calculation results in λ producing consistently lower values than Goodman and Kruskal's tau. More researchers are preferring Goodman and Kruskal's tau over λ, which is deemed often to be an underestimate of PRE. A good discussion of procedures and the differences between λ and τ can be found in Reynolds (1984).

To compute λ and τ in SPSS we return to the *Data Editor:* click *Analyze* and then *Descriptive Statistics* on the drop-down menu. Then slide over and select *Crosstabs*. When the *Crosstabs* window opens, highlight and move the *condition* variable to the *Row(s)* area and the *score* variable to the *Column(s)* area (Figure 6.27). Then click on the *Statistics* button. When the *Crosstabs: Statistics* window opens, check *Lambda* (Figure 6.28) and then click *Continue*. When you return to the *Crosstabs* window, select the *Bootstrap* button. When the *Bootstrap* window opens, check the *Perform bootstrapping* and *Set seed for Mersenne Twister* boxes, and then click *Continue*. When you return to the *Crosstabs* window, click *OK*.

Below the *Bootstrap Specification*, the *Case Processing Summary*, and the *condition * score Crosstabulation* tables in the output window is the *Directional Measures* table (Figure 6.29). The first row of interest to us is the one where *score* is identified as the dependent (criterion) variable in the *Lambda* area. Not surprisingly, the value is 0.000 and the probability is not reported. As mentioned above, this is because both modal categories of *score* are at the same level of *condition*. Next of interest is the *score Dependent* row in the *Goodman and Kruskal tau* area. The computational problem has been avoided and a τ-value of 0.074 with a *p*-value of 0.037 is reported, indicating a weak association and weak reduction in the errors of predicting *score* using *condition*.

Examining the bootstrapping results (Figure 6.30), we find the same *lambda* and *tau* values. When the lower limit of the 95% confidence intervals is 0.000 this suggests independence is a possibility. The upper limit indicates the estimate of the maximum strength of the association. In the current example, the Goodman and Kruskal tau for *score* as the dependent variable ranges from near independence (0.001) to nearly a moderate association (0.258).

One final qualification of λ and τ should be made. Both measures often underestimate the proportion of the reduction in error. That is, they underestimate the strength of the directional association between the predictor and the criterion. The more skewed one of the variables is, the more λ in particular underestimates the association. Skewness in the case of nominal variables is related to the relative

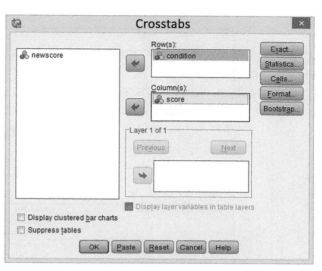

Figure 6.27

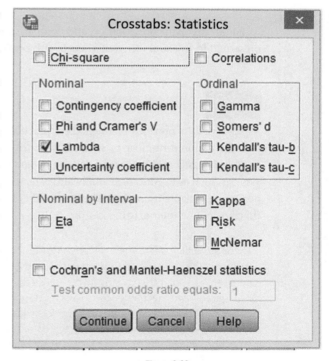

Figure 6.28

frequencies in the two categories. In the case of the 3-D line-drawing data, there is considerable skewness in *score*: one category has a frequency of 15 and the other a frequency of 45.

Directional Measures

			Value	Asymp. Std. Error[a]	Approx. T[b]	Approx. Sig.
Nominal by Nominal	Lambda	Symmetric	.122	.085	1.309	.190
		condition Dependent	.192	.134	1.309	.190
		score Dependent	.000	.000	[c]	[c]
	Goodman and Kruskal tau	condition Dependent	.074	.067		.037[d]
		score Dependent	.074	.068		.037[d]

Figure 6.29

Bootstrap for Directional Measures

			Value	Bootstrap[a]			
				Bias	Std. Error	95% Confidence Interval	
						Lower	Upper
Nominal by Nominal	Lambda	Symmetric	.122	-.008	.084	.000	.306
		condition Dependent	.192	-.020	.121	.000	.417
		score Dependent	.000	.012	.045	.000	.174
	Goodman and Kruskal tau	condition Dependent	.074	.012	.068	.001	.258
		score Dependent	.074	.012	.068	.001	.258

Figure 6.30

For an excellent presentation and comparison of the many measures of strength of association presented in this and other chapters in this book, see Liebetrau (1983).

6 ● 8 POWER, SAMPLE SIZE, AND THE χ^2 TEST OF INDEPENDENCE

As discussed in previous chapters, best practice would dictate that we address the issue of power and the required number of subjects prior to collecting data. With observational research, this is frequently easier said than done. Often the data may have been collected by others. In many applied settings, such as in education and health care, it may take a considerable amount of time or money to obtain appreciably more data. These and other factors mean that researchers have little choice other than to analyse their existing sample. If they wish to maintain power = 0.80, they may be limited to testing for strong associations: $\phi > 0.5$. Having said this, the basic principles of power remain the same.

There are online sites which allow you to quickly calculate the χ^2 test of independence without entering all your observations into a data editor. You merely need the frequencies for each category. These can be quick ways of performing at least the basic analyses without entering the data into an editor. More comprehensive software packages such as SPSS are usually required for a complete analysis. The link provided here is for a reliable site which is easy to navigate.

http://vassarstats.net/newcs.html

As a researcher increases the number of observations, the *observed* relative frequencies will be closer to the population's true relative frequencies. Remember, this trend is what we expect on average. Due to chance alone, there are occasions when, as n increases, the observed relative frequencies may move further away from their population counterparts, even when H_0 is true and the two variables are independent. Second, for any given n, it is possible incorrectly to reject a true H_0: make a Type I error. This of course will happen 5% of the time, when H_0 is true.

The sixth row of the sample size table in Appendix B (Table B.2) corresponds to a χ^2 test with $df = 1$, regardless of whether it is a test of goodness of fit or a test of independence. As we see in the first row under the column for a large effect size, power = 0.80, and $\alpha = 0.05$, 26 subjects are required; for a medium effect size 87 subjects are required; and for a small effect size 785 subjects are required. We assume that the sample is representative of the population to which the researcher wishes to generalize.

    ⟡ Web Link 6.10 for an interactive demonstration of the effect that both sample size and effect size have on the power of a χ^2 test of independence.

For an extensive discussion of power, sample size, and the χ^2 test of independence, see Kraemer and Thiemann (1987, Chapter 9).

6 ● 9 THE THIRD-VARIABLE PROBLEM

In this section we discuss one of the most common limitations of the χ^2 test of independence: the third-variable problem. Despite the name, however, there can be a fourth-, fifth-, sixth-, etc., variable problem.

All research results are tentative; this is particularly important to bear in mind when the research design is observational rather than experimental in nature. Recall the *amalgamation paradox* described in Chapter 1. In this chapter we will refer to a version of that paradox as the *third-variable problem*. The third-variable problem highlights the importance for the researcher to know the most appropriate statistical test to employ, to understand the phenomenon under investigation, and to be familiar with the relevant literature.

Imagine you are an educational psychologist exploring the possible association between early childhood education and reading competency among first-year primary school students. Previous research revealed that early childhood education (age 4 and 5) was positively related to a number of other educational measures. To explore the association between early childhood education and reading competency you obtain permission to test 400 first-year primary school students from two schools. Half of the children were enrolled the previous year in early childhood education programmes: 0 = not enrolled, 1 = enrolled. Each child's reading competency is assessed and deemed to be either above or below average: 0 = below average, 1 = above average. The data file for this hypothetical study is found on the book's web page.

    ⟡ Web Link 6.11 as a link to the *earlychildeducation.sav* data set.

You began by testing for an association between early childhood education (*EarlychildEd*) and reading competency (*ReadHiLo*). You analysed the 2 × 2 contingency table with a χ^2 test of independence. The data set contains 400 valid cases and no missing data. The *EarlychildEd * ReadHiLo Crosstabulation* table (Figure 6.31) breaks down the observations into the observed cell frequencies (*Count*) along with their corresponding expected frequencies (*Expected Count*).

EarlychildEd * ReadHiLo Crosstabulation

			ReadHiLo		
			.00	1.00	Total
EarlychildEd	.00	Count	100	100	200
		Expected Count	100.0	100.0	200.0
	1.00	Count	100	100	200
		Expected Count	100.0	100.0	200.0
Total		Count	200	200	400
		Expected Count	200.0	200.0	400.0

Figure 6.31

As would be expected from the *EarlychildEd * ReadHiLo Crosstabulation* table, the *Chi-Square Tests* table (Figure 6.32) discloses no difference between the expected and the observed frequencies. Further, the *Symmetric Measures* table (Figure 6.33) reveals a 0.000 association between *EarlychildEd* and *ReadHiLo*. Early childhood education and reading competency among the first-year primary school students appear to be completely independent of each other.

Before you attempt to publish your findings, however, your research assistants inform you they have one more piece of information about the students which may be relevant. They know the income status of the families: below or above average. This information is reflected in the variable *IncomeHiLo* in the

Chi-Square Tests

	Value	df	Asymp. Sig. (2-sided)	Exact Sig. (2-sided)	Exact Sig. (1-sided)
Pearson Chi-Square	.000[a]	1	1.000		
Continuity Correction[b]	.000	1	1.000		
Likelihood Ratio	.000	1	1.000		
Fisher's Exact Test				1.000	.540
Linear-by-Linear Association	.000	1	1.000		
N of Valid Cases	400				

a. 0 cells (0.0%) have expected count less than 5. The minimum expected count is 100.00.

Figure 6.32

Symmetric Measures

		Value	Approx. Sig.
Nominal by Nominal	Phi	.000	1.000
	Cramer's V	.000	1.000
	Contingency Coefficient	.000	1.000
N of Valid Cases		400	

Figure 6.33

SPSS data set: below average income = 0 and above average income = 1. You now wonder if the effect of early childhood education is different for the two income groups. Perhaps low-income students benefit from early childhood education, while high-income students are hindered. Consequently, when data from the two income groups were amalgamated the differential effects cancelled out each other. To further explore this possibility you analyse the data from the two income groups separately.

If you are following along in SPSS, use the following instructions. **With the *Data Editor* for *earlychildeducation.sav* file open, click *Data* from the menu and then slide down and click *Select Cases*. When the *Select Cases* window opens, select *If condition is satisfied* (Figure 6.34) and then click on the *If* button below it. When the *Select Cases: If* window opens, move the *IncomeHiLo* variable over to the empty window, insert '= 0' (Figure 6.35), and then click *Continue*. When you return to the *Select Cases* window, click *OK*. Rerun the x^2 test of independence with the *EarlychildEd* and *ReadHiLo* variables.**

The *Case Processing Summary* table (Figure 6.36) shows that there are 200 valid cases of students in the below-average-income group. The *EarlychildEd * ReadHiLo Crosstabulation* table (Figure 6.37) indicates that 62 of the 200 students from the low-income group are not enrolled in early childhood education. Of those 62 students, 10 are above average in terms of reading competency. Of the 138 from the low-income group who are enrolled in early childhood education students, 48 are above average in terms of reading competency.

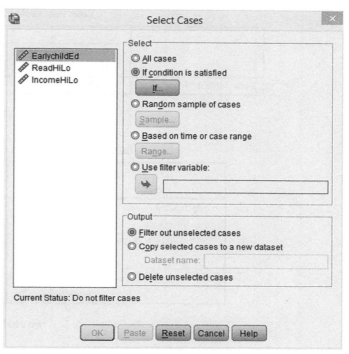

Figure 6.34

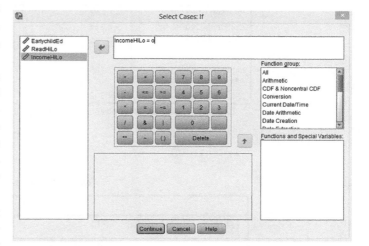

Figure 6.35

Pearson's x^2 test of independence and with all of its variations, found in the *Chi-Square Tests* table (Figure 6.38), are significant, indicating that there is an association between early childhood

Case Processing Summary

	Cases					
	Valid		Missing		Total	
	N	Percent	N	Percent	N	Percent
EarlychildEd * ReadHiLo	200	100.0%	0	0.0%	200	100.0%

Figure 6.36

EarlychildEd * ReadHiLo Crosstabulation

			ReadHiLo		Total
			.00	1.00	
EarlychildEd	.00	Count	52	10	62
		Expected Count	44.0	18.0	62.0
	1.00	Count	90	48	138
		Expected Count	98.0	40.0	138.0
Total		Count	142	58	200
		Expected Count	142.0	58.0	200.0

Figure 6.37

Chi-Square Tests

	Value	df	Asymp. Sig. (2-sided)	Exact Sig. (2-sided)	Exact Sig. (1-sided)
Pearson Chi-Square	7.230[a]	1	.007		
Continuity Correction[b]	6.352	1	.012		
Likelihood Ratio	7.756	1	.005		
Fisher's Exact Test				.007	.005
Linear-by-Linear Association	7.193	1	.007		
N of Valid Cases	200				

a. 0 cells (0.0%) have expected count less than 5. The minimum expected count is 17.98.

Figure 6.38

Symmetric Measures

		Value	Approx. Sig.
Nominal by Nominal	Phi	.190	.007
	Cramer's V	.190	.007
	Contingency Coefficient	.187	.007
N of Valid Cases		200	

Figure 6.39

education and reading competency. Close examination of the *Crosstabuation* table reveals that where only 16% (10/62) of those who are not enrolled in early childhood education are above average in terms of reading competency, 35% (48/138) of those who are enrolled are above average in terms of reading competency. The *Symmetric Measures* table (Figure 6.39) indicates a weak but significant ($\phi = 0.19$) association between early childhood education and reading competency for students from low-income families.

Thus, there is evidence that early childhood education fosters reading competency in students from low-income families. The question remains: does early childhood education hinder the development of reading competency in the high-income children? If this is the case, it may explain why, when the data from low-income and high-income students are amalgamated, there appears to be no relation between early childhood education and reading competency. Return to the *Select Cases: If* window (Figure 6.35), change the *IncomeHiLo = 0* to *IncomeHiLo = 1*, and then rerun the analysis.

The *Case Processing Summary* table (Figure 6.40) shows that there are 200 valid cases of students in the high-income group. The *EarlychildEd * ReadHiLo Crosstabulation* table (Figure 6.41) indicates that 138 of these 200 students are not enrolled in early childhood education. Of those 138 students, 90 are above average in terms of reading competency. Sixty-two students from the high-income group are enrolled in early childhood education. Of those 62 students, 52 are above average in terms of reading competency.

The tests of independence found in the *Chi-Square Tests* table (Figure 6.42) are significant, indicating that there is an association between early childhood education and reading competency. Note that the values of the test statistics are identical to those found for the low-income group.

Case Processing Summary

	Cases					
	Valid		Missing		Total	
	N	Percent	N	Percent	N	Percent
EarlychildEd * ReadHiLo	200	100.0%	0	0.0%	200	100.0%

Figure 6.40

EarlychildEd * ReadHiLo Crosstabulation

			ReadHiLo		
			.00	1.00	Total
EarlychildEd	.00	Count	48	90	138
		Expected Count	40.0	98.0	138.0
	1.00	Count	10	52	62
		Expected Count	18.0	44.0	62.0
Total		Count	58	142	200
		Expected Count	58.0	142.0	200.0

Figure 6.41

Chi-Square Tests

	Value	df	Asymp. Sig. (2-sided)	Exact Sig. (2-sided)	Exact Sig. (1-sided)
Pearson Chi-Square	7.230[a]	1	.007		
Continuity Correction[b]	6.352	1	.012		
Likelihood Ratio	7.756	1	.005		
Fisher's Exact Test				.007	.005
Linear-by-Linear Association	7.193	1	.007		
N of Valid Cases	200				

a. 0 cells (0.0%) have expected count less than 5. The minimum expected count is 17.98.

Figure 6.42

Symmetric Measures

		Value	Approx. Sig.
Nominal by Nominal	Phi	.190	.007
	Cramer's V	.190	.007
	Contingency Coefficient	.187	.007
N of Valid Cases		200	

Figure 6.43

Further examination of the *Crosstabluation* table reveals that 65% (90/138) of those high-income students who are not enrolled in early childhood education are above average in terms of reading competency. Surprisingly, 84% (52/62) of those who are enrolled were above average in terms of reading competency. The *Symmetric Measures* table (Figure 6.43) indicates that the association between early childhood education and reading competency for the high-income group is identical to that of the low-income group: $\phi = 0.19$.

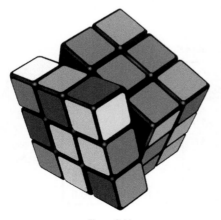

Figure 6.44

There is evidence that early childhood education fosters reading competency not only in low-income students, but also in students from high-income families. You initially thought that low-income students might benefit from early childhood education, while the high-income students might be hindered, and when the data from the two groups were amalgamated the differential effects would cancel out each other. Almost like magic, however, you find both income groups benefit from early childhood education. As you now see, it is not easy to predict what will happen to the association between rows and columns when another row or column is taken into account (Figure 6.44).

━━━━━━━━━ CHALLENGE QUESTION ━━━━━━━━━

Examine the early childhood/reading competency data closely, both when amalgamated and when separated by income level. What is the key factor that makes the surprising result possible?

 Web Link 6.12 for a discussion of and answer to the challenge question.

6 ◗10 MULTI-CATEGORY NOMINAL VARIABLES

Thus far in this chapter we have dealt with the possible association between two binary nominal variables. That is, both variables have had only two possible outcomes or categories (e.g., above- versus below-average reading competency and enrolled versus not enrolled in early childhood education). Although such designs and analyses are not uncommon, often one or both of the nominal variables has more than two categories. In this section we examine a design where one variable is binary and the other has three categories: a 2 × 3 contingency table. The primary question remains the same: is there an association between the two variables? The difference between a 2 × 3 analysis and the analysis of a 2 × 2 design is what is done following the discovery of a significant association.

Imagine you are an instructor searching for a way to improve test performance in a required course in a medical technology programme. It is a pass–fail (*outcome*) course which all students must pass prior to their accreditation as a medical technician. Most students find the course challenging and end up taking the course several times before passing. The programme coordinator finds this to be a drain on resources and expensive for the students. She asks you as the instructor to find a way to improve the student outcomes: fail = 0 and pass = 1. In search of a solution, you decide to divide the current class into three groups called preparation styles. The first group, as usual, is left to its own devices (*nothing*: group = 1); the second group attends a study-skills seminar (*study*: group = 2); the

> For 100 years there has been evidence that practice testing facilitates learning more than simply increasing study time (Gates, 1917). This has come to be called the *testing effect* (Roediger & Karpicke, 2006).

third group is administered a practice examination two-thirds of the way through the course (*test*: group = 3). After reviewing the literature, you feel there is reason to believe that the practice *test* group will outperform the other two groups on the examination.

With a 2 × 3 design there are 2 degrees of freedom: $(2 − 1)(3 − 1) = 2$. The seventh row of the sample size table in Appendix B (Table B.2) corresponds to a x^2 test with $df = 2$. As we see in the seventh row under the column for a large effect size, power = 0.80, and $\alpha = 0.05$, 39 subjects are required; for a medium effect size 107 subjects are required; and for a small effect size 964 subjects are required. Thus, you have enough students only for detecting a large effect (power = 0.80). Should you wish to follow along in SPSS, the data for this hypothetical study are found on the book's web page.

 Web Link 6.13 to the *twobythreechisq.sav* data set.

When you open the data file and run a x^2 test of independence on the two variables (*outcome* and *group*) be sure to select *Chi-Square, Phi and Cramer's V*, and *Lambda* in the *Crosstabs: Statistics* window. Also be sure to select the *Observed* and *Expected* boxes in the *Counts* area of the *Crosstabs: Cell Display* window. Additionally, select *Adjusted standardized* in the *Residuals* area of the *Crosstabs: Cell Display* window.

The *Case Processing Summary* table (Figure 6.45) shows that there were 60 valid cases. The *outcome * group Crosstabulation* table (Figure 6.46) reveals that there were 19 students in group 1 (*nothing*), 16 in group 2 (*study*), and 25 in group 3 (*test*). Of those 19 students in group 1, 6 passed (outcome =1). Of the 16 students in group 2, 8 passed. And of the 25 students in group 3, 21 passed.

Case Processing Summary

	Cases					
	Valid		Missing		Total	
	N	Percent	N	Percent	N	Percent
outcome * group	60	100.0%	0	0.0%	60	100.0%

Figure 6.45

outcome * group Crosstabulation

			group			Total
			1.00	2.00	3.00	
outcome	.00	Count	13	8	4	25
		Expected Count	7.9	6.7	10.4	25.0
		Adjusted Residual	2.9	.8	-3.4	
	1.00	Count	6	8	21	35
		Expected Count	11.1	9.3	14.6	35.0
		Adjusted Residual	-2.9	-.8	3.4	
Total		Count	19	16	25	60
		Expected Count	19.0	16.0	25.0	60.0

Figure 6.46

The tests of independence found in the *Chi-Square Tests* table (Figure 6.47) are all significant, indicating that there is an association between *group* (preparation style) and *outcome* (course performance). The *Symmetric Measures* table (Figure 6.48) indicates that there is very nearly a strong association between outcome and group: ϕ and Cramér's V are both equal to 0.462.

Recall that λ indicates the percentage increase in the ability to predict one variable (treated as the dependent variable or criterion) using another variable (treated as the independent or predictor), given the baseline of dependent variable alone. In the current case, we will treat *group* as the predictor variable and outcome as the *criterion* variable. The λ of 0.28 (*outcome Dependent*) found in the *Directional Measures* table (Figure 6.49) indicates that when you take *group* into account, you increase your ability to predict *outcome* by 28%, which is considered a moderate effect.

Chi-Square Tests

	Value	df	Asymp. Sig. (2-sided)
Pearson Chi-Square	12.829[a]	2	.002
Likelihood Ratio	13.640	2	.001
Linear-by-Linear Association	1.633	1	.201
N of Valid Cases	60		

Figure 6.47

Symmetric Measures

		Value	Approx. Sig.
Nominal by Nominal	Phi	.462	.002
	Cramer's V	.462	.002
N of Valid Cases		60	

Figure 6.48

Directional Measures

			Value	Asymp. Std. Error[a]	Approx. T[b]	Approx. Sig.
Nominal by Nominal	Lambda	Symmetric	.267	.128	1.863	.062
		outcome Dependent	.280	.201	1.197	.231
		altgroup Dependent	.257	.102	2.275	.023
	Goodman and Kruskal tau	outcome Dependent	.214	.099		.002[c]
		altgroup Dependent	.120	.059		.001[c]

Figure 6.49

Now that you have a 2 × 3 contingency table, rather than the 2 × 2, it is not as obvious where the important differences in the frequencies reside. Where is the *difference* responsible for the *association*? Or stated otherwise, where is the crucial difference between what is *expected* and what is *observed*? Are the two frequencies in group 1 different from what would be expected if *outcome* and *group* were independent? The same can be asked of the other two groups. There are several ways to address these questions; we will examine one of them. For a detailed discussion of such procedures, see MacDonald and Gardner (2000).

To begin with, look back at the *outcome * group Crosstabulation* table (Figure 6.46). The third row in each of the cells is the *Adjusted Residual*. Although the labels are inconsistent, this is the *Adjusted standardized* that you selected when designing the analysis. Adjusted residuals are equivalent to *z*-values. Knowing that a *z*-score greater than ±1.96 has a *p*-value of less than 0.05, you might be inclined to simply examine the adjusted residuals and conclude that those with values greater than ±1.96 indicate observed frequencies that are significantly different from the expected, if *outcome* and *group* were independent.

When we conduct multiple tests we need to reduce the *p*-value threshold required for significance to compensate for the increase in the probability of a Type I error. We can hold the Type I error rate constant by dividing 0.05 by the number of tests we are making. In our case we are testing six adjusted residuals. Thus, the threshold for significance for any one of them becomes 0.05/6 or 0.008. SPSS provides an easy way to determine the *p*-value of the adjusted residuals.

• • • • •

We previously hinted at this issue of the familywise error rate (FWER) in Chapter 5 when we discussed a problem with a 'fishing expedition'. FWER is a simple function of your starting alpha (usually $\alpha = 0.05$) and the number of tests that you run: FWER $= \alpha \times$ no. of tests. In our current example, we have six cells we are testing with their adjusted residual. Our FWER would be $0.05 \times 6 = 0.30$. That is, we would have a 30% chance of making at least one Type I error. This is certainly unacceptable.

As the equivalent to a z-score, an adjusted residual can be viewed as the number of standard deviations the *observed frequency* deviates from the *expected frequency* in a given cell. It also happens that $z^2 = x^2$. This conversion can be used to examine the role each cell plays in the association between two variables by computing an accurate estimate of our six x^2 values.

To accomplish this, we must open a new *Data Editor* window and enter our six adjusted residuals into the first column. Enter in the order of outcome = 0 for groups 1, 2, and 3 and the outcome = 1 for groups 1, 2, and 3. Next, under the *Transform* option on the menu select *Compute Variable*. In the *Target Variable* box (Figure 6.50) enter a new name (e.g., *chisq*). Then in the *Numeric Expression* box enter 'VAR00001 * VAR00001'. After clicking *OK* and returning to the *Data Editor* window, you will find the new variable, which is the x^2 values that correspond to the adjusted residuals (Figure 6.51).

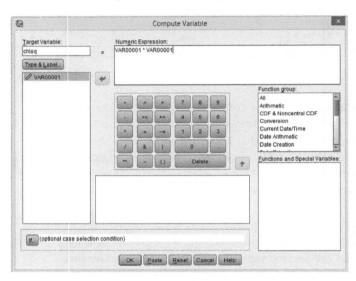

Figure 6.50

	VAR00001	chisq
1	2.90	8.41
2	.80	.64
3	-3.40	11.56
4	-2.90	8.41
5	-.80	.64
6	3.40	11.56
7		

Figure 6.51

Next we compute the *p*-values that correspond to the six x^2 values. Again, in the *Compute Variable* window (Figure 6.52), scroll down the *Function group* options and select *Significance*. Then double-click on *Sig.Chisq* in the *Functions and Special Variables* area. SIG.CHISQ(?) appears in the *Numeric Expression* area. Move the *chisq* variable over into the expression and also enter ',1' and click *OK*. The new variable will appear in the *Data Editor*. Then in the bottom left of the *Data Editor* select *Variable View*. Then in the *Decimals* column change the '2' to a '4' in the *pval* variable (Figure 6.53) and return to the *Data View* window.

Finally, the *p*-values in the *pval* variable can be compared to our critical value we computed earlier, 0.05/6 or 0.008. You find the frequency of the pass category for the *nothing* group 1 (row 4) is significantly smaller ($p = 0.0037$) than expected (Figure 6.54), if *outcome* and *group* were independent. The frequency of the pass category for *practice examination* group (row 6) is significantly greater than expected. There was no significant difference with respect to the study-skills group. These results allow you to report to the programme coordinator that there is sufficient evidence supporting the idea that practice examinations will improve performance on your course.

What would you conclude about the effect of the study-skills seminar? Does no difference here actually indicate that there was no effect? What if you only had the data from the *nothing* and the *study-skills* groups?

Web Link 6.14 for a discussion and an answer to the challenge question.

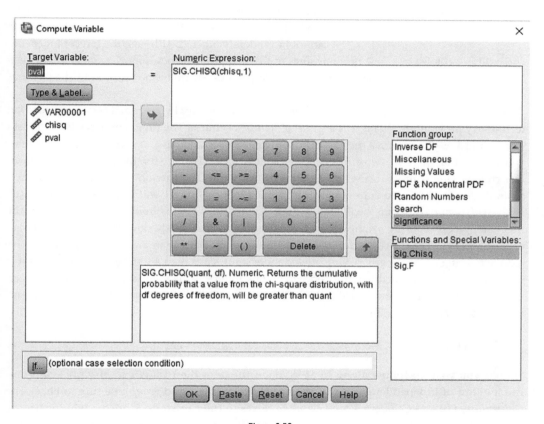

Figure 6.52

	Name	Type	Width	Decimals	Label	Values	Missing	Columns	Align	Measure	Role
1	VAR00001	Numeric	8	2		None	None	8	Right	Scale	Input
2	chisq	Numeric	8	2		None	None	10	Right	Scale	Input
3	pval	Numeric	8	4		None	None	10	Right	Scale	Input
4											

Figure 6.53

	VAR00001	chisq	pval
1	2.90	8.41	.0037
2	.80	.64	.4237
3	-3.40	11.56	.0007
4	-2.90	8.41	.0037
5	-.80	.64	.4237
6	3.40	11.56	.0007
7			

Figure 6.54

6 11 TESTS OF INDEPENDENCE WITH ORDINAL VARIABLES

So far we have analysed categorical data that are nominal in nature. In such cases where the numbers assigned to the levels of the variables are merely names, it does not matter how the categories in the rows or columns are ordered. When we consider categorical data that are ordinal in nature, the numbers assigned to the levels of the variable indicate relative magnitude as well as a name. Thus, the categories of a variable cannot be randomly ordered. Although the tests of independence will not change, we have new measures of the strength of association: *gamma*, *Kendall's tau-b* and *Kendall's tau-c*. Let us imaginatively create a version of the problem discussed in the previous section.

Again you are searching for a way to improve test performance in a required course in a medical technology programme. Again it is a pass–fail (*outcome*) course. The programme coordinator asks you to find a way to improve the student outcomes (fail = 0 and pass = 1) on this difficult course. You are told that there are two effective study-skills seminars that are run by the academic services department. One seminar focuses on note-taking skills and the other on exam-writing skills. You again decide to divide the current class into three groups. Group 1 will not attend either of the study-skills seminars; group 2 will attend a note-taking-skills group; group 3 will attend both the note-taking-skills and the exam-writing seminars. In this case, study skills can be considered an ordinal variable. Those in group 2 are offered more study skills than are those in group 1, who receive nothing. Those in group 3 are offered more study skills than are those in group 2, but it is impossible to say that the difference between groups 1 and 2 is the same as the difference between groups 2 and 3. All that can be said is that a '2' is greater than a '1' and that a '3' is great than a '2' in terms of offered study skills.

Web Link 6.15 to the *twobythreechisq.sav* data set used in this example.

Should you wish to follow along in SPSS, open the data file *twobythreechisq.sav* again and run a X^2 test of independence on the two variables (*outcome* and *group*). Be sure to check the *Chi-square*, *Phi* and *Cramer's V*, and *Lambda* boxes in the *Crosstabs: Statistics* window in the *Nominal* window and the *Gamma*, *Kendall's tau-b* and *Kendall's tau-c* boxes in the *Ordinal* area.

The data used in this example are those used in the previous section. The nature of the group variable is conceptually changed to create an ordinal factor.

Because these are the same data you analysed in the previous section, nothing will have changed in the *outcome * group Crosstabulation*, the *Chi-Square Tests* (Figure 6.55), and the *Directional Measures* tables. The same is true for the *Nominal by Nominal* area in the *Symmetric Measures* table. There is an addition to the *Symmetric Measures* table (Figure 6.56), however: the *Ordinal by Ordinal* area. There you will find three new measures: *Kendall's tau-b* (τ-b), *Kendall's tau-c* (τ-c), and *Gamma* (Γ).

Similar to the nominal measures of association, Kendall's tau-b, Kendall's tau-c, and gamma range in value from 0 to 1, but these values have the additional property of being either positive or negative. The terms *positive* and *negative* do not indicate the quality of the association, but rather the nature of the ordinal association's *trend*. A positive association indicates that increased relative frequencies found in higher-level categories of one variable are associated with higher levels of the other variable; a negative association indicates that increased relative frequencies found in higher-level categories of one variable are associated with lower levels of the other variable. A re-examination of the *outcome * group Crosstabulation* table illustrates a positive trend (Figure 6.57). As we move from group 1 to group 2 and to group 3, there is an increase in the relative frequency of passing (*outcome* = 1). Do not allow the ordering of the outcome variable in the table (.00 above 1.00) to confuse you regarding the higher level of outcome. The '.00' level may be above the '1.00,' but the '1.00' is the higher level of outcome.

The *Ordinal by Ordinal* area in the *Symmetric Measures* table reveals that τ-b and τ-c are more similar to each other than they are to Γ. τ-b is an appropriate measure of association when there is an equal number of rows and columns in the contingency table, which is not the case in this example. When the numbers of rows and columns are unequal, τ-c is the appropriate choice. In this example τ-c = 0.490 ($p < 0.001$), indicating a strong association between *outcome* and *group*. Usually the best choice for estimating associations between ordinal variables, however, is Γ. In your example it is

Chi-Square Tests

	Value	df	Asymp. Sig. (2-sided)
Pearson Chi-Square	12.829[a]	2	.002
Likelihood Ratio	13.640	2	.001
Linear-by-Linear Association	12.328	1	.000
N of Valid Cases	60		

Figure 6.55

Symmetric Measures

		Value	Asymp. Std. Error[a]	Approx. T[b]	Approx. Sig.
Nominal by Nominal	Phi	.462			.002
	Cramer's V	.462			.002
	Contingency Coefficient	.420			.002
Ordinal by Ordinal	Kendall's tau-b	.434	.104	4.144	.000
	Kendall's tau-c	.490	.118	4.144	.000
	Gamma	.680	.128	4.144	.000
N of Valid Cases		60			

Figure 6.56

even stronger than τ-c: $\Gamma = 0.680$. Thus, you have evidence to conclude that the more academic skills seminars a student attends, the more likely he or she is to pass the course.

Göktaş and İşçi (2011) have examined the average accuracy of these three measures of ordinal association. Both τ-b and τ-c tend to underestimate an ordinal association, particularly when the total number of observations (n) is 50 or less. As n increases up to 100 or greater, the extent of the underestimation diminishes, but continues. Γ, on the other hand, is on average the most accurate estimate of the association. But as n increases beyond 100, Γ begins to overestimate the association. Therefore, it is prudent to report both Γ and τ.

One important qualification must be made regarding all measures of ordinal association. They estimate what we will provisionally refer to as a *linear* association. Such measures are insensitive to other possible associations that are *curvilinear* in nature. Once again examine the *outcome * group*

outcome * group Crosstabulation

			group			
			1.00	2.00	3.00	Total
outcome	.00	Count	13	8	4	25
		Expected Count	7.9	6.7	10.4	25.0
		Adjusted Residual	2.9	.8	-3.4	
	1.00	Count	6	8	21	35
		Expected Count	11.1	9.3	14.6	35.0
		Adjusted Residual	-2.9	-.8	3.4	
Total		Count	19	16	25	60
		Expected Count	19.0	16.0	25.0	60.0

Figure 6.57

outcome * group Crosstabulation

			group			
			1.00	2.00	3.00	Total
outcome	.00	Count	13	8	4	25
		Expected Count	7.9	6.7	10.4	25.0
		Adjusted Residual	2.9	.8	-3.4	
	1.00	Count	6	8	21	35
		Expected Count	11.1	9.3	14.6	35.0
		Adjusted Residual	-2.9	-.8	3.4	
Total		Count	19	16	25	60
		Expected Count	19.0	16.0	25.0	60.0

Figure 6.58

Crosstabulation table (Figure 6.58). In group 1, (6/19) 31% of the students passed the course. In group 2, (8/16) 50% of the students passed. In group 3, (21/25) 84% of the students passed. Although the increases in relative frequency are not equal, both changes represent increases and they are quite similar.

> The precise nature of a *linear* association will be discussed in great detail in the next chapter which addresses the association between two measurement variables.

Reversing the outcomes for groups 2 and 3 dramatically changes the values of these ordinal measures. The *outcome * altgroup Crosstabulation* table (Figure 6.59) depicts the change in the data. The *Chi-Square Tests* table (Figure 6.60) reveals no change in the test statistics or their *p*-values. As well, the *Directional Measures* table (Figure 6.61) reveals that there is no change in the lambda (0.280, $p = 0.062$) or Goodman and Kruskal's tau (0.214, $p = 0.002$) values for *outcome Dependent*. And finally, there is no change in the *Nominal by Nominal* values in the *Symmetric Measures* table (Figure 6.62). There is a substantial difference in the *Ordinal by Ordinal* measures, however. For example, Γ has been reduced from

outcome * altgroup Crosstabulation

			altgroup			
			1.00	2.00	3.00	Total
outcome	.00	Count	13	4	8	25
		Expected Count	7.9	10.4	6.7	25.0
	1.00	Count	6	21	8	35
		Expected Count	11.1	14.6	9.3	35.0
Total		Count	19	25	16	60
		Expected Count	19.0	25.0	16.0	60.0

Figure 6.59

Chi-Square Tests

	Value	df	Asymp. Sig. (2-sided)
Pearson Chi-Square	12.829[a]	2	.002
Likelihood Ratio	13.640	2	.001
Linear-by-Linear Association	1.633	1	.201
N of Valid Cases	60		

Figure 6.60

Directional Measures

			Value	Asymp. Std. Error[a]	Approx. T[b]	Approx. Sig.
Nominal by Nominal	Lambda	Symmetric	.267	.128	1.863	.062
		outcome Dependent	.280	.201	1.197	.231
		altgroup Dependent	.257	.102	2.275	.023
	Goodman and Kruskal tau	outcome Dependent	.214	.099		.002[c]
		altgroup Dependent	.120	.059		.001[c]

Figure 6.61

Symmetric Measures

		Value	Asymp. Std. Error[a]	Approx. T[b]	Approx. Sig.
Nominal by Nominal	Phi	.462			.002
	Cramer's V	.462			.002
	Contingency Coefficient	.420			.002
Ordinal by Ordinal	Kendall's tau-b	.166	.134	1.240	.215
	Kendall's tau-c	.188	.151	1.240	.215
	Gamma	.260	.206	1.240	.215
N of Valid Cases		60			

Figure 6.62

0.680 to 0.260. The cell frequencies associated with the different groups are unchanged, as are the nominal measures of association. Knowing group memberships reduces the amount of error in predicting *outcome*. What has changed is the nature of the shape of the relation between the rows (*outcomes*) and the columns (*groups*). To avoid confusion, the differences in the various measures of association must be clearly understood.

This example illustrates the importance of closely examining the contingency table prior to going any further in the analysis of categorical data. When there is a nonlinear association between two ordinal variables, it is best to report one of the nominal measures of association.

One final issue we will address in this section is the assignment of values to the levels of an ordinal variable. We know that because the variable is ordinal, a larger number must represent more of something than is represented by a smaller number; a 2 means more of something than does a 1. We also know that unlike in an ordinal scale, in an interval scale the intervals between adjacent values are all equal. That is, the difference between a 2 and a 1 is the same as the difference between a 3 and a 2. It may be asked if the specific values chosen for an ordinal variable will affect the strength of the measures of association. For example, how would the results change if all of the 3s in the *group* variable in the current data set were transformed into 9s (*twobythreechisq. sav*)? Should you make the transformation and repeat the analysis, you will find that all of the test statistics and all of the measures of association remain unchanged.

Why do all the test statistics and symmetric measures remain unchanged when we transform the values of an ordinal variable, as long as we maintain ordinality?

 Web Link 6.16 for an answer to the challenge question.

6 12 CHAPTER SUMMARY

The current chapter focused on testing and reporting a possible *association* between two *categorical* variables. The chapter began with an extension of the x^2 goodness-of-fit procedure and the examination of nominal data. The primary difference between the x^2 goodness-of-fit procedure and the x^2 test of independence is the manner in which the latter's *expected frequencies* are derived. The x^2 test of independence expected frequencies are based on the assumption that the two variables are independent. Variations and alternatives to the standard x^2 test statistic were also discussed: Yates's *continuity correction*, the *likelihood ratio*, and Fisher's *exact test*. Each has its appropriate uses and its limitations. Along with the tests of independence, we discussed various standardized measures of the strength of the association between the two categorical variables. For nominal variables, when analysing a 2×2 contingency table, ϕ is the best measure of the strength of the association. With larger contingency tables, *Cramér's V* and the *contingency coefficient* are more appropriate. For ordinal variables, *gamma* (Γ) is usually considered the best index. If the contingency table has an equal number of rows and columns, *Kendall's tau-b* is an alternative. If the number of rows and columns are unequal, *Kendall's tau-c* is the alternative. It must be kept in mind that the x^2 test of independence assumes the observations are independent. This is best guaranteed by ensuring that there is only one observation per subject. To avoid bias in the results, none of the *expected frequencies* should be less than 5. Finally, researchers need to avoid the error of *nonoccurrence* by ensuring all independent observations that were collected are included in the analysis.

6 13 RECOMMENDED READINGS

Kraemer, H. C., & Thiemann, S. (1987). *How many subjects? Statistical power analysis in research.* London: Sage.

This book provides a simple yet detailed introduction to power determination and sample size. Chapter 9 is dedicated to contingency table analysis.

MacDonald, P. L., & Gardner, R. C. (2000). Type I error rate comparisons of post hoc procedures for $I \times J$ chi-square tables. *Educational and Psychological Measurement, 60,* 735–754.

This article provides a useful description and analysis of the various strategies researchers may use for following up significant tests of independence with contingency tables with more than two rows and two columns.

Reynolds, H. T. (1984). *Analysis of nominal data.* London: Sage.

This book contains useful discussions of measures of strength association for nominal data. Of particular relevance is the comparison of Goodman and Kruskal's tau and lambda.

6●14 CHAPTER REVIEW QUESTIONS

Multiple-choice questions

1 The null hypothesis of the x^2 test of independence assumes _____.

    a   all the cells have an equal number of observations

    b   all the cells have an unequal number of observations

    c   the rows and columns have different totals

    d   rows and columns are unrelated

    e   None of the above

2 Yates's correction to the standard Pearson x^2 test of independence results in _____.

    a   a reduction in the squared differences between observed and expected frequencies

    b   a reduction in the overall x^2

    c   an increase in the probability of x^2

    d   a decreases in the chance of rejecting H_0

    e   All of the above

3 What is the critical value for a x^2 with 3 degrees of freedom ($\alpha = 0.05$)?

    a   3.841

    b   44.00

    c   7.815

    d   5.991

    e   9.348

4 How many subjects are required to ensure power of 0.80 for a x^2 test of independence with 4 df when the researcher wishes to test for a medium effect size ($\alpha = 0.05$)?

    a   133

    b   87

    c   100

    d   48

    e   50

5 If an observed x^2 value was 6.57 and there were 50 total observations, the corresponding ϕ coefficient is _____.

    a   0.36

    b   0.13

    c   6.57

    d   0.63

    e   None of the above

6 Which of the following is *not* an assumption of the x^2 test of independence?

    a   The independence of the observations

    b   The independence of the variables

    c   A minimum expected frequency of 5 in all cells

    d   Inclusion of cases of non-occurrence

    e   All of the above are assumptions

7   When analysing a 3×4 contingency table with nominal data, which measure of strength of symmetrical association is most appropriate to report?

a   The ϕ coefficient
b   Cramér's V
c   Goodman and Kruskal's tau
d   Lambda
e   Any of the above are appropriate

8   When analysing a 2×3 contingency table with nominal data, which measure of strength of asymmetrical or directional association is most appropriate to report?

a   The ϕ coefficient
b   Cramér's V
c   Goodman and Kruskal's tau
d   Lambda
e   None of the above are appropriate

9   Usually the most appropriate choice for estimating associations between ordinal variables is _____.

a   Kendall's tau-b
b   Kendall's tau-c
c   Gamma
d   Lambda
e   None of the above are appropriate

10 As the total number of observations increases, the difference between the values of a standard Pearson x^2 test of independence and of the corresponding Yates's correction _____.

a   increases
b   decreases
c   remains the same
d   is unpredictable
e   is zero

Short-answer questions

1   What is the difference between a x^2 *goodness-of-fit test* and a x^2 *test of independence*?
2   How are the expected frequencies for the x^2 test of independence derived?
3   Why is the ϕ coefficient an inappropriate measure of strength of association for a contingency table with more than two rows and columns?
4   What is the third-variable problem and how might it be addressed?
5   What is a limitation of lambda as a measure of the strength of an ordinal association?

Data set questions

1   If an observed x^2 value was 7.20 ($df = 1$, $p = 0.007$) and all of the expected frequencies were 5, what were the observed frequencies in the four cells?

2   Marco d'Naldo was reading about the caloric differences between standard ice cream and gelato. He wondered if the choice of ice cream versus gelato is related to whether the person is on a diet. One day Marco goes to an ice cream parlour (which also serves gelato) and surveys the customers. His data are summarized in the contingency table in Figure 6.63.

   (a)   What is the null hypothesis?
   (b)   What are the expected frequencies?
   (c)   What is the observed x^2 value?
   (d)   How many degrees of freedom are there?
   (e)   What is the critical x^2 value?
   (f)   Would Marco d'Naldo reject the null hypothesis?
   (g)   What is the effect size?

	Ice cream	Gelato	Total
On Diet	10	30	40
Not on Diet	30	30	60
Total	40	60	100

Figure 6.63

3   Dr. Head, a clinical psychologist, claims that the recidivism rate (the likelihood that a patient will be readmitted) for a given psychological disorder is unrelated to age group (young, middle-aged, and elderly). To test his claim he randomly checked the files of three age categories: 40 young patients, 110 middle-aged patients, and 50 elderly patients who had had the disorder. Of these patients, the total number of patients who had been readmitted to hospital with their disorder was 100. Of these 30 were young and 40 were middle-aged.

   (a)   Do the clinician's findings support his claim?
   (b)   What is the best estimate of the strength of the association between age group and recidivism?
   (c)   If there is a significant association, where is the important difference(s) between the observed and expected frequencies?
   (d)   How would you best describe the relation between age group and recidivism?

4   Create two data sets for 2 × 2 contingency tables. Both of the data sets should produce a significant x^2 test of independence. When the two data sets are amalgamated, however, the x^2 test of independence for the combined data set should be non-significant.

Don't forget to use the online resources! Meet your supporting stats tutor through an **introductory video**, review your maths skills with a **diagnostic pre-test**, explore statistical principles through **interactive simulations**, practice analysis techniques with **SPSS datasets**, and check your work with **answers to all in-text questions**.

https://study.sagepub.com/bors

7

Chapter contents

OBSERVATIONAL STUDIES: TWO MEASUREMENT VARIABLES

KEY CONCEPTS: linear relation, scatterplot, covariance, correlation coefficient, regression coefficient.

7.1 PURPOSE

The purpose of this chapter is to explore the statistical procedures used to determine whether two *measurement* variables are *associated* with each other and, if so, to what degree. A lack of association means that the two variables are independent with respect to each other. For example, I suspect that the marks on a statistics examination are independent of the students' shoe sizes, but examination marks are related to the number of hours students have studied. Much of this chapter, like the previous chapter, is an extension of the discussion of *independence* found in Chapter 3 (see p. 90).

The current chapter is Chapter 6's sister chapter. The nature of the research *question* is unchanged, but there is a change in the type of *data* to be analysed. It is the change in the type of data that is responsible for the different formulae contained in the two chapters. Recall our orienting framework. Statistical tests can be loosely segregated into four families that are based on the intersection of one of two types of research questions and one of two types of data. In this chapter we have a family of procedures based on the intersection of (1) a question of *relation* (or association) and (2) *measurement* data. Of specific concern will be the Pearson product moment correlation, the ordinary least squares regression, and indices of effect size. Finally, in addition to material from Chapter 6, connections will be made with other topics previously covered, such as z-scores and the t-test. (For a review for a discussion of the differences between measurement and categorical data, see p. 29 in Chapter 2.)

7.2 INTRODUCTION

Examination of a possible *association* between two measurement variables begins with the construction of a *scatterplot*. A scatterplot is a graphic portrayal of the data. A scatterplot's descriptive function is parallel to

1   a *contingency table* used when assessing the question of *association* with *frequency* data (Chapter 6, p. 228), and
2   a *bar graph* used when assessing the *difference* between groups with *measurement* data (Chapter 5, p. 185).

Much of the material in this chapter revolves around the key concept of *covariance*. Covariance expresses the extent to which the observed values of one variable change systematically with the observed changes in the values of another variable. Covariance alone is not very informative and is typically standardized in two ways. The first standardized form is the *correlation coefficient*. This *standardized estimate* of the strength or degree of association between two variables is analogous to the ϕ coefficient and to Cramér's V discussed in Chapter 6. The second standardized form of covariance is the *regression coefficient*, which is used to predict the value of one variable (the criterion) when the value of a second variable is known (the predictor). Figure 7.1 summarizes the relations among covariance, correlation, and regression coefficient.

• • • • •

Unstandardized scores are raw scores, expressed in the units in which the variable was initially measured. For example, unstandardized quiz marks are the original marks assigned by the instructor, and hours worked are the number of hours worked during the week.

Standardized scores typically are unstandardized scores that have been divided by a fixed quantity, transforming the original values into a fraction of the standardizing quantity. For example, z-scores are standardized scores. A z-score is the difference between a score and the mean of the scores divided by (standardized on) the standard deviation in the original scores. For example, quiz scores can be expressed as z-scores, the number of standard deviations that each student's mark is above or below the group's mean.

You will find that our old friend the *t-test* is used to assess the statistical *significance* (reliability) of these two coefficients. Thus, the *t-test* plays a role analogous to that of the χ^2 and the *likelihood ratio* discussed in Chapter 6. Although this chapter is restricted to the analysis of two *measurement* variables (*simple regression*), the material covered here forms the basis for the analyses of the more complex cases where there are multiple *predictor variables* (Chapter 12). Finally, the important issue of the relation between correlation and causation will be discussed. Keep in mind that in this chapter, as in the previous one, the researcher has two pieces of information (or a pair of scores) for each source or subject. A psycholinguist may have the age of subjects and their score on a standardized vocabulary test, or a sociologist may have the average income of the citizens living in major cities along with each city's crime rate. (For a discussion of ordinal variables and measures of association see p. 258 in the previous chapter.)

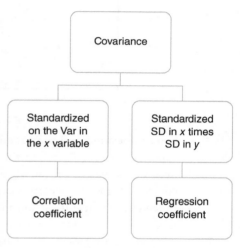

Figure 7.1

The discussion of the association between two *ordinal* variables in Section 6.11 provides a conceptual segue to the material covered in the present chapter. Just as the values of *nominal* measures of association range from 0 to 1, so do the values of *ordinal* measures of association, such as *gamma* (Γ). Additionally, Γ and other measures of ordinal association have the property of being signed, either positively or negatively. Where the numerical value of Γ indicates the strength of the association, the sign indicates the nature or direction of the ordinal association's *trend* (see the discussion of Γ on p. 258 in Chapter 6.)

Ordinal measures of association estimate the degree of a systematic increase or decrease in the relative frequencies of one variable across the increasing levels of the other variable; this trend is what was provisionally referred to in the previous chapter as a *linear* relation (see the discussion of a *linear trend* on p. 260).

The *outcome * group Crosstabulation* table presented in the previous chapter and reproduced in Figure 7.2 illustrates a positive orientation or trend. As we move from group 1 to group 2 and on to group 3, there is a general increase in the relative frequency in the *passing* category (*outcome* = 1): 6/19, 8/16, and 21/25.

As with the other tests of association we have explored, resolving the question of a possible association between two measurement variables requires establishing what is *expected* when there

outcome * group Crosstabulation

			group			
			1.00	2.00	3.00	Total
outcome	.00	Count	13	8	4	25
		Expected Count	7.9	6.7	10.4	25.0
		Adjusted Residual	2.9	.8	-3.4	
	1.00	Count	⑥	⑧	㉑	35
		Expected Count	11.1	9.3	14.6	35.0
		Adjusted Residual	-2.9	-.8	3.4	
Total		Count	⑲	⑯	㉕	60
		Expected Count	19.0	16.0	25.0	60.0

Figure 7.2

is no association and the variables are random with respect to each other. In Chapter 6, this expectation was reflected in the *expected frequencies* reported in the contingency table. We will need an alternative scheme when analysing measurement data. Furthermore, as in Chapter 6, the conclusion that two variables are not random with respect to each other can be translated into statements about a reduction in the amount of error when making predictions. Knowing that there is an association between two variables signifies that there is an improvement (less error) in our predictions. Finally, as in Chapter 6, we need to be concerned with the issue of *power* and the *third-variable* problem.

 TESTS OF ASSOCIATION FOR CATEGORICAL DATA REVIEWED

In this section we review the logic of the tests of association used with categorical data and consider its worth and limitations when applied to measurement data. Chapter 6 was introduced through a fictional study examining the association between the shading of geometrical figures and performance on a test with 3-D line-drawings. In that introduction we saw how a question of association might be framed in terms of an independent-samples *t*-test. In this chapter we continue drawing connections by reframing the question of an association between two *measurement* variables as if it were a question of an association between two *categorical* variables.

Imagine that you are a literature professor and believe that performance on your weekly quiz is related to the number of hours per week a student works outside of the university. You consider it a matter of increasing pressure on the students' struggle to manage their time. You hypothesize that the more the student works, the less time the student has for the assigned readings for your class and, as a consequence, the lower his or her quiz mark will be. Prior to the next quiz you asks your students ($n = 40$) to record the number of hours they have worked outside of the university that week. The data you collect for this imaginary study are in the SPSS file *workandquizmark.sav* on the book's web page. (Note: For the moment ignore the variables *Zquizmark* and *Zhoursworked*.)

🗚 Web Link 7.1 to the SPSS file *workandquizmark.sav*.

The descriptive statistics for your 40 students reveal (Figure 7.3) that the mean number of hours your students worked per week (*hoursworked*) was 13.15 (median = 13.5). The mean quiz mark (*quizmark*) was 6.45 (median = 7). With this information and having read Chapter 6, you might consider transforming the measurement data into categorical data and then resort to the tests and indices you used in Chapter 6 to answer the current question of a possible association between *hoursworked* and *quizmark*. This strategy is reasonable and would show resourcefulness on your part.

Statistics

		quizmark	hoursworked
N	Valid	40	40
	Missing	0	0
Mean		6.4500	13.1500
Median		7.0000	13.5000
Minimum		3.00	8.00
Maximum		10.00	18.00

Figure 7.3

One way to transform the measurement data into categorical data is to use the medians to create two binary variables: *hourcat* and *quizcat*. Those students with fewer hours worked per week (13.5 and below) can be assigned an *hourcat* score of 0 and those with more hours worked (above 13.5) can be assigned a 1. Those students with a below-median quiz mark (7 and below) can be assigned a *quizcat* of 0 and those with a mark above the median (above 7) can be assigned a 1. You then could create a 2 × 2 contingency table. This transformation of the original measurement data into categorical variables can be found in the variables *quizcat* and *hourcat* in the data file. **Next you would run the SPSS *Crosstabs* and select *Chi-square*, *Phi and Cramer's V*, *Lambda*, *Gamma*, and *Kendall's tau-b* from the *Crosstabs: Statistics* window. From the *Crosstabs: Cell Display* window also select *Observed* and *Expected* in the *Counts* area.**

The *quizcat * hourcat Crosstabulation* table (Figure 7.4) displays the *expected* and *observed* frequencies for the four cells. It reveals a difference in the relative frequency of *quizcat* = 1 for the two levels of *hourcat*: 11/19 versus 4/21. If there were no association between the two variables, you would expect to find no difference between the *observed* and the *expected* frequencies. The discrepancies between the *expected* and *observed* frequencies in the table, however, do suggest an association. It appears as if the more a student works, the more likely the student will receive a mark below the median. Is it feasible that the *observed differences* between the *expected* and *observed* frequencies are due to chance or *sampling error* alone? Are the observed differences reliable? Recalling a vital assumption necessary for χ^2 analysis, note that none of the expected frequencies are less than 5. (See *sampling error* in Chapter 5 and Chapter 6.)

quizcat *hourcat Crosstabulation

			hourcat .00	hourcat 1.00	Total
quizcat	.00	Count	8	17	25
		Expected Count	11.9	13.1	25.0
	1.00	Count	(11)	(4)	15
		Expected Count	7.1	7.9	15.0
Total		Count	(19)	(21)	40
		Expected Count	19.0	21.0	40.0

Figure 7.4

REVIEW QUESTION

What are two other assumptions necessary for conducting a x^2 test of independence? Do your data satisfy the assumptions?

Web Link 7.2 for an answer to the review question.

The *Chi-Square Tests* output (Figure 7.5) reveals that all tests of association are significant ($p < 0.05$), suggesting a reliable association between *quizcat* and *hourcat* (e.g., Pearson chi-square = 6.423, $p = 0.011$).

Chi-Square Tests

	Value	df	Asymp. Sig. (2-sided)	Exact Sig. (2-sided)	Exact Sig. (1-sided)
Pearson Chi-Square	6.423[a]	1	(.011)		
Continuity Correction[b]	4.872	1	(.027)		
Likelihood Ratio	6.611	1	(.010)		
Fisher's Exact Test				(.021)	.013
Linear-by-Linear Association	6.262	1	(.012)		
N of Valid Cases	40				

a. 0 cells (0.0%) have expected count less than 5. The minimum expected count is 7.13.

Figure 7.5

The *Symmetrical Measures* output (Figure 7.6) reveals that both nominal indices of the strength of the association (*phi* and *Cramér's V* = 0.401) are deemed to be in the moderate range and are also significant ($p < 0.05$). Both ordinal indices are also significant, with gamma (-0.708) indicating a strong negative association. The additional information you gain from the ordinal indices is that the nature of the association is negative. This is consistent with your hypothesis: the more students work outside of the university, the lower their quiz marks tend to be.

Symmetric Measures

		Value	Asymp. Std. Error[a]	Approx. T[b]	Approx. Sig.
Nominal by Nominal	Phi	.401			.011
	Cramer's V	.401			.011
Ordinal by Ordinal	Kendall's tau-b	.401	.144	-2.733	.006
	Gamma	-.708	.181	-2.733	.006
N of Valid Cases		40			

Figure 7.6

The results reported in the *Directional Measures* output (Figure 7.7) are more ambiguous. If we were to identify *quizcat* as the dependent variable and evaluate *lambda* (0.200), there does not appear to be much improvement in prediction from knowing *hourcat* ($p = 0.489$). We find, however, that the *Goodman and Kruskal tau* (0.161) is significant ($p = 0.012$). Thus, the proportion reduction in error (PRE) estimates range from 16% to 20% when you use *hourcat* to predict *quizcat*. (For a discussion of PRE see p. 243 in Chapter 6.)

Directional Measures

			Value	Asymp. Std. Error[a]	Approx. T[b]	Approx. Sig.
Nominal by Nominal	Lambda	Symmetric	.294	.191	1.367	.172
		quizcat Dependent	.200	.260	.692	.489
		hourcat Dependent	.368	.162	1.886	.059
	Goodman and Kruskal tau	quizcat Dependent	.161	.115		.012[c]
		hourcat Dependent	.161	.115		.012[c]

Figure 7.7

Although these analyses may provide you with evidence that there is an association between the number of hours worked per week and quiz performance, and they may indicate that the association is negative and probably moderate in nature, these are not the preferred or the most appropriate analyses when examining measurement data. Also keep in mind that you have observational data, not experimental data. Thus you need to be very careful when elaborating your findings into causal statements. As much as it might appear to be obvious, you do *not* have evidence that working more outside of the university causes students to have lower quiz marks. Your students were not randomly assigned to the high and low number of hours worked conditions.

When faced with measurement data, a possible association between two variables would not be posed in terms of the difference between *expected* and *observed* categorical frequencies. Rather, the null hypothesis (H_0) now pertains to scores on the *y*-variable being random with respect to scores on the *x*-variable. Alternatively, the researcher hypothesizes (H_1) that there is a discernible increase or decrease in the scores on one variable as the scores on the other variable increase. This systematic increase or decrease is in the *value* of the scores, not in the relative *frequencies* of the different categories. Thus in your case, you are hypothesizing that as the number of hours worked per week increases, your students' marks will tend to decrease.

━━━━━━━━━━ CHALLENGE QUESTION ━━━━━━━━━━

You have transformed your measurement data into a form where they could be analysed as categorical data. Can you further transform the analysis to a *t*-test? (*Hint*: We did something like this in the introduction to Chapter 6.) What are the consequences of doing so?

👆 Web Link 7.3 for a discussion of and answer to the challenge question.

When investigating a possible association between two measurement variables we begin with descriptive statistics and by examining the data for outliers. Then we graphically portray data and introduce the scatterplot. Next we examine in some detail the index of *covariance*. As stated above, covariance is crucial because it is the basis for both determining the strength of an association between two measurement variables (correlation coefficient) and making future predictions.

As always, we are concerned with assumptions and the limitations of these procedures. Foremost of these is the proviso that, unless otherwise stated, this chapter is concerned with linear associations, that is associations best characterized by a straight line.

7 ● 4 THE SCATTERPLOT

In this section we introduce the *scatterplot*. A scatterplot is a graphic portrayal of the relation between two variables which subsequently is further described and tested numerically by statistics discussed throughout this chapter. It is always best to begin any statistical procedure by examining the descrip-

> Should you need to review the procedures for running this version of the descriptive statistics, see Chapter 3.

tive statistics separately for the individual variables: *quizmark* and *hoursworked*. When you run the SPSS descriptive statistics for these variables, be sure and check the *Save standardized values as variables* box. In addition to the *minima, maxima,* and *means* we saw above, the *Descriptive Statistics* output provides us with *standard deviations, variances,* and *skewnesses* of the two variables.

The mean *quizmark* of 6.45 in the SPSS *Descriptive Statistics* table (Figure 7.8) is not unreasonable for a quiz with a maximum mark of 10. Hours worked has a range from one full day (8 hours) to more than two full days (18 hours). Most importantly, there is little skewness in either of the variables. Later we will see how skewness can result in distorted estimates of both the nature and the strength of an association.

Descriptive Statistics

	N	Minimum	Maximum	Mean	Std. Deviation	Variance	Skewness	
	Statistic	Statistic	Statistic	Statistic	Statistic	Statistic	Statistic	Std. Error
quizmark	40	3.00	10.00	6.4500	2.21822	4.921	-.071	.374
hoursworked	40	8.00	18.00	13.1500	2.71322	7.362	-.191	.374
Valid N (listwise)	40							

Figure 7.8

Now turn your attention to the previously discussed problem of univariate outliers. When you return to your data file in the SPSS *Data Editor* window and examine the two new additional variables (*Zquizmark* and *Zhoursworked*), which were created by the *Save standard values as variables* command when you ran the descriptive statistics, you will find that there are no z-scores greater than 4, which is the default threshold we are using for identifying univariate outliers. Had an outlier been detected (z-score of 4.0 or greater), there are several strategies you may use to correct the problem. (For a discussion of outliers and possible correction strategies see p. 182 in Chapter 5.)

═══════ REVIEW QUESTION ═══════

What does a z-score of 4.0 represent and how might outliers be related to the problem of extreme skewness?

Web Link 7.4 for answer to the review question.

The next step in examining your data is to create a graphic representation. In the previous chapter where we asked whether the rows were independent of the columns, we first examined a contingency table. With measurement data we are asking if the *scores* plotted along the y-axis of a Cartesian graph are independent of their x-axis values. Reporting the frequencies in the various categories is replaced by the plotting of pairs of scores in their Cartesian coordinates. The rows and columns become the y-axis and the x-axis values. Each subject is plotted in two-dimensional space according to the student's two scores, in your current example, his or her quiz mark and hours per week worked (Figure 7.9).

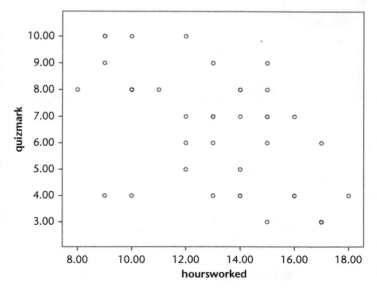

Figure 7.9

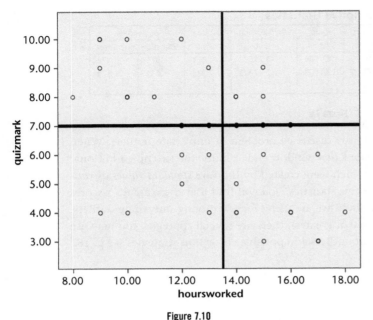

Figure 7.10

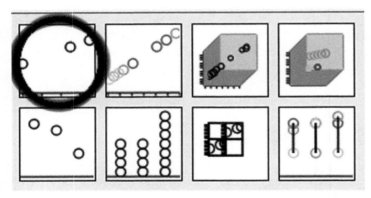

Figure 7.11

If you look at the scatterplot and imagine a vertical line at the 13.5 value on the x-axis and a horizontal line across from the value of 7 on the y-axis (Figure 7.10), you may begin to transform the scatterplot into the 2 × 2 contingency table you analysed in the previous section. All you need to do is count the number of observations in each of the four cells, and you have the contingency table.

Converting a scatterplot into a contingency table

In Figure 7.10 most of the observations above the horizontal line are to the left of the vertical line while most of the observations below the horizontal line are to the right of the vertical line. This pattern of relative frequencies in the four cells is responsible for the negative gamma (−0.708) you saw earlier when you conducted the χ^2 test of independence on the transformed data. Dwelling on this imaginary contingency table for a moment, you may see why it is not desirable to reduce our measurement data to categorical data. The drawback is that all of the points in a given cell are reduced to a single score, even though they are all different. Simply put, we unnecessarily lose potentially important information.

CHALLENGE QUESTION

What if we created a 10 × 10 contingency table using the deciles of the variables as category boundaries and then examined the frequencies? Would that more closely approximate the *measurement* nature of the observations? What if we made each possible score on the x-axis and y-axis a category and treated the data as ordinal? What serious problem immediately emerges from such strategies?

Web Link 7.5 for discussion of and answer to the challenge question.

To create a scatterplot with SPSS, from the *Graphs* option on the *Data Editor* menu bar slide down and select *Chart Builder*. When the *Chart Builder* window opens (Figure 7.12) click *OK* and a second *Chart Builder* window will open (Figure 7.13). In the lower left-hand area highlight the *Scatter/Dot* option. In the area just to the right, click and drag the upper left-hand example (see Figure 7.11) up into the empty area called *Chart preview uses example data* (Figure 7.13).

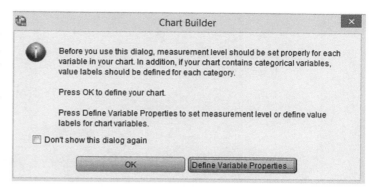

Figure 7.12

Once that is complete the window changes with the *x*-axis and *y*-axis labels appearing (Figure 7.14).

Click and drag *quizmark* into the *y*-axis rectangle and *hoursworked* into the *x*-axis rectangle and then click *OK*. The scatterplot we saw above appears in the output window (Figure 7.15).

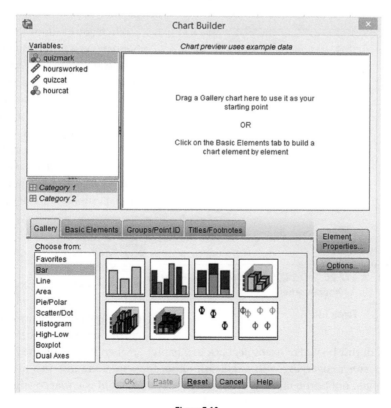

Figure 7.13

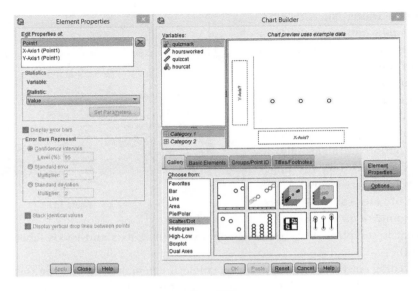

Figure 7.14

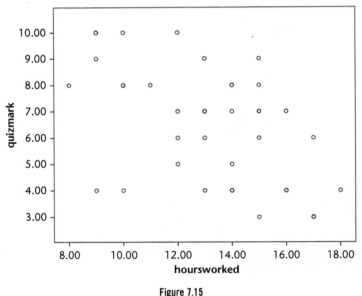

Figure 7.15

When you examine the scatterplot of your data, you find that as the observed *x*-values increase, the *y*-values decrease: higher *x*-values tend to be paired with lower *y*-values. Such an *association* is referred to as *negative*; as the scores on one axis decrease, the scores on the other axis increase. We can also replace the word *association* with the word *covariation*; *quizmark* appears to *covary* with *hoursworked* in a negative manner.

7 5 COVARIANCE

In this section we explore the key concept of *covariance*, which underlies much of what is discussed in this chapter. In fact, covariance underlies most statistical tests in this book. For example, back in Chapter 5, when discussing the *t*-test, we might have spoken of *scores* covarying with *conditions*, rather than speaking in terms of a difference in means. This should not be too much of a surprise to you, since I told you that covariance is another way to express the notion of an association, and questions of *differences* can be translated into questions of *association*.

More specifically, covariance (*cov*) is an *unstandardized* statistic that describes the extent to which two variables change together, or 'co'-'vary'. Its value can range from 0 to infinity and its sign can be either negative or positive. It is calculated by

> There may be different families of statistical tests, but, as with human families, when you push lineage back far enough all families are related.

$$cov_{xy} = \frac{\Sigma(x - \bar{x})(y - \bar{y})}{n - 1},$$

where x is an individual's x-score, $\bar{x}$ is the mean of the x-scores, y is the individual's y score, $\bar{y}$ is the mean of the y-scores, and n is the number of subjects or pairs of scores.

We can refer to $x - \bar{x}$ and $y - \bar{y}$ as *difference scores* or *d-scores*. Reflecting on the formula, we see the following possibilities. If a subject has an above-average x-score, he or she will have a positive d-score for x. If a subject has a below-average x-score, he or she will have a negative d-score for x. Correspondingly, if a subject has an above-average y-score, he or she will have a positive d-score for y. If a subject has a below-average y-score, he or she will have a negative d-score for y.

Therefore, there are two circumstances which result in the product of an individual's d-scores being positive: when both of the subject's d-scores are positive or both d-scores are negative. There are two circumstances which result in the product of an individual's scores being negative: when one of the d-scores is positive and the other is negative. Disregarding the issue of

Sub	x	x–d	y	y–d	(x–d)(y–d)
Panel 1					
1	100	−200	20	10	−2000
2	200	−100	15	5	−500
3	300	0	10	0	0
4	400	100	5	−5	−500
5	500	200	0	−10	−2000
Panel 2					
1	100	−200	0	−10	2000
2	200	−100	5	−5	500
3	300	0	10	0	0
4	400	100	15	5	500
5	500	200	20	10	2000
Panel 3					
1	100	−200	10	4	−800
2	200	−100	5	−1	100
3	300	0	0	−6	0
4	400	100	5	−1	−100
5	500	200	10	4	800

Figure 7.16

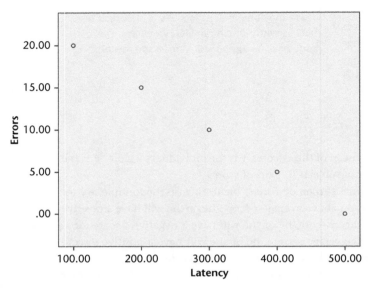

Figure 7.17

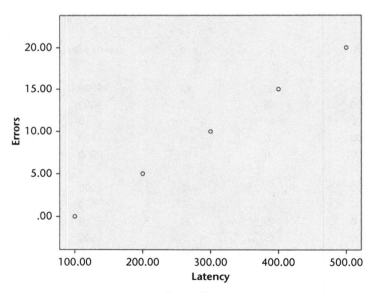

Figure 7.18

statistical significance for the moment, when we sum those products across all subjects, if the total is positive, it indicates a positive association. If the preponderance of the values of the products of the d-scores is negative, it indicates a negative association. If the sum of the products of the d-scores is 0 (the probability of this happening with real data is itself close to 0) then the y-scores are random with respect to the x-scores. The question we must answer is whether or not cov_{xy} is far enough from 0 for us to conclude that there is evidence of an association, or whether it should be considered chance covariance and due simply to sampling error. (To review sampling error, see Chapters 5 and 6.)

Figure 7.16 illustrates the three types of outcomes using three fictitious small data sets of five subjects each. Subjects were instructed to answer 100 simple addition items as quickly as possible. The x-variable represents a subject's average response latency in milliseconds (ms) on the test. The y-variable represents the number of errors the subject committed. In Panel 1 the sum of the products of the d-scores across the five subjects is –5000 ($cov =$ –1250), indicating a negative association between response latency and the number of errors. In other words, there is a trend that the more time a subject takes on average to respond, the fewer errors he or she commits. In Panel 2 the sum of the products of the d-scores is +5000 ($cov = 1250$), indicating a positive association between response latency and the number of errors. In this case there is a trend that the more time a subject takes on average to respond, the more errors he or she commits. In Panel 3 the sum of the products of the d-scores is 0 ($cov = 0$), indicating that there is no association between response latency and the number of errors committed. Response latency and error rates appear to be completely random with respect to each other.

It is instructive to examine the scatterplots from the data in the three panels of Figure 7.16. Figure 7.17 is a scatterplot depicting the data from Panel 1. It illustrates a negative linear trend. Figure 7.18 is a scatterplot of the data from Panel 2, and a positive linear trend is evident. The scatterplot in Figure 7.19 is a different story. The *cov* associated with the data in Panel 3 was found to be 0. It would be easy to conclude that there was no association between latency and error rates. Figure 7.19 illustrates the necessity of examining scatterplots, however. Although there is

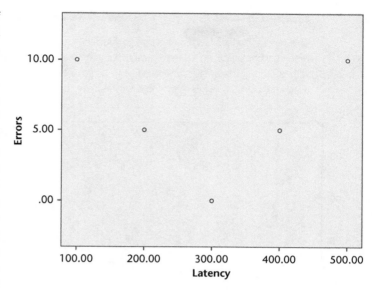

Figure 7.19

no *linear* trend to be discerned, there is a clear relation that can be described. As latency increases, error rates begin to fall. But as latency continues to increase beyond 300 ms, error rates then begin to increase. Such an association is referred to as *quadratic* in nature. Such associations are not unheard of in psychology and other disciplines. The Yerkes–Dodson law (Yerkes & Dodson, 1908), which describes the relation between arousal and performance, is a classic example of a quadratic function. Remember, in this chapter we are concerned primarily with linear associations. Having said this, it is important to recognize that other associations are possible.

Sub	x	x–d	y	y–d	(x–d)(y–d)
Panel 1					
1	1	–4	5	–8	32
2	3	–2	13	0	0
3	5	0	9	–4	0
4	7	2	17	4	8
5	9	4	21	8	32
Panel 2					
1	1	–4	300	–480	–1920
2	3	–2	780	0	0
3	5	0	540	–240	0
4	7	2	1020	240	480
5	9	4	1260	–480	1920

Figure 7.20 Covariance and issues of scale

The Yerkes–Dodson law dictates that performance on many psychological and behavioural tasks increases with physiological or mental arousal, but only up to a certain point. When levels of arousal become too high, performance then decreases. Research has shown that different tasks require different levels of arousal for optimal performance to be reached.

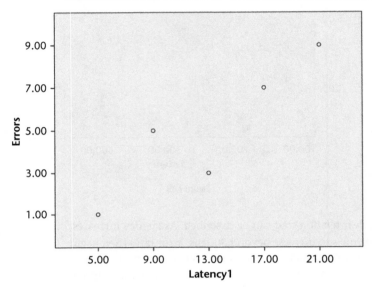

Figure 7.21

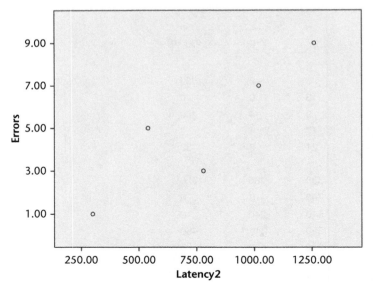

Figure 7.22

As stated above, covariance is an *unstandardized* statistic that reflects the degree to which two variables change together, or covary. Its value can range from 0 to infinity and its sign can be either negative or positive. To say that it is unstandardized is to say that it is the product of the units in which the two variables were measured. In the example of panels, these were milliseconds and number of errors.

Figure 7.19 illustrates how covariance is sensitive to the units of measurement and how the size of covariance is largely irrelevant and can be misleading. If we calculate *cov* from the data in Panel 1 of Figure 7.20 we find that

$$cov = \frac{32 + 0 + 0 + 8 + 32}{5 - 1} = 72.$$

If we calculate *cov* from the data in Panel 2 of Figure 7.20 we find that

$$cov = \frac{1920 + 0 + 0 + 480 + 1920}{5 - 1}$$

$$= 4320.$$

From the two covariances alone, we might be inclined to conclude that there is a stronger association in Panel 2 than there is in Panel 1. Examination of the two scatterplots produced from the two panels, however, reveals otherwise. Figures 7.21 and 7.22 reveal that it is only in terms of the units of measurements on the *x*-axis that the two scatterplots differ. The association between *errors* and *latency* depicted in the two scatterplots is identical. In the first panel *latency* was recorded in seconds; in the second panel *latency* was recorded in milliseconds. Just as we used indices such as ϕ, Cramér's V, and Γ, to standardize the association between two categorical variables, we need an index for standardizing the association between two measurement variables.

THE PEARSON PRODUCT MOMENT CORRELATION COEFFICIENT

In this section we will examine:

1   the Pearson product moment correlation coefficient or r,
2   how r is related to z-scores,
3   how r can be transformed into an index of the reduction of error in prediction,
4   how to test the significance of r, and
5   nonparametric alternatives to r.

Where ϕ and Γ are standardized measures of the association between two categorical (nominal and ordinal) variables, the *Pearson product moment correlation coefficient* (r) (often simply referred to as the *correlation*) is the most common index of a linear association between two measurement variables.

> The word 'correlation' comes from two words in Latin, *cor (com)* meaning 'together' and *relatio* which means relation.

Like the other measures of association we have discussed, r can take any value between 0 and 1. And like the ordinal Γ, r can be either negative or positive. One way to begin to understand r is to define it as the covariance of the two variables standardized on the product of the standard deviations of the two variables:

$$r = \frac{cov_{xy}}{s_x s_y}.$$

From the formula for r, it can be seen that as the covariance of the two variables approaches the product of their standard deviations, r approaches 1. As the covariance of the two variables approaches 0, r approaches 0. Stated another way, r is the ratio between the amount of observed covariation between two variables and the amount of covariation that would be observed if the two variables were perfectly associated with one another. 'Perfectly associated' means that if you knew the value of one variable, you would be able to predict the value of the other variable without any error. When two variables are perfectly associated the product of the standard deviations is the maximum possible covariance that can be observed between those two variables. Thus, r can be written as

$$r = \frac{\text{amount of observed covariance}}{\text{maximum possible covariance}}.$$

There is even an easier way to grasp the nature of r. Recall from Chapter 3 the discussion of a linear transformation and z-scores. Linear transformations, such as z-scores, are merely a change in the units in which scores are expressed, as in the above example involving seconds and milliseconds. In the case of z-scores the unit of measurement is the standard deviation of the variable; a z-score represents the number of standard deviations a raw score is above or below the variable's mean. That is, the difference between each score and the mean is standardized on the variable's standard deviation. (For a discussion of linear transformation and z-scores see p. 109 in Chapter 3.)

If we again examine the formula for *r*, we see that *r* is actually the average product of the z-scores for *x* and the z-scores for *y*:

$$r = \frac{cov_{xy}}{s_x s_y} = \frac{\dfrac{\Sigma(x-\bar{x})(y-\bar{y})}{n-1}}{\sqrt{\dfrac{\Sigma(x-\bar{x})^2}{n-1}}\sqrt{\dfrac{\Sigma(y-\bar{y})^2}{n-1}}} = \frac{\Sigma z_x z_y}{n-1}.$$

When formulated in this manner, it is easier to think of 0 as the expected product of the z-scores, if there is no association between the two variables. The total of the negative products is perfectly counterbalanced by the total of the positive products. Of course, when dealing with samples, the probability of the average product of the z-scores being 0 is close to 0. The question is: how much greater than 0 must *r* (the average product of the z-scores) be before we conclude that there is enough evidence to assume an association between the two variables?

If you were ambitious enough and calculated the correlation for *quizmark* and *hoursworked* in your SPSS data file (*workandquizmark.sav*), you would have found *r* = −0.544. The negative sign indicates that as the number of hours worked per week increases, scores on the quiz tend to decrease. As with other indices of association, we assign qualitative meanings to the quantitative value. Correlations between 0 and 0.10 are said to indicate no association. Correlations between 0.10 and 0.30 are said to indicate a weak association. Correlations between 0.30 and 0.50 are said to indicate a moderate association. Correlations of 0.60 or above are said to indicate a strong association. The particular ranges must be taken loosely.

It is interesting to note that the correlation between *quizmark* and *hoursworked* (*r* = −0.544) falls between the values we obtained earlier when we transformed the measurement data in categorical variables (*quizcat* and *hourcat*): Kendall's tau-b = −0.401 and Γ = −0.708.

If you calculate the correlation using the z-scores for the two variables (*Zquizmark* and *Zhoursworked*), not surprisingly, you will find that *r* = −0.544. In fact, if you use the z-scores to calculate *r*, you will find that *cov* = −0.544. Again, looking at the formula for *r*, we see that the denominator must be 1 when z-scores are analysed, and thus *cov* (the numerator) will equal *r*:

$$r = \frac{\dfrac{\Sigma(x-\bar{x})(y-\bar{y})}{n-1}}{\sqrt{\dfrac{\Sigma(x-\bar{x})^2}{n-1}}\sqrt{\dfrac{\Sigma(y-\bar{y})^2}{n-1}}} = \frac{cov_{xy}}{s_x s_y} = \frac{cov_{xy}}{1} - cov_{xy}.$$

Remember that when any set of scores is transformed into z-scores they will have a μ of 0, an *S* of 1.0, and an S^2 of 1.

Testing *r* for significance

At this point it might be reasonable to inquire about testing the reliability or significance of *r*. In Chapter 6 you first tested the assumption of independence with x^2, Yates's *continuity correction*, or the *likelihood ratio* and then calculated and reported the indices of association. Here we have calculated the index of association (*r*) but have not yet tested its reliability or significance. A *t*-test is more than a test for a *difference* between two means. It can be reconceptualized as a test of the amount of reduction in the error related to a prediction.

In Chapter 5, the null hypothesis (H_0) revolved around the question of the observations being random with respect to the two conditions. We now rephrase our current H_0 as a question of the values on the *y*-axis (*quizmark*) being random, with respect to the *x*-axis (*hoursworked*). To the extent that the values are not random you are able to reduce the errors in any prediction.

To test *r* for significance, we calculate *t* as

$$t = \frac{r\sqrt{n-2}}{\sqrt{1-r^2}},$$

where *r* is the correlation and *n* is the number of subjects. For the quiz marks and hours worked data,

$$t = \frac{-0.544\sqrt{40-2}}{\sqrt{1-(-0.544)^2}} = \frac{3.3534}{0.8608} = 3.896.$$

This *t*-value is tested with $n-2$ degrees of freedom ($df = 38$). One *df* is lost for each sample mean used to estimate a variance. There was a mean and variance for both the *x* (*quizmark*) and the *y* (*hoursworked*) scores. Using the table in Appendix D, you will not find an entry for $df = 38$, so the closest smaller entry is used (i.e., $df = 30$). You will find that your observed *t*-value (3.896) is much greater than the critical value at $\alpha = 0.05$ (2.024). You can conclude that there is sufficient evidence to reject the assumption of independence (H_0) and that there is support for your hypothesis (H_1) of an association between quiz marks and the number of hours worked during the week.

Remember, the level of the *p*-value is not an index of the importance of your findings or the size of the effect. The *p*-value is only used for deciding whether or not to reject H_0, which indirectly is about the likelihood of replicating your findings. Also remember that some researchers will not be interested in the outcome of the *t*-test and the resulting *p*-value. Rather, they will be interested in the estimate of the effect size. In correlational analyses, r^2 is one estimate of the effect size.

━━━━━━━━━━ REVIEW QUESTION ━━━━━━━━━━

What would your *t*-value be if there were only 10 subjects in your study? What would you conclude? How do you explain any change?

Web Link 7.6 for a discussion of and answer to the review question.

To calculate correlation coefficients in SPSS, from the *Analyze* option on the *Data Editor* menu bar scroll down and select *Correlate* and slide over to and click *Bivariate*.

• • • • •

The prefix *bi* comes from the Latin and is derived from the Greek *di* and means two, in our case two variables. Common words with these prefixes are *bi*cycle and carbon *di*oxide (CO_2). Our descriptive statistics, such as means, variance, and skewness, are univariate. The prefix *un(i)* again comes from the Latin and Greek and means *one* or *made one*. Common words with this prefix are *uni*corn and *un*animous.

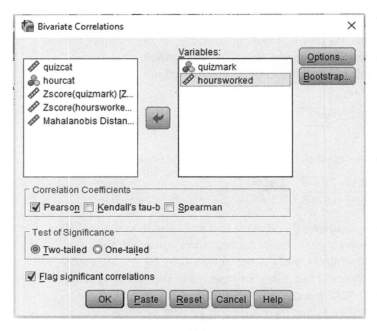

Figure 7.23

When you do so the **Bivariate Correlations** window will open. When it does, select and move **quizmark** and **hoursworked** over to the **Variables** area (Figure 7.23) and then click **OK**. In the SPSS output window a **Correlations** table appears (Figure 7.24).

quizmark correlated with itself and *hoursworked* correlated with itself are both 1. This is necessarily the case because any variable will perfectly predict itself. For example, it is hardly a surprise that you can perfectly predict the *quizmark* of one of your students from his or her *quizmark*. The correlation between *quizmark* and *hoursworked* is –0.544. The table also reports N, the number of subjects, and the estimated probability or *p*-value of *r*, *Sig. (2-tailed)*. The value reported of the significance is 0.000. This does not mean that there is no chance at all of the two variables being independent. When SPSS calculates a probability to be less than 0.001 it reports it as 0.000.

Because the *p*-value is less than 0.05, you can reject H_0 and conclude that there is sufficient evidence of at least a moderate association between your students' quiz marks and the number of hours they worked during the week. Squaring *r*, you can report that 29.6% of the variance in the quiz marks is associated with the number of hours worked.

REVIEW QUESTION

Why are the correlations between *quizmark* and *Zquizmark* and between *hoursworked* and *Zhoursworked* 1? What are the correlations between *quizmark* and *Zhoursworked* and between *Zquizmark* and between *hoursworked*? Why?

Web Link 7.7 for a discussion of and answer to the review question.

Correlations

		quizmark	hoursworked
quizmark	Pearson Correlation	1	-.544[**]
	Sig. (2-tailed)		.000
	N	40	40
hoursworked	Pearson Correlation	-.544[**]	1
	Sig. (2-tailed)	.000	
	N	40	40

**. Correlation is significant at the 0.01 level (2-tailed).

Figure 7.24

Adjusted r

Once you have concluded that there is an association between quiz marks and the number of hours students worked during the week, there remains one step for you to take concerning r. Although r should be reported in any publication of your findings, it is not an unbiased estimate of the population correlation (i.e., all of the students who have taken or will take your course), as a sample statistic r tends to overestimate the association that exists in the population. For a discussion of sample statistics versus population parameters, see p. 46, in Chapter 2, and for a discussion of unbiased estimators see p. 69 in Chapter 2.

To correct for the bias, an adjusted r (r_{adj}) should be reported. The adjustment is easy to make:

$$r_{adj} = \sqrt{1 - \frac{(1-r^2)(n-1)}{n-k-1}} ,$$

where r^2 is the square of the correlation coefficient, n is the number of subjects, and k is the number of predictor variables (one variable is often referred to as the outcome or criterion variable and the other is referred to as the predictor), which is always 1 in case of simple regression.

The greater the number of subjects, the smaller the correction. r_{adj} is deemed to be the best estimate of the association between two variables. When r_{adj} is calculated for your results you find

$$r_{adj} = \sqrt{1 - \frac{(1-0.296)(40-1)}{40-1-1}} = -0.526.$$

Because your sample size is not small there is only a small adjustment to your correlation.

Bootstrapping *r*

The bootstrapping option introduced in other chapters is also available for correlation coefficients. (See the discussion of bootstrapping in Chapters 4 and 5.)

Bootstrapping can be selected from the *Bivariate Correlations* window. If you do so, you will find that the correlation coefficients and their probabilities are unchanged (Figure 7.25). One advantage of the bootstrapping analysis is that 95% confidence intervals are reported for correlations. In the case of the correlation between *quizmark* and *hoursworked* the lower limit is −0.263 and upper limit is −0.754. The fact that zero is outside of the 95% confidence interval reflects the fact that the correlation will be found to be significant, $\alpha = 0.05$.

Nonparametric correlation

Like other parametric statistics, *r* has a nonparametric version. Spearman's (1904a) ρ (rho), sometimes denoted by r_s, is the most common nonparametric alternative. Spearman's rho is based on

Correlations

				quizmark	hoursworked
quizmark	Pearson Correlation			1	-.544[**]
	Sig. (2-tailed)				.000
	N			40	40
	Bootstrap[c]	Bias		0	.009
		Std. Error		0	.127
		95% Confidence Interval	Lower	1	-.754
			Upper	1	-.263
hoursworked	Pearson Correlation			-.544[**]	1
	Sig. (2-tailed)			.000	
	N			40	40
	Bootstrap[c]	Bias		.009	0
		Std. Error		.127	0
		95% Confidence Interval	Lower	-.754	1
			Upper	-.263	1

[**]. Correlation is significant at the 0.01 level (2-tailed).

c. Unless otherwise noted, bootstrap results are based on 1000 bootstrap samples

Figure 7.25

converting the raw scores for each variable into their rank-ordered positions and then using these converted variables in the usual r formula. The formula is

> The transformation of measurement data into ordinal data was used in the nonparametric alternative to the t-test in Chapter 5.

$$r_S = \frac{cov(rg_x, rg_y)}{\sigma_{rgx}\sigma_{rgy}},$$

where $cov(rg_x, rg_y)$ is the covariance between the rank-ordered scores, and σ_{rgx} and σ_{rgy} are the standard deviations of the two rank-ordered variables.

If you return to the SPSS *Bivariate Correlations* window, you will see in the *Correlation Coefficients* field the *Spearman* option. If you select it (Figure 7.26) and rerun the correlations, you will find an additional *Correlations* table under the heading of *Nonparametric Correlations* (Figure 7.27).

Comparing the two correlations (Pearson's product moment and Spearman's rho), we see that the original correlations ($r = -0.544$)

> r^2 is also known as the *coefficient of determination*.

are all slightly augmented ($r_S = -0.556$). When outliers are removed and the assumptions for r have been met or corrected, the difference between r and ρ (rho) is usually minimal.

r^2 as the proportion of shared variance

An estimate of the strength of the association between two variables is provided by r. By squaring r you obtain an estimate of the proportion of the variance one of the variables shares with the other. Squaring the r for your quiz marks and hours worked data yields $r^2 = (-0.544)^2 = 0.296$. This proportion is often expressed in various ways. It may be said that the number of hours worked per week *accounts for, is shared with*, or *explains* 29.6% of the variance in your students' quiz marks. We will return to these expressions later in the chapter, but it must be kept in mind that our data were not experimental in nature and we must use great care when attempting to attribute causality or directionality.

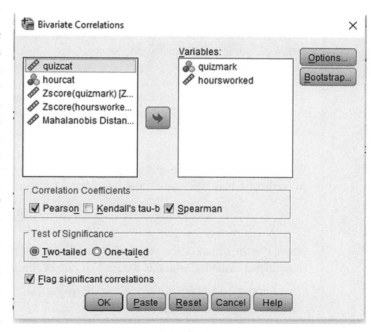

Figure 7.26

Nonparametric Correlations

[DataSet1] D:\statstext\NEWchapters\NewChapter8\chapter8spssfi.

Correlations

			quizmark	hoursworked
Spearman's rho	quizmark	Correlation Coefficient	1.000	-.556[**]
		Sig. (2-tailed)	.	.000
		N	40	40
	hoursworked	Correlation Coefficient	-.556[**]	1.000
		Sig. (2-tailed)	.000	.
		N	40	40

[**]. Correlation is significant at the 0.01 level (2-tailed).

Figure 7.27

• • • • •

Karl Pearson, who developed what we now call the correlation coefficient or r, warned against overinterpreting the associations revealed by r: correlation does not equal causation. Based on common sense (often nonsense) and for theoretical reasons, however, it is easy to slip from correlation to causation. Pearson himself was guilty of this sin when correlational data revealed that Jews and other groups (living in crowded ghettos in England) had higher rates of certain illnesses and thus should be prevented from immigrating into the country (Pearson, 1901a). On a less serious note, while my age over the last 50 years may be strongly correlated with real estate prices is London, New York, and Hong Kong, my ageing is not responsible for the increase in real estate prices. Nor, on the other hand, are the increases in real estate prices responsible for my ageing.

Recall from above that r is not an unbiased estimate of the population correlation and you needed to correct for bias. The same is the case for r^2. The adjustment again is easy to make:

$$r_{adj}^2 = 1 - \frac{(1-r^2)(n-1)}{n-k-1},$$

where r^2 is the square of the correlation coefficient, n is the number of subjects, and k is the number of predictor variables, which is always 1 in case of simple regression. For our data set,

$$r_{adj}^2 = 1 - \frac{(1-0.296)(40-1)}{40-1-1} = 0.277.$$

The r_{adj}^2 estimates that 27.7% of the variance in the quiz marks in your course is associated with hours worked, slightly less than the original estimate of 29.6%. Both the unadjusted and adjusted versions should be reported in any publication of your findings.

Effect size and power

In Chapter 6 where we were comparing the means of two conditions using a t-test we reported the effect size in terms of Cohen's d. In correlational analyses effect sizes are estimated by r^2. It is easy to convert r^2 to d, should that be desired. The following formula provides one simple conversion:

$$d = \frac{2r}{1-r^2}.$$

For your quiz marks and hours worked data,

$$d = \frac{2r}{1-r^2} = \frac{2(-0.544)}{1-0.296} = 1.545.$$

Note that neither form of reporting the effect size is insensitive to p-value. The p-value associated with a correlation is irrelevant for any purpose other than for making a decision concerning H_0.

The test for the significance of a correlation is best understood as a test for a particular effect size, rather than a test for the abstract presence or absence of an association between the two variables. The t-test for your $r = -0.544$ is a test for a moderate to large effect. Regarding correlations, according to Cohen (1992) you need a minimum of 85 subjects (Appendix B) to have the requisite power (0.80) to test for a medium effect ($\alpha = 0.05$). Because you have 40 students in your class, you are only able to test for a large effect, which requires 26 subjects. You are testing for the presence or total absence of an association. Using the tables in Appendix B, if you were interested in testing for a small effect ($r = 0.10$) you would need 783 students in your class. Ideally, you should predetermine the effect size that is important to you, either theoretically or practically, and then set your sample size accordingly. But often, as in this case of examining the possible association between quiz marks and hours worked, sample size is out of your control. In such cases, you are limited to testing a particular effect size. This must be kept in mind when drawing conclusions, particularly if the t-test is found to be non-significant. You need to be careful that you do not attempt to interpret Type II errors. Had your correlation been 0.30, your test of significance would have yielded a non-significant t-value (1.95) and you might have drawn the wrong conclusion, if H_0 was false.

 Web Link 7.8 for sample size and power version of the correlation (ball/line) demonstration.

7 ● 7 SIMPLE REGRESSION ANALYSIS

In this section we examine another statistic related to correlational analysis, the ordinary least squares (OLS) regression line and the regression coefficient or *slope* (B). OLS refers to the aim of producing a line that minimizes the sum of the squared deviations. Where r indicates the strength of the association between two variables, B is used to make predictions. The analysis is called a *simple* regression because there is only one predictor variable. For example, your data comprise one criterion variable (*quizmark*) and one predictor variable (*hoursworked*). *quizmark* is deemed the criterion and *hoursworked* the predictor because you suspect that the hours worked during the week influence the quiz mark, not the other way around.

> Keep in mind that in this chapter we are dealing only with straight lines when we speak of possible associations and predictions.

Imagine you wish to use your data to predict future quiz marks from knowing the number of hours students have worked. Or you may wish to warn your new students of a possible negative effect of working too many hours. From your correlational analysis you have already concluded there is a substantial negative association between quiz marks and the number of hours worked ($r = -0.544$, $r_{adj} = -0.526$) and you can account for 27.7% ($r^2 = 0.296$, $r^2_{adj} = 0.277$) of the variance in quiz marks. In discussions with your students you may wish to express this association in concrete or everyday terms. For example, what is the predicted change in quiz marks that accompanies each additional hour of work outside of the university?

The straight line

Let us begin with a review of the definition of a straight line. In addition to the x-axis values and the y-axis values, the equation for a straight line contains a slope (B) and a y-intercept (a):

$$y = Bx + a,$$

where y is the y-axis value that is paired with an x-axis value (x), B is the slope of the line, and a is the point on the y-axis intercepted by the line. When we examine Figure 7.28 it is easy to determine the slope and y-intercept. The slope, or B, is the amount of change in the y-value for each unit increase in the x-value:

$$B = \frac{\Delta y}{\Delta x} = \frac{y_2 - y_1}{x_2 - x_1},$$

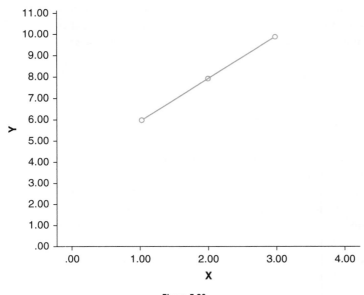

where Δ or 'delta' signifies 'the change in'.

Examining the simple example in Figure 7.28, we see that for a single-unit increase in the x-value there is a change of two units in the y-value (e.g., a change in the x-value from 1 to 2 is related to a change in the y-value from 6 to 8). Therefore, $B = 2$. The y-intercept, or a, is the y-value that corresponds to an x-value of 0. If we imagine an extension of the line in Figure 7.27 we find it intercepts the y-axis at $y = 4$. The definition of our line is $y = 2x + 4$. Thus, if someone has an x-value of 1.5, using B and a, we predict a y-value of $y = 2(1.5) + 4$, or 7. It is always important to return to the figure to confirm that such a prediction visually makes sense, which it does in this case.

Figure 7.28

When all of the points fall on a straight line and the association is perfect, there is no error at all when predicting the y-values from the x-values. In psychology, biology, education, and the social sciences rarely, if ever, are associations perfect. Associations in these disciplines are less than perfect and are seldom stronger than that depicted by your scatterplot of *quizmark* and *hoursworked* ($r = -0.544$). Under these circumstances we need a line that portrays or 'best fits' the data points in the scatterplot. (For the quizmark–hoursworked scatterplot see p. 276 in this chapter.)

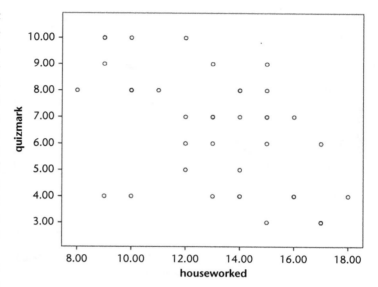

Figure 7.29

It is evident from Figure 7.29 that the slope of the line (B) that best captures the general trend in your *quizmark–hoursworked* data will be negative in nature. The higher values of *quizmark* tend to cluster at the lower values of *hoursworked*, whereas the lower values of *quizmark* tend to cluster at the higher values of *hoursworked*. Furthermore, it appears that the y-intercept will be near 9. An approximation of such a line is found in Figure 7.30. Contrarily, the line depicted in Figure 7.31 certainly would not be the best linear summary of your data. Although a few points are very close to the line in Figure 7.31, most of the points are quite remote. The line actually appears to run counter to the general trend in your data. The obvious question is: what makes one line a better 'fit' than another?

The ordinary least squares regression line

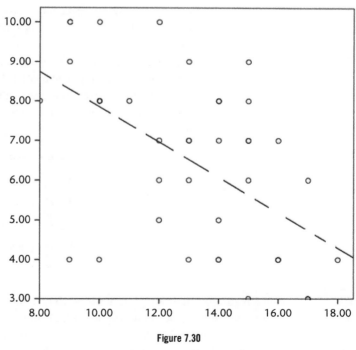

Figure 7.30

What determines which line will best capture the general trend in your *quizmark–hoursworked* data and allow you to make reasonable predictions about future performance on your quizzes with the minimum of error possible? First,

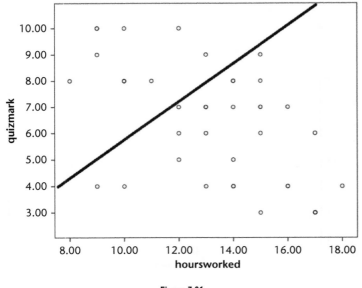

Figure 7.31

Y	X
2	1
3	2
4	3
4	4
5	5
7	6

Figure 7.32

we describe the ordinary least squares (OLS) regression line and then its relation to sample mean will be described. Next, we illustrate how the OLS line can be used for making predictions and how to estimate the error that will be inherent to those predictions. Then we divulge the surprising relationship between the slope of the OLS regression line (B) and r. We end the section with a discussion of how B is tested for statistical significance.

Before we return to your *quizmark–hoursworked* data, let us examine a simple example with six subjects whose data are found in Figure 7.32. Each subject has an x-score and a y-score. For example, the first subject has an x-score of 2 and a y-score of 1, and the sixth subject has an x-score of 7 and a y-score of 6.

The scatterplot of the data for those six subjects (Figure 7.33) reveals that the points do not fall on a perfectly straight line. When this is the case the definition of the line (B and a) will differ for the various pairs of adjacent point. For example, the slope that defines the relation between the y-values associated with $x = 2$ and $x = 3$ is 1, but the slope that defines the relation between the y-values associated with $x = 3$ and $x = 4$ is 0. Another way to express this problem is that there are no values for B and a that will simultaneously satisfy the following six linear equations that describe the data:

$$2 = B \times 1 + a,$$

$$3 = B \times 2 + a,$$

$$4 = B \times 3 + a,$$

$$4 = B \times 4 + a,$$

$$5 = B \times 5 + a,$$

$$7 = B \times 6 + a.$$

The OLS regression line can be understood to be a moving mean. Recall from Chapter 2 that the mean of a variable is the value or point which minimizes the sum of the squared deviations of the *scores* about that *value*. Any value other than the mean will result in an increase in the sum of the squared deviations. The OLS regression line is the 'moving mean' (line) which minimizes the squared deviations (*least squares*) of the *points* in the scatterplot. Any other line will result in a greater sum of the squared deviations. The formula for such a line can be written as

$$\hat{y} = Bx + a,$$

in which $\hat{y}$ represents predicted values of y rather than the actual values.

There is a simple way to derive the slope of the OLS regression line (B) by using *cov*:

$$B = \frac{\frac{\sum(x - \bar{x})(y - \bar{y})}{n - 1}}{\frac{\sum(x - \bar{x})^2}{n - 1}}$$

where we recognize that the numerator is the covariance between x and y and the denominator is the variance in x. Thus,

$$B = \frac{cov_{xy}}{S_x^2}.$$

For the data from the six subjects,

$$B = \frac{3.10}{3.5} = 0.89.$$

The y-intercept (a) also is obtained easily:

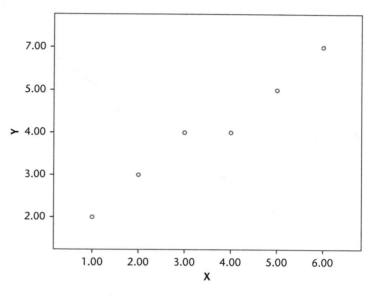

Figure 7.33

For those interested, web Link 7.9 describes how the best-fitting line can be derived by obtaining first and second normal equations and solving them simultaneously. The procedure can be long and torturous, even with a data set of only 20 subjects. Fortunately, we have an algebraically equivalent procedure that is simpler and is based on the covariance.

$$a = \bar{y} - B\bar{x}.$$

Again, with our example of six subjects

$$a = 4.17 - 0.89 \times 3.5 = 1.05.$$

If B is positive, a will be below $\bar{y}.$; if B is negative, a will be above $\bar{y}.$.

For our simple example of six subjects, the OLS regression line is depicted in Figure 7.34 as

$$\hat{y} = 0.89x + 1.05.$$

Looking back at the scatterplot of the data from the six subjects, a slope close to 1.0 and a y-intercept near 1.0 appear to be reasonable values.

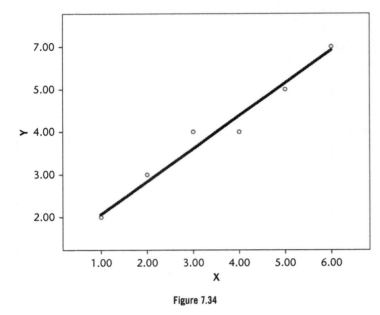

Figure 7.34

If you wish to warn your students about working during the week and its effect on quiz marks, you certainly will wish to ensure that the effect is reliable, or statistically significant at $\alpha = 0.05$. At this point you may note that the correlation has already been tested and found to be significant. And you would be correct if you thought that testing *B* is redundant once *r* has been tested. This follows from the fact that when the scores are standardized, *B* and *r* are revealed to be the same thing – the slope is also the strength of the association. Examining the *t*-test for *B*, however, may offer additional insights into the nature of *cov*, *r*, and *B*.

The null hypothesis for the test of the reliability of *B* is based on the expectation that $B = 0$, that there is no slope. When H_0 is true, $B = 0$ and $\hat{y} = Bx + a$, is reduced to $\hat{y} = a$. Furthermore, because $a = \bar{y} - B\bar{x}$ and $B = 0$, *a* is reduced to $a = \bar{y}$. This implies that the 'moving mean' does not move, but is a constant across all levels of the *x*-variable. If we return to the SPSS data set used in Chapter 5 (*independentsamplesttest.sav*) and rerun the *t*-test and then run a linear regression analysis using *score* as the criterion and *condition* as the predictor, interesting results emerge. (For a review of running the independent-samples *t*-test in SPSS, see p. 177 in Chapter 5.)

To perform a regression analysis in SPSS and calculate *B* and *a*, return to SPSS. From the *Analyze* option on the *Data Editor* menu bar scroll down and select *Regression* and slide over to and click *Linear*. When you do so the *Linear Regression* window (Figure 7.35) will open. When it does, select and move *score* to the *Dependent* area and move *condition* to the *Independent(s)* zone. Then click *OK*.

Examining the *Independent Samples Test* table (Figure 7.36) and the *Coefficients* table (Figure 7.37), we find that:

1 The *t*-values are identical (1.652).
2 The mean difference in the *Independent Samples Test* table and the *B* in the *Coefficients* table are identical, except for the sign (1.038).
3 The standard error terms are identical to three decimal places (0.629).
4 The significance *p*-values (*Sig. 2-tailed* and *Sig.*) are identical (0.105).

From this we find that your *t*-test for a difference between two means in Chapter 5 can be reconceptualized as a test of *B* with *score* regressed on *condition*. Conversely, we can understand your test

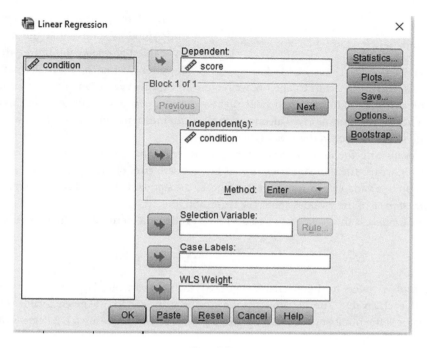

Figure 7.35

Independent Samples Test

		Levene's Test for Equality of Variances		t-test for Equality of Means						95% Confidence Interval of the Difference	
		F	Sig.	t	df	Sig. (2-tailed)	Mean Difference	Std. Error Difference		Lower	Upper
score	Equal variances assumed	.014	.906	-1.652	50	.105	-1.03846	.62875		-2.30134	.22442
	Equal variances not assumed			-1.652	49.981	.105	-1.03846	.62875		-2.30135	.22443

Figure 7.36

Coefficients^a

Model		Unstandardized Coefficients		Standardized Coefficients	t	Sig.	Correlations		
		B	Std. Error	Beta			Zero-order	Partial	Part
1	(Constant)	4.962	.994		4.991	.000			
	condition	1.038	.629	.227	1.652	.105	.227	.227	.227

a. Dependent Variable: score

Figure 7.37

of *B* when *quizmark* is regressed on *hoursworked* as a test for any difference in the means in *quizmark* that accompany changes in *hoursworked*, with the proviso that that change would need to be linear in nature.

Again we see how questions and tests of association can be reframed in terms of questions and tests of differences, and vice versa.

The H_0 of the regression therefore can be understood as stating that the mean of the y-variable (*quizmark*) minimizes the squared deviations better than any alternative regression line. As with any *t*-test in Chapter 5, we require an expected value, an observed value, and the amount of variability in the observed value that we would expect due to chance alone. In Chapter 5 the difference between the *observed* mean and the *expected* mean in a one-sample *t*-test was evaluated against the standard error in the mean (see p. 180).

When evaluating the difference between the *observed* slope (*B*) of the regression line and the *expected B* (0), we use the standard error of *B*. As the standard error of the mean is based on the standard deviation of a variable's scores about their mean, the standard error of *B* is based on the *standard error of the estimate* of the y-values about the regression line.

Residual variance is the *average* squared deviation of the data points about that moving mean (*B*):

$$S_{y.x}^2 = \frac{\sum(y-\hat{y})^2}{n-2}.$$

The subscript *y.x* refers to the *y*-variable regressed on the *x*-variable. The *y* represents the *y*-value paired with each *x*-value, The $\hat{y}$ represents the *expected* value of *y* for the given *x*-value. The *n* in the denominator is the number of subjects or pairs of observations. There are *n* – 2 degrees of freedom,

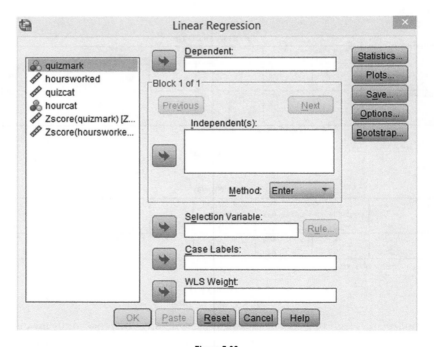

Figure 7.38

rather than $n - 1$, because there are two means ($\bar{x}$ and $\bar{y}$.) involved in estimating the predicted value of y or $\hat{y}$.

The *standard error of the estimate* is the square root of the residual variance:

$$S_{y.x} = \sqrt{\frac{\sum(y - \hat{y})^2}{n - 2}}.$$

The standard error of B is then

$$S_B = \frac{S_{y.x}}{S_x\sqrt{n-1}}.$$

The *t*-test then for evaluating B is

$$t = \frac{B - 0}{S_B},$$

where B is the observed slope and S_B is the standard error of B.

Let us now return to your *quizmark* and *hoursworked* data and regress *quizmark* on *hoursworked* using SPSS.

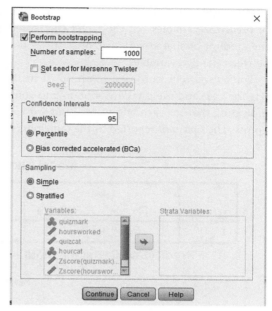

Figure 7.39

To perform a regression analysis in SPSS and calculate B and a, return to SPSS and the **workandquizmark.sav** file. From the *Analyze* option on the *Data Editor* menu bar scroll down and select *Regression* and slide over to and click *Linear*. The *Linear Regression* window (Figure 7.38) will open. When it does, select and move *quizmark* to the *Dependent* area and move *hoursworked* to the *Independent(s)* area. Click the *Bootstrap* button, select *Perform bootstrapping* when the *Bootstrap* window opens (Figure 7.39), and then click *Continue*. Then click *OK*.

> As we will find in Chapter 12, there can be more than one independent/predictor variable. R in the *Model Summary* table is the correlation between the criterion (dependent) variable and all predictors. At this point we have only one.

The first entries to appear in the output window are the *Bootstrap Specifications* table and the *Variables Entered/Removed* table which shows that *hoursworked* is the predictor variable.

Next appears the *Model Summary* table (Figure 7.40). With only one predictor, R is identical to r; in your study $R = r = -0.544$. Again, because there is only one predictor in your study of *quizmark* and *hoursworked*, R *Square* is equivalent to $r^2 = 0.296$. The *Adjusted R Square* ((R^2_{adj} corrects for the number of predictors relative to the number of subjects and is computed using the following formula:

$$R^2_{adj} = 1 - \frac{(1 - R^2)(n - 1)}{n - k - 1},$$

where n is the number of subjects and k is the number of predictor variables.

The greater the number of subjects (n), the smaller the correction; the greater the number of predictor variables (k), the larger the correction. (R^2_{adj} is deemed to be the best estimate of the amount of shared variance, once it has been concluded that there is a reliable association between the two variables.

For our current purposes, jump down in the SPSS output window to the *Coefficients* table (Figure 7.41) and the row corresponding to your *hoursworked* variable. Here you see *B* (the slope), indicating that for each additional hour worked, the quiz mark is expected to decline by 0.445 points. The *Constant* reported in the table refers to the *y*-intercept or *a*.

Model Summary

Model	R	R Square	Adjusted R Square	Std. Error of the Estimate
1	.544[a]	.296	.277	1.88554

a. Predictors: (Constant), hoursworked

Figure 7.40

• • • • •

It can be tricky to interpret *y*-intercepts, because they often are impossible values. They can be impossible in the sense that the score they represent is impossible, given the nature of the variable being studied. In your case, the maximum quiz mark is 10, but the *y*-intercept (Constant) is 12.299. The *y*-intercept is indispensable for predicting future *y*-scores, however.

The standard error of *B* (*Std. Error*) reported in the table is 0.111. Recall that *t* is *B* divided by the standard error of *B*. The resulting *t*-value (in the *Coefficients* table) is –3.997, with a *p*-value (*Sig.*) less than 0.001. The *Standardized Coefficient* (–0.544) is the value of *B* if you had converted *quizmark* and *hoursworked* into *z*-scores prior to running the regression. Note that the value (–0.544) is the value of the correlation between *quizmark* and *hoursworked*, again illustrating the nature of the relationship between *B* and *r*.

If *r* and the *Standardized Coefficient (Beta)* are one and the same thing, you may ask, what is the need for the original or unstandardized *B*? Earlier in this section, you were interested in informing

Coefficients[a]

Model		Unstandardized Coefficients		Standardized Coefficients	t	Sig.
		B	Std. Error	Beta		
1	(Constant)	12.299	1.493		8.236	.000
	hoursworked	-.445	.111	-.544	-3.997	.000

a. Dependent Variable: quizmark

Figure 7.41

your students of the potential effect that working during the week would have on their quiz marks. You and your students would be able to understand the slope (*B*) in terms of their quiz marks if they worked for 17 hours this week,

$$\hat{y} - Bx + a = -0.445 \times 17 + 12.299 = 4.734.$$

You would predict the students' mark to be 4.734. Returning to the scatterplot of your data, you see that the prediction appears plausible and is in keeping with the trend of the data. But if you report the predicted quiz marks in terms of standard deviations (*Standardized Coefficient*), who would comprehend or be able to interpret the severity of the problem associated with working during the week?

● ● ● ● ●

It is important when predicting future *y*-variable values to distinguish between interpolation and extrapolation. Predicting *y*-values for *x*-values within the original range of scores on the *x*-axis is called *interpolation* and is considered safe. In terms of your data, *hoursworked* ranged from 8 to 18. Predicting outside of the original *x*-axis range is called *extrapolation*. The further the extrapolation goes outside of the original *x*-axis range, either above or below, the more likely it is that the original *B* and *a* may no longer provide the line of best fit. Thus there is a danger of seriously misleading results.

The final table in the SPSS output is labelled *Bootstrap for Coefficients* (Figure 7.42). There is little to no difference between the *B*, standard error, and significance found in the OLS regression and the bootstrapping versions. The *Bias* statistic found in the table represents the difference between the reported original *B* (–0.445) and the average value of *B* across all 1000 iterations of the analysis during the bootstrapping procedure. With a *B* of –0.445 and a bias of 0.004 there is very little bias in the statistic: 0.004 is a very small percentage of 0.445 (approximately 1%).

From what we have seen so far, you may *tentatively* rest comfortably when reporting your findings to your students and perhaps to the university's counselling centre. Note the word 'tentatively'.

As with other forms of parametric statistics we have discussed, there are nonparametric alternatives. Nonparametric regression does not assume that the criterion and predictor variables are associated in a linear or any other particular form. Instead, analogous to ordinal tests

Bootstrap for Coefficients

Model		B	Bootstrap[a]					
			Bias	Std. Error	Sig. (2-tailed)	95% Confidence Interval		
						Lower	Upper	
1	(Constant)	12.299	-.046	1.548	.001	9.045	15.097	
	hoursworked	-.445	.004	.113	.001	-.645	-.210	

a. Unless otherwise noted, bootstrap results are based on 1000 bootstrap samples

Figure 7.42

of association, nonparametric approaches are based on calculating different mean values for the criterion variable at different segments of the predictor variable. These different means can then be connected by lines, regardless of resulting shape. These analytic techniques are outside of the scope of this book. But for those who are interested, they are clearly developed in Fox (2000).

7●8 THE ASSUMPTIONS NECESSARY FOR VALID CORRELATION AND REGRESSION COEFFICIENTS

In this section we examine the assumptions that are necessary for r and B to be valid estimates of the strength and nature of the association between two measurement variables. Some of these assumptions have already been alluded to earlier in this chapter. Of course, r and B can always be computed regardless of any violation of these assumptions, but the resulting values may be extremely misleading. It is perhaps unfortunate that SPSS automatically does not test these assumptions and report the results. Therefore, it is incumbent upon the researcher to be vigilant in this respect. The ancient Latin expression *ignorantia legis neminen excusat* (ignorance of the law excuses no one) also holds for statistical assumptions. There are four general assumptions which need to be examined:

1 The normality of the distributions of both the *X*- and *Y*-variables.
2 Homoscedasticity.
3 Linearity of association.
4 Although it is not formally an assumption, the third-variable problem which was addressed in Chapter 6 (see p. 247) is also a potential source of concern in OLS regression with respect to the reliability and validity of *B* and *r*.

Normality

In previous chapters, particularly in Chapters 2 and 5, we addressed the assumption of normality and how it is easily examined using a histogram.

Although r and B enjoy relative immunity from low and moderate levels of skewness, r and B are susceptible to considerable distortions when distributions are significantly skewed. Kendall and Stuart (1958) showed that skewness levels of 2.0 and above cause serious attenuation problems. That is, the skewness tended to lead to severe underestimates of the associations.

Figures 7.43 and 7.44 show the histograms for your *quizmark* and *hoursworked* data, with a normal curve superimposed. Although neither distribution perfectly adheres to a normal distribution, with only 40 observations and a relatively wide range of values for both variables, a perfectly normal distribution is unexpected. In terms of your data, neither *quizmark* nor *hoursworked* appears so abnormal as to call into question the integrity of r and B. Acceptance of the assumption of normality

When the ratio of the number of observations to number of possible responses is small, it is not unusual to have gaps in the frequency distribution, as can be seen in Figure 7.43.

of your data is supported by the fact that little skewness was found in the two variables: –0.071 and –0.191.

Related to the issue of normality is the possible presence of outliers. Outliers need not create statistically significant skewness for them to have distorting effects on r and B, and it is incumbent upon the researcher to be vigilant with respect to *univariate* outliers. We also face the possible problem of *bivariate* outliers, where it is the combination of a subjects' x-score and y-score that creates the distorting effect.

For example, in Figure 7.45 it is only because of the subject with a score of 9 on the x-axis and a score of 10 on the y-axis that the data appear to be anything other than a random swarm lacking any trend. When that one data point is included the resulting correlation is 0.61. When it is removed the resulting correlation is attenuated to –0.10.

In Figure 7.46, if it were not for the one subject with a score of 10 on the x-axis and a score of 1 on the y-axis, the data would appear to reveal a strong positive trend. In fact, when that one data point is removed, the resulting correlation is 0.74. When it is included, the resulting correlation is attenuated to 0.46.

These two examples of bivariate outliers underscore the necessity of inspecting scatterplots prior to judging and reporting correlation coefficients. In addition to visually inspecting scatterplots, Mahalanobis (1936) developed a numerical index (distance) used for the identification of bivariate outliers – data points that have an excessive influence on B and r. Unlike the case with univariate outliers, when a bivariate outlier is identified our only course is to remove that subject from the data.

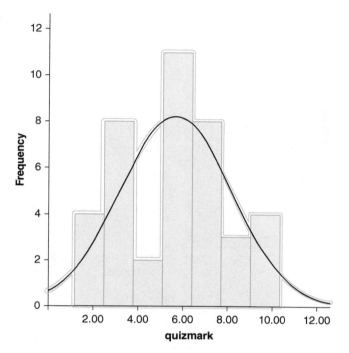

Figure 7.43

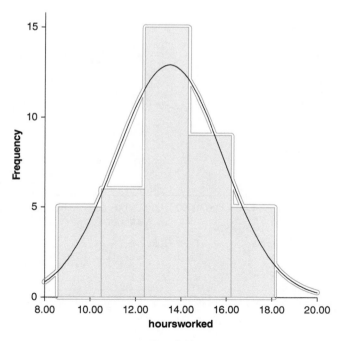

Figure 7.44

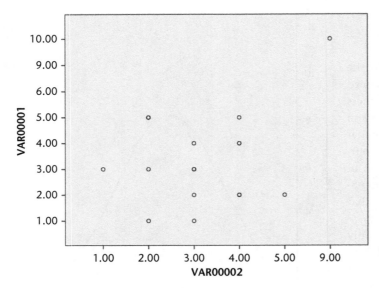

Figure 7.45

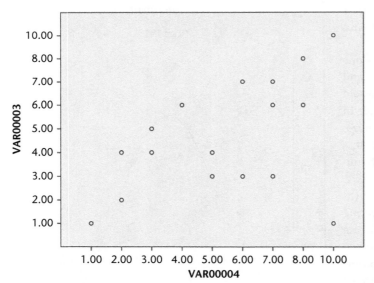

Figure 7.46

Mahalanobis values are often evaluated against a critical value at $\alpha = 0.001$. Most researchers will use a more conservative α of 0.01, as we will.

Mahalanobis distance is distributed as χ^2, and an observed value with a probability less than 0.01 typically is used to indicate that a subject is a *bivariate outlier* and should be removed, and the analysis rerun. The degrees of freedom for the test are the number of predictor variables, which in the current chapter is always 1. From the χ^2 table in Appendix C, with $df = 1$ we find that the critical value for $\alpha = 0.01$ is 6.635. That is, any subject with a Mahalanobis distance greater than 6.635 will need to be removed from the data set and the analysis rerun.

If you are following along in SPSS, return to your regression analysis (see Figure 7.47). This time click *Save* to open the *Linear Regression: Save* window (Figure 7.47) and choose the *Mahalanobis* option in the *Distances* box. Click *Continue* to return to the *Linear Regression* window and click *OK*.

In practice, prior to examining the results of your regression analysis you should examine your data for possible bivariate outliers. If you return to the SPSS *Data Editor* (Figure 7.49) you will find that a new variable (*MAH_1*) has been created. If you examine the column of χ^2 values (a sample from your data is presented here), you will find that none of your subjects exceeds the critical value of 6.63. There are no identifiable bivariate outliers found in your data.

Web Link 7.9 for an interactive demonstration exploring the effect of bivariate outliers on slopes and correlations.

For a detailed discussion of evaluating and addressing potential bivariate outliers, see Cook and Weisberg (1982) and Stevens (2002).

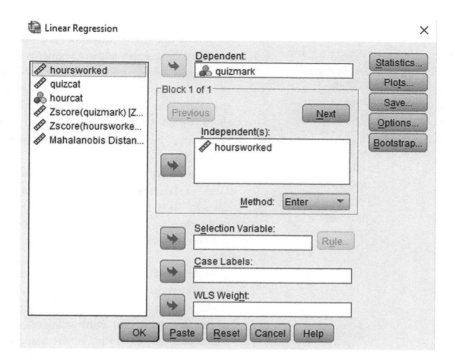

Figure 7.47

Homoscedasticity

In Chapter 5 we addressed the assumption of *homogeneity of variance* (see p. 184) and how violations affect the integrity of the *t*-test.

• • • • •

The term 'homoscedasticity' is Greek in origin, with *homo* meaning 'same' and *skedasis* meaning 'scatter'.

The assumption of homoscedasticity can be viewed as an extension of the assumption of homogeneity of variance – or the assumption of homogeneity of variance can be viewed as a simplification of the assumption of homoscedasticity. In the case of regression and correlation analysis, rather than having two means for the dependent variable, as was the case with the *t*-test in Chapter 5, there are now a large number or an infinite number of means. There is a different mean for the dependent/criterion variable (point on the regression line) for each possible value on the *x*-axis. We assume that the variance in the *y*-values is a constant along the regression line (homoscedastic) and is unrelated to the *x*-values.

Let us segment a regression line into three parts: the low *x*-values, the medium *x*-values, and the high *x*-values. Using this simple model, a violation of the assumption of homoscedasticity

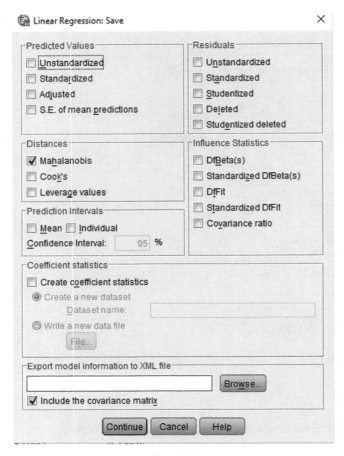

Figure 7.48

(heteroscedasticity) would be indicated by the variability about the regression line differing substantially across the three segments.

Figure 7.50 illustrates one common form of heteroscedasticity. There is little variance in the y-scores at the low values on the x-axis, there is more variance at the medium x-axis values, and there is great variance at the high x-axis values.

Figure 7.51 illustrates another common form of heteroscedasticity. There is little variance in the y-scores at both the low and high values on the x-axis, but there is considerably more variance at the medium x-axis values.

Heteroscedasticity produces two primary and related distortions. First, the correlation coefficient will underestimate the strength of the association for some segments of the x-axis and will overestimate the association at other segments. Remember, visually r is a function of how near the points in the scatterplot are to the regression line. Second, the amount of error (standard error of the estimate) related to predictions will be underestimated for some segments of the x-axis and will be overestimated at other segments. For

quizmark	hoursworked	quizcat	hourcat	Zquizmark	Zhoursworked	MAH_1
7.00	15.00	.00	1.00	.24795	.68185	.46492
3.00	17.00	.00	1.00	-1.55530	1.41898	2.01351
4.00	16.00	.00	1.00	-1.10449	1.05041	1.10337
8.00	15.00	1.00	1.00	.69876	.68185	.46492
10.00	12.00	1.00	.00	1.60038	-.42385	.17965
8.00	14.00	1.00	1.00	.69876	.31328	.09815
7.00	13.00	.00	.00	.24795	-.05528	.00306
9.00	13.00	1.00	.00	1.14957	-.05528	.00306
4.00	18.00	.00	1.00	-1.10449	1.78755	3.19532
4.00	13.00	.00	1.00	-1.10449	-.05528	.00306
7.00	14.00	.00	1.00	.24795	.31328	.09815
8.00	10.00	1.00	.00	.69876	-1.16098	1.34788

Figure 7.49

a detailed discussion of the detection and the effects of heteroscedasticity, see Kaufman (2013).

Linearity

As repeatedly stated, this chapter is concerned solely with linear associations: associations which are best captured and summarized by a straight line. There are other types of associations that may describe the relations between two variables and they have their related statistical procedures (Seber & Wild, 1989), but they are beyond the scope of this book. (For graphs of linear and quadratic scatterplots, see Figures 7.17–7.19.)

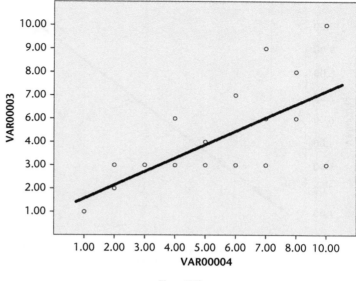

Figure 7.50

Figure 7.52 depicts a scatterplot where the trend clearly is best described by a straight line. One important characteristic of a linear association is that it is *monotonic*.

• • • • •

Like other technical terms used in statistics, the word is Greek and Latin in origin. *Monos* means 'single' or 'alone' and *tonic* comes from the verb *teinein* meaning 'to stretch' or 'to hold', as in holding a string at a given length which musically produces a single tone. Thus we derive the word *monotony*, which refers to hearing a single tone over and over again.

Statistically, *monotonicity* means that the shape of the regression line is one single stretch; it does not change direction either up or down, which would require a stoppage and a second stretch. Clearly the scatterplot in Figure 7.52 requires only a single stretch to capture its trend. In Figure 7.53 the single stretch (straight line) does not do a very good job of capturing the nature of the trend. The two stretches (lines) in Figure 7.54 do a much better job in depicting the nature of the association between those two variables.

Why is the assumption of linearity important for OLS regression? Using an OLS line to make predictions in Figure 7.52, at all levels of *x*-axis values we are nearly as likely to overestimate as we are to underestimate the observed values. If, however, we use a single OLS line to make prediction from the data in Figure 7.53, we are more likely to produce overestimates than we are to

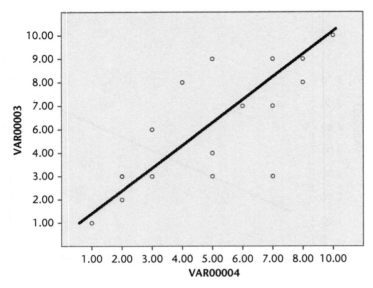

Figure 7.51

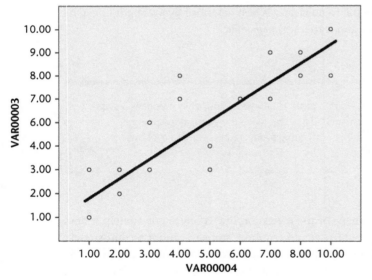

Figure 7.52

produce underestimates at low values on the x-axis, but we are more likely to produce underestimates at the intermediate x-axis values.

Rarely do data perfectly conform to the assumptions of homoscedasticity and linearity. Often scatterplots are a bit ambiguous as are your data concerning quiz marks and the number of hours worked (Figure 7.55). It is those two data points in the lower left-hand corner of the scatterplot that would be responsible for any possible violations.

When there are questions as to the extent of the effect of any violation, it is best for you to complete the analysis both with and without the dubious data points. When you reanalyse your data without those two subjects, you will find no substantial change in the general results or the conclusions you would draw. Both B and r have been somewhat augmented: B from -0.45 to -0.54 and r from -0.54 to -0.68. As n increases, the influence of one or two such errant data points quickly dissipates. For example, if you had 80 rather 40 students, and if the general trend remained the same and the two data points were again removed, the increase in B would only be from -0.45 to -0.50 and in r from -0.54 to -0.60. The influence of the two questionable points would be substantially reduced.

The third-variable problem

Although the third-variable problem is not formally an assumption, being able to identify a relevant third variable(s) and account for its effects is crucial. In Chapter 6 we discovered the third-variable problem to be a serious limitation which accompanies the test of independence. The third-variable problem is also a threat to the validity of *B* and *r*. Although called the third-variable problem, as you already know, there can be a fourth-, fifth-, sixth-, etc., variable problem.

Remember, I warned you that your results and conclusion concerning quiz marks and the number of hours worked are tentative, as are all research results. This caveat is particularly important to bear in mind when the research design is *observational* rather than *experimental* in nature. The third-variable problem highlights the importance for the researcher not only to know the most appropriate statistical test to employ, but also to be able to identify potential third-variable problems and how to eventually control for their effects. An in-depth discussion of controlling for the effects of third variables must wait until Chapter 12, however.

If you return to your SPSS data file (*workandquizmark.sav*) you will find in the *Data Editor* one final variable: *group*. Imagine that you now realize that students in your literature class belong to one of two groups. Members of group 1 are those students who are native English speakers. Members of group 2 are students whose native language is other than English. I have chosen native versus non-native speakers because it is a clear example of how the third variable can present serious problems for interpreting simple correlation and regression studies.

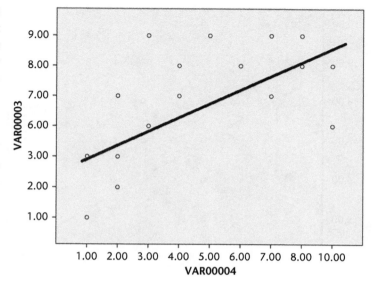

Figure 7.53

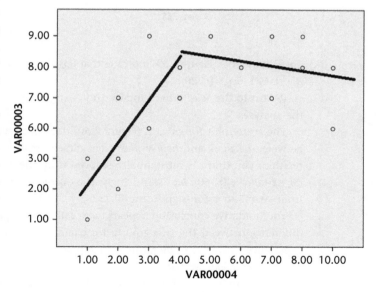

Figure 7.54

The question you now face is whether or not the group variable interferes in any way with your tentative conclusions concerning quiz marks and the number of hours worked. The simplest way to answer your question is to conduct the analyses on each group separately.

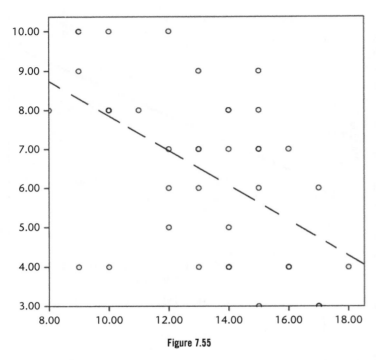

Figure 7.55

If you are following along in SPSS, proceed as follows. From within the SPSS *Data Editor* select *Data* from the menu and then slide down and click *Select Cases*. When the Select Cases window opens (Figure 7.56), select *If condition is satisfied* and click on the *If* button below it. When the *Select Cases: If* window opens (Figure 7.57) move the *group* variable over to the empty window, insert '= 1', and then click *Continue*. When you return to the *Select Cases* window, click *OK*. Rerun the scatterplot, the correlation, and the regression analysis.

The scatterplot for group 1 (Figure 7.58) does not reveal much of a trend or association between *quizmark* and *hoursworked*. After rerunning the correlation analysis, you find *r* is greatly reduced from the original –0.544 to –0.083 (*Sig. 2-tailed* = 0.720). Not surprisingly, the *Coefficients* table (Figure 7.59) indicates that *B* is also greatly reduced from –0.445 to a non-significant *B* = –0.071 (*Sig.* = 0.720).

Return to the *Select Case* window and change the '*group* = 1' selection to '*group* = 2' and rerun the analyses.

The scatterplot for *group* 2 (Figure 7.60) does not reveal much more of a trend or association between *quizmark* and *hoursworked* than did the scatterplot for *group* 1. After rerunning the correlation, you find *r* is substantially reduced from the original –0.544 to a non-significant –0.222 (*Sig. 2-tailed* = 0.360). Not surprisingly, the *Coefficients* table (Figure 7.61) reveals that *B* is reduced from –0.445 to a non-significant –0.252 (*Sig.* = 0.360).

Your tentative conclusion appears to be called into question. It now appears there may be some difference between the two groups; for example, facility with the English language or previous experience with English literature, which may play a vital role in the apparent association between *quizmark* and *hoursworked*.

Close examination of the *y*-axis and *x*-axis on the two individual scatterplots reveals more specifics about the possible source of the apparent strength of the association between *quizmark* and *hoursworked*. Group 1 has on average a higher quiz mark than group 2. Group 2 worked more hours than did group 1.

Two independent-sample *t*-tests help to clarify the picture. As can be seen from the *quizmark Group Statistics* table (Figure 7.62), the mean *quizmark* for group 1 (7.7619) was 2.762 marks higher than the mean for group 2 (5.000). The observed *t*-value of 4.997 (*df* = 38) has a *p*-value (*Sig. 2-tailed*) of less than 0.001.

Figure 7.56

As seen from the *hoursworked Group Statistics* table (Figure 7.63), the mean number of hours worked for group 1 (11.2381) is 4.025 hours fewer than the mean for group 2 (15.2632). The observed *t*-value of −7.088 (*df* = 38) has a *p*-value (*Sig. 2-tailed*) less than 0.001. The results of these two *t*-tests support the interpretation that it is an amalgamation of two heterogeneous groups that is responsible for what appeared at first to be an association between weekly quiz marks and the number of hours worked during the week.

Although this has been a fictitious study from beginning to end, it does illustrate the questions and the pitfalls common to simple OLS regression and correlational studies.

═══ CHALLENGE QUESTION ═══

Create a data set where taking a third variable into account can increase the strength of the correlation rather than attenuate it. Are there other outcomes that you can imagine?

🔍 Web Link 7.10 for an answer to the challenge question and a discussion.

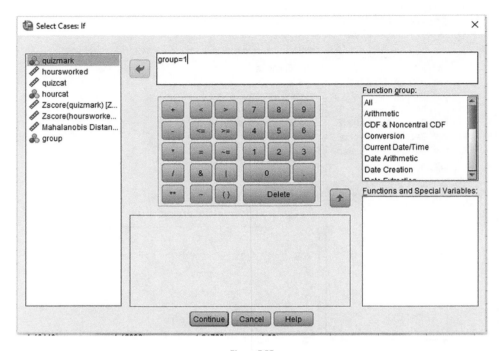

Figure 7.57

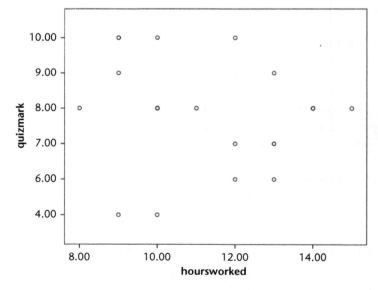

Figure 7.58

An excellent discussion of the above assumptions and other factors influencing r can be found in Goodwin and Leech (2006).

7 • 9 CHAPTER SUMMARY

The current chapter focused on testing for a possible *association* between two *measurement* variables. We saw that the question of *association* between two measurement variables is not far removed from the question of the association between two categorical variables, particularly those on an ordinal scale. The primary difference between categorical measures of association and measures of association

Coefficients[a]

Model		Unstandardized Coefficients		Standardized Coefficients	t	Sig.
		B	Std. Error	Beta		
1	(Constant)	8.560	2.230		3.838	.001
	hoursworked	-.071	.195	-.083	-.363	.720

a. Dependent Variable: quizmark

Figure 7.59

designed for measurement variables is that the latter are based on fitting a straight line. The foundational statistic for both correlation and the regression coefficients is *covariance*, an *unstandardized* statistic that describes the extent to which two variables change together, or covary. The correlation coefficient *r* provides a standardized estimate of the strength of the association between two measurement variables, while r^2 provides an estimate of the proportion of the variance that one variable shares with the other. Because neither *r* nor r^2 is unbiased, it is important to report their adjusted values. The regression coefficient (*B*), along with the *y*-intercept (*a*), allows the researcher to predict future values

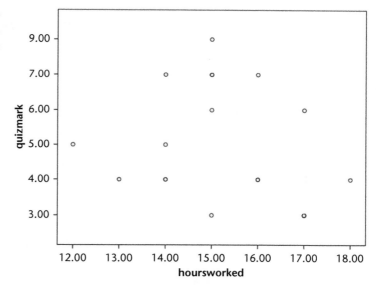

Figure 7.60

of one variable (the criterion) based on knowledge of the other variable (the predictor). There are important assumptions that require examination prior to considering *r* and *B* to be trustworthy estimates: normality, homoscedasticity, and linearity. As it is with respect to the test of independence, the third-variable problem is often a source of concern with respect to the validity of *B* and *r*.

Coefficients[a]

Model		Unstandardized Coefficients		Standardized Coefficients	t	Sig.
		B	Std. Error	Beta		
1	(Constant)	8.843	4.106		2.154	.046
	hoursworked	-.252	.268	-.222	-.941	.360

a. Dependent Variable: quizmark

Figure 7.61

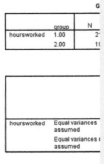

	group	N
quizmark	1.00	21
	2.00	19

quizmark	Equal variances assumed	
	Equal variances not assumed	

Figure 7.62 *quizmark t*-test

	group	N
hoursworked	1.00	2
	2.00	1

hoursworked	Equal variances assumed	
	Equal variances assumed	

Figure 7.63 *hoursworked t*-test

The problem highlights the importance of being familiar with the phenomenon being studied and with previous relevant research.

7 ● 10 RECOMMENDED READINGS

Cook, R. D., & Weisberg, S. (1982). *Residuals and influence in regression.* New York: Chapman & Hall.

This book provides a detailed discussion of numerous strategies and addresses potential bivariate outliers. It contains various approaches to computing the extent of an outlier and its statistical effect on the analysis.

Fox, J. (2000). *Nonparametric simple regression.* London: Sage.

This book, particularly the first few chapters, provides a clear and detailed description of a general nonparametric approach to regression analysis. The author also argues that this approach can, in most circumstances, replace the traditional parametric OLS analysis and offers enhanced fidelity to the actual nature of the association between the criterion and the predictor.

Goodwin, L. D., & Leech, N. L. (2006). Understanding correlation: Factors that affect the size of *r*. *Journal of Experimental Education, 74*, 251–266.

The authors discuss six factors that affect the size of the correlation. Additionally, they present various ways of determining the extent of the effect of these factors.

Kaufman, R. L. (2013). *Heteroskedasticity in regression*. Thousand Oaks, CA: Sage.

Kaufman provides an excellent discussion of heteroscedasticity, a topic that is often ignored. In addition to discussing the effects, he offers a practical guide for the detection of the violation and strategies for correction.

Seber, G. A. F., & Wild, C. J. (1989). *Nonlinear regression*. New York: John Wiley & Sons.

For those who are interested, Seber and Wild provide a detailed description of the rationale and methods for conducting and interpreting nonlinear regression analysis.

7 ● 11 CHAPTER REVIEW QUESTIONS

Multiple-choice questions

1   Covariance will always _____.

    a   be a positive number

    b   be greater than the product of the variance of the two variables

    c   be equal to or less than 1.0

    d   be less than either of the variances

    e   reflect the direction of the association

2   A correlation coefficient estimates _____.

    a   the strength of the association between two variables

    b   the *y*-variable values for a specific *x*-variable value

    c   the *x*-variable values for a specific *y*-variable value

    d   the change in the *y*-variable values associated with changes in the *x*-variable values

    e   None of the above

3   A newspaper headline writer found that the more adjectives she put in the titles of her articles, the greater the number of newspapers sold that day. This association between the number of adjectives and the number of newspapers sold is said to be _____.

    a   significantly positive

    b   significantly negative

    c   positive

    d   negative

    e   quadratic

4   The null hypothesis in a correlational study is that _____.

    a $B = 0$

    b $a = 0$

    c $r < 1$

    d $r > 1$

    e $r = 0$

5   The relationship between the number of cups of coffee consumed (x) and caffeine levels found in the blood (y) was investigated in 100 University of Toronto students. The data resulted in the regression equation $\hat{y} = 2x + 0.05$.

This equation indicates _____.

a   each cup of coffee increases caffeine levels by 5%
b   it takes 18 cups of coffee to increase caffeine levels by one unit
c   for each cup of coffee caffeine levels increase by two units
d   All of the above
e   None of the above

6   In ordinary least squares regression, which of the following is (are) assumed?

a   The relationship between the x- and the y-variables is linear
b   There is equal variance of the y-values about the regression line
c   The distributions of the x- and y- variables is roughly normal
d   All of the above are assumed
e   None of the above are assumed

7   Covariance can never _____.

a   be equal to the product of the two standard deviations
b   be greater than the product of the two standard deviations
c   be less than the product of the two standard deviations
d   be greater than 1.0
e   There are no limitations on the covariance

8   In a regression analysis, if the predictor variable is measured in millilitres, the criterion variable _____.

a   can be in any units
b   must also be measure in millilitres
c   cannot be measured in millilitres
d   must be standardized
e   must be measured in some units of volume

9   The minimum number of subjects required for statistical power of 0.80 when testing for a correlation of 0.50 or greater is _____ .

a   783
b   28
c   50
d   80
e   40

Short-answer questions

1   What are the two primary distortions associated with the problem of heteroscedasticity?
2   What is the third-variable problem and how is it relevant to correlation and OLS regression analysis?
3   Why is linearity a necessary assumption of both correlational and regression analysis?
4   Why is homoscedasticity an assumption of both correlational and regression analysis?
5   How are the ϕ coefficient and r related? How are they different?

Data set questions

1   The manager of the Toronto United soccer club is interested in the number of matches his starting 11 players missed due to injury. It seemed to him that those who missed more matches than the others one year also missed more matches the next year. To test his suspicion he recorded the number of days the 11 players missed due to injury for two years. The data are reported in Figure 7.64. Do the data support the manager's suspicion? Be sure to create a scatterplot and any necessary test of significance.

2   How would the results change if player no. 11 had missed nine matches in year 2 rather than two?

3   How would the results change if player no. 9 had missed 19 matches in year 1 and 28 matches in year 2? (Return player no. 11's year 2 number of missed matches to two.)

4   Are there any univariate or bivariate outliers in the data used in Questions 2 and 3?

5   What do Questions 2 and 3 illustrate?

6   A cultural anthropologist suspected that those who watched more home renovation programmes on television would also be those who watched more cooking programmes. To test out her hypothesis she asked 10 of her neighbours to keep track of the number of home renovation and cooking programmes they watched for a week. The data are reported in Figure 7.65.

Player	Year 1	Year 2
1	4	6
2	5	5
3	3	4
4	7	6
5	3	5
6	6	8
7	8	7
8	2	4
9	9	5
10	6	4
11	1	2

Figure 7.64

Neighbour	Home renovation programmes	Cooking programmes
1	6	5
2	3	3
3	3	4
4	7	6
5	3	5
6	6	8
7	8	7
8	5	4
9	8	6
10	5	4

Figure 7.65

7   Create two data sets where the correlation coefficients are significant. When the two data sets are amalgamated, however, the resulting correlation coefficient should be non-significant. Use 10 subjects in each of the data sets. The x- and y-variables should be the same in both of the original data sets.

8   If another neighbour watched 4 hours of home renovation programmes during a week, how many hours would you predict this neighbour would watch cooking programmes? Include in your answer a scatterplot and any necessary tests of significance.

Don't forget to use the online resources! Meet your supporting stats tutor through an **introductory video**, review your maths skills with a **diagnostic pre-test**, explore statistical principles through **interactive simulations**, practice analysis techniques with **SPSS datasets**, and check your work with **answers to all in-text questions**.

https://study.sagepub.com/bors

8

Chapter contents

TESTING FOR A DIFFERENCE: MULTIPLE BETWEEN-SUBJECTS CONDITIONS (ANOVA)

KEY CONCEPTS: one-way analysis of variance (ANOVA), between-subjects design, sum-of-squares total, sum-of-squares within-conditions (error), sum-of-squares between-subjects (treatment), mean square error, mean square treatment, *F*-test, Kruskal–Wallis test.

8.1 PURPOSE

The immediate purpose of this chapter is to examine statistical tests used to determine if more than two groups of scores likely arise from a single population. Its broader purpose is to build the foundation for the next three chapters. Furthermore, looking back, we will find that the *t*-test presented in Chapter 5 is only an algebraically equivalent and special case of the analysis of variance (ANOVA) *F*-test described in this chapter. This is not to diminish the value of the *t*-test. It will become clear over the next four chapters that a variant of the *t*-test is an essential instrument for dissecting data, be they experimental, quasi-experimental, or observational. As was the case with the *t*-test, the ANOVA *F*-test may be used to analyse data from either a *between-subjects* or a *within-subjects* design. (For a review of between-subjects or within-subjects factors, see p. 195 in Chapter 5.)

Having said this, the current chapter is concerned with the analysis of one-way, between-subjects designs. Although ANOVA can accommodate multiple independent variables, 'one-way' refers to those designs where there is only one independent variable. Although ANOVA is used to analyse both between-subjects and within-subjects data, this chapter is restricted to between-subjects designs where subjects are randomly assigned to conditions. (For a review of the distinctions among *experimental, quasi-experimental, and observational* data, see p. 16 in Chapter 1.)

As usual, we begin by making logical and analytical links with previously covered procedures. The stage is set for the chapter through a review of the between-subjects (independent samples) *t*-test and the χ^2 test of independence. The core of the chapter is an in-depth examination of the logic of ANOVA through a detailed consideration of a simple example. Once more we examine the *third-variable problem*. This time, however, we discover that in certain instances it is an asset rather than a hindrance: analysis of covariance (ANCOVA). Finally, we explore an alternative procedure, the Kruskal–Wallis *H*-test, used in circumstances either where parametric assumptions required by ANOVA are violated or where the data are ordinal or nominal in nature. (For a discussion of parametric versus nonparametric analyses, see Chapter 5.)

Again, recall our orienting framework. As in Chapter 5, in this chapter we are primarily concerned with a family of tests based on the intersection of (1) a research question of *difference* and (2) *measurement* data. Where in Chapter 5 the analyses only accommodated an independent variable with two levels, in the current chapter the tests allow the independent variable to have multiple levels or conditions.

8.2 INTRODUCTION

Imagine that you are an animal psychologist wanting to examine the effects of early social environment on the personality of rodents. Anyone who has had a rodent as a pet, such as a hamster or a guinea pig, knows that, like human beings, no two rodents are identical in appearance or in temperament.

Personality is a big and widely debated topic; therefore, you restrict your investigation to a more concrete and circumscribed dimension. If you have had several pet hamsters, you will have noticed individual differences in their willingness to explore their surroundings when freed from their cage. Some hamsters move tentatively and keep to the walls, while

> Rodents rule! Over 4000 species of rodents have been identified. They are divided into three groups. First, there is the Sciuromorpha group, characterized best by the squirrels. Second, there is the Myomorpha group that is typified by mice and rats. Finally, there is the Hystricomorpha group that includes guinea pigs and porcupines.

others freely wander out into the middle of the floor. Perhaps there have been periods when you have had more than one hamster. If so, you may have noted that hamsters housed with cage-mates appear to be more explorative when let loose than are those hamsters housed alone. As an animal psychologist you hypothesize (H_1) that rodents, and in particular hamsters, will be more explorative the more social their early housing experience. Specifically, the more cage-mates the hamsters have, the more explorative they will be.

To test your hypothesis, you randomly assign 12 young hamsters to one of three housing conditions: four hamster to each condition. In the first condition (*cage 1*) the four hamsters are housed for 30 days in isolation (one hamster per cage); in the second condition (*cage 2*) the hamsters are housed two per cage; and in the third condition (*cage 4*) all four hamsters are housed in a single cage. All 12 hamsters are kept in their assigned cages for 30 days prior to testing.

To determine their willingness to explore, after the 30 days the hamsters were individually tested in a standard *open-field apparatus*, which is quite a misnomer. The open-field apparatus is anything but open and is not located in a field. It is an enclosed box found in the laboratory. The floor of the box is marked off in 16 (4×4) equal squares (see Figure 8.1 for an overhead view). The perimeter lines of the large square represent the 30.5 cm (12 inch) high walls of the box. The four central squares, those not adjacent to a wall, are considered middle squares. A camera records the hamster's activity.

> What about the issues of *power* and *sample size*, you may correctly ask? As discussed earlier, normally we would consider the desired *effect size* for which we wished to test (small, medium, or large) and then determine the required sample size. For demonstration purposes, however, we will keep this data set small ($n = 12$).

Because hamsters, like other rodents, have a tendency to avoid open areas, especially when lit, the number of middle squares a hamster enters is considered an index of their 'willingness to explore'. The more middle squares the hamster enters during a two-minute testing session, the more explorative the hamster is considered to be. That is, the *operational definition* of 'willingness to explore' is the number of middle squares the hamster enters. Because of the behaviour of rodents in the wild, this operational definition does appear to have some *ecological validity* (see p. 19).

──────── **REVIEW QUESTION** ────────

In this experiment, what is the independent variable? What is the dependent variable?

Web Link 8.1 for an answer to the review question.

• • • • •

The open-field apparatus has been used for decades to test a rodent's willingness to explore. The research apparatus has been employed not only in enrichment studies, such as Bors and Vigneau (2001), but also in many other areas, such as psychopharmacology. Smith's (1972) study of enrichment, open-field behaviour, and learning in rats is a good example of the early work that set the pattern for the research that followed up to this day. The current data to be analysed are a small fictional version of those reported in Bors and Vigneau (2001).

As usual, the first step in data analysis is to compute and report descriptive statistics. Figure 8.2 presents the data you collected. Each row in the table represents a hamster. The first column (*cage*) is the condition under which the young hamsters were housed (independent variable). The second column (*midsquares*) reports the number of middle squares that the hamsters entered (dependent variable).

To follow along in SPSS, go to the data file *onewayenriched.sav* found on the book's web page and produce the descriptive statistics using SPSS.

Web Link 8.2 for SPSS data set *onewayenriched.sav*.

In Chapter 5 we used one SPSS data file to compute descriptive statistics for the between-subjects analysis and another data file to complete the *t*-test. In this chapter we introduce

cage	midsquares
1.00	3.00
1.00	1.00
1.00	4.00
1.00	4.00
2.00	5.00
2.00	4.00
2.00	2.00
2.00	5.00
4.00	6.00
4.00	9.00
4.00	7.00
4.00	10.00

Figure 8.1   Overhead view of the open-field apparatus

Figure 8.2

another approach which uses a single file for both purposes. From the menu across the top of the *SPSS Data Editor* window, click on the *Data* tab and slide down to and choose the *Select Cases* option. When the *Select Cases* window opens (Figure 8.3), choose the *If condition is satisfied* option and click on the *IF* button.

When the *Select Cases: If* window opens, highlight and move the variable *cage* over to the empty rectangle, enter '= 1' (Figure 8.4) and click *Continue*. When returned to the *Select Cases* window, click *OK*. This will allow you to produce descriptive statistics for the *cage 1* hamsters' *midsquares* separately. Under *Analyze* in the *Data Editor* slide down to *Descriptive Statistics*, then over to and select *Descriptives* (not *Frequencies*). After moving *midsquares* over to the *Variable(s)* area, click *Options* and select *Variance* and *Skewness*. Also click the box *Save standardized values as variables* in the *Descriptives* window prior to clicking *OK*. The procedure of using the *Data/Select Cases* functions can be repeated for producing the descriptive statistics for the *cage 2* and *cage 4* hamsters. Once this is completed, be sure to return to the *Select Cases* window and select the *All cases* option.

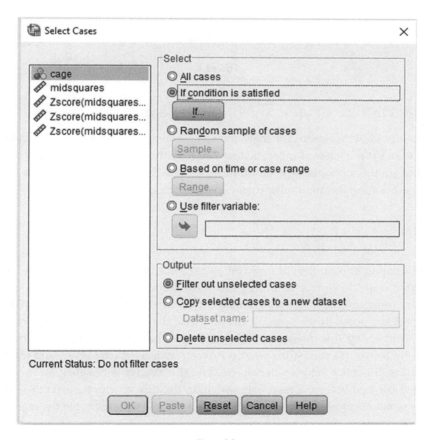

Figure 8.3

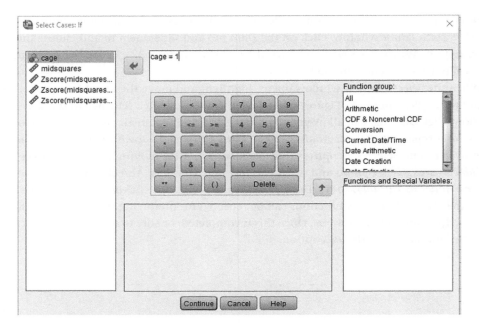

Figure 8.4

3 REVIEWING THE T-TEST AND THE χ^2 TEST OF INDEPENDENCE

In this section is a brief review of the logic and some assumptions underlying the independent-samples t-test and the χ^2 test of independence and how they might be applied to your hamster data. It is also another opportunity to illustrate how the differences between the families of tests are more superficial and less substantial than they first appear.

Applying the t-test

As stated in Chapter 4, regardless of how complicated our research designs may be, the crucial questions often come down to examining pairs of conditions: were the scores in one condition influenced by something that did not influence the scores in another condition? This evokes the model problem posed in the opening chapter: were the 10 scores randomly sorted into the two groups? Answering this question involves (1) determining what to *expect* if the numbers were randomly sorted, (2) comparing what is *expected* with what is *observed*, and (3) determining whether the difference between the *expected* and the *observed* is too great for us to continue assuming that the numbers were randomly sorted. In the case of your hamster experiment, are the numbers of middle squares entered by the hamsters random with respect to the cage conditions (number of cage-mates)?

━━━━━━ REVIEW QUESTION ━━━━━━

Can you formulate the null hypothesis (H_0) and the alternative hypothesis (H_1) both in terms of *differ-ence* and in terms of *association*?

🔖 Web Link 8.3 for an answer to the review question.

While the names of the three new variables in the *Data Editor* differ (*Zmidsquares*, *ZSco01*, and *StdZ01*), they all three represent the *z*-scores of the *midsquares*, one column or variable for each condition.

cage	midsquares	filter_$	Zmidsquares	ZSco01	StdZ01
1.00	3.00	0	.00000	.	.
1.00	1.00	0	-1.41421	.	.
1.00	4.00	0	.70711	.	.
1.00	4.00	0	.70711	.	.
2.00	5.00	0	.	.70711	.
2.00	4.00	0	.	.00000	.
2.00	2.00	0	.	-1.41421	.
2.00	5.00	0	.	.70711	.
4.00	6.00	1	.	.	-1.09545
4.00	9.00	1	.	.	.54772
4.00	7.00	1	.	.	-.54772
4.00	10.00	1	.	.	1.09545

Figure 8.5

If you return to the SPSS *Data Editor* you will see that three new variables have been created, one for each cage condition: the by-condition *z*-scores for *midsquares* (Figure 8.5). Recall that an outlier is identified by a *z*-score greater than ±4.00. As can be seen from the *z*-scores in the three new variables (*Zmidsquares*, *ZSco01*, and *StdZ01*), there are no outliers in any of the three cage conditions.

Figure 8.6 summarizes the descriptive statistics for the three cage conditions. The means for the three cage conditions are 3, 4, and 8. The corresponding variances of 2.0, 2.0, and 3.3 suggest that we may provisionally assume homogeneity of variance. (For a discussion of assuming homogeneity of variance, see p. 202.)

Using what you have learned in Chapter 5, you might answer your research question through a series of independent-samples *t*-tests, comparing *cage 1* with *cage 2*, *cage 1* with *cage 4*, and *cage 2* with *cage 4*. For example, a *t*-test comparing *cage 1* with *cage 2* results in the following *t*-value:

$$t = \frac{\bar{y}_1 - \bar{y}_2}{\sqrt{\frac{s_1^2}{n_1} + \frac{s_2^2}{n_2}}} = \frac{3 - 4}{\sqrt{\frac{2}{4} + \frac{2}{4}}} = -1.$$

Cage	Mean	Variance
1	3	2.0
2	4	2.0
4	8	3.3

Figure 8.6

t-test	t-value	df	p-value
Cage 1 vs Cage 2	−1.00	6	.356
Cage 2 vs Cage 4	−3.46	6	.013
Cage 1 vs Cage 4	−4.33	6	.005

Figure 8.7

Figure 8.7 reports the three t-tests, their degrees of freedom, and their p-values. Using $\alpha = 0.05$ for decision-making purposes, we conclude that there is insufficient evidence to presume that there is a difference between the *cage 1* and the *cage 2* conditions (failure to reject H_0), but that there is sufficient evidence to presume that there is a difference between *cage 2* and *cage 4* and between *cage 1* and *cage 4* (reject H_0).

What might you conclude about your hypothesis concerning the number of cage-mates and its effect on a hamster's 'willingness to explore'? It appears to be a bit complicated. You might be tempted to say that your original hypothesis (as the number of cage-mates increased, so would the hamsters' willingness to explore) was not fully confirmed. There appears to be no change in a hamster's willingness to explore simply because it was housed with one other hamster. Being caged with three others, however, does appear to increase the hamster's willingness to explore an open field. Note that there was a difference in the means between *cage 1* and *cage 2*: an increase from 3 to 4. This change is consistent with your hypothesis. As you know by now, the issue may be one of power. The difference may be real, but you may not have a sufficient number of observations (hamsters) for the difference to be significant. Concluding that there is no difference between *cage 1* and *cage 2* may be an instance of a Type II error.

═══ CHALLENGE QUESTION ═══

What is the effect size associated with the difference between *cage 1* and *cage 2*? How many hamsters would you require in each of those conditions to find an effect of that size to be significant at $\alpha = 0.05$ with a desired *power* of 0.80?

Web Link 8.4 for an answer to the challenge question.

Interpretations can be more uncertain the more complicated the research design becomes, with not only additional levels of the independent variable (IV) but also additional IVs. Moreover, performing multiple statistical tests raises the issue of the *familywise* Type I error rate which will be discussed in detail in Chapter 10. Simply stated, if you compute three t-tests on your hamster data, you will need to reduce the per-test α level. With such a necessary reduction in α and the related reduction in power, you may not find that there is sufficient evidence to conclude that there is a statistically significant difference between *cage 2* and *cage 4*, for example.

The reduction in power related to running multiple *t*-tests could be avoided if there was a test that could simultaneously examine the differences among conditions, regardless of their number (levels of the IV). The tests of our focus in this chapter do just that, but as we will see, such tests come at a price.

Applying the X^2 test of independence

Your data (dependent variable: *midsquares*) are *measurement* in nature, and your research question concerns possible *differences* in the effects of the *cage* conditions. With a bit of imagination the data can be made *categorical* in nature and the research question translated into one of *association*. Once this conjuring trick has been performed, you may recognize that you have already covered a statistical test which addresses your H_1. An analogous transformational strategy was already used in Section 7.3.

First, using the median (4.5) of the 12 *midsquares* scores, you can create a new dependent variable (*hiloexplore*). (This new dependent variable already appears in the SPSS data file.) Those hamsters with *midsquares* scores below 4.5 are assigned a 1 and those with *midsquares* above 4.5 are assigned a 2. Next, the research question can be changed from one of *differences* to one of *association*: is there an association between *hiloexplore* and *cage* condition? Furthermore, when *cage* condition is considered to be at least ordinal in nature, your H_1 concerning 'willingness to explore' and the number of cage-mates translates easily into a χ^2 test of independence followed by a Γ (gamma) index for a possible ordinal trend. To follow along in SPSS, conduct a χ^2 test of independence using *cage* and *hiloexplore* as the two variables.

The *hiloexplore * cage Crosstabulation* table (Figure 8.8) shows the *expected* and *observed* (count) frequencies for the six cells. The *Chi-Square Tests* table (Figure 8.9) reveals a significant Pearson χ^2 (8.0, *p*-value 0.018). Except for a problem with the expected frequencies which we will address, these results would allow you to conclude that *hiloexplore* is influenced by *cage* condition.

If we examine the *Symmetric Measures* table (Figure 8.10), we find that Γ (1.0) indicates a perfect ordinal association between *hiloexplore* and *cage* condition. This appears to provide you with very

hiloexplore * cage Crosstabulation

			cage			
			1.00	2.00	4.00	Total
hiloexplore	1.00	Count	4	2	0	6
		Expected Count	2.0	2.0	2.0	6.0
	2.00	Count	0	2	4	6
		Expected Count	2.0	2.0	2.0	6.0
Total		Count	4	4	4	12
		Expected Count	4.0	4.0	4.0	12.0

Figure 8.8

Chi-Square Tests

	Value	df	Asymp. Sig. (2-sided)
Pearson Chi-Square	8.000[a]	2	.018
Likelihood Ratio	11.090	2	.004
Linear-by-Linear Association	7.333	1	.007
N of Valid Cases	12		

Figure 8.9

> Along with the loss of information that accompanies the transformation from measurement data to categorical data, there is usually a loss of power. This does not appear to be an issue with your data. The gamma cannot be any stronger.

strong evidence for your initial H_1, that willingness to explore increased with an increase in the number of cage-mates.

Before you become too excited, two points should be made. Looking back at the *hilo-explore * cage Crosstabulation* table reveals a violation of a vital assumption. The χ^2 test requires that all cells must have a minimum *expected frequency* of 5. Unfortunately, none of your six cells meets this requirement. Furthermore, as mentioned in the previous chapter, when measurement data are transformed into categorical data, information is lost. In the case of your hamster data, the specific *midsquares* scores are reduced to being either a 1 or 2. The loss of such information can often result in reduced *power*.

As a consequence of these and other issues, researchers use related but specifically devised statistical procedures for analysing measurement data from experiments with more than two treatment conditions. ANOVA and its *F*-test are the focus of a large portion of this chapter. Most of the tests described back in Chapter 5 are streamlined variations and algebraic equivalents of the tests described in the current chapter. The *F*-test is designed to simultaneously compare multiple conditions, thus allowing you to draw a single, general conclusion from a single test. For example, is there sufficient evidence to reject the assumption that the *midsquares* scores are random with respect to the *cage* conditions (H_0)? As you will discover, such test have a drawback. Such a test will not fully address your hypothesis and there will be a need to return to our old friend the *t*-test, albeit in a modified form, in Chapter 10. Such is the price for the single test.

Symmetric Measures

		Value	Asymp. Std. Error[a]	Approx. T[b]	Approx. Sig.
Ordinal by Ordinal	Gamma	1.000	.000	9.798	.000
N of Valid Cases		12			

Figure 8.10

8 ● 4 THE LOGIC OF ANOVA: TWO UNBIASED ESTIMATES OF σ^2

We begin this section by reviewing the model we developed in Chapter 5 that was used for partitioning a score and extending it for our presentation of the one-way ANOVA F-test. We then introduce the logic underlying the F-test and the notion of two independent estimates of population variance (σ^2). The goal of this section is to provide you with an understanding of how the formula for the F-test arises directly from how we partition a single score into its components.

In Chapter 5 (see Section 5.5) we presented the basic model for a score from the perspective of the general linear model:

$$y_i = \mu + \tau_k + e_i,$$

where y_i is the ith score, μ is the population mean, τ_k is the treatment effect for a given condition, and e_i is the error associated with the ith score. We used this model to compare two treatment conditions. With only two conditions, if H_0 is true and $\tau_1 = \tau_2$, the *expected* value of $\bar{y}_1 - \bar{y}_2$ is 0.0.

In this chapter we extend the logic to include multiple conditions. With three conditions, if H_0 is true and $\tau_1 = \tau_2 = \tau_3$, the *expected* difference among all combinations of condition means is 0. Because we are dealing with a sample and not the population, the probability of the *observed* differences among the condition means all being 0 is itself close to 0, regardless of the veracity of H_0. As a consequence, we require a procedure for simultaneously testing if the *observed* differences among the means is too great to be assumed to be 0. This test is based on computing two independent estimates of the population variance (σ^2) from which the sample was drawn. We assume that the subjects in the sample were randomly *assigned* to the different conditions. One estimate of σ^2 is based on the average within-condition variance. The other estimate of σ^2 is based on the variance among the condition means.

The first estimate of σ^2

The first estimate of σ^2 is based on the average within-condition variance. To understand this estimate we must start by examining the nature of data associated with a between-subjects design. Assume that we select N subjects from a population which is normally distributed and we randomly assign them to one of three groups (conditions). At this point assume that the three groups have not received differential treatment. We could

> Note the assumptions of random assignment to conditions. It is key to the sample variances being unbiased estimators (see p. 75).

calculate a sample mean and a sample variance for each condition: $\bar{y}_1$, s_1^2; $\bar{y}_2$, s_2^2; and $\bar{y}_3$, s_3^2. Because the subjects were *randomly* assigned to the three conditions, without differential treatment these conditions represent three samples drawn from a single population. Thus, $\bar{y}_1$, $\bar{y}_2$, and $\bar{y}_3$ are unbiased estimates of a single μ. Also, s_1^2, s_2^2, and s_3^2 are three unbiased estimates of a single σ^2.

Remember that N refers to the total size of a sample drawn from a population and n refers to the number of observations or subjects in a given condition (a subset of the overall sample of N).

When there are three estimates of the same population parameter, all of which are inevitably different from the true value of the parameter, the average of the three estimates is the best estimate. Thus, our first estimate of σ^2 when the ns are equal is $\frac{1}{3}\left(s_1^2 + s_2^2 + s_3^2\right)$. To generalize the formula, we find the best estimate of σ^2 to be $\frac{1}{k}\Sigma s_j^2$, where s_j^2 is the variance in the jth condition and k is the number of conditions.

━━━━━ REVIEW QUESTION ━━━━━

If the ns are unequal, how would you calculate the average or best estimate of σ^2. *Hint*: We have already addressed this problem in an earlier chapter.

👆 Web Link 8.5 for an answer to the challenge question.

At this point we have our first unbiased estimate of σ^2.

The second estimate of σ^2

A second estimate of the σ^2 from which the observations were drawn can be derived from the variability among the subsample or condition means. To do so we return to our earlier discussions of the sampling distribution of the mean (see p. 192).

The fact that several sample variances are all unbiased estimates of a single population variance does not guarantee that the assumption of homogeneity of variance will be satisfied. The assumption of homogeneity will always require testing.

Examining the formula for the sampling distribution of the mean ($\sigma_{\bar{y}}^2 = s^2 / n$), we find it possible to obtain a second estimate of σ^2, one independent of the first. Remember, s^2 is an estimate of σ^2. By solving for σ^2 in place of computing its estimate (s^2) and with a bit of algebra we see that

$$\sigma^2 = n\,s_{\bar{y}}^2.$$

Rather than estimating $s_{\bar{y}}^2$ using s^2, we can calculate the variance among the means directly:

$$s_{\bar{y}}^2 = \frac{\Sigma(\bar{y} - GM)^2}{k-1},$$

where GM represents the mean of the condition means and k represents the number of conditions. The individual observations are irrelevant here. Here the condition means are in effect the observations.

Putting all this together, our second independent estimate of σ^2 is

$$\sigma^2 = n\frac{\sum(\bar{y} - GM)^2}{k-1},$$

where n is the number of observations in a condition. This version of the formula assumes that all ns are equal.

━━━━━ REVIEW QUESTION ━━━━━

If the ns were unequal how would $\sigma^2 = n\sum(\bar{y} - GM)^2 / (k-1)$ be transformed?

🔖 Web Link 8.6 for the answer to the review question.

What does it actually mean to say that the two estimates of σ^2 are *independent*? As we have pointed out, independence means that two things are *unrelated, uncorrelated,* and are *random* with respect to each other. Returning to your hamster data for a moment, the four *midsquares* scores in the *cage 1* condition were 3, 1, 4, and 4. The mean and variance of *cage 1* were 3 and 2.0, respectively. If we were to add the constant of 100 to those four scores and transform them to 103, 101, 104, and 104, we would *linearly transform* the mean from 3 to 103, but the variance would remain 2.0. (For the discussion of linear transformation, see p. 120 in Chapter 3.)

🔖 Web Link 8.7 for an interactive demonstration of the independence of mean and variance.

By adding a constant to the scores in the three conditions – even by adding a different constant in each condition – we discover that the average variance is *unrelated* to the changes in the means. Conversely, we can conclude that the variance among the condition means is *random* with respect to the within-condition variances and their average. Thus, we have two *independent* procedures for estimating σ^2.

🔖 Web Link 8.8 for an interactive demonstration of the independence of multiple means and variances.

There is one important proviso that must be placed on the second estimate, $\sigma^2 = n\sum(\bar{y} - GM)^2 / (k-1)$. This is an unbiased estimate of σ^2 when and *only when* H_0 is true. That is, the second estimate of σ^2 based on the variability among the condition means is unbiased if, and only if, the condition means are estimates of the same μ. To the extent that that there is any differential treatment effect (e.g., *cage* condition has an effect), this second estimate of σ^2 will tend to be an overestimate. The estimate of σ^2 based on the average within-condition variance, however, is an unbiased estimate of σ^2 regardless of the veracity of H_0, because it is independent of any changes differential treatment may create in the condition means. Therein resides the basis for the logic of the F-test.

━━━━━━━━━━ **REVIEW QUESTION** ━━━━━━━━━━

Construct two data sets comprising 15 whole numbers. Sort the 15 scores into three equal groups (treatment conditions). In the first data set the resulting estimate of the population variance based on the variance among the condition means should be greater than the estimate based on the average within-condition variance. In the second data set the resulting estimate of the population variance based on the variability among the condition means should be less than the estimate based on the average within-condition variance. There is one important proviso. All six condition variances should be a constant.

🔖 Web Link 8.9 for a discussion of and answer to the review question.

• • • • •

To the extent that there is a treatment effect, the estimate of σ^2 based on the variability among the conditions means will *tend* to be an overestimate. There is a reason for the word 'tend' in that statement. Because we are dealing with samples there always will be sample-to-sample variability in (1) the average within-condition variance and (2) the variance among the condition means. Remember that the average within-condition variance and the variance among the means are independent. As a consequence, simply due to chance alone, the estimate of σ^2 based on the variance among the condition means may be smaller than the estimate based on the average within-condition variance, even when there is a treatment effect. Granted, the probability is low, but it can and will happen. Such an outcome is an example of a Type I error.

We now can put these two independent estimates of σ^2 together with our partitioning of a score and derive the formula for the *F*-test. As you recall, the model for a score in a between-subjects design is $y = \mu + \tau_i + e_i$. These are population parameters for which we need estimates:

- μ is estimated by the average of our sample means, $\bar{y}/k$, where k is the number of condition means.
- τ_i, or condition/treatment effect, is estimated by $\bar{y}_j - GM$.
- The error in an individual's score (e_i) is estimated by the difference between the individual's score and the condition mean, $y - \bar{y}$.

Thus, the model can be rewritten as

$$Y_i = GM + (\bar{y}_j - GM) + (Y_i - \bar{y}_j).$$

Each score is composed of an estimate of the population mean, an estimate of the treatment effect, and an estimate of the error associated with that score. Further, we can describe the nature of the difference between an individual score and the population mean, which is estimated by the difference between the score and *GM*. The difference between an individual score and *GM* has two components: an estimate of the treatment effect and an estimate of the error associated with that score:

$$(Y_i - GM) = (\bar{y}_j - GM) + (Y_i - \bar{y}_j).$$

As can be seen from the formula, within a condition the *treatment effect* is a constant for all subjects: $(\bar{y}_j - GM)$. The difference between two scores within the same condition is solely the difference in their errors: $(Y_i - \bar{y}_j)$. Remember, *error* is not a mistake. It is the product of all those uncontrolled variables which influence a score. The difference between two scores in different conditions is the difference in their *error* plus the difference in *treatment effects*, if there is one. If we did not assume that treatment was a constant within a condition, this additive model and the analysis which follows from it would be inappropriate. This graphic representation of the model illustrates spatially how the difference between an individual score and the *GM* score is composed of (1) the deviation of the score from the mean of its condition and (2) the deviation of the mean of its condition from the *GM*.

For example, it can be seen how the *midsquares* score of 1 in the *cage 1* condition can be partitioned into the score's distance from its condition mean (*m*)

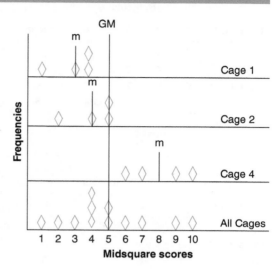

Figure 8.11

and the distance between its condition mean and the *GM* (Figure 8.11).

If we apply this model to the first hamster in the *cage 1* condition ($y = 3$) we find

$$(Y_i - GM) = (\bar{y}_j - GM) + (Y_i - \bar{y}_j)$$

$$(3 - 5) = (3 - 5) + (3 - 3) = -2.$$

The above model of estimates is the basis for the ANOVA *F*-test's formula. We have illustrated its component terms for one hamster; we need to repeat this for all of the hamsters and sum the components. Recall from our initial discussion of variance in Chapter 2(p. 59), however, that the sum of such differences about their mean will always be 0. This is one reason why we square the differences prior to summing across subjects:

$$(3 - 5)^2 = (3 - 5)^2 + (3 - 3)^2 = 4.$$

Figure 8.12 depicts your 12 hamsters, four in each treatment condition. The rightmost column reports the three *cage* condition means and the bottom row provides the overall or grand mean of all 12 *midsquares* scores.

Figure 8.13 shows the 12 *midsquares* scores after *GM* has been removed from each of them, which is the $(Y_i - GM)$ component of the model. Note that the new *GM* is 0, as it must be after the

	Subjects				
Treatment	1	2	3	4	Mean
Cage 1	3	1	4	4	3
Cage 2	5	4	2	5	4
Cage 4	6	9	7	10	8
				GM =	5

Figure 8.12

	Subjects				
Treatment	1	2	3	4	Mean
Cage 1	-2	-4	-1	-1	-2
Cage 2	0	-1	-3	0	-1
Cage 4	1	4	2	5	3
				GM =	0

Figure 8.13

	Subjects			
Treatment	1	2	3	4
Cage 1	4	16	1	1
Cage 2	0	1	9	0
Cage 4	1	16	4	25
				Total = 78

Figure 8.14

original GM was subtracted from all of the scores. Also note that although the condition means have changed, the absolute differences among them have not changed.

Figure 8.14 shows the 12 *midsquares* score after the GM has been removed and the differences have been squared. The total of 78 we will call the *sum-of-squares total*: SS_{total}. Recall that variance is the sum of squares divided by the corresponding *df*. For the moment we are only concerned with the sum of squares (SS). We can summarize this procedure with the following formula:

$$SS_{total} = \Sigma(y - GM)^2.$$

For all hamsters we have completed squaring and summing one side of the equation: $(y_i - GM)^2$.

	Subjects				
Treatment	1	2	3	4	Mean
Cage 1	3	1	4	4	3
Cage 2	5	4	2	5	4
Cage 4	6	9	7	10	8
				GM =	5

Figure 8.15

Now we will address the other side of the equation: $(\bar{y}_j - GM) + (Y_i - \bar{y}_j)$. As we did on the first side of the equation, we begin with the original data (Figure 8.15).

Figure 8.16 portrays the 12 *midsquares* scores after the mean of each *cage* condition has been subtracted from each score in its condition. Because each treatment condition mean also contains the GM, the GM is simultaneously removed from each score as well.

· · · · ·

What are the constituents of a given condition mean? First of all, $\bar{y}$ is an estimate of μ, which itself is estimated by the GM. Second, there is the treatment effect, if there is one. Furthermore, the *average error* of the subjects in that particular condition will alter $\bar{y}$. Thus when we subtract $\bar{y}$ from a given score within that condition, we are subtracting everything that goes into $\bar{y}$, including GM.

Note that all of the condition means now are 0. If the *GM* and the treatment means have been removed from the *midsquares* scores, what remains? Because an individual score is made up of μ (estimated by the *GM*), τ_j (estimated by the difference between $\bar{y}_j$ and the *GM*), and e_i (estimated by the difference between y_i and $\bar{y}_j$), it is only this last term that the remaining values in Figure 8.16 represent.

Figure 8.17 shows the 12 *midsquares* scores after their treatment condition means have been subtracted and the differences have been squared. The total of 22 we will call the *sum-of-squares error*: SS$_{error}$. We can summarize this procedure with the following formula:

$$SS_{error} = \Sigma\Sigma(y_i - \bar{y}_j)^2.$$

	Subjects				
Treatment	**1**	**2**	**3**	**4**	**Mean**
Cage 1	0	−2	1	1	0
Cage 2	1	0	−2	1	0
Cage 4	−2	1	−1	2	0
				GM =	0

Figure 8.16

	Subjects			
Treatment	1	2	3	4
Cage 1	0	4	1	1
Cage 2	1	0	4	1
Cage 4	4	1	1	4
			Total =	22

Figure 8.17

The double-summation notation denotes that once a condition mean has been subtracted from each score in its condition and each difference squared, you move to the next condition and repeat the process until all conditions have been completed.

Because the total value on one side of an equals sign must be the total value on the other side, we can derive the sum of squares for the remaining component $(\bar{Y}_j - GM)^2$ as a residual, by subtracting SS$_{error}$ from SS$_{total}$ (56). This difference will be called the sum-of-squares treatment: SS$_{treatment}$. Or we can subtract the *GM* from each subject's condition mean, square each of the differences, and sum across all subjects. Or we can subtract the *GM* from each condition mean, square the differences, sum these squared differences, and multiple the total by n. This is summarized in the following formula:

$$SS_{treatment} = n\Sigma(\bar{y} - GM)^2,$$

where n is the number of subjects in a condition, assuming that n is a constant. If the ns are unequal the formula changes to

$$SS_{treatment} = \Sigma n(\bar{y} - GM)^2.$$

Figure 8.18 Sir Ronald Fisher, statistician and biologist, who developed ANOVA for analysing crop experiments.

We have completed computing the three primary components of ANOVA and the two independent estimates of σ^2.

8 ● 5 ANOVA AND THE *F*-TEST

We can now proceed with the logic of the *F*-test developed by Sir Ronald Fisher (1935), pictured in Figure 8.18. SS_{error} and $SS_{treatment}$ are the sums of squares that correspond to our two estimates of σ^2: one based on the average within-condition variance and the other based on the variability among the condition means. These sums of squares can be transformed into variances by dividing them by their appropriate degrees of freedom (*df*).

● ● ● ● ●

Fisher did not 'invent' ANOVA out of the blue in the twentieth century. As Stigler (1986) points out, Laplace and Gauss were developing the least squares method 100 years earlier. Pierre-Simon Laplace was a French scholar who made important contributions to physics and astronomy. We met the German mathematician Johann Carl Friedrich Gauss during our discussion of the normal distribution in Chapter 2. Fisher introduced the term 'variance' and formalized the method of analysis.

Remember, when computing variance one *df* is lost because $\bar{y}$ is only an estimate of μ. Each *cage* condition's s^2 is based on its corresponding $\bar{y}$, thus each *cage* condition has $n - 1 = 4 - 1 = 3$ *df*. With three *cage* conditions, there are $(4 - 1) + (4 - 1) + (4 - 1) = 9$ *df* associated with SS_{error}. Turning to the $df_{treatment}$, the *GM* is the overall mean of the three condition means, thus the *df* associated with $SS_{treatment}$ are $K - 1 = 3 - 1 = 2$ *df*. Viewed another way, for computing your $MS_{treatment}$, the *GM* is said to be based on three observations, the three conditions means. The individual scores in the conditions are irrelevant and can be ignored.

Regarding your hamster data we find the following two independent estimates of σ^2:

$$MS_{treatment} = SS_{treatment}/df_{treatment} = 56/2 = 28.0,$$
$$MS_{error} = SS_{error}/df_{error} = 22/9 = 2.4.$$

Remember that MS_{error} is an unbiased estimate of σ^2 regardless of the veracity of the H_0. $MS_{treatment}$ is only an unbiased estimate of σ^2 when H_0 is true: that is, when there is no treatment effect. When there is a treatment effect, $MS_{treatment}$ as an estimate of σ^2 will be inflated.

• • • • •

Recall the discussion of the source of variance found in Chapter 3. The variance associated with a score is the sum of the variances in the individual factors which influence that score (assuming that they are independent of each other). When H_0 is true, MS_{error} and $MS_{treatment}$ are influenced by the same set of factors and their *expected values* (E) are the same. When H_0 is false, however, $MS_{treatment}$ is influenced by an additional factor. Thus, the size of the treatment effect will produce a corresponding inflation of $MS_{treatment}$, and $E(MS_{treatment})$ will be greater than $E(MS_{error})$.

To summarize, then, when H_0 is true

$$E(MS_{error}) = \sigma^2 \quad \text{and} \quad E(MS_{treatment}) = \sigma^2 .$$

Thus,

$$E(MS_{error}) = E(MS_{treatment}).$$

When H_0 is false,

$$E(MS_{error}) = \sigma^2 ,$$

but

$$E(MS_{treatment}) = \sigma^2 + \sigma^2_{treatment} .$$

Thus,

$$E(MS_{error}) < E(MS_{treatment}).$$

This provides us with a key to the *F*-test. We know what to expect if H_0 is true. The *F*-test is based on the ratio of the observed $MS_{treatment}$ to that observed MS_{error}. Thus, when H_0 is true the expected value of the *F*-ratio is 1.

Reviewing assumptions

Before returning to your hamster data, computing the *F*-value, rejecting or failing to reject H_0, and drawing a conclusion, we should review the important assumptions that apply to ANOVA and the *F*-test. Earlier when we examined the descriptive data for the three *cage* conditions, we provisionally concluded that we could assume homogeneity of variance. Here we will more formally test the assumption. In Chapter 5 we introduced Hartley's F_{max} test (Hartley, 1950). To compute F_{max} we simply divide the largest of the variances (*cage 4*: $s_1^2 = 3.3$) by the smallest (in your case, *cage 1* or *cage 2*: $s_2^2 = 2.0$). For your hamster data the resulting *observed* F_{max} value is 1.65. Our H_0 regarding

Does this sound familiar? There is a ratio of variances (MSs). It is the logic of the ANOVA F-test. The reason for a separate F_{max} table (Appendix E) resides in the fact that you have not randomly decided which variances to compare. Further discussion of the logic behind the F_{max} table and the derivation of its critical values can be found in Hartley (1950).

homogeneity of variance is that the sample variances are estimating the same population variance: the *expected* $F_{max} = s^2_{largest} / s^2_{smallest} = 1$.

Because the three condition variances are averaged when computing the F-value, if the assumption of homogeneity of variance is violated, you must rectify the situation by either transforming your data or using an alternative statistical test. The table in Appendix E contains the F_{max} critical values. If the *observed* F_{max} exceeds the corresponding critical value, then H_0 is rejected. The columns in the F_{max} table represent the number of conditions (k) and the rows represent the df associated with a single condition. The table assumes that the df are constant across conditions. In the present case $k = 3$ and $df = 3$. We find that the critical value for $k = 3$ and $df = 3$ is 27.8.

• • • • •

Note that, in the F_{max} table, as the df increase, the critical values decrease. This is because, as n increases, the *efficiency* of the estimate increases and the sample estimates of σ^2, on average, will cluster nearer to the true value of σ^2. Conversely, as k (the number of conditions) increases, the critical values in the F_{max} table increase. This is because, as the number of condition variances to be calculated increases, the probability of accidentally obtaining a somewhat abnormal variance in one of the conditions increases. What is the real concern? The real concern is that one or more of the conditions is not an unbiased estimator of σ^2. The problem is not simply that a variance may be abnormally large or small, but that it contains more or fewer sources of variance than do the other condition variances. As a consequence, you are not averaging apples of somewhat different sizes, but rather you are trying to average apples and oranges.

Because your observed F_{max} value of 1.65 is less than the critical value of 27.8, you fail to reject H_0 and may continue to assume homogeneity of variance. Often SPSS will provide an exact probability for a test of homogeneity of variance or provide you with an alternative p-value for your statistical test.

Should you be unable to safely assume homogeneity of variance, there are various ways to transform your data that will decrease the severity of the problem. Howell (2002) describes a number of such strategies: taking the logarithm, the reciprocal, or the square root of all of your observations. Each strategy is linked to a particular relationship between the size of the variances or standard deviations and the size of their respective condition means. Often, if one transformation sufficiently reduces the problem of heterogeneity of variance, the other transformations will do so as well.

The drawback associated with such transformations of data is that the findings cannot be expressed and discussed in terms of the original units of measurement. For example, after transforming the data you may need to express your findings in terms of the log of the number of squares entered by the hamsters. More specifically, effect size estimates become particularly difficult to interpret. There is at least one circumstance under which one particular transformation is preferable, while it also avoids the problem of uninterpretable units of measurement. When latency is the dependent variable, and there is an indication of heterogeneity of variance, it is best to transform the scores (latencies) with their reciprocals. Transforming latency with its reciprocal creates no problem with respect to discussing the results or interpreting a standardized measure of effect size. You merely need to change your presentation from 'time' to 'speed': speed is the reciprocal of latency.

The other important assumption is that of normality. In Chapters 2 and 5 we discussed using a frequency histogram as one way to examine the normality of data. With small data sets, such as your 12 hamsters, examining a histogram is of little value. There are only one or two observations for most, if not all, scores. Under such circumstances the identification of possible outliers becomes even more important. As we saw above from the saved z-scores for *midsquares*, your data are free of outliers. That said, as we saw in Chapters 2 and 5, with small *n*s it is highly unlikely that what appear to be extreme scores will meet the criterion for being outliers. In the end, the researcher with a small sample size is left to rely on previous research that sampled from similar populations as a guide to the distributional nature of the dependent variable.

ANOVA and bar charts

It is always valuable to graphically depict your data, even with rather simple designs such as your hamster study. The picture provides the visual portrayal of the results, the 'greater than' and 'less than' representations of the *differences* or *associations*. The subsequent statistical tests provide the numerical estimates concerning the reliability of the visual portrayal. When experimental studies are to be analysed with an *F*-test, a bar chart with error bars based on 1 standard error of the condition means is typically displayed. If necessary, review in Chapter 5 the creation of bar charts with SPSS using the *Chart Builder* accessed from within the *Data Editor*

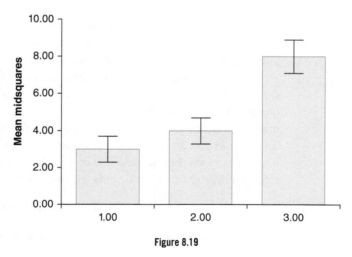

Figure 8.19

window. Examining the bar chart of your hamster data, in addition to a general increase in *midsquares* entered across *cage* conditions, we see that the *cage 4* condition is considerably different from the other two *cage* conditions (Figure 8.19).

• • • • •

As a rule of thumb, in a between-subjects design, when the error bars of one condition do not overlap with those of another condition, as is the case with the *cage* 4 error bars, it is highly likely that the *F*-test will be significant at $\alpha = 0.05$.

Calculating the *F*-test for your hamster data, we find the *F*-ratio to be

$$F = \frac{\text{observed MS}_{\text{treament}}}{\text{observed MS}_{\text{error}}} = \frac{28.0}{2.4} = 11.6.$$

ANOVA Summary Table

Source	SS	df	MS	F	p-value
Treatment	56.0	2	28.0	11.6	< .05
Error	22.0	9	2.4		
Total	78.0	11			

Figure 8.20

Your *observed F*-ratio is 11.6 times greater than *expected* (1.0), if H_0 was true. The question remains: because we have a sample and not the population, is 11.6 within the range of *F*-values that would be *expected due to chance alone*? As when we evaluated *t*-values, the probability associated with an *observed F*-value is contingent upon the *df*. When evaluating an *observed t*-value, we were concerned with only the *df* associated with the *standard error of the difference between the means*. When evaluating an *F*-value, those *df* correspond to the df_{error}. What appears to be an addition when evaluating the *F*-value are the *df* associated with $MS_{\text{treatment}}$. There are *df* associated with *treatment* when we evaluated a *t*-value, but there is no need to include them in the table of critical values. When there are only two treatment conditions, as is the case with *t*-tests, treatment will always have only 1 *df*.

ANOVA results are often reported in table form. Figure 8.20 is typical of the reporting, both in publications and in statistical software outputs.

It illustrates several important characteristics of the analysis. The most important characteristic is the additive nature of the sum of squares (SS) and the degrees of freedom (*df*). This is a consequence (1) of the fact that the two estimates of σ^2 are independent and (2) of the assumptions made concerning the components of a score. As a result, the SS_{total} and the df_{total} can be partitioned into their SS and *df* components: treatment and error. From this partitioning, it can again be seen how the term on the left-hand side of the following equation is the basis of the SS_{total}, and the two terms on the right-hand side of the equation are the basis of the $SS_{\text{treatment}}$ and SS_{error}:

$$(Y_i - GM) = (\bar{y}_j - GM) + (Y_i - \bar{Y}_j).$$

In the formula we see the full additive nature of the sum of squares:

$$\Sigma(y - GM)^2 = \Sigma\Sigma(\bar{y} - GM)^2 + \Sigma\Sigma(y_i - \bar{y}_j)^2.$$

The double-summation signs in front of the treatment and error terms indicate that the procedure is repeated for all subjects across all conditions. Because $\bar{y}$ is a constant for all of the subjects in a given condition, the summing within a condition can be replaced by multiplying by

n: $\Sigma n(\bar{y} - GM)^2$. Furthermore, when n is a constant it can be moved outside of the remaining summation sign and executed only once:

$$\Sigma(y - GM)^2 = n \, \Sigma(\bar{y} - GM)^2 + \Sigma\Sigma(y_i - \bar{y}_j)^2.$$

Figure 8.21 illustrates in detail the scores of your 12 hamsters as well as how each score is partitioned and contributes to each component sum of squares.

	Hamster	Score	$(y{-}GM)^2$	$(\bar{y}_j{-}GM)^2$	$(y{-}\bar{y}_j)^2$
Cage 1	1	3	4	4	0
	2	1	16	4	4
	3	4	1	4	1
	4	4	1	4	1
Cage 2	1	5	0	1	1
	2	4	1	1	0
	3	2	9	1	4
	4	5	0	1	1
Cage 4	1	6	1	9	4
	2	9	16	9	1
	3	7	4	9	1
	4	10	25	9	4
	Totals		78	56	22

Figure 8.21

Not only are the sums of squares additive, but so are the corresponding df. You have 12 hamsters in your study. The GM of all 12 of the *midsquares* scores is the basis for the SS_{total}. If you calculate the variance of all 12 scores, you would have $N - 1 = 12 - 1 = 11$ df. These df_{total} can be partitioned into the $df_{treatment}$ and the df_{error}. In calculating the $SS_{treatment}$ there were three condition means ($k = 3$). The GM can be seen as the mean of these three observations (condition means). Thus, the $df_{treatment}$ is $k - 1 = 3 - 1 = 2$. Should you wish to avoid computing the df_{error}, you could derive it as a residual: $df_{total} - df_{treatment} = 11 - 2 = 9$. The df_{error} are based on the sum of the df associated with the variance for each *cage* condition. There are $n - 1$ df in each of three conditions, $k(n - 1) = 3 + 3 + 3 = 9$.

The formula for the $SS_{treatment}$, $n\Sigma(\bar{y} - GM)^2$, only works when n is a constant, when there are the same number of subjects in all conditions. When there is inequality among the ns, the formula is modified to $\Sigma n_j(\bar{y}_j - GM)^2$, and the squared difference between each treatment condition mean and the GM is multiplied by each condition's particular n.

It is apparent from Figure 8.19 that mean square (MS) is another name for variance. The MSs are the quotients of the SSs divided by their corresponding df. Finally, as seen in Figure 8.20, F represents the ratio of the two MSs, or the two independent estimates of σ^2. If you are not using a software package to complete the analysis, you can consult the F-table for $\alpha = 0.05$ in

Appendix G (Table G.1). Along the columns are the $df_{treatment}$ and the rows are the df_{error}. Locating the intersection of 2 $df_{treatment}$ and 9 df_{error} we find the critical value of 4.26. Because your *observed* F-value (11.6) is greater than 4.26, you reject the H_0 and conclude that the number of *midsquares* the hamsters entered was influenced by the *cage* condition in which they were housed. Assuming that *midsquares* is a *valid* index of a hamster's willingness to explore, you may wish to go a step further and conclude that willingness to explore was influenced by *cage* condition. (For the discussion of validity see p. 16 in Chapter 1.)

> The word 'omnibus' arises from the Latin word *omnis,* meaning 'all'. Omnibus may be translated as 'for all'. In our case it indicates that the test is a single comprehensive test *for all* means simultaneously. Interestingly, in British English, the original word for a bus (form of transportation) was omnibus (for all).

When you look at the means of the three *cage* conditions (3, 4, and 8), you may be inclined to draw additional conclusions. For example, it may appear that as the number of cage-mates increases, so does the hamsters' willingness to explore, which was your initial hypothesis. Or, alternatively, you may conclude that the number of cage-mates makes no difference unless there are more than two hamsters per cage. The current significant F-test, however, does not provide the evidence necessary for drawing either of those possible conclusions. This significant F-test – which we will call the *omnibus F* – only tells you there is more variability among the condition means than you would have expected due to chance alone. It does not specify where among the condition means the crucial difference or differences are located.

Of what value, then, is the omnibus F-test? First and foremost, it provides an overall test of the treatments. Under certain circumstances, particularly when research designs are more complicated, this can be quite useful. Sometimes, particularly early in a research project, it is important to establish that a particular variable influences the dependent measure. Furthermore, some authors, such as Fisher himself, have argued that it is inappropriate to further examine or analyse data when the omnibus F is non-significant.

8 ● 6 STANDARDIZED EFFECT SIZES AND THE *F*-TEST

When we obtain a significant test statistic, such as t or r, it is incumbent upon us to provide a standardized estimate of the effect size. Calculating the omnibus F is a step in the calculation of a standardized estimate of the effect size. One common estimate reported when the omnibus F-value is found to be significant is η^2 (eta squared):

$$\eta^2 = \frac{SS_{total} - SS_{error}}{SS_{total}} = \frac{SS_{treatment}}{SS_{total}} \, .$$

η^2 is a correlation coefficient (like r) that will swerve to fit the condition means. Because it is a squared value, unlike r it cannot be negative. And like r, η^2 can range from 0 to 1. As Howell (2002) has pointed out, η^2 also can be considered a proportion reduction in error (PRE) measure, which was discussed in Chapter 6 (see p. 243).

For the hamster data, η^2 = 56/76 = 0.72. This value can be interpreted as saying that you have reduced the errors in predicting midsquares activity in the hamsters by 72%. The SS_{total} (78) reflects the error associated with predicting midsquares activity when you know nothing about the cage conditions of the hamsters. When you take the hamsters' cage condition into account, the error in your prediction is reduced to the SS_{error} (22), or by 72%. The popularity of η^2 waxes and wanes, and it is often criticized as biased towards overestimating the effect size.

A popular alternative to η^2 was developed by Fleiss (1969): ω^2 (omega squared):

$$\omega^2 = \frac{SS_{treatment} - (k-1)MS_{error}}{SS_{total} + MS_{error}}.$$

Fleiss's formula was designed to correct the tendency in η^2 to overestimate the effect size. As seen in the formula, ω^2 will necessarily be less than η^2. How much less? Examining the two formulae, as MS_{error} becomes larger, the correction becomes greater, and ω^2 will be smaller relative to η^2. The same relations are true for k, the number of conditions.

For your hamster data,

$$\omega^2 = \frac{56 - (3-1)2.44}{78 + 2.44} = 0.64,$$

which represents a 64% reduction in the errors associated with predicting *midsquares* activity.

With respect to your hamster data, using either estimate of effect size, you would conclude that the number of cage-mates has a large effect on the hamsters' willingness to explore, as operationally defined by *open-field* behaviour. This should not surprise you. Because the *F*-test was significant despite the very small sample size, it would be impossible to obtain simultaneously a small effect size estimate and statistical significance.

Imagine that you conducted the research in the proper manner. Again, you hypothesize that the housing conditions (number of cage-mates) influence the hamsters' willingness to explore. You add the proviso that you are only interested in medium effect sizes or greater. According to Cohen (1992), for a medium effect size for a one-way ANOVA with three treatment conditions, with power = 0.80 (an 80% chance of finding the effect), at α = 0.05 you would need 52 hamsters per condition rather than the 4 per condition in your current data set.

--- REVIEW QUESTION ---

Construct two data sets of 15 whole numbers. Sort the 15 scores into three equal groups (treatment conditions). From one of the data sets the resulting *F*-ratio should be significant and from the other data set the resulting *F*-ratio should be non-significant. Do this while keeping the within-condition variance equal across all *six* groups or conditions. Also, keep the two grand means the same.

Web Link 8.10 for an answer to the review question.

When the *F*-value is non-significant (greater than 0.05), η^2 often is not reported. When you fail to reject H_0 you will need to consider the possibility of a Type II error. Stated differently, you must question the power you had to reject H_0, if it were false, and determine an appropriate sample size. It is fairly straightforward to convert η^2 to Cohen's f and consult his effect size and sample size tables.

● ● ● ● ●

For purposes of using Cohen's table (Appendix B) for determining the necessary number of subjects, η^2 can be easily be converted into Cohen's f:

$$f = \sqrt{\frac{\eta^2}{1 - \eta^2}} = \sqrt{\frac{0.72^2}{1 - 0.72^2}} = 1.04 .$$

Similar to effect size measure, Cohen's f is based on proportion of variance explained. Examining

Cohen's effect size table, an f of 1.04 would be a very large effect. Examining his sample size table, you find that a large effect of an ANOVA with three groups requires 21 subjects per condition to ensure that power equals 0.80, meaning that you have an 80% chance of rejecting a false H_0. Because your analysis was significant, however, there is no question of lack of power, nor is there a need to calculate sample size.

 8 7 USING SPSS TO RUN AN ANOVA *F*-TEST: BETWEEN-SUBJECTS DESIGN

🖰 Web Link 8.2 for SPSS data set *onewayenriched.sav*.

From within the *Data Editor*, select *Analyze* from the menu along the top and drop down and select *Compare Means*. Next, select the *One-Way ANOVA* option that appears in the new window. In the *One-Way ANOVA* window, highlight and move the dependent variable (*midsquares*) to the *Dependent List* box. Then move the independent variable (*cage*) to the *Factor* box (Figure 8.22). Note that SPSS does not support the *Bootstrap* option for the omnibus *F*-test. Only the descriptive statistics are bootstrapped. Click *OK* to run the analysis. The results appear in the SPSS output window.

In a similar manner to the ANOVA table we created earlier, the SPSS *ANOVA* output box (Figure 8.23) reports the results of the ANOVA *F*-test. The first row, labelled *Between Groups,* corresponds to what we referred to as *treatment* (*cage*). The second row, labelled *Within Groups,* corresponds to what we have referred to as *error*. The primary difference between

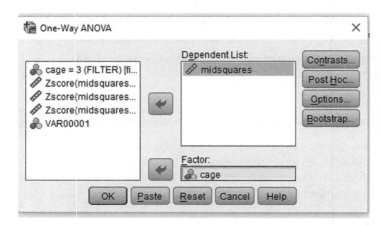

Figure 8.22

ANOVA

midsquares

	Sum of Squares	df	Mean Square	F	Sig.
Between Groups	56.000	2	28.000	11.455	.003
Within Groups	22.000	9	2.444		
Total	78.000	11			

Figure 8.23

this table and the one we created earlier is that the SPSS version has an estimate of the exact p-value ($Sig.$ = 0.003), rather than a comparison with a critical value at a given α. Practically speaking, however, rejecting an H_0 with $p < 0.05$ or with $p = 0.003$ has no significance (pun intended). It is imperative to bear in mind that a p-value reveals nothing about the effect size or the importance of the finding.

===== CHALLENGE QUESTION =====

What is the minimum number of pieces of information you would need in the ANOVA table to complete all of the other pieces? For example, it is not possible to complete the entire table with only the $SS_{treatment}$ and the F-value.

⟋ Web Link 8.11 for an answer to the challenge question.

Often in a publication the ANOVA results are reported in a sentence such as: 'The effect of *cage* was found to be significant; $F(2, 9) = 11.455$, $MS_{error} = 2.444$, $\omega^2 = 0.64$.' Here the (2, 9) following the F refers to the df (treatment and error).

As mentioned above, an analysis of a very small sample presents distinct complications regarding the testing of assumptions and for the identification of outliers. With small data sets there comes an additional worry. Researchers may understandably be anxious about their results and conclusions, particularly when the rejection of H_0 rests on a single observation. It is difficult to argue for your conclusions and interpretation when your story may stand or fall on the presence of a single score. One approach I suggest for use in such circumstances is first to remove either the highest or the lowest score in the data set, whichever appears to be the most extreme, and then to rerun the analysis. For example, in the case of your hamsters, you could remove the hamster with a *midsquares* score of 10 and rerun the ANOVA. As seen in the *ANOVA* table in Figure 8.24, although the $MS_{treatment}$ and the F-value are substantially diminished, as would be expected, the F-value remains significant: $F = 8.175$, $p < 0.05$ ($Sig.$ = 0.012). At least now you know that your finding does not rest solely on the presence of a single hamster.

Once you conclude that *cage* condition or the number of cage-mates influences the number of *midsquares* entered, you can turn your attention back to your original H_1: as the number of

ANOVA

midsquares

	Sum of Squares	df	Mean Square	F	Sig.
Between Groups	34.061	2	17.030	8.175	.012
Within Groups	16.667	8	2.083		
Total	50.727	10			

Figure 8.24

cage-mates increases, so will the hamsters' willingness to explore. Finding the omnibus F to be significant and knowing that the *cage* condition of the hamsters reduces the error in predicting *midsquares* by 72%, however, does not fully address your H_1. As mentioned earlier, at this point you only know that there is more variability among the condition means than you would have expected due to chance alone. It does not confirm that there is a systematic increase in *midsquares* entered with an increase in the number of cage-mates. Nor does it confirm that the number of cage-mates makes no differences unless there are more than two hamsters per cage. That the number of cage-mates affects the hamsters' open-field behaviour is all you may conclude at this point. To go beyond this, we will need to wait until Chapter 10.

⚲ Web Link 8.12 for an interactive demonstration of ANOVA and the relationships among sample size, within-condition variance, and variability among the means.

8 ● 8 THE THIRD-VARIABLE PROBLEM: ANALYSIS OF COVARIANCE

Already in previous chapters we have addressed typical problems that unidentified third variables can create when they remain unidentified and are left unaddressed. Once such third variables are controlled, significant *differences* or *associations* may magically appear or disappear. (For a discussion of third-variable problems, see Chapters 5, 6, and 7.)

In this section we will discuss how a third variable, one that is usually a nuisance and is undermining your *power*, can be converted into an asset that potentially increases your statistical power. The basis of this procedure, known now as *analysis of covariance* (ANCOVA), was first published by Fisher (1927) in the *Journal of Agricultural Science*. Like all statistical tests, ANCOVA will rest on further assumptions. In this section we will continue with your hamster SPSS data set.

Your hamster experiment contains three *cage* conditions based on the number of hamsters housed in a single cage and the hamsters' performances in the open-field apparatus. Now imagine that prior to testing you noticed that the weights of the hamsters varied greatly. As a consequence, you weighed and recorded each animal's weight (in grams), suspecting that it may be of use at some point during your analysis. Specifically, you suspect that the heavier hamsters are more physically and psychologically mature and, as a consequence, may be more willing

The SPSS bootstrapping option when conducting an ANOVA does not bootstrap the *F*-value, only the descriptive statistics for the treatment conditions. To obtain the bootstrapping results for the descriptive statistics you must select the *Bootstrapping* option on the *One-Way ANOVA* page and then check the *Perform bootstrapping* box in the *Bootstrap* window (Figure 8.25). Furthermore, you will need to check the *Descriptive* box in the *One-Way ANOVA: Options* window (Figure 8.26).

The output window provides you with the descriptive statistics for each condition, the bias, standard errors, and 95% confidence intervals, as discussed in Chapter 2.

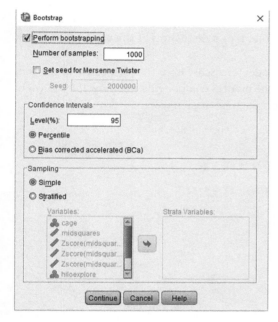

Figure 8.25

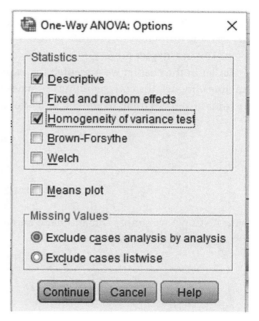

Figure 8.26

and able to explore open areas. Thus, you are hoping that weight is associated with *midsquares*. An important assumption for ANCOVA is that although weight (called the *covariate*) is free to be associated with *midsquares*, it must be random or independent with respect to the *cage* condition. Crucially, the covariate must be independent of the *independent variable*. The *independent* variable must be *independent* to avoid possible *confounding*. The assumption can be translated into a question of *difference*.

Do the *cage* conditions differ in terms of the hamsters' weights? If on average the weights of the hamsters are no different across the *cage* conditions, weight can assumed to be independent of cage condition. Recalling our discussion of the *variance sum law*, if weight is associated with *midsquares*, then weight is a variable that contributes to the overall variance in *midsquares*.

It is the overall variability in *midsquares* minus the variance associated with the variability associated with treatment that defines MS_{error}. If weight is unrelated to *cage* condition but it is related to *midsquares*, variance in *midsquares* associated with *weight* can be removed from the error term.

The value of the covariate is spatially depicted in Figures 8.27–8.29. In Figure 8.27 no covariate has been identified and the total variance is split 50–50 between treatment and error. In Figure 8.28 a covariate has been identified by the researcher and the percentage of the variance associated with error has been somewhat reduced, improving the ratio of treatment variance to error variance. In Figure 8.29, the researcher again has identified a covariate; this one greatly reduces the variance associated with error. The greater the influence of the covariate on the dependent variable, the greater the increase in power, as long as the covariate is unrelated to the independent variable. (For a discussion of the variance sum law, see p. 179 in Chapter 5.)

Earlier in the chapter we presented the basic model for a score from the perspective of the general linear model, the corresponding estimates of the model's components, and how the sources of the sum-of-squares total, treatment, and error are contained in each score:

$$y_i = \mu + \tau_k + e_i,$$

$$y_i = GM + (\bar{y}_j - GM) + (Y_i - \bar{y}_j)$$

$$(Y_i - GM) = (\bar{y}_j - GM) + (Y_i - \bar{y}_j).$$

With ANCOVA we simply add another component:

$$y_i = \mu + \tau_k + cov + e_i,$$

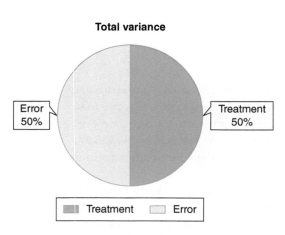

Figure 8.27

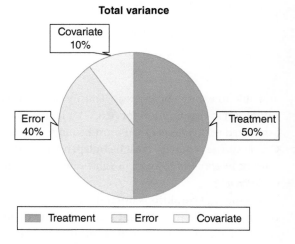

Figure 8.28

$$= GM + (\bar{y}_j - GM) + cov(Y_{cov} - \bar{y}_j) + (Y_i - \bar{y}_j)$$

$$(Y_i - GM) = (\bar{y}_j - GM) + cov(Y_{cov} - \bar{y}_j) + (Y_i - \bar{y}_j),$$

where y_i is the ith score, μ is the population mean, τ_k is the treatment effect for a given condition, cov is the score on the covariate for the ith subject, and e_i is the error associated with the ith score. SS_{error} now is the residual once $SS_{treatment}$ and SS_{cov} have been subtracted from SS_{total}.

We can estimate cov by the subject's score on the covariate minus the mean of the subject's treatment condition. Just as all variability around the GM is error until we can partition out treatment, we can also partition out other sources of variance once it is known and measured.

We return to your hamster data to examine the role that weight might play in your experiment. Figure 8.30 depicts the means of the weights for the hamsters in the three *cage* conditions. The figure shows some variability in the mean weights of the three conditions. The probability of the three conditions having exactly the same mean weight is virtually 0. The essential question is: are the *observed* differences in the means too great for you to assume that they are due to chance alone?

A one-way ANOVA using *weight* as the dependent variable and *cage* as the independent variable indicates that the *observed* differences in weight across the three *cage* conditions can be assumed to be due to chance alone; $F(2, 9) = 0.423$, $p = 0.667$ (*Sig.* in Figure 8.31).

You are now free to replace your ANOVA with an ANCOVA and remove the variance in the error term that is associated with the hamster's *weight*. To do so you will need to use a

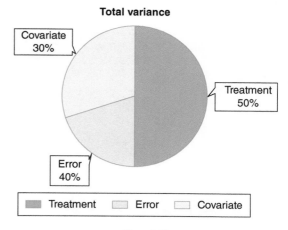

Total variance

Covariate 30%

Treatment 50%

Error 40%

Treatment ⬚ Error ⬚ Covariate

Figure 8.29

Weight:

cage	mean
1	412.25
2	335.00
4	390.00

Figure 8.30

ANOVA

weight

	Sum of Squares	df	Mean Square	F	Sig.
Between Groups	12650.167	2	6325.083	.423	.667
Within Groups	134554.750	9	14950.528		
Total	147204.917	11			

Figure 8.31

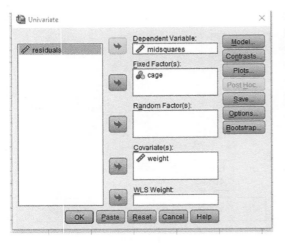

Figure 8.32

Between-Subjects Factors

		N
cage	1.00	4
	2.00	4
	4.00	4

Figure 8.33

new procedure in SPSS. Scroll down the *Analyze* tab in the SPSS *Data Editor* to the *General Linear Model*, then open, slide over, and select *Univariate*. When the *Univariate* window opens, move the *midsquares* variable to the *Dependent Variable* area, move *cage* to the *Fixed Factor(s)* area, and move *weight* to the *Covariate(s)* area (Figure 8.32). Then click *OK* to run the analysis.

The first table in the SPSS output window is the *Between-Subject Factors* table (Figure 8.33) which lists your treatment conditions (*cages*) or the levels of your *factor* along with the number of subjects in each condition.

Next in the output window you will find the *Test of Between-Subjects Effects* table (Figure 8.34). For your purposes the first row of concern is the third (for the covariate *weight*). The sum of squares associated with *weight* reflects the reduction in the sum-of-squares error in your earlier ANOVA. The 1 *df* associated with *weight* also was removed from the error term, and it is the price you pay for being able to extract the SS_{weight}. The $F(1, 8)$ of 9.577 ($p = 0.015$) relates to the significant contribution *weight* made to the *midsquares* scores. It is the subsequent reduction in the MS_{error} that is responsible for the substantial increase in the F-value (22.488) in comparison to that found in the earlier ANOVA ($F = 11.455$). Although in your earlier ANOVA the effect

Tests of Between-Subjects Effects

Dependent Variable: midsquares

Source	Type III Sum of Squares	df	Mean Square	F	Sig.
Corrected Model	67.987[a]	3	22.662	18.106	.001
Intercept	1.756	1	1.756	1.403	.270
weight	11.987	1	11.987	9.577	.015
cage	56.293	2	28.147	22.488	.001
Error	10.013	8	1.252		
Total	378.000	12			
Corrected Total	78.000	11			

Figure 8.34

of *cage* was already found to be significant, this example does help to illustrate how a third variable can be a benefit rather than a hindrance. The effective use of a covariate or covariates depends on identifying them during the design phase of the experiment. Simple subject variables such as age and gender can frequently be effective covariates, as long as they are random across the treatment conditions.

● ● ● ● ●

In the ANCOVA *Test of Between-Subjects Effects* table you may notice slight changes in the $SS_{treatment}$ and $MS_{treatment}$ from those values in the initial ANOVA. This is a result of the fact that, although weak and non-significant, there were small difference in the mean weights among the *cage* conditions. To the extent that a covariate is associated with treatment, the ANCOVA procedure makes corresponding and necessary changes to the treatment sum of squares. For a complete presentation and discussion of ANCOVA and how these changes are made, see Rutherford (2001).

In addition to the assumptions of normality and homogeneity of variance, there are two other crucial assumptions that accompany ANCOVA. First, there is the assumption that the covariate is linearly related to the dependent variable. Stated another way, ANCOVA removes the variance in the dependent variable that is linearly associated with the covariate. If the covariate and the dependent variable are related nonlinearly, the error variance attributed to the covariate will be biased. Second, ANCOVA assumes that the regression coefficient for the dependent variable regressed on the covariate is the same for all treatment conditions. When the sample size is relatively small, as is yours, researchers usually rely on a rough scatterplot of the dependent variable on covariate and testing for a mean difference in the covariate across the treatment conditions. We already found no significant difference in your covariate *weight* across the three cage conditions. Figure 8.35 is a scatterplot of *midsquares* regressed on the covariate *weight*. The figure appears to illustrate a general positive linear trend between *midsquares* and weight.

There are other more controversial uses of ANCOVA. For example, often researchers attempt to adjust for pre-existing differences in *non-equivalent* groups. This is an attempt to correct for initial group differences where subjects cannot be made equal through random assignment, so a covariate is used to adjust the scores and make the subjects more similar. For example, non-equivalent groups frequently are found in clinical psychology where patient

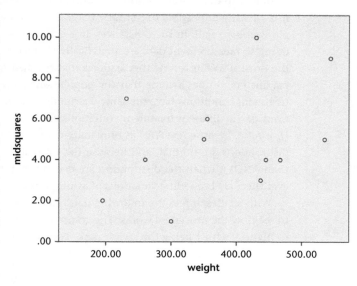

Figure 8.35

and control groups cannot be constituted through random assignment. Typically such research is not experimental but rather quasi-experimental in nature. However, even with the application of a covariate, it is highly unlikely that groups which are surely unequal on almost any measure can be equated (Miller & Chapman, 2001).

8 ● 9 NONPARAMETRIC ALTERNATIVES

The parametric tests discussed thus far in this chapter (ANOVA and ANCOVA) are appropriate for measurement data, and require the assumption that the observations to be analysed are either interval or ratio in nature. Parametric tests are 'parametric' because they involve estimating particular population *parameters* (e.g., μ and σ^2).

REVIEW QUESTION

Is your hamster data interval or ratio in nature? Why?

Web Link 8.13 for an answer to the review question.

In this section we will examine the most common nonparametric alternative to the one-way, between-subjects ANOVA: the Kruskal–Wallis (*H*) test. The Kruskal–Wallis test is designed for use with nominal data. It is also often used when the data are measurement in nature, but the researcher is concerned that the assumption of normality is markedly violated. As we saw earlier in the chapter, it is virtually impossible to test for violations of normality and the presence of outliers when sample sizes are small. In such instances, it is common to replace the ANOVA with Kruskal–Wallis. In doing so measurement data are analytically transformed into ordinal and nominal data. Although the Kruskal–Wallis test neither assumes that the distributions are normal nor estimates population parameters, it does assume that the populations represented by the observations in the different treatment conditions have the same distribution. In other words, the test assumes that the distributions of the different treatment conditions are identical and will only differ in some regard when H_0 is false. Because ANOVA has only marginally more *power* than the Kruskal–Wallis test when the distributions are normal, and because the Kruskal–Wallis test often has considerably more *power* than ANOVA when the distribution are non-normal, the Kruskal–Wallis test is appropriate whenever there are borderline violations of assumptions or whenever assumptions are difficult to test.

With small samples the following hand calculations are easily used. This also gives us a chance to see how the procedure works. The computation is based on first ranking the scores from lowest to highest, with 1 being the lowest rank. The formula for *H* is as follows:

$$H = \frac{12}{N(N+1)}\sum\frac{R_j^2}{n_j} - 3(N+1).$$

Figure 8.36 contains the reaction times (RTs) of 14 subjects in three treatment conditions. Because RT is often highly skewed, the researcher deems Kruskal–Wallis to be the appropriate test. Figure 8.37 contains the reaction times (RT) of 14 subjects after they have been ranked.

RTs in Milliseconds		
Condition 1	**Condition 2**	**Condition 3**
96	82	115
128	124	149
83	132	166
61	135	147
101	109	

Figure 8.36

Ranked RTs		
Condition 1	**Condition 2**	**Condition 3**
4	2	7
9	8	13
3	10	14
1	11	12
5	6	

Figure 8.37

We now sum the ranks in each condition and substitute them into the formula for H:

$$H = \frac{12}{14(14+1)}\left[\frac{22^2}{5} + \frac{37^2}{5} + \frac{46^2}{4}\right] - 3(14+1)$$
$$= 6.4.$$

H is distributed as χ^2 with $(k-1)$ df, where k is the number of conditions. From the χ^2 table in Appendix C, we find that the critical value for 2 df at $\alpha = 0.05$ is 5.99. Because the researcher's *observed H* is greater than the critical value, he or she rejects H_0 and concludes there is sufficient evidence to suggest that condition influences RT. As was the case with ANOVA, H only provides an omnibus test. It does not provide information concerning where the crucial difference(s) might be. It is interesting to note that at the heart of the formula for H is the χ^2 test, albeit modified with a correction factor. In effect, the Kruskal–Wallis may begin with a transformation of measurement data into ordinal data (ranks), but then it transforms the ranks into nominal data (frequencies). We have come full circle during the chapter.

• • • • •

The original purpose of the Kruskal–Wallis test was the analysis of nominal data in multiple treatment conditions. It is also generally used for ordinal data, such as patients rating their pain on a scale of 1 to 10. Some authors have argued that even with measurement data, unless you have a large sample size and can clearly demonstrate that your data are normal, the Kruskal–Wallis test should always be used as a safe alternative to ANOVA. Others have argued, however, that the one-way ANOVA is very robust and rather insensitive to typical deviations from normality. This latter group of researchers maintains that the Kruskal–Wallis test should only be used as an alternative to ANOVA in extreme circumstances and should be reserved for use with nominal and ordinal data.

Hypothesis Test Summary

	Null Hypothesis	Test	Sig.	Decision
1	The distribution of midsquares is the same across categories of cage.	Independent-Samples Kruskal-Wallis Test	.017	Reject the null hypothesis.

Asymptotic significances are displayed. The significance level is .05.

Figure 8.38

We now return to your hamster data. Because your sample size is small and you are concerned with possible violations of ANOVA assumptions, you have decided that the Kruskal–Wallis H is the most appropriate test for your data.

To run the Kruskal–Wallis test in SPSS, scroll down the *Analyze* tab in the SPSS *Data Editor* to the *Nonparametric Tests*, then open, slide over, and select *Independent Samples*. When the *Nonparametric Tests: Two or More Independent Samples* window opens, select the *Fields* tab at the top. When the next window opens, move the *midsquares* variable to the *Test Fields* area and move *cage* to the *Group* area. Next, select the *Settings* tab at the top. At this point, we will leave the *Automatically choose the tests based on the data* option unchanged. To run the analysis, click on the *Run* button at the bottom of the window.

In the output window a *Hypothesis Test Summary* box appears (Figure 8.38). The first area in the box describes the H_0 that is being tested. As described above, this is not a test of differences in the condition means, but rather a test for any difference at all in the distributions of the cage conditions. The next area identifies the test: the Kruskal–Wallis test for independent samples. The final area indicates the *Decision*: you should reject H_0 at the $\alpha = 0.05$ level.

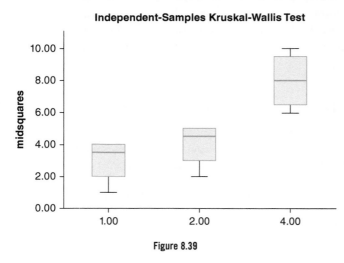

Independent-Samples Kruskal-Wallis Test

Figure 8.39

If you double-click the *Decision* area, another window will open displaying box-and-whisker plots and the summary statistics. Analogous to the bar chart for the hamster data that accompanied your ANOVA, the box-and-whiskers plot (Figure 8.39) shows that the distribution of *cage* condition 3 does not overlap with those of the other two cage conditions. The summary statistics table (Figure 8.40) reports the total number of observations (*N*), the χ^2 (*Test Statistic*), the degrees of freedom, and calculated p-value of 0.017 (*Asymptotic Sig.*).

It is interesting to note that the results of all omnibus tests (ANOVA, ANCOVA, and

Kruskal–Wallis) employed to analyse your hamster data were significant. Even the χ^2 test of independence used at the outset of the chapter following the transformation of the measurement data into nominal data was significant. With moderate to large effect sizes, such parallel findings are quite common. Remember, these tests are all related. Finding these omnibus tests to be significant, however, does not fully address your H_1: do the number of *midsquares* entered increase with an increase in the number of cage-mates?

Total N	12
Test Statistic	8.142
Degrees of Freedom	2
Asymptotic Sig. (2-sided test)	.017

Figure 8.40

At this point you may be reminded of the initial analyses you performed on the hamster data: a series of three *t*-tests. We will find in Chapter 11 that *t*-tests, albeit in a modified form, will provide one approach to getting closer to a more complete evaluation of your research hypothesis. Recall what was stated in this and other chapters: regardless of how complicated our research designs may be, the crucial questions often come down to examining pairs of conditions, in terms of either their differences or associations.

8 ● 10 CHAPTER SUMMARY

The purpose of this chapter was to examine the most common statistical tests (ANOVA, ANCOVA, and Kruskal–Wallis) designed to determine whether the observations in more than two conditions arise from a single population. This question is often phrased as 'is there any treatment effect?' Our primary focus was on a one-way, between-subjects ANOVA which is based on two independent estimates of σ^2. We again examined the *third-variable problem*. This time, however, we discovered that when the *third variable* was random with respect to the independent variable it may be an asset by reducing the error variance: ANCOVA. ANOVA, and the other discussed tests were used as *omnibus* tests. That is, the tests could only indicate the presence or absence of a treatment effect, not the effect's specific location or nature. When the ANOVA or the ANCOVA omnibus *F*-values are significant, the results only indicate that the condition means are spread out more than would be expected due to chance alone. The significant *F* does not specify where among the means the spread is too great.

In circumstances where either parametric assumptions required by ANOVA are violated or when the data are categorical in nature, the nonparametric Kruskal–Wallis *H*-test is preferred. When the *H*-test is significant, the results only indicate that in one way or another the distributions of the treatment conditions are too dissimilar to be considered the result of mere chance. As with ANOVA, a significant Kruskal–Wallis *H* does not reveal which distribution(s) is dissimilar from the others.

It should be becoming clearer that the underlying 'plot' has remained the same. There is a research question that is posed in terms of either *difference* or *association*, and these questions are interchangeable. The researcher has collected either *categorical* or *measurement* data, and the latter can be transformed into the former. Finally, a *difference* or an *association* is evaluated in terms of (1) the difference between what is *expected* and what is *observed* and (2) what can be expected due to chance alone. Finally, regardless of the test used and the sample size, Type I and Type II errors are always possible. There is no substitute for independent replication of results to demonstrate their reliability.

 ## RECOMMENDED READINGS

Corder, G. W., & Foreman, D. I. (2014). *Nonparametric statistics: A step-by-step approach* (2nd ed.). Hoboken, NJ: Wiley.

The first six chapters in this book provide a detailed description of the logic, the need for, and the computations used in nonparametric tests.

Miller, G. A., & Chapman, J. P. (2001). Misunderstanding analysis of covariance. *Journal of Abnormal Psychology*, *110*(1), 40–48.

This article is a good summary of ANCOVA and the questionable uses to which it has been put.

Rutherford, A. (2001). *Introduction to ANOVA and ANCOVA: A GLM approach.* London: Sage.

This is an excellent introduction to ANCOVA and how it is used with traditional ANOVA. It also contains a useful discussion of the relationship between regression and ANCOVA and the GLM approach.

 ## CHAPTER REVIEW QUESTIONS

Multiple-choice questions

1 An estimate of σ^2 based on the variability among the condition means is unbiased _____.

   a   regardless of the veracity of the null hypothesis
   b   if the null hypothesis is false
   c   if there is no variability among the condition means
   d   if the null hypothesis is true
   e   if there is a large sample size

2 An estimate of σ^2 based on the average within-condition variance is unbiased _____.

   a   regardless of the veracity of the null hypothesis
   b   if the null hypothesis is false
   c   if there is no variability among the condition means
   d   if the null hypothesis is true
   e   if there is a large sample size

3 According to the model we have used in this chapter, which is *not* a component of an individual score?

   a   The population variance
   b   The population mean
   c   The treatment effect
   d   The difference between the individual score and its condition mean
   e   They are all components of an individual score

4   Treatment effect or τ_j is estimated by _____.

   a   the difference between a score and the grand mean

   b   the difference between a score and the condition mean

   c   the difference between the condition mean and the grand mean

   d   the difference between the score and the condition variance

   e   None of the above: a treatment effect cannot be estimated

5   If a one-way ANOVA has four treatment conditions, how many degrees of freedom treatment are there?

   a   3

   b   4

   c   1

   d   0

   e   It depends on the number of subjects in the treatment conditions

6   If a one-way ANOVA has four treatment conditions, how many degrees of freedom error are there?

   a   3

   b   4

   c   1

   d   0

   e   It depends on the number of subjects in the treatment conditions

7   With a one-way ANOVA what is the required sample size for a researcher to test for a large effect size at $\alpha = 0.5$ and a power of 0.80?

   a   38

   b   95

   c   76

   d   100

   e   It depends on the number of treatment conditions

8   If there were initially 3 $df_{treatment}$, 16 df_{error}, and 19 df_{total} associated with an ANOVA, what would be the resulting treatment, error, and total dfs if a covariate were added to the analysis?

   a   3 $df_{treatment}$, 16 df_{error}, and 19 df_{total}

   b   2 $df_{treatment}$, 16 df_{error}, and 19 df_{total}

   c   3 $df_{treatment}$, 15 df_{error}, and 18 df_{total}

   d   3 $df_{treatment}$, 15 df_{error}, and 19 df_{total}

   e   2 $df_{treatment}$, 16 df_{error}, and 18 df_{total}

9   Following a one-way, between-subjects ANOVA, if the sum-of-squares treatment was 45 and the sum-of-squares error was 55, what is the accompanying η^2?

   a   0.45

   b   0.55

   c   45

   d   0.82

   e   There is insufficient information to determine the η^2

10 Which of the following is not an assumption necessary for conducting an ANCOVA?

a   The covariate is linearly related to the dependent variable

b   The covariate is linearly related to the independent variable

c   The regression coefficient for the dependent variable regressed on the covariate is the same for all treatment conditions

d   Homogeneity of variance

e   All of the above are assumptions necessary for conducting an ANCOVA

Short-answer questions

1   With a one-way, between-subjects design, why is the expected value of the F-ratio equal to 1, if the null hypothesis is true?

2   On average, what happens to the F-ratio if the null hypothesis is false? Why?

3   What is responsible for the sums of squares that make up the sum-of-squares *error*?

4   Complete the missing value in the ANOVA summary table in Figure 8.41.

Source	SS	df	MS	F
Treatment		2	5	.5
Error				
Total	100			

Figure 8.41

5   Given the descriptive statistics in Figure 8.42, what is the resulting F-value?

	Cond. 1	Cond. 2	Cond. 3
$\bar{Y}$	11	9	13
S^2	10	8	6
n	10	10	10

Figure 8.42

Data set questions

1   A psychologist hypothesized that meditation prior to a memory test would improve scores. To test her hypothesis, she randomly assigned 15 subjects to 3 conditions: condition 1 (no meditation), condition 2 (5 minutes of meditation), and condition 3 (10 minutes of meditation). Do the data in Figure 8.43 support her hypothesis? The scores are the number of items correctly recalled. Be sure to include all tests of assumptions (with conclusions), descriptive statistics, an appropriate graph, ANOVA summary table, and state and test the overall null hypothesis. Complete the analysis two ways: first, assuming that you can make the parametric assumptions; and second, assuming that you cannot make those assumptions. Draw the appropriate conclusions from both analyses.

Cond. 1	Cond. 2	Cond. 3
5	6	8
10	15	4
7	11	16
9	13	12
2	3	14

Figure 8.43

2 First, imagine an analysis where the sum-of-squares total, treatment, and error are 73.6, 19.6, and 54, respectively. The degrees of freedom are 14, 2, and 12, respectively. Assuming a between-subjects design, what is the resulting F-value and what do you conclude? Now imagine a covariate that accounts for 50% of the sum-of-squares total. What is the new resulting F-value and what do you conclude?

3 Construct a data set of 15 whole numbers between 5 and 20. Separate them into three equal groups (treatment conditions) twice, once where the resulting F-ratio would be significant and once where the resulting F-ratio would not be significant. Try to keep the within-group variances as similar as possible across all *six* groups.

Don't forget to use the online resources! Meet your supporting stats tutor through an **introductory video**, review your maths skills with a **diagnostic pre-test**, explore statistical principles through **interactive simulations**, practice analysis techniques with **SPSS datasets**, and check your work with **answers to all in-text questions**.

https://study.sagepub.com/bors

9

Chapter contents

TESTING FOR A DIFFERENCE: MULTIPLE RELATED SAMPLES

KEY CONCEPTS: within-subjects design, randomized block design, repeated-measures ANOVA, sum-of-squares block, sum-of-squares subject, sphericity, partial eta squared, Friedman's two-way ANOVA by ranks test.

9 ● 1 PURPOSE

As was the case with the previous chapter, the purpose of this chapter is to examine several statistical tests that are used to determine whether two or more sets of scores (treatment conditions) are likely to be members of a single population. Whereas the previous chapter focused on *between-subjects* designs, the current chapter addresses *related-samples* and *within-subjects* designs. *Related-samples* is the most comprehensive term, which denotes designs where the observations in one condition are *not* independent of the observations in the other conditions. Subjects are not randomly assigned to conditions; in fact all subjects may be tested in all conditions. As in the previous chapter, we will be concerned only with one-way analyses, designs with only one independent variable. Typically, the data are *measurement* in nature and the designs are *experimental* rather than *observational*. (For a review of the distinctions among *experimental, quasi-experimental,* and *observational* data in, see p. 18 in Chapter 1.)

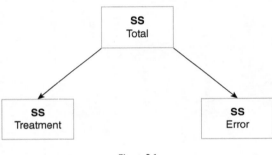

Figure 9.1

Connections will be made with material previously covered, such as homogeneity of variance, repeated-measures or paired-samples *t*-test, ANCOVA, standardized effect size, *power*, and nonparametric tests. We will begin with a review of the logic underlying a one-way ANOVA and then the related-samples *t*-test. We will explore the most universal form of a related-samples ANOVA: the *randomized block* design. In a randomized block design, although there are different subjects in each condition, groups of subjects across the conditions are related in some fashion. This is followed by an examination of the most common variant of the randomized block analysis: a *repeated-measures* design where all subjects are tested in all conditions. Finally, we will explore an alternative nonparametric procedure: Friedman's two-way analysis of variance by ranks. As we were in Chapters 5 and 8, in this chapter we are primarily concerned with a family of tests based on the intersection of (1) a research question of *difference* and (2) *measurement* data.

Figure 9.1 depicts the partitioning of the sum-of-squares total (SS_{total}) for a one-way, between-subjects ANOVA

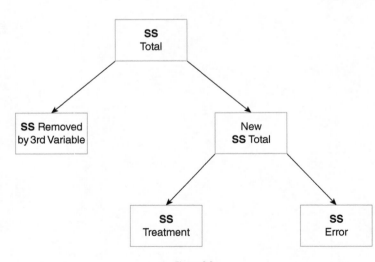

Figure 9.2

that was the focus of Chapter 8. Figure 9.2 depicts the partitioning of SS_{total} when a covariate was present. Figure 9.2 also depicts the related-samples analysis which is the focus of this chapter. In a randomized block analysis, the sum of squares (SS) *removed by the third variable* will correspond to SS_{block}. In a repeated-measures analysis, the *SS removed by the third variable* will correspond to $SS_{subject}$. As was the case with ANCOVA, the purpose of a randomized block design and of repeated measures is to reduce the error term and increase power. Finally, this chapter illustrates even more than the previous one that although steam, water, ice, and snow may look and feel very different, they are all forms of H_2O.

9 ● 2 INTRODUCTION

In the previous chapter we imaginatively explored hamster 'personality'. Now envision yourself as an animal psychologist wanting to examine the effects of early housing environment on hamster intelligence. As was the case with hamster personality, anyone who has had pet hamsters knows that some appear to be 'smarter' or more 'intelligent' than others.

- - - - -

The noun *intelligence* is derived from the Latin verb *intelligere*, which means 'to comprehend' or 'to understand'. Historically the term had more to do with wisdom than with empirical knowledge. In modern psychology over the past 150 years, there have been, and continue to be, a broad range of definitions: the ability to reason, plan, solve problems, deal with complex ideas, learn quickly, quickly process information, apply information, think abstractly, and pay attention, to name just a few. Some would argue that the concept is both theoretically and practically useless. For a comprehensive history of the notion of intelligence in psychology, see Cianciolo and Sternberg (2004). Tests of intelligence have varied in content at least as much as have the definitions. Regardless of the position one chooses, reliable individual differences in performance on almost any task, in both humans and hamsters, can be observed. These reliably observed individual differences in hamster and human performance are what gives rise to our notions of intelligence.

Assume you have noted that hamsters housed with cage-mates appear to be quicker to find things than those housed in isolation, particularly finding ways of escaping their cage. Furthermore, from previous research you know that forms of enrichment, including cage conditions, have been shown to facilitate learning in rodents. Your pets and

> As in the previous chapter, you may be concerned with issues of *power* and *sample size*. Normally we would determine the desired *effect size* for which we wished to test (small, medium, or large) and then determine the required sample size. For demonstration purposes, however, we will keep this data set small ($n = 12$).

past research have piqued your scientific curiosity. After careful consideration, you hypothesize (H_1) that hamsters will be more intelligent, the more social (number of cage-mates) their early housing experience.

To test your hypothesis, you randomly assign 12 young hamsters, 6 from each of two litters, to one of three housing conditions for 30 days. As in your previous experiment (Chapter 8), in the first condition (*cage 1*) the four hamsters are housed in isolation (one hamster per cage); in the second condition (*cage 2*) the hamsters are housed two per cage; and in the third condition (*cage 4*) all four hamsters are housed in a single cage.

After the 30 days, your 12 hamsters are individually tested in a T-maze (Figure 9.3). The testing begins with the hamster being placed in the opening of the maze (bottom of the T). During each trial food is available at one arm of the T, the arm behind the light blue door. The arm of the T with the grey door and the food is randomized from trial to trial. Each day the hamster is given 10 trials. The score for each hamster (*days*) is the number of days required for the hamster to master the maze. Mastering the maze is operationally defined as the hamster correctly choosing the door on 9 out of the 10 trials on a given day. Whatever the validity of the T-maze, you can be certain that there could be countless other operational definitions of hamster intelligence.

=== **REVIEW QUESTION** ===

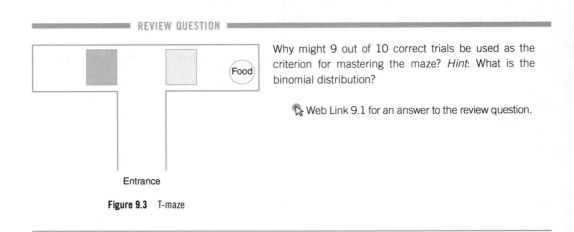

Why might 9 out of 10 correct trials be used as the criterion for mastering the maze? *Hint*: What is the binomial distribution?

⭠ Web Link 9.1 for an answer to the review question.

Figure 9.3 T-maze

• • • • •

Maze learning has been used for many decades to test rodents' cognitive capabilities. The apparatus has been employed in the field of learning and in many other areas of research, such as neuroscience and psychopharmacology. It also has been frequently used in enrichment studies, such as that of Bors and Forrin (1996). For a review of some of the earlier literature using simple T and Y mazes, see Olton (1979). The current data to be analysed are a small, fictional version of those reported in Bors and Forrin (1996).

As usual, the first step in data analysis is to compute and present your descriptive statistics (Figure 9.4). Each row in the figure represents a hamster. The first column (*days*) reports the number of days required for the hamster to reach the criterion for mastering the maze (dependent variable). The second column (*cage*) is the condition under which the young hamster was housed

days	cage
8.00	1.00
6.00	1.00
19.00	1.00
19.00	1.00
3.00	2.00
7.00	2.00
13.00	2.00
17.00	2.00
4.00	4.00
2.00	4.00
10.00	4.00
12.00	4.00

Figure 9.4

days	cage	Zdays	ZSco01	StdZ01
8.00	1.00	-.71673	.	.
6.00	1.00	-1.00342	.	.
19.00	1.00	.86007	.	.
19.00	1.00	.86007	.	.
3.00	2.00	.	-1.12572	.
7.00	2.00	.	-.48245	.
13.00	2.00	.	.48245	.
17.00	2.00	.	1.12572	.
4.00	4.00	.	.	-.63013
2.00	4.00	.	.	-1.05021
10.00	4.00	.	.	.63013
12.00	4.00	.	.	1.05021

Figure 9.5

(independent variable). To follow along in SPSS, go to the data set (*randomblock.sav*) found on the book's web page and produce the descriptive statistics using SPSS.

Web Link 9.2 for SPSS data set *randomblock.sav*.

As in the previous chapter, from the menu across the top of the *SPSS Data Editor* window click on *Data* and slide down and choose the *Select Cases* option. When the *Select Cases* window opens, choose the *If condition is satisfied* option and click on the *IF* button. When the *Select Cases: If* window opens, highlight and move the variable *cage* over to the empty rectangle and enter '= 1'. Then click *Continue*. When returned to the *Select Cases* window, click *OK*. This will allow you to separately produce descriptive statistics for the *cage 1* hamsters. When doing so be sure to select *Options* and then click on all of the options including *skewness*. Also check the box labelled *Save standardized values as variables*. This procedure of using the *Data/ Select Cases* functions can be repeated for separately producing the descriptive statistics for the *cage 2* and *cage 4* hamsters. Once this is completed, be sure to return to the *Select Cases* window and select the *All cases* option.

Web Link 9.3 for a review of the instructions for computing descriptive statistics in SPSS in Chapter 2.

The difficulties related to the testing of assumptions and the identification of outliers with small sample sizes that were discussed in the previous chapter are also relevant here, as are the strategies for addressing the problems.

Cage	Mean	Variance
1	13.00	48.67
2	10.00	38.67
4	7.00	22.67

Figure 9.6

For a review of Hartley's F_{max} test, see p. 184 in Chapter 5.

The three new z-score variables you will find in the SPSS *Data Editor* indicate that there are no outliers: no z-scores greater than ± 4.00 (Figure 9.5).

The means and variances for the three cage conditions are found in Figure 9.6. Consistent with your H_1, as the number of cage-mates increases there is a decrease in the mean number of days required for mastering the T-maze. Using the F_{max} test, there is insufficient evidence to reject the assumption of homogeneity of variance: 48.67/22.67 = 2.15 (the critical value with three conditions and 3 *df* is 27.8).

9 ● 3 REVIEWING THE BETWEEN-SUBJECTS ANOVA AND THE *T*-TEST

In this section we will briefly review the logic of the one-way, between-subjects ANOVA and the paired-samples *t*-test, as well as how these tests might be applied to your current hamster data. This is also another opportunity to illustrate the differences between the independent-samples (between-subjects) and related-samples (within-subjects) designs.

In the previous chapter we examined the underlying logic of a between-subjects ANOVA. We presented a model used for partitioning a score into its component parts and the related notion of two independent estimates of population variance (σ^2). The first estimate is based on the within-condition variance (error) and the second is based on the variability among the condition (treatment) means:

$$y_i = \mu + \tau_k + \varepsilon_i,$$

where y_i is the *i*th score, μ is the population mean, τ_k is the treatment effect for a given condition, and ε_i is the error associated with the *i*th score.

The parameter components are estimated by the following statistics:

$$Y_i = GM + (\bar{y}_j - GM) + (Y_i - \bar{Y}_j),$$

where the subscript *j* refers to the *j*th condition.

● ● ● ● ●

μ is estimated by the *GM*.

τ_k is estimated by $(\bar{y}_j - GM)$.

ε_i is estimated by $(Y_i - \bar{Y}_j)$.

For the discussion in Chapter 8 of the two independent estimates of population variance (σ^2) and their role in the *F*-test, see p. 331.

Your experimental or alternative hypothesis (H_1) is that an increase in the number of cage-mates will decrease the number of *days* it takes hamsters to master the T-maze. Your H_0 is that the number of cage-mates will not influence maze mastering. Your results, after conducting a between-subjects ANOVA, are found in Figure 9.7. The figure shows that the resulting F-value of 0.982 with 2 df treatment (between groups) and 9 df error (within groups) is non-significant with a p-value greater than 0.05 (*Sig.* = 0.411). As a consequence, you fail to reject H_0 and conclude that there is insufficient evidence to infer that cage condition influences hamster intelligence, as operationalized by T-maze mastery.

> For the sake of brevity, we will forgo the formal examination of assumptions and the creation of a bar chart. Remember, the testing of assumptions and pictorial representations of the data are necessary components when reporting all data analyses.

ANOVA

days

	Sum of Squares	df	Mean Square	F	Sig.
Between Groups	72.000	2	36.000	.982	.411
Within Groups	330.000	9	36.667		
Total	402.000	11			

Figure 9.7

Of course you may be making a Type II error, which is an understandable concern, because of your sample size. Normally you would first consider the minimum desired *effect size* for which you wished to test (small, medium, or large) and then determine the required sample size. As in the previous chapter, for demonstration purposes, we have kept the data set small ($n = 12$).

> As we saw in Chapter 8, a third variable need not always be a source of apprehension, as it was in Chapters 6 and 7.

Now imagine that after you found that your H_1 was not supported by the data, you are informed that your research assistant used hamsters from two litters and, furthermore, he randomly assigned an equal number of hamsters from each litter to each of the three cage conditions. Although the results of your experiment failed to support your hypothesis, a curious third-variable issue has complicated matters. As you will see, this third variable may turn into a tool that breathes hope into your data.

Applying the t-test

In this subsection we review the repeated-measures t-test, its logic, and its possible relevance to your current data. As stated in Chapter 5, we discussed t-tests for both independent samples and related or paired samples. The potential advantage of the paired-samples t-tests is that the variance associated with individual differences can be removed from the denominator or error term by subtracting each subject's second score from his or her first score. This procedure also corrects for the violation of independence of observations. These differences (d-scores) then are tested against the expected value of 0 using the variability in the d-scores in the error term. (For the discussion of repeated measures and the violation of the assumption of independence of observations, see p. 190 in Chapter 5.)

As was stated, repeated-measures is not the only form of related-samples design. Any design where the scores in one conditions can be related to the scores in another condition is a form of related-samples design. On the basis of the fact that you have hamsters from two litters, we can reconstruct your data file to create a related-samples design. Hamsters from the same litter are likely to be more similar than hamsters from different litters. The rows in a data file can be made related (correlated) by ensuring that all of the observations in each row are from the same litter. Figure 9.8 depicts such a reconstruction. The scores in rows 1 and 2 comprise hamsters from litter 1, while rows 3 and 4 comprise hamsters from litter 2. The columns are the *cage* conditions. Recall that the independent-samples t-test assumes that the observations are random across conditions. Figure 9.9 illustrates the strong correlations among the conditions that exist once we have ordered the data by litter, a violation of the assumption of independence.

Once this is completed we can compute the three possible paired-samples t-tests. We correct the dependence by creating d-scores, as we did in Chapter 5. For example, to test for a difference between *cage 1* and *cage 2*, we first derive the four d-scores (5, –1, 6, and 2) and calculate their standard deviation (3.16). The t-value can be calculated as follows:

> Creating d-scores not only corrects for the lack of independence of observations, but also can result in increased power. Bear in mind that an increase in power – the ability to reject a false null hypothesis (H_0) – is only possible when H_0 is false. When H_0 is true, rejecting H_0 constitutes a Type I error.

cage1	cage2	cage4
8.00	3.00	4.00
6.00	7.00	2.00
19.00	13.00	10.00
19.00	17.00	12.00

Figure 9.8

Correlations

		cage1	cage2	cage4
cage1	Pearson Correlation	1	.891	.984*
	Sig. (2-tailed)		.109	.016
	N	4	4	4
cage2	Pearson Correlation	.891	1	.901
	Sig. (2-tailed)	.109		.099
	N	4	4	4
cage4	Pearson Correlation	.984*	.901	1
	Sig. (2-tailed)	.016	.099	
	N	4	4	4

*. Correlation is significant at the 0.05 level (2-tailed).

Figure 9.9

$$t = \frac{\bar{d} - \mu}{s_d/\sqrt{n}} = \frac{3 - 0}{3.16/2} = 1.90.$$

===== REVIEW QUESTION =====

How are a *paired-samples* t-test and *one-sample* t-test similar?

Web Link 9.4 for an answer to the review question.

Figure 9.10 reports the results from your three t-tests. The p-value for the three t-tests reveals mixed results. Using $\alpha = 0.05$, you do not find the results fully supportive of your H_1 that there will be a reduction in the number of days required to master the maze as the number of cage-mates increases.

In addition to the somewhat complicated picture presented by the results, there are two complications that make this approach to analysing your data inappropriate. The first problem is one we encountered with the multiple t-test approach in the previous chapter: the more tests a researcher conducts at $\alpha = 0.05$, the greater the risk of committing a Type I error, if H_0 is true. Although this problem is neither insurmountable nor the approach entirely misplaced, the second problem is fatal. If you closely examine the *litter* and *cage* condition affiliations of the 12 scores, you will discover there are more ways than one to reconstruct the data set into a repeated-measures design. The scores in rows 1 and 2 can be switched within one or two of the columns, and the same is true for the scores in rows 3 and 4. For example,

t-test	t-value	df	p-value
Cage 1 vs Cage 2	1.90	3	.1.54
Cage 2 vs Cage 4	2.12	3	.124
Cage 1 vs Cage 4	4.90	3	.016

Figure 9.10

cage1	cage2	cage4
8.00	7.00	2.00
6.00	3.00	4.00
19.00	17.00	12.00
20.00	13.00	10.00

Figure 9.11

t-test	t-value	df	p-value
Cage 1 vs Cage 2	2.47	3	.090
Cage 2 vs Cage 4	2.12	3	.124
Cage 1 vs Cage 4	3.78	3	.032

Figure 9.12

Figure 9.11 shows an alternative reconstruction. With this reconstruction, the condition means remain the same but the t-values for the three t-tests are changed. Figure 9.12 reports the three t-tests for this reconstruction of the data set. The fact that the resulting p-values can vary depending upon how the reconstruction is completed makes this approach unsound.

===== REVIEW QUESTION =====

If the condition (treatment) means remain unchanged, how is it possible that the t-values change?

Web Link 9.5 for a discussion of and answer to the review question.

9 ● 4 THE LOGIC OF THE RANDOMIZED BLOCK DESIGN

In this section we find how your knowledge of the hamsters' litter affiliation might be used in an ANOVA to reduce your SS_{error} and increase your *power* in a similar manner as did knowing the weights of your hamsters in the previous chapter. The ANOVA of a randomized block design will be shown to be a special case of ANCOVA discussed in the previous chapter. As you may recall, ANCOVA adds a further component (the covariate, *cov*) to our initial model of a score:

$$y_i = \mu + \tau_k + cov + \varepsilon_i.$$

With respect to the randomized block design, the variance in *y* (dependent variable) associated with a covariate is now associated with a blocking variable (β), in your case the *litter*:

$$y_i = \mu + \tau_k + \beta_j + \varepsilon_i,$$

where y_i is the *i*th score, μ is the population mean, τ_k is the treatment effect for a given condition, β_j is the block effect for a given block, and ε_i is the error associated with the *i*th score.

The parameters can be estimated as follows:

$$y_i = GM + (\bar{y}_j - GM) + (\bar{Y}_{\beta j} - GM) + (Y_i - \bar{Y}_j - \bar{Y}_{\beta j} + GM),$$

where y_i is the *i*th score, *GM* is the mean of all scores in the sample regardless of condition or block, $\bar{y}_j$ is the mean of the *y*-scores in a given condition or treatment, and $\bar{Y}_{\beta j}$ is the mean of the *y*-scores in a given block.

We see that the difference between an individual score and the *GM* has three components: an estimate of the treatment effect, an estimate of the block effect, and an estimate of the error associated with the particular score. The error term now also contains not only the removal of the treatment effect from the score, but also the removal of the block effect. Computationally, the error term contains the addition of the *GM*. Because both a treatment mean and a block mean contain the *GM*, the addition of the *GM* compensates for the double removal of the *GM* in the error term:

$$(Y_i - GM) = (\bar{y}_j - GM) + (\bar{Y}_{\beta j} - GM) + (Y_i - \bar{Y}_j - \bar{Y}_{\beta j} + GM).$$

● ● ● ● ●

What makes up a given block mean? First of all, the mean of a block is an estimate of μ, which is estimated by the *GM*. There is also the true effect of being in the particular block. Furthermore, the average error of all the subjects in that particular block will alter the mean of the block. Thus when we subtract the mean *y*-score of a particular block from a score within that block, we are subtracting everything that goes into the mean of the block, including *GM* and the average error.

● ● ● ● ●

Treatment effects and block effects are assumed to be constants, within a treatment condition and within a block. If treatment condition and block are independent:

1   The difference between two scores in two different treatment conditions is the difference in *error* plus a difference in the *treatment effects*, if there is one. The block effects cancel themselves out.

2   The difference between two scores in two different blocks is the difference in *error* plus a difference in the *block effects*, if there is one. The treatment effects cancel themselves out.

3   The difference between two scores in the same treatment condition and the same block is only the difference in *error*.

If we did not assume that treatment and block effects were constants and independent, this additive model and the analysis that follows from it would be inappropriate.

Figure 9.13 reproduces your hamster data (*days*) along with the *GM*, the conditions means, and the block means.

Cage 1	Cage 2	Cage 4		
8	3	4		
6	7	2	Block mean =	5.00
19	13	10		
19	17	12	Block mean =	15.00
Cage mean = 13.00	Cage mean = 10.00	Cage mean = 7.00		
			GM =	10.00

Figure 9.13

If we apply the new model to the first hamster in the *cage 1* condition ($y = 8$) we find

$$(Y_i - GM) = (\bar{Y}_j - GM) + (\bar{Y}_{\beta j} - GM) + (Y_i - \bar{Y}_j - \bar{Y}_{\beta j} - GM)$$

$$(8 - 10) = (13 - 10) + (5 - 10) + (8 - 13 - 5 + 10).$$

The above component estimates are the basis for the ANOVA *F*-test with a blocking variable. Recall that these terms need to be squared:

$$(8 - 10)^2 = (13 - 10)^2 + (5 - 10)^2 + (8 - 13 - 5 + 10)^2.$$

These calculations now need to be repeated for all hamsters and summed:

$$\Sigma\Sigma\,(Y_i - GM)^2 = \Sigma\Sigma(\bar{Y}_j - GM)^2 + \Sigma\Sigma(\bar{Y}_{\beta j} - GM)^2 + \Sigma\Sigma(Y_i - \bar{Y}_j - \bar{Y}_{\beta j} + GM)^2.$$

The double-summation signs in front of the treatment, block, and error terms indicate that the calculation is repeated for all subjects across all conditions. Because $\bar{y}_j$ is a constant for all of the subjects in a given treatment condition and $\bar{Y}_{\beta j}$ is a constant for all of the subjects in a given block, the summing within a condition and block can be replaced by multiplying by n and bn: $\sum n(\bar{y} - GM)^2$ and $\sum bn(\bar{Y}_{\beta j} - GM)$, where n is the number of subjects within a treatment condition and bn is the number of subjects within a block. Furthermore, when n is a constant across all treatments it can be moved outside of the remaining summation sign and the multiplication executed only once. Similarly, when bn is a constant across all blocks, which it must be, it can be moved outside of the remaining summation sign and the multiplication completed only once:

$$\Sigma\Sigma(Y_i - GM)^2 = n\Sigma(\bar{y}_j - GM)^2 + bn\Sigma(\bar{Y}_{\beta j} - GM)^2 + \Sigma\Sigma(Y_i - \bar{Y}_J - \bar{Y}_{\beta j} + GM)^2.$$

Figure 9.14 shows the 12 scores (*days*) after the GM has been removed, the $(Y_i - GM)$ component of the model. Note: the new GM is 0, as it must be after the original GM was subtracted from all of the scores. Also note that although the condition means and block means have changed, the absolute differences among them have not changed.

Cage 1	Cage 2	Cage 4		
−2	−7	−6		
−4	−3	−8	Block mean =	−5.00
9	3	0		
9	7	2	Block mean =	+5.00
Cage mean = 3.00	Cage mean = 0.00	Cage mean = −3.00		
			GM =	0.00

Figure 9.14

Cage 1	Cage 2	Cage 4
4	49	36
16	9	64
81	9	0
81	49	4
	Total =	402

Figure 9.15

Figure 9.15 depicts the 12 scores (*days*) after the GM has been removed and the differences have been squared to create the *sum-of-squares total*. The calculation of the total of 402 (SS_{total}) is expressed by the following formula:

$$SS_{total} = \Sigma\Sigma(y - GM)^2.$$

We have completed squaring and summing one side of the equation. Now we focus on the other side of the equation: $n\Sigma(\bar{y}_j - GM)^2 + bn\Sigma(\bar{Y}_{\beta j} - GM)^2 + \Sigma\Sigma(Y_i - \bar{Y}_J - \bar{Y}_{\beta j} - GM)^2$. We begin again with your original data in Figure 9.13.

We start, as we did in Chapter 8, by removing the *cage* condition mean from each score. Because the treatment condition means also contain the GM, it is simultaneously removed from each score as well. Figure 9.16 shows the outcome of this step. All three condition means now are 0. If the *GM* and the treatment means have been removed from the scores (*days*), what remains? In Chapter 8, when analysing a within-subjects design, all that remained after this step was error. Currently, however, in addition to error there remains a difference in the two blocks (*litter*). This difference in the litters is in part responsible for differences among the 12 scores.

Cage 1	Cage 2	Cage 4		
−5	−7	−3		
−7	−3	−5	Block mean =	−5.00
6	3	3		
6	7	5	Block mean =	+5.00
Cage mean = 0	Cage mean = 0	Cage mean = 0		
			GM =	0.00

Figure 9.16

REVIEW QUESTION

Why are the block means in Figure 9.16 different from those found in Figure 9.13?

Web Link 9.6 for an answer to the review question.

Figure 9.17 depicts the scores in Figure 9.16 after their being squared. In a between-subjects (independent-samples) analysis, these squared values summed to SS_{error}. In the current case, however, the values still contain the effect of block.

Compare SS_{error} in the independent-samples ANOVA conducted on the data at the outset of the chapter (330) with the total in Figure 9.17 (330). They are identical. But in the earlier case, you were unaware of the possibility of removing the effect of a blocking variable (*litter*).

Return to Figure 9.16. The effect of the blocking variable – disclosed by the difference in the two block means – remains a component of the 12 scores. As we removed the effect of treatment we can also remove the effect of block by subtracting the mean of a block from all of the observations in that block. The resulting 12 scores are shown in Figure 9.18. The *GM*, the condition means, and the block means are all 0.

Cage 1	Cage 2	Cage 4
25	49	9
49	9	25
36	9	9
36	49	25
	Total =	330

Figure 9.17

Cage 1	Cage 2	Cage 4		
0	−2	2		
−2	2	0	Block mean =	0.00
1	−2	−2		
1	2	0	Block mean =	0.00
Cage mean = 0	Cage mean = 0	Cage mean = 0		
			GM =	0.00

Figure 9.18

Cage 1	Cage 2	Cage 4
0	4	4
4	4	0
1	4	4
1	4	0
	Total =	30

Figure 9.19

The squares of the scores found in Figure 9.18 are reported in Figure 9.19. Now that the *GM*, the treatment effect, and the block effect have been removed, the total of those values (30) is the new SS_{error}. This is summarized by the formula $\Sigma\Sigma(Y_i - \bar{Y}_j - \bar{Y}_{\beta j} - GM)^2$.

Figure 9.20 illustrates in detail the scores of your 12 hamsters as well as how each score is partitioned and squared and contributes to each component sum of squares.

Recall the ANOVA you performed on your data without the blocking variable (Figure 9.21). After reviewing Figures 9.6 and 9.18, it is easy to construct an ANOVA table that includes the blocking variable (Figure 9.22). Besides the row for the blocking variable, the crucial difference between the two tables is that of the *p*-value related to the effect of *days*.

	Hamster	Litter	days	$(y-GM)^2$	$(\bar{y}_j-GM)^2$	$(\bar{y}_\beta-GM)^2$	$(y - \bar{y}_j - \bar{y}_\beta +GM)^2$
Cage 1	1	1	8	4	9	25	0
	2	1	6	16	9	25	4
	3	2	19	81	9	25	1
	4	2	19	81	9	25	1
Cage 2	1	1	3	49	0	25	4
	2	1	7	9	0	25	4
	3	2	13	9	0	25	4
	4	2	17	49	0	25	4
Cage 4	1	1	4	36	9	25	4
	2	1	2	64	9	25	0
	3	2	10	0	9	25	4
	4	2	12	4	9	25	0
			Totals	402	72	300	30

Figure 9.20

In the independent-samples ANOVA reported in Figure 9.21, the observed F-value (0.982) is less than the critical value found in the $\alpha = 0.05$ table in Appendix G (Table G.1) for 2 and 9 df (4.26). You fail to reject H_0 and conclude that there is insufficient evidence to support the notion that *cage* condition influences T-maze mastery. On the other hand, in Figure 9.22, where the variance in *days* accounted for by *litter* has been removed from the error term, the observed F-value (9.60) is greater than the critical value found in the $\alpha = 0.05$ table in Appendix G for 2 and 8 df (4.46). Now you reject H_0 and conclude there is sufficient evidence to support your hypothesis that *cage* condition influences T-maze mastery.

In the randomized block analysis (Figure 9.22) the $SS_{treatment}$, the $df_{treatment}$, and the $MS_{treatment}$ are unchanged from those in Figure 9.21. The reduction in SS_{error} produced a reduction in the size of MS_{error}. Because $MS_{treatment}$ remains unchanged, the reduction in MS_{error} produced an increase in the F-value. Results from a randomized block design analysis are frequently reported as they are in Figure 9.22 or they may be embedded in the text of a report. In a scientific publication the results are reported in a sentence such as the following: 'After analysing the randomized block design the effect of cage condition was found to be significant: $F(2, 8) = 9.60$, $MS_{error} = 3.750$, $p < 0.05$.'

	Sum of Squares	df	Mean Square	F	p-value
Days/Treatment	72.000	2	36.000	.982	> .05
Error	330.000	9	36.667		
Total	402.000	11			

Figure 9.21

	Sum of Squares	df	Mean Square	F	p-value
Block/Litter	300.000	1	300.000	104.800	
Days/Treatment	72.000	2	36.000	9.60	< .05
Error	30.000	8	3.750		
Total	402.000	11			

Figure 9.22

The reduction in SS_{error} is not free, however. The cost is the loss of df_{error}. How many are lost?

• • • • •

Examine the $\alpha = 0.05$ table in Appendix G. Examine how, within a column ($df_{treatment}$), the critical values are augmented as df_{error} decreases and diminished as df_{error} increases. Thus, there is a trade-off, a loss of degrees of freedom is the price for a reduction in the sum of squares.

Analogously to computing the $df_{\text{treatment}}$, the df_{block} is the number of blocks minus one. When the SS_{block} is calculated, the GM is conceptually based solely on the means of the blocks; in your case, there are only two block means. The values of the individual observations in each block are irrelevant at this point, only the number of individual observations matters. If we denote the number of blocks as b, then $df_{\text{block}} = b - 1$, in your case $2 - 1$ or $1\ df_{\text{block}}$.

CHALLENGE QUESTION

Given SS_{total} and $SS_{\text{treatment}}$, how few SS_{block} would there need to be in your hamster data for there to have been a decrease in power rather than an increase?

Web Link 9.7 for an answer to the challenge question.

Rarely would you find a blocking variable that would reduce your error term to the extent found in your hamster data, but this fictional example illustrates the advantages of identifying useful third variables when designing your research.

As was the case with the covariate in the previous chapter, the value of the blocking variable can be spatially depicted. In Figure 9.23 no blocking variable is present and the total variance is split 50–50 between treatment and error. In Figure 9.24 a blocking variable has been used by the researcher and the percentage of the variance associated with error has been somewhat reduced, improving the ratio of treatment variance to error variance. In Figure 9.25 the researcher again has employed a blocking variable, this time greatly reducing the variance associated with error. The greater the association between the blocking variable and the dependent variable, the greater the increase in power.

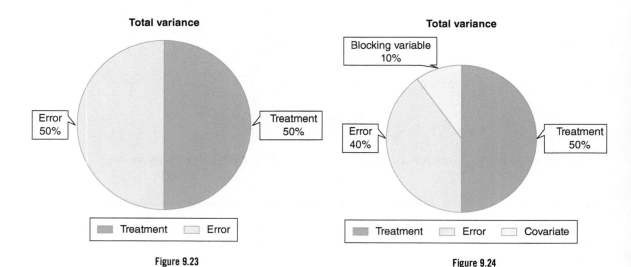

Total variance

Error 50%

Treatment 50%

Treatment   Error

Figure 9.23

Total variance

Blocking variable 10%

Error 40%

Treatment 50%

Treatment   Error   Covariate

Figure 9.24

Reviewing assumptions

Earlier in the chapter we used Hartley's F_{max} test (Hartley, 1950) to test the assumption of homogeneity of variance and found that we had insufficient evidence to reject H_0. That is, you were free to continue assuming homogeneity of variance. Using z-scores, we examined your data for outliers and found none. Another important assumption is that of normality. As discussed in the previous chapter, with small data sets, such as your 12 hamsters, trying to examine the shape of the distribution with a histogram is of little value. If you wish to continue to treat your data as measurement in nature, you will need to rely on previous research for information about the distribution of hamster mastery of the T-maze. (For a discussion of testing for normality with small sample sizes, see p. 341, Chapter 8.)

In this section we describe two new assumptions necessary for a randomized block analysis. Perhaps the most important new assumption accompanying the use of a blocking variable is that the blocking variable must be *independent* of the independent variable (IV). This is necessary for us to assume that all of the SS_{block} may be removed from the error term (SS_{error}). As stated earlier, your research assistant randomly assigned 12 young hamsters, *six from each of two litters*, to one of three housing conditions: four hamsters to each condition. The way to ensure that treatment (IV) and block are unrelated (independent) is to assign an equal number of subjects (hamsters) from each block (*litter*) to each treatment (*cage*) condition. Examining Figure 9.26, you find that your assistant assigned an equal number of hamsters from each litter to each cage condition. Each *cage* condition has two hamsters from each of the two *litters*. This ensures perfect independence of *cage* and *litter*. Remember that perfect independence means a zero correlation. If you open the SPSS file *randomblock.sav* and compute the correlation (bivariate) between *cage* and *litter*, you will find the Pearson correlation coefficient (r) to be 0.00. You could return to the formula in Chapter 7 and carry out the calculation of r by hand (with the use of a calculator).

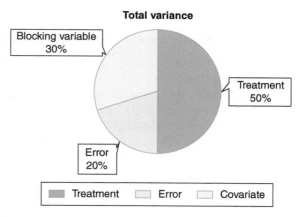

Total variance

Blocking variable 30%

Treatment 50%

Error 20%

Treatment   Error   Covariate

Figure 9.25

days	cage	litter
8.00	1.00	1.00
6.00	1.00	1.00
19.00	1.00	2.00
19.00	1.00	2.00
3.00	2.00	1.00
7.00	2.00	1.00
13.00	2.00	2.00
17.00	2.00	2.00
4.00	4.00	1.00
2.00	4.00	1.00
10.00	4.00	2.00
12.00	4.00	2.00

Figure 9.26

See Chapter 7 for instructions for computing a correlation coefficient with SPSS. Ensure that the *Measurement type in the Variable View* for the two variables is changed to *Scale* for the correlation analysis.

• • • • •

Recall that in Chapter 3, while presenting the laws of probability, the notion of independence was introduced. It was discussed in terms of the relative frequency of one event (e.g., eye colour) at different levels of a second variable (e.g., gender). In the case of your hamster data, the proportion of hamsters from litter 1 (50%) is constant across all three cage conditions. Thus, *litter* and *cage* are perfectly independent. In Chapter 6 we used x^2 to examine the issue of independence. We might use that approach here. You could construct a 2 × 3 *litter * cage Crosstabulation* contingency table (Figure 9.27) and look at the frequencies in each cell. All of the observed frequencies (counts) and expected frequencies (expected counts) are 2. Thus it is not surprising that the Pearson x^2 value in the *Chi-Square Tests* table (Figure 9.28) is 0.000, indicating no association at all (i.e., perfect independence).

The agreement of these approaches to independence illustrates that when we speak of *independence* we are always speaking of the same concept, regardless of how the data are understood (measurement or categorical) or how the test is conducted (parametric or nonparametric).

litter * cage Crosstabulation

			cage 1.00	cage 2.00	cage 4.00	Total
litter	1.00	Count	2	2	2	6
		Expected Count	2.0	2.0	2.0	6.0
	2.00	Count	2	2	2	6
		Expected Count	2.0	2.0	2.0	6.0
Total		Count	4	4	4	12
		Expected Count	4.0	4.0	4.0	12.0

Figure 9.27

Chi-Square Tests

	Value	df	Asymptotic Significance (2-sided)
Pearson Chi-Square	.000[a]	2	1.000
Likelihood Ratio	.000	2	1.000
Linear-by-Linear Association	.000	1	1.000
N of Valid Cases	12		

a. 6 cells (100.0%) have expected count less than 5. The minimum expected count is 2.00.

Figure 9.28

Another new assumption pertains to how subjects within a block are assigned to treatment conditions. Although subjects cannot be completely randomized with respect to treatment condition, which would likely result in an unequal number of observations from each block in each condition, they must be randomly (quasi-randomly) assigned to treatment conditions within the block. Thus, all subjects within a block have *roughly* an equal chance of being assigned to each of the treatment conditions. Each block might be viewed as a separate between-subjects experiment. What is gained from merging multiple blocks into a single analysis is the ability to remove from the error term variance associated with block. This source of error (block) can only be identified when more than one block is present. (For a discussion of random versus quasi-random assignment, see p. 15 in Chapter 1.)

Randomized block designs have been around since Fisher (1927) developed ANOVA, but they have been used too infrequently in psychology and the social sciences. A number of areas of applied research, such as educational outcomes (Andrade, 2013), however, are beginning to take advantage of the benefits of the technique. It should be pointed out that, like ANOVA and ANCOVA, the randomized block analysis is only an omnibus test. It does not specify the specific type or location of the effect, only that there is evidence that an effect is present.

Randomized block designs and bar charts

It is always important to graphically depict your data. There have been various approaches to graphically depicting the results of a randomized block analysis. When the design includes only one IV and one blocking variable, a bar or line graph depicting the condition means is almost always used. Any differences in approach usually focus on the question of error bars. In Chapter 8, with a simple one-way, independent-samples ANOVA we used one standard error of the means as the basis for the error bars. This approach is often used with the randomized block design as well, but there are more revelatory graphs in use. We will illustrate one that can be produced simultaneously with the analysis in SPSS.

9 ● 5 RUNNING A RANDOMIZED BLOCK DESIGN WITH SPSS

 Web Link (reinsert) 9.2 for SPSS data set *randomblock.sav.*

To introduce the analysis of the randomized block design using SPSS we will run a simple independent-samples ANOVA using an alternative option in SPSS. This also will afford us an opportunity to introduce a few additional SPSS features related to *standardized effect size* and *power.*

From within the ***Data Editor***, select ***Analyze*** from the menu and drop down to ***General Linear Model.*** Then slide over and select the ***Univariate*** option that appears to the right. In the ***Univariate*** window, highlight and move the dependent variable (*days*) to the ***Dependent Variable*** box. Then move the IV (*cage*) to the ***Fixed Factor(s)*** box (Figure 9.29). Next click ***Options***.

When the *Univariate: Options* window appears, click on *Estimates of effect size, Observed power,* and *Homogeneity tests* in the lower *Display* area (Figure 9.30). Then click *Continue*. After you are returned to the main *Univariate* screen click *OK* to run the analysis. The results appear in the SPSS output window.

The first area in the SPSS output window, the *Between-Subjects Factors* table (Figure 9.31), reports the number of observations per *cage* condition: four hamsters in each. The second area in the output window, *Levene's Test* (Figure 9.32), reports the results of the test for homogeneity of variance. The H_0 is that the variances across the three *cage* conditions are the same. The reported *p*-value (*Sig.*) of 0.248, which is greater than 0.05, indicates that you fail to reject H_0 and may continue to assume homogeneity of variance.

The third area in the output window reports the results of an independent-samples ANOVA: *Tests of Between-Subjects Effects* (Figure 9.33). This output table is a bit more cluttered than the ANOVA table produced when you analysed your data with the *Compare Means* option under *Analyze*. The first column, *Source*, identifies the source of the sum of squares. The rows of interest to you are

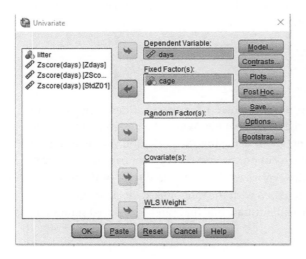

Figure 9.29

Figure 9.30

Between-Subjects Factors

		N
cage	1.00	4
	2.00	4
	4.00	4

Figure 9.31

Levene's Test of Equality of Error Variances[a]

Dependent Variable: days

F	df1	df2	Sig.
1.636	2	9	.248

Tests the null hypothesis that the error variance of the dependent variable is equal across groups.

Figure 9.32

cage, Error, and *Corrected Total* (which is SS_{total} as we have computed it). The other rows are beyond the scope of this book. The second column (*Type III Sum of Squares*) identifies the method used for partitioning the SS_{total}. Type III is the method that we have been describing throughout this chapter and Chapter 8. This method is the most common, particularly when *n* is a constant across all conditions. It computes the SS for each component (be they independent variables or blocking variables) by holding the others constant. Other methods, such as Type I and Type II sums of squares, carve up the SS_{total} somewhat differently and require additional assumptions. For a summary of the use of Type I, II, and III sum-of-squares, see Langsrud (2003).

Tests of Between-Subjects Effects

Dependent Variable: days

Source	Type III Sum of Squares	df	Mean Square	F	Sig.	Partial Eta Squared	Noncent. Parameter	Observed Power[b]
Corrected Model	72.000[a]	2	36.000	.982	.411	.179	1.964	.171
Intercept	1200.000	1	1200.000	32.727	.000	.784	32.727	.999
cage	72.000	2	36.000	.982	.411	.179	1.964	.171
Error	330.000	9	36.667					
Total	1602.000	12						
Corrected Total	402.000	11						

a. R Squared = .179 (Adjusted R Squared = -.003)

b. Computed using alpha = .05

Figure 9.33

The SS_{total} (now called the *Corrected Total*, 402), SS_{cage} (72.000), and SS_{error} (330.000) are identical to those reported in the previous analysis, as are their corresponding *df*. The MS_{cage} (36.000) and the MS_{error} (36.667) are also unchanged, as are the resulting *F*-value (0.982) and its *p*-value (*Sig.* = 0.411). Finally, as you did earlier, you would fail to reject H_0.

Recall that had you rejected H_0 and concluded that there was evidence that *cage* condition influences T-maze mastery, you would need to report a standardized effect size measure. The seventh column in the *Tests of Between-Subjects Effects* table reports a *Partial Eta Squared*. For one-way, independent-samples designs, such as yours, the eta squared (η^2) that was discussed earlier and the partial eta squared are equivalent. Because you failed to reject H_0, there is no need to report η^2. Under normal circumstances, when you fail to reject an H_0 it is important to examine your *power*. That is, what was the probability of your rejecting H_0 with the given effect size? Your observed power is reported in the final column of the table: 0.171. Stated differently, you had a 17.1% chance of rejecting H_0, if the true differences among the means are reflected in the sample means. If you were testing for that specific effect size and H_0 was false, you would be better off flipping a coin as a decision-making strategy than collecting and analysing those few observations. (For the earlier analysis of these data, see Figure 9.21 and the accompanying text.)

> For a detailed discussion of Type I, II, and III sums of squares and their appropriate uses, see Carlson and Timm (1974).

We now return to SPSS to execute a randomized block analysis of your hamster data taking *litter* into account. From within the *Data Editor*, select *Analyze* from the menu and drop down to *General Linear Model*. Then slide over and select the *Univariate* option that appears to the right. In the *Univariate* window, highlight and move the DV (*days*) to the *Dependent Variable* box. Then move the IV (*cage*) and the blocking variable (*litter*) to the Fixed *Factor(s)* box (Figure 9.34). Next, click on the *Model* button. When the *Univariate: Model* screen opens, select the *Custom* button and then switch the *Build Term(s) Type* option in the centre of the screen from *Interaction* to *Main Effects*. Next highlight and move *cage* and *litter* into the *Model* area (Figure 9.35) and click *Continue*. When you return to the main *Univariate* screen click the *Plots* button. When the *Univariate: Profile Plots* screen opens (Figure 9.36), move *cage* to the *Horizontal Axis* area and *litter* to the *Separate Lines* area and then click *Add* followed by *Continue*. Click the *Options* button. When the *Univariate: Options* window opens, select *Estimates of effect size*, *Observed power*, and *Homogeneity tests* in the lower *Display* area (Figure 9.37). Then click *Continue*. When you return to the main *Univariate* screen click *OK*. The results appear in the SPSS output window.

The first area in the SPSS output window is be the *Between-Subjects Factors* table (Figure 9.38) that reports the number of observations by *cage* and by *litter*. The second reports the results of Levene's test for homogeneity of variance (Figure 9.39). The reported *p*-value (*Sig.*) of 0.746, which is greater than 0.05, signifies that you are free to assume homogeneity of variance.

Regarding Levene's test, note that the *df* associated with the randomized block analysis ($df1 = 5$, $df2 = 6$) are different from those associated with the previous ANOVA without the blocking variable ($df1 = 2$, $df2 = 9$). Both sets sum to 11, the df_{total}. The difference is that the test for homogeneity of variance in the randomized block design is examining six conditions (5 *df*) rather than three: *cage 1/litter 1*, *cage 1/litter 2*, *cage 2/litter 1*, *cage 2/litter 2*, *cage 3/litter 1*, and *cage 3/litter 2*. In this design the H_0 is that the variances within all six of those conditions are estimating the same σ^2.

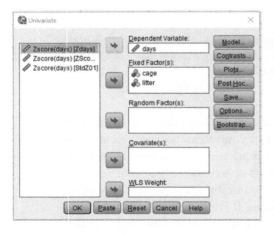

Figure 9.34

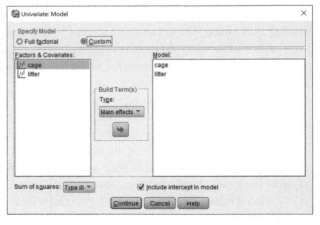

Figure 9.35

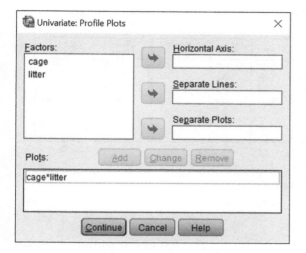

Figure 9.36

Figure 9.37

• • • • •

The model for the randomized block design is a general formula which may be used when there is more than one independent variable. The algorithm does not *know* that one is merely a blocking variable. Thus it *sees* six experimental conditions that are defined by a combination of *cage* and *litter*: *cage1/litter1*, *cage1/litter2*, *cage2/litter1*, *cage2/litter2*, *cage3/litter1*, and *cage3/litter2*. Thus, with six conditions there are six condition variances estimating σ^2, each with its own condition mean. As a result, Levene's test sees 5 *df* treatments (6 − 1), which leaves only 6 *df* for error. The fact that the ANOVA has different *df* from those of Levene's test relates to our changing the *Build Term(s) Type* option from *Interaction* to *Main Effects*.

Between-Subjects Factors

		N
cage	1.00	4
	2.00	4
	4.00	4
litter	1.00	6
	2.00	6

Figure 9.38

Levene's Test of Equality of Error Variances[a]

Dependent Variable: days

F	df1	df2	Sig.
.533	5	6	.746

Tests the null hypothesis that the error variance of the dependent variable is equal across groups.

Figure 9.39

Tests of Between-Subjects Effects

Dependent Variable: days

Source	Type III Sum of Squares	df	Mean Square	F	Sig.	Partial Eta Squared	Noncent. Parameter	Observed Power[b]
Corrected Model	372.000[a]	3	124.000	33.067	.000	.925	99.200	1.000
Intercept	1200.000	1	1200.000	320.000	.000	.976	320.000	1.000
cage	72.000	2	36.000	9.600	.007	.706	19.200	.903
litter	300.000	1	300.000	80.000	.000	.909	80.000	1.000
Error	30.000	8	3.750					
Total	1602.000	12						
Corrected Total	402.000	11						

a. R Squared = .925 (Adjusted R Squared = .897)

b. Computed using alpha = .05

Figure 9.40

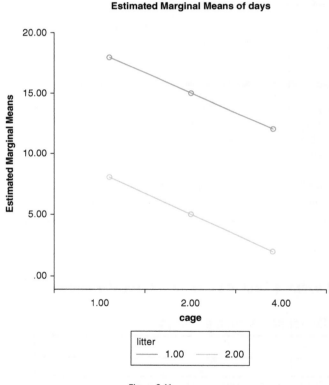

Estimated Marginal Means of days

Figure 9.41

The *Test of Between-Subjects Effects* table (Figure 9.40) reports the result of your randomized block design analysis. As in the previous analysis, this table contains more information than is necessary for our purposes. The rows of interest to you are *cage, litter, Error,* and *Corrected Total*. Again, the *Corrected Total* is what we have been referring to SS_{total} and df_{total}. First notice that SS_{cage}, SS_{litter}, and SS_{error} sum to SS_{total}, as the df_{cage}, df_{litter}, and df_{error} sum to df_{total}. These values, along with their corresponding MSs, are consistent with your findings in Figure 9.22. The only *F*-value of interest to you is the one associated with *cage*, which is also identical to that found in Figure 9.22. The *p*-value (*Sig.*) of 0.007 is less than 0.05 and is consistent with Figure 9.22 ($p < 0.05$). Again you reject H_0 and conclude that there is sufficient evidence to support the notion that *cage* condition influences T-maze mastery.

As you already know, when you obtain a significant test *F*-value it is incumbent upon you to provide a standardized estimate of the effect size. As discussed in the previous chapter, the most common estimate reported when the omnibus *F*-value is found to be significant is η^2 (eta squared). η^2 is considered by some authors to be problematic when the analysis includes more than one IV, even if the additional variable is merely a blocking variable (Tabachnick & Fidell, 2012). (See the presentation of η^2 on p. 344 in Chapter 8.)

The problem is that the original formula for η^2 ($SS_{treatment}/SS_{block}$) does not take into account the effect of other identified variables, in your case the effect of *litter*. To address this concern SPSS reports a standardized effect measure called *partial eta squared*, given by

$$\text{partial eta squared} = \frac{SS_{effect}}{SS_{effect} + SS_{error}}.$$

In your case partial eta squared is

$$\text{partial eta squared} = \frac{SS_{cage}}{SS_{cage} + SS_{error}} = \frac{72}{72 + 30} = 0.706.$$

This value takes into account the effect of other variables by customizing the denominator for each effect. When there is more than one independent variable, SS_{effect} plus SS_{error} will not equal SS_{total}.

There are problems associated with interpreting partial eta squared, however. As pointed out by Levine and Hullett (2002), the sum of a set of partial eta squared values may end up being greater than 1; that is, greater than 100% of the variance. Looking at your *Test of Between-Subjects Effects* table, you can see that this is the case with your results. The partial eta squared for *cage* is 0.706 and for *litter* is 0.909. If you were thinking in terms of the total variance explained, the two variables would explain 162% of the total variance in days, which is impossible. It is usually best practice to report either η^2 or η^2 together with partial eta squared. Beware that different disciplines and specific journals have their own preferences regarding the reporting of standardized effects.

The fact that in the table power (*Observed Power*) is reported for *cage* (0.903) is irrelevant. Because you have rejected H_0 there is no chance of making a Type II error. Power and the corresponding probability of making a Type II error (1.000 – 0.903) are only an issue when you fail to reject H_0. Because you have rejected H_0, the issue is whether or not you are making a Type I error. If H_0 is *true*, the probability of that is 0.05 (α). (For the discussion of Type I and Type II errors, see p. 141 in Chapter 4.)

The randomized block design represents the second time we have seen how a *third variable* can be of benefit to a researcher. Several times it has been mentioned how the randomized block analysis is similar to ANCOVA. Actually, the randomized block analysis is an algebraically equivalent, special case of ANCOVA. The apparent difference between them is all in the number scale of the third variable. A covariate is usually a measurement variable, either ratio or interval in nature. The blocking variable is typically categorical, usually nominal in nature. With ANCOVA, we assume that the covariate (measurement in scale) is independent of the independent variable, although the two will never be perfectly uncorrelated ($r = 0$). In the case of the randomized block design, we ensure their complete independence by assigning an equal number of subjects from each block to each treatment condition. (For the discussion of number scales, see p. 25 in Chapter 2.)

To demonstrate the linkage between the two forms of analysis, let us conduct an ANCOVA using your hamster data from the randomized block design example. We will use *litter* as the covariate. Notice that the output (*Tests of Between-Subjects Effects*, Figure 9.42) from the ANCOVA, with respect to the rows of interest, is identical to that of the above randomized block analysis. (For instructions on running an ANCOVA, see p. 348 in Chapter 8.)

If we consider a randomized block analysis a special case of ANCOVA, our next test can be considered a special case of the randomized block design.

Tests of Between-Subjects Effects

Dependent Variable:　days

Source	Type III Sum of Squares	df	Mean Square	F	Sig.	Partial Eta Squared	Noncent. Parameter	Observed Power[b]
Corrected Model	372.000[a]	3	124.000	33.067	.000	.925	99.200	1.000
Intercept	30.000	1	30.000	8.000	.022	.500	8.000	.698
litter	300.000	1	300.000	80.000	.000	.909	80.000	1.000
cage	72.000	2	36.000	9.600	.007	.706	19.200	.903
Error	30.000	8	3.750					
Total	1602.000	12						
Corrected Total	402.000	11						

a. R Squared = .925 (Adjusted R Squared = .897)

b. Computed using alpha = .05

Figure 9.42　ANCOVA output

9 ● 6　THE LOGIC OF THE REPEATED-MEASURES DESIGN

In this section we explore the most common form of randomized block design: repeated-measures analysis. As mentioned in Chapter 1, in a repeated-measures design all subjects are tested in all conditions. Although the terminology, the notation, and the presentation of the output are different from that of the randomized block analysis, the two analyses are computationally identical. In a repeated-measures analysis each subject is a block, with one observation per block (subject) per treatment condition.

Like hamsters, all subjects are unique, regardless of species. Consequently, there is a unique effect for you being you and for me being me. In terms of research methodology, this uniqueness is referred to as *individual differences*. The SS_{block} now will be called $SS_{subject}$ (or sum of squares between subjects). With reference to Figure 9.2, *subject* now is the third variable capable of effectively shrinking the SS_{total}, thereby reducing the SS_{error}.

In this section we discover how testing all subjects in all conditions can be used in an ANOVA to reduce your SS_{error} and increase your *power* in a similar manner as with ANCOVA and the randomized block design. With the randomized block design we substituted *block* (β) for the *covariate* (*cov*) in our model of a score:

$$y_i = \mu + \tau_k + \beta + \varepsilon_i,$$

With the repeated-measures design, the variance in y associated with our new blocking variable (subject) is identified by the parameter ς, for subject effect:

$$y_i = \mu + \tau_k + \varsigma_j + \varepsilon_i,$$

where y_i is the ith score, μ is the population mean, τ_k is the treatment effect for a given condition, ς_j is the effect for being that particular subject, and ε_i is the error associated with the ith score.

* * * * *

We have now used three different versions of the Greek letter sigma. The upper case Σ indicates the summation procedure. The lower case σ denotes population standard deviation. And ς, which is used when a sigma is the last letter of a word, denotes subject.

Within a single observation the parameters can be estimated as follows:

$$y_i = GM + (\bar{y}_j - GM) + (\bar{Y}_{\varsigma j} - GM) + (Y_i - \bar{Y}_j - \bar{Y}_{\varsigma j} + GM),$$

where y_i is the ith score, GM is the mean of all scores in the sample regardless of condition or block, $\bar{y}_j$ is the mean of the scores in a given condition or treatment, and $\bar{Y}_{\varsigma j}$ is the mean of the scores for a given subject.

The difference between an individual score and the GM again has three components: an estimate of the treatment effect, an estimate of the subject effect, and an estimate of the error associated with the particular score. The error term now involves not only the removal of the treatment effect from the score, but also the removal of the effect for being that particular subject:

$$(y_i - GM) = (\bar{y}_j - GM) + (\bar{Y}_{\varsigma j} - GM) + (Y_i - \bar{Y}_j - \bar{Y}_{\varsigma j} + GM).$$

Analogous to the case of the randomized block analysis, computationally, the error term contains the addition of the GM (see the discussion of the randomized block error term earlier in this chapter).

The components for each observation must be squared and summed:

$$\Sigma\Sigma(Y_i - GM)^2 = n\Sigma(\bar{Y}_j - GM)^2 + \varsigma n(\bar{Y}_{\varsigma j} - GM)^2 + \Sigma\Sigma(Y_i - \bar{Y}_j - \bar{Y}_{\varsigma j} + GM)^2.$$

■■■■■ • • • • • ■■■■■

What makes up a given subject's mean? First of all, the subject's score is an estimate of μ, which is estimated by the *GM*. Then there is the true effect for being that particular subject. Furthermore, the average error across all of that subject's scores alters the subject's mean. Thus when we subtract the mean of the subject's scores from each of his or her individual scores, we are subtracting everything that goes into the mean for that subject.

■■■■■ • • • • • ■■■■■

Treatment effects and subject effects are assumed to be constants. If treatment effects and subject effects are independent:

1   The difference between two scores from a single subject in two different treatment conditions is the difference in *error* plus a difference in the *treatment effect*, if there is one.
2   The difference between two scores from two different subjects in the same treatment condition is the difference in *error* plus a difference in the *subject effect*, if there is one.

If we did not assume that treatment and subject effects were constants and were independent, this additive model and the analysis that follows from it would be inappropriate.

For an example of a repeated-measures design, we will leave the realm of hamsters and use first-year undergraduate students as your subjects. This imaginative data set is based on the findings of MacLeod and Kampe (1996). Although the imaginary data do not do full justice to their important work and to the work of other researchers in the area, they reflect one aspect of their results. For demonstration purposes, we will use a sample size, $n = 5$, much smaller than would normally be required.

Imagine you are a cognitive psychologist studying memory. You have just read a colleague's paper reporting findings from a study of *word frequency* and recall. Subjects were first asked to read a three-page article. Subsequently, after a brief distraction task, subjects were asked to *recall* as many of the nouns as they could from the article. There were three categories of nouns in the article. *High-frequency* nouns are those that are very common, such as *window*. *Medium-frequency* nouns, such as *rejection*, are somewhat less common in everyday speech but are not unusual. Finally, *low-frequency* nouns, such as *defenestration*, are rare and often unfamiliar to the subject. Your colleague reported that subjects were most likely to recall the high-frequency nouns and were least likely to recall the low-frequency nouns. From other relevant literature you are also aware that the results of *recall* memory tasks and *recognition* memory tasks often produce contradictory results. Putting your colleague's findings together with the other literature, you suspect that subjects will be most likely to recognize low-frequency words and least likely to recognize high-frequency words.

To test your hunch you repeat your colleague's experiment, replacing the *recall task* with a *recognition task*. The task consists of a list of 120 nouns, half of which were in the article and half of which were not. Of the 60 nouns that had appeared in the article, 20 were high-frequency, 20 were medium-frequency, and 20 were low-frequency in nature.

The data from your experiment are reported in Figure 9.43. Each row reports the three scores for a single subject. For example, subject 1 recognized 7 of the low-frequency nouns, 3 of the medium-frequency nouns, and 3 of the high-frequency nouns. Your experimental hypothesis was that low-frequency nouns would be the most likely to be recognized and high-frequency nouns would be the least likely to be recognized. By simply scanning the pattern of recognition scores in Figure 9.43 we see that all subjects had their best performance in the *low*-frequency category. The picture with the *medium*-frequency and *high*-frequency categories is a bit more complicated. As was the case with *block* in the previous section, each subject might be viewed as a mini-experiment. As will be seen later in the chapter, viewing the data in such a manner is not entirely unreasonable.

What if you were unaware of the fact that this was a repeated-measures design and thought they were scores from 15 subjects who had been randomly assigned to the three categories of noun frequencies? The data would then be better depicted as in Figure 9.44.

If you computed the descriptive statistics for the three frequency conditions you would find the means to be 12, 9, and 8 for the low-, medium-, and high-frequency conditions, respectively. This is consistent with your hypothesis. If you saved the *z*-scores when calculating the descriptive statistics, there would be no indication of any outliers. Next you would produce a bar graph of the data which depicts the trend that you hypothesized (Figure 9.45).

A between-subjects, independent-samples ANOVA fails to support your hypothesis, however (Figure 9.46). Remember that the rows of interest in the SPSS *Test of Between-Subjects Effects* table are *frequency* (treatment), *Error*, and *Corrected Total*.

Frequency	Low	Medium	High
Subject 1	7	3	3
Subject 2	14	10	10
Subject 3	13	10	7
Subject 4	18	15	13
Subject 5	8	7	7

Figure 9.43

Subject #	Frequency	Recognition
1	1	7
2	1	14
3	1	13
4	1	18
5	1	8
6	2	3
7	2	10
8	2	10
9	2	15
10	2	7
11	3	3
12	3	10
13	3	7
14	3	13
15	3	7

Figure 9.44

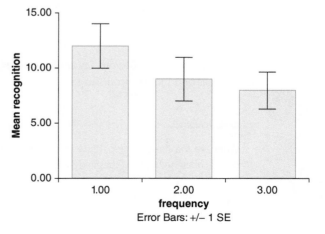

Error Bars: +/– 1 SE

Figure 9.45

The F-value associated with *frequency* effect is 1.204 with a *p*-value (*Sig.*) of 0.334. Thus, you fail to reject H_0 and conclude that you have insufficient evidence that word frequency influences noun recognition. There are two matters to be considered: power and the standardized effect size. The partial eta squared of 0.167 (which in this case is equivalent to the normal η^2) indicates a large effect, when converted into Cohen's *f*. The final column in the table (*Observed Power*) indicates that *if* H_0 were false and *if* the effect were of the size reported, then your chance of correctly rejecting H_0 would be 0.214 or 21.4%. You could consult Cohen's tables and determine how many subjects you would require to have an 80% chance of correctly rejecting H_0.

Tests of Between-Subjects Effects

Dependent Variable: recognition

Source	Type III Sum of Squares	df	Mean Square	F	Sig.	Partial Eta Squared	Noncent. Parameter	Observed Power[b]
Corrected Model	43.333[a]	2	21.667	1.204	.334	.167	2.407	.214
Intercept	1401.667	1	1401.667	77.870	.000	.866	77.870	1.000
frequency	43.333	2	21.667	1.204	.334	.167	2.407	.214
Error	216.000	12	18.000					
Total	1661.000	15						
Corrected Total	259.333	14						

a. R Squared = .167 (Adjusted R Squared = .028)

b. Computed using alpha = .05

Figure 9.46

• • • • •

As we saw in the previous chapter, for purposes of using Cohen's table for determining the necessary number of subjects, η^2 can be easily converted into Cohen's *f*:

$$f = \sqrt{\frac{\eta^2}{1-\eta^2}} = \sqrt{\frac{0.167^2}{1-0.167^2}} = 0.45.$$

Examining Cohen's effect size table, an *f* of 0.45 would be a large effect. Examining his sample size table, you find that for a large effect of an ANOVA with three groups, 21 subjects per condition are required to ensure that power equals 0.80, corresponding to an 80% chance of rejecting a false H_0.

What is the source of your failure to reject H_0? Everything appeared to be consistent with your hypothesis and looked promising.

■■■■■ REVIEW QUESTION ■■■■■

What are the three principal factors that influence *power*, and how do they operate? How do these factors relate to the two independent estimates of population variance?

Web Link 9.8 for an answer to the review question.

The simple answer is that you have proportionately far more variance within the conditions than you have between the means of the conditions. This proportionality is also apparent from the relative size of the error bars in the bar graph. If you consider the scores to be grouped into five blocks with one observation from each block (subject) in each of the three frequency conditions, you could apply the randomized block approach to the analysis (Figure 9.47).

The SPSS output *Test of Between-Subjects Effects* table (Figure 9.48) now reveals a different outcome. By treating *subject* as a blocking variable you were able to associate much of the variance in the *recognition* scores with the blocking variable. Thus, blocking reduced the sum-of-squares error by 206.667. You paid for that reduction with 4 *df* (df_{block}). Although the *df* for the error term was reduced from 12 to 8, the reduction in the sum of squares was proportionately far greater such that MS_{error} was reduced from 18 to 1.167. These changes created by the blocking variable resulted in the *frequency* effect becoming statistically significant, $F(2, 8) = 18.571$, $MS_{error} = 1.167$, $p = 0.001$. H_0 is rejected and you may conclude that there is sufficient evidence to support the idea that noun frequency would affect recognition performance.

In the *Test of Between-Subjects Effects* partial eta squared is reported to be 0.823. Partial eta squared is now no longer equivalent to η^2 and it no longer represents the proportion of the total variance explained by word frequency. η^2 remains unchanged at 0.167. Partial eta squared represents the portion of the total variance explained by *frequency*, *after* the variance explained by the blocking variable has been removed.

Subject no.	Frequency	Recognition	Block
1	1	7	1
2	1	14	2
3	1	13	3
4	1	18	4
5	1	8	5
6	2	3	1
7	2	10	2
8	2	10	3
9	2	15	4
10	2	7	5
11	3	3	1
12	3	10	2
13	3	7	3
14	3	13	4
15	3	7	5

Figure 9.47 Subject as block

Tests of Between-Subjects Effects

Dependent Variable: recognition

Source	Type III Sum of Squares	df	Mean Square	F	Sig.	Partial Eta Squared	Noncent. Parameter	Observed Power[b]
Corrected Model	250.000[a]	6	41.667	35.714	.000	.964	214.286	1.000
Intercept	1401.667	1	1401.667	1201.429	.000	.993	1201.429	1.000
frequency	43.333	2	21.667	18.571	.001	.823	37.143	.995
block	206.667	4	51.667	44.286	.000	.957	177.143	1.000
Error	9.333	8	1.167					
Total	1661.000	15						
Corrected Total	259.333	14						

a. R Squared = .964 (Adjusted R Squared = .937)

b. Computed using alpha = .05

Figure 9.48

Repeated-measures ANOVA

The above randomized block analysis is actually a repeated-measures design. The answer to the question concerning the source of your failure to reject H_0 is somewhat more specific. The source of much of the error variance is clearly the *individual differences* in overall recognition performance. Some subjects appeared to perform better than others, regardless of condition. You are not interested in these individual differences, but rather in the possible differences between the frequency conditions.

Returning to Figure 9.43, we can compute the means for the five subjects: 4.33, 11.33, 10.00, 15.33, and 7.33. Just as a randomized block design removes the variance in the dependent variable associated with *block*, so too repeated-measures ANOVA removes the variance associated with individual differences in the subjects. In fact, as we will see, the differences between a randomized block analysis and a repeated-measures analysis are only in the presentation, not in the actual analysis.

Figure 9.49 reproduces your noun frequency (low, medium, high) data with the addition of the condition means, the mean for each subject, and the *GM*. Figure 9.50 depicts the 15 individual scores and means after subtracting the *GM* from them all. The *GM* is now 0. The condition means and subject means have changed, but the absolute differences among them are unchanged. The sum of the squared residuals reported in Figure 9.51 represents the SS_{total}. The value is the same, save for rounding differences, as we saw in the previous two analyses of your data. The SS_{total} always will be the same, regardless of the design: independent-samples, randomized block, or repeated-measures.

━━━━━━━━ REVIEW QUESTION ━━━━━━━━

Why will the SS_{total} remain the same, regardless of the type of ANOVA that is performed on your data?

 Web Link 9.9 for an answer to the review question.

Subject no.	Low	Medium	High	Subject mean
1	7	3	3	4.33
2	14	10	10	11.33
3	13	10	7	10.00
4	18	15	13	15.33
5	8	7	7	7.33
Condition Means	12	9	8	GM = 9.66

Figure 9.49

Now that we have addressed the SS_{total} we can address its components: $SS_{treatments}$, $SS_{subject}$, and SS_{error}. We begin as we did with the randomized block analysis by subtracting the means of three frequency conditions from the five scores in each condition. The results are shown in Figure 9.52. The condition means along with the *GM* are all now 0. The subject means are changed from their original values (Figure 9.49), but the differences among them remain unchanged. Recall from the randomized

Subject no.	Low	Medium	High	Subject mean
1	−2.66	−6.66	−6.66	−5.33
2	4.34	.34	.34	1.67
3	3.44	.34	−2.66	.34
4	8.34	5.34	3.34	5.67
5	−1.66	−2.66	−2.66	−2.33
Condition Means	2.34	−.66	−1.66	GM = 0.00

Figure 9.50

Low	Medium	High
7.08	44.36	44.36
18.84	.12	.12
11.16	.12	7.08
69.56	28.52	11.16
2.76	7.08	7.08
		Total = 259.40

Figure 9.51

block analysis that the *GM* will be removed simultaneously with the condition means. As in the randomized block analysis, what remain in the 15 individual scores are (1) error and (2) the effect of the blocking variable, which is now the subject effect or individual differences.

Next we remove the individual differences by subtracting each subject's mean in Figure 9.52 from all three of his or her scores (Figure 9.53). The *GM*, the condition means, and the subject means now have all been removed from the individual scores.

Subject#	Low	Medium	High	Subject mean
1	−5.00	−6.00	−5.00	−5.33
2	2.00	1.00	2.00	1.67
3	1.00	1.00	−1.00	.34
4	6.00	6.00	5.00	5.67
5	−4.00	−2.00	−1.00	−2.33
Condition Means	0.00	0.00	0.00	GM = 0.00

Figure 9.52

The squares of the remaining values in the matrix of 15 scores reflect all of the unexplained variance or error (Figure 9.54). The total represents SS_{error} (9.37) which, except for a minor rounding difference, is equal to the SS_{error} (9.33) from your randomized block analysis.

Figure 9.55 illustrates in detail how the three scores of each of your five subjects are partitioned and contribute to each component sum of squares. Using the information in Figure 9.55, you can construct an ANOVA summary table (Figure 9.56). Note the initial partitioning of the sum of squares between and within subjects, along with their corresponding degrees of freedom.

Subject#	Low	Medium	High	Subject mean
1	.33	−.67	−.33	0.00
2	.33	−.67	.33	0.00
3	.66	.66	−1.34	0.00
4	.33	.33	−.67	0.00
5	−1.67	.33	1.33	0.00
Condition Means	0.00	0.00	0.00	0.00
				GM = 0.00

Figure 9.53

Subject	Low	Medium	High
1	.12	.45	.12
2	.12	.45	.12
3	.44	.44	1.80
4	.12	.12	.45
5	2.80	.12	1.70
		Total =	9.37

Figure 9.54

	Subject	recognition	$(y - GM)^2$	$(\bar{y}_i - GM)^2$	$(\bar{y}_c - GM)^2$	$(y - \bar{y}_i - \bar{y}_c + GM)^2$
Frequency 1	1	7	7.08	5.48	28.41	.12
	2	14	18.84	5.48	2.79	.12
	3	13	11.16	5.48	.12	.44
	4	18	69.56	5.48	32.15	.12
	5	8	7.08	5.48	5.43	2.80
Frequency 2	1	3	44.36	.44	28.41	.45
	2	10	.12	.44	2.79	.45
	3	10	.12	.44	.12	.44
	4	15	28.52	.44	32.15	.12
	5	7	7.08	.44	5.43	.12
Frequency 3	1	3	44.36	2.76	28.41	.12
	2	10	.12	2.76	2.79	.12
	3	7	7.08	2.76	.12	1.80
	4	13	11.16	2.76	32.15	.45
	5	7	7.08	2.76	5.43	1.70
	Total		**259.40**	**43.40**	**206.66**	**9.37**

Figure 9.55

ANOVA Summary Table

Source	Sum-of-Squares		df	Mean Square	F	Sig.
Between-Sub.	206.66		4			
Within-Sub.	52.77		10			
Frequency		43.40	2	21.70	18.55	< .05
Error		9.37	8	1.17		
Total	**259.40 (rounding)**		**14**			

Figure 9.56

● ● ● ● ●

Degrees of freedom can be partitioned in the same manner as the sum of squares. There are 15 observations, thus 14 *df* in total. There are five subjects, thus 4 $df_{\text{between subjects}}$. Consequently, there are $14 - 4 = 10\ df_{\text{within subjects}}$. There are three treatment conditions, thus 2 $df_{\text{treatment}}$. Consequently, there are $10 - 2 = 8\ df_{\text{error}}$.

The within-subjects sum of squares and *df* are then partitioned into *frequency* (treatment) and error. Mean squares are computed by dividing sums of squares by their respective *df*. The resulting *F*-value (18.55) with 2 and 8 *df* is greater than the critical value found in the $\alpha = 0.05$ table in Appendix G (4.46). Thus, you reject H_0 and conclude that there is sufficient evidence to support your suspicion that word frequency affects noun recognition. Comparing this summary table with the *Test of Between-Subject Effects* table from the randomized block analysis of your data, you find that with respect to (1) *frequency*, (2) *between subjects* (block), and (3) *error*, the sums of squares, the *df*, the mean squares, and the *F* are all identical, save for rounding differences.

Remember that the repeated-measures ANOVA and the randomized block analysis, like the other tests examined in this and the previous chapter, are omnibus tests. They only indicate that there is sufficient evidence to conclude that the treatment conditions differ, but not specifically where and how they differ.

RUNNING A REPEATED-MEASURES DESIGN WITH SPSS

To execute a repeated-measures analysis of your *noun recognition* data using SPSS, open the *repeatedmeasures1.sav* SPSS file on the book's web page.

From within the **Data Editor**, select **Analyze** from the menu along the top and drop down to **General Linear Model**. Then slide over and select the **Repeated Measures** option that appears to the right. In the **Repeated Measures Define Factor(s)** window (Figure 9.57) enter '3' into the **Number of Levels** box and click **Add** and then **Define**. When the **Repeated Measures** window opens, highlight and move your three variables into the **Within-Subjects Variables** window (Figure 9.58). Click **Options**. When the **Repeated Measures: Options** window (Figure 9.59) appears, click on **Estimates of effect size**, **Observed power**, and **Homogeneity tests** in the lower **Display** area. Then click **Continue**. When you are returned to the **Repeated Measures** window click **OK**. The results appear in the SPSS output window.

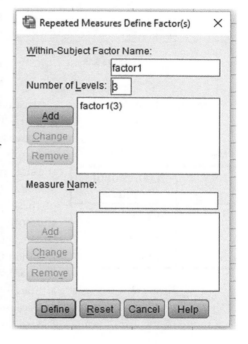

Figure 9.57

The first area to appear in the output window is the *Within-Subjects Factors* table (Figure 9.60). This lists your three within-subjects variables or repeated-measures: *low*, *medium*, and *high* word frequencies. To the next area, *Multivariate Tests* (Figure 9.61), we will return shortly.

The third area is central for deciding how to examine the output tables, draw conclusions, and interpret the results of your repeated measures ANOVA (Figure 9.62). *Mauchly's Test of Sphericity* (Mauchly, 1940) is addressed in more detail shortly; for now it is enough to note that the *p*-value (*Sig.* = 0.630) is greater than 0.05. Thus, you fail to reject the null hypothesis and may continue to make a critical assumption related to homogeneity of variance. Had the *p*-value been less than 0.05, returning to the *F*-values in the above *Multivariate Test* table would be one solution to the violation of the assumption.

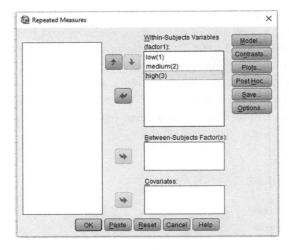

Figure 9.58

Figure 9.59

Within-Subjects Factors

Measure: MEASURE_1

factor1	Dependent Variable
1	low
2	medium
3	high

Figure 9.60

Because those multivariate tests usually have less power than the 'normal' repeated-measures ANOVA, they are reserved for cases involving violations of the assumption of sphericity. Each row in the *Multivariate Tests* table (Figure 9.61) reports the statistics of a distinct multivariate test: *Pillai's Trace, Wilks' Lambda, Hotelling's Trace,* and *Roy's Largest Root*. For each of these tests, the *F*-value, *df*, and the *p*-value are provided. Currently most researchers consider Wilks' lambda test to be the most appropriate, when Mauchly's test has a *p*-value less than 0.05. Note that in the case of your data all four tests have a *p*-value of 0.036, which would allow you to reject H_0, although you need not resort to these multivariate tests.

Because Mauchly's test was non-significant, you may use the tests found in the *Test of Within-Subjects Effects* table (Figure 9.63). Each row in the top half of the table corresponds to $SS_{treatment}$, $df_{treatment}$, and $MS_{treatment}$, along with the *F*-value each of the four tests. Each row in the bottom half of the table reports their corresponding error terms: SS_{error}, df_{error}, MS_{error}.

Multivariate Tests[a]

Effect		Value	F	Hypothesis df	Error df	Sig.	Partial Eta Squared	Noncent. Parameter	Observed Power[c]
factor1	Pillai's Trace	.890	12.188[b]	2.000	3.000	.036	.890	24.375	.709
	Wilks' Lambda	.110	12.188[b]	2.000	3.000	.036	.890	24.375	.709
	Hotelling's Trace	8.125	12.188[b]	2.000	3.000	.036	.890	24.375	.709
	Roy's Largest Root	8.125	12.188[b]	2.000	3.000	.036	.890	24.375	.709

a. Design: Intercept
   Within Subjects Design: factor1

Figure 9.61

Mauchly's Test of Sphericity[a]

Measure: MEASURE_1

Within Subjects Effect	Mauchly's W	Approx. Chi-Square	df	Sig.	Epsilon[b]		
					Greenhouse-Geisser	Huynh-Feldt	Lower-bound
factor1	.735	.925	2	.630	.790	1.000	.500

Tests the null hypothesis that the error covariance matrix of the orthonormalized transformed dependent variables is proportional to an identity matrix.

Figure 9.62

Tests of Within-Subjects Effects

Measure: MEASURE_1

Source		Type III Sum of Squares	df	Mean Square	F	Sig.	Partial Eta Squared	Noncent. Parameter	Observed Power[a]
factor1	Sphericity Assumed	43.333	2	21.667	18.571	.001	.823	37.143	.995
	Greenhouse-Geisser	43.333	1.581	27.415	18.571	.003	.823	29.355	.981
	Huynh-Feldt	43.333	2.000	21.667	18.571	.001	.823	37.143	.995
	Lower-bound	43.333	1.000	43.333	18.571	.013	.823	18.571	.889
Error(factor1)	Sphericity Assumed	9.333	8	1.167					
	Greenhouse-Geisser	9.333	6.323	1.476					
	Huynh-Feldt	9.333	8.000	1.167					
	Lower-bound	9.333	4.000	2.333					

a. Computed using alpha = .05

Figure 9.63

When Mauchly's test is non-significant, most researchers report the *Sphericity Assumed* test. Note that the sum of squares, the *df*, the mean squares, and the *F*-value for the sphericity assumed that tests are equivalent to those in your above repeated-measures ANOVA summary table (Figure 9.56). The three other tests reported in the *Tests of Within-Subjects Effects* table are tests a researcher may choose to correct for any minor violation regarding the sphericity assumption, even when Mauchly's test is non-significant. As seen from the table, the corrections are made through modifications in the *df*. These changes in the *df* then change the probabilities associated with the *F*-values. The *Huynh-Feldt* test is considered the least conservative and the *Lower-bound* test the most conservative.

> The computational difference between a repeated-measures ANOVA and the multivariate tests centres on the computation of SS_{error}. Scheiner and Gurevitch (2001) offer a good overview of the topic.

• • • • •

The contents of all of these tables would not be reported in a published article. You may write something like the following: 'After finding Mauchly's *W* (0.735) to be non-significant ($p = 0.63$), a significant repeated-measures ANOVA (sphericity assumed) of *frequency* provided evidence that the word frequency of nouns affected recognition memory: $F(2, 8) = 18.571$, $MS_{error} = 1.167$, $p = 0.001$.'

Because the ANOVA was significant, it is incumbent upon you to report a standardized measure of effect size. The *Test of Within-Subject Effects* table reports a partial eta squared of 0.823 for the assumed sphericity test. This partial eta squared, remember, is not the proportion of total variance explained by *frequency*, rather it is $SS_{frequency}/(SS_{frequency} + SS_{error})$. If you wished to report the η^2, you would use SS_{total} in the denominator: $43.333/(43.333 + 206.667) = 0.17$. The SS_{total} (206.667) used in the calculation is the $SS_{between\ subjects}$ found hidden as the *Type III Sum of Squares* error in the SPSS *Test of Between-Subjects Effect* table (Figure 9.64).

Tests of Between-Subjects Effects

Measure: MEASURE_1
Transformed Variable: Average

Source	Type III Sum of Squares	df	Mean Square	F	Sig.	Partial Eta Squared	Noncent. Parameter	Observed Power[a]
Intercept	1401.667	1	1401.667	27.129	.006	.872	27.129	.967
Error	206.667	4	51.667					

a. Computed using alpha = .05

Figure 9.64

A new assumption for repeated measures

> There are no SPSS options for bootstrapping when conducting a repeated-measures ANOVA, not even with respect to the descriptive statistics. Bootstrapping of the descriptive statistics would need to be conducted through the SPSS *Descriptive Statistics* option as in Chapter 2. It is possible to conduct bootstrapping for the design, however. For a full discussion of how to do so, and the issues of which you should be aware, see Berkovits et al. (2000).

Subject #	d-score (low–medium)	d-score (low–high)	d-score (medium-high)
1	4	4	0
2	4	4	0
3	3	6	3
4	3	5	2
5	1	1	0
Variances =	1.5	3.5	2.0

Figure 9.65

With each new variation of ANOVA we encounter new assumptions. In addition to the assumptions of reasonable normality and homogeneity of variance with respect to the treatment conditions, with repeated-measures analysis comes the critical assumption of *sphericity*. Sphericity refers to the circumstance when the *variances* of the *differences* in the scores (*d*-scores) between all possible pairs of the treatment conditions are equal. If sphericity cannot be assumed, then the variance calculations for the treatment conditions are likely to be biased in a manner that tends to inflate the *F*-value. Thus, if H_0 is true, a violation of sphericity may increase the probability of committing a Type I error (Hinton et al., 2004). As the number of levels of the IV increases, the risk of violating the assumption of sphericity also increases: the more sets of *d*-scores you have, the greater the chance that one set could be significantly different from the others. Similarly to testing other assumptions, such as homogeneity of variance and normality, when the sample size is small, as is yours, Mauchly's test has been shown to be insensitive to violations. Figure 9.65 lists your three possible sets of *d*-scores and their variances. You could think of Mauchly's test as being analogous to the F_{max} test. If you divide the smallest (*d*-score) variance by the largest variance (3.5/1.5 = 2.33) and consider the F_{max} table for 4 *df* error and three treatments (critical value = 15.5), you fail to reject H_0 and you are able to assume sphericity.

9 8 NONPARAMETRIC ALTERNATIVES

The two new parametric tests discussed thus far in this chapter (randomized block and repeated-measures ANOVA) are appropriate for measurement data, and thus make the assumption that the observations are either interval or ratio in nature. There are many cases where a researcher's data are not measurement in nature and other instances where the assumptions cannot be met or violations not easily corrected.

REVIEW QUESTION

Are your *noun recognition* data interval or ratio in nature? Why?

Web Link 9.10 for an answer to the review question.

In this section we examine the most common nonparametric alternative to the repeated-measures ANOVA: Friedman's (1937, 1939) test for *k* related samples: *Friedman's two-way analysis of variance by ranks*. Friedman's test is designed for use with ordinal data. It also is used when the data are measurement in nature, but the researcher believes that the assumption of normality is seriously violated. As we saw earlier in this chapter and in the previous one, it is virtually impossible to test for violations of normality and the presence of outliers when sample sizes are small. In such instances, it is common to replace the repeated-measures ANOVA with Friedman's test. Friedman's test is also considered an alternative to ANOVA when sphericity is violated. As discussed in the previous section, under such circumstances multivariate tests are often judged viable alternatives. If you wish to avoid making the assumptions required by the multivariate alternatives, Friedman's test is a suitable substitute.

There are two types of circumstances where the data clearly require a nonparametric approach. Unfortunately, researchers often inappropriately analyse such data with a repeated-measures ANOVA. In the first circumstance the data represent subject ratings. For example, a social psychologist may be interested in facial expression and asks subjects to rate photographs of three faces in terms of happiness on a scale from 1 to 7. In the second circumstance subjects are asked to rank-order stimuli. For example, our social psychologist may ask subjects to rank the three faces in terms of their perceived happiness: the most, the middle, and the least. In both of these cases it is wishful thinking to assume that the scales used by the subjects are equal interval in nature. Furthermore, the distributions of ratings are likely to be skewed to such an extent as to render the assumption of normality unrealistic.

Friedman's test is similar to the Wilcoxon test discussed in Chapter 5. Where the Wilcoxon test was limited to two related samples (conditions), Friedman's test allows for the analysis of

Subject	Low	Medium	High
1	7 (3)	3 (1.5)	3 (1.5)
2	14 (3)	10 (1.5)	10 (1.5)
3	13 (3)	10 (2)	7 (1)
4	18 (3)	15 (2)	13 (1)
5	8 (3)	7 (1.5)	7 (1.5)

Rankings are in brackets.

Figure 9.66

1	2	3
1	3	2
2	3	1
3	1	3
3	1	2
3	2	1

Possible Ranking Patterns

Figure 9.67

more than two related samples. Like the Kruskal–Wallis test, Friedman's test begins by ranking the responses. But where the Kruskal–Wallis test ranks all scores across all conditions, Friedman's test rank-orders the scores separately within each subject. For example, if there are three conditions, as is the case with your noun recognition data, each subject has a score of 1 (his or her lowest score), and 2 (their middle score), and 3 (their highest score). Figure 9.66 depicts your original five subjects' noun recognition scores and their corresponding within-subject rankings. Should there be a tie between two of a subject's scores, as there is in the cases of subjects 1, 2, and 5, then the average of the two adjacent rankings is used for both subjects.

The H_0 is that the rankings are random with respect to column or word frequency. Looked at in more detail, with three conditions there are six possible patterns of rankings (Figure 9.67). Stated another way, the H_0 is that the six possible patterns are all equally probable, that is they are randomly present.

There are various algebraically equivalent ways to calculate Friedman's test statistic, all of which are evaluated on the χ^2 distribution with $k-1$ df, where k is the number of treatment conditions. In one version, at the heart of the matter there is a type of χ^2 formula with a correction:

$$\chi^2_{\text{Friedman}} = \frac{12}{nk(k+1)} \Sigma R_j^2 - 3n(k+1),$$

where n is the number of subjects, k is the number of conditions, and R_j is the total of the ranks in a given condition. For your noun recognition data,

$$\chi^2_{\text{Friedman}} = \frac{12}{5 \times 3(3+1)}(15^2 + 8.5^2 + 6.5^2) - 3(5)(3+1) = 7.9.$$

In a second version, we can glimpse at how the nonparametric test resembles the parametric ANOVA:

$$\chi^2_{\text{Friedman}} = \frac{n\Sigma\left(\bar{y}_{rj} - GM_r\right)^2}{k(k+1)/12}.$$

First, we again calculate the total ranks for each condition. Then we calculate the mean rank for each condition: the sum of the ranks for each condition divided by the number of subjects. For your data the mean ranks ($\bar{y}_{rj}$, mean ranks for the jth condition) for the three conditions are 3 (15/5), 1.7 (8.5/5), and 1.3 (6.5/5). Next we calculate the grand mean (GM_r) of the ranks across all columns: $(k+1)/2$. For your data, $GM_r = [(3+1)/2] = 2$. Next we calculate what appears to be – and in effect is – $SS_{\text{treatment}}$, which we will call SS_{ranks}:

$$SS_{\text{ranks}} = n\Sigma(\bar{y}_{rj} - GM_r)^2.$$

For your data we find

$$SS_{ranks} = 5[(3 - 2)^2 + (1.7 - 2)^2 + (1.3 - 2)^2] = 7.9.$$

This is divided by $k(k + 1)/12$, which will always be 1 when the number of conditions is 3:

$$\chi^2_{Friedman} = \frac{7.9}{1} = 7.9.$$

Again, $\chi^2_{Friedman}$ is evaluated against the χ^2 distribution of critical values with $k - 1$ df. With 2 df, at $\alpha = 0.05$ the critical value is 5.99 (Appendix C). Therefore you reject the null hypothesis that the distributions of ranks are random. As was the case after the repeated-measure ANOVA, you may conclude that the word frequency of nouns influences recognition memory. Remember, one of the limitations of a nonparametric test is that it is difficult to make specific quantitative statements concerning the differences between the conditions – that is, there is no way to state on which specific *parameter* of their distribution they differ. It may be the means, it may be the variances, or it may be another parameter.

Running Friedman's test in SPSS

To run Friedman's test in SPSS, scroll down the *Analyze* tab in the SPSS *Data Editor* to *Nonparametric Tests*, open, slide over, and select *Related Samples*. When the *Nonparametric Tests: Two or More Related Samples* window opens, (Figure 9.68) select the *Fields* tab at the top. When the next window opens, move the *low, medium,* and *high* variables to the *Test Fields* area. Next select the *Settings* tab at the top. At this point, we will leave the *automatically 'choose the tests based on the data'* option unchanged. To run the analysis, click the *Run* button at the bottom of the window.

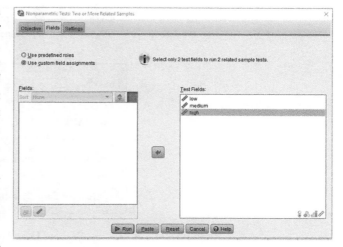

Figure 9.68

In the output window a *Hypothesis Test Summary* box (Figure 9.69) appears. The leftmost area in the box defines the H_0 that is being tested. As described above, this is not a test of differences in the condition means, but rather a test for any dissimilarity in the distributions of the word *frequency* conditions. The next area in the window designates the test: the Friedman's test for related samples. The third area reports the p-value (*Sig.* = 0.010). The final area suggests a *Decision*: you may reject H_0 at the $\alpha = 0.05$ level.

If you double-click the *Decision* area, another window will open displaying graphs and summary statistics (Figure 9.70). Analogous to the bar chart for the word frequency data that accompanied your earlier ANOVA, the three horizontal bar graphs show the frequencies of the

Hypothesis Test Summary

	Null Hypothesis	Test	Sig.	Decision
1	The distributions of low, medium and high are the same.	Related-Samples Friedman's Two-Way Analysis of Variance by Ranks	.010	Reject the null hypothesis.

Asymptotic significances are displayed. The significance level is .05.

Figure 9.69

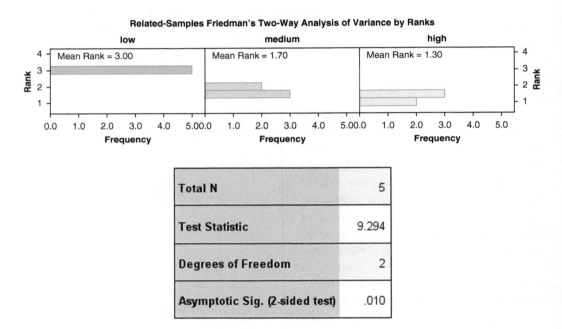

Related-Samples Friedman's Two-Way Analysis of Variance by Ranks

Total N	5
Test Statistic	9.294
Degrees of Freedom	2
Asymptotic Sig. (2-sided test)	.010

Figure 9.70

rankings in each of the three word *frequency* conditions. For example, the *medium* condition has two ranks of 2 and three ranks of 1.5.

The summary statistics table below the graphs reports the number of subjects (*Total N* = 5), the χ^2 (*Test Statistic* = 9.294), the degrees of freedom (2), and the calculated *p*-value of 0.010 (*Asymptotic Sig.*). As was the case with the randomized block ANOVA and the repeated-measures ANOVA, Friedman's test is an omnibus test. It only tells you there is sufficient evidence to conclude that the conditions differ, but not where and how they differ.

● ● ● ● ●

You may have noticed that the χ^2 we calculated twice earlier (7.9) in the chapter is slightly different from the one reported in the SPSS output summary statistics (9.294). The reason for the difference is related to the presence of ties in your ranked data. Most textbooks usually provide one of the two formulae we used for our hand calculations. These formulae are shortcuts and work perfectly well when no ties are present. The greater the number of ties, however, the greater the discrepancy in the estimate of the χ^2. A more complete formula for the Friedman test that avoids the distortion even further resembles the formula for a parametric ANOVA:

$$\chi^2_{\text{Friedman}} = \frac{n\Sigma\left(\bar{y}_{rj} - GM_r\right)^2}{\frac{1}{n(k-1)}\Sigma\left(r_{ij} - GM_r\right)^2}$$

where r_{ij} is the ith rank in the jth condition. In addition to the correction factor prior to the summation sign, the basis of the denominator is now the sum of the squared differences of all individual rankings about their GM. Using this formula for your recognition data will produce a χ^2 identical to that found in the SPSS output. For a detailed discussion, see Daniel (1990).

As in the previous chapter, it is interesting to note that the results of all your omnibus tests (randomized block ANOVA, repeated-measures ANOVA, and Friedman's test) employed to analyse your noun recognition data yielded very similar p-values: 0.001, 0.001, and 0.010, respectively. In this case, it appears that the parametric test had somewhat more power, if H_0 is false. Finding these omnibus tests to be significant, however, does not fully address your H_1: are low-*frequency* nouns more readily recognized than are high-*frequency* nouns? We will find in the next chapter that t-tests, albeit in a modified form, along with their nonparametric alternatives, will provide two approaches for getting closer to a more complete evaluation of your hypothesis.

9 ● 9 CHAPTER SUMMARY

The purpose of this chapter was to examine the most common statistical tests (randomized block ANOVA, repeated-measures ANOVA, and Friedman's two-way analysis of variance by ranks) used to determine if the observations in more than two related conditions can be considered to be members of a single population (H_0). This chapter further illustrates the common nature of all of the statistical tests presented thus far, beginning with the χ^2 goodness-of-fit test, through the t-tests, the χ^2 test of independence, and in particular the tests covered in these last two chapters. The apparent multiplicity of forms (tests) can be seen to have an underlying unity, of which each test is a variation designed for particular circumstances.

Specifically in this chapter, we discovered how the randomized block design is a variant of ANCOVA and how repeated-measures ANOVA is a particular form of the randomized block design. All of these analyses, through the use of a third variable, are intended to trade off *df* for a reduction in SS_{error} and thus increase power:

$$y_i = \mu + \tau_k + \text{third variable} + \varepsilon_{i'}$$

$$y_i = \mu + \tau_k + cov + \varepsilon_{i'}$$

$$y_i = \mu + \tau_k + \beta_j + \varepsilon_{i'}$$

$$y_i = \mu + \tau_k + \varsigma_j + \varepsilon_i.$$

The parallel nature of the above designs was captured also by Figure 9.2 at the outset of this chapter. As we saw in Chapter 8, it is virtually impossible for a *covariate* to be completely independent of the independent variable ($r = 0$). The randomized block design produces total independence by ensuring an equal number of observations from each block at all levels of the independent variable. By extension, this is also true for the repeated-measures analysis where each subject is a block. A new important assumption is added with the repeated-measures ANOVA: *sphericity*. Sphericity refers to the assumed equality of the *variances* of the *differences* in the *d*-scores between all possible pairs of the treatment conditions. If sphericity cannot be assumed, then the researcher must use either a multivariate approach or Friedman's test.

As in the previous chapter, all three of the primary analyses discussed are *omnibus* tests. That is, they test for the possible presence of a treatment effect, not for the location of the effect. When the omnibus *F*-value is significant, the results only indicate that, relative to the error variance, the condition means are spread out more than would be expected due to chance alone. When the nonparametric Friedman's test is significant, the results only indicate that in one way or another the distributions of the within-subjects rankings across the treatment conditions are too dissimilar to be considered the result of mere chance. How and which distribution(s) is dissimilar from the others is not identified. Going beyond the omnibus test will be addressed in the next chapter.

9 ● 10 RECOMMENDED READINGS

Daniel, W. W. (1990). *Applied nonparametric statistics* (2nd ed.). Boston, MA: PWS-Kent.
The chapter entitled 'Friedman's two-way test of analysis of variance by ranks' provides a clear and detailed exposition of Friedman's test and its relation to other nonparametric tests we have covered in previous chapters.

Girden, E. R. (1992). *ANOVA: Repeated measures*. Newbury Park, CA: Sage.
This book is an excellent extension of this chapter. It fills in important details that are beyond our scope, and it extends the coverage to more complicated designs researchers are likely to encounter.

Scheiner, S. M., & Gurevitch, J. (2001). *Design and analysis of ecological experiments* (2nd ed.). Oxford: Oxford University Press.
Although this book is directed at researchers in the area of ecology, Chapters 4, 5, and 8 provide an in-depth coverage of ANOVA, ANCOVA, and repeated-measures analyses that goes beyond what can be covered here.

9 ● 11 CHAPTER REVIEW QUESTIONS

Multiple-choice questions

1   According to the model we have used in this chapter, which is *not* a component of an individual score in a randomized block design?

a   The population variance
b   The population mean
c   The treatment effect
d   The block effect
e   They are all components of an individual score

2   The block effect is estimated by _____ .

a   the difference between a score and the grand mean
b   the difference between a score and the condition mean
c   the difference between the block mean and the grand mean
d   the difference between the score and the block variance
e   A block effect cannot be estimated

3   In a randomized block design, what is the result of subtracting the sum-of-squares error and the sum-of-squares block from the sum-of-squares total?

a   Mean square error
b   Mean square block
c   Sum-of-squares covariate
d   Sum-of-squares treatment
e   Sum-of-squares error from an ANOVA with a blocking variable

4   If there is no true variance attributable to treatment, then the expected *F*-value for the treatment factor in a randomized block design is _____.

a   1
b   indeterminate
c   0
d   It depends on the variance associated with the blocking variable
e   It depends on the variance associated with the error term

5   Which of the following is *not* an assumption necessary for conducting a related-samples ANOVA?

a   Reasonable normality of the treatment condition distributions
b   Homogeneity of variance with respect to the treatment conditions
c   Sphericity
d   The independence of the observations
e   All of the above are assumptions necessary for conducting an ANCOVA

6   How is the sum of squares between subjects computed?

a   By subtracting the grand mean from each of the subject means, squaring the differences, summing them, and multiplying the sum by the number of treatments
b   By subtracting the condition means from each of the subject means, squaring the differences, and summing them

c   By subtracting the grand mean from each of the condition means, squaring the differences, and summing them

d   By subtracting the sum-of-squares error from the sum-of-squares total

e   By subtracting the sum-of-squares treatment from the sum-of-squares total

7   In a randomized block design, the difference between two scores in two different treatment conditions is _____ .

a   the difference in *error* plus the difference in the *treatment effect,* if there is one

b   the difference in error plus the difference in the block effect, if there is one

c   the difference between the errors in the two treatment conditions

d   the difference between the errors in the blocks

e   All of the above differences are related to the difference between two scores in two different treatment conditions

8   In a repeated-measures design where there are four treatment conditions and 20 total observations, how many degrees of freedom in total are there?

a   15

b   3

c   4

d   12

e   19

9   The critical *F*-value for evaluating an observed *F*-value ($\alpha = 0.05$) in a repeated-measures ANOVA with four treatment conditions and 20 total observations is ____.

a   1.96

b   3.49

c   3.10

d   3.13

e   3.26

10   Which of the following is (are) assumptions for *Friedman's two-way analysis of variance by ranks*?

a   Normality of the condition distributions

b   Homogeneity of variance

c   Independence of observations

d   Sphericity

e   None of the above are necessary assumptions of *Friedman's two-way analysis of variance by ranks*

Short-answer questions

1   From the model approach we have taken, given a repeated-measures design (one treatment variable), an individual observation in a given condition is composed of what components?

2   How are the components from Question 1 estimated?

3   What comprises the sum of squares between subjects in a repeated-measures analysis?

4   Complete the repeated-measures ANOVA summary table in Figure 9.71.

5   What could happen to the sums of squares, the mean squares, the degrees of freedom (total, treatment, and error), and the *F*-ratio if a data set that was first analysed as a between-subjects design

Source		SS	DF	MS	F
Between-Subjects			9		
Within-Subjects		560			
	Treatment			2	
	Error	360		20	
Total		1000			

Figure 9.71

was subsequently reanalysed as a repeated-measures design? (Be sure to cover all categorically different outcomes.)

6   How do we ensure that block and treatment are kept independent in a randomized block design? Why is that necessary?

7   When is it most appropriate to use Friedman's nonparametric test for related samples?

Data set questions

1   Imagine an analysis of a data set with three conditions and five observations in each condition. The sums-of-squares total, treatment, and error are 73.6, 19.6, and 54, respectively. The degrees of freedom are 14, 2, and 12, respectively. Assuming a between-subjects design, what is the resulting F-value and what do you conclude? Now imagine a blocking variable that accounts for 50% of the sums-of-squares total. What is the new resulting F-value and what do you conclude?

2   Construct a data set of 15 whole numbers between 5 and 20. Separate them into three equal groups (treatment conditions) twice. In the first data set, the resulting between-subjects F-value should be non-significant but the repeated-measures analysis of the data should be significant. In the second data set, the resulting between-subjects F-value should be significant but the repeated-measures analysis of the data should be non-significant.

3   Figure 9.72 shows five subjects who rated (on a 1 to 10 scale) a melody played three different ways: once in a major key, once in a minor key, and once in a double-harmonic minor key. Because the subjects were of Hungarian origin the researcher thought that the double-harmonic minor version of the melody would be rated the highest. Do the data support her hypothesis?

	Melody type		Double harmonic
Subject#	Major	Minor	Minor
1	7	6	9
2	6	7	5
3	9	4	7
4	4	4	5
5	6	2	5

Figure 9.72

4   A psychologist noticed that, relative, to the number of cars on the road, there were more accidents
     in the afternoon than in the morning or midday. He suspected that time of day affected reaction time
     (RT), and slightly slower RTs were responsible for more accidents. He suspected that people were
     'psychologically' tired by the afternoon. To test his hypothesis, he tested the simple RTs of five subjects
     at 9 am, 1 pm, and 5 pm. The data are presented in Figure 9.73. Do the data support the idea that RT
     is sensitive to time of day? RT is recorded in milliseconds. The greater the RT, the slower the subject.
     Be sure to include all tests of assumptions (with conclusions), descriptive statistics, appropriate figures,
     tests of overall null hypothesis, and ANOVA summary table.

	Time of day		
Subject#	**9.00 am**	**1.00 pm**	**5.00 pm**
1	190	210	275
2	210	240	320
3	201	220	290
4	175	170	200
5	240	235	300

Figure 9.73

Don't forget to use the online resources! Meet your supporting stats tutor through an **introductory
video**, review your maths skills with a **diagnostic pre-test**, explore statistical principles through
interactive simulations, practice analysis techniques with **SPSS datasets**, and check your
work with **answers to all in-text questions**.

https://study.sagepub.com/bors

10

Chapter contents

TESTING FOR SPECIFIC DIFFERENCES: PLANNED AND UNPLANNED TESTS

KEY CONCEPTS: *a priori* tests, *post hoc* test, per-comparison α, familywise α, linear contrasts, orthogonal contrasts, Bonferroni–Dunn test, Studentized range statistic (q), Newman–Keuls test, Tukey's HSD and WSD, quantitative versus qualitative independent variable, test of polynomial trends.

10●1 PURPOSE

The purpose of this chapter is introduce some of the more common forms of follow-up tests researchers use to evaluate their data. As you will see, some evaluations are pre-planned, such as your hypothesis concerning the effect of *cage* condition on the open-field behaviour of hamsters, and some are not pre-planned. In this chapter we discuss one of the reasons why some view statistical analyses as akin to alchemy, as mentioned in Chapter 1. There appear to be so many incantations (formulae) one can employ for producing silver or gold (possible significant results). Plus, the incantations (formulae) are different for within-subjects designs than they are for between-subjects designs. By the end of the chapter, however, we discover there is basically one incantation, but with many incarnations.

10●2 INTRODUCTION

In Chapter 8 (see p. 322) you tested the effect of *cage* condition (the number of cage-mates) on a hamster's willingness to explore an 'open field' (the number of *midsquares* entered).

Finding the omnibus *F*-test to be significant, however, did not fully address your H_1: as the number of cage-mates increases, so will a hamster's willingness to explore. Figure 10.1 reiterates the results of your independent-samples (between-subjects) ANOVA. As mentioned in Chapter 8, all you know from the significant omnibus F ($F = 11.455$, $p = 0.003$) is that the *observed* variability among the condition means is greater than what would be *expected* due to chance alone. The omnibus F cannot confirm that a systematic increase in the number of cage-mates accompanies a corresponding increase in the number of *midsquares* entered. Nor can it confirm that the number of cage-mates makes no differences unless there are more than two hamsters per cage, which was a possible alternative interpretation of the results. In order to answer a researcher's H_1 it is usually necessary to conduct multiple follow-up tests.

But before turning our attention back to your original overall H_1 and beginning to evaluate it, we need to recognize the consequences of conducting multiple tests on a single data set and address two important issues.

ANOVA

midsquares

	Sum of Squares	df	Mean Square	F	Sig.
Between Groups	56.000	2	28.000	11.455	.003
Within Groups	22.000	9	2.444		
Total	78.000	11			

Figure 10.1

10 ● 3 *A PRIORI* VERSUS *POST HOC* TESTS

In this section we will describe the difference between *planned* (*a priori*) and *unplanned* (*post hoc*) tests. This distinction has implications for evaluating the results of multiple follow-up tests. One recurring theme throughout this book has been the interrelated issues of Type I errors, Type II errors, and *power*. As we proceed through this chapter, bear in mind that one reason for the variety of tests, particularly those which are *post hoc* in nature, is the tension between a need to avoid discovering 'hens' teeth' (committing a Type I error), when H_0 is true, and the desire to have sufficient statistical power to avoid committing a Type II error, when H_0 is false. It is the status of H_0 that is in question and is the reason for empirical research. The complicated mixture of possible outcomes when conducting multiple follow-up tests is summarized in Figure 10.2. Keep in mind that all we know is whether or not H_0 has been rejected; we do not know whether H_0 is true or false.

K in Figure 10.2 is the total number of follow-up tests; TK is the number of follow-up tests when H_0 is true; $K - TK$ is the number of follow-up tests when H_0 is false; R is the total number of rejections of H_0; $K - R$ is the number of failures to reject H_0. TR is the number of Type I errors; FR is the number of correct rejections of H_0; TFR is

	H_0 is true	H_0 is false	Total
Reject H_0	TR	FR	R
Fail to reject H_0	TFR	FFR	K − R
Total	TK	K − TK	K

Figure 10.2

the number of correct failures to reject H_0; FFR is the number of Type II errors. While we know the totals for the two centre rows (R and $K - R$), we do not know the totals for the two centre columns (TK and $K - TK$).

When you either (1) reject all of the null hypotheses or (2) fail to reject all of the null hypotheses, the table simplifies and the results are easier to interpret. A mix of rejections and failures to reject complicates the matter. In the first case, the researcher only needs to be concerned with either Type I or Type II errors, but not both. In the latter case, with a mix of rejections and failures to reject, the researcher needs to be open to the presence of both Type I and Type II errors.

● ● ● ● ●

Because the omnibus *F*-test rarely answers the researcher's questions, it has been argued by some that it can often be ignored and that researchers can move directly to more analytical follow-up tests (e.g., Wilcox, 1987). In the past, I once intentionally failed to report the omnibus *F* when submitting an article to a scientific journal for possible publication. The editor immediately informed me that I must report the omnibus *F*, regardless of its relevance. With respect to the reporting of results, editorial customs often carry considerable weight.

Rarely upon completion of the omnibus *F*-test is the researcher's overall question(s) fully answered. This is particularly true when the research design is as complex as those discussed in Part III of this book. To fully address the overall question (H_1), the researcher will need to statistically dissect his or her data, which will necessitate testing a more limited and specific H_0. Before discussing the logic and the 'how to' of dissecting a data set, it is necessary to make two important distinctions: *a priori* versus *post hoc* comparisons and the *per-comparison* Type I error rate versus the *familywise* Type I error rate.

A priori in Latin literally means 'from the earlier' or 'from the prior'. In terms of follow-up statistical tests it implies that in light of previous research and knowledge of the topic, and prior to data collection, there was the intent of conducting particular follow-up tests. In fact, the intended *a priori* tests were probably instrumental in the design of the experiment. Your prior knowledge may have several dimensions. It may be theories concerning hamster behaviour, it may be your previous experience with hamsters, or it may be previous research reported by others. The important point is that the intent to make particular comparisons arose *before* you collected the data. *A priori* follow-up tests are also referred to as planned *comparisons* or planned *contrasts*.

● ● ● ● ●

Recall from Chapter 1 that one of the important differences between experimental and observational studies is the design of the research. In an experiment the researcher has control over which variables will be included, how the dependent and independent variables will be operationally defined, how subjects will be assigned to conditions, and other important elements of the data collection procedures. One of these elements is that he or she is able to ensure, albeit incompletely, that the design allows for his or her predictions to be appropriately examined. That is, the researcher's design can incorporate knowledge of the planned comparisons necessary for answering his or her questions.

Post hoc is the abbreviated form of the Latin phrase *post hoc, ergo propter hoc*, meaning 'after this, therefore because of this'. With respect to follow-up tests the phrase implies that the thought of making a particular comparison(s) did not arise until the researcher, at least cursorily, examined the collected data. We might call these 'after the fact' comparisons. The important point is that the intent of making the comparison(s) did not arise out of prior theoretical or empirical knowledge. At best, conducting *post hoc* tests is an attempt to explore some promising ideas that emerged after the data were collected and scrutinized. At its worst, conducting *post hoc* comparisons can be viewed as a 'fishing expedition' where any catch will do.

The results of *post hoc* tests must be reported as such. In the next section we shall see why. Unfortunately some researchers have reported *post hoc* tests as if they were *a priori* by scripting an after-the-fact story to give the appearance that the tests were planned. These tests may be planned, but that plan is applicable to future data collection. If you think that you have found something of interest with *post hoc* tests, then you should design another experiment to test out this new idea before publishing your findings.

10 ● 4 PER-COMPARISON VERSUS FAMILYWISE ERROR RATES

In this section we will describe the difference between per-comparison and familywise Type I error rates. We will see the distinction has implications for (1) the choice of follow-up tests and (2) the determination of the critical value (or the p-value) to be used for rejecting specific null hypotheses. We also explore how the per-comparison α (pcα) can be modified to maintain a desired familywise α (fwα).

The first issue to be faced when conducting multiple comparisons is how to deal with the Type I error rate, α. Thus far in this book, we have concentrated on the *per-comparison* Type I error rate, with the exception of a brief mention of the *familywise* rate in Chapters 5 and 8. The identification of this distinction and its importance are largely attributed to Tukey (1953). The per-comparison Type I error rate is the probability of concluding that a given H_0 is false, when in fact it is true. The vital point is that the per-comparison rate is a statement about an individual test, planned or unplanned. Once we are conducting multiple tests on a single data set, however, it is the familywise error rate that is of prime concern.

The pcα we use for decision-making purposes is $\alpha = 0.05$. That is, the *observed* test statistic (t-value, r, X^2, or F-value) requires a probability of less than 0.05 for us to reject H_0. To understand the implications of multiple tests, it is necessary to recall the laws of probability. If we have an incredibly complicated research design and are conducting 100 follow-up tests with each test using $\alpha = 0.05$, then we would *expect* 5 of those tests to be found to be significant by chance alone. We can deconstruct the problem with the following four statements:

1   The probability of making a Type I error is pcα.
2   The probability of *not* making a Type I error is $1 -$ pcα.
3   The probability of *not* making a Type I error with c follow-up tests is $(1 - \text{pca})^c$.
4   The probability of making *at least* one Type I error with c tests is $1 - (1 - \text{pca})^c$

(See the discussion of the laws of probability on p. 94 in Chapter 3.)

The issue that must be faced, and is too often avoided in the social and behavioural sciences (Frane, 2015), is statement 4, which is the familywise error rate. Statement 4 reveals that if we used a pcα of 0.05 and conducted two tests, the chances of making at least one Type I error (if H_0 were false) would be $1 - (1 - 0.05)^2$ or 0.0975. The Type I error rate in this case has almost doubled. The familywise Type I error rate is always greater than the per-comparison rate, unless the family has only one member. If we conducted 10 follow-up tests using a pcα of 0.05, the chances of making at least one Type I error (if all the H_0 were false) would be 0.4013. It should be clear that we need to worry about discovering an abundance of hens' teeth (hens don't have teeth). That is, how many of our significant results are Type I errors? Consequently, it must be asked, upon how many false leads are we constructing our interpretation and planning our future studies? As pointed out by Jaccard et al. (1984), historically, there have been too many published research reports involving *post hoc* tests with inadequate protection against an escalating familywise Type I error rate.

Here we see the dilemma that researchers face. If H_0 is false, we need enough *power* to be able to correctly reject H_0. That is, we legitimately worry about missing an effect that exists (Type II error). On the other hand, as our research design includes more and more follow-up tests, we worry about claiming to have found effects that are not really there (Type I error). The problem is that we do not know the status of each H_0, but that is the reason for our research in the first place. From previous work in the area we may have an educated guess about its status, but in terms of how it applies to our data, we can never be sure.

For any one of our multiple follow-up tests H_0 may be true or it may be false. If it is true, we can either correctly *fail to reject* or incorrectly reject it (Type I error). If it is false, we can either correctly reject or incorrectly *fail to reject* it (Type II error).

As mentioned above, the problem is complicated by the fact that the multiple H_0 need not all be true or all be false. The outcomes can be mixed: some of the specific H_0 in the *family* may be true and others false, which is often the case. Given this complicated picture, it is incumbent to keep the familywise Type I error rate as close to 0.05 as possible.

Obviously we need to define the term *family* for purposes of the familywise Type I error rate. A *family* is a related set of tests conducted on a single set of data. If you have a set of planned (*a priori*) comparisons, the family is composed of those and only those specific comparisons. In terms of your specific hypotheses concerning *cage* condition and *midsquares* entered, you might have the following planned comparisons:

H_1: *cage 1 < cage 2*,

H_2: *cage 2 < cage 4*.

Therefore, there is a family of two planned comparisons. If, after your initial results you decided to test for a difference between *cage 1* and *cage 4*, that test would be a *post hoc*. Under such conditions, to run a *post hoc* test on one pair of means implies that you are running tests on all possible pairs of means, whether or not you actually do so. Why? Because you only decided to compare the one pair of means after viewing the data and your initial results. Implicitly, even when you merely scan the results you are testing all possible pairs. Thus, the *post hoc* family is composed of all possible pairs. *Post hoc* tests are like crisps (potato chips): once you have opened the bag it is open. You might as well eat them all, because you are going to pay for the full bag. In this possible *post hoc* scenario there is a family of three pairwise comparisons:

> Some researchers will consider the omnibus *F* as a member of the family; most researchers think otherwise. Most would exclude the omnibus *F* from the family – or at best consider it to be a distant relative – unless the omnibus *F* itself is necessary for evaluating one of the specific planned hypotheses. In the case of your open-field data, the omnibus *F* offers nothing that would not be tested with your planned comparisons.

H_{0-1}: *cage 1 = cage 2,*

H_{0-2}: *cage 1 = cage 4,*

H_{0-3}: *cage 2 = cage 4.*

As the number of follow-up tests increases, be they *a priori* or *post hoc*, and if the pcα remains at 0.05, the familywise Type I error rate will balloon to an indefensible size. In terms of *a priori* tests, the easiest rule of thumb for compensating for the increasing familywise error rate is to reduce the pcα by dividing 0.05 by the number of planned comparisons. Usually the number of planned comparisons is equal to or less than $df_{treatment}$. For example, because you have two planned comparisons you could use a *p*-value of 0.025 or the corresponding critical value

> Appendix G contains tabled critical values corresponding to a pcα of 0.05, 0.025, and 0.01. The same is true for Appendix D.

in the *t*-table or *F*-table as the revised threshold for significance for both comparisons. If you had a more complicated design which contained 3, 4, or 5 planned comparisons, many researchers often would use a per-comparison α of 0.01 for all comparisons.

• • • • •

The differences between *a priori* and *post hoc* tests are summarized in Figure 10.3.

A priori **tests**	*Post hoc* **tests**
Designed prior to data collection.	Considered only after data collection.
Explicit question: Do these particular pairs of means differ?	Implicit question: Which of these pairs of means differ?
Testing of a theory or specific informed hypotheses.	Empirical summary of the differences among the means.
Omnibus *F*-test is not necessary.	Omnibus *F*-test must be significant.
Number of comparisons usually equal to or less than $df_{treatment}$.	Number of comparisons usually greater than $df_{treatment}$.

Figure 10.3

10 ● 5 PLANNED COMPARISONS: *A PRIORI* TESTS

In Chapter 8 we attempted to answer your overall research hypothesis that as the number of cage-mates (*cage* condition) increased, so would the number of *midsquares* entered in an open-field apparatus, indicating an increasing willingness on the part of young hamsters to explore. We first attempted to evaluate your overall H_1 by analysing the data from your 12 hamsters with a series of three t-tests. Due to what we now know as the issue of a familywise Type I error rate, we subsequently turned to Fisher's F-test (ANOVA). Although the significant omnibus F-value from the ANOVA was helpful and indicated that *cage* condition did affect open-field behaviour, an omnibus test is not specific about the details of the effect. Ironically, we will now revisit the t-test, albeit in a revised form. The t-test conventionally has been the most common form of planned comparisons.

Fisher's LSD

Fisher's (1935) least significant difference (LSD) test can be considered either an *a priori* or a *post hoc* test. In many ways it has been a model and a foil for many of the tests, particularly *post hoc* comparisons, which were subsequently developed. The chief criticism of the LSD is that it does not provide adequate protection against inflating the familywise Type I error rate. Fisher based his protection on the omnibus F. His strategy was simple. If the result of the omnibus F was significant, then the researcher was free to explore follow-up tests. If the result of the omnibus F was non-significant, then no further testing was permitted. There was no clear distinction made between *a priori* and *post hoc* test procedures and there was no discussion of a need to change the pcα. This latter problem can be easily resolved, however, as we will see.

Fisher's LSD involves using the t-test formula to compute the smallest difference between two means necessary for statistical significance, using a pcα of 0.05. The key difference between the t-tests described in Chapter 5 and Fisher's LSD is the error term (denominator). Fisher recognized that when it comes to computing an unbiased estimate of population variance, the more data, the merrier. Therefore the MS_{error} from the omnibus F-test would be superior to the estimates for the specific comparisons of particular pairs of means. Using your hamster data from Chapter 8 (see Figure 10.1) which had four hamsters in each of three *cage* conditions ($df_{error} = 9$) and an MS_{error} of 2.4 as an example, we find the following (see p. 324 for the hamster data analysis in Chapter 8):

$$t = \frac{\bar{y}_1 - \bar{y}_2}{\sqrt{\dfrac{s_1^2}{n_1} + \dfrac{s_2^2}{n_2}}} \text{ is replaced with } t = \frac{\bar{y}_1 - \bar{y}_2}{\sqrt{\dfrac{MS_{error}}{n_1} + \dfrac{MS_{error}}{n_2}}} = \frac{\bar{y}_1 - \bar{y}_2}{\sqrt{\dfrac{2.4}{4} + \dfrac{2.4}{4}}}.$$

Next, we solve for the minimum absolute difference (LSD) between the mean that will be critical at $\alpha = 0.05$. For 9 df the critical t-value (LSD) found in Appendix D is 2.262:

$$LSD = \text{critical } t_{(9)} \sqrt{\frac{2.4}{4} + \frac{2.4}{4}} = 2.262 \sqrt{\frac{2.4}{4} + \frac{2.4}{4}} = 2.48.$$

For your data, the difference between any pair of means must be greater than 2.48 to be considered significant at $\alpha = 0.05$. Figure 10.4 represents the absolute differences between the three pairings of the means from your hamster data in Chapter 8.

When the three differences are compared with the LSD of 2.48 we find the difference between *cage* conditions 1 and 2 ($|-1| < 2.48$) to be non-significant, and the difference between *cage* conditions 2 and 4 ($|-4| > 2.48$) to be significant. As was the case in Chapter 8 (see p. 326), the use of the LSD (*t*-test) provides only limited support for your overall hypothesis: as the number of cage-mates increases, so will a hamster's willingness to explore.

Cage conditions	Difference
1 versus 2	−1
1 versus 4	−5
1 versus 4	−4

Figure 10.4

Two points must be made. First, the two planned comparisons were made at the per-comparison α of 0.05. Because there were two comparisons to be tested, a pcα of 0.025 would be more appropriate. Although Fisher did not call for such a strategy, there is nothing incompatible between Fisher's LSD and changing the critical value to one that is more appropriate for the number of planned comparisons. Using the $\alpha = 0.025$ column in Appendix D, we find the critical value of 2.685. Recalculating the LSD using this value, we find a difference of 2.941 or greater is required for two means to be considered significantly different. This does not change the pattern of significance for your planned comparisons, nor does it change your conclusion of partial support.

The second point to be made regards power and interpreting failures to reject an H_0. As discussed in Chapters 1 and 4, failing to reject an H_0 (in your case, comparing *cage* condition 1 versus 2) does not prove the H_0 to be true. Bear in mind that although the difference appears relatively small, the direction of the difference is consistent with your prediction: the mean of *cage* condition 2 (4) is greater than the mean of *cage* condition 1 (3). It may be a matter of having insufficient power for an effect of that size. Recall that the effect size for a difference between two independent means is

$$d = \frac{\bar{y}_1 - \bar{y}_2}{\sigma},$$

where σ is estimated by s, the best estimate of population standard deviation in this case being the square root of MS_{error} from the omnibus *F*-test ($\sqrt{2.4}$),

$$d = \frac{3-4}{1.55} = 0.65.$$

Examining Cohen's effect size table (Table B.1 in Appendix B), we find this to be a medium size effect. Furthermore, we find from Cohen's required sample size table (Table B.2 in Appendix B) that 64 subjects per condition are required to ensure that power is at least 0.80 ($\alpha = 0.05$). Thus, it is clear that it is risky to conclude there is no difference whatsoever between *cage* conditions 1 and 2.

It would be easier to evaluate your overall hypothesis about the relation between *cage* condition and willingness to explore if both of your *a priori* comparisons had been significant. It also would be easier if both comparisons were non-significant, although, as you can see, with your small sample size the issue of power would remain. It is easiest to interpret results when all of your planned comparisons are significant. But as research designs become more complicated the probability of such an outcome is less and less likely. Data are often messy and outcomes are frequently mixed. This is even more often the case when you have insufficient power for medium size effects.

Finally, with respect to the LSD analysis, when a planned comparison is found to be significant it is incumbent upon the researcher to report a standardized effect size. In your case Cohen's d is appropriate. Using the formula for d, we find that the standardized effect for the difference between *cage* conditions 2 and 4 is

$$d = \frac{4-8}{1.55} = 2.58,$$

which is an extremely large effect. From Cohen's effect size table (Table B.1 in Appendix B), we see that a large effect size for the difference between two independent means is a d of 0.80. Remember, this is an imaginary data set. Rarely, if ever, do we come across real effect sizes of such magnitude.

● ● ● ● ●

The other alternative hypothesis you generated after examining the data was that hamsters required more than two cage-mates for *cage* condition to affect a hamster's willingness to explore an open field. You constructed this alternative hypothesis after examining the condition means. That is, this is a *post hoc* hypothesis. As such it will be examined in Section 10.7.

Multiple *t*-tests

As Howell (2013) points out, perhaps the simplest method for evaluating planned comparisons is the multiple *t*-test approach. The multiple *t*-test approach is simply (1) using Fisher's idea concerning the most appropriate error terms for the individual *t*-tests, (2) restricting the comparisons to those that are planned, and (3) using a *p*-value appropriate to the number of comparisons.

There are three points that multiple *t*-tests are based upon as follows:

1 All sample variances in your study are unbiased estimators of the population variance, regardless of the veracity of H_0.
2 The more unbiased estimates you have of a population parameter (e.g., variance), the more efficient your estimate.
3 The greater the *df* error, the greater the test's power. This is reflected in the *t*-table and *F*-tables by the fact that as the *df* error increases, the critical value decreases.

Assuming homogeneity of variance, you can use the MS_{error} and df_{error} from your independent-samples ANOVA (Figure 10.1) for all follow-up tests rather than the error terms and *df* specific to the conditions being compared. For example, to test your first planned comparison (*cage 1 < cage 2*) we use

$$t = \frac{\bar{y}_1 - \bar{y}_2}{\sqrt{\dfrac{MS_1^2}{n_1} + \dfrac{MS_2^2}{n_2}}} = \frac{3-4}{\sqrt{\dfrac{2.44}{4} + \dfrac{2.44}{4}}} = -0.91.$$

For your second planned comparison (*cage 2 < cage 4*),

$$t = \frac{\bar{y}_1 - \bar{y}_2}{\sqrt{\dfrac{MS_1^2}{n_1} + \dfrac{MS_2^2}{n_2}}} = \frac{4-8}{\sqrt{\dfrac{2.44}{4} + \dfrac{2.44}{4}}} = -3.62.$$

If you are running the tests using SPSS, as we will see shortly, a specific *p*-value will be reported for each comparison. If you are computing the two *t*-tests by hand, you will need to use the critical values in Appendix D for evaluating significance. Because the variances from all three conditions are used in the error term for your two comparisons, you use all 9 *df* and the $\alpha = 0.025$ column from Appendix D for testing the significance: critical value = 2.685. Using this critical value as the threshold for significance, we fail to reject the H_0 from the first comparison and find that there is insufficient evidence to conclude that the performances of hamsters in *cage 2* were different from those in *cage 1*. There is, however, sufficient evidence to conclude that open-field performance in *cage 4* was greater than performance in *cage 2*. Figure 10.5 allows for a comparison between two of the standard independent-sample *t*-tests and the multiple *t*-tests performed here on your two planned comparisons.

Cage Comparison	*t*	Standard *t*-tests			*t*	Multiple *t*-tests		
		Std Error	df	*p-value*		Std Error	df	*p-value*
1 versus 2	−1.0000	1.0000	6	> .05	−.91	1.1055	9	> .025
1 versus 4	−3.464	1.1547	6	< .05	−3.62	1.1055	9	< .025

Figure 10.5

The first difference to be noted between the standard independent *t*-tests and the multiple *t*-tests relates to the *t*-values themselves. Because the differences in the means do not change, the changes in the *t*-values must be the result of other changes: the *standard errors* and the *df*. Where the standard errors for the standard *t*-tests are constructed on the basis of the variances of the two particular conditions being compared, the multiple *t*-tests use the variances from all three *cage* conditions to construct the standard errors. Consequently, for the two multiple *t*-tests a single standard error is used for both comparisons (1.1055). The differences in the *df* reflect the differences in the number of observations comprising the different *standard errors*.

Because the *standard error* for the multiple *t*-tests is based on an average of all three variances some comparisons will gain *power*, due to a smaller error term (*cage 2* versus *cage 4*), while other comparisons will lose power (*cage 1* versus *cage 2*). This change in the standard error term produced the change in the three *t*-values. On the other hand, the change in the *df* from 6 to 9 increases the power for both comparisons by reducing the critical value. At $\alpha = 0.025$: with 6 *df* the critical *t*-value is 2.969, and with 9 *df* the critical *t*-value is 2.685.

• • • • •

Remember, power is influenced by three factors: the size of the effect (difference in means), the variance, and *n* or *df*. In our example, there are no changes in the differences between the three means. As the variance (reflected in the standard error for a comparison) decreases, the *t*-value increases and power increases. As the standard error increases, the *t*-value decreases and power decreases. As the *df* increases, power increases by lowering the critical value.

Bonferroni and Dunn's multiple *t*-tests

Figure 10.6   Carlo Emilio Bonferroni

$$P\left(\bigcup_{i=1}^{t} E_i\right) \leq \sum_{i=1}^{n} P(E_i)$$

Figure 10.7

The rationale for a multiple *t*-test procedure controlling the familywise error rate was developed by the Italian mathematician Carlo Emilio Bonferroni (1936), who is pictured in Figure 10.6, and further developed by Olive Jean Dunn (1961). The rule of thumb we introduced earlier for the division of the pcα of 0.05 is based on Bonferroni's inequality,

$$P\left(\bigcup_{i=1}^{t} E_i\right) \leq \sum_{i=1}^{n} P(E_i),$$

which arises from the laws of probability we discussed in Chapter 3 (see p. 194).

Bonferroni's inequality (Figure 10.7) states that the probability of one or more events, such as a Type I error, cannot be greater than the sum of their individual probabilities. As a consequence, if we set the pcα at 0.05 divided by the number of planned comparisons, the familywise error rate will not exceed 0.05. Dunn's major contribution was a table of critical values based on the number of contrasts conducted. Today when computer software, such as SPSS, is used, exact *p*-values for all tests are routinely reported. Thus, the need for the tables has been largely eliminated. For example, if you are conducting three planned contrasts, the *p*-value of your observed *t*-value must be less than 0.05/3 = 0.017; if you are conducting four contrasts, the *p*-value of your observed *t* must be less than 0.05/4 = 0.013. As mentioned above, when 3, 4, or 5 contrasts are made, 0.01 is routinely used as the critical *p*-value. This likely is related historically to the nature of the tables of critical values.

• • • • •

The Dunn–Šidák test (Šidák, 1967) is a slightly different version of the multiple *t*-test and the corresponding table of critical values. The difference between this test and the Bonferroni–Dunn version arises from Šidák's variation on the Bonferroni inequality formula. Using Bonferroni's formula we produce a pcα by dividing the desired fwα by the number of comparisons. Using Šidák's variation, we produce a pcα via the formula pc$\alpha = 1 - (1 - \text{fw}\alpha)^{1/c}$, where *c* is the number of comparisons.

For two planned comparisons, using Bonferroni, we find that pc$\alpha = 0.05/2 = 0.0250$. The comparisons must have a probability less than 0.0250 to be considered significant. Using Šidák's variation we find that pc$\alpha = 1 - (1 - 0.05)^{1/2} = 0.0253$. As you can see, the Dunn–Šidák test makes it slightly easier to reject H_0. Despite this, the test based on the standard Bonferroni formula is the more commonly used of the two.

As should be apparent, as the number of planned comparisons grows, the statistical *power* for any one comparison is correspondingly reduced: a greater difference between two means is required for their observed *t*-value to produce the smaller required *p*-value. This trend produces the tension that was mentioned earlier resulting from the desire to simultaneously avoid a Type I error and a Type II error. This tension motivated the development of the Holm–Bonferroni multistage procedure (Holm, 1979). Holm based the specific testing procedure on a logic described in Marcus et al. (1976). The Holm–Bonferroni multistage procedure is a multiple *t*-test with a twist, allowing for a systematic reduction in the operative size of the family of comparisons, thus altering the pcα. The procedure is straightforward:

1   Calculate all of the planned *t*-tests using the multiple *t*-test formula.
2   Arrange the observed *t*-values from largest to smallest in magnitude.
3   Compare the *p*-value of the largest of the observed *t*-values to the appropriate critical *p*-value. The appropriate critical *p*-value is the desired fwα, typically 0.05, divided by the number of planned multiple *t*-tests in the family (*family size*).
4   If *and only if* the observed *t*-value has a *p*-value less than the critical *p*-value for that particular *family size* do you advance to test the next largest *t*-value.
5   If the previous *t*-value had a *p*-value less than the critical *p*-value, then reduce the *family size* by one and return to step 4.
6   If you reach an observed *t*-value with a *p*-value greater than the critical *p*-value, then you conclude that this contrast and all contrasts with smaller *t*-values are non-significant.

For example, the fictitious findings in Figure 10.8 illustrate how the Holm–Bonferroni multistage procedure works with five *a priori* contrasts and $df_{\text{error}} = 16$ and a familywise α of 0.05. The *t*-values have already been rank-ordered. The table reports the family size associated with each test, the observed *t*-values, their associated observed *p*-values, the applicable critical *p*-values for each family size, along with the appropriate conclusion concerning significance. As found in the table, tests 1 and 2 have observed *p*-values less than their corresponding critical *p*-values and thus are deemed significant. The observed *p*-value for test 3, however, is greater than its corresponding critical *p*-value, and is thus deemed non-significant. Test 4 is of interest. Although its observed

t-test	Family size	Observed *t*-value	Observed *p*-value	Critical *p*-value	Significant?
#1	5	4.11	.0010	.0100	Yes
#2	4	3.56	.0026	.0125	Yes
#3	3	2.58	.0201	.0167	No
#4	2	2.57	.0205	.0250	No
#5	1	1.91	.0742	.0500	No

Figure 10.8

p-value is less than its corresponding critical *p*-value, the comparison is considered non-significant. This is because of the rule stated in step 6: if you reach an observed *t*-value with a *p*-value greater than the critical *p*-value, then all contrasts with smaller *t*-values are deemed non-significant. In Figure 10.8, test 3 is non-significant, thus tests 4 and 5 are automatically non-significant. This rule holds regardless of whether those subsequent *t*-tests would be considered significant on their own. This is the price to be paid for allowing a systematic reduction in the family size and accompanying increase in the statistical power.

To summarize what we have covered thus far:

1　The change from the standard independent-samples *t*-test to the multiple *t*-test does not involve a change in the condition means. The numerator of the *t*-test remains the same.
2　As a result of averaging the variances, the multiple *t*-test does involve a change in the standard errors (the numerator of the *t*-test).
3　By increasing the *df*, the change from the standard to the multiple *t*-tests involves an increase in the power for evaluating the individual *t*-values.

At this point, the results of your follow-up analyses of your data remain ambiguous. Frustrating as it is, there is only partial support for your hypothesis that an increase in the number of cage-mates would produce an increase in the hamsters' willingness to explore an open-field. Given the 'more of this, more of that' nature of your hypothesis, we may yet find a more appropriate follow-up test.

Linear contrasts

In this subsection we will discover the following:

1　What makes a linear contrast linear?
2　How is the multiple *t*-test procedure a special case of a linear contrast (Howell, 2013)?
3　What are orthogonal linear contrasts and what makes them special?

As discussed by Howell (2013), the multiple *t*-test procedure is actually only a special case of a more general procedure called a *linear contrast*. Although, like a *t*-test, a linear contrast will always have 1 *df* treatment, it allows for a number of diverse comparisons. Linear contrasts allow us to compare:

- one condition mean against another condition mean;
- one condition mean against an amalgamation of other condition means;
- one group of amalgamated condition means against another group of amalgamated condition means.

At first the formula for a linear contrast may look unfamiliar. The formula, however, is in fact a variation on the ANOVA *F*-test that was analysed in detail in Chapter 8. What makes for the apparent difference is the use of *weighting coefficients* that are introduced and subsequently removed from the calculation. These weighting coefficients are used to identify the two terms to be contrasted.

> Weighting coefficients can be positive or negative, as well as fractions or whole numbers, depending on the comparison of interest. Linear contrasts may be used to test both simple and complex hypotheses. In essence, each contrast (set of weighting coefficients) defines and tests a particular pattern of differences among the means.

What makes a linear contrast a 'linear contrast' is that, regardless of the number of positive and negative coefficients, the sum of the weighting coefficients equals 0 (Abdi & Williams, 2010). We use the letter *c* to symbolize weighting coefficients. At the heart of a linear contrast is the 1 *df* comparison of those conditions with negative weightings coefficients against those conditions with positive weighting coefficients. We begin with the simplest set of weighting coefficients. For example, if you wished to contrast *cage* condition 1 with *cage* condition 2, you might weight the mean of *cage* condition 1 with a '–1', weight *cage* condition 2 with a '+1' and weight *cage* condition 4 with a '0': $\Sigma = -1 + 1 + 0 = 0$. In the case of a between-subjects design, the means are multiplied by (weighted by) the coefficients. The sum of these *weighted means* is usually labelled *L*. In your current example,

$$L = \Sigma c\bar{y}_j = -1(3) + 1(4) + 0(8) = 1.$$

=== REVIEW QUESTION ===

If the coefficient for *cage* condition 1 were –0.5 and the weighting coefficient for *cage* condition 4 were –0.5, what must be the weighting coefficient for *cage* condition 2 for the contrast to be linear?

Web Link 10.1 for an answer to the review question.

L is then used to calculate $SS_{treatment}$, now called $SS_{contrast}$. Next, square *L* and multiply it by the number of subjects (hamsters) in each condition. Squaring the difference between the positive and negatively weighted groups and multiplying by *n* looks very much like the standard ANOVA formula for $SS_{treatment}$. It is, however, augmented by the weighting coefficients. Consequently, their influence must be removed. This is accomplished by dividing by the sum of the squared weighting coefficients: Σc_j^2. We arrive at the following formula for $SS_{contrast}$ for our example:

$$SS_{contrast} = \frac{nL^2}{\Sigma c_j^2} = \frac{4(1)^2}{-1^2 + 1^2 + 0^2} = 2.$$

Recall that $MS_{treatment}$, now $MS_{contrast}$, is equal to $MS_{contrast}/df_{contrast}$. Linear contrasts, by nature, always contrast two conditions or two sets of conditions. That is, a linear contrast involves two means or an amalgamation of two groups of means: one with negative weightings and one with positive weightings. Thus, a linear contrast always has only 1 df and $MS_{contrast}$ always equals $SS_{contrast}$. For your contrast of *cage 1* with *cage 2*,

$$MS_{contrast} = \frac{SS_{contrast}}{df_{contrast}} = \frac{2}{1} = 2.$$

Next is the issue of the appropriate error term. With a between-subjects design the appropriate error term for all contrasts is the average within-condition variance:

$$\frac{SS_{error}}{df_{error}} = \frac{22}{9}.$$

MS_{error} is unchanged (2.44) from (see the omnibus F-test for this data on p. 344 in Chapter 8.)

The linear contrast is expressed as an F-ratio and evaluated with 1 df contrast (treatment) and the df associated with the error term. For our example we find the following F-value:

$$F_{(1, 9)} = \frac{MS_{contrast}}{MS_{error}} = \frac{2}{2.444} = 0.82.$$

The critical value for an observed F-value with 1 and 9 df at $\alpha = 0.025$ is 7.21. Thus, you fail to reject H_0 and conclude that there is insufficient evidence to support the restricted H_1 of a difference between those two cage conditions.

The example illustrates how a multiple t-value is simply the square root of the F-value from the parallel linear contrast, or how the F-value from the linear contrast is merely the square of the multiple t. If we take the square root of your obtained F-value from the above linear contrast, we find it to be 0.905, which was the t-value obtained from your multiple t-test procedure comparing *cage 1* and *cage 2*. This is one way to see that t is a square root and a special case of F, when the F-test has 1 $df_{treatment}$. Furthermore, the square root of the critical value for $F_{(1, 9)}$ (7.21) as found in Appendix G ($\alpha = 0.025$, Table G.2) is 2.69, which is the critical t-value with 9 df (Appendix D, $\alpha = 0.025$).

In Chapter 5 the t-value was found to be a variation of the z-table value (+1.96, $\alpha = 0.05$) after correcting for the fact that we had a sample and df_{error} rather than a population. In this chapter we find the F-value (1 $df_{treatment}$)to be a squared variation of the z-table value correcting for the fact that we may have both df_{error} and $df_{treatment}$. The critical t-value (pc$\alpha = 0.05$) when the df are infinite is 1.96 and the critical F-value (pc$\alpha = 0.05$) when the df_{error} are infinite is 3.8416 (1.96²). We are always assuming a two-tailed test, unless otherwise told.

■■■ • • • • • ■■■

If you examine the formula for $SS_{contrast}$ you will see that what complicates the computation for this version of 'sum-of-squares' treatment/contrast is the presence of the weighting coefficients. In cases such as the one we have been examining the weighting coefficients can be eliminated, however, and the two means being compared can be treated as if they were the only treatment conditions. You then could compute $SS_{treatment/contrast}$ as follows.

The mean of *cage* condition 1 is 3. The mean of *cage* condition 2 is 4. The $GM = 3.5$. Then

$$SS_{treatment/contrast} = n\Sigma(\bar{y} - GM)^2 = 4[(3 - 3.5)^2 + (3 - 3.5)^2] = 2.0.$$

The corresponding $MS_{treatment/contrast}$ equals $SS_{treatment/contrast}$ (2.0) divided by MS_{error} (2.444). The resulting F-value of 0.82 is identical to the one produced using the weighting coefficients. The weighting coefficients are only necessary when the contrasts are more than simple comparisons between two means. Again we find that apparent differences in formulae are just that, apparent differences. Steam and ice are found to be variants of H_2O.

In the case of your other planned comparison (*cage* condition 2 versus *cage* condition 4), we find

$$L = \Sigma c\bar{y}_j = 0(3) - 1(4) + 1(8) = 4,$$

$$SS_{contrast} = \frac{nL^2}{\Sigma c_j^2} = \frac{4(4)^2}{(-1)^2 + 1^2} = 32,$$

$$MS_{contrast} = \frac{SS_{contrast}}{df_{contrast}} = \frac{32}{1} = 32,$$

$$F = \frac{32}{2.444} = 13.09,$$

which is greater than the critical value of 7.21.

As you hypothesized, there is sufficient evidence that hamsters in *cage 4* will enter

> The F-value from this second linear contrast (13.09) is again the square of the corresponding multiple t-value found above (3.62).

more *midsquares* than will hamsters in *cage 2*. The results of your study remain mixed with respect to your original hypothesis. Do not lose faith now; there may yet be another twist in this story.

■■■ • • • • • ■■■

There is nothing special about using the values of −1, 1, and 0 in your first contrast. Nor is there anything special about using 0, −1, and 1 for the weighting coefficients in your second contrast. You could have used −100, 100, and 0 or −0.0023, +0.0023, and 0. The only requirement is that $\Sigma cj = 0$. Because we correct for the value of the weighting coefficients by dividing by the sum of the squared weighting coefficients ($nL^2/\Sigma c_j^2$), the particular weightings will not influence the resulting $SS_{contrast}$. Let us recompute your first contrast using −2, 2, and 0 as the weighting coefficients:

(Continued)

(*Continued*)

$$L = \Sigma\, c\bar{y}_i = -2(3) + 2(4) + 0(8) = 2,$$

$$SS_{contrast} = \frac{nL^2}{\Sigma\, c_j^2} = \frac{4(2)^2}{(-2)^2 + 2^2 + 0^2} = \frac{16}{8} = 2,$$

$$MS_{contrast} = \frac{SS_{contrast}}{df_{contrast}} = \frac{2}{1} = 2,$$

$$F_{(1,\,9)} = \frac{MS_{contrast}}{MS_{error}} = \frac{2}{2.444} = 0.82.$$

There is no change in $MS_{contrast}$ nor in the resulting F-value.

For the sake of example, assume your original H_1 is that there is no difference in the hamsters' willingness to enter *midsquares* unless they are housed more than two per cage. This idea is *post hoc*, but ignore that for the sake of this example. We have already found no significant difference between *cage 1* and *cage 2*. A plausible second planned comparison might be to compare *cage 1* and *cage 2* combined against *cage 4*. The key issue is the assignment of the weighting coefficients. Remember, they must sum to 0. If we are to weight *cage 1* and *cage 2* equally, and the absolute value of their combined weight is equal to that of *cage 4*, the simplest assignments might be –0.5, –0.5, and +1, respectively. The contrast then becomes

$$L = \Sigma\, c_i\bar{y}_i = -0.5(3) + (-0.5)(4) + 1(8) = 4.5,$$

$$SS_{contrast} = \frac{nL^2}{\Sigma\, c_j^2} = \frac{4(4.5)^2}{(-0.5)^2 + 0.5^2 + 1^2} = 54,$$

$$MS_{contrast} = \frac{SS_{contrast}}{df_{contrast}} = \frac{54}{1} = 54,$$

$$F = \frac{54}{2.444} = 22.09,$$

which is greater than the critical value of 7.21 at 1 and 9 *df*.

In this example, you would conclude that there is evidence supporting your H_1 that hamsters' willingness to explore an open field increases when they are housed more than two per cage. But remember, this was not an *a priori* hypothesis of yours; it was *post hoc*. As stated earlier in this chapter, ideas that emerge from *post hoc* analyses should be tested with follow-up data collection, prior to drawing conclusions.

━━━━━━━ CHALLENGE QUESTION ━━━━━━━

Why might you wish to combine *cage* conditions 1 and 2 for a contrast with *cage* condition 4 rather than comparing *cage* conditions 1 and 2 separately against *cage* condition 4? *Hint*: You might reflect on the reasoning behind the multiple *t*-test MS_{error}.

Web Link 10.2 for an answer to the challenge question.

Orthogonal contrasts

At this point in the text the term *orthogonal* should be familiar to you. From Chapter 1 on we have seen that *orthogonality, independence, uncorrelated,* and *unrelated* are synonyms. We might have labelled this subsection *independent contrasts* or *uncorrelated contrasts.* Historically, however, 'orthogonal contrasts' has been the moniker for the topic. This subsection has four primary objectives:

1 How are orthogonal contrasts defined?
2 How do we test for orthogonality?
3 How many pairs of orthogonal contrasts are possible?
4 Of what value are orthogonal contrast?

Simply put, orthogonal contrasts are a pair of contrasts that are unrelated or independent of each other. Where the term *linear contrast* is a description of an individual contrast, orthogonality is a description of the relation between two contrasts. Recall what *independence* meant in terms of probability theory in Chapter 3 (see p. 90).

Two events are independent if the outcome of one event does not influence the outcome of the other. Analogously, two linear contrasts are independent if the outcome of one contrast (significance versus non-significance) does not influence the outcome of the other (significance versus non-significance).

If the term 'orthogonal contrasts' denotes that two linear contrasts are uncorrelated, then the obvious way to test for orthogonality is to compute a correlation. The two variables now in question are the two sets of weighting coefficients. For example, let us correlate the two sets of weighting coefficients from your two planned comparisons. Figure 10.9 depicts the two sets of weighting coefficients associated with each *cage* condition. The two contrasts are the two variables that we wish to correlate.

The means of both variables (sets of contrast weightings) are 0. The two standard deviations are 1. Recall from Chapter 7 that a correlation coefficient is equal to the covariance of the two variables divided by the product of the standard deviations:

$$cov_{xy} = \frac{\Sigma(x - \bar{x})(y - \bar{y})}{n - 1},$$

where x represents the weighting coefficients for the first contrast and y the weighting coefficients for the second contrast. Because the means of both variables are 0, the covariance

Cage Condition	Contrast Cond 1 vs 2	Contrast Cond 2 vs 4
1	−1	0
2	1	−1
3	0	1

Figure 10.9

can be easily computed: $-1/2 = -0.5$. The two standard deviations are 1, thus their product is 1. We find that the correlation between the two sets of weighting coefficients is

$$r = \frac{cov_{xy}}{S_x S_y} = \frac{-0.5}{1.0} = -0.5.$$

Because the correlation is not 0, the pair contrasts are not orthogonal.

If you slowly walk through our computations for the correlation, you will find that for decision-making purposes the procedure can be reduced to the sum of the products of the paired weighting coefficients. This is illustrated in Figure 10.10. The sum of the product of the weighting coefficients represents the numerator in the formula for covariance. Once it is divided by $n - 1$, we then have the covariance (-0.5). Thus, only when the product of the paired weighting coefficient is 0 will covariance be 0; only then will the correlation be 0; and only then will the two contrasts be orthogonal. In summary, the *expected* value of the sum of the products of the paired weighting coefficients is 0. Any *observed* value other than 0 indicates non-orthogonal or correlated contrasts.

Cage Condition	Contrast Cond 1 vs 2	Contrast Cond 2 vs 4	Product of coefficients
1	−1	0	0
2	1	−1	−1
3	0	1	0
Sum			−1

Figure 10.10

For the sake of another example, assume for some strange reason your two planned comparisons were that (1) *cage* conditions 1 and 4 would be different and (2) *cage* condition 2 would be different from *cage* conditions 1 and 4 combined. The weighting coefficients for the two are reported in Figure 10.11. Note that the sum of the products of the weighting coefficients is 0, indicating that the two contrasts are orthogonal.

Cage Condition	Contrast Cond 1 vs 4	Contrast Cond 2 vs 1 + 4	Product of coefficients
1	−1	−1	1
2	0	−2	0
3	1	−1	−1
Sum			0

Figure 10.11

Because the only limitation on a linear contrast is that their weighting coefficients sum to 0, for any given data set an infinite number of linear contrasts are possible. The number of pairs of orthogonal contrasts is limited, however. The source of the limitation is the number of treatment conditions, or the $df_{treatment}$.

If you apply the weighting coefficients found in Figure 10.11 to your hamster data, you find that the two $SS_{contrast}$ values sum to 56: they are 50 and 6, respectively. If you return to the results of the original ANOVA of your data reproduced at the outset of this chapter, you find that $SS_{treatment}$ was 56. There are three indicators that you have reached the maximum number of orthogonal contrasts for your data set. First, your orthogonal contrasts have fully accounted for $SS_{treatment}$. Second, you are unable to find another set of weighting coefficients that will be orthogonal to the other contrasts already identified as being orthogonal to each other. Finally, the maximum number for a set of orthogonal contrasts is equal to the $df_{treatment}$ found in the omnibus ANOVA *F*-test. There were 2 $df_{treatment}$ in your omnibus *F*-test. Thus, you will not find a third contrast orthogonal to the two you have already computed.

• • • • •

Two points should be made here. First, if you had 3 $df_{treatment}$ then you could have a set of three contrasts that would be orthogonal to each other. Remember, however, that each contrast must be orthogonal to all others. Only then will the $SS_{contrast}$ sum to the $SS_{treatment}$ from the omnibus *F*. Second, even for an experiment such as yours with only three treatment conditions, there are an infinite number of possible pairs of orthogonal contrasts. Once you have conducted a first contrast, there always will be a second contrast that is orthogonal to the first. When you have only three treatment conditions, however, there is only one possible orthogonal contrast. For example, if your first contrast has weighting coefficients –1, 1, and 0, then the only orthogonal contrast that will complete the set of two will have weighting coefficients –1, –1, and 2.

CHALLENGE QUESTION

Assume that you have 3 $df_{treatment}$. Also assume that you have made your first linear contrast using the following weighting coefficients: condition 1 (–3), condition 2 (–1), condition 3 (1), and condition 4 (3). The contrast is linear: –3 –1 + 1 + 3 = 0. What two additional linear contrasts would complete the full set of orthogonal contrasts?

Web Link 10.3 for an answer to the challenge question.

Now we know what makes orthogonal contrasts different from any other set of linear contrasts. Simply put, it is the fact that the contrasts are independent and the outcome of one of the contrasts (e.g., a Type I error) will not alter the probability of the outcome on any subsequent contrasts within the set. When two contrasts are non-orthogonal, however, a Type I or Type II error on one contrast will increase the probability of the same error on an ensuing non-orthogonal contrast. How much will the probability of the same error increase? It depends on the strength of the correlation between the two contrasts.

Having pointed out the advantage of orthogonal contrasts, it should be noted that researchers do not design their experiments solely on the basis of ensuring that their planned comparisons are orthogonal. In fact, except for special questions, researchers rarely consider the issue of orthogonality when designing experiments. Even when they do, orthogonality is almost an accidental side effect of the planned comparisons. Other issues that were mentioned in Chapter 1, such as levels of the independent variable, appropriate controls, within-subjects versus between-subjects designs, and power, tend to dominate researchers' concerns. There is nothing wrong with orthogonality not being the primary concern. In certain circumstances, however, it becomes an issue after the data have been analysed. Should all of your planned comparisons be significant, the issue of orthogonality is immaterial. The same is true when all of your planned comparisons are non-significant. Orthogonality is an issue when the researcher's design is complex and the results are mixed, as illustrated in Figure 10.2. If all of the significant or non-significant contrasts are non-orthogonal, then the researcher may be concerned that the results might not be as promising, or as disappointing, as they appeared at first. For example, if only two of the five planned contrasts are significant and they are non-orthogonal to each other, but are orthogonal to the other three contrasts, then I might be somewhat concerned that I am making two Type I errors. I would not have the same level of concern if those two significant contrasts were orthogonal.

Linear contrasts using SPSS

In SPSS linear contrasts for *a priori* comparisons are reported as *t*-values. These *t*-values, as you will recall, are the square roots of the *F*-values. To run your planned linear contrast, return to the *onewayenriched.sav* file in the SPSS *Data Editor*. Under *Analyze* choose *Compare Means* and then the *One-Way ANOVA* option. When the *One-Way ANOVA* window opens, move *cage* to the *Factor* area and *midsquares* to the *Dependent List* area. Then click *Contrasts*. We will first enter the weighting coefficients for contrasting *cage 1* against *cage 2*. The three coefficients are entered one at a time in the *Coefficients* area using the *Add* button (Figures 10.12 and 10.13). After entering those three coefficients (–1, +1, and 0) as in Figure 10.14, click *Next*. A new window will open and the weighting coefficients for your second planned comparison (0, –1, and +1) can be entered in the same manner as the previous contrast (Figure 10.15). Then click *Continue*, which returns you to the main *One-Way ANOVA* window. Click *Options*. When the *Options* window opens, check *Homogeneity of variance test* (Figure 10.16). Click *Continue* to return to the main *One-Way ANOVA* window. Click *OK* to run the analysis.

The first table we see in the output window is the Levene *Test of Homogeneity of Variance* table (Figure 10.17). Because the probability is greater than 0.05 (*Sig.* = 0.569) you may continue to assume homogeneity of variance. Next is the *ANOVA* table which we saw in Chapter 8 (Figure 10.18). Recall that the row labelled *Between Groups* corresponds to what we called *treatment* and that the row labelled *Within Groups* corresponds to what we referred to as *error*. The significant *p*-value (*Sig.*) of 0.003 tells you that there is evidence that *cage* condition influenced the number of *midsquares* the hamsters entered. Next you find the *Contrast Coefficients* table (Figure 10.19). Rows labelled *1* and *2* report the weighting coefficients corresponding to your two planned comparisons. The *Contrast Tests* table (Figure 10.20) reports the results of the two linear contrasts, one assuming equal condition variances and one correcting for any inequalities in the variance.

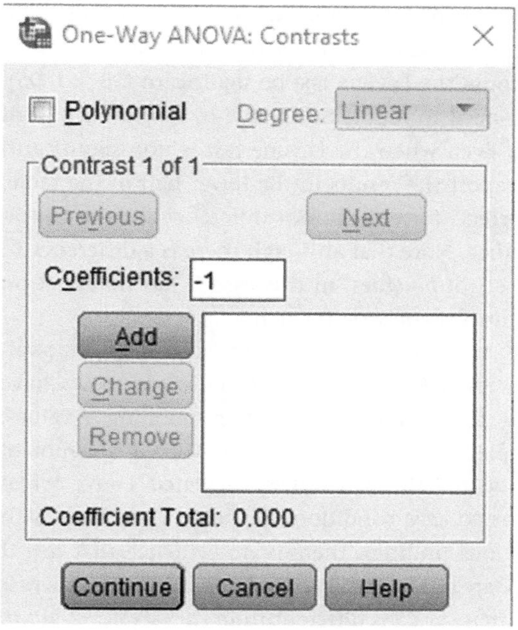

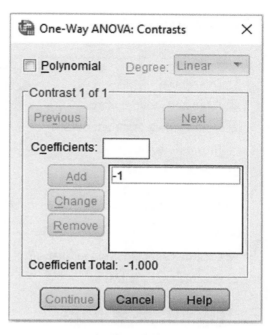

Figure 10.12

Figure 10.13

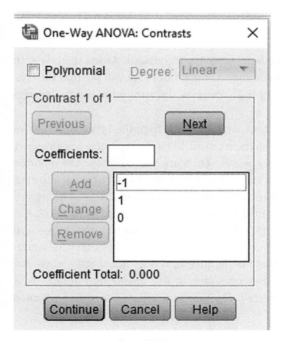

Figure 10.14

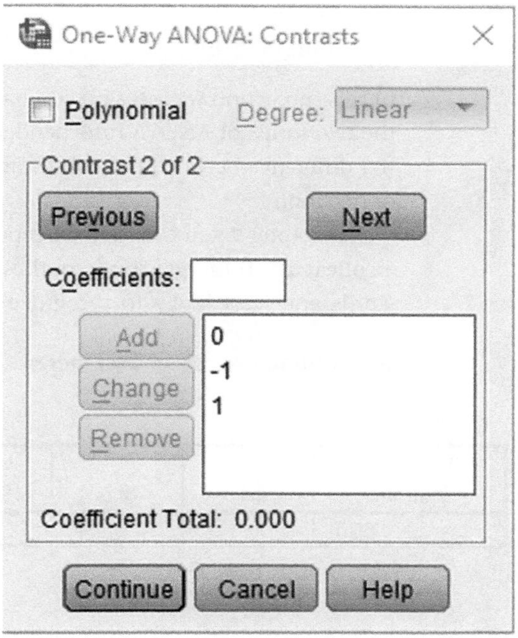

Figure 10.15

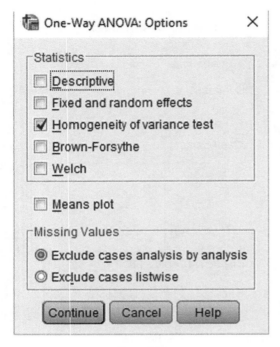

Figure 10.16

When the Levene test is non-significant, as yours is, you typically report the two rows that assume equal variances. Should the Levene test be significant (*Sig.* < 0.05), then you need to report that value in the lower half of the table. Even when the Levene test is non-significant, you can report the results in the lower half of the table, which corrects for even minor differences in the condition variance. Note that although there is a difference in the two sets of *p*-values, in this case it has no effect on the conclusions you would reach.

Notice that SPSS reports linear contrasts in *t*-values rather than *F*-values. These *t*-values are, as we have seen, the square root of the corresponding *F*-values; for example, the *t*-value of 0.905 is the square root of the *F*-value (0.818) which we calculated above when we contrasted *cage* conditions 1 and 2. Consistent with your previous findings, there is no evidence that *cage 1* and *cage 2* are different (*Sig.* *(2-tailed)* = 0.389), but there is evidence that *cage 2* is different from *cage 4* (*Sig.* *(2-tailed)* = 0.006). (For proving *F* is equal to *t* squared see: http://stats.stackexchange.com/questions/55236/prove-f-test-is-equal-to-t-test-squared.)

Repeated-measures linear contrasts

In this subsection we focus on conducting repeated-measures linear contrasts. As was the case with the two forms of ANOVA (independent-samples and repeated-measures), we will see that the central difference between the two forms of linear contrasts involves the error term and the degrees of freedom.

In Chapter 9 you conducted a repeated-measures analysis to test a hypothesis that arose out of a colleague's findings. You hypothesized that subjects are most likely to recognize *low-frequency* words and least likely to recognize *high-frequency* words. The data you collected are reported in Figure 10.21 and the results of your omnibus *F*-test are reproduced in Figure 10.22. The significant (*Sig.* < 0.05) *F*-value for word *frequency* (2, 8 *df* = 18.55) indicates that noun *frequency* influenced noun recognition. Again, although the omnibus *F* is significant, it does not specify where the differences among the means may reside. Your overall H_1 can be translated into two planned

Test of Homogeneity of Variances

midsquares

Levene Statistic	df1	df2	Sig.
.600	2	9	.569

Figure 10.17

ANOVA

midsquares

	Sum of Squares	df	Mean Square	F	Sig.
Between Groups	56.000	2	28.000	11.455	.003
Within Groups	22.000	9	2.444		
Total	78.000	11			

Figure 10.18

Contrast Coefficients

	cage		
Contrast	1.00	2.00	3.00
1	-1	1	0
2	0	-1	1

Figure 10.19

Contrast Tests

		Contrast	Value of Contrast	Std. Error	t	df	Sig. (2-tailed)
midsquares	Assume equal variances	1	1.0000	1.10554	.905	9	.389
		2	4.0000	1.10554	3.618	9	.006
	Does not assume equal variances	1	1.0000	1.00000	1.000	6.000	.356
		2	4.0000	1.15470	3.464	5.647	.015

Figure 10.20

comparisons with two planned null hypotheses. First, because the *high-frequency* nouns are predicted to be the least recognized, your first contrast involves a comparison of the *medium-frequency* ($\bar{y} = 9.0$) and *high-frequency* ($\bar{y} = 8.0$) conditions. Next, because the *low-frequency* nouns are predicted to be the most recognized, your second contrast involves a comparison of the *low-frequency* ($\bar{y} = 12.0$) and *medium-frequency* ($\bar{y} = 9.0$) conditions. (For a description of the experiment and results, see p. 390 in Chapter 9.)

In Chapter 9 we saw that $SS_{treatment}$, $df_{treatment}$, and $MS_{treatment}$ resulting from a repeated-measures analysis do not differ from those produced by independent-samples ANOVA of the same data. The difference between a related-samples analysis and an independent-samples analysis regards their error terms and the corresponding degrees of freedom.

There are various approaches to computing linear contrasts with repeated-measures, depending upon the assumptions you wish to make. The simplest approach is to think of your planned comparisons as a

Subject #	Low	Medium	High	Subject mean
1	7	3	3	4.33
2	14	10	10	11.33
3	13	10	7	10.00
4	18	15	13	15.33
5	8	7	7	7.33
Condition Means	12	9	8	
				GM = 9.66

Figure 10.21

AVOVA Summary Table

Source	Sum-of-Squares	df	Mean Square	F	Sig.
Between-Sub.	206.66	4			
Within-Sub.	52.77	10			
Frequency	43.40	2	21.70	18.55	< .05
Error	9.37	8	1.17		
Total	259.40 (rounding)	14			

Figure 10.22

Subject no.	Medium	High	Subject mean
1	3	3	3.00
2	10	10	10.00
3	10	7	8.50
4	15	13	14.00
5	7	7	7.00
Condition Means	9	8	
			GM = 8.5

Figure 10.23

set of autonomous repeated-measures ANOVAs. For example, your overall H_1 implies noun recognition scores in the high-frequency condition will be inferior to that of their scores in the medium-frequency condition and subjects' recognition scores in the medium-frequency condition will be inferior to those of their scores in the low-frequency condition.

You might first conduct a repeated-measures ANOVA as if only the medium-frequency and the high-frequency conditions existed. Figure 10.23 depicts the data for the analysis along with the subject means and the grand mean specific for this contrast.

Figure 10.24 is the summary table of the ANOVA that functions as the contrast between the medium-frequency and the high-frequency conditions. Note that the error terms (SS_{error}, df_{error}, and

MS_{error}) differ from those found in the omnibus ANOVA (Figure 10.22). They are specific to this contrast. The observed *F*-value (2.50) is less than the critical value found in the *F*-table for $\alpha = 0.025$ (Table G.2 in Appendix G) with 1 $df_{contrast}$ and 4 df_{error} (12.22) Thus, you fail to reject H_0 and conclude that there is insufficient evidence to support the idea that high-frequency noun recognition is more difficult than medium-frequency noun recognition.

AVOVA Summary Table

Source	Sum-of-Squares		df	Mean Square	F	Sig.
Between-Sub.	130.00		4			
Within-Sub.	6.5		5			
Frequency		2.50	1	2.50	2.50	> .05
Error		4.00	4	1.00		
Total	136.50		9			

Figure 10.24

You conduct a second repeated-measures ANOVA with only the low-frequency and the medium-frequency conditions. Figure 10.25 depicts the data for the analysis along with the subject means and the grand mean specific for this contrast.

Subject no.	Low	Medium	Subject mean
1	7	3	5.00
2	14	10	12.00
3	13	10	11.50
4	18	15	16.50
5	8	7	7.50
Condition Means	12	9	
		GM =	10.50

Figure 10.25

Figure 10.26 is the ANOVA summary table that functions as the contrast between the low-frequency and the medium-frequency conditions. Again, note that the error terms (SS_{error}, df_{error}, and MS_{error}) differ from those found in the omnibus ANOVA (Figure 10.21) and are specific to this particular contrast. The observed *F*-value (30.00) is greater than the critical value found in the *F*-table for $\alpha = 0.025$ (Table G.2 in Appendix G) with 1 $df_{contrast}$ and 4 df_{error} (12.22). You can reject H_0 and conclude that there is sufficient evidence to support the idea that low-frequency noun recognition is easier than medium-frequency noun recognition.

The df_{error}, SS_{error}, and MS_{error} for repeated-measures linear contrasts go by various names, including $df_{subject \times contrast}$, $SS_{subject \times contrast}$, and $MS_{subject \times contrast}$.

AVOVA Summary Table

Source	Sum-of-Squares	df	Mean Square	F	Sig.
Between-Sub.	157.00	4			
Within-Sub.	25.5	5			
Frequency		22.50	1	22.50	30.00	< .05
Error		3.00	4	0.75		
Total	**182.50**	**9**			

Figure 10.26

━━━━━━━━━━ REVIEW QUESTION ━━━━━━━━━━

Why do the two repeated-measures $SS_{contrast}$ values (Figures 10.2 and 10.16) not sum to the $SS_{treatment}$ for the omnibus repeated-measures ANOVA in Figure 10.22?

🖰 Web Link 10.4 for the answer to the review question.

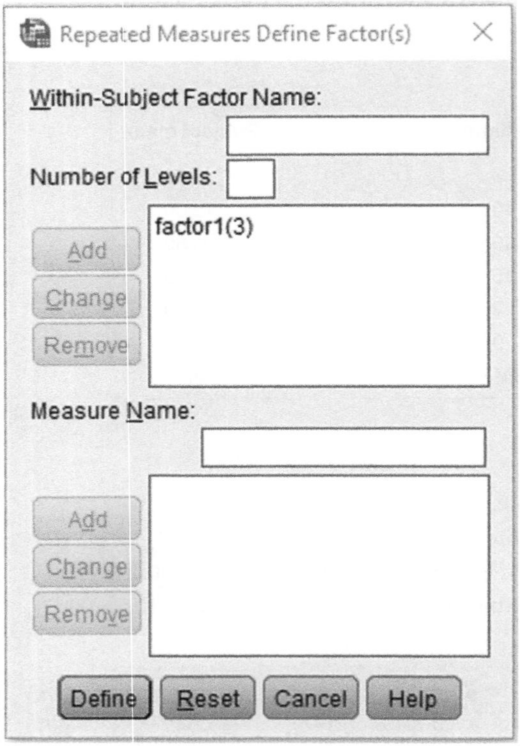

Repeated Measures Define Factor(s) ✕

Within-Subject Factor Name:

Number of Levels:

factor1(3)

Add
Change
Remove

Measure Name:

Add
Change
Remove

Define Reset Cancel Help

Figure 10.27

To execute these two planned contrasts with your *recognition* data using SPSS, return to the *repeatedmeasures1.sav* SPSS file on the book's web page. **From within the *Data Editor*, select *Analyze* from the menu along the top and drop down to *General Linear Model*. Then slide over and select the *Repeated Measures* option that appears to the right. In the *Repeated Measures Define Factor(s)* window enter 3 into the *Number of Levels* box and click the *Add* button (Figure 10.27). Click on the *Define* button at the bottom of the window. When the *Repeated Measures* window opens, highlight and move your three variables into the *Within-Subjects Variables* window (Figure 10.28). Next, click *Options*. When the *Repeated Measures: Options* window appears select *Estimates of effect size*, *Observed power*, and *Homogeneity tests* in the lower *Display* area. Then click *Continue*. (See Figures 10.26 and 10.27.)**

Next, select the *Contrasts* button. When the *Repeated Measures: Contrasts* window opens, change the *Contrast* option to *Repeated*, click *Change* (Figure 10.29), and then *Continue*. After you are returned to the *Repeated Measures* window click *OK*. The results appear in the SPSS output window.

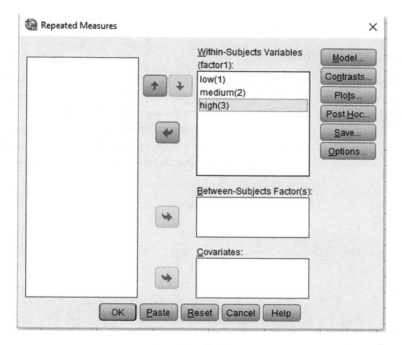

Figure 10.28

Figure 10.29

▬▬▬▬ ● ● ● ● ● ▬▬▬▬

Contrast Name	Description
Deviation (first or last)	Contrasts each condition other than the first or the last with the overall effect.
Simple (first or last)	Contrasts each condition with either the first or the last condition.
Repeated	Contrasts each condition with the previous condition.
Helmert	Contrasts each condition with the average effect of all subsequent conditions.
Difference	Contrasts each condition with the average effect of all previous conditions.
Polynomial	Tests for all possible polynomial trends, limited by the total degrees-of-freedom treatment.

Figure 10.30

In addition to (*Repeated*), in the *Contrast* window SPSS makes a number of standard contrasts available (Figure 10.30).

Most of what appears in the SPSS output window was reported in Chapter 9 (see Section 9.6) with the omnibus *F*-test and will only be summarized here.

The first area to appear in the output window is the *Within-Subjects Factors* box which lists your three within-subjects variables. The next area, *Multivariate Tests*, is of use when the assumption of sphericity is violated. The third area reports *Mauchly's Test of Sphericity*. Because the *p*-value (*Sig.* = 0.630) is greater than 0.05 we can continue to assume sphericity. Because Mauchly's test was non-significant, you may use the tests found in the *Test of Within-Subjects Effects* table. When Mauchly's test is non-significant, most researchers report the *Sphericity Assumed* test: $F(2, 8) = 18.571$, $MS_{error} = 21.667$, $p = 0.001$.

Next we find the *Tests of Within-Subjects Contrasts* table (Figure 10.31), which is new and of immediate interest us. The first panel (*factor1*) provides us with information on the contrast terms: SS, *df*, MS, *F*-value, and *p*-value (*Sig.*). Level 1 versus level 2 corresponds to our contrast of the low- and medium-*frequency* conditions. Level 2 versus level 3 corresponds to our contrast of the medium- and high-*frequency* conditions. The second panel provides us with information on their corresponding error terms: SS, *df*, and MS. There are three things to note. First, and most importantly, the observed *F*-values are identical to those we computed above by hand. Second, the pattern of significance is thus unchanged. Third, and surprisingly, SS and MS for both the contrast and the error terms are much greater than they were when we calculated them by hand. Keep in mind that the resulting *F*-values are unchanged. If you closely analyse our earlier calculations you will discover that SPSS has retained the factor of the weighting coefficients in its computations of SS.

Tests of Within-Subjects Contrasts

Measure: MEASURE_1

Source	factor1	Type III Sum of Squares	df	Mean Square	F	Sig.
factor1	Level 1 vs. Level 2	45.000	1	45.000	30.000	.005
	Level 2 vs. Level 3	5.000	1	5.000	2.500	.189
Error(factor1)	Level 1 vs. Level 2	6.000	4	1.500		
	Level 2 vs. Level 3	8.000	4	2.000		

Figure 10.31

TESTING FOR POLYNOMIAL TRENDS

In this section we will discuss how a linear contrast becomes a test for a polynomial trend. As you will see, you have already learned how to compute tests for polynomial trends. Next we shall explore the usefulness of such trends. Finally, we shall see how the test for two particular polynomial trends may at last provide you with a direct test of your hypothesis concerning *cage* condition and the willingness of your hamsters to explore an open field.

Before examining the nature and usefulness of polynomial trends, a distinction must be made between *qualitative* and *quantitative* independent variables (IVs). A qualitative IV is categorical in nature, where the treatment levels represent differences in kind. For example, a researcher may have a hypothesis concerning the different forms of treatment for depression. The IV may be composed of different forms of psychotherapy, such as cognitive behavioural therapy (CBT), interpersonal therapy (IT), mindfulness-based therapy (MBT), and psychoanalysis (PSY). Or the IV may involve different antidepressants, such as Cymbalta, Lexapro, and Zoloft. Numbers can be assigned to such treatments: CBT = 1, IT = 2, MBT = 3, and PSY = 4. These numbers are nominal, however; they can be changed arbitrarily with no consequences for the analysis. (For discussion of numerical scales, see p. 25 in Chapter 2.)

On the other hand, the numbers associated with a quantitative IV are not arbitrary. As a parallel example to the above qualitative IV, a researcher's quantitative IV might be the number of hours of CBT the patients received: condition 1 = 6 hours, condition 2 = 12 hours, condition 3 = 18 hours, and condition 4 = 24 hours. As a quantitative parallel to the above antidepressant example, a researcher may have a hypothesis concerning the dosage of Cymbalta: condition 1 = 0 mg/day of Cymbalta, condition 2 = 20 mg/day of Cymbalta, and condition 3 = 40 mg/day of Cymbalta. In the examples of a quantitative IV the differences in treatment are differences in the amount of a single 'kind', whereas in the examples of a qualitative IV the differences in treatment are differences between kinds (categorical differences). The numbers relating to the quantitative IV are not arbitrary, but are *measurement* in nature. Your IV (*cage* condition) is quantitative in nature; it reflects the number of cage-mates.

Polynomial trends are an important application of orthogonal linear (1 $df_{treatment}$) contrasts. Mathematically, polynomial functions are often described as first-order, second-order, third-order, etc., functions. In statistics we usually name them linear, quadratic, cubic, etc. The *order* simply designates the number of times a line appears to change direction. Figures 10.32, 10.33, and 10.34 illustrate the linear, quadratic, and cubic trends, respectively, where the IV is the dosage of a fictional substance.

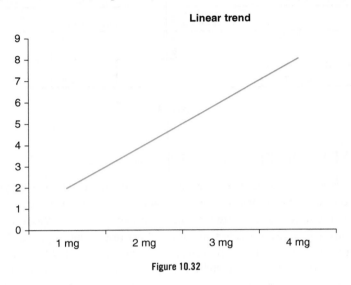

Figure 10.32

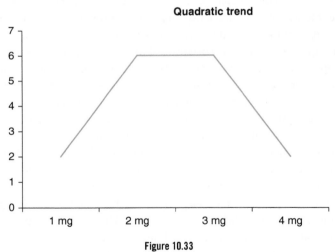

Figure 10.33

In addition to a single $df_{contrast}$ for a linear contrast to be a test of a polynomial trend, it must meet two requirements. First, the IV must be quantitative in nature. For example, in Figures 10.32–10.34 the IV is the number of milligrams of a single substance. Second, the tests for polynomial trends require defining weighting coefficients. The specifics of the weighting coefficients are such that they reflect the nature of the number of changes in direction of the trend: linear (a straight line/ no change in direction), quadratic (one curve/one change in direction), cubic (two curves/two changes in direction), etc. For most purposes in the social, psychological, and biological sciences only the linear and quadratic trends are of consequence.

Cubic trend

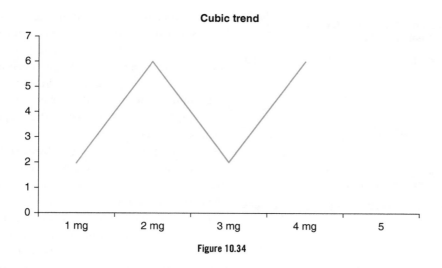

Figure 10.34

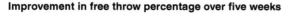

Often the researcher expects both a significant linear trend and a significant quadratic trend. The linear trend indicates, for example, an improvement in performance. The additional quadratic trend may indicate that asymptotic performance has been reached. Imagine a group of new basketball players learning to shoot free throws. Every day we record the number of successes. You can imagine a pattern over time similar to that depicted in Figure 10.35. At first there is steady improvement. At some point the rate of improvement slows until the line flattens out, indicating that asymptotic performance has been attained – that is, not much more improvement can be expected.

Improvement in free throw percentage over five weeks

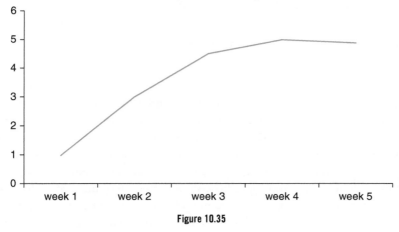

Figure 10.35

Invert the chart and change weeks to days and you might have a reduction in the symptoms of an infection after five days of treatment with an antibiotic.

**Weighting Coefficients for
3 Treatments Levels**

Trend	Level 1	Level 2	Level 3
linear	−1	0	1
quadratic	1	−2	1

Figure 10.36

**Weighting Coefficients for
4 Treatments Levels**

Trend	Level 1	Level 2	Level 3	Level 4
linear	−3	−1	1	3
quadratic	1	−1	−1	1
cubic	−1	3	−3	1

Figure 10.37

Of further importance regarding the weighting coefficients is that they are orthogonal; for example, testing for a linear trend is independent of testing for a quadratic trend or testing for a cubic trend. This implies that finding a significant linear trend is not mutually exclusive with finding a significant quadratic trend. In fact, it does not alter the chances one way or another. Because the weighting coefficients are orthogonal to each other, like any set of orthogonal linear contrasts, there can be as many tests of polynomial trends as there are df in the omnibus F-test.

The weighting coefficients for designs with 3 and 4 $df_{treatment}$ are found in Figures 10.36 and 10.37, respectively. When the IV is qualitative rather than quantitative, the linear contrasts defined in Figure 10.10, for example, no longer test polynomial trends. The contrast merely compares level 1 against level 3. The contrast labelled quadratic merely contrasts level 2 against the average of levels 1 and 3 combined. This is necessarily the case, because when the IV is qualitative, the numbers are merely nominal and do not represent an increase in an amount.

═══ REVIEW QUESTION ═══

What are the correlations among the three polynomial trends in Figure 10.37? Why?

⌕ Web Link 10.5 for an answer to the review question.

Using the weighting coefficients in Figures 10.36 and 10.37 for tests of polynomial trends assumes that the intervals between all treatment levels are equal and that the number of observations in all conditions are the same. The number of observations per condition are the same in all three of your *cage* conditions, but the two intervals between the levels of your IV are unequal. There is one hamster per cage in the first condition, two per cage in the second condition, and four per cage in the third condition. The difference between the *cage 2* and *cage 4* conditions is twice that between *cage 1* and *cage 2* conditions. This requires the calculation of customized weighting coefficients. Once we have done so, we simply apply the derived weighting coefficients and conduct the usual linear contrast.

When the intervals of the IV are unequal the weighting coefficients (c) for a test of linear trend can be easily calculated. All we need are (1) the values of the IV (Figure 10.38), and (2) a set of equations (Figure 10.39).

After summing the number of Ks and the values of the IV, we arrive at the equation at the bottom of Figure 10.38 which, as a linear contrast, must equal 0. Rearranging the equation and solving for K we find that $K = -7/3 = -2.333$. Then the new weighting coefficients can be calculated by inserting the value of K (−2.333) into the equations in the table.

Thus, the weighting coefficients for a test for a first-order polynomial trend (linear) for your data are −1.333, −0.333, and +1.333, which sum to 0, as required. The calculations for the second-order polynomial trend (quadratic) are a bit more challenging and unnecessary for our purposes. Fortunately, SPSS will recognize unequal intervals and make the necessary compensations to the

K		IV value	
K	+	1	
K	+	2	
K	+	4	
3K	+	7	= 0.0

Figure 10.38

K		IV value	c
−2.333	+	1	= −1.333
−2.333	+	2	= −.333
−2.333	+	4	= +1.666
Total			= 0.0

Figure 10.39

weighting coefficients when you request the tests for polynomial trends.

$$L = \Sigma c_j \bar{y}_j = -1.33(3) + (-0.333)(4) + 1.666(8) = 8.005,$$

$$SS_{contrast} = \frac{nL^2}{\Sigma c_j^2} = \frac{4(8.005)^2}{(-1.333)^2 + (-0.333)^2 + 1.666^2} = 54.92,$$

$$MS_{contrast} = \frac{SS_{contrast}}{df_{contrast}} = \frac{54.92}{1} = 54.92,$$

$$F = \frac{54.92}{2.444} \; 22.47,$$

which is greater than the critical value of 7.21 at 1 and 9 *df* found in the *F*-table.

When the *F*-value for a test of a polynomial trend is significant, it means that the trend accounts for a substantial amount of the variance in the DV. In other words, your hamster data support your hypothesis that there is a linear increase in the number of *midsquares* entered in the open field as the number of cage-mates increases. (Remember, I hinted earlier that there may be a more straightforward (pun intended) test of your hypothesis.) The test for a linear trend is the most direct test of your hypothesis, and the significant result is the strongest possible evidence in support of your hypothesis. But the story is not yet concluded. Finding a significant linear trend does not preclude the presence of a quadratic trend; remember, tests for polynomial trends are independent. Although it was made *post hoc*, another interpretation also seemed reasonable: more than two hamsters per *cage* condition are needed to increase their open-field activity. In combination with the three *cage* condition means (3, 4, and 8), this hypothesis would be supported by the presence of a significant quadratic trend. There does appear to be something of a curve in the effect across the conditions.

In cases where there are 2 $df_{treatment}$ there can be no more than two orthogonal contrasts. Recall as well that the $SS_{contrast}$ for a complete set of orthogonal contrasts (in your case 2) must sum to the $SS_{treatment}$ found in the omnibus *F*-test. Once you have tested for a linear trend, there is only one contrast that will complete the orthogonal set, the contrast testing for a quadratic trend. Following this logic, you need not calculate the weighting coefficients for the quadratic trend. The $SS_{contrast}$ for the quadratic trend can be derived as the difference between the $SS_{treatment}$ from the omnibus *F*-test and the $SS_{contrast}$ from the contrast testing for the linear trend: $56.00 - 54.92 = 1.08$. With 1 $df_{treatment}$ the $MS_{treatment}$ is 1.08. The resulting $F = 1.08/2.444 = 0.44$, which is less than the critical value (7.21) for 1 and 9 *df*. Therefore, there is insufficient evidence to support the notion that there must be more than two hamsters per *cage* condition for *cage* condition to affect open-field activity.

> Although SPSS reports linear contrast as *t*-values, it reports the tests for polynomial trend (which are themselves linear contrasts) as *F*-values. We have already seen that the *t*-values are merely the square root of the 1 $df_{treatment}$ *F*-values.

Using SPSS to test for polynomial trends

Let us return to your *cage* condition/open-field independent-samples data set and use SPSS to test for the polynomial trends mentioned above. We begin by again opening the SPSS *onewayenriched.sav* file.

To run your polynomial contrast, under the *Analysis* tab choose *Compare Means* and then the *One-Way ANOVA* option. When the *One-Way ANOVA* window opens, move *cage* to the *Factor* area and *midsquares* to the *Dependent List* area as we did above and in Chapter 8. Then click *Contrasts*. When the *One-Way ANOVA: Contrasts* window opens (Figure 10.40), check *Polynomial* in the upper left-hand corner. Then change the *Degree* setting to *Quadratic*. This will produce tests for both the linear and the quadratic trends. Then click *Continue*, which returns

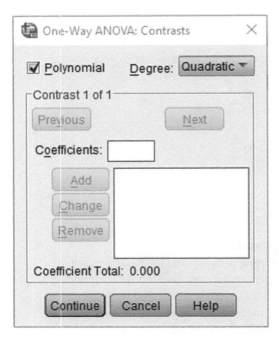

Figure 10.40

you to the main *One-Way ANOVA* window. We will not bother with repeating the testing for homogeneity of variance. Click *OK* to run the analysis.

The first line of the SPSS ANOVA table in Figure 10.41 (*Between Groups (Combined)*) details the total (omnibus) treatment effect. The second line (*Linear Term*) reports the test for a linear trend. The third line (*Deviation*) reports the residual treatment after removing the linear component. The fourth line (*Quadratic*) reports the test for a quadratic trend. The fifth line (*Within Groups*) is the error term or the average within-condition variance.

ANOVA

midsquares

			Sum of Squares	df	Mean Square	F	Sig.
Between Groups	(Combined)		56.000	2	28.000	11.455	.003
	Linear Term	Contrast	54.857	1	54.857	22.442	.001
		Deviation	1.143	1	1.143	.468	.511
	Quadratic Term	Contrast	1.143	1	1.143	.468	.511
Within Groups			22.000	9	2.444		
Total			78.000	11			

Figure 10.41

REVIEW QUESTION

Why are the statistics for the *Deviation* and *Quadratic Term Contrast* lines identical in the ANOVA table?

Web Link 10.6 for an answer to the review question.

The $MS_{BetweenGroups}$ divided by the $MS_{WithinGroups}$ results in an observed *F*-value of 11.455 with a *p*-value (*Sig.*) of 0.003. This is a recapitulation of your earlier omnibus test of the data (see Figure 10.1). The $MS_{LinearTerm}$ divided by the $MS_{WithinGroups}$ results in an observed *F*-value of 22.442 with a *p*-value (*Sig.*) of 0.001. The $MS_{QuadraticTerm}$ divided by the $MS_{WithinGroups}$ results in an observed *F*-value of 0.468 with a *p*-value (*Sig.*) of 0.511. The *F*-values are identical to those we calculated above.

• • • • •

Bear in mind that there is a danger associated with attempting to extrapolate beyond your IV's range of values (1 to 4). I assume that if you increase the number of *cage* conditions to where you have a large number of hamsters per cage, at some point you will likely discover a quadratic trend (i.e., the open-field activity will level off). Furthermore, this may be one of those occasions when a quadratic trend might illustrate a reversal of the effect. That is, perhaps it is possible to have too many hamsters per cage, which results in the hamsters becoming less willing to explore. This situation would be analogous to the example depicted in Figure 10.33.

To demonstrate testing for polynomial trends with related samples, let us reopen your *repeated-measures1.sav* file. From within the *Data Editor*, select *Analyze*, drop down to *General Linear Model*, and slide over and select the *Repeated Measures* option. As earlier, in the *Repeated Measures Define Factor(s)* window enter '3' into the *Number of Levels* box, click *Add*, and then click *Define* at the bottom of the window. When the *Repeated Measures* window opens, highlight and move your three variables into the *Within-Subjects Variables* window and click *Options*. Next select the *Contrasts* button. When the *Repeated Measures: Contrasts* window opens (Figure 10.42) ensure that the *Factors* box shows *factor1(Polynomial)* and click *Continue*. After you are returned to the *Repeated Measures* window click *OK*. The results appear in the SPSS output window.

The SPSS output is nearly identical to what we found earlier. The one difference regards the change in one table: *Test of Within-Subjects Contrasts* (Figure 10.43). Rather than the contrasts of the adjacent frequency conditions which were reported in the earlier linear contrast analysis, here the tests for the linear and quadratic polynomial trends are reported. The test for a linear trend is significant: $F(1, 4) = 22.857$, $MS_{error} = 1.750$, p (*Sig.*) = 0.009. This finding, together with the graphic representation of the data found in Chapter 9, support your hypothesis that there is a linear decrease in noun recognition with an increase in word frequency.

Figure 10.42

The test for a quadratic trend is non-significant: $F(1, 4) = 5.714$, $MS_{error} = 0.583$, $p = 0.075$. Thus, there is insufficient evidence to support the presence of a quadratic trend.

Both the independent-samples and the repeated-measures examples used in this section demonstrate how the tests for polynomial trends can play a crucial role in analysing and interpreting data when the IV is quantitative in nature.

Tests of Within-Subjects Contrasts

Measure: MEASURE_1

Source	factor1	Type III Sum of Squares	df	Mean Square	F	Sig.
factor1	Linear	40.000	1	40.000	22.857	.009
	Quadratic	3.333	1	3.333	5.714	.075
Error(factor1)	Linear	7.000	4	1.750		
	Quadratic	2.333	4	.583		

Figure 10.43

10 ● 7 UNPLANNED COMPARISONS: *POST HOC* TESTS

This section is intended to be an introduction to *post hoc* tests. Because there are numerous *post hoc* procedures and many disputes around the topic, we will need to limit the discussion. The focus will be on the Studentized range statistic (q) and the most common procedures which have evolved from it. Additionally, we shall concentrate on those procedures that compare pairs of condition means. As will become evident, we will never stray very far from the basic *t*-test. Because of the controversy surrounding *post hoc* testing of repeated-measures designs, particularly with respect to appropriate error terms, we are only concerned with between-subjects designs in this section.

> Note that SPSS does not permit *post hoc* tests to be selected following a repeated-measures ANOVA. *Post hoc* testing of repeated-measures designs is usually conducted with the linear contrast procedures presented in the previous section.

Post hoc or 'after the fact' tests are those that the researcher did not formulate prior to the initial examination of his or her data. In the previous section the tension between the desire to avoid a Type I error when H_0 is true and to avoid a Type II error when H_0 is false was expressed in the nature of the Holm–Bonferroni multistage procedure. The tension is even greater in the case of *post hoc* testing and is reflected in the multitude of *post hoc* testing procedures. The first way in which the tension is dealt with regards the outcome of the omnibus tests. Typically, researchers follow Fisher's (1935) stricture that post *hoc tests* be conducted only if the omnibus test is significant.

Studentized range statistic

The historical and computational basis for most *post hoc* testing procedures is the Studentized range statistic, q (Student, 1927). Similar to Fisher's (1935) LSD, q provides a minimum difference used to evaluate the observed difference between two means. With q, however, the number of means being compared is taken into account. Initially q is used to test for a difference between the largest and smallest mean, while compensating for the number of possible comparisons:

$$q_k = \frac{\bar{y}_{\text{largest}} - \bar{y}_{\text{smallest}}}{\sqrt{MS_{\text{error}}/n}}$$

where k = the number of conditions in the experiment, $\bar{y}_{\text{largest}}$ is the largest of the rank-ordered condition means, $\bar{y}_{\text{smallest}}$ the smallest of the condition means, MS_{error} the mean squared error from the omnibus ANOVA, and n is the number of observations per condition.

Using your *cage* condition/open-field data as an example, we find the observed q to be

$$q_3 = \frac{8-3}{\sqrt{2.444/4}} = 6.39.$$

Appendix H provides a table of critical q-values based on the number of conditions and the df_{error}. The columns of the table represent the number of means in the experiment and the rows represent the df_{error} from the omnibus test. Your experiment had 3 conditions and 9 df_{error}. The corresponding critical q-value is 3.95. Because your observed q is greater than the critical q, you reject H_0 and conclude that the hamsters in *cage* conditions 1 and 4 differ in terms of their open-field behaviour. Substituting the mean of *cage* condition 2 for that of *cage* condition 4, not surprisingly you find the observed q (1.28) to be less than the critical value (3.95). And, consistent with your previous analyses, you fail to reject H_0 and conclude that there is insufficient evidence to support the hypothesis that hamsters in *cage* conditions 1 and 2 differ in terms of their open-field activity.

$$q_3 = \frac{4-3}{\sqrt{2.444/4}} = 1.28.$$

Rather than being a stand-alone test, the formula for the q-statistic has been used primarily for establishing minimum significant differences to be used in other procedures. With a bit of manipulation,

$$q_k = \frac{\bar{y}_{\text{largest}} - \bar{y}_{\text{smallest}}}{\sqrt{MS_{\text{error}}/n}}$$

becomes

$$\bar{y}_{\text{largest}} - \bar{y}_{\text{smallest}} = q_{(k, df)}\sqrt{\frac{MS_{\text{error}}}{n}},$$

where $\bar{y}_{\text{largest}} - \bar{y}_{\text{smallest}}$ now represents the minimum difference required for the difference between two means to be significant; $q_{(k, df)}$, the critical q-value, is obtained from Appendix H.

Again, using your *cage* condition/open-field data as the example,

$$\bar{y}_{\text{largest}} - \bar{y}_{\text{smallest}} = 3.95\sqrt{\frac{2.44}{4}} = 3.09.$$

In your experiment, pairs of means must differ by 3.09 for a difference to be considered significant.

●●●●●

A quick comparison of the formula for q and the formula for the t-test reveals only a small difference:

$$q_k = \frac{\bar{y}_{\text{largest}} - \bar{y}_{\text{smallest}}}{\sqrt{MS_{\text{error}}/n}} \quad \text{and} \quad t = \frac{\bar{y}_1 - \bar{y}_2}{\sqrt{2MS_{\text{error}}/n}}.$$

The only substantial difference is that MS_{error} is multiplied by 2 in the t-test formula. In fact, when there are only two experimental conditions, the probabilities associated with q and t are identical.

Newman–Keuls test

The Newman–Keuls (NK) or Student–Newman–Keuls test is based on an application of the q-statistic by Newman (1939) and Keuls (1952). There are several ways to describe the procedure and how to calculate it. It is hoped that the current approach is not more confusing than the others. The NK test is a stepwise procedure which, like the Holm–Bonferroni test, can be understood to involve a systematic reduction in the family size being considered. A different minimum difference is computed for each family size.

The first step in the procedure is to rank-order all of the condition means. Using your hamster data again, we have the order of 3, 4, and 8. Defining family size is the central feature of the NK. In this context a family is the number of means in the rank ordering bracketed by the two means which are being compared. The two means being compared are included in the count. If you are comparing the mean of 3 with the mean of 8, the family size is 3. If you are comparing the mean of 3 with the mean of 4, then the family size is 2. If you are comparing the mean of 4 with the mean of 8, then the family size also is 2. Family size then is used as the k in Appendix H for obtaining the critical q-value.

Next you need to compute a minimum difference (min. diff.) for each family size. For your data we need a min. diff. for a family of 3 and a family of 2. Again, using Appendix H, we find the critical q for $k = 3$ with 9 df is 3.95. Thus, the minimum required difference for a family of 3 is

$$\text{min. diff.} = 3.95 \sqrt{\frac{2.44}{4}} = 3.09.$$

Using Appendix H, we find the critical q for $k = 2$ with 9 df is 3.20. Thus, the minimum required difference for a family of 2 is

$$\text{min. diff.} = 3.20 \sqrt{\frac{2.44}{4}} = 2.50.$$

Figure 10.44 summarizes the results of the NK tests. In terms of the pattern of significance, the results are no different from those of our previous series of *t*-tests conducted on your data. Such consistency is typically the case when there are fewer than five conditions. We might further describe the results of your NK analysis in terms of groups of means, which is how SPSS presents the results. One group is formed by *cage* conditions 1 and 2, because they are not found to be different from each other; however, both are found to be different from *cage* condition 4, which forms a group of its own.

Cage Conditions	Absolute Difference Between Means	k	Critical Min. Diff.	$\alpha = .05$ Significance
1 versus 2	1	2	2.50	No
1 versus 4	5	3	3.09	Yes
2 versus 4	4	2	2.50	Yes

Figure 10.44

━━━━━━━━━━━━ REVIEW QUESTION ━━━━━━━━━━━━

Assume the following data summary. There are four conditions with means of 4, 2, 5, and 8. There are five subjects in each of the conditions. The MS_{error} from the omnibus ANOVA is 2.50. Conduct an NK *post hoc* analysis of the data. How do the conditions appear to group themselves?

 Web Link 10.7 for an answer to the review question.

Of all the *post hoc* tests the NK test offers the most power but the least familywise Type I error rate protection. That is, in comparison to other *post hoc* tests, if an H_0 is false the NK test affords the researcher the greatest chance of correctly rejecting the H_0. On the other hand, if an H_0 is true the NK test unfortunately gives the researcher the greatest chance of incorrectly rejecting the H_0. Today, the NK test is considered by many researchers to be a test to avoid and to be a symptom of the 'fishing expedition' mentioned at the outset of this chapter.

Tukey's honest significant difference

As a correction for the lack of Type I error protection provided by the NK test, Tukey (1949) offered a simple solution. He proposed eliminating the stepwise reduction in the family size and in the corresponding critical minimum difference. The largest of the minimum differences should be used for all comparisons of pairs of means, regardless of where they are in the rank ordering. While the NK test provides little protection against an inflating familywise error rate, the Tukey honest significant difference (HSD) provides the least amount of power, should the H_0 be false. Again we see a manifestation of the tension that accompanies having multiple follow-up tests.

Tukey's wholly significant difference

As a compromise between the extremes of the NK test and HSD, Tukey proposed the wholly significant difference (WSD). The WSD uses the arithmetic average of the minimum differences that would be used for the NK test and the HSD. An example using your data is found in Figure 10.45. The three sets of critical minimum differences reflect the range of trade-offs found in a host of *post hoc* tests that are available in SPSS and other statistical software packages.

Cage Conditions	Absolute Difference Between Means	k	Critical N-K Min. Diff.	Critical HSD Min. Diff.	Critical WSD Min. Diff.
1 versus 2	1	2	2.50	3.09	2.80
1 versus 4	5	3	3.09	3.09	3.09
2 versus 4	4	2	2.50	3.09	2.80

Figure 10.45

Using SPSS to conduct *post hoc* comparisons

To run a *post hoc* test, return to the *onewayenriched.sav* file in the SPSS *Data Editor*. Under *Analyze* choose *Compare Means* and then *One-Way ANOVA*. As before, move *cage* to the *Factor* area and *midsquares* to the *Dependent List* area. Then click *Post Hoc*. A new window, *One-Way ANOVA: Post Hoc Multiple Comparisons*, with a large selection of tests, will appear (Figure 10.46). In the *Equal Variances Assumed* area select *S-N-K, Tukey, and Tukey's-b* (which is the WSD). In the *Equal Variances Not Assumed* area select *Games-Howell*. Click *Continue* to return to the main *One-Way ANOVA* window. Click *OK* to run the analysis.

The first table we see in the output is the ANOVA summary table for the omnibus *F*-test and recapitulates the results we saw earlier for these data. Next we find the *post hoc* tests *Multiple Comparisons*

table (Figure 10.47). This table reports the results of the Tukey HSD and the Games–Howell test. There are three panels in the HSD area; each reports the given *cage* condition contrasted with the other two. The difference between the pair of means, the standard errors of the difference, and the *p*-values are reported. Significance (indicated by an *) for the *post hoc* test is based on the critical values (usually *q*) at $\alpha = 0.05$ and reflects the correction employed by the particular test. Additionally, the 95% confidence intervals are reported. As we have seen previously, with 95% confidence intervals, when 0 does not fall within the region

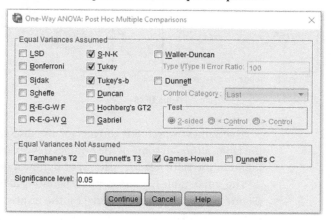

Figure 10.46

Multiple Comparisons

Dependent Variable: midsquares

	(I) cage	(J) cage	Mean Difference (I-J)	Std. Error	Sig.	95% Confidence Interval Lower Bound	95% Confidence Interval Upper Bound
Tukey HSD	1.00	2.00	-1.00000	1.10554	.651	-4.0867	2.0867
		4.00	-5.00000*	1.10554	.004	-8.0867	-1.9133
	2.00	1.00	1.00000	1.10554	.651	-2.0867	4.0867
		4.00	-4.00000*	1.10554	.014	-7.0867	-.9133
	4.00	1.00	5.00000*	1.10554	.004	1.9133	8.0867
		2.00	4.00000*	1.10554	.014	.9133	7.0867
Games-Howell	1.00	2.00	-1.00000	1.00000	.603	-4.0683	2.0683
		4.00	-5.00000*	1.15470	.013	-8.6080	-1.3920
	2.00	1.00	1.00000	1.00000	.603	-2.0683	4.0683
		4.00	-4.00000*	1.15470	.034	-7.6080	-.3920
	4.00	1.00	5.00000*	1.15470	.013	1.3920	8.6080
		2.00	4.00000*	1.15470	.034	.3920	7.6080

*. The mean difference is significant at the 0.05 level.

Figure 10.47

Homogeneous Subsets

midsquares

| | cage | N | Subset for alpha = 0.05 | |
			1	2
Student-Newman-Keuls[a]	1.00	4	3.0000	
	2.00	4	4.0000	
	4.00	4		8.0000
	Sig.		.389	1.000
Tukey HSD[a]	1.00	4	3.0000	
	2.00	4	4.0000	
	4.00	4		8.0000
	Sig.		.651	1.000
Tukey B[a]	1.00	4	3.0000	
	2.00	4	4.0000	
	4.00	4		8.0000

Means for groups in homogeneous subsets are displayed.

Figure 10.48

bracketed by the lower and upper bounds, the test inevitably is significant at $\alpha = 0.05$ level. For example, 0 falls within the lower and upper bounds of *cage* condition 1 contrasted with *cage* condition 2, −4.0867 and 2.0867, but not within the lower and upper bounds of *cage* condition 1 contrasted with *cage* condition 4, −8.0867 and −1.9133.

The Games–Howell test is a *post hoc* test often preferred when homogeneity of variance cannot be assumed. Recall that when the sample is small, as is yours, it is difficult to reliably test for homogeneity of variance. Thus, even though the Levene test is non-significant, it may be prudent not to assume homogeneity of variance. (See p. 343 in Chapter 8 regarding the difficulties encountered testing assumptions when the sample size is small.)

The Games–Howell test corrects for any discrepancy among the condition variances. As seen in the table, although some of the *p*-values have been substantially attenuated in comparison to those found in the HSD area, the pattern of significance is unchanged.

The final table in the output window defines *Homogeneous Subsets* of condition means (Figure 10.48). This table is based on the results of the (Student–)Newman–Keuls, the Tukey HSD (selected as Tukey), and the Tukey WSD. As we found above, your three *cage* conditions segregate into two groups. The first group contains *cage* conditions 1 and 2. The second group comprises *cage* condition 4 alone. The pattern is the same for all three tests. This table provides no information beyond that found in the previous table; the difference between the two tables is merely one of form.

Choosing a *post hoc* test

As you can see in the SPSS *Post Hoc Multiple Comparisons* window, there is a plethora of *post hoc* tests from which to choose. The basic choice revolves around two decisions. The first decision concerns the issue of homogeneity of variance. If the Levene test was significant or if you have any concerns regarding homogeneity of variance, then I suggest that the Games–Howell test is the appropriate choice. If homogeneity of variance is not an issue, the choice then centres on the trade-off between potential Type I error rate protection and statistical power. The Tukey WSD is a common compromise. If you do not treat the *post hoc* tests as the final word on your results, the choice of test is not crucial.

Remember the advice offered earlier in this chapter. First, the results of *post hoc* tests always must be reported as such. Second, the results of *post hoc* tests should be used primarily to inform future research. If you think that you have found something of interest with *post hoc* tests, then before publicly reporting your findings you should design another experiment to test out your new idea in a planned manner.

NONPARAMETRIC FOLLOW-UP COMPARISONS

The follow-up tests discussed thus far in this chapter, both *a priori* and *post hoc*, are appropriate for measurement data. In this section we will examine the most common nonparametric alternatives to those procedures.

Independent samples

We begin with the independent-samples design. The Kruskal–Wallis test, as discussed in Chapter 8, is designed for use with independent samples when the data are nominal. It is also often used when the data are measurement in nature, but the researcher has concerns regarding assumptions, such as normality. In Chapter 8 the Kruskal–Wallis test was presented as an alternative to the independent-samples omnibus ANOVA. In this section we shall see how we can extend its use as a follow-up test.

REVIEW QUESTION

Why might you consider using a nonparametric test to analyse your *cage* condition/open-field hamster data?

Web Link 10.8 for an answer to the review question.

After opening the *onewayenriched.sav* file, to run the Kruskal–Wallis in SPSS scroll down the *Analyze* tab to *Nonparametric Tests*. Then slide over and select *Independent Samples*. When the *Nonparametric Tests: Two or More Independent Samples* window opens (Figure 10.49) select the *Fields* tab at the top. When the next window opens, move the *midsquares* variable to the *Test Fields* area and move *cage* to the *Group* area. Next select the *Settings* tab at the top. When the *Settings* window opens, click on the *Customized tests* button. Next check the *Kruskal-Wallis 1-way ANOVA (k samples)* option. The *Multiple comparisons* drop-down box should indicate *All pairwise*. To run the analysis, click *Run*.

In the output window a *Hypothesis Test Summary* box appears (Figure 10.50). This is an omnibus test for any difference in the distributions of the three *cage* conditions and it was discussed in Chapter 8. (For the discussion of the *Hypothesis Test Summary* box, see p. 356.)

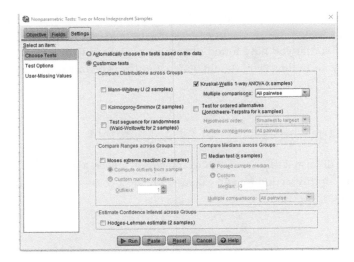

Figure 10.49

Hypothesis Test Summary

	Null Hypothesis	Test	Sig.	Decision
1	The distribution of midsquares is the same across categories of cage.	Independent-Samples Kruskal-Wallis Test	.017	Reject the null hypothesis.

Asymptotic significances are displayed. The significance level is .05.

Figure 10.50

Related-Samples Friedman's Two-Way Analysis of Variance by Ranks

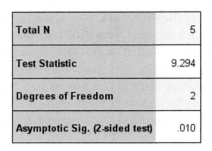

Total N	5
Test Statistic	9.294
Degrees of Freedom	2
Asymptotic Sig. (2-sided test)	.010

Figure 10.51

Pairwise Comparisons of cage

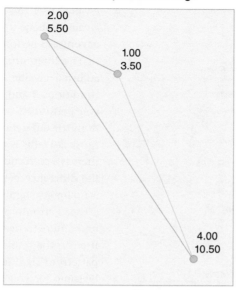

Each node shows the sample average rank of cage.

Sample1-Sample2	Test Statistic	Std. Error	Std. Test Statistic	Sig.	Adj.Sig.
1.00-2.00	-2.000	2.527	-.791	.429	1.000
1.00-4.00	-7.000	2.527	-2.770	.006	.017
2.00-4.00	-5.000	2.527	-1.979	.048	.144

Each row tests the null hypothesis that the Sample 1 and Sample 2 distributions are the same.
Asymptotic significances (2-sided tests) are displayed. The significance level is .05.

Figure 10.52

Double-clicking in the *Decision* area will open another window with box-and-whisker plots and a test statistic summary (Figure 10.51). At the bottom of the window there is a box labelled *View* that indicates *Independent Samples Test View*. By clicking the small down arrow *View* can be changed to *Pairwise comparisons*. This will open another window: *Pairwise Comparisons of cage* (Figure 10.52).

The figure at the top of the window graphically displays three pairwise comparisons along with the corresponding sets of average rankings. The table at the bottom of the window reports the Kruskal–Wallis results for the three comparisons: the test statistic, the standard error, the standardized test

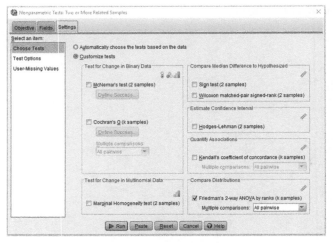

Figure 10.53

Hypothesis Test Summary

	Null Hypothesis	Test	Sig.	Decision
1	The distributions of low, medium and high are the same.	Related-Samples Friedman's Two-Way Analysis of Variance by Ranks	.010	Reject the null hypothesis.

Asymptotic significances are displayed. The significance level is .05.

Figure 10.54

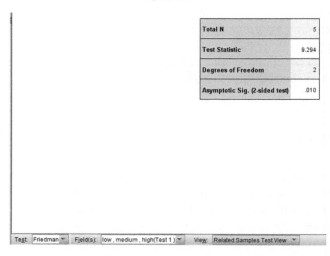

Total N	5
Test Statistic	9.294
Degrees of Freedom	2
Asymptotic Sig. (2-sided test)	.010

Figure 10.55

statistic, the *p*-value (*Sig.*), and the adjusted *p*-value (*Adj. Sig.*). The adjustment in the *p*-value is made to compensate for the number of contrasts performed.

The interesting aspect of the table is the adjusted *p*-value for the comparison of *cage* conditions 2 and 4. In all the other analyses you performed comparing these two conditions the difference was significant. When the Kruskal–Wallis is used as a follow-up test and there is a correction for multiple comparisons, the difference between these two conditions is no longer significant. Either you have made a Type I error in previous analyses, or the current failure to reject the H_0 constitutes a Type II error, the result of insufficient power. This pattern of significant findings must be troublesome for you because it fits neither your original H_1 nor the alternative that more than two hamsters per cage are required to produce an effect on the animals' willingness to explore the open-field apparatus.

Related samples

Friedman's test, as discussed in Chapter 9, is the usual choice for both the omnibus and follow-up nonparametric tests for related samples. You can run the related-samples (repeated-measures) nonparametric follow-up test using your noun frequency data.

After opening the *repeatedmeasures1. sav* SPSS file, to run Friedman's test in SPSS scroll down the *Analyze* tab in the SPSS *Data Editor* to *Nonparametric Tests*. Then slide over and select *Related Samples*. When the *Nonparametric Tests: Two or More Related Samples* window opens (Figure 10.53) select the *Fields* tab at the top. As you did in Chapter 9, when the next window opens move the *low, medium,* and *high* variables to the *Test Fields* area. Next select

Pairwise Comparisons

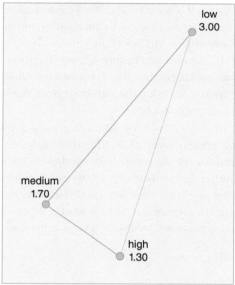

Each node shows the sample average rank.

Sample1-Sample2	Test Statistic	Std. Error	Std. Test Statistic	Sig.	Adj.Sig.
high-medium	.400	.632	.632	.527	1.000
high-low	1.700	.632	2.688	.007	.022
medium-low	1.300	.632	2.055	.040	.119

Each row tests the null hypothesis that the Sample 1 and Sample 2 distributions are the same.

Asymptotic significances (2-sided tests) are displayed. The significance level is .05.

Figure 10.56

the *Settings* tab and then select *Customize tests* at the top of the new window. At the bottom right of the window, check the *Friedman's 2-way ANOVA by ranks (k samples)* option. Be sure that the *Multiple comparisons* option is set at *All pairwise*. To run the analysis, click *Run*.

In the output window a *Hypothesis Test Summary* box appears (Figure 10.54). This is the omnibus test for any difference at all in the distributions of the noun frequency conditions which we discussed in Chapter 9.

If you double-click the *Decision* area, another window will open displaying graphs and summary statistics as seen in Chapter 9 (Figure 10.55). The *View* box indicates *Independent Samples Test View*. By clicking the small down arrow *View* can be changed to *Pairwise comparisons*. This will open another window: *Pairwise Comparisons* window (Figure 10.56).

The figure at the top of the window graphically displays the three pairwise comparisons along with the corresponding mean rankings. The table at the bottom reports the Friedman's test results for the three comparisons: the test statistics, the standard errors, the standardized test statistic, the *p*-values (*Sig.*), and the adjusted *p*-values (*Adj. Sig.*).

The noteworthy aspect of this table is the adjusted *p*-value for the comparison of the low-frequency and medium-frequency conditions. In the other analyses you performed on these data comparing these two conditions the difference was significant. With the nonparametric follow-up and a correction for multiple comparisons, the difference between these two conditions is no longer significant. As was the case with your *cage* condition data, either you have made a Type I error in previous analyses, or the current failure to reject the H_0 constitutes a Type II error. These findings also highlight the dangers associated with small sample sizes.

CHAPTER SUMMARY

In this chapter we surveyed the logic of the most common forms of follow-up tests. Important distinctions were made between *a priori* and *post hoc* tests and between per-comparison and familywise Type I error rates. Both *a priori* and *post hoc* tests can be seen as variants of the *t*-test or of the *F*-test. Once more we found that the multitude of formulaic appearances is reducible to a common, underlying structure. Furthermore, the *t*-test and *F*-test formulae are incarnations of the general structure regarding (1) what is expected, (2) what is observed, and (3) what is expected due to chance alone? The crucial difference between *a priori* and *post hoc* tests revolves around the presumed family size. When contrasts are planned, the family is defined by the number of tests designed prior to collecting the data. When the contrasts are unplanned, the family is defined by the total number of tests that are possible of that type (e.g., all possible pairs of means). Once homogeneity of variance is assumed, the choice of *post hoc* test is made on the basis of a compromise between an acceptable familywise Type I error rate and the desired level of statistical power.

After the long journey through these last three chapters, we can now summarize your two primary data sets and draw conclusions. We begin with your *cage* condition/open-field data and your H_1 that as the number of cage-mates increased so would hamsters' willingness to explore. Back in Chapter 8 you computed descriptive statistics, tested assumptions, constructed a graphic representation of the data, and conducted an omnibus test where it was concluded that *cage* condition (number of cage-mates) affected willingness to explore (open-field activity). Until this chapter you were able to specify the nature of the effect produced by *cage* condition. Although several planned and unplanned comparisons indicated possible ways to specify the effect, it was the test for polynomial trends that most directly evaluated your H_1. The significant linear trend provided direct support for your H_1. You may conclude that there is evidence that as the number of cage-mates increased so did hamsters' willingness to explore. The same can be said for the analyses of your data from your within-subjects design experiment regarding word frequency and noun recall. Again the significant linear trend supported your H_1 that as the word frequency of the nouns increased, recall performance would be adversely affected. The results from both fictitious studies illustrate the important role that tests of polynomial trends can play when the experimental design involves a quantitative independent variable.

Finally, the need to control the familywise Type I error rate inevitably results in a loss of statistical power. The more conditions there are in an experiment, the more contrasts are likely to be made, and the greater the loss of power. Some *post hoc* tests are associated with a greater loss of power than are others. In your two data sets, switching from parametric to nonparametric tests changed little with respect to the omnibus test found in Chapters 8 and 9, but the switch did result in a considerable change with respect to the follow-up tests discussed in this chapter. Remember, if you think that you have found something of interest with *post hoc* tests, before getting excited, design and conduct another experiment specifically for testing your new idea.

 ## RECOMMENDED READINGS

Abdi, H., & Williams, L. J. (2010). *Post hoc* analysis. In N. Salkind (ed.), *Encyclopedia of research design*. Thousand Oaks, CA: Sage.
This chapter offers a readable introduction to the logic behind linear contrasts and *post hoc* comparisons. The chapter also provides a useful comparison of a *priori* and *post hoc* contrasts.
Hochberg, Y., & Tamhane, A. C. (1987). *Multiple comparison procedures*. New York: John Wiley & Sons.
This is one of the most comprehensive and detailed books available that deals with both *a priori* and *post hoc* comparisons.
Klockars, A. J., & Sax, G. (1986). *Multiple comparisons*. Beverly Hills, CA: Sage.
This nice little book provides a detailed discussion of multiple comparisons and the issue of statistical power. The authors make effective use of the classic Solomon Asch group conformity experiment.

 ## CHAPTER REVIEW QUESTIONS

Multiple-choice questions

1   If the per-comparison alpha was set at 0.05 and a set of eight comparisons was made, what would be the familywise alpha?

   a   0.34
   b   0.66
   c   0.95
   d   0.50
   e   0.05

2   A researcher studied the effects of three common groundwater pollutants on arctic voles by comparing each of the three pollutants against the control of plain, clean water. How many contrasts were there in the family?

a   5

b   9

c   3

d   6

e   4

3   Another researcher studied four airborne pollutants on arctic voles. There were five groups of voles: one group for each of the airborne pollutants and one control group. She had no idea if one or more of the pollutants would adversely affect the voles or whether the pollutants would be equally detrimental. How may contrasts were there in the family?

a   10

b   5

c   50

d   4

e   12

4   If you had a family of four planned comparisons, what would be your best choice of a per-comparison α?

a   0.05

b   0.005

c   0.01

d   0.001

e   0.04

5   Which of the following is not a characteristic of an *a priori* test?

a   It is designed prior to data collection

b   It tests a theory of a specific informed hypothesis

c   The explicit questions is: Do these particular means differ?

d   The number of comparisons is usually greater than the $df_{treatment}$

e   All are characteristics of an *a priori* test

6   Which of the following is a principle(s) upon which multiple *t*-tests are based?

a   All sample variances in the study are unbiased estimators of the population variance, regardless of the veracity of H_0

b   The more estimates (unbiased) you have of the population variance, the better

c   The greater the df_{error}, the greater the test's power

d   All of the above are principles upon which multiple *t*-tests are based

e   None of the above are principles upon which multiple *t*-tests are based

7   In terms of the Studentized range statistic (q), what is the minimum difference required for two means to be significantly different, if there are four treatment conditions and five subjects in each condition?

a   1.96

b   3.84

c   3.56

d   4.05

e   3.96

8   Linear contrasts allow us to compare _____.

a   One condition mean against another condition mean

b   One condition mean against an amalgamation of other condition means c   One group of amalgamated condition means against another group of amalgamated condition means

   d   All three of the above comparisons

   e   Only a and b

9   Which set of weighting coefficients does not represent a linear contrast?

   a   +1, −0.5, −0.5

   b   −1, 0, −1

   c   −3, +0.5, +2.5

   d   0, −1, +1

   e   All of the above represent linear contrasts

10 Two linear contrasts are made by a researcher and the first has the weighting coefficients of 0, −1, and +1. What set of weighting coefficients would allow a second contrast to be orthogonal to the first?

   a   −2, 0, +2

   b   +2, 0, −2

   c   −2, +1, +1

   d   +2, −1, −1

   e   −1, +2, −1

Short-answer questions

1   What is the difference between *a priori* and *post hoc* follow-up tests?

2   As a follow-up test, what advantage does the *multiple t-test* procedure have over simply carrying out a series of standard *t*-tests?

3   In terms of their minimum difference values, what is the difference between the Newman–Keuls, Tukey's HSD, and Tukey's WSD tests? What statistical issues are behind the development of these tests?

4   What is the Holm–Bonferroni multistage procedure and how is it different from the standard multiple *t*-test procedure?

5   Why are tests for polynomial trends not possible when the independent variable is qualitative in nature?

Data set questions

1   Using 30 subjects (10 in each of three conditions), a psychologist tested the effects of caffeine on the Klutz Hand–Eye Coordination Test. In condition I subjects were given no caffeine. In condition II subjects were given 10 mg of caffeine. In condition III subjects were given 20 mg of caffeine. The psychologist wished to know if scores would simply improve linearly as the dosage was increased or if performance would suffer at higher dosages. The means for condition 1, 2, and 3 were 20, 70, and 40, respectively (the higher the score, the better the performance). The mean squared error from the overall analysis was 125. There is no need to test assumptions or make a figure. You need only carry out the statistical tests necessary to answer the psychologist's questions and draw appropriate conclusions.

2   A driving safety officer tested the effect of sleeplessness on driving errors. She suspected that the longer drivers go without sleep after 24 hours, the more likely they are to make errors. She did not think that there would be an increase in errors until the 24 hours. She had 12 young adult drivers stay awake for 18 hours (condition 1), 24 hours (condition 2), and 30 hours (condition 3). She then tested

each of them on a driving simulator. Figure 10.57 shows the number of errors committed by each driver. Using a nonparametric test, do the data support her suspicion?

3 A student completing a master's degree in Animal Science is interested in the social behaviour of cats. From his previous experience he believes that cats that were previously outdoor cats and later became indoor cats would want more attention from their owner than cats that had always been indoor cats. Furthermore, he thinks that cats that were always indoor cats but were the only cat in the household

Conditions	# Errors
1	30
1	11
1	40
1	44
2	52
2	41
2	20
2	58
3	63
3	90
3	71
3	100

Figure 10.57

would want more attention than cats that lived with litter-mates. To test his ideas, the student asked five cat owners in each of the conditions to observe and report the number of times the cat sought attention over a 24-hour period. Do the data in Figure 10.58 support the student's suspicions? The scores represent the number of times during a 24-hour period the cat sought attention from its owner. Be sure to start with descriptive statistics, tests of assumptions, a graph, and an omnibus test. This is to be followed up with appropriate *a priori* tests.

Outdoor To Indoor	Lone Indoor	Indoor with Litter-mates
18	3	10
14	10	3
19	10	7
18	15	12
20	7	7

Figure 10.58

Don't forget to use the online resources! Meet your supporting stats tutor through an **introductory video**, review your maths skills with a **diagnostic pre-test**, explore statistical principles through **interactive simulations**, practice analysis techniques with **SPSS datasets**, and check your work with **answers to all in-text questions**.

https://study.sagepub.com/bors

PART III

ANALYSING COMPLEX DESIGNS

In Part II of the book we focused on applying the tools and the general concepts covered in Part I to simple, yet realistic, research questions. In this final part of the book we apply those same general concepts and extend the tools and strategies we developed in Part II to more complex designs. The key change found in this part is in the inclusion of additional independent (predictor) variables (factorial design ANOVAs and multiple regression). In the final chapter the distinction between independent and dependent variables is eliminated (factor analysis). There is little that is genuinely new in these final three chapters. The challenge to the reader is in following the integration and extension of the previously covered material. By the end of each chapter, the student should (1) appreciate the most common research designs in each of the three chapters, (2) know how to determine and conduct the appropriate analyses, and (3) understand the accompanying limitations. Chapter 11 addresses the two most common forms of *factorial experimental design* (ANOVA). Chapter 12 provides an in-depth example of an observational study and the use of *multiple regression*. Finally, Chapter 13 provides an introduction to *factor analysis*, where the researcher is concerned with the pattern of relationships among a set of variables, rather than predicting the outcome of one variable. Although the designs presented in these three chapters may become substantially more complex in actual laboratory and field research, the logic and the general analytic strategies should remain the same.

> The word 'factor' gives an active character to the IV. Factor originates from the Latin word *factor* which can mean 'doer', 'creator', or 'maker'. In terms of research design it implies that the factor (IV) is a producer of change in the DV. It is used interchangeably with IV and *predictor variable*.

11

Chapter contents

TESTING FOR DIFFERENCES: ANOVA AND FACTORIAL DESIGNS

KEY CONCEPTS: main effects, interaction effect, simple effects, fixed factors, random factors, proportionality.

11●1 PURPOSE

The purpose of this chapter is to introduce the two most common experimental designs and their appropriate forms of analysis. For the simplicity of the demonstration, both designs will be restricted to two independent variables (IVs). In our first example, both IVs are between-subjects in nature; in the second example (*split-plot* or *mixed-design*) one IV is between-subjects in nature and the other IV is a within-subjects variable. With the introduction of a second IV a new element emerges: an *interaction*. When an interaction is significant it requires its own category of follow-up analysis: *simple effects*. In this chapter we also discuss the important distinction between *fixed* and *random* independent IVs and address their importance with respect to computations and generalization. Finally, we will briefly discuss the limited nonparametric alternatives that are available when assumptions are violated or the data are categorical. In addition to introducing the concept of interaction, in this chapter we will identify the appropriate error terms necessary for testing particular treatment terms and follow-up tests.

=== REVIEW QUESTION ===

How are MS_{error} and $MS_{treatment}$ the same and how are they different? Relate the components to the constituents of variance.

Web Link 11.1 for an answer to the review question.

11●2 INTRODUCTION

In Chapters 8 and 9 we extended the logic of the *t*-test and we were able to evaluate designs where the IV had more than two levels. Although a significant *F*-test indicates that the IV influenced performance on the DV, it does not specify the location or the nature of the effect. The answer to that question required the follow-up tests described in Chapter 10. In this chapter the presence of a second IV (a *factorial design*) makes things somewhat more complicated. You may ask why the researcher does not merely run two experiments, one for each IV, and keep things simple. Although under certain circumstances this may be appropriate, there are two reasons why the more complicated two-IV design is preferable (Keppel & Wickens, 2004).

First, by using one sample of subjects to test both IVs simultaneously, you gain efficiency. Depending upon the design, the total number of subjects required for two separate experiments is likely to approach twice that required for the single factorial design. This is often not a trivial matter. Some forms of research may cost up to $500 per subject, particularly research requiring functional magnetic resonance imaging data.

Second, and more importantly, by including both IVs in a single experiment the researcher can test for the presence of an interaction, and interactions are often theoretically or practically decisive.

Qualitatively speaking, the presence of an interaction requires you to begin describing your results with the phrase 'it depends'. Statistically speaking, the presence of an interaction means that the *effects* of the IVs are not *independent*. For example, imagine you are interested in two of the factors that affect acquiring a new language. From the literature you know that (1) time spent in a language lab and (2) being bilingual facilitate the acquisition of a new language. After reading the related literature, you hypothesize that (1) bilingual students will outperform those who are not bilingual, and (2) the effect will be even greater the more time bilingual students spend in a language lab. That is, you suspect that the effect of time spent in the language lab on acquiring a new language in part *depends* on whether or not the student is bilingual. You will need to design an appropriate experiment and determine an appropriate statistical test for the two IVs and for the interaction. Furthermore, you will find that interactions are like omnibus tests. They can alert us to the presence of an effect, but can rarely specify its location or its nature. As such, as with significant omnibus tests, significant interactions require follow-up tests. Such follow-up tests have a particular name (simple effects), but a rose is a rose regardless of the name or variety.

11●3 REVIEWING THE INDEPENDENT-SAMPLES ANOVA

In this section we will briefly review the basic logic of a one-way, independent-samples ANOVA as described in detail in Chapter 8.

> Remember, 'one-way' refers to the fact that the experiment has only one independent variable.

The independent-samples ANOVA is based on (1) computing two independent estimates of the population variance (σ^2) and (2) subjects being randomly *assigned* to the different treatment conditions:

- One estimate of σ^2 is based on the average within-condition variance. This is what we expect to observe in terms of variability.
- The other estimate of σ^2 is based on the variance among the condition means. This observation is compared with the average within-condition variance.

The first estimate is an unbiased estimate regardless of the veracity of H_0, but the second estimate is an unbiased estimate only when H_0 is true. The F-ratio is the second esti-

> Remember, the probability of an observed F-value is also relative to the $df_{treatment}$ and df_{error}.

mate divided by the first estimate. The expected value of the ratio is 1, when the H_0 is true. As the F-ratio increases in size, the probability of an F-value of that magnitude or greater being due to chance alone decreases, and the chances of H_0 being true are reduced.

Since Chapter 5 we have used a simple model of a score and variations on that model for depicting various designs and forms of analysis. The simplest form is $y_i = \mu + \tau_k + e_i$, where y_i is the *i*th score, μ is the population mean, τ_k is the treatment effect for a given condition, and e_i is the error associated with the *i*th score. Using the estimates of the parameters and solving for the difference between a score and the grand mean (*GM*) provides the components for the two estimates of σ^2: $(Y_i - GM) = (\bar{Y}_j - GM) + (Y_i - \bar{Y}_j)$. This chapter explores the consequences of the addition of a second IV. Previously we saw the addition of other variables. In Chapter 8 we saw the addition of a covariate (see p. 349); in Chapter 9 we saw the addition of both a blocking variable and a subject variable (see p. 372).

In those cases the insertion of the additional variable into the design was specifically for the purpose of reducing error variance and increasing the power for testing the lone treatment variable. Although an increase in power is often an advantage of a factorial design, at least for one of the IVs, this is not the design's primary purpose. The additional variable in a factorial design is a true second IV, whose effect we are as interested in determining as we are in determining the effect of the first IV. More importantly, the purpose of a factorial design is to allow for the evaluation of a possible interaction. Thus, the model of the difference between a score and the *GM* will take on another term – an interaction:

$$\text{score} - GM = \text{effect of IV}_1 + \text{effect of IV}_2 + \text{effect of interaction between IV}_1 \text{ and IV}_2 + \text{error.}$$

Building on the model of a score, Figure 11.1 depicts the partitioning of SS_{total} for a factorial design with two between-subjects factors. The computations for the four components, although requiring additional steps, entail little that is new. The key additions in this chapter are conceptual rather than computational. It is essential to understand that all of the following outcomes are possible:

1 Both IVs as well as the interaction are found to be non-significant.
2 One IV is found to be significant while the other IV and the interaction are both found to be non-significant.
3 Both IVs are found to be significant while the interaction is found to be non-significant.
4 Both IVs as well as the interaction are found to be significant.
5 Although neither IV is significant, the interaction is found to be significant.

Figure 11.1

 ## THE LOGIC OF THE FACTORIAL DESIGN: TWO BETWEEN-SUBJECTS INDEPENDENT VARIABLES

In this section we introduce the logical and procedural adjustments to ANOVA necessary for its application to a factorial design which has two between-subjects IVs. As in Chapter 8, we assume that the subjects are randomly assigned to conditions. At the level of the omnibus test, there are three elements to be added to the logic found in Chapter 9:

1 The partitioning of the $SS_{treatment/total}$ and $df_{treatment/total}$ into component elements.
2 The definition of the interaction component and deriving it as a residual.
3 The appropriate *F*-ratio for the testing of the new components.

Let us begin with a simple example. Figure 11.2 displays a 2 × 2 factorial design (two rows and two columns) with three subjects in each of four cells or conditions. The two rows (*A1* and *A2*) represent the two levels of IV *A* and the columns represent the two levels of IV *B* (*B1* and *B2*). If we forget about the factorial aspect of the design for a moment, you have an experiment with four treatment conditions. As such you might return to the one-way independent-samples ANOVA, with four conditions: *B1-A1, B1-A2, B2-A1, B2-A2*.

We begin by compiling descriptive statistics (Figure 11.3), looking for outliers, and testing for homogeneity of variance. The standard errors of the means are used to produce the error bars in a bar graph. The variances are used for testing homogeneity of variance. With all variance being equal, there is no question of violating the assumption of homogeneity. The standard deviation is used to test for outliers: values four standard deviations or more above or below their condition mean. No outliers are to be found. The four skewnesses (0.0) indicate that there is no problem with the assumption of normality.

	B1	B2	
A1	10	8	A1
	9	7	
	8	6	$\bar{Y} = 8$
	$\bar{Y} = 9$	$\bar{Y} = 7$	
A2	6	2	A2
	5	1	
	4	0	$\bar{Y} = 3$
	$\bar{Y} = 5$	$\bar{Y} = 1$	
	$B1\ \bar{Y} = 7$	$B2\ \bar{Y} = 4$	$GM = 5.5$

Figure 11.2

REVIEW QUESTION

After a cursory examination of Figure 11.3, what would be the MS_{error} for a one-way independent-samples (four treatment conditions) ANOVA on the data depicted in Figure 11.2? (No calculator is required.)

Web Link 11.2 for an answer to the review question.

Descriptive Statistics

	$\bar{Y}$	$S_{\bar{y}}$	S^2	S	Skewness
B1-A1	9	0.58	1.0	1.0	0.0
B1-A2	5	0.58	1.0	1.0	0.0
B2-A1	7	0.58	1.0	1.0	0.0
B2-A2	1	0.58	1.0	1.0	0.0

Figure 11.3

REVIEW QUESTION

Conduct a one-way (four treatment conditions) independent-samples ANOVA on the data depicted in Figure 11.2.

Web Link 11.3 for an answer to the review question.

If you completed the above review questions, you will have found the observed $F(3, 8)$ of 35.00 to be greater than the critical value 4.07, and thus H_0 is rejected. Three other aspects of your analysis to take note of are the SS_{total}, $SS_{treatment}$, and SS_{error}, which were 113, 105, and 8, respectively.

Recall that the numbers in the brackets following an F (in the current example $F(3, 8)$) indicate the $df_{treatment}$ and the df_{error}, respectively.

Now we return to the factorial model. It is most informative to begin as you did with the one-way analysis. In fact, most statistical software packages begin the analysis of factorial designs in this manner. Each of the four cells is considered a condition. Descriptive statistics are then produced for the four conditions. These are already available in Figures 11.2 and 11.3. Next we search for outliers and test for homogeneity of variance, as we did above. Once we have made any corrections, which were unnecessary in the current case, we proceed with constructing a graphic representation of the data. Figure 11.4 represents the four conditions clustered into pairs. The pair of bars on the left of the graph compares *B1* with *B2* at level 1 of *A*. The pair of bars on the right compares *B1* with *B2* at level 2 of *A*. The error bars represent one standard error of the mean for each condition. From the table it appears that the *B1* condition is superior to the *B2* condition at both levels of factor *A*. Furthermore, the average of *B1* and *B2* at *A1* is clearly greater than the average of *B1* and *B2* at *A2*. This difference indicates that the performance of *A1* is superior to that of *A2*. These two visual comparisons would indicate that both factor *A* and factor *B* influence the DV (i.e., *score*).

Finally, there is the issue of a possible interaction. That is, in order to answer the question about the effect of factor *B*, do we need to start with the phrase 'it depends'? Does it appear in Figures 11.3 and 11.4 that the differences between *B1* and *B2* are dissimilar at the two levels of *A*? The difference in their means at *A1* is 2 (9 − 7) and their difference at *A2* is 4 (5 − 1). The answer at this point is 'possibly'. A more definitive answer will require a statistical test. The question of the interaction can also be phrased with respect to the differences between *A1* and *A2* at the two levels of *B*. This alternative orientation or clustering is depicted in Figure 11.5. The difference in the means of *A1* and *A2* at *B1* is 4 (9 − 5) and the difference at *B2* is 6 (7 − 1). Should the interaction be significant when the conditions are clustered one way, the interaction is significant when the conditions are clustered the other way. The appropriate clustering for presentation and discussion is determined by the researcher's questions.

==================== REVIEW QUESTION ====================

How is the standard error of the mean calculated? What does it represent? Why do the error bars all appear to be identical in Figure 11.3?

Web Link 11.4 for an answer to the review question.

We begin partitioning the sum of squares as usual by computing the SS_{total}. There is no change in the formula used in Chapter 8:

$$SS_{total} = \Sigma(y_{cell\,j} - GM)^2,$$

The notation indicates the *GM* is subtracted from all scores within all of the cells, each difference is squared, and the squared differences are summed.

After subtracting the *GM* (5.0) from all 12 scores in Figure 11.2 and summing the square differences, you find the SS_{total} to be 113. Not surprisingly, this is what you found earlier when you conducted the one-way ANOVA on the four conditions. Despite the fact that we transformed the one-way ANOVA into a 2 × 2 (two rows and two columns) factorial design the data do not change, nor does the *GM*. Thus, the SS_{total} remains the same.

Next we compute the SS_{error}. There are two approaches to this, one forwards and one backwards. When we consider that the design may be regarded as a one-way ANOVA with four conditions, our best error term is the average within-condition variance. Cell *B1A1* is unaffected by any *B* effect, and it is also unaffected by any *A* affect. Both the *B* effect and the *A* effect are constants within any given cell. All we have within a cell are individual differences. Examining the *B1A1* and *B1A2* combined scores reveals that the variance within the column is far greater than the variance in *B1A1* and *B1A2* considered separately. This increase in the spread of the scores when *B1A1* and *B1A1* are combined is the product of the different *A* means in the two combined cells. Because we are in search of an estimate of population variance free of identifiable influences, it is the within-cell variance that is the best unit for estimating the SS_{error}. Therefore, we can compute it as we did in Chapter 8: $SS_{error} = \Sigma\Sigma(y_{cell\ j} - \bar{y}_j)^2$, where the mean of each cell is subtracted from all scores in that cell, and the differences are squared and summed. The process is repeated for all cells. As we saw in Chapter 8, we also can derive the SS_{error} by working backwards from the MS_{error}. It is the average within-cell (within-condition) variance. From Figure 11.3 we find

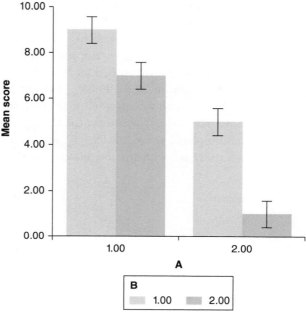

Figure 11.4

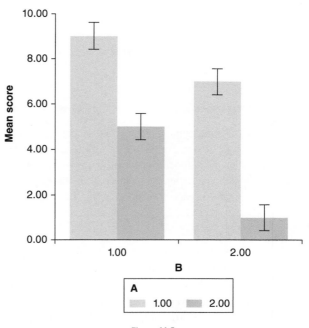

Figure 11.5

that in the present case it is $(1 + 1 + 1 + 1)/4 = 1$. Because $MS_{error} = SS_{error}/df_{error}$, we can easily solve for SS_{error} by multiplying the MS_{error} by the df_{error}. With three observations in each cell, there are 2 df per cell because the mean specific to each cell is used to calculate the variance. With four cells, there are a total of 8 df_{error}. Again, not surprisingly, this is what you found earlier when you conducted the one-way ANOVA on the four conditions (cells). The data within the cells did not change, nor did the cell means. Thus, the SS_{error} remains the same. (For discussion of MS_{error} being the average within-condition variance, see p. 331 in Chapter 8.)

We move on to the issue of the $SS_{treatment}$, now called the $SS_{treatment/total}$. In the one-way ANOVA you completed above, the $SS_{treatment}$ was 105. We now recognize that we have two IVs or factors: one associated with the row means and the other with the column means. We have used the term 'IV', but are they really independent? As usual, the term *independent* can be rephrased as *uncorrelated*. But which two variables in this case are uncorrelated? The two variables are the row and column designations. For row and column to be *independent* or *random* with respect to each other, the probability of an observation being a *B1* should be the same regardless of whether the observation is in an *A1* or an *A2* row. In terms of a correlation, all subjects can be assigned a score on the two variables: either a 1 or a 2 for their *A* condition and either a 1 or a 2 for their *B* condition (Figure 11.6). *A* and *B* can then be correlated. The result will be $r = 0$. (For a review of computing a correlation coefficient, see Chapter 7.)

Subject	A	B
1	1	1
2	1	1
3	1	1
4	1	2
5	1	2
6	1	2
7	2	1
8	2	1
9	2	1
10	2	2
11	2	2
12	2	2

Figure 11.6

· · · · ·

All of the computations in this section assume an equal number of observations in all conditions (cells). When the number of observations varies across cells, alterations to the computations can be made, but they are beyond the scope of this book. Statistical software packages, such as SPSS, have a standard method for correcting such imbalances. David Howell has an excellent description of the problem on his website: https://www.uvm.edu/~dhowell/StatPages/More_Stuff/Unequal-ns/unequal-ns.html

We now focus on partitioning the $SS_{treatment/total}$ into its components as depicted in Figure 11.7. Because the two treatment factors (*A* and *B*) are uncorrelated, they make independent contributions to the overall treatment. As such, you can analyse them separately. At this point we are about to conduct two one-way ANOVAs, one that ignores column distinction and one that ignores row distinction. To compute the SS_A we simply employ our standard formula for the $SS_{treatment}$. The means of interest in Figure 11.2 are those of *A1* (8) and *A2* (3). Substituting these means into the formula we find that

$$SS_A = n\Sigma(\bar{y}_{Aj} - GM)^2,$$

where $\bar{y}_{Aj}$ is the mean of the *A* scores in the *j*th *A* condition, and *n* is now the number of observations in an *A* condition (6). Thus,

$$SS_A = 6\Sigma[(8 - 5.5)^2 + (3 - 5.5)^2 = 75.$$

To compute the SS_B we again use our standard formula for $SS_{treatment}$. The means now of interest in Figure 11.2 are those of *B1* (7) and *B2* (4). Substituting these means into the formula we find

$$SS_B = n\Sigma(\bar{y}_{Bj} - GM)^2,$$

where $\bar{y}_{Bj}$ is the mean of the *B* scores in the *j*th *B* condition, and *n* is the number of observations in a *B* condition (6). The resulting $SS_B = 27$.

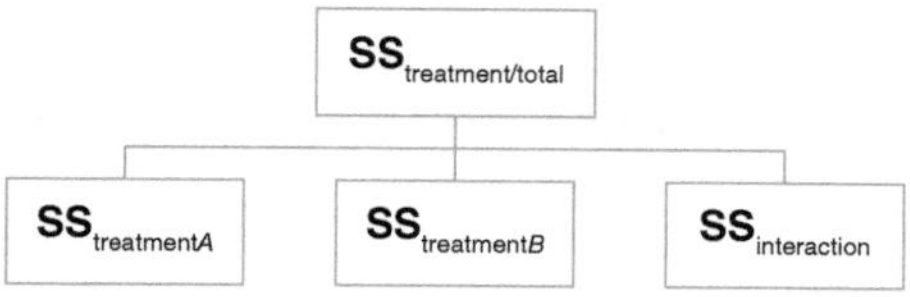

Summing the SS_A (75) and the SS_B (27) yields a total of 102. Recall that the one-way analysis resulted in $SS_{treatment} = 105$ (see p. 474).

Where is the difference of 3 hiding? When the SS_A and SS_B are subtracted from the $SS_{treatment/total}$, the residual, as it is often called, is the SS_{AB} or the $SS_{interaction}$. We have identified the sum of squares associated with the four components of SS_{total} as depicted in Figure 11.1.

Figure 11.7

There are two major components that comprise the difference between a score and the *GM*: treatment and error. Treatment in the case of a two-factor design is made of up three effects: the individual effects of each factor (*A* and *B*) plus the residual called the *interaction* (Figure 11.7).

The coefficient outside the Σ in all formulae always represents the number of observations that were used to calculate the first term in the binomial on the right of the Σ. When calculating the SS_{total} there appears to be no coefficient. When a coefficient is not present it is assumed to be 1.

Note that if the number of observations per cell varies, the correlation between the two factors will not be 0, and corrections to the computation of $SS_{treatment}$ will need to be made. When the conditions are correlated, the effect of one factor can spill over and influence the observed effect of the other factor. There are various methods used to address the problem. Howell (2013) neatly describes the problem, its consequences, and the default solution used by SPSS.

We can now complete an ANOVA summary table (Figure 11.8) for your 2×2 factorial design. As was the case with the earlier one-way analysis, the SS_{total} (113) comprises $SS_{treatment/total}$ (105) and SS_{error} (8). If you are interested in the overall treatment effect, you find a significant observed F-value of 35 ($\alpha = 0.05$). The critical value for an $F(3, 8)$ with 3 $df_{treatment}$ and 8 df_{error} is 4.07. Treatment is then partitioned into its three additive components. Notice that the SSs and the dfs for the three components sum to the $SS_{treatment/total}$ and the $df_{treatment/total}$. With two levels of factor A there is 1 $df_{treatment\ A}$; with two levels of factor B there is 1 $df_{treatment\ B}$. That leaves 1 $df_{interaction}$ derived as a residual. The MSs for the three treatment components are computed as usual by dividing the SS by the df.

As seen in the ANOVA summary table (Figure 11. 8), using the critical value for an F with 1 $df_{treatment}$ and 8 df_{error} (5.32), you reject H_0 in the case of the two IVs (A and B) and conclude that both factor A (($F(1, 8) = 75$, $MS_{error} = 75$, $p < 0.05$) and factor B ($F(1, 8) = 27$, $MS_{error} = 27$, $p < 0.05$) affect the DV. With respect to the interaction (AB), you do not reject H_0: $F(1, 8) = 3$, $MS_{error} = 3$, $p > 0.05$. You must conclude that there is insufficient evidence of an interaction. Bear in mind that Cohen's effect size and sample size tables (Appendix B) report values for only one-way ANOVAs. It is more challenging to calculate those values for factorial designs, particularly with respect to interaction effects. Although a thorough discussion is beyond the scope of this chapter, a detailed treatment of the issue can be found in Bausell and Li (2002).

The simplest strategy for estimating power or the necessary sample size for an interaction is to reduce the problem to a point where Cohen's table and values for a one-way ANOVA may be consulted. An interaction represents a difference in differences. That difference in differences can be considered the basis for calculating the f for the effect size. Similarly, the researcher can begin by determining how large an interaction effect is desired (small, medium, or large) for either theoretical or practical purposes. Then Cohen's sample size table (Table B.2) in Appendix B can be consulted to determine the required sample size for power of 0.80.

Interactions can come in two basic forms: *disordinal* and *ordinal*. Disordinal interactions involve a crossover and are difficult to explain. An interaction is disordinal if, for example, *B1* is superior to *B2* at one level of factor *A*, but *B1* is inferior to *B2* at another level of factor *A*. Ordinal interactions do not exhibit a cross-over, at least not within the value range of the IVs investigated. For example, *B1* may be only slightly superior to *B2* at one level of *A*, but may be greatly superior to *B2* at another level of *A*. We will explore both ordinal and disordinal interactions in more detail in the following sections.

---

11 ● 5   MAIN AND SIMPLE EFFECTS

We begin this section by differentiating between *main* and *simple* effects (McBurney & White, 2009). We then discuss the modifications to our ANOVA formulae necessary for testing simple effects.

ANOVA SUMMARY TABLE

Source		SS	df	MS	F	p-value (sig.)
Treatment total		105	3	35	35	< .05
	A	75	1	75	75	< .05
	B	27	1	27	27	< .05
	AB	3	1	3	3	ns
Within cell Error		8	8	1		
Total		**113**	**11**	**11**		

Figure 11.8

Main effects are the overall effects of each factor (IV) and are reported in the ANOVA summary table. For example, the tests for the effects of factors A and B in Figure 11.8 are examples of main effects. Stated another way, a main effect sums across all levels of the other factor(s) and is a test of marginal means. For example, in Figure 11.2 the main effect of A is the comparison of $A1$ ($\bar{y} = 8$) against $A2$ ($\bar{y} = 3$) and the main effect of B is the comparison of $B1$ ($\bar{y} = 7$) against $B2$ ($\bar{y} = 4$), which we have already computed.

Simple effects are the effects of one factor at individual levels of another factor. Testing the simple effects is a standard procedure when an interaction is found to be significant. Although in the current example the interaction is non-significant, for demonstration purposes we will proceed with testing the simple effects. There are two simple effects of factor A (Figure 11.2). The first is the difference between $A1$ ($\bar{y} = 9$) and $A2$ ($\bar{y} = 5$) at $B1$. The second is the difference between $A1$ ($\bar{y} = 7$) and $A2$ ($\bar{y} = 1$) at $B2$. There are also two simple effects of factor B. The first is the difference between $B1$ ($\bar{y} = 9$) and $B2$ ($\bar{y} = 7$) at $A1$ and the second is the difference between $B1$ ($\bar{y} = 5$) and $A2$ ($\bar{y} = 1$) at $A2$. Usually only one set of simple effects is tested, the set linked to the researcher's theoretical or practical question.

Simple effects require a conceptual reversal. They are analogous to conducting a one-way ANOVA. In terms of treatment, when we test for a simple effect of A at $B1$ we are acting as if the $B2$ column did not exist. We are only comparing $A1$ ($\bar{y} = 9$) and $A2$ ($\bar{y} = 5$) at $B1$ and thus require a GM specific to those two conditions. Because the ns are equal in the two conditions, in the current example the GM is $(9 + 5)/2$ or 7. The formula for the treatment term for the simple effect is, as usual,

$$SS_{A \text{ at } B1} = n\Sigma(\bar{y}_{Aj} - GM)^2 = 3\Sigma[(9 - 7)^2 + (5 - 7)^2] = 24.$$

Note that there are now four observations per condition.

In order to compute the $MS_{A \text{ at } B1}$ you require the appropriate df. There are two condition means, thus there is 1 $df_{A \text{ at } B1}$. This results in an $MS_{A \text{ at } B1}$ of 24.

All that is left is to determine the appropriate error term. If this were a simple one-way between-subjects ANOVA, you would use the average of the two within-condition variances for the error term. But, using the logic described in Chapter 10 for deriving the error terms for linear contrasts, why use only two estimates when you have four (the four condition variances)? (For a discussion of the logic for the appropriate SS and df for linear contrasts with a between-subjects design, see p. 427 in Chapter 10.)

Thus, the appropriate SS_{error} and the corresponding df_{error} are those used in Figure 11.8: 8 and 8, respectively. Thus $MS_{error} = 1$. The resulting observed $F(1, 8) = MS_{A \text{ at } B1} / MS_{error} = 24/1$ or 24. Because you have a family of two simple effects, the critical F-value in the 0.025 table is most appropriate. For 1 $df_{treatment}$ and 8 df_{error} the corresponding critical F-value is 7.57. Because your observed F-value (24) is greater than the critical value, you reject H_0 and conclude that there is a difference between the $A1$ and $A2$ conditions at the $B1$ level.

The same procedure is used to calculate the sample effect of A at level 2 of factor B. The difference is in the treatment term, in particular, in determining the appropriate GM. Because you are only comparing $A1$ ($\bar{y} = 7$) and $A2$ ($\bar{y} = 1$) at $B2$ the appropriate GM for calculating $SS_{A \text{ at } B2}$ is 4. The SS_{error} remains the same (8). The df for both the simple effect (1) and error (8) are unchanged. Thus,

$$SS_{A \text{ at } B2} = n\Sigma(\bar{y}_{Aj} - GM)^2 = 3\Sigma[(7-4)^2 + (1-4)^2] = 54.$$

The resulting observed $F(1, 8) = \dfrac{MS_{A \text{ at } B2}}{MS_{error}} = 54/1$ or 54. Again, because you have a family of two simple effects, you use the critical F-value in the 0.025 table (7.57). Because the observed F-value of 54 is greater than the critical value, you reject H_0 and conclude that there is a difference between the $A1$ and $A2$ at the $B2$ level.

━━━━━━━━━ REVIEW QUESTION ━━━━━━━━━

Complete the simple effects for the B factor at the two levels of factor A.

↘ Web Link 11.5 link for the answer to the review question.

11 ● 6   TWO BETWEEN-SUBJECTS FACTORIAL ANOVA WITH SPSS

Let us return to your hypothetical study on acquiring a new language described at the outset of the chapter. The literature indicates that (1) time spent in a language lab and (2) being bilingual both facilitate the acquisition of a new language. You hypothesize that the more time students spend in a language lab, the faster they will acquire a new language (main effect). You also hypothesize that bilingual students will acquire the new language faster (main effect). Furthermore, you hypothesize that the positive effect of the language lab will be greater for bilingual students than it will be for non-bilingual students (interaction). Your test for the two main effects is an attempt to replicate previous studies you have read. Replicating previous findings is important prior to testing new, hypothesized effects. The interaction effect is your new hypothesis.

To answer your research questions you recruit 30 undergraduate students from an introductory French course, half of whom are bilingual. Five students from each group are not offered a language lab session you have organized; five students from each group are assigned one hour per week in the language lab; and five students are assigned two hours per week. After six weeks the students are administered a mid-term examination. The students' marks are your DV. As usual, we begin with descriptive statistics and a graphical representation of the data. To follow along with the SPSS instructions, open the *langlearn2between.sav* SPSS data file on the book's web page.

Under *Analyze* in the SPSS *Data Editor* window, slide down to *General Linear Model,* then over and select *Univariate.* When the *Univariate* window opens, move *marks* to the *Dependent Variable* area and *bilingual* and *hourlanglab* to the *Fixed Factor(s)* area (Figure 11.9). Click *Options.* When the *Univariate: Options* window opens, check *Descriptive statistics, Estimates of effect size, Observed power,* and *Homogeneity tests* (Figure 11.10) and then click *Continue.* When you return to the *Univariate* window, click *Bootstrap.* When the *Bootstrap* window opens check *Perform bootstrapping* and *Set seed for Mersenne Twister* (Figure 11.11) and then *Continue.* When you return to the *Univariate* window, click *OK* to run the analysis.

The first table in the SPSS output window provides the *Bootstrapping Specifications*: the number of samples (1000) and the range of the confidence intervals (95%). The second table (*Between-Subjects Factors,* Figure 11.12) indicates the number of observations per level of each of the two between-subjects factors.

The first three columns of the next table (Figure 11.13) report the basic *Descriptive Statistics* (mean and standard deviation) by condition. In the next four columns the bootstrapping values are reported for the descriptive statistics. The nature of these bootstrapping statistics has been described in Chapters 2 and 4.

As mentioned in Chapter 8, the SPSS bootstrapping option available for an ANOVA only pertains to the descriptive statistics and not to the test statistics (e.g. *F*-values).

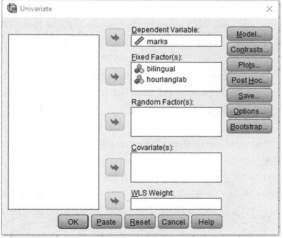

Figure 11.9

Figure 11.10

Figure 11.11

Between-Subjects Factors

		N
bilingual	.00	15
	1.00	15
hourlanglab	.00	10
	1.00	10
	2.00	10

Figure 11.12

Recall from previous chapters that what SPSS output labels *Type III Sum of Squares* is equivalent to what we have simply referred to as 'sum of squares'.

More detailed descriptive statistics are available through the *Descriptive Statistics* option under *Analyze* in the SPSS *Data Editor* window. These procedures were described in detail in Chapter 2. The primary use for the descriptive statistics at this point is to test for outliers, of which you find none in this data set.

The next table in the output window provides the results of Levene's test of homogeneity of variance (Figure 11.14). Because the p-value (*Sig.* = 0.462) is greater than 0.05, you can assume homogeneity of variance and no corrections need to be made.

Before examining the final table in the output window, it is appropriate to create a graphic representation of the data.

In the SPSS *Data Editor* window, select *Graphs* and click on *Chart Builder*. When the *Chart Builder* window opens (Figure 11.15), click *OK*.

When the next *Chart Builder* window opens, drag the second *Bar* example in the top row of the row of the choices into the *Chart preview* area above it (Figure 11.16). Then drag the DV (*marks*) from the *Variable* window to the *y-axis* area, drag *bilingual* to the *x-axis* area, and drag *hourlanglab* to the *Cluster on X* area. In the *Element Properties* panel to the side check *Display error bars*, select the *Standard error* option, and change the *Multiplier* from 2 to 1. Then click *Apply* at the bottom of the panel and then *OK* in the *Chart Builder* panel to produce the graph.

The graph appears in the SPSS output window (Figure 11.17). You can see from the graph that the bilingual students (bilingual 1.00), regardless of language lab condition, performed in general better than did the non-bilingual students (bilingual 0.00).

Next let us examine the *Tests of Between-Subjects Effects* table in the SPSS output (Figure 11.18). A few terminological issues should be cleared up before addressing issues of significance. The values in the top row of the table (*Corrected Model*) refer to what we have called $SS_{treatment/total}$, $df_{treatment/total}$ and $MS_{treatment/total}$. The values in the row labelled *Error* correspond to the SS_{error}, df_{error} and MS_{error} as we have also referred to them. The values in the bottom row (*Corrected Total*) and *not* in the row labelled *Total* represent what we have referred to as SS_{total}, df_{total} and MS_{total}. The $SS_{treatment/total}$ plus the SS_{error} sum to the SS_{total} (*Corrected Total*), as they should. The same is true for their corresponding degrees of freedom. Additionally, the $SS_{bilingual}$, the $SS_{hourlanglab}$, and the $SS_{bilingual \times hourlanglab}$ (interaction) sum to the $SS_{treatment/total}$ (*Corrected Model*). The same is also true for their corresponding degrees of freedom.

Descriptive Statistics

Dependent Variable: marks

bilingual	hourlanglab		Statistic	Bootstrap[a]			
				Bias	Std. Error	95% Confidence Interval	
						Lower	Upper
.00	.00	Mean	20.4002	.0473[b]	1.0094[b]	18.5000[b]	22.3401[b]
		Std. Deviation	2.30212	-.38902[g]	.74109[g]	.00063[g]	3.21455[g]
		N	5	0[b]	2[b]	2[b]	9[b]
	1.00	Mean	34.2000	-.0316[d]	2.1218[d]	29.6667[d]	38.2033[d]
		Std. Deviation	4.76445	-.74510[i]	1.58726[i]	.61348[i]	6.63024[i]
		N	5	0[d]	2[d]	1[d]	9[d]
	2.00	Mean	46.8000	-.1267[f]	2.0595[f]	42.3333[f]	50.5000[f]
		Std. Deviation	4.65833	-.82801[h]	1.58434[h]	.50000[h]	6.50641[h]
		N	5	0[f]	2[f]	1[f]	9[f]
	Total	Mean	33.8001	.0284	3.0669	28.0021	39.9959
		Std. Deviation	11.77882	-.54735	1.42871	8.22307	13.73305
		N	15	0	3	10	20
1.00	.00	Mean	49.4000	.0188[e]	1.2413[e]	46.6667[e]	52.0000[e]
		Std. Deviation	2.88097	-.43912[h]	.80483[h]	.50000[h]	3.78343[h]
		N	5	0[e]	2[e]	1[e]	9[e]
	1.00	Mean	64.6000	.0740[e]	3.4184[e]	57.8272[e]	71.5000[e]
		Std. Deviation	7.63544	-1.43896[j]	2.50113[j]	.00000[j]	10.39230[j]
		N	5	0[e]	2[e]	1[e]	9[e]
	2.00	Mean	90.8000	-.0362[e]	2.4070[e]	86.0000[e]	95.0000[e]
		Std. Deviation	5.63028	-.89942[k]	1.89453[k]	.57735[k]	8.15935[k]
		N	5	0[e]	2[e]	1[e]	10[e]
	Total	Mean	68.2667	.1505	4.7888	58.7783	78.0000
		Std. Deviation	18.47572	-.80262	2.12734	12.66621	21.37313
		N	15	0	3	10	20
Total	.00	Mean	34.9001	.0455	4.8014	25.4029	44.1992
		Std. Deviation	15.48069	-.91236	1.92206	10.18707	16.93771
		N	10	0	3	5	15
	1.00	Mean	49.4000	.0323	5.2426	39.3333	59.8861
		Std. Deviation	17.10880	-1.00506	2.33816	11.03572	19.91625
		N	10	0	3	5	15
	2.00	Mean	68.8000	-.0372	7.4999	54.0000	83.6193
		Std. Deviation	23.69623	-1.45415	2.99867	15.22400	26.22389
		N	10	0	3	5	16
	Total	Mean	51.0334	.1522	4.1990	43.5676	59.7333

Figure 11.13

Levene's Test of Equality of Error Variances[a]

Dependent Variable: marks

F	df1	df2	Sig.
.959	5	24	.462

Tests the null hypothesis that the error variance of the dependent variable is equal across groups.

a. Design: Intercept + bilingual + hourlanglab + bilingual * hourlanglab

Figure 11.14

As seen in the *Tests of Between-Subjects Effects* table, the bilingual students significantly outperformed their monolingual counterparts: $F(1, 24) = 361.20$, $MS_{error} = 24.667$, $p < 0.001$. SPSS reports a partial eta squared of 0.938. If you wish to report the standard η^2 instead of the partial eta squared, you simply need to divide the $SS_{bilingual}$ by the SS_{total} (*Corrected Total*):

$$\eta^2 = \frac{8909.594}{15630.896} = 0.569.$$

As also seen in the table, the number of hours spent in the language lab (*hourlanglab*) significantly improved performance on the exam: $F(2, 24) = 117.285$, $MS_{error} = 24.667$, $p < 0.001$. SPSS reports a partial eta squared of 0.907. Finally, the interaction (bilingual × hourlanglab) is significant: $F(2, 24) = 6.958$, $MS_{error} = 24.667$, $p = 0.004$. SPSS reports a partial eta squared of 0.367. Thus, the main effects we have reported must be qualified. For example, if someone were to ask you what the effect of being bilingual is on acquiring another language, you would need to say, 'it depends'. It depends on how much time they spend in a language lab.

═══ REVIEW QUESTION ═══

What is a potential problem with reporting partial eta squared? How might it pertain to your current findings?

Web Link 11.6 for an answer to the review question.

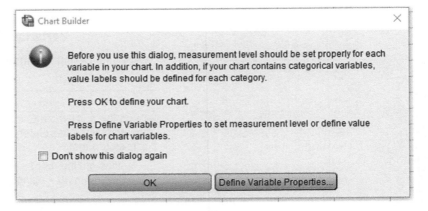

Figure 11.15

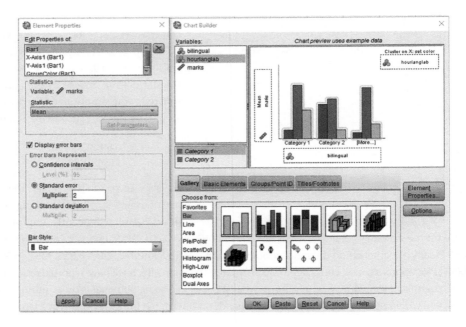

Figure 11.16

As stated above, significant interactions are similar to omnibus tests; they tell you there is an effect, but not necessarily the nature or the location of the effect. If we re-examine the graph of your data, it appears that the interaction has something to do with the performance of the bilingual students in the 2 hours per week language lab condition. That cell stands out. In fact, sometimes interactions are called 'cell' effects, while row and column effects are called 'main' effects. If we further compare the means of the bilingual and monolingual students across the three *hourlanglab* conditions (0, 1, and 2) separately, we find that the differences are 29.0, 30.4, and 44.0, respectively. It is very likely that the difference in the *hourlanglab* = 2 condition is the source of the interaction. But this neither fully describes the interaction nor is it a statistical test. More detailed analyses of simple effects will be provided later in the chapter in the section on mixed designs.

The interaction found in your language acquisition data is an example of an *ordinal* interaction. Ordinal interactions do not exhibit a cross-over. That is, the ordinal rankings of the levels of one variable do not change across levels of another variable. For example, in your data the bilingual students outperformed the monolingual students across all levels of the *hourlanglab* factor.

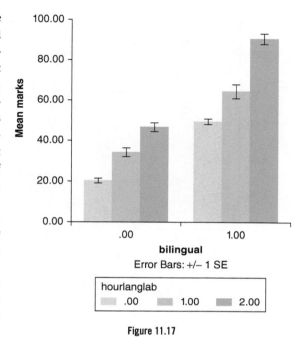

Figure 11.17

Tests of Between-Subjects Effects

Dependent Variable: marks

Source	Type III Sum of Squares	df	Mean Square	F	Sig.	Partial Eta Squared	Noncent. Parameter	Observed Power[b]
Corrected Model	15038.897[a]	5	3007.779	121.937	.000	.962	609.686	1.000
Intercept	78132.149	1	78132.149	3167.524	.000	.992	3167.524	1.000
bilingual	8909.594	1	8909.594	361.200	.000	.938	361.200	1.000
hourlanglab	5786.030	2	2893.015	117.285	.000	.907	234.569	1.000
bilingual * hourlanglab	343.273	2	171.636	6.958	.004	.367	13.916	.890
Error	591.999	24	24.667					
Total	93763.045	30						
Corrected Total	15630.896	29						

a. R Squared = .962 (Adjusted R Squared = .954)

b. Computed using alpha = .05

Figure 11.18

• • • • •

It is difficult to analyse simple effects in SPSS without needing to actually do a bit of programming. For those who are interested in how it is done, the Institute for Digital Research and Education has worked through an example on the web page http://www.ats.ucla.edu/stat/spss/faq/sme.htm

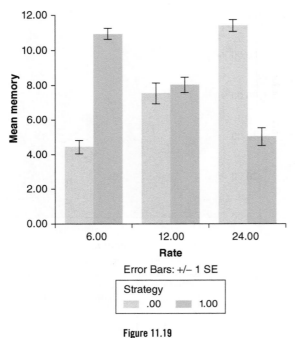

Error Bars: +/– 1 SE

Figure 11.19

Figure 11.19 illustrates a strong cross-over or *disordinal* interaction. Imagine the data depicted in the figure represent a memory experiment involving a paired-associate paradigm. During the experiment's study phase, subjects are presented with a list of pairs of words (e.g., alligator–thermometer). During the test phase subjects are presented with the first member of each pair and are asked to recall the second member. There are two factors or IVs: *strategy* and *rate*. The *strategy* factor has two levels. The first consists of a group of subjects who are told to simply repeat the pairs of words over and over again (*strategy* = 0). The second group are told to create a sentence using the pair of words (*strategy* = 1). The *rate* factor pertains to how many pairs of words were presented per minute during the study phase. There are three rates: 6, 12, and 24 pairs per minute. The DV is the number of words correctly recalled (*memory*) when subjects are presented with the first half of the pairing.

As can been seen from Figure 11.19, at the slowest *rate* (6) subjects in the *strategy* 1 condition correctly recalled more words than those subjects in the *strategy* 0 condition. At the fastest *rate* (24) subjects in the *strategy* 1 condition correctly recalled far fewer words than did subjects in the *strategy* 0 condition.

Tests of Between-Subjects Effects

Dependent Variable: memory

Source	Type III Sum of Squares	df	Mean Square	F	Sig.	Partial Eta Squared
Corrected Model	210.424[a]	5	42.085	43.435	.000	.900
Intercept	1869.393	1	1869.393	1929.352	.000	.988
Strategy	.311	1	.311	.321	.576	.013
Rate	1.558	2	.779	.804	.459	.063
Strategy * Rate	208.555	2	104.277	107.622	.000	.900
Error	23.254	24	.969			
Total	2103.071	30				
Corrected Total	233.678	29				

a. R Squared = .900 (Adjusted R Squared = .880)

Figure 11.20

At the intermediate *rate* (12), there was little difference in the recall between the subjects in the two *strategy* conditions. Combining the data from the two strategies within the three rates gives the impression that on average the performances of the subjects were no different at the different rates. We would be left with the impression that neither of the two factors influenced the *memory* performance.

The *Test of Between-Subjects Effects* table (Figure 11.20) illustrates how the apparent absence of main effects can be very misleading. Neither main effects factor (*strategy*, *rate*) was significant. This is confirmed by the means of the two *strategy* conditions in the *Descriptive*

Descriptive Statistics

Dependent Variable: memory

Strategy	Rate	Mean	Std. Deviation	N
.00	6.00	4.4334	.85483	5
	12.00	7.5350	1.34160	5
	24.00	11.4079	.72799	5
	Total	7.7921	3.09775	15
1.00	6.00	10.9500	.69160	5
	12.00	8.0200	.99124	5
	24.00	5.0169	1.13669	5
	Total	7.9956	2.65952	15
Total	6.00	7.6917	3.51191	10
	12.00	7.7775	1.14104	10
	24.00	8.2124	3.48649	10
	Total	7.8939	2.83864	30

Figure 11.21

Statistics table (Figure 11.21): for *strategy* 0, $\bar{y}$ = 7.7921; for *strategy* 1, $\bar{y}$ = 7.9956. The *rate* means produce a similar picture: *rate* 6, $\bar{y}$ = 7.6917; *rate* 12, $\bar{y}$ = 7.7775; *rate* 24, $\bar{y}$ = 8.2124. Nearly all of the $SS_{treatment/total}$ (*Corrected Model*, 210.424) is accounted for by the $SS_{strategy \times rate}$ (interaction, 208.555).

In such a case of substantial cross-over effects, it is misleading to say that the primary factors (*strategy* and *rate*) have no effect. They do have an effect. Their effects are *conditional*, however, analogously to the way we spoke of *conditional probabilities* in Chapter 3. In this study, the strategy of constructing a sentence had a strong positive effect in the slow rate condition. On the other hand, at the fastest rate with increased time pressure the strategy was quite detrimental. Knowing how other variables might conditionalize the effect of important factors can be especially revealing when the researcher is concerned with ecological validity.

━━━━━━━ CHALLENGE QUESTION ━━━━━━━

Run two one-way, between-subjects ANOVAs on the data in the *Descriptive Statistics* table: one analysis using *strategy* as the IV and the other using *rate*. How do the SS_{total}, $SS_{treatment}$ (for the factor being analysed), and SS_{error} for your one-way analyses compare to those in the *Test of Between-Subjects Effects* table from the factorial analysis?

↘ Web Link 11.7 for an answer to the challenge question.

• • • • •

Factorial designs are not limited to two factors. Designs with three or more factors are not uncommon. The more factors, the more complicated the interaction picture becomes. For example, with three factors, there can be a significant three-way interaction, which must be understood in terms of the possible significant two-way interactions that underlie it before the tests of simple effects become relevant.

11 ● 7 FIXED VERSUS RANDOM FACTORS

In this section we distinguish between *fixed* and *random* factors or IVs. The distinction has implications for (1) the computation of *F*-values and (2) the limitations placed on the generalization of the experiment's findings. The distinction between fixed and random factors is related to the concepts of *sample* and *population*. To all intents and purposes, when the IV is a fixed factor we have the entire population of IV levels. When the IV is a random factor we have only a sample of the population of IV levels.

Most experimental research involves fixed factors. In the previous example, you wished to explore the effects of *study strategy* and *rate of presentation* on recall. You decided *a priori* which two strategies you would test: repetition and sentence construction. You also decided *a priori* the rates at which the pairs of words would be presented. The key Latin phrase in both of the previous sentences is *a priori*. When the levels of the IV are decided upon *a priori* by the researcher, the factor is fixed. There are usually practical or theoretical reasons for the chosen levels of the IVs. That is why most experimental IVs are fixed in nature.

If a researcher *randomly* chooses the levels of the IV from the possible levels then the factor is random. Random factors are more common in applied areas of research. Imagine that you wish to test for a difference between two specific study guides in first-year calculus. You are at a large university that offers 10 sections of the course. You plan to use only four sections in your study. If you choose the four sections because the instructors of those sections are your friends, or are all women, or are of any other category, the factor is fixed. On the other hand, if you write down the 10 section numbers and drop them in a bag and then reach in and pull four out, then *section* is a random variable.

There are clear implications for generalizing the researcher's results. When the factor is fixed, strictly speaking, you, the researcher, may only generalize to those levels you included in the experiment (e.g., you can only speak of the relative effectiveness of those two particular study guides). When the factor is random, as it would have been had you selected your instructors out of a bag, then you would be freer to generalize to other instructors who were not selected. There are designs where generalization of the results related to a fixed factor may be extended. Such cases involve a quantitative IV. Imagine an experiment where dosage of an anxiolytic drug is a fixed factor: 0 mg, 5 mg, and 10 mg. The DV was the reported severity of panic attack symptoms. If the researcher found that, as dosage increased, the severity of reported symptoms declined and there was a significant linear polynomial trend, then he or she would be free to interpolate the results. That is, generalizing the results to dosages within the range studied (e.g., 2.5 mg) is usually deemed admissible. Extrapolating the results is usually considered inappropriate. That is, generalizing the findings to dosages well above the highest dosage (10 mg) would not be admissible. It cannot be assumed that the linear function will continue *ad infinitum*.

The implications for the calculation of the *F*-value are contradictory to what is often assumed. Only a cursory treatment of the topic is within the scope of this book. Those wishing a detailed description of the issues involved when a random IV is included in an experimental design should consult Jackson and Brashers (1994). Assuming a between-subjects design with two factors, the presence of a random IV alters the error term that is appropriate for the fixed factor. When the fixed-factor condition means are calculated they are summing across a sample of the effects of the random factor, rather than across the population of effects of another fixed factor. As a consequence, the expected value of the $MS_{fixedfactor}$ includes both the effect of the fixed factor (if there is any) and error, and any fixed-factor–random-factor interaction (if there is any). This problem does not exist for the random factor because its means are summed across the population of the fixed-factor effects, which will sum to zero.

Figure 11.22 shows the components of the expected values of the two factors and the interaction term. The general principle for choice of an error term is that it should contain all components of the treatment term being evaluated except for the one element being tested. Thus, if H_0 is true (the element identified with the treatment factor has no effect) then $E(F) = 1$. As seen in the table, the appropriate error term for testing the random factor and the interaction term is the usual error term. The appropriate error term for the fixed factor, however, is the interaction term! If H_0 is true the *F*-ratio is composed of

$$\frac{\text{interaction plus error}}{\text{interaction plus error}},$$

and $E(F) = 1$. If H_0 is false the *F*-ratio is composed of

$$\frac{\text{effect of fixed factor} + \text{interaction plus error}}{\text{interaction plus error}},$$

and $E(F) > 1$.

Because the degrees of freedom associated with the interaction term are usually substantially fewer than those associated with the standard error term, testing the fixed factor with the interaction term involves a considerable loss of power. There are various approaches to correcting this shortcoming, some of which are described in Jackson and Brashers (1994).

E(MS)	Treatment (fixed)	Treatment (random)	interaction	error
E(fixed)	yes	no	yes	yes
E(random)	no	yes	no	yes
E(interaction)	no	no	no	yes
E(error)	no	no	no	yes

Figure 11.22

11 ● 8 THE SPLIT-PLOT OR MIXED-DESIGN ANOVA

The split-plot factorial design is also referred to as a mixed-design ANOVA. Regardless of the name, in this design there are two factors (IVs): one of them is a between-subjects factor (group) and the other is a within-subjects factor (repeated measures). Subjects are randomly assigned to groups, but all subjects are tested in multiple treatment conditions. This leads to the first complication concerning the error term. We can no longer use the average within-condition variance as the MS_{error}. As will be seen, the average within-condition variance will be inappropriate for testing the (1) within-subjects factor main effect, (2) the between-subjects factor main effect, as well as (3) the interaction.

As we saw in Section 11.3, the additional variable in a factorial design is a true IV. Furthermore, the factorial design allows us to explore possible interactions. In the mixed-design ANOVA there is an additional feature. One of the IVs is a between-subjects factor and the other IV is a within-subjects factor. This additional feature makes the presentation of the partitioning of the difference between a score and the GM slightly more complex. The difference between a score and the GM may still be described as

> If you are thinking that the term 'split-plot' is agricultural in origin, you are correct. The term's origins can be traced back to the splitting of the plots of farmers' fields into sections in order to test both fertilizer and different seed types simultaneously (two factors). All seed types are used in each plot, with one fertilizer per plot. Fertilizer represents the between-subjects factor and seed type represents the within-subjects factor.

$$\text{score} - GM = \text{effect of IV}_1 + \text{effect of IV}_2 + \text{effect of interaction between IV}_1 \text{ and IV}_2 + \text{error.}$$

The complication is that within the error component there are two categories of error.

Figure 11.23 depicts the partitioning of the SS_{total} for a split-plot design. The computations for the three components of the $SS_{treatment/total}$ are unchanged from the two between-subjects analysis. They cannot change. The condition means, the GM, and the number of observations per condition remain the same, regardless of the design. The important modification in the computations concerns the two error terms we now have. This is not surprising since, as we saw in Chapter 5 with respect to t-tests and in Chapter 8 with respect to ANOVAs, the error terms for between-subjects designs and within-subjects designs are different. It is important to understand the following points with respect to the mixed design:

> Bear in mind that the SS_{total} cannot change. Both the scores and the GM remain the same, regardless of how the design is conceived.

1 The SS_{total} is no different from what it would have been had the experiment been a two between-subjects design.

2 The $SS_{treatment/total}$ will be the sum of the $SS_{factor\ 1/group}$, $SS_{factor\ 2/treatment}$ and $SS_{interaction}$, and is no different from what it would have been had the experiment been a two between-subjects design.

3   SS_{error} *in total* is no different from what it would have been had the experiment been a two between-subjects design.

4   In a mixed design, the total SS_{error} is split: a portion will be associated with the between-subjects factor (now called *group*) and the remainder will be associated with the within-subjects factor (often called *treatment*).

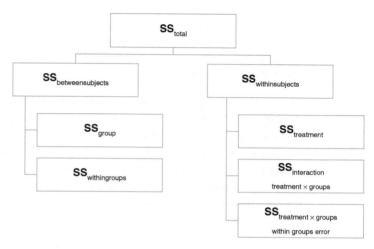

Figure 11.23

As can be seen from Figure 11.23, just as in Chapter 9, when there is a repeated-measures (within-subjects) IV, the first step in the analysis, after computing descriptive statistics and testing assumptions, will be to separate the between-subjects sum of squares from the within-subjects sum of squares. The difference between the mixed-design analysis and the one-way repeated-measures analysis is that in the mixed design we have an error term on the between-subjects side of the partition. The other point of interest is that the interaction term is identified as a within-subjects factor. It could not be otherwise. At a simple level, on the between-subjects side of the partition, the subjects have only one score, averaged across all treatment conditions. On the within-subjects side of the partition, each subject has multiple scores and the group effect is different for different groups of subjects. For a more detailed analysis of partitioning of the treatment sum of squares in a split-plot design, see Girden (1992, Chapter 5).

Although your computer and SPSS can do the work for you, it is worthwhile to walk through the formulae to get an understanding of the logic, the typical names of the components, and how they all fit together into the whole. Figure 11.24 parallels Figure 11.23 and inserts the formulae. Before walking through Figure 11.24 we need to compute a familiar calculation: $SS_{treatment/total}$, which is labelled $SS_{trt/tot}$ in the diagram. As you will recall, $SS_{treatment/total} = n\Sigma(\bar{y} - GM)^2$, where the GM is subtracted from each of the condition (or cell) means, the differences are squared, the squared differences are summed, and then multiplied by the number of observations in a condition. Remember that, for purposes of this chapter, a condition is a *cell*, not a row or column.

$$SS_{total} = \Sigma\Sigma\Sigma(y - GM)^2$$

$$SS_{bs} = n\Sigma(\bar{y} - GM)^2 \qquad SS_{ws} = SS_{total} - SS_{bs}$$

$$SS_{grp} = n\Sigma(\bar{y}_{grp} - GM)^2 \qquad SS_{trt} = n\Sigma(\bar{y}_{trt} - GM)^2$$

$$SS_{wrgp} = SS_{bs} - SS_{grp} \qquad SS_{int} = SS_{trt/tot} - SS_{grp} - SS_{trt}$$

$$SS_{trt\times grp/error} = SS_{ws} - SS_{trt} - SS_{int}$$

Examining Figure 11.24, the first logical step is to compute the SS_{total}. As always, the GM is subtracted from

Figure 11.24

All of the computations in this section, as in the section on between-subjects designs, assume an equal number of observations in all conditions, in all rows (groups), and in all columns (treatments).

all observations in all conditions (cells) in all rows and in all columns; that is, from *all* observations. This is indicated by the triple summation sign outside of the brackets. When there is a repeated-measures factor, the next step is to segregate the between-subjects and the within-subjects sums of squares. The simplest strategy is to compute the sum-of-squares between subjects (SS_{bs}) and then subtract that from the SS_{total}. This in effect creates two one-way ANOVAs, one on each side of the partitioning, one a between-subjects ANOVA (on the left-hand side), and one a repeated-measures ANOVA with a twist (on the right-hand side). The twist is the presence of the interaction term. Each side of the partitioning has its own new sum-of-squares total: $SS_{total/between}$ and $SS_{total/within}$. These two new sum-of-squares totals correspond to the SS_{bs} and SS_{ws} in Figure 11.24.

Between-subjects analysis

We first address the between-subjects side. Previously in Chapter 9 when we had a one-way repeated-measures design we similarly partitioned off the SS_{bs}. This is done to remove the correlation between the treatment conditions and simultaneously increase the statistical power by reducing the SS_{error}. (See Chapter 5 for a discussion of the error term of repeated-measures *t*-test and Chapter 9 for a discussion of the repeated-measures ANOVA error term.)

In the present case, however, rather than only individual differences on the between-subjects side of the partition, there are also differences *between groups* of subjects. Once we have more than one group, we can calculate the sums of squares associated with a possible group effect. These sums of squares are identified in Figure 11.24 by SS_{grp}: the *GM* is subtracted from each of the group means, the differences are squared and summed, and the total is multiplied by the number of observations in each group. Recall, from above, that group (grp) is one of our treatment components. If we treat $SS_{total/between}$ as the new SS_{total} and SS_{grp} as sum-of-squares treatment, and if we subtract the latter from the former, we obtain the SS_{error}, labelled SS_{wgrp} in Figure 11.24. Structurally, we have the equivalent of a one-way, between-subjects ANOVA.

The next task is to determine the associated degrees of freedom. Recall, from Chapters 5 and 9, that the degrees of freedom 'lost' to the between-subjects side of the partition are the number of subjects minus one, $(n - 1)$; this is considered the new $df_{grp/total}$. Next we can easily derive the df_{grp} (our treatment term) by subtracting one from the number of groups (treatment conditions) we have: $k - 1$. Finally, the df_{wgrp} (our error term) can be derived as a residual: $df_{grp/total} - df_{grp} = (n - 1) - (k - 1)$.

All that is left is to compute the MSs by dividing SS_{grp} by df_{grp} and by dividing SS_{wgrp} by df_{wgrp}. The observed *F*-value for the *group* factor is MS_{grp}/MS_{wgrp}. The resulting *F* is evaluated with df_{grp} (treatment) and df_{wgrp} (error) in the $\alpha = 0.05$ *F*-table (Table G.1 in Appendix G). Notice that all of this is done to obtain the appropriate error term (SS, df, and MS) for testing the *group* factor.

Within-subjects side

We now turn our attention to the within-subjects side of the partition. The correlation between the repeated-measures treatment conditions – a violation of a critical assumption – has been eliminated by removing the sums of squares associated with the individual differences and moving them to the between-subjects side of the partition. Save for the matter of the interaction, we can now treat this side of the partition as a one-way, between-subjects design (yes, a between-subjects design). The new SS_{total} is the SS_{ws} as depicted in Figure 11.24. The $SS_{treatment}$ (now labelled SS_{trt} in the figure) is calculated as any treatment effects are calculated: the GM is subtracted from each of the treatment means, the differences are squared and summed, then the total is multiplied by the number of observations in each treatment. Next we deal with the twist mentioned above, the interaction term. It can be derived as a residual, just as it was when we examined the two between-subjects factors design. The sums of squares from the two treatment effects (now referred to as the group and the treatment factors) are subtracted from the sum of squares treatment total which we calculated at the outset of this analysis: $SS_{treatment/total} = n\Sigma(\bar{y} - GM)^2$, where the GM is subtracted from each of the condition (or cell) means, the differences are squared, summed, and then multiplied by the number of observations in a condition (cells). Thus, the sum-of-squares interaction is

$$SS_{int} = SS_{trt/tot} - SS_{grp} - SS_{trt},$$

as defined in Figure 11.24.

Finally, the $SS_{trt \times grp/error}$ (our error term) is derived as a residual:

$$SS_{ws} - SS_{grp} - SS_{int}.$$

Now we need to determine the associated degrees of freedom. We begin with the df_{total}. The degrees of freedom associated with the between-subjects side of the partition were $n - 1$. Thus, $df_{ws} = df_{total} - df_{bs} = df_{ws} = df_{total} - n - 1$. This represents the new total df for our analysis on the within-subjects side of the partition. The df associated with the treatment factor (df_{trt}) is derived as usual, the number of treatments minus one: $k - 1$. The df associated with the interaction (df_{int}) term are derived in the same manner as was the sum of squares for the interaction:

$$df_{int} = df_{trt/tot} - df_{grp} - df_{trt}.$$

The df from the two treatment effects (now referred to as the group and treatment factors) are subtracted from the df treatment total. The $df_{treatment/total}$ are the number of cells (conditions) minus one. Finally, the $df_{trt \times grp/error}$ (our error term) are derived as a residual:

$$df_{trt \times grp/error} = df_{ws} - df_{trt} - df_{int}.$$

■■■■ ● ● ● ● ● ■■■■

Another way to think of the $df_{\text{treatment/total}}$ is first to consider the design as a one-way analysis. How many conditions are there? The number of conditions (k) equals the number of row conditions times the number of column conditions. The $df_{\text{treatment/total}}$ are $k - 1$, as in any one-way analysis. The row df are the number of rows minus 1. The column df are the number of columns minus 1. Thus, the df_{int} are $df_{\text{treatment/total}} - df_{\text{row}} - df_{\text{column}}$.

All that remains is to compute (1) the MS_{trt} by dividing SS_{trt} by df_{trt}, (2) the MS_{int} by dividing SS_{int} by df_{int}, (3) the $MS_{\text{trt} \times \text{grp/error}}$ by dividing $SS_{\text{trt} \times \text{grp/error}}$ by $df_{\text{trt} \times \text{grp/error}}$. The observed F-value for the *treatment* factor is $MS_{\text{trt}}/MS_{\text{trt} \times \text{grp/error}}$, and the observed F-value for the *interaction* term is $MS_{\text{int}}/MS_{\text{trt} \times \text{grp/error}}$. The *treatment* F is evaluated with df_{trt} (treatment) and $df_{\text{trt} \times \text{grp/error}}$ (error) using the F-table for $\alpha = 0.05$ (Table G.1 in Appendix G). The *interaction* F is evaluated with df_{int} (treatment) and $df_{\text{trt} \times \text{grp/error}}$ (error) in the same table. Notice that all of this is done to obtain the appropriate error term (SS, df, and MS) for testing the *treatment* and *interaction* factors. Other than changing labels, such as *factor A* for *group* factor, all calculations remain unchanged. In terms of the differences within the treatment terms, we know the *expected values*. The H_0 is that scores are random by condition – that there are no differences among the condition means. This section is needed to illustrate how to determine *what is expected due to chance alone* (the error term) for evaluating the treatment terms on the two sides of the partition.

11 ● 9 ANALYSING A MIXED-DESIGN ANOVA WITH SPSS

For the purposes of this section you will analyse a fictitious experiment. The data for this example are found on the book's web page: SPSS file *furelisesplitplot.sav*.

Imagine that you teach piano in the music department at your university. The problem of performance anxiety has always been around and has impaired the performance of many piano students. You have noticed that although almost all of your students report being anxious about performing in public, not all appeared negatively affected. Furthermore, from observing your students playing in practice rooms, you suspect that performance anxiety has little effect on non-public playing. You have developed the idea that the public performance of students with severe performance anxiety will be affected negatively, while those with less severe cases of performance anxiety show little or no effect during public performance.

To test your suspicions you administer the self-report Performance Anxiety Test (PAT) to your current cohort of 19 piano students. From the 19, you select those 5 students with the lowest PAT scores (group 1) and those 5 students with the highest PAT scores (group 2). The higher the PAT score, the greater the self-reported performance anxiety. You now have two groups of piano students: low and high PAT. You then test all 10 under two conditions. In the first treatment condition (*nonpublic*), you have all 10 students, alone in a practice room, playing and recording Beethoven's *Für Elise*, a piece all of your students have played with little difficulty for several years.

In the second treatment condition (*public*), all students play and record *Für Elise* in front of the class of 19 students. You then have a colleague listen to each student's recording and count the number of errors made during the three-minute piece of music. Figure 11.25 depicts the data from the 10 piano students as they appear in the SPSS *Data Editor* window. The DV recorded in the *nonpublic* and *public* columns is the number of errors the student made.

The reporting of descriptive statistics and the testing of assumptions can almost entirely be accomplished during the running of the mixed-design analysis in SPSS.

To conduct the analysis in SPSS, select *Analyze* at the top of the *Data Editor* window, move down to *General Linear Model*, and slide over to and click on *Repeated Measures*. When the *Repeated Measures Define Factor(s)* window opens (Figure 11.26) enter a '2' in the *Number of Levels* box, click *Add*, and then *Define*. When the *Repeated Measures* window opens (Figure 11.27) highlight and move the variable *nonpublic* to the first line in the *Within-Subjects Variables (factor1)* area and then highlight and move the variable *public* to the second line. Then highlight and move the variable *Group* to the *Between-Subjects Factor(s)* area. Here we have identified the treatment or repeated-measures factor (*nonpublic–public*) and the between-subjects group factor (*Group*).

Next select the *Options* button. When the *Univariate: Options* window opens, check *Descriptive statistics, Estimate of effect size, Observed power,* and *Homogeneity tests* (Figure 11.28). Click *Continue.* When you return to the *Repeated Measures* window, click *Plots*. When the *Repeated Measures: Profile Plots* window opens (Figure 11.29), highlight and move the variable *Group* to the *Separate Lines* area, then move the variable *factor1* (which is the *nonpublic–public* within-subjects variable) to the *Horizontal Axis* area, click *Add*, and then *Continue.* When you return to the main *Repeated Measures* window, click *OK* to run the analysis.

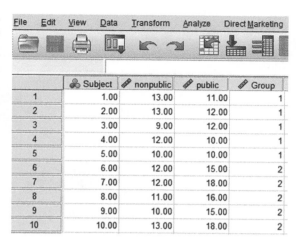

	Subject	nonpublic	public	Group
1	1.00	13.00	11.00	1
2	2.00	13.00	12.00	1
3	3.00	9.00	12.00	1
4	4.00	12.00	10.00	1
5	5.00	10.00	10.00	1
6	6.00	12.00	15.00	2
7	7.00	12.00	18.00	2
8	8.00	11.00	16.00	2
9	9.00	10.00	15.00	2
10	10.00	13.00	18.00	2

Figure 11.25

Figure 11.26

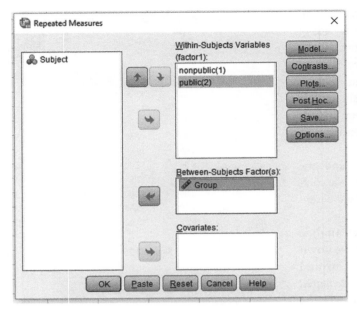

Figure 11.27

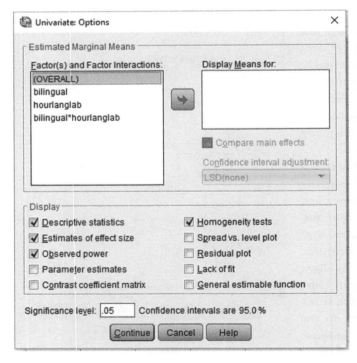

Figure 11.28

The first table in the output window (Figure 11.30) describes the levels of the within-subjects or repeated-measures factor. The next table (Figure 11.31) describes the categories of the between-subjects or group factor. The third table provides basic descriptive statistics by cell, row, and column (Figure 11.32).

A tentative conclusion based on a cursory examination of the condition (cell) means in the table appears to confirm your prediction regarding the difference in the performances of the two groups in the *public* condition: *Group* 1 = 11.0 and *Group* 2 = 16.4. The descriptive statistics can be used to test for the presence of outliers. Recall that an outlier is a score that is more than four standard deviations above or below its condition mean. For example, the standard deviation for the *Group* 1 students in the *public* condition is 1.0 and the mean of their scores is 11.00. Thus, a score in *Group* 1 in the *public* condition must be above 15 or below 8 to be considered an outlier. After examining Figure 11.25, you find no outliers. Tests of other important assumptions are reported later in the SPSS output.

The next table in the output reports Box's test of the equality of the within-group covariance matrices across the two groups of subjects (Figure 11.33). The test has been described as problematic in both directions. Most importantly, the test can be very sensitive to small deviations and often an α of 0.001 is suggested for the rejection of H_0. Failure to reject means you may assume equality of the covariance matrices. For a detailed discussion of Box's test see Tabachnick and Fidell (2012). The table reports an F of 3.343 with a *p*-value (*Sig.*) of 0.487.

Figure 11.29

Within-Subjects Factors

Measure: MEASURE_1

factor1	Dependent Variable
1	nonpublic
2	public

Figure 11.30

Between-Subjects Factors

		N
Group	1	5
	2	5

Figure 11.31

Descriptive Statistics

	Group	Mean	Std. Deviation	N
nonpublic	1	11.4000	1.81659	5
	2	11.6000	1.14018	5
	Total	11.5000	1.43372	10
public	1	11.0000	1.00000	5
	2	16.4000	1.51658	5
	Total	13.7000	3.09300	10

Figure 11.32

Thus, even with an α of 0.05, you are able to assume equality of covariance matrices across your two groups.

Before proceeding further with your test results it is appropriate to examine the graphic depiction of your data. This SPSS module produces line graphs. We gave SPSS instructions such that each group's performance across treatment factor levels (1 = *nonpublic* and 2 = *public*) is connected by a line (Figure 11.34). Examining the graph, in comparison to the *nonpublic* condition, we see that the number of errors made by the *Group* 1 (low PAT score) students did not increase when they performed in the *public* condition. If anything, they slightly decreased. On the other hand, the number of errors made by the *Group* 2 (high PAT score) students increased dramatically when they performed in the *public* condition. Furthermore, if you visually estimate where on the *x*-axis the means for the two groups of subjects might fall (14 and 11), there is a strong indication the groups are appreciably different. As were the descriptive statistics, the graph is consistent with your predictions.

We now return to the statistical tests. The table after Box's test reports the multivariate tests (Figure 11.35). Recall from Chapter 9 how these multivariate tests are used primarily when Mauchly's test of sphericity is significant and sphericity cannot be assumed.

Box's Test of Equality of Covariance Matrices[a]

Box's M	3.343
F	.812
df1	3
df2	11520.000
Sig.	.487

Tests the null hypothesis that the observed covariance matrices of the dependent variables are equal across groups.

Figure 11.33

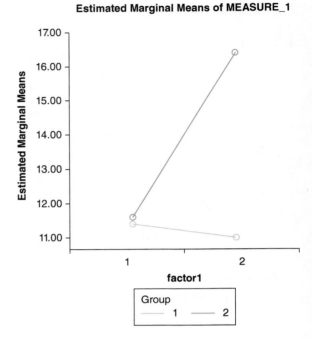

Estimated Marginal Means of MEASURE_1

factor1

Group
—— 1 —— 2

Figure 11.34

Multivariate Tests[a]

Effect		Value	F	Hypothesis df	Error df	Sig.	Partial Eta Squared	Noncent. Parameter	Observed Power[c]
factor1	Pillai's Trace	.688	17.600[b]	1.000	8.000	.003	.688	17.600	.955
	Wilks' Lambda	.313	17.600[b]	1.000	8.000	.003	.688	17.600	.955
	Hotelling's Trace	2.200	17.600[b]	1.000	8.000	.003	.688	17.600	.955
	Roy's Largest Root	2.200	17.600[b]	1.000	8.000	.003	.688	17.600	.955
factor1 * Group	Pillai's Trace	.754	24.582[b]	1.000	8.000	.001	.754	24.582	.990
	Wilks' Lambda	.246	24.582[b]	1.000	8.000	.001	.754	24.582	.990
	Hotelling's Trace	3.073	24.582[b]	1.000	8.000	.001	.754	24.582	.990
	Roy's Largest Root	3.073	24.582[b]	1.000	8.000	.001	.754	24.582	.990

Figure 11.35

Mauchly's Test of Sphericity[a]

Measure: MEASURE_1

Within Subjects Effect	Mauchly's W	Approx. Chi-Square	df	Sig.	Greenhouse-Geisser	Huynh-Feldt	Lower-bound
factor1	1.000	.000	0	.	1.000	1.000	1.000

Epsilon[b] spans the Greenhouse-Geisser, Huynh-Feldt, and Lower-bound columns.

Tests the null hypothesis that the error covariance matrix of the orthonormalized transformed dependent variables is proportional to an identity matrix.

Figure 11.36

Mauchly's test of sphericity (for a detailed discussion of sphericity and Mauchly's test, see p. 397) is the next table in the output (Figure 11.36). Note the perplexing df (= 0) and no reported p-value. Recall from the discussion in Chapter 9 that Mauchly's test is based on the differences in sets of difference scores. When there are only two levels of a repeated-measures factor there can only be one set of difference scores. Thus, there cannot be any difference in the differences, the test cannot be computed, and sphericity is not a concern.

The next table (*Test of Within-Subjects Effects*, Figure 11.37) provides a test of your two within-subjects factors: treatment (*nonpublic* versus *public*) and the treatment × group interaction terms. Recall that, when sphericity is assumed, the *Sphericity Assumed* lines in the table are usually reported. They are the first line in each panel of the table. The test for a main effect of *factor1* addresses your repeated-measures factor: *nonpublic* versus *public*. The error term is reported in the first line (*Sphericity Assumed*) of the third panel: what we referred to as $SS_{trt \times grp/error}$, $df_{trt \times grp/error}$ and $MS_{trt \times grp/error}$. As suggested by the descriptive statistics and the graph, there is a significant overall difference between the *nonpublic* and *public* conditions: $F(1, 8) = 17.60$, MS_{error} 1.375, $p = 0.003$. The H_0 is rejected and you can conclude that overall the students made more errors during the public performance for *Für Elise* than they did during their non-public performance. The first line in the next panel of the table, however, qualifies the main effect. The treatment × group interaction (*factor1 * Group*) is also significant: $F(1, 8) = 24.582$, MS_{error} 1.375, $p = 0.001$. The H_0 is rejected and you can conclude that there is an interaction between the repeated-measures factor (*nonpublic* versus *public*) and the group factor (low PAT score versus high PAT score). If you are asked what the effect is of the level of self-reported performance anxiety on piano performance, you need to say, 'it depends'. Putting together these findings, the significant interaction, and the graph, you can tentatively state that levels of performance anxiety make no difference in non-public performance. However, where high levels of performance anxiety appear to greatly harm performance, low levels of performance anxiety appear to make no difference.

Because you have only two levels of your repeated-measures factor, the next table in the SPSS output merely recapitulates what we have observed in the previous table. The next table, *Levene's Test*

Tests of Within-Subjects Effects

Measure: MEASURE_1

Source		Type III Sum of Squares	df	Mean Square	F	Sig.	Partial Eta Squared	Noncent. Parameter	Observed Power[a]
factor1	Sphericity Assumed	24.200	1	24.200	17.600	.003	.688	17.600	.955
	Greenhouse-Geisser	24.200	1.000	24.200	17.600	.003	.688	17.600	.955
	Huynh-Feldt	24.200	1.000	24.200	17.600	.003	.688	17.600	.955
	Lower-bound	24.200	1.000	24.200	17.600	.003	.688	17.600	.955
factor1 * Group	Sphericity Assumed	33.800	1	33.800	24.582	.001	.754	24.582	.990
	Greenhouse-Geisser	33.800	1.000	33.800	24.582	.001	.754	24.582	.990
	Huynh-Feldt	33.800	1.000	33.800	24.582	.001	.754	24.582	.990
	Lower-bound	33.800	1.000	33.800	24.582	.001	.754	24.582	.990
Error(factor1)	Sphericity Assumed	11.000	8	1.375					
	Greenhouse-Geisser	11.000	8.000	1.375					
	Huynh-Feldt	11.000	8.000	1.375					
	Lower-bound	11.000	8.000	1.375					

a. Computed using alpha = .05

Figure 11.37

Levene's Test of Equality of Error Variances[a]

	F	df1	df2	Sig.
nonpublic	2.753	1	8	.136
public	2.549	1	8	.149

Tests the null hypothesis that the error variance of the dependent variable is equal across groups.

Figure 11.38

of *Equality of Error Variances* (Figure 11.38), is the test for homogeneity of variance necessary for testing your between-subjects or group factor. Because the two *p*-values are greater than 0.05, the table indicates you can assume homogeneity across the two groups.

The last table in the SPSS output, *Test of Between-Subjects Effects* (Figure 11.39), confirms that, as suggested by the descriptive statistics and the graph, there is a significant overall difference in the number of errors made by the two groups (low PAT versus high PAT scores): $F(1, 8) = 15.223$, $MS_{error} = 2.575$, $p = 0.005$. The H_0 is rejected and you can conclude that there was a difference in the performance of the two groups of piano students.

Tests of Between-Subjects Effects

Measure: MEASURE_1

Transformed Variable: Average

Source	Type III Sum of Squares	df	Mean Square	F	Sig.	Partial Eta Squared	Noncent. Parameter	Observed Power[a]
Intercept	3175.200	1	3175.200	1233.087	.000	.994	1233.087	1.000
Group	39.200	1	39.200	15.223	.005	.656	15.223	.926
Error	20.600	8	2.575					

a. Computed using alpha = .05

Figure 11.39

The crucial aspect of your results is the significant interaction. As mentioned in the section on two between-subjects factors, SPSS does not offer an easy way to test simple effects. Given the significant interaction and the picture offered by the graph, it would be important to know if there was a significant simple effect of *group* in the *public* condition but not in the *nonpublic* condition. The means, the graph, and the significant interaction certainly indicate that this might be the case. There are SPSS procedures for testing these simple effects (Braver & MacKinnon, 2003). We will use a variation that simplifies the matter, but it will require you to engage in a little addition and division by hand. As we said at the outset of the chapter, the problem is always deriving the appropriate error term.

To test the simple effects, you begin by conducting two one-way between-subjects analyses, one comparing the two groups' performances in the *nonpublic* condition and one comparing their performances in the *public* condition. These can be run as the one-way between-subjects ANOVAs were run in Chapter 9.

From within the *Data Editor*, select *Analyze* from the menu along the top and drop down to select *Compare Means* and select the *One-Way* ANOVA option. In the *One-Way ANOVA* window, highlight and move the dependent variable (*nonpublic*) to the *Dependent List* box and the independent variable (*Group*) to the *Factor* box. Click *OK* to run the analysis. The results appear in the SPSS output window.

(For more detailed review of the instructions for the ANOVA, see p. 346 in Chapter 8.)

First you test the two groups using their errors in the *nonpublic* condition. The ANOVA table in the output window (Figure 11.40) confirms your suspicion that there is little if any difference between the high PAT and the low PAT students when they perform privately (*nonpublic*): $F(1, 8) = 0.043$, $MS_{error} = 2.30$, $p = 0.840$. You fail to reject H_0 and conclude that there is insufficient evidence to support the idea of a performance difference between low and high PAT scorers when they perform privately.

Oneway

ANOVA

nonpublic

	Sum of Squares	df	Mean Square	F	Sig.
Between Groups	.100	1	.100	.043	.840
Within Groups	18.400	8	2.300		
Total	18.500	9			

Figure 11.40

Next you compare the two groups using their errors in the *public* condition (Figure 11.41). The ANOVA table again confirms your suspicion that there is a difference between the high PAT and the low PAT students when they perform publicly (*public*): $F(1, 8) = 44.182$, $MS_{error} = 1.65$, $p < 0.001$. You reject H_0 and conclude that there is sufficient evidence to support the idea of a performance difference between low and high PAT scorers when they perform publicly.

Oneway

ANOVA

public

	Sum of Squares	df	Mean Square	F	Sig.
Between Groups	72.900	1	72.900	44.182	.000
Within Groups	13.200	8	1.650		
Total	86.100	9			

Figure 11.41

There is one problem that needs to be addressed: have you used the most appropriate error term when testing the two simple effects?

═══ REVIEW QUESTION ═══

What is the appropriate error term for a set of linear contrasts in a one-way between-subjects design?

Web Link 11.8 for the answer to the review question.

Bear in mind that your comparisons are between-subjects in nature: the low versus the high PAT groups. These tests of simple effects are no different than the linear contrast you conducted in Chapter 8. The most appropriate error term then was based on the average within-condition variance. The same is true here. In a mixed-design ANOVA, however, the within-condition variance has been partitioned, with part going with the between-subjects sum of squares and the remainder with the within-subjects sum of squares. We can restore the sums of squares and degrees of freedom by summing those associated with the test of within-subjects factors and those associated with the test of the between-subjects factor (group).

Returning to the table of *Test of Within-Subject Effects*, we find that the sum of squares and the degrees of freedom (sphericity assumed) error were 11.00 and 8, respectively. Returning to the table of *Test of Between-Subject Effects* we find that the error sum of squares error and the degrees of freedom error were 20.60 and 8, respectively. The new $SS_{error/composite}$ and the new $df_{error/composite}$ are 31.6 and 16, respectively. The new $MS_{error/composite} = SS_{error/composite}/df_{error/composite} = 1.975$. To confirm this, return to the data's *Descriptive Statistics* table, square the four standard deviations, and then divide the sum of the four resulting variances by 4. The resulting average variance will be 1.975.

▬▬▬▬▬ REVIEW QUESTION ▬▬▬▬▬

What would this average variance represent, had both of your factors been between-subjects?

🔖 Web Link 11.9 for the review question answer.

We now return to your two tests of simple effects and insert the more appropriate error terms: $SS_{error/composite}$ (31.60), $df_{error/composite}$ (16), and $MS_{error/composite}$ (1.975). The new resulting F-values for the two simple effect are:

$$\text{simple effect } (\textit{nonpublic}), F(1,16) = \frac{0.1000}{1.975} = 0.051.$$

$$\text{simple effect } (\textit{public}), F(1,16) = \frac{72.900}{1.975} = 36.911.$$

The resulting observed F-values have changed slightly, but the pattern of significance has not. Although we are unable to compute new p-values, you can consult the critical value in the F-table for $\alpha = 0.01$ (Table G.3 in Appendix G). As expected, when you compare the new observed F-values against the critical value of 8.53 you reject the H_0 for the simple effect of PAT for public performance but you fail to reject the H_0 for the simple effect for non-public performance.

▬▬▬▬ • • • • • ▬▬▬▬

You might summarize your results as follows.

In your mixed-design experiment you examined the effects of low versus high levels of performance anxiety on public versus non-public performances of university piano students. Both main effects were significant. Students made significantly more errors in the public performance condition ($\bar{y} = 13.70$) than they did in the non-public condition ($\bar{y} = 11.50$), $F(1, 8) = 17.60$, $MS_{error} = 1.375$, $p = 0.003$, partial eta squared = 0.688. Students who reported low levels of performance anxiety ($\bar{y} = 11.20$) made significantly fewer errors than did students who reported high levels of performance anxiety ($\bar{y} = 14.00$), $F(1, 8) = 15.22$, $MS_{error} = 2.575$, $p = 0.005$, partial eta squared = 0.656. The central finding, however, was the significant interaction: $F(1, 8) = 24.58$, $MS_{error} = 1.375$, $p = 0.001$, partial eta squared = 0.754. In the *nonpublic* condition piano students who reported low levels of performance anxiety performed no differently than did those students who reported high levels of performance anxiety, $F(1, 16) = 0.051$, $MS_{error} = 1.975$, $p > 0.05$. However, students who reported low levels of performance anxiety made fewer errors in the *public* condition than did those students who reported high levels of performance anxiety, $F(1, 16) = 36.911$, $MS_{error} = 1.975$, $p < 0.01$. All results are consistent with your hypotheses.

Alternative simple effects

Although the previous two tests of simple effects were appropriate, given the significant interaction and your research hypotheses concerning the difference between two groups of piano students, another pair of simple effects is possible. You may have wished for a difference between the private (non-public) and public conditions at different levels of reported performance anxiety.

Because of the nature of your design, testing these simple effects is not difficult. Testing the simple effects for your repeated-measures factor is possible without having to write SPSS code (Braver & MacKinnon, 2003). You run two one-way repeated-measures ANOVAs. In the first ANOVA you ignore the *Group* 2 students (high PAT scorers) and their data, and you run a one-way repeated-measures ANOVA as you did in Chapter 9, (see p. 397). The appropriate error term is the specific *subject × treatment/error* term specific to that analysis. Following this, you ignore

Figure 11.42

the *Group* 1 students (low PAT scorers) and their data and run the one-way repeated-measures analysis on the *Group* 2 data (high PAT scorers). The appropriate error term is the specific *subject × treatment/error* term specific to that analysis. Hopefully it is becoming clear that this chapter is primarily about identifying appropriate error terms.

We begin by ignoring the group 2 students. We do this by selecting cases starting in the SPSS *Data Editor* as we did in Chapter 2. **Open the file *furelisesplitplot.sav*. Click the *DATA* option and scroll down and select *Select Cases*. When the *Select Cases* window opens (Figure 11.42), in the *Select* area, change the choice from *All Cases* to *If condition is satisfied* and click on the *If* button.**

When the *Select Cases: If* window opens, move the variable *Group* from the area on the left to the empty area in the top right, then add ' = 1' after it, and click *Continue* (Figure 11.43). When you return to the *Select Case* window, click *OK*. When you do so you will see that the group 2 subjects have been removed from the analysis by the slash in front of their data in the SPSS *Data Editor* window (Figure 11.44). The new variable (*filter_$*) created indicates the data to be used by a value of 1 and the data to be ignored by a value of 0.

Now you can conduct a one-way, repeated-measures analysis on the *Group* 1 piano students separately. From within the *Data Editor*, select *Analyze* from the menu along the top and drop down to *General Linear Model*. Then slide over and select the *Repeated Measures* option that appears to the right. In the *Options* window be sure to select *Estimates of effect size* and *Observed power*.

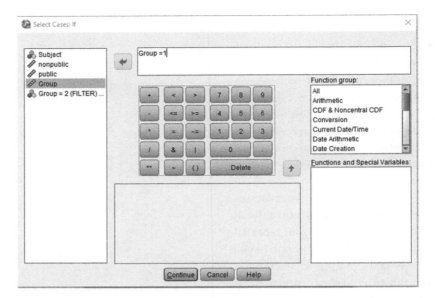

Figure 11.43

	Subject	nonpublic	public	Group	filter_$
1	1.00	13.00	11.00	1	1
2	2.00	13.00	12.00	1	1
3	3.00	9.00	12.00	1	1
4	4.00	12.00	10.00	1	1
5	5.00	10.00	10.00	1	1
6	6.00	12.00	15.00	2	0
7	7.00	12.00	18.00	2	0
8	8.00	11.00	16.00	2	0
9	9.00	10.00	15.00	2	0
10	10.00	13.00	18.00	2	0

Figure 11.44

The only table of interest to you in the SPSS output is the table of *Test for Within-Subjects Effects* (Figure 11.45). We are concerned with the line labelled *Sphericity Assumed*. In the table we see that *factor1* (non-public versus public) is non-significant: $F(1, 4) = 0.186$, $MS_{error} = 2.15$, $p = 0.688$. Because you are only analysing the five low PAT students (*Group* 1), there are only 4 *df* error: $df_{error\ (factor1)}$. You fail to reject H_0 and you conclude that there is insufficient evidence to support a difference in the two conditions (public versus non-public) among the *Group* 1 students.

Tests of Within-Subjects Effects

Measure: MEASURE_1

Source		Type III Sum of Squares	df	Mean Square	F	Sig.	Partial Eta Squared	Noncent. Parameter	Observed Power[a]
factor1	Sphericity Assumed	.400	1	.400	.186	.688	.044	.186	.063
	Greenhouse-Geisser	.400	1.000	.400	.186	.688	.044	.186	.063
	Huynh-Feldt	.400	1.000	.400	.186	.688	.044	.186	.063
	Lower-bound	.400	1.000	.400	.186	.688	.044	.186	.063
Error(factor1)	Sphericity Assumed	8.600	4	2.150					
	Greenhouse-Geisser	8.600	4.000	2.150					
	Huynh-Feldt	8.600	4.000	2.150					
	Lower-bound	8.600	4.000	2.150					

a. Computed using alpha = .05

Figure 11.45

Now repeat the *Select Cases* procedure and change 'Group = 1' to 'Group = 2' and rerun the one-way repeated-measures ANOVA, this time on the high PAT students (Group 2). We are only concerned with the line labelled *Sphericity Assumed*. In Figure 11.46 you can see that *factor1* (*nonpublic* versus *public*) is significant: $F(1, 4) = 96.00$, $MS_{error} = 0.60$, $p = 0.001$. Because you are only analysing the five high PAT students (*Group 2*), there are only 4 *df* error: $df_{error\ (factor1)}$. You reject H_0 and you can conclude that there is sufficient evidence to support a difference in the two conditions among high PAT piano students. In fact, because of the means (non-public = 11.60 and public = 16.40), you can conclude that the high PAT piano students make more errors when playing publicly than they make when playing non-publicly.

Tests of Within-Subjects Effects

Measure: MEASURE_1

Source		Type III Sum of Squares	df	Mean Square	F	Sig.	Partial Eta Squared	Noncent. Parameter	Observed Power[a]
factor1	Sphericity Assumed	57.600	1	57.600	96.000	.001	.960	96.000	1.000
	Greenhouse-Geisser	57.600	1.000	57.600	96.000	.001	.960	96.000	1.000
	Huynh-Feldt	57.600	1.000	57.600	96.000	.001	.960	96.000	1.000
	Lower-bound	57.600	1.000	57.600	96.000	.001	.960	96.000	1.000
Error(factor1)	Sphericity Assumed	2.400	4	.600					
	Greenhouse-Geisser	2.400	4.000	.600					
	Huynh-Feldt	2.400	4.000	.600					
	Lower-bound	2.400	4.000	.600					

a. Computed using alpha = .05

Figure 11.46

=== CHALLENGE QUESTION ===

As more and more of the SS_{total} is associated with the SS_{bs}, what happens to the statistical power for testing the between-subjects and the within-subjects effects?

Web Link 11.10 for an answer to the challenge question.

A priori and *post hoc* tests

A priori and *post hoc* follow-up tests can be used with factorial designs. Other than simple effects, typically follow-up tests are restricted to evaluating the marginal mean (the means associated with the main effects). The appropriate error terms, except for unusual circumstances, are those that were discussed in Chapter 8 for between-subjects factors and those discussed in Chapter 9 for repeated-measures factors.

Experiments versus quasi-experiments

Before we leave your study of public versus non-public piano performance of *Für Elise*, there is a question that needs to be answered. Was this actually an experiment? More specifically, did it involve independent variables? The answer is 'yes' and 'no' to both questions. Remember, for a 'predictor variable' to be a true 'independent variable' you must be able to randomly assign subjects to the various levels or test them at all levels. This is certainly the case with your repeated-measures factor. Students played both publicly and privately. In this respect, your study was experimental. In terms of your group variable, however, the story is different. You can neither assign students to high or low performance anxiety, nor can you test each of them at both levels. Self-reported performance anxiety, like personality traits, IQ, gender, first language spoken, are all subject variables. In this respect, your study was quasi-experimental and has the associated limitations (Morgan et al., 2000). At best, self-reported performance anxiety is a marker for many other variables on which the two groups of students inevitably vary, one or more of which may be the important factor(s) responsible for the observed difference in the performances of the two groups.

11●10 NONPARAMETRIC ALTERNATIVES

The simplest approach, and the least satisfying, is to analyse the main effects with a nonparametric test which we discussed in Chapters 9 and 10. The Kruskal–Wallis test would be used for the between-subjects factors and the Friedman test for the within-subjects factors. These tests, as we saw, can also be applied in SPSS for follow-up specific comparisons. The problem is that there is no simple way to directly test for an interaction. Sokal and Rohlf (2012) discuss an extension of the Kruskal–Wallis test which closely approximates a factorial ANOVA; it is, however, quite complicated and cannot be completed entirely in SPSS.

11●11 CHAPTER SUMMARY

In this chapter we combined material covered in the previous three chapters for the purpose of analysing more complex designs. The factorial ANOVA and two of the most common experimental designs along with their appropriate forms of analysis were introduced. In our first example, both IVs were between-subjects in nature; in our second example (*split-plot* or *mixed-design*) one IV was between-subjects in nature and the other IV was a (within-subjects) repeated-measures variable. With the introduction of a second IV there emerges the possibility of a statistical interaction between the two factors (IVs). An interaction implies that the size of the effect of one IV is contingent upon the level of the other IV. Stated otherwise, a significant interaction indicates that a statement about a factor's effect on the DV needs to be qualified.

The factorial design also necessitates partitioning the $SS_{treatment}$. As the SS_{total} can be partitioned into the additive components of the $SS_{treatment}$ and SS_{error}, in a factorial design the $SS_{treatment/total}$ can be partitioned into the additive components of the $SS_{factor\,A}$, $SS_{factor\,B}$, and the $SS_{AB/interaction}$. Interactions, when significant, require their own category of follow-up analysis. These follow-up analyses are different in name from those covered in Chapter 10, but not in nature. These follow-up tests reflect the distinction between *main* and *simple* effects.

In the chapter's presentation of the split-plot or mixed-design, we found that not only the overall treatment effect could be partitioned, but so also could the error term. In a mixed design where there is at least one between-subjects factor and at least one repeated-measures factor, the total error is partitioned between the between-subjects side of the analysis and the within-subjects side. Once the between-subjects and within-subjects sums of squares have been partitioned, the analysis takes on the character of two separate one-way ANOVAs, each with its own error term.

In many respects, this chapter has been about identifying the appropriate error terms for particular designs and tests. Finally, although the chapter was restricted to factorial designs with only two factors, the basic logic of factorial ANOVA has been established. This logic can be directly applied to designs with three or more factors (Iversen & Norpoth, 1987).

11●12 RECOMMENDED READINGS

Braver, M. C., & MacKinnon, D. P. (1993). *Levine's guide to SPSS for analysis of variance* (2nd ed.) Mahwah, NJ: Erlbaum.

This book provides step-by-step descriptions of how to use SPSS to analyse complex designs, including most follow-ups. Simple effects are given attention. Learning to use SPSS coding is required in some sections.

Bausell, R. B., and Li, Y. (2002). *Power analysis for experimental research: A practical guide for the biological, medical and social sciences*. New York: Cambridge University Press.

This book contains an excellent discussion of power and sample size calculations. It is also a handy guide for estimating sample size requirements necessary for designs from the simple to the complex.

Cardinal, R. N., & Aitken, M. R. (2006). *ANOVA for the behavioral science researcher*. Mahwah, NJ: Erlbaum.

This book provides a detailed elaboration of the two basic designs presented in this chapter. Of particular interest will be the discussion in Chapter 2 of the difference between a covariate and a true second independent variable. Also of interest is the authors' comprehensive examination of both the within-subjects and the between-subjects assumptions.

Jaccard, J. (1999). *Interaction effects on factorial analysis of variance.* London: Sage.

This book provides an in-depth description of forms of interaction and the problems researchers face in both analysing and interpreting them. The issue of unequal samples sizes is dealt with in detail.

11 ● 13 CHAPTER REVIEW QUESTIONS

Multiple-choice questions

1 Which of the following are advantages of a factorial design?

 a By using one sample of subjects to test more than one IV simultaneously, you gain efficiency

 b By including more than one IV in a single experiment the researcher is able to test for the presence of interactions

 c By using one sample of subjects to test more than one IV simultaneously, you gain necessarily power for testing both main effects

 d Both a and b

 e Both b and c

2 In a 2 × 3 factorial design, how many conditions are there?

 a 3

 b 6

 c 5

 d 9

 e 1

3 Which of the following terms refers to the circumstance where the effect of one independent variable in a factorial design is contingent upon the level of the other independent variable?

 a Confounding

 b Dependent variable

 c Interaction

 d Non-significant

 e All of the above are possible

4 In a factorial design with one between-subjects factor and one within-subjects factor, what is the appropriate error term for testing the simple effects for the within-subjects factor?

 a The error term for each one-way, repeated-measures ANOVAs at each level of the between-subjects factor

 b The error term for each one-way, between-subjects ANOVAs at each level of the within-subjects factor

 c The error term for each one-way, repeated-measures ANOVAs at each level of the within-subjects factor

 d The error term from the within-subjects analysis: $MS_{trt \times grp/error}$

 e None of the above are appropriate

5 The correct error term for testing the fixed factor in a design where there is one fixed factor and one random factor is _____.

   a MS_{error}

   b $MS_{interaction}$

   c $MS_{randomfactor}$

   d $MS_{error} + MS_{randomfactor}$

   e   None of the above are appropriate

6 The correct error term for testing the random factor in a design where there is one fixed factor and one random factor is _____.

   a MS_{error}

   b $MS_{interaction}$

   c $MS_{randomfactor}$

   d $MS_{error} + MS_{randomfactor}$

   e   None of the above are appropriate

7 The only difference between the SSs, *df*s, and MSs for a factorial ANOVA with two between-subjects factors and an ANOVA with one between-subjects factor and one within-subjects factor is in terms of_____.

   a   the treatment total divided into component parts: *A*, *B*, and *AB*

   b   factor *A*

   c   factor *B*

   d   the interaction

   e   the error divided into between-subjects and within-subjects parts

8 When subject variables are used in an experiment, they are best described as _____?

   a   predictor variables

   b   independent variables

   c   outcome variables

   d   confounding variables

   e   third variables

9 In a factorial design what is a potential problem with reporting partial eta squared rather than η^2?

   a   The partial eta squared values may sum to zero

   b   The partial eta squared values may sum to more than 100%

   c   The partial eta squared values may sum to less than 100%

   d   There is no problem because the partial eta squared values will always sum to η^2

   e   There is no problem because the partial eta squared values will always sum to the sum of the corresponding η^2 values

10 In a factorial design the $SS_{treatment\ A}$, $SS_{treatment\ B}$, and $SS_{treatment\ AB/interaction}$ will sum to the $SS_{treatment/total}$ _____.

   a   only when all three effects are significant

   b   only when none of the three effects are significant

   c   only when the interaction is non-significant

   d   always

   e   never

Short-answer questions

1 From the model approach we have used, what are the components of an individual score in a 2×2 factorial design? Assume both factors are between-subjects in nature.

2 What is the difference between a *main effect* and a *simple effect*? In a factorial design with one between-subjects factor and one within-subjects factor, how do you test the simple effects for the between-subjects factor?

3 Complete the ANOVA summary table in Figure 11.47 from a factor analysis of a two between-subjects design.

Source	SS	df	MS	F
Treatment Total		5		11
A		1		
B	120			
AB			200	
Error			10	
Total	**1090**	**59**		

Figure 11.47

4 How can a factorial design with one between-subjects factor and one within-subjects factor be viewed as two one-way ANOVAs? What is the major qualification that must be made?

5 As more and more of the SS_{total} is associated with the SS_{bs}, what happens to the statistical power for testing the between-subjects and the within-subjects effects? Why?

Data set questions

1 A psychologist suspected that sleep prior to a memory test would improve scores for both graduate and undergraduate students, and that, within the range examined, the more one sleeps, the more improvement there would be in memory scores. He also thought that in general graduate students would do better than undergraduates on the memory test. To test his hypotheses, he randomly assigned 12 graduate students to three conditions: condition 1 (no sleep), condition 2 (4 hours of sleep), and condition 3 (8 hours of sleep); and 12 undergraduates to those same three conditions. Do the data in Figure 11.48 support his hypothesis? The scores are the number of items correctly recalled. Be sure to include all tests of assumptions (with conclusions), descriptive statistics, appropriate graph, test of null hypotheses, experimental conclusion, as well as the appropriate follow-up (power or effect size) procedures.

2 Another psychologist suspected that sleep prior to an abstract reasoning test would improve scores for both graduate and undergraduate students, and that, within the range examined, the more one sleeps, the more improvement there would be in memory scores. She also thought that in general graduate students would do better than undergraduates on the abstract reasoning test. To test her hypotheses,

Student type	Cond.1	Cond.2	Cond.3
Graduate	10	11	17
Graduate	13	15	15
Graduate	10	21	19
Graduate	15	3	13
Undergraduate	2	6	10
Undergraduate	6	4	8
Undergraduate	4	8	6
Undergraduate	0	6	8

Figure 11.48

she tested four graduate students in three conditions: condition 1 (2 hours of sleep), condition 2 (5 hours of sleep), and condition 3 (8 hours of sleep); and four undergraduates in those same three conditions. Do the data in Figure 11.49 support her hypothesis? The scores are the number of items answered correctly. Be sure to include all tests of assumptions (with conclusions), descriptive statistics, appropriate graph, test of null hypotheses, experimental conclusion, as well as the appropriate follow-up (power or effect size) procedures.

Student type	Cond.1	Cond.2	Cond.3
Graduate	20	25	26
Graduate	18	16	17
Graduate	9	14	25
Graduate	8	13	26
Undergraduate	12	20	23
Undergraduate	6	14	16
Undergraduate	10	12	14
Undergraduate	5	12	13

Figure 11.49

3   An error has been made regarding the design of the experiment in Question 2 concerning abstract reasoning. The design did not contain one between-subjects variable (graduate versus undergraduate students) and one within-subjects variable (hours of sleep). Both variables in fact were within-subjects in nature. Both variables were between-subjects in nature. There were 12 graduate students and 12 undergraduate students. Rerun the complete analysis. What differences are there? Why?

Don't forget to use the online resources! Meet your supporting stats tutor through an **introductory video**, review your maths skills with a **diagnostic pre-test**, explore statistical principles through **interactive simulations**, practice analysis techniques with **SPSS datasets**, and check your work with **answers to all in-text questions**.

https://study.sagepub.com/bors

12

Chapter contents

MULTIPLE REGRESSION

KEY CONCEPTS: ordinary least squares (OLS) method, multivariate outliers, Mahalanobis test, Kolmogorov–Smirnov test, Shapiro–Wilk test, missing completely at random (MCAR), missing at random (MAR), imputation, R, R^2, partial correlation, semi-partial correlation, multicollinearity, tipping effect, mediating variable, moderating variable, bilinear interaction.

12 1 PURPOSE

The aim of this chapter is to familiarize you with the basic design, assumptions, forms of analysis, and typical problems associated with *multiple regression*. There are many forms of multiple regression, too many to be covered in a single chapter. Our focus will be on an extension of Chapter 8 and on the ordinary least squares (OLS) method. As in Chapter 7, we have procedures based on the intersection of (1) a question of *relation* (or association) and (2) *measurement* data. Unlike in Chapter 7, however, the designs covered in this chapter will contain more than one *independent variable*, referred to as the *predictor variables* or, simply, *predictors*.

This chapter represents a culmination and an integration of material covered in previous chapters. As in previous chapters, there is a single *dependent variable*, now best referred to as the *criterion variable* or, simply, the *criterion*. Particular attention is paid to the key assumptions and to the annoying problems that are typically encountered when the predictors are not independent of one another. This lack of independence is commonplace when the data are *observational* in nature, rather than *experimental*.

The analysis of variance (ANOVA) of experimental data generated by factorial designs as described in Chapter 11 is actually a special case of OLS multiple regression. For a detailed treatment of the relation between ANOVA and regression, see Vik (2014). In a true experiment the predictor variables are, by design, *independent* of each other, and the analysis is simplified. Also, in an experiment there are a small number (usually between two and five) of values (called *conditions*) for each independent variable. At least ideally, there are an equal number of observations or subjects in each of the conditions. Finally, experimental designs can be within-subjects, between-subjects, or a combination of both in nature.

Multiple regression is the most common form of analysis associated with observational research. The design is completely within-subjects in nature, even when there are different groups of subjects (e.g., men and women or treatment and no treatment). Ideally, all subjects have a score for all observed variables, both the criterion and the predictors. Some of the subjects may have *missing data*, a potentially thorny problem researchers must address. Unlike in an experiment, in observational research the predictors tend to be correlated (*not* independent). When predictors are substantially correlated the researcher faces the task of resolving the problem of *multicollinearity*, a topic covered in detail in this chapter. Finally, frequent limitations related to the conclusions and the interpretation of results are presented.

12 2 INTRODUCTION

We all have met people who claim a sure-fire way for predicting certain events, such as forecasting the weather. They are nearly always using a single indicator (variable). For example, my neighbour maintains that when the wind allows him to see the underside of the leaves on his maple tree, it will rain. Among my friends and family we frequently wager on the Kentucky Derby; the winner is given the privilege of buying dinner for all the losers. Everyone has a favourite scheme for picking a winner. Again, it is almost always a single variable. These variables can range from being quantitative (e.g., the horse with the greatest number of previous wins) to qualitative (e.g., the colour of the jockey's togs). My strategy is different. Having taught statistics for over three decades, I have a habit of collecting and analysing data. First, I scan the racing form (a compendium which provides all the statistics you would ever want, and, more, about every horse). Second, I select several variables I deem important for making my pick: for example, the number of races the horse has won, the number of races the horse's jockey has won, and how many *hands* the horse is (height). Next, I devise a method for combining the information for all of the horses. Finally, I predict the order of finishing. Of course, the second step is crucial. I need to decide which variables in the racing form are relevant and which can be ignored; otherwise I would be swamped with distracting or useless information. Knowing what to include and what to ignore requires knowing your area of research, in this case,

> Although the method described in this chapter (multiple regression) is often associated with observational research, it can be – and in fact is – used for analysing experimental data. This is true even when a simple *t*-test might be used.

hippology and the *hippodrome*. The test of my strategy is the accuracy of my predictions. After a few races and after failing to predict any better than my family and friends, I revert to my childhood method of wagering on the horse with the grooviest name. It is clear from this anecdote that in this chapter we are not dealing with laboratory experiments with a high level of control and random assignment.

Web Link 12.1 for a demonstration of when the independent-samples *t*-test used in Chapter 5 and the simple one-predictor regression used in Chapter 7 are one and the same analysis and yield identical results, albeit reported in different formats.

After years of such experiences with horses and rarely paying for the family meal, I reached several conclusions. First, never wager more than a *toonie* (a Canadian two-dollar coin) on a race. Second, any one variable found in the racing form is as good – or as bad – as any other for predicting the order of finishing. Furthermore, no single variable appears to be more reliable than simply drawing the horses' names out of a hat. The winners appear to be random with respect to everyone's scheme. There are occasions where someone's strategy appears to be working, but eventually it is found to be a Type I error. Third, if I am to do better than chance, I remain convinced of the need to take multiple variables into account. But I never have enough data or time (statistical power) to develop a model

> I thought that *Northern Dancer, Unbridled,* and *Animal Kingdom* were great names, and they *won* the Kentucky Derby!

that is more reliable than the grooviest name. Finally, it is clear that few can predict horse races with more accuracy than fortune tellers who read tea leaves.

The third conclusion reflects the topic of this chapter: multiple regression. Multiple regression differs from the simple form of regression discussed in Chapter 7 in terms of the number of predictors in the model. Increasing the number of predictors greatly increases the complexity of the analysis, as revealed by the above imaginary attempt to predict the outcome of a horse race.

12 ● 3 REGRESSION REVISITED

We begin by briefly revisiting OLS *simple regression* as discussed in Chapter 7. Let us consider a hypothetical study which will allow us to review some of the terminology and assumptions associated with OLS regression.

Imagine you are interested in exploring the relationship between ingenuity and honesty. You *expect* that the relationship is *not random*. You suspect that the ingenious person finds ways to justify dishonest behaviour and hypothesize that the more ingenious someone is, the less honest they will tend to be. To test your H_1 and to examine just how much of an effect ingenuity has on dishonesty, you administer the Malus Ingenium (*ingenium*) test of ingenuity and the Mendax–Mendax Test of Honesty (*mendax*) to 15 volunteers from your Ethics in Research course. The higher the *ingenium* score, the higher the subject's ingenuity. The higher the *mendax* score, the more honest the subject is deemed to be. The data in Figure 12.1 can be entered into the SPSS *Data Editor* so you may review the SPSS procedures. Each row represents a subject, and for each subject there are two scores.

For the purpose of this study, ingenuity and honesty are operationally defined by the Malus Ingenium (*ingenium*) test of ingenuity and the Mendax–Mendax Test of Honesty (*mendax*). We will need to assume that these scales are reliable and appropriate for the population the students represent.

As usual, we begin with descriptive statistics. When using the SPSS *Descriptives* module be sure to check the *Save standardized values as variables* box. The *Statistics* output (Figure 12.2) indicates no concerns with two distributions. When you return to the SPSS *Data Editor*, you will find that two new variables (*Zingenium* and *Zmendax*) have been created. As discussed in Chapter 7, outliers can have distorting effects on regression and correlation coefficients. Using a distance of four standard deviations (*z*-score greater than 4) as the criterion to evaluate the new variables reveals no univariate outliers.

As you will recall from Chapter 7, when computing regression (OLS) and correlation coefficients it is also important to examine the scatterplot (see p. 276). OLS regression and correlation coefficients assume a linear relation between the two variables. Furthermore, it is important to remember that when a regression coefficient (*B*), also referred to as the *slope*, or a correlation coefficient is found to be non-significant, it does not necessarily mean that there is no relation at all between the two variables. It only indicates that there is insufficient evidence to conclude that there

Student	Ingenium	Mendax
1	22	21
2	45	18
3	36	15
4	40	18
5	28	21
6	32	17
7	39	10
8	18	23
9	26	19
10	22	15
11	30	16
12	34	9
13	28	13
14	17	19
15	43	7

Figure 12.1

is a *linear* relation between the two variables of the magnitude observed. Such tests reveal nothing about other possible relations (e.g., quadratic).

Using the *Graphs* option in the SPSS *Data Editor* window, you can produce a scatterplot (Figure 12.3) with *ingenium* as the predictor (*x*-axis) and *mendax* as the criterion (*y*-axis). If *mendax* is random with respect to *ingenium*, you would *expect* no discernible pattern to emerge from the scatterplot. As can be seen in the scatterplot, however, there appears to be a negative relation between *ingenium* and *mendax*. The relation also appears generally to be linear in nature. Furthermore, the scatterplot indicates that we can assume *homoscedasticity*. That is, the variance in *mendax* does not appear to vary greatly at different levels of *ingenium*. As discussed in Chapter 7, a violation of the assumption of homoscedasticity (*heteroscedasticity*) most notably results in misleading results.

Statistics

		ingenium	mendax
N	Valid	15	15
	Missing	0	0
Mean		30.6667	16.0667
Std. Deviation		8.82097	4.65168
Variance		77.810	21.638
Skewness		.045	-.584
Std. Error of Skewness		.580	.580

Figure 12.2

Remember that each dot in a scatterplot represents two observations (in this case, an *ingenium* score and a *mendax* score) from a single subject. The 15 dots represent the data from the 15 subjects in Figure 12.1.

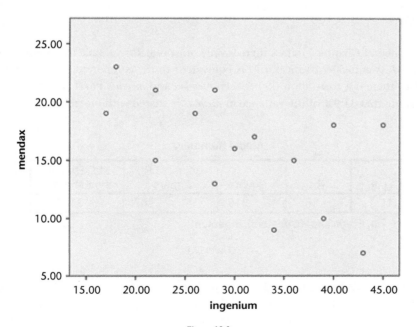

Figure 12.3

Typically, Mahalanobis values are evaluated against a critical value at $\alpha = 0.001$. Some researchers will use a more conservative α of 0.01. By 'conservative' what is meant is that by using an α of 0.01 it is more likely for a subject to be considered a bivariate outlier. When the sample size is large (over 100) and there are few predictors (5 or fewer), the choice of α is rarely consequential with respect to the regression outcome. In this chapter we will use an α of 0.01 for the Mahalanobis test.

Remember, when we speak of the relation between variables in terms of their variance, the phrases 'proportion of shared variance', 'proportion of variance in common', 'proportion of variance accounted for' and 'proportion of variance explained' all refer to the same affair.

When using the *Linear* option from *Regression* under the *Analyze* menu on the SPSS *Data Editor*, be sure to enter the *Save* window and choose the *Mahalanobis* option in the *Distances* box. After running the regression, if you return to the SPSS *Data Editor*, you will find that another new variable (*MAH_1*) has been created. Recall from Chapter 7 that this new variable indicates the distance between a subject's *observed* score and his or her *expected* score, given the observations for all subjects. This *Mahalanobis* distance is distributed as χ^2 and an observed value with a probability less than 0.01 indicates the subject is a *bivariate outlier*. From the χ^2 table in Appendix C, with $df = 1$ (one predictor variable) we find that the critical value for $\alpha = 0.01$ is 6.63. As expected from viewing the scatterplot, none of the subjects has a Mahalanobis value of 6.63 or greater, and you need not worry about distortions due to bivariate outliers.

Web Link 12.2 for the interactive demo for exploring the effect of bivariate outliers on slopes and correlations.

As mentioned in Chapter 7, when there is only one predictor variable in a regression analysis, the multiple R is equivalent to r and R^2 is equivalent to r^2. As reported in the *Model Summary* (Figure 12.4), there is a correlation (R) between *mendax* and *ingenium* of 0.565 and r^2 (*R Square*) is 0.319, meaning that 31.9% of the variance in *mendax* is shared with *ingenium*.

Model Summary

Model	R	R Square	Adjusted R Square	Std. Error of the Estimate
1	.565[a]	.319	.267	3.98236

a. Predictors: (Constant), ingenium

Figure 12.4

The current ANOVA table (Figure 12.5) is no different in essence from the ANOVA tables used in previous chapters for analysing experimental data. The row labels of *Regression* and *Residual* simply replace the labels of *Treatment* and *Error*. The ANOVA table shows that the relation between *mendax* and *ingenium* is significant: $F(1,13) = 6.101$, $p = 0.028$.

ANOVA[a]

Model		Sum of Squares	df	Mean Square	F	Sig.
1	Regression	96.764	1	96.764	6.101	.028[b]
	Residual	206.169	13	15.859		
	Total	302.933	14			

a. Dependent Variable: mendax

b. Predictors: (Constant), ingenium

Figure 12.5

Coefficients[a]

Model		Unstandardized Coefficients		Standardized Coefficients			95.0% Confidence Interval for B	
		B	Std. Error	Beta	t	Sig.	Lower Bound	Upper Bound
1	(Constant)	25.207	3.840		6.564	.000	16.910	33.503
	ingenium	-.298	.121	-.565	-2.470	.028	-.559	-.037

a. Dependent Variable: mendax

Figure 12.6

The *Coefficients* table (Figure 12.6) shows that the y-intercept (constant) is 25.207 and the B is –0.298. As suggested by the scatterplot, the negative slope is significant: $t = -2.470$, $p = 0.028$. Note that the absolute value of the t (2.470) for the regression coefficient is the square root of the F (6.101) reported for the overall model fit in the ANOVA table and the two corresponding p-values are identical. This equality will only occur when there is only one predictor in the regression model.

The significant results of the tests of the overall model and of the individual B support your suspicions: ingenuity appears to be negatively related to honesty. Remember, however, that the conclusion is limited by the appropriateness of the operation definitions. Furthermore, recall from Chapter 7 the limitation related to the issue of interpolation versus extrapolation.

━━━━━ CHALLENGE QUESTION ━━━━━

What questions might be raised with respect to the issue of interpolation versus extrapolation?

Web Link 12.3 for a discussion of the challenge question.

The B of –0.298 means that a one-point increase in a subject's *ingenium* score predicts a 0.298-point decrease in his or her *mendax* score. The *Coefficients* table also provides the 95% confidence limits of the regression coefficient (B): from –0.559 to –0.037. Analogously to evaluating the difference between two means, when 0 is not within the 95% confidence limits, B will be significant at $\alpha = 0.05$.

Throughout this chapter we will use $p < 0.05$ for t-tests and F-tests in regression analyses where there is a single predictor variable. We will use $p < 0.01$ for those models that include more than one predictor. Where p-values other than these are used for determining significance, it will be stated.

With a constant (*y*-intercept) of 25.207 and a *B* of −0.298 you are able to predict a student's *mendax* score, if you know his or her *ingenium* score:

$$mendax = -0.298(ingenium) + 25.207.$$

For example, if someone has an *ingenium* score of 25, we predict a *mendax* score of

$$mendax = -0.298(25) + 25.207 = 17.757.$$

Again recall from Chapter 7 that the predicted scores are what we *expect* to find, if we repeatedly select subjects from the same population and administer the *ingenium* and *mendax* scales. Of course the probability of our *expectation* being *observed* is close to 0.

12 ● 4   INTRODUCING A SECOND PREDICTOR

When researchers attempt to predict an outcome from information gathered in a non-experimental setting, the process can at times be challenging. Imagine how meteorologists feel when they face their neighbours (Figure 12.7). We begin our exploration of multiple regression by examining three simple examples of what could happen when a second predictor variable is added.

Figure 12.7 'Trust me, it will be beautiful today' (B. L. U. Sky, PhD, meteorologist)

In this section we use fictional data illustrating the issues faced when attempting to predict the finishing order in a horse race (*finish*) using two of three predictors: the number of previous wins for the horse (*horsewins*), the number of previous wins by the jockey (*jockwins*), and the height of the horse as measured in *hands*. A hand is 4 inches or 10.16 centimetres. The predictors are used in different combination in the following three examples. The circles used in the figures represent population variances. For the purposes of analysis we are randomly sampling 20 observations. In real research we would hope for a larger sample size.

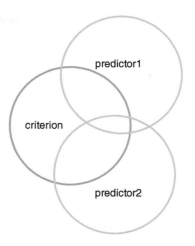

Figure 12.8

Example 1

The first example is depicted in Figure 12.8. In this case we have the criterion (*finish*) and two predictors: *jockwins* and *hands*. The lower the number in *finish*, the better the performance: 1 equals finishing first, 2 equals finishing second, etc. The greater the number of *hands,* the taller the horse, and *jockwins* is the number of previous wins by the jockey. The fact that the two predictors overlap with roughly a third of the criterion indicates they each share approximately a third of the criterion's variance. The fact that *jockwins* and *hands* do not overlap, however, indicates that at a population level they are uncorrelated. The data for this example are available on the book's web page: *horserace1.sav*.

   Web Link 12.4 for the *horserace1.sav* data set.

Descriptive statistics (including the means, standard deviations, variances, and skewness) and scatterplots are the usual first steps in any regression analysis. Also when the regressions are run, save the Mahalanobis values so that any bivariate outliers can be identified. For this example and the next two examples the descriptive statistics and scatterplots can be produced using SPSS, the instructions for which were covered in Chapter 3.

First, let us examine individually the results of two one-predictor regressions. For the sake of brevity, we will examine only one scatterplot to review its importance regarding regression assumptions. The scatterplot for regressing the criterion (*finish*) on *jockwins* (Figure 12.9) suggests a moderate negative relation, with an increase in *jockwins* associated with a decrease in *finish*. Horses ridden by jockeys with a relatively high number of wins tend to finish ahead of horses ridden by jockeys with relatively fewer wins. The relation appears to conform generally to the assumption of linearity. Finally, there appears to be roughly the same amount of variance in *finish* at each level of *jockwins*: homoscedasticity. As mentioned in Chapter 7, it is often difficult to detect violations of linearity and homoscedasticity when the sample size is small, as it is in this example.

The *Model Summary* table (Figure 12.10) reports a correlation between *finish* and *jockwins* of 0.607 and that *jockwins* is associated with 36.9% of the variance ($R^2 = 0.369$) in *finish*. R^2_{adj}, the *Adjusted R Square*, given by

$$R^2_{adj} = 1 - \frac{(1 - R^2)(n - 1)}{n - 1 - k}$$

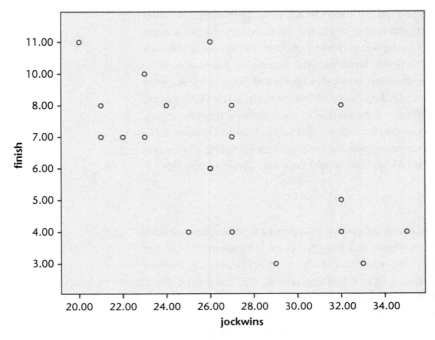

Figure 12.9

(where *n* is the sample size and *k* is the number of predictors), estimates the percentage of the variance the model would likely account for if the population rather than the sample were analysed. R^2_{adj} is sensitive to both sample size and the number of predictors. Note that the R in Figure 12.10 is positive. As can be seen in Figure 12.12 from the zero-order correlation (–.607) and from the scatter plot in Figure 12.9, the relation is actually negative (–.607).

Model Summary

Model	R	R Square	Adjusted R Square	Std. Error of the Estimate
1	.607[a]	.369	.334	2.00785

a. Predictors: (Constant), jockwins

Figure 12.10

ANOVA[a]

Model		Sum of Squares	df	Mean Square	F	Sig.
1	Regression	42.384	1	42.384	10.513	.005[b]
	Residual	72.566	18	4.031		
	Total	114.950	19			

a. Dependent Variable: finish
b. Predictors: (Constant), jockwins

Figure 12.11

The *ANOVA* table (Figure 12.11) reports a test of R (the fit of the overall model) with an *F*-statistic:

$$F = \frac{R^2}{1 - R^2} \frac{N - K - 1}{K}$$

where *N* is the number of subjects and *K* is the number of predictors. The table confirms the significance of the model using only *jockwins* as the predictor: $F(1,18) = 10.513$, $p = 0.005$. In cases where there is only one predictor variable, $R = r$, $R^2 = r^2$, and the *F*-test is equivalent to the *t*-test used in Chapter 7 for testing the significance of a correlation.

The *Coefficients* table (Figure 12.12) reports that for each unit increase in *jockwins* there is a −0.339 unit change (decrease) in *finish* (which is an improvement). Horses with jockeys who have more previous wins are faster than horses with jockeys who have fewer previous wins. The *standardized coefficient*, which is based on all data being transformed into *z*-scores prior to analysis, will

Coefficients[a]

Model		Unstandardized Coefficients		Standardized Coefficients	t	Sig.	95.0% Confidence Interval for B		Correlations			Collinearity Statistics	
		B	Std. Error	Beta			Lower Bound	Upper Bound	Zero-order	Partial	Part	Tolerance	VIF
1	(Constant)	15.549	2.811		5.531	.000	9.642	21.455					
	jockwins	-.339	.105	-.607	-3.242	.005	-.559	-.119	-.607	-.607	-.607	1.000	1.000

a. Dependent Variable: finish

Figure 12.12

be addressed in greater detail later in the chapter. The zero-order correlation reported in the table, or the Pearson product moment correlation coefficient (*r*), is −0.607. The partial and part correlations will be discussed shortly. Finally, the table reports that the slope was significantly different from 0: $t = -3.242$, $p = 0.005$. If we squared this *t*-value, we would find it to be the *F*-value reported in the ANOVA table. This is the case when the overall model contains only one predictor.

We now turn our attention to the second predictor: *hands*. The *Model Summary* (Figure 12.13) shows us that the correlation between *finish* and *hands* is 0.625 and that the predictor is associated with 39.1% of the variance in the criterion. The *ANOVA* table (Figure 12.14) confirms the significance of the overall model: $F(1,18) = 11.538$, $p. = 0.003$.

The *Coefficients* table (Figure 12.15) illustrates that for each unit increase in *hands* there is a −0.678 unit improvement in *finish*. The taller the horse, the faster the horse. Note that the zero-order correlation and the part correlation coefficient are both −0.625. Finally, the table shows us that the test of B was significant: $t = -3.397$, $p = 0.003$.

We now perform our first multiple regression. In doing so, we regress *finish* on *jockwins* and *hands* simultaneously. A multiple regression gives us an estimate of each predictor's effect on the criterion when all other predictors are simultaneously statistically controlled. The details of how

Model Summary

Model	R	R Square	Adjusted R Square	Std. Error of the Estimate
1	.625[a]	.391	.357	1.97272

a. Predictors: (Constant), hands

Figure 12.13

ANOVA[a]

Model		Sum of Squares	df	Mean Square	F	Sig.
1	Regression	44.901	1	44.901	11.538	.003[b]
	Residual	70.049	18	3.892		
	Total	114.950	19			

a. Dependent Variable: finish

b. Predictors: (Constant), hands

Figure 12.14

Coefficients[a]

Model		Unstandardized Coefficients		Standardized Coefficients	t	Sig.	95.0% Confidence Interval for B		Correlations			Collinearity Statistics	
		B	Std. Error	Beta			Lower Bound	Upper Bound	Zero-order	Partial	Part	Tolerance	VIF
1	(Constant)	15.869	2.779		5.711	.000	10.031	21.707					
	hands	-.678	.200	-.625	-3.397	.003	-1.097	-.259	-.625	-.625	-.625	1.000	1.000

a. Dependent Variable: finish

Figure 12.15

In an experiment, the predictor variables, called *independent variables*, are controlled for by the nature of the design. Review factorial designs in Chapter 1 and 11, if necessary. In the case of most observational research the *predictor variables* are rendered orthogonal or independent (controlled) through statistical procedures.

this statistical control is actually accomplished mathematically are beyond the scope of this book, but those who are interested will find an effective discussion in Berk (2004, Chapter 7). The model is similar to what has been used throughout this book:

$$finish = b(jockwins) + b(hands) + a.$$

On the book's web page click on the file labelled *horserace1.sav*. When the SPSS *Data Editor* opens, scroll down the *Analyze* menu to *Regression,* then over, and select *Linear.* When the *Linear Regression* window opens, move *finish* to the *Dependent* box and *jockwins* and *hands* to the *Independent(s)* box (Figure 12.16).

Now click *Statistics.* When the *Linear Regression: Statistics* window opens, ensure that *Estimates, Confidence intervals, Model fit, Part and partial correlations,* and *Collinearity diagnostics* are selected (Figure 12.17). Then click *Continue.* When you return to the *Linear Regression* window, click *Save.* When

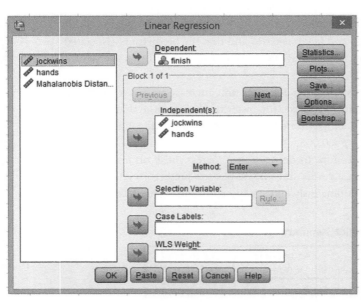

Figure 12.16

the *Linear Regression: Save* window opens, select the *Mahalanobis* option in the *Distances* box (Figure 12.18) and click *Continue*. Upon returning to the *Linear Regression* window, click *OK*.

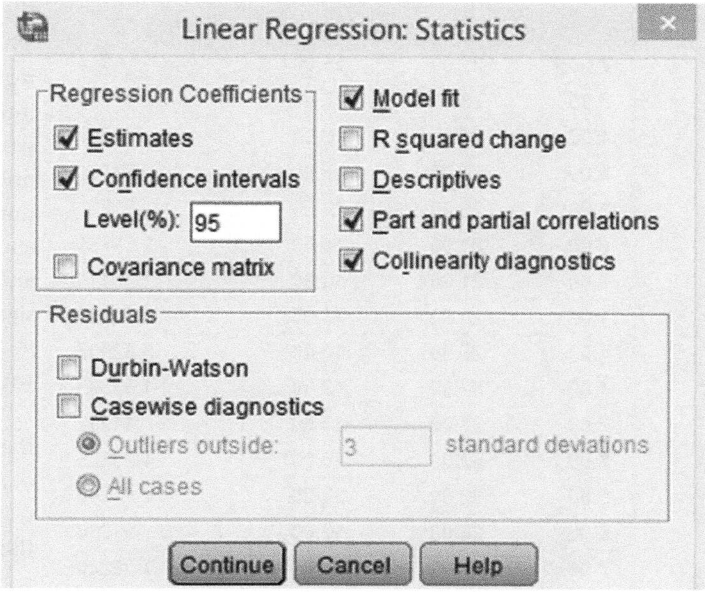

Prior to examining the results always examine the data for possible multivariate outliers. If you selected *Save standardized values as variables* when using SPSS to produce descriptive statistics and examined the new variables, you would not have found any univariate outliers in the data. If you used SPSS to conduct the two individual single-predictor regressions and saved the Mahalanobis values, you would have failed to identify any bivariate outliers. Failure to find bivariate outliers, however, does not preclude the presence of multivariate outliers when two or more predictors are used in a single regression. For example, height and weight may be used to predict a rugby coach's index of athleticism. There may not be any univariate outliers with respect to the three measures. And there may not be any bivariate outliers when athleticism is regressed on height and weight individually. There may be someone whose height and weight combination makes him or her an outlier with respect to athleticism. For example, in combination, someone may be unusually heavy and short for his or her level of athleticism.

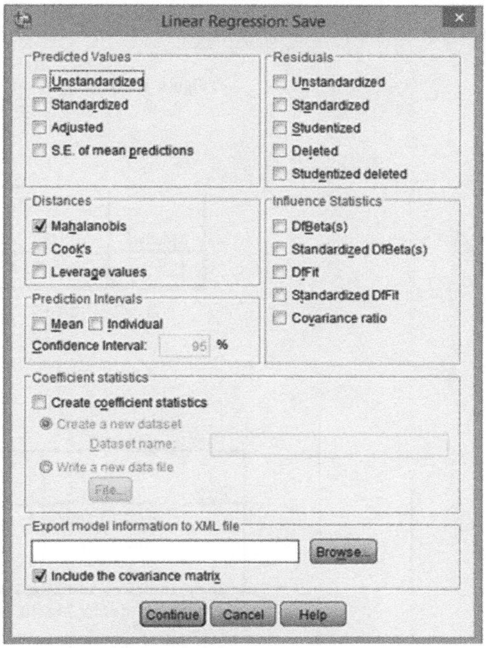

To examine the data for the presence of such multivariate outliers, return to the SPSS *Data Editor* and examine the new variable created during the regression (Figure 12.19). Recall that Mahalanobis values are distributed as χ^2. Returning to the table in Appendix C, we find the critical value for $df = 2$ is 9.21 at $\alpha = 0.01$. Examining the *MAH_1* values for our 20 subjects, we find no outliers.

Turning to the *Model Summary* table (Figure 12.20), we find $R = 0.874$ and $R^2 = 0.764$. Together *jockwins* and *hands* account for 76.4% of the variance in *finish*. Looking back at the results of the individual regressions, *jockwins* accounted for 36.9% of

Figure 12.17

Figure 12.18

finish	jockwins	hands	MAH_1
7.00	23.00	15.00	.94690
3.00	29.00	17.00	2.37277
4.00	27.00	16.00	.99582
8.00	24.00	15.00	.63440
11.00	26.00	12.00	.61214
8.00	21.00	14.00	1.59664
7.00	21.00	13.00	1.70114
11.00	20.00	13.00	2.32528
4.00	25.00	18.00	3.62607
4.00	32.00	13.00	1.63363
7.00	27.00	13.00	.11932
8.00	32.00	10.00	4.23625
5.00	32.00	12.00	2.11240
6.00	26.00	12.00	.61214
7.00	22.00	15.00	1.36240
8.00	27.00	11.00	1.47881
6.00	26.00	15.00	.31839
3.00	33.00	17.00	4.22329
10.00	23.00	10.00	3.40005
4.00	35.00	14.00	3.69214

Figure 12.19

the variance in *finish* and *hands* accounted for 39.1%. The sum of R^2 values of the individual regressions roughly equals that of the R^2 of the multiple regression. This equality only occurs when the *predictor variables* are effectively uncorrelated. In our sample, the actual correlation between *jockwins* and *hands* is −0.007. As above, the *ANOVA* table (Figure 12.21) reports an *F*-test of the overall model, confirming the significance of the model: $F(2,17) = 27.571$, $p < 0.001$. Thus, we reject the null hypothesis with respect to our overall model.

The *Coefficients* table (Figure 12.22) reveals that the slopes (*Unstandardized Coefficients*) of *jockwins* and *hands* are −0.341 and −0.682, respectively. Again, these slopes are virtually the coefficients we found in the individual regressions. As was the case with R^2, this equality will only occur when the predictor variables are uncorrelated. The fact that the two predictors are uncorrelated is reflected in the fact that the part correlations are essentially equal to their zero-order counterparts. The part correlation for *jockwins* is the square root of R^2 from the multiple regression minus

Model Summary

Model	R	R Square	Adjusted R Square	Std. Error of the Estimate
1	.874[a]	.764	.737	1.26229

a. Predictors: (Constant), hands, jockwins

Figure 12.20

ANOVA[a]

Model		Sum of Squares	df	Mean Square	F	Sig.
1	Regression	87.863	2	43.931	27.571	.000[b]
	Residual	27.087	17	1.593		
	Total	114.950	19			

a. Dependent Variable: finish

b. Predictors: (Constant), hands, jockwins

Figure 12.21

Coefficients[a]

Model		Unstandardized Coefficients		Standardized Coefficients	t	Sig.	95.0% Confidence Interval for B		Correlations			Collinearity Statistics	
		B	Std. Error	Beta			Lower Bound	Upper Bound	Zero-order	Partial	Part	Tolerance	VIF
1	(Constant)	24.989	2.499		9.999	.000	19.716	30.262					
	jockwins	-.341	.066	-.611	-5.193	.000	-.480	-.203	-.607	-.783	-.611	1.000	1.000
	hands	-.682	.128	-.629	-5.343	.000	-.951	-.413	-.625	-.792	-.629	1.000	1.000

a. Dependent Variable: finish

Figure 12.22

R^2, also known as the *coefficient of determination,* is the amount of variance in the criterion accounted for by changes in the predictors. It can be expressed as the sum of the squares about the regression line divided by the sum of the squares associated with the variance in the criterion (remember that variance is the sum of the squares divided by the degrees of freedom):

$$R^2 = 1 - \frac{\text{sum of the squares in the criterion about the regression line}}{\text{sum of the squares in the criterion about the mean of the criterion}}.$$

A ratio of 0 means that the criterion is completely *random* with respect to the predictors. A ratio of 1 means that the criterion is totally predictable by some combination of the predictors. In practice you will never encounter these two outcomes.

the R^2 from the regression of *finish* on *hands* alone: $\sqrt{0.764 - 0.391}$. The part correlation for *hands* is the square root of R^2 from the multiple regression minus R^2 from the regression of the criterion on *jockwins*. At this point simply note the *Collinearity Statistics* in the table. The *Tolerance* and *VIF* (variance inflation factor) are both 1.000 for both predictors. We will return to these two statistics shortly.

Web Link 12.5 for a detailed discussion of part and partial correlation coefficients.

The *Sig.* column reveals that the null hypotheses regarding the two predictors can be rejected. Because the overall model is significant it does not imply that both predictors are necessarily significant. Because both coefficients are significant, the coefficients and the intercept (constant) may be used to predict future *finish* scores. For example, if a horse's *jockwins* and *hands* scores were 35 and 17, respectively, we would predict the following *finish* score:

$$finish = (-0.341)35 + (-0.682)17 + 24.989 = 1.46.$$

That is, we predict that the horse will finish either first or second.

Example 2

Results and interpretations are somewhat more complicated when the predictors are correlated. The next example is depicted in Figure 12.23. In this case again we have a criterion (*finish*) and

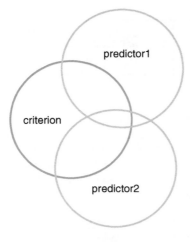

Figure 12.23

two predictors (*horsewins* and *hands*). The fact that a horse's number of previous wins and a horse's height overlap with about a third of *finish* in the figure indicates they each share roughly a third of the criterion's variance. The fact that the two predictors overlap slightly indicates they are somewhat correlated and not completely independent of each other: $r = 0.214$. The data for this example are available on the book's web page: *horserace2.sav*.

Web Link 12.6 for data set: *horserace2.sav*.

Again we begin by examining the two individual one-predictor regressions. If you wish, run the SPSS descriptive statistics and scatterplots to explore relevant assumptions and then the regressions. The *Model Summary* (Figure 12.24) shows us the correlation between *finish* and *horsewins* (0.596) and that the predictor is associated with 35.5% of the variance in the criterion. The *ANOVA* table (Figure 12.25) confirms the significance of the model: $F(1,18) = 9.964$, $p = 0.005$. The *Coefficients* table (Figure 12.26) illustrates that for each unit increase in *horsewins* there is a –0.246 unit decrease in

Model Summary

Model	R	R Square	Adjusted R Square	Std. Error of the Estimate
1	.596[a]	.355	.319	1.59737

a. Predictors: (Constant), horsewins

Figure 12.24

ANOVA[a]

Model		Sum of Squares	df	Mean Square	F	Sig.
1	Regression	25.370	1	25.370	9.964	.005[b]
	Residual	45.830	18	2.546		
	Total	71.200	19			

a. Dependent Variable: finish
b. Predictors: (Constant), hands

Figure 12.25

Coefficients[a]

Model		Unstandardized Coefficients		Standardized Coefficients	t	Sig.	95.0% Confidence Interval for B		Correlations			Collinearity Statistics	
		B	Std. Error	Beta			Lower Bound	Upper Bound	Zero-order	Partial	Part	Tolerance	VIF
1	(Constant)	13.887	2.155		6.445	.000	9.360	18.414					
	horsewins	-.246	.078	-.596	-3.147	.006	-.411	-.082	-.596	-.596	-.596	1.000	1.000

a. Dependent Variable: finish

Figure 12.26

finish, which is an improvement. Horses with relatively more previous wins tend to be faster than those horses with relatively fewer wins. The table shows us that B is significant: $t = -3.147, p = 0.006$.

When we regress *finish* on *hands* alone, the *Model Summary* (Figure 12.27) shows us that the correlation between the *finish* and *hands* is 0.597 and that the predictor is associated with 35.6% of the variance in the criterion. The *ANOVA* table (Figure 12.28) reveals the significance of the model: $F = 9.964$, $p = 0.005$. In the *Coefficients* table (Figure 12.29) we see that for each unit increase in *hands* there is a -0.693 unit change or improvement in *finish*. Again, relatively taller horses tend to be faster than relatively shorter horses. Finally, the *Coefficients* table shows us that B is significant: $t = -3.157, p = 0.005$.

Model Summary

Model	R	R Square	Adjusted R Square	Std. Error of the Estimate
1	.597[a]	.356	.321	1.59565

a. Predictors: (Constant), hands

Figure 12.27

ANOVA[a]

Model		Sum of Squares	df	Mean Square	F	Sig.
1	Regression	25.370	1	25.370	9.964	.005[b]
	Residual	45.830	18	2.546		
	Total	71.200	19			

a. Dependent Variable: finish

b. Predictors: (Constant), hands

Figure 12.28

Coefficients[a]

Model		Unstandardized Coefficients		Standardized Coefficients	t	Sig.	95.0% Confidence Interval for B		Correlations			Collinearity Statistics	
		B	Std. Error	Beta			Lower Bound	Upper Bound	Zero-order	Partial	Part	Tolerance	VIF
1	(Constant)	17.182	3.182		5.399	.000	10.496	23.867					
	hands	-.693	.220	-.597	-3.157	.005	-1.155	-.232	-.597	-.597	-.597	1.000	1.000

a. Dependent Variable: finish

Figure 12.29

Next we regress the *finish* on *horsewins* and *hands* simultaneously. Turning to the *Model Summary* table (Figure 12.30), we find that $R = 0.765$ and $R^2 = 0.586$. That is, the correlation between *finish* and the combined predictors is 0.765. Together *horsewins* and *hands* account for 58.6% of the variance in the *criterion*. Looking back at the result of the individual regressions, *horsewins* accounted for 35.5% of the variance in *finish* and *hands* accounted for 35.6%. The sum of these two individual percentages (71.1%) is greater than the percentage accounted for by the multiple regression (58.6%). Why? Look at Figure 12.23. If we sum the individual R^2 values the portion of the overlap between the two predictors that overlaps with *finish* is counted twice. The *ANOVA* table (Figure 12.31) shows that the overall model is significant: $F(2,17) = 12.015$, $p = 001$.

Model Summary

Model	R	R Square	Adjusted R Square	Std. Error of the Estimate
1	.765[a]	.586	.537	1.31730

a. Predictors: (Constant), hands, horsewins

Figure 12.30

ANOVA[a]

Model		Sum of Squares	df	Mean Square	F	Sig.
1	Regression	41.700	2	20.850	12.015	.001[b]
	Residual	29.500	17	1.735		
	Total	71.200	19			

a. Dependent Variable: finish

b. Predictors: (Constant), hands, horsewins

Figure 12.31

We see in the *Coefficients* table that the slopes (*Unstandardized Coefficients*) of *horsewins* and *hands* are –0.203 and –0.571, respectively. Unlike when the predictors were uncorrelated, although still statistically significant, these coefficients are reduced from those we saw in the individual regressions: –0.246 and –0.693. Remember, the coefficients in the multiple regression are the coefficients associated with each predictor after controlling for the other predictor. Statistically controlling other predictors is analogous to creating linear independence. The idea behind multiple regression is that by including other relevant variables (which are statistically controlled) the researcher is provided with a more accurate idea of the effect of any given variable in a more realistic context.

Coefficients[a]

Model		Unstandardized Coefficients		Standardized Coefficients	t	Sig.	95.0% Confidence Interval for B		Correlations			Collinearity Statistics	
		B	Std. Error	Beta			Lower Bound	Upper Bound	Zero-order	Partial	Part	Tolerance	VIF
1	(Constant)	20.927	2.897		7.224	.000	14.815	27.039					
	horsewins	-.203	.066	-.490	-3.068	.007	-.342	-.063	-.596	-.597	-.479	.954	1.048
	hands	-.571	.186	-.492	-3.077	.007	-.963	-.180	-.597	-.598	-.480	.954	1.048

a. Dependent Variable: finish

Figure 12.32

The attenuation of the part correlations in comparison to their zero-order counterparts reflects the degree to which the two predictors are correlated. The part correlation for *horsewins* is the square root of R^2 from the multiple regression minus the R^2 from the regression of *finish* on *hands* alone: $\sqrt{0.586 - 0.356} = 0.479$.

Note the *Collinearity Statistics* in the *Coefficients* table. The *Tolerance* and *VIF* are no longer 1 for both predictors. Tolerance is 1 minus the multiple R^2 for each predictor regressed on the other. In other words, tolerance indicates how redundant a predictor is with respect to the other predictor(s), or the degree of *collinearity*. If you return to the SPSS *Data Editor* and use *horsewins* as the dependent variable and *hands* as the independent variable you will find the resulting R^2 is 0.046. When 0.046 is subtracted from 1.0 we have the value that is reported as the tolerance for *horsewins*: 0.954. The VIF is 1/tolerance. Thus, the VIF for *horsewins* is 1/0.954 = 1.048. The square root of the VIF is the factor by which the standard error of the estimate used to evaluate that predictor's regression coefficient is inflated: 1.024. Because we have only two predictors in our current model, we need not calculate the tolerance and VIF for *hands*. The *R* and R^2 for *hands* regressed on *horsewins* can be no different from that of *horsewins* regressed on *hands*. The inflated standard error reduces the *power* of the tests of the slopes (coefficients). This is one of the prices paid for having collected observational data outside of the laboratory. It is often argued, however, that the benefit in terms of ecological validity more than compensates for such costs.

Example 3

In this third example (depicted in Figure 12.33), once more we have two predictors that overlap. Whereas in the previous example the two predictors slightly overlapped, in the current example they substantially overlap. Each predictor (*jockwins* and *horsewins*) shares roughly a quarter of the criterion's (*finish*) variance. The substantial overlap of the two predictors is reflected in their strong correlation: $r = 0.744$. The data for this example are available on the book's web page: *horserace3.sav*.

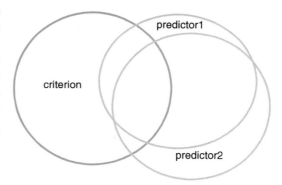

Figure 12.33

Web Link 12.7 for data set: *horserace3.sav*.

As usual, we begin by examining the two individual simple one-predictor regressions. The *Model Summary* (Figure 12.34) reports the correlation between the *finish* and *jockwins* (0.463), and that *jockwins* is associated with 21.4% of the variance in the *finish*. Note that although the R (.463) in Figure 12.34 is positive, the relation is actually negative (–.463), as reported in the zero-order correlation in Figure 12.36. The *ANOVA* table (Figure 12.35) reveals that the model is significant: $F(1,18) = 4.9$, $p = 0.04$. The *Coefficients* table (Figure 12.36) shows us that for each unit increase in *jockwins* there is a significant –0.498 unit improvement in *finish*: $t = -2.214$, $p = 0.04$.

Model Summary

Model	R	R Square	Adjusted R Square	Std. Error of the Estimate
1	.463[a]	.214	.170	1.67891

a. Predictors: (Constant), jockwins

Figure 12.34

ANOVA[a]

Model		Sum of Squares	df	Mean Square	F	Sig.
1	Regression	13.813	1	13.813	4.900	.040[b]
	Residual	50.737	18	2.819		
	Total	64.550	19			

a. Dependent Variable: finish

b. Predictors: (Constant), jockwins

Figure 12.35

Coefficients[a]

Model		Unstandardized Coefficients		Standardized Coefficients	t	Sig.	95.0% Confidence Interval for B		Correlations			Collinearity Statistics	
		B	Std. Error	Beta			Lower Bound	Upper Bound	Zero-order	Partial	Part	Tolerance	VIF
1	(Constant)	19.718	5.690		3.465	.003	7.764	31.673					
	jockwins	-.498	.225	-.463	-2.214	.040	-.970	-.025	-.463	-.463	-.463	1.000	1.000

a. Dependent Variable: finish

Figure 12.36

═══════ REVIEW QUESTION ═══════

Why are the *p*-values (0.040) for the *F* in the *ANOVA* table and for the *t* for *jockwins* in the *Coefficients* table identical? When will they not be identical?

Web Link 12.8 for a discussion of and answer to the review question.

As we have seen and will continue to see, the R value reported in the SPSS Model Summary tables can be positive when the relation is actually negative in nature. Thus, it is crucial to examine the B and the zero-order correlations in the Coefficients table to determine the nature of the relation (negative or positive).

When we regress *finish* on *horsewins* the *Model Summary* (Figure 12.37) shows us the correlation between the criterion and the predictor (−0.531) and that *horsewins* is associated with 28.2% of the variance in *finish*. The *ANOVA* table (Figure 12.38) reveals that the model is significant: $F(1,18) = 7.078$, $p = 0.016$. The *Coefficients* table (Figure 12.39) shows that for each unit increase in *horsewins* there is a −0.624 unit significant change in *finish*: $t = -2.66$, $p = 0.016$.

Finally, *finish* is regressed on *jockwins* and *horsewins* simultaneously. We see from the *Model Summary* table (Figure 12.40) that $R = 0.541$ and $R^2 = 0.292$. Together the two predictors account for 29.2% of the variance in *finish*. Recalling the results of the individual regressions, *jockwins* accounted for 21.4% of the variance in the *finish* and *horsewins* accounted for 28.2%. The sum of R^2

Model Summary

Model	R	R Square	Adjusted R Square	Std. Error of the Estimate
1	.531[a]	.282	.242	1.60436

a. Predictors: (Constant), horsewins

Figure 12.37

ANOVA[a]

Model		Sum of Squares	df	Mean Square	F	Sig.
1	Regression	18.219	1	18.219	7.078	.016[b]
	Residual	46.331	18	2.574		
	Total	64.550	19			

a. Dependent Variable: finish

b. Predictors: (Constant), horsewins

Figure 12.38

Coefficients[a]

Model		Unstandardized Coefficients		Standardized Coefficients	t	Sig.	95.0% Confidence Interval for B		Correlations			Collinearity Statistics	
		B	Std. Error	Beta			Lower Bound	Upper Bound	Zero-order	Partial	Part	Tolerance	VIF
1	(Constant)	16.759	3.629		4.617	.000	9.134	24.384					
	horsewins	-.624	.235	-.531	-2.660	.016	-1.117	-.131	-.531	-.531	-.531	1.000	1.000

a. Dependent Variable: finish

Figure 12.39

Model Summary

Model	R	R Square	Adjusted R Square	Std. Error of the Estimate
1	.541[a]	.292	.209	1.63914

a. Predictors: (Constant), horsewins, jockwins

Figure 12.40

ANOVA[a]

Model		Sum of Squares	df	Mean Square	F	Sig.
1	Regression	18.875	2	9.437	3.512	.053[b]
	Residual	45.675	17	2.687		
	Total	64.550	19			

a. Dependent Variable: finish

b. Predictors: (Constant), horsewins, jockwins

Figure 12.41

Coefficients[a]

Model		Unstandardized Coefficients		Standardized Coefficients	t	Sig.	95.0% Confidence Interval for B		Correlations			Collinearity Statistics	
		B	Std. Error	Beta			Lower Bound	Upper Bound	Zero-order	Partial	Part	Tolerance	VIF
1	(Constant)	18.827	5.593		3.366	.004	7.027	30.628					
	jockwins	-.162	.329	-.151	-.494	.628	-.855	.531	-.463	-.119	-.101	.447	2.239
	horsewins	-.492	.359	-.419	-1.373	.188	-1.249	.264	-.531	-.316	-.280	.447	2.239

a. Dependent Variable: finish

Figure 12.42

values of the individual regression (49.6) is almost double that of the R^2 of the multiple regression (29.2). Moreover, as reported in the *ANOVA* table (Figure 12.41), unlike in the two individual regressions, the *R* from the multiple regression is non-significant: $F(2,17) = 3.512, p = 0.053$.

We see in the *Coefficients* table (Figure 12.42) that the coefficients associated with *jockwins* and *horsewins* are −0.162 and −0.492, respectively. This is a dramatic reduction from the coefficients found in the individual regressions: −0.498 and −0.624. Neither of the current coefficients is statistically significant; note the increase in the standard errors. It is the attenuation in the coefficients and the increased standard errors that are responsible for the increase in *p*-values. The highly correlated nature of the two predictors is reflected in the fact that the part correlations are greatly attenuated in comparison to their zero-order counterparts.

The *Collinearity Statistics* in the *Coefficients* table are revealing of the issue. The *Tolerance* and *VIF* are no longer 1 for both predictors. The tolerances are 0.447, indicating that the two predictors are largely a linear function of each other. The VIFs are greater than 2.0, meaning that the error terms used for evaluating the slopes are 1.5 times what they were for the two individual one-predictor regressions. If we simply ran this last analysis and did not examine the tolerance and VIF values, we would conclude that *jockwins* and *horsewins* were unimportant variables for predicting the finishing position of horses in a race. Take note that the collinearity diagnostics are *not* automatically provided in SPSS, they must be selected by the researcher.

Following the second example, it was noted how the correlations among predictors can reduce the power of statistical tests. This third example illustrates how, when predictors are highly correlated, not only is there a problem with power, but also distortions in the results and in the corresponding conclusions are probable. Later in the chapter we examine the problem of *multicollinearity* in more detail and explore strategies for reducing its effects.

> ⌕ Web Link 12.9 for an interactive demonstration that allows the student to systematically manipulate various degrees of overlap between a criterion and two predictors and examine the accompanying changes in the results.

The bootstrapping option for simple regression described in Chapter 7 may also be used for multiple regression analysis. When the data from the third example are analysed with the bootstrapping option which is accessed from the *Linear Regression* window, there is little change in the results (Figure 12.43). While the *B*s remain the same, there are slight changes in their *p*-values, with both remaining non-significant.

Bootstrap for Coefficients

Model		B	Bootstrap[a]				
			Bias	Std. Error	Sig. (2-tailed)	95% Confidence Interval	
						Lower	Upper
1	(Constant)	18.827	-.208	5.090	.004	7.345	27.893
	jockwins	-.162	.041	.375	.674	-.744	.757
	horsewins	-.492	-.053	.422	.270	-1.436	.161

a. Unless otherwise noted, bootstrap results are based on 1000 bootstrap samples

Figure 12.43

12 ● 5 A DETAILED EXAMPLE

From the above examples some of the complications which often emerge when more than one predictor is used in a regression analysis are seen. The remainder of this chapter is devoted to working through a large example that illustrates many of these and other issues as well as exploring the techniques researchers use to address them. The data set to be analysed is found on the book's web page: *multipleregressiondataset.sav*.

☞ Web Link 12.10 for data set: *multipleregressiondataset.sav*.

Descriptive statistics and outliers

The data used in this section were collected by the author and are a subset of a larger set collected in an undergraduate introductory psychology course (Bors et al., 2006). The variables include standardized final examination score (*score*), Raven's Advanced Progressive

> If necessary, return to Chapter 2 to review the instructions for using SPSS to produce descriptive statistics and graphs. Remember to select the *Save standardized values as variables* option.

Matrices (*raven*), the student's gender (*gender*), whether or not the student is a native English speaker (*natv_spk*), and Spielberger et al.'s (1980) Test Anxiety Inventory (TAI). Consistent with Spielberger's description of the test, the TAI scale is split into an emotionality score (*Etai*) and a worry score (*Wtai*). According to Spielberger, academic performance is related to *Wtai* but not *Etai*. Some researchers, however, report various relations between *Etai* and academic performance (Cassady & Johnson, 2002; Zhang & Henderson, 2014).

Although it was not the original purpose of the research, the goal of the current analysis is to find, given the available data, the best model for predicting performance on the introductory psychology final examination (*score*). The proviso of 'given the available data' is an important one, as we shall see. At this point, simply recall a statement from the chapter's opening anecdote, 'I need to decide which variables in the racing form are relevant and which can be ignored'. The analysis begins, as usual, with descriptive statistics.

Of the 539 students tested, 362 were women and 384 were native English speakers. As seen in the *N* column in the *Descriptive Statistics* table (Figure 12.44), not all subjects have a score for all variables. The bottom row (*Valid N (listwise)*) indicates there are 503 complete cases or subjects. We will address the issue of missing data shortly. Returning to the SPSS *Data Editor* window, we find four new variables: *Zscore, Zraven, ZEtai,* and *ZWtai*. Recall that the values for these variables are z-scores, and any value greater than 4.0 will be considered a univariate outlier. Examination of the four new variables in the *Data Editor* window (which is too large to reproduce here) does not reveal the presence of any univariate outliers (z-score > 4.0). The skewness of both *Etai* and *Wtai* reported in the *Descriptive Statistics* table indicates that both variables are positively skewed.

Descriptive Statistics

	N	Minimum	Maximum	Mean	Std. Deviation	Variance	Skewness	
	Statistic	Statistic	Statistic	Statistic	Statistic	Statistic	Statistic	Std. Error
score	531	-2.50	2.71	.0285	.98198	.964	.201	.106
raven	516	.00	12.00	7.1744	2.26853	5.146	-.341	.108
Etai	534	8.00	32.00	18.1573	5.45539	29.761	.533	.106
Wtai	535	8.00	31.00	14.7626	4.66336	21.747	.736	.106
Valid N (listwise)	503							

Figure 12.44

12 ● 6 ISSUES CONCERNING NORMALITY

The four frequency histograms in Figure 12.45 indicate that while *score* and *raven* have relatively normal distributions, *Etai* appears to be moderately skewed, and *Wtai* substantially skewed.

There is considerable discussion around the assumption of normality as it pertains to multiple regression. Yes, skewness will attenuate the correlations between pairs of variables (Goodwin & Leech, 2006) and affect the fit of the overall model. As discussed in Chapter 7, if one variable is substantially skewed its correlation with another variable will likely underestimate the degree of their relation.

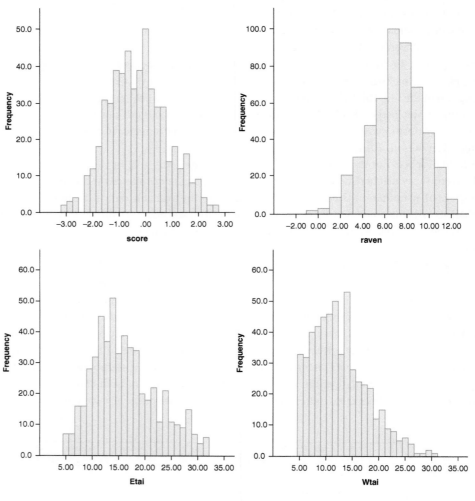

Figure 12.45

With respect to regression coefficients, the normality of the variables themselves is not an assumption required for multiple regression (Allison, 1999). Under certain circumstances extreme skewness can distort the results, however. In particular, when the skewness is the result of a *ceiling* or *basement* effect due to a limitation of the measuring device, the estimates of R, of R^2, and of the individual coefficients can be attenuated or even augmented. The issue revolves around the researcher's *expectation* concerning the shape of the variable's underlying population distribution. If he or she assumes that the underlying distribution is skewed, then the problem is minimal. If he or she assumes the underlying distribution is normal and only the *observed* distribution is skewed, the potential complications can be far-reaching. Such complications typically exist when a measuring instrument is inappropriate for the population from which the subjects are sampled (e.g., a test that is either too difficult or too easy for those being tested). For example, examine *regressionandskewness.sav* found on the book's web page.

Web Link 12.11 to data set *regressionandskewness.sav*.

Begin by regressing *criterion* on *predictor1* and *predictor2* and examining the R, R^2, and *B*s. Assume that for some reason there was a basement effect and the scores on *predictor1* could not fall below 33. Accordingly, create a new variable in the *Data Editor* reflecting that limitation. (Simply copy the values from *predictor1* into a new variable and change all scores below 33 to 33.) Then regress *criterion* on the new *predictor1* (*VAR00001*) and *predictor2*. In the first analysis the R^2 was 0.704 and coefficients of *predictor1* and *predictor2* were 0.502 ($p < 0.001$) and 0.591 ($p < 0.001$), respectively. After raising the scores on *predictor1* that were below 33 up to 33 the results change. In this second analysis the R^2 drop to 0.544 and coefficients of the new *predictor1* (*VAR00001*) and *predictor2* change to 0.584 ($p = 0.016$) and 0.577 ($p = 0.002$). It is interesting to note that although the slope of *VAR00001* increased, the *p*-value would no longer be considered significant using $\alpha = 0.01$. If we compare the scatterplot of *criterion* regressed on *predictor1* with the scatterplot of *criterion* regressed on *VAR00001* (Figure 12.46), we find that the basement effect distorts the linear nature of the relation between the two variables and produces heteroscedasticity.

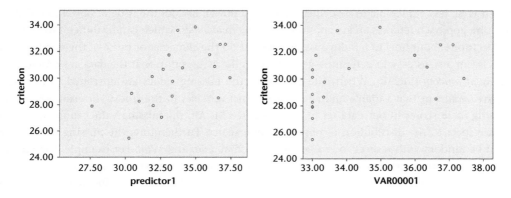

Figure 12.46

How do the violations of linearity and homoscedasticity affect specific aspects of regression analysis?

 Web Link 12.12 for a discussion of the review question.

> To the extent that skewness reflects a problem with the reliability of a measure, it also undermines the validity of the measure and attenuates the measure's observed association with other variables. The critical issue of the relative reliabilities of the variables is discussed later in the chapter.

There is another form of normality that is unquestionably assumed in OLS multiple regression and it will be addressed later in the chapter.

MISSING DATA

As the descriptive statistics reveal, there are some students who are missing responses on one or more variables. There can be many reasons for missing data. Subjects may simply refuse to answer a question. It is not uncommon for subjects to refuse to provide personal information, such as annual income, level of education, or religious affiliation. Subjects may accidentally overlook a question. Particularly with long questionnaires, subjects accidentally skip over items. At times subjects are unsure of their response and intend to return to the item, but forget to do so. Certain questions are inapplicable for some subjects.

Historically, the conventional solution to missing data has been *listwise deletion*. That is, if any subject is missing any data, he or she is removed from all subsequent analyses. Only subjects whose data are 'complete' are included. This is not always a desirable strategy, however. When the researcher's sample size is small and power is of concern, the loss of even a few subjects can be troublesome. Recall from previous chapters how sample size is an important determinant of *power*. The *t*-test for an individual *B* is no different from the *t*-test for the difference between two means and it is no less vulnerable to inadequate statistical power. Besides the issue of power, the listwise deletion approach requires an assumption regarding *randomness* which can be difficult to verify.

Decisions about how to handle missing data rest on the character or cause of the missing data. This is not always easy to determine. First, there is the assumption that the data are *missing completely at random* (MCAR). When data are MCAR the missing values are unrelated to the other *observed values* of that variable and all other *observed variables* in the study. For example, for the missing *raven* scores in our data set to be considered MCAR, the missing values must be *random* with respect to the distribution of observed *raven* scores. Furthermore, the missing *raven* scores must be random with respect to *gender*, *natv_spk*, *score*, *Etai*, and *Wtai*. For example, the missing *raven* scores cannot be more frequent among men than among women, nor can the average *Wtai* be significantly higher or lower for those with missing *raven* scores than it is for those who are not missing their *raven* score.

The most frequently used test of MCAR is that developed by Little (1988). **This test is available in SPSS. Under *Analyze* in the *Data Editor* window, scroll down and click *Missing Values Analysis*.**

When the *Missing Values Analysis* window opens, move the variables of interest to the *Quantitative Variables* box (*score, raven, Etai,* and *Wtai*) and the *Categorical Variables* box (*gender* and *natv_spk*) as in Figure 12.47. Next choose a type of *Estimation*. The most common and often considered the best choice is *EM* (expectation maximization), thought to be less susceptible to the biases associated with the other forms of estimation. Finally, click *OK*.

Univariate Statistics is the first box to appear in the output window (Figure 12.48). There is a row for each of the selected variables. The most important columns are under the label *Missing*. *Count* reveals the number of missing

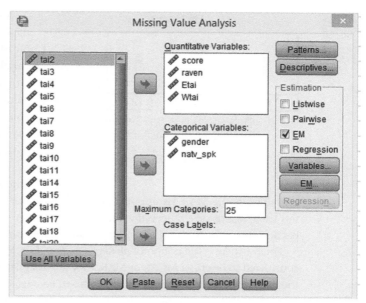

Figure 12.47

values for each variable and *Percent* expresses the count as a percentage of the total sample size. Particularly with large sample sizes, such as ours, 2.0% or less missing data is not uncommon and usually of little concern. When the percentage exceeds 2.0%, particularly as it approaches 5% or more, it is imperative to ascertain the nature of the missing data. Is it MCAR? In the current data set, we should be concerned with missing *raven* scores (4.3% missing).

The next two boxes report further descriptive statistics, comparing statistics for those cases without missing data against the corresponding statistics derived through EM. The next three boxes under the title *EM Estimated Statistics* all provide the key χ^2 test, albeit expressed in different forms. The first box (*EM Means*, Figure 12.49) reveals that χ^2 ($df = 20$) = 18.543, $p = 0.552$, indicating the null hypothesis is *not* to be rejected: $p > 0.05$. Failing to reject means that there is insufficient evidence to reject the assumption of MCAR. This leaves several options open for addressing our missing data.

Univariate Statistics

	N	Mean	Std. Deviation	Missing		No. of Extremes[a]	
				Count	Percent	Low	High
score	531	.0285	.98198	8	1.5	0	1
raven	516	7.1744	2.26853	23	4.3	5	0
Etai	534	18.1573	5.45539	5	.9	0	0
Wtai	535	14.7626	4.66336	4	.7	0	15
gender	538			1	.2		
natv_spk	538			1	.2		

a. Number of cases outside the range (Q1 - 1.5*IQR, Q3 + 1.5*IQR).

Figure 12.48

EM Means[a]

score	raven	Etai	Wtai
.0276	7.1653	18.1442	14.7568

a. Little's MCAR test: Chi-Square = 18.543, DF = 20, Sig. = .552

Figure 12.49

A second and weaker assumption is that the data are *missing at random* (MAR), which is a bit of a misnomer. When data for a particular variable are MAR the missing data are deemed random with respect to the variable's observed values, after controlling for the other variables used in the analysis. For example, *raven* scores could be assumed MAR if those subjects with missing *raven* scores do *not* have on average higher or lower *raven* scores than subjects whose data are not missing. It is impossible to actually test the MAR assumption because we do not know the missing values, thus we cannot test them against the observed values. There are other strategies for considering data MAR that are beyond the scope of this book, but they are summarized well in Allison (2002).

Finally, there is the notion of *missing not at random* (MNAR). In practice, if missing data cannot be considered to be either MCAR or MAR, they are designated as MNAR. In cases where data are MNAR the missing observations are presumed also to be related to other (third) variables omitted from the study. When this is the case, it is extremely difficult to address the missing values with any degree of confidence. It is always possible to make further assumptions and to replace the missing values, but the results of the regression are highly contingent upon those assumptions. On the other hand, subjects with missing data cannot simply be discarded. Recall, removing subjects with missing data from the analyses makes an assumption. That assumption is MCAR. Of course, the fewer the missing values relative to the sample size, the smaller the potential bias in the results, regardless of the assumption made.

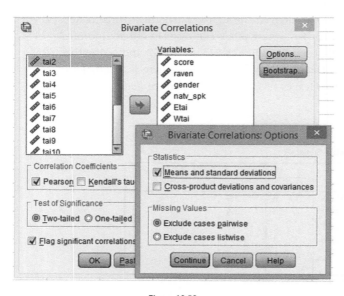

Figure 12.50

Strategies for addressing missing data

There are several standard strategies for addressing missing data: listwise deletion, pairwise deletion, and imputation. As mentioned above, listwise deletion of subjects with missing data is a common strategy. Many researchers fail to recognize that listwise deletion often biases the results when the assumption of MCAR is violated. Thankfully, unless more than 10% of the data is missing, listwise deletion is reasonably robust with respect to violations of MAR assumptions. For demonstration purposes we will use listwise deletion and one other strategy (imputation), and compare the results. Because of our relatively large sample and the small percentages of missing data, listwise deletion should result in little distortion of the results.

A second strategy is pairwise deletion. This approach is based on the fact that linear regression analysis can be conducted without the raw data. All that is required are the means, standard deviations, and the correlation matrix. If we run correlations and select the *Means and standard deviations* option (Figure 12.50), we have all we need to complete our multiple regression. (See p. 287 for the detailed instructions in Chapter 7 for using SPSS to produce correlation coefficients.)

Notice that the descriptive *Statistics* table and the *Correlations* table report the number of observations upon which each statistic is based. This allows for each statistic to be based on as much information as is available. If the missing data are MCAR, then a pairwise deletion solution will produce somewhat more efficient regression estimates than a listwise deletion solution. Pairwise deletion can be selected in the *Linear Regression: Options* window (Figure 12.51).

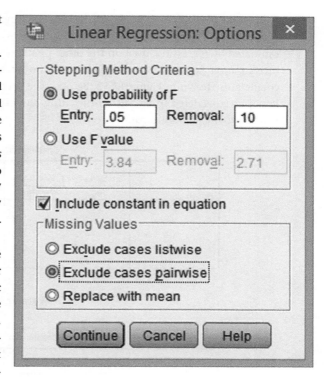

Figure 12.51

The third strategy, *imputation*, is actually a collection of techniques. 'Impute' comes from the Latin verb *imputare*, which means to assign or attribute. Today it often means 'pointing the finger'. In statistics, imputation means replacing missing data with a reasonable estimate. Historically one of the first forms of imputation was to replace any missing value with the *observed* mean of that variable. Today this technique is rarely used, since it has been shown to result in biased estimates of variance (Haitovsky, 1968).

CHALLENGE QUESTION

As randomly as possible, create a data set of 20 values between 0 and 100. Calculate the mean and variance. Now, randomly remove one of the values and recalculate the mean based on only 19 observations. Then replace the 'missing' value with the mean and recalculate the mean and variance. Repeat this process with 5 and then 10 'missing' values from the original data set. What pattern do you see? What is the problem with using the mean of a variable as a replacement for missing data?

Web Link 12.13 for a discussion of the challenge question.

Another form of imputation involves conducting a multiple regression(s) to replace the missing data prior to running your intended multiple regression. For example, the missing *raven* scores are estimated by regressing *raven* on the other predictors. This provides a formula for estimating each missing *raven* score. When we regress *raven* on *gender, natv_spk, score, Etai,* and *Wtai* we find the coefficients shown in Figure 12.52. Because the coefficient associated with *Etai* is non-significant, it can be considered irrelevant for imputing *raven* scores. We might rerun the regression without *Etai* to provide a more accurate model.

Coefficients[a]

Model		Unstandardized Coefficients		Standardized Coefficients	t	Sig.
		B	Std. Error	Beta		
1	(Constant)	9.024	.418		21.580	.000
	gender	-.629	.214	-.130	-2.941	.003
	natv_spk	-.432	.223	-.086	-1.939	.053
	Etai	.007	.026	.017	.272	.786
	Wtai	-.085	.032	-.175	-2.712	.007

a. Dependent Variable: raven

Figure 12.52

Coefficients[a]

Model		Unstandardized Coefficients		Standardized Coefficients	t	Sig.
		B	Std. Error	Beta		
1	(Constant)	9.088	.396		22.959	.000
	gender	-.611	.211	-.127	-2.891	.004
	natv_spk	-.447	.220	-.089	-2.030	.043
	Wtai	-.080	.022	-.165	-3.707	.000

a. Dependent Variable: raven

Figure 12.53

The second model provides the coefficients shown in Figure 12.53. A subject's missing *raven* value can now be estimated by the following equation:

$$raven = -0.611(gender) - 0.447(natv\_spk) - 0.080(Wtai) + 9.088,$$

where *gender* is either 0 (men) or 1 (women), *natv_spk* is either 0 (Non-English) or 1 (English), and *Wtai* is the subject's worry score. For example, for a woman who is a native English speaker with a *Wtai* of 15 we would impute a *raven* score of

$$-0.611(1) - 0.447(1) - 0.08(15) + 9.088 = 6.83.$$

This approach is complicated when several variables have missing data, particularly so when the variables are missing more than 2% of the observations. As summarized by Allison (2002), such imputation strategies typically result in underestimates of the standard errors of the coefficients and, consequentially, overestimates of the *t*-test values.

Today the preferred method of imputation is an extension of the regression method described above: *multiple imputation*. Multiple imputation incorporates two additions to ameliorate the biases associated with the standard regression technique. First, random error, based on the variability in the variable in question, is added to each imputation. Second, the imputation is repeated several times. Because of the random error that is added, the imputed values for each missing score will differ somewhat with each iteration. Finally, the average of each imputed value for each missing score is then used in place of the missing value. The SPSS instructions will be described shortly, but first a crucial question must be answered.

There is debate over whether to include the criterion variable in the multiple imputation of missing predictor values. The safest approach is to include the criterion in the multiple imputation of predictor variables, but then listwise delete those subjects with missing criterion scores from the final analysis (von Hippel, 2007). Excluding the criterion from the imputation assumes that the imputed predictor has no relation with the criterion, and thus biases relations with the criterion towards 0. Should you include the criterion in the imputation, you make no assumption about the relation.

We have already used Little's test and have determined that we can assume that our missing data are MCAR. We can use the listwise deletion strategy or opt for multiple imputations. Multiple imputations are produced in SPSS from the *Data Editor* window.

Under *Transform* scroll down and select *Random Number Generators*. When the *Random Number Generators* window (Figure 12.54) opens, select *Set Active Generator* and the *Mersenne Twister* option as the method of random generation. Then select *Set Starting Point* and *Fixed Value* and click *OK*.

Under *Analyze* in the *Data Editor* window, scroll down to *Multiple Imputation* and slide over and select *Impute Missing Data Values*. When the *Impute Missing Data Values* window opens, click on the *Variables* tab (Figure 12.55). Move the variables *score, raven, gender, natv_spk, score, Etai*, and *Wtai* over into the *Variables in Model* box and then click on the *Method* tab

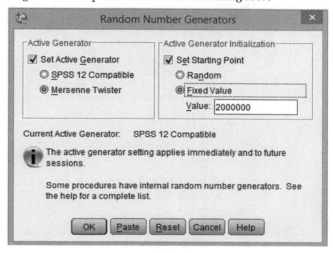

Figure 12.54

Figure 12.55

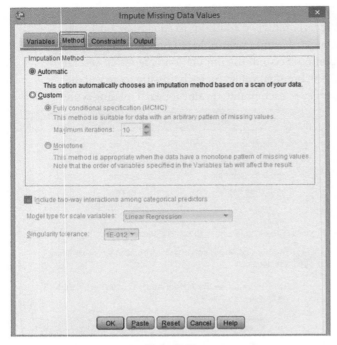

Figure 12.56

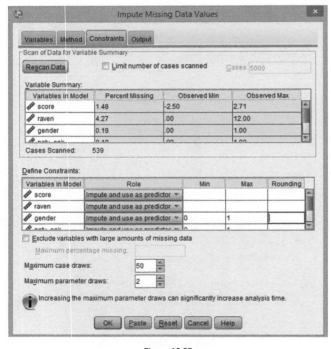

Figure 12.57

(Figure 12.56). Selecting *Automatic* allows SPSS to decide which form of imputation is best, given the nature of the missing data. Then click on the *Constraints* tab. When the new window opens (Figure 12.57), click *Rescan Data*. This reiterates descriptive statistics for the variables included in the model. The *Define Constraints* box allows you to set upper and lower limits on the imputed values. For example, we wish to limit *gender* and *natv_spk* to 0 and 1. Then click on the *Output* tab (Figure 12.58). In the *Display* box select *Imputation model* and *Descriptive statistics for variables with imputed values*. Finally, click *OK*.

The SPSS summary output for the imputed values and a discussion are available on the book's web page.

Web Link 12.14 for the output and discussion of the imputation output summary.

Under the *Window* option in the SPSS *Data Editor* scroll down and locate the file you created for your new data file containing imputed data. Selecting that file will open it in a new *Data Editor* window (Figure 12.59). You will notice a new first variable: *Imputation*. The new file actually contains six data sets or sub-files. The first is the original, denoted with a 0 in the imputation column, which contains missing data. As you scroll down through the file you come to the sub-files, denoted by a 1, 2, 3, 4, and 5 in the *Imputation* column. These represent the five iterations of the imputation procedure. When statistical analyses are performed on this file, results are reported separately for the original data, each imputed iteration, and on the average of the five imputed iterations. Save this file with the new name you assigned to it. We shall return to this file later in the chapter.

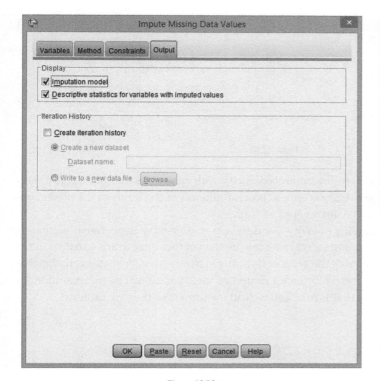

Imputation_	score	raven
0	-1.21	7.00
0	-1.29	3.00
0	.11	5.00
0	.80	.
0	.76	7.00
0	-.92	8.00
0	-1.19	3.00
0	2.38	7.00
0	-.50	9.00
0	-.22	7.00

Imputation_	score	raven
	.50	4.00
5	-1.21	7.00
5	-1.29	3.00
5	.11	5.00
5	.80	6.00
5	.76	7.00
5	-.92	8.00
5	-1.19	3.00
5	2.38	7.00
5	-.50	9.00
5	-.22	7.00

Figure 12.58   Figure 12.59

12 ● 8 TESTING FOR LINEARITY AND HOMOSCEDASTICITY

Return to the *Data Editor* window for the original data set: *multipleregressiondataset.sav*. Like simple regression described in Chapter 7, multiple regression assumes linear relations between the variables, as well as homoscedasticity. Thus it is important to examine the individual scatterplots of the criterion regressed on all predictors individually. We can exclude *gender* and *natv_spk* from this because they have only two values and the relation can only be linear. Using the SPSS *Graphs Chart Builder*, produce scatterplots for *score* against *raven, Etai,* and *Wtai*.

The pattern emerging from all three relevant scatterplots (Figure 12.60) is not uncommon in large-scale observational research in many disciplines. In all three, although there is no distinct relation between the criterion and the predictor, if there is a relation, it appears to be linear (positive or negative).

🔍 Web Link 12.15 for an advanced-topic presentation on testing for the presence of nonlinear relations between the criterion and the predictors.

The scatterplots also suggest little problem with heteroscedasticity, with the possible exception of the *score–Wtai* scatterplot. This possibility regarding the *score–Wtai* scatterplot was suggested in the above discussion regarding the *Wtai* histograms and the issue of normality. Although some

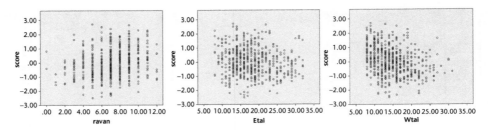

Figure 12.60

researchers maintain there is a need for homoscedasticity with respect to the individual predictors, others argue that homoscedasticity is only important in terms of the errors in the predictions related to the final overall model (Williams et al., 2013).

Once we are comfortable assuming linearity, our next step is to examine the correlations among all of the variables of interest. In doing so, we recall my problem of 'deciding which variables in the racing form are relevant' for predicting the order of finishing in a horse race. Predictor variables that are random (have no zero-order correlation) with respect to the criterion will be irrelevant for our final model. There are exceptions to this rule, and we will mention how they are explored.

12 ● 9 A MULTIPLE REGRESSION: THE FIRST PASS

The instructions for generating a correlation matrix can be found in Chapter 7. Examining the correlation matrix in Figure 12.61, while *raven* appears somewhat positively related to *score*, *Etai*

Correlations

		score	raven	gender	natv_spk	Etai	Wtai
score	Pearson Correlation	1	.224**	-.059	.071	-.123**	-.286**
	Sig. (2-tailed)		.000	.176	.104	.005	.000
	N	531	509	530	530	527	527
raven	Pearson Correlation	.224**	1	-.158**	-.064	-.124**	-.167**
	Sig. (2-tailed)	.000		.000	.147	.005	.000
	N	509	516	515	515	512	513
gender	Pearson Correlation	-.059	-.158**	1	.036	.187**	.146**
	Sig. (2-tailed)	.176	.000		.399	.000	.001
	N	530	515	538	537	533	534
natv_spk	Pearson Correlation	.071	-.064	.036	1	-.074	-.165**
	Sig. (2-tailed)	.104	.147	.399		.090	.000
	N	530	515	537	538	533	534
Etai	Pearson Correlation	-.123**	-.124**	.187**	-.074	1	.718**
	Sig. (2-tailed)	.005	.005	.000	.090		.000
	N	527	512	533	533	534	530
Wtai	Pearson Correlation	-.286**	-.167**	.146**	-.165**	.718**	1
	Sig. (2-tailed)	.000	.000	.001	.000	.000	
	N	527	513	534	534	530	535

**. Correlation is significant at the 0.01 level (2-tailed).

Figure 12.61

and *Wtai* appear somewhat negatively related to *score*, and *gender* and *natv_spk* are likely to be unrelated to *score*. Furthermore, the strong correlation between *Etai* and *Wtai* warns us of a problem regarding their collinearity. Earlier in the chapter we saw the complication that could arise when predictors are substantially correlated.

REVIEW QUESTION

What happens when you regress *score* on *Etai* and *Wtai* separately and then jointly as we did in our earlier three examples?

Web Link 12.16 for an answer to the review question.

• • • • •

Reversals in the nature of the association between a criterion and a predictor, such as those found in the answer to the review question, are examples of *Lord's paradox* (Lord, 1967) or the *suppression effect*. The paradox may also manifest itself as a change from an absence of association to a significant association. These are versions of Simpson's paradox which was discussed in Chapter 1. The difference between Lord's paradox and Simpson's paradox concerns the *scale of measurement* to which each is historically linked: categorical versus measurement. There has been considerable debate about how to understand and interpret such paradoxical effects. One thing these paradoxes undoubtedly illustrate, however, is the need for a thorough understanding of (1) the topic being researched, (2) the previous research findings, (3) the population from which the sample was drawn, and (4) the appropriateness of the measures employed.

Even though the correlations between *score* and *gender* and between *score* and *natv_spk* are nonsignificant, these two predictors are retained for at least the first pass of the regression. As we saw in Chapters 6 and 7, when other predictors (third variables) are controlled, the relations between individual predictors and the criterion can change substantially. When running the regression in SPSS be sure to select *Confidence intervals, Part and partial correlations,* and *Collinearity diagnostics* from the *Linear Regression: Statistics* window. By not changing any *Options*, we are using a listwise deletion approach to missing values.

The *Model Summary* (Figure 12.62) reveals an R^2 of 0.124 and an R_{adj}^2 of 0.115, indicating the model accounts for only between 11% and 12% of the variance in *score*. The *ANOVA* table

Model Summary

Model	R	R Square	Adjusted R Square	Std. Error of the Estimate
1	.352[a]	.124	.115	.92721

a. Predictors: (Constant), Wtai, gender, natv_spk, raven, Etai

Figure 12.62

(Figure 12.63) reveals that the model is significant, $F(5, 495) = 13.981$, $p < 0.001$, however. As mentioned in previous chapters, the p-value is *not* an indicator of the *worth* or *usefulness* of the model. The tests for the individual predictors in the *Coefficients* table (Figure 12.64) confirm that *gender* and *natv_spk* are likely to be irrelevant for predicting *score*. The *Tolerance* and *VIF* values reported in the table also confirm a multicollinearity issue with *Wtai* and *Wtai*.

ANOVA[a]

Model		Sum of Squares	df	Mean Square	F	Sig.
1	Regression	60.096	5	12.019	13.981	.000[b]
	Residual	425.557	495	.860		
	Total	485.653	500			

a. Dependent Variable: score

b. Predictors: (Constant), Wtai, gender, natv_spk, raven, Etai

Figure 12.63

Coefficients[a]

Model		Unstandardized Coefficients		Standardized Coefficients	t	Sig.	95.0% Confidence Interval for B		Correlations			Collinearity Statistics	
		B	Std. Error	Beta			Lower Bound	Upper Bound	Zero-order	Partial	Part	Tolerance	VIF
1	(Constant)	.002	.244		.008	.994	-.477	.481					
	raven	.082	.019	.187	4.330	.000	.045	.119	.223	.191	.182	.946	1.057
	gender	.013	.091	.006	.140	.889	-.166	.192	-.051	.006	.006	.940	1.064
	natv_spk	.075	.094	.034	.797	.426	-.110	.260	.072	.036	.034	.958	1.044
	Etai	.029	.011	.161	2.588	.010	.007	.051	-.128	.116	.109	.459	2.179
	Wtai	-.077	.013	-.360	-5.729	.000	-.103	-.050	-.278	-.249	-.241	.447	2.235

a. Dependent Variable: score

Figure 12.64

Before proceeding, however, *gender* and *natv_spk* are removed and the regression repeated. It is important to remove irrelevant predictors; they contribute little to predicting the criterion, while inflating the standard errors. Prior to our second regression, select *Mahalanobis* in the *Distances* box from the *Save* options.

An examination of the new variable (*MAH_1*) in the *Data Editor* reveals four subjects with values slightly greater than the critical χ^2 with 3 *df* and $\alpha = 0.01$ (11.35). They could be considered multivariate outliers. But because there are so few of them, relative to the sample size, and because they only slightly exceed the critical χ^2 value, we shall proceed with evaluating the analysis. In comparison to the first pass, the *Model Summary* (Figure 12.65) discloses a trivial decrease in R^2 but a slight

Model Summary

Model	R	R Square	Adjusted R Square	Std. Error of the Estimate
1	.351[a]	.123	.118	.92414

a. Predictors: (Constant), Wtai, raven, Etai

Figure 12.65

increase in R^2_{adj}. These shifts signify that *gender* and *natv_spk* contributed almost nothing to overall prediction of *score*, but they contributed to the amount of adjustment made in R^2.

● ● ● ● ●

Remember that R^2_{adj} estimates the percentage of the variance for which the model would likely account if the population rather than the sample had been studied and is sensitive to the number of predictors. From the formula,

$$R^2_{adj} = 1 - \frac{(1 - R^2)(n - 1)}{n - 1 - k}$$

(where n is the sample size and k is the number of predictors), it is seen that those variables which do not increase R^2 will only reduce R^2_{adj} by increasing k.

The decrease in the regression degrees of freedom in the *ANOVA* table (from 5 to 3, Figure 12.66) reflects the removal of the two irrelevant predictors. The increases in the *residual* and *total* degrees of freedom are a result of an increase in the sample size. After removing *gender* and *natv_spk* from the analysis, two subjects with previously missing data (*gender* or *natv_spk*) were returned to the sample.

Comparing the two *Coefficient* tables (Figures 12.64 and 12.67), we see negligible changes in the individual *B*s and all three remain significant, $\alpha = 0.01$. The *Tolerance* and *VIF* of *Etai* and *Wtai* remain questionable.

ANOVA[a]

Model		Sum of Squares	df	Mean Square	F	Sig.
1	Regression	59.857	3	19.952	23.363	.000[b]
	Residual	426.159	499	.854		
	Total	486.016	502			

a. Dependent Variable: score

b. Predictors: (Constant), Wtai, raven, Etai

Figure 12.66

Coefficients[a]

Model		Unstandardized Coefficients		Standardized Coefficients			95.0% Confidence Interval for B		Correlations			Collinearity Statistics	
		B	Std. Error	Beta	t	Sig.	Lower Bound	Upper Bound	Zero-order	Partial	Part	Tolerance	VIF
1	(Constant)	.088	.215		.411	.681	-.334	.511					
	raven	.080	.018	.184	4.327	.000	.044	.116	.224	.190	.181	.973	1.027
	Etai	.030	.011	.166	2.712	.007	.008	.051	-.126	.121	.114	.469	2.133
	Wtai	-.079	.013	-.370	-6.004	.000	-.104	-.053	-.279	-.260	-.252	.464	2.157

a. Dependent Variable: score

Figure 12.67

12 ● 10 ADDRESSING MULTICOLLINEARITY

Advice varies concerning the point at which too small a tolerance or too great a VIF becomes a serious issue. Some say that you can tolerate tolerance as low as 0.1. In practice, the threshold depends upon your variables, the assumptions made about them, and their interrelations. In the current case, we assumed that *Wtai* would predict academic performance (*score*) and that *Etai* would not. We also assumed *Wtai* and *Etai* were two relatively independent variables, but they appear to be virtually one. We saw earlier in the chapter how a correlation similar to the one between *Etai* and *Wtai* (0.718) could affect results. Even though the tolerances are greater than 0.40, we may wish to explore the nature and effect of their multicollinearity.

There are several circumstances that produce low tolerance in a predictor variable. When a predictor is a perfect linear function of other predictors, the computations for the analysis become impossible. Remember, the *B* for one predictor is computed while controlling the others. Controlling can be regarded as holding them constant. As the linear function approaches being perfect (tolerance decreases), controlling the other predictors gets closer and closer to controlling (holding constant) the variable for which you are calculating the coefficient. Once the variance in a predictor is completely accounted for by other predictors, there is no variance left to associate with the criterion. Consequently, there can be no relation. When a predictor is a perfect linear function of others the problem is evident, because the calculations are impossible and SPSS will so inform you. It is those instances where the multicollinearity is not total, but where the results may be distorted, that need to be identified and assessed. There are four circumstances that produce multicollinearity:

1   A predictor variable is highly correlated with one other predictor in the model. A glance at the tolerances and then back at the correlation matrix discloses that this is the situation in our current analysis. Both *Etai* and *Wtai* have somewhat problematic tolerances. *Etai* and *Wtai* are strongly correlated with each other and are weakly correlated with *raven*.
2   A predictor variable is moderately correlated with a few other predictors.
3   A predictor variable is somewhat correlated with a number of other predictors.
4   Some combination of the above three is also possible.

The consequences are more severe, the greater the extent of the multicollinearity:

1   The standard error for the predictor is exaggerated, as we have seen.
2   Consequently, there is a reduction in statistical power.
3   The predictor may look less important than it actually is.
4   The confidence interval around the slope will enlarge.
5   The results become sensitive to minor differences in error or to violations of other assumptions.

Probably the most dramatic possible consequence of multicollinearity is the *tipping effect*. Allison (1999) presents a clear example of the tipping effect and how it can be obscured by extreme multicollinearity. This example is situated within the context of our ongoing horse race saga. Examine the correlation matrix in Figure 12.68. Note the correlations between the three predictors and the criterion. *Horsewins* has the strongest relation with the criterion (*finish*) and *hands* has the weakest relation with *finish*. Also note the strong correlation between *jockwins* and *horsewins*.

Correlation Matrix

	Jockwins	Hands	Horsewins	Finish
Jockwins	1.00			
Hands	−.15	1.00		
Horsewins	.90	−.20	1.00	
Finish	.35	−.23	.37	1.00

Figure 12.68

When the model includes all three predictors, surprising results emerge (Figure 12.69). Neither *jockwins* nor *horsewins* is found to have a significant *B*. Thus, it is unexpected when the coefficient for *hands*, the predictor with the weakest zero-order correlation with *finish*, is found to be significant.

Regression Table

	Coefficient	t-value	Significant?	VIF
Jockwins	0.12	0.67	No	5.29
Hands	−0.17	−2.15	Yes	1.05
Horsewins	0.23	1.33	No	5.39

Figure 12.69

━━━━━ REVIEW QUESTION ━━━━━

What are the tolerances of the three predictors in Figure 12.69?

🖈 Web Link 12.17 for an answer to the review question.

Figure 12.70 reports the results for a model with *Horsewins* removed. The effect on *jockwins'* regression is dramatic, both in comparison to its coefficient found in the first model and relative to the coefficient for *hands*. *Jockwins* suddenly appears to be an important predictor, more so than *hands*.

Regression Table

	Coefficient	t-value	Significant?	VIF
Jockwins	0.32	4.21	Yes	1.04
Hands	−0.18	−2.37	Yes	1.02

Figure 12.70

Similar results are found when *jockwins* is removed and *horsewins* is returned to the model, as reported in Figure 12.71.

Regression Table

	Coefficient	t-value	Significant?	VIF
Hands	−0.16	−2.11	Yes	1.04
Horsewins	0.34	4.38	Yes	1.04

Figure 12.71

● ● ● ● ●

Comparing regression coefficients, particularly unstandardized regression coefficients, to determine their relative practical or theoretical importance is tricky. Once we reach a final model for our current data set we will address this issue in some detail. Bear in mind one question I had earlier concerning the racing form in our opening anecdote: which pieces of information should I include in my attempt to construct a model for predicting the Kentucky Derby? We might add, have I left out anything of importance?

There are several standard strategies for addressing possible problems arising from multicollinearity. The choice of strategy depends upon the circumstances responsible for the multicollinearity and the assumptions made about the nature of the relevant variables. After locating the source of the multicollinearity, the ideal solution is to find a replacement predictor variable(s) and collect new data. With observational research, starting over is rarely feasible. There are times when increasing the sample size helps. When this helps, it often requires greatly increasing the sample size: a doubling or a tripling of n. For theoretical or practical reasons, sometimes there is no other choice but to leave the model as it is, despite the multicollinearity. Additionally, there are five strategies researchers employ to reduce the effects of multicollinearity:

1   If there is only one predictor variable with a very low tolerance, then remove that variable from the model. This strategy is most often used when the source of a variable's problem is a pattern of moderate correlations with several other predictors.

2   If the source of the problem is a single high correlation with one other predictor, then one of the two variables may be excluded from the model. When the correlation between two variables exceeds 0.80, unless there is reason to think otherwise, the two variables may be considered to be two measures of a single construct.

3   Alternatively, if the source of the problem is a single high correlation with one other predictor, the two variables may be combined. This requires that the two variables are scaled in the same manner (e.g., number of correct responses).

4   Predictive redundancies that result from multicollinearity may also be addressed through a *stepwise* regression. Up to this point we have been regressing the criterion on the predictors *simultaneously*. Simultaneous analysis is the default *Method* in the *Linear Regression* window and is labelled *Enter* (Figure 12.72). In a stepwise regression, variables are added to the model in the order of their additive contribution to the prediction of the criterion. More will be said on this below.

5   When variables are interrelated, a new predictor variable can be derived from the original correlated predictors. This is done through a bit of 'linear magic' called *factor analysis* which is discussed in greater detail in the next chapter.

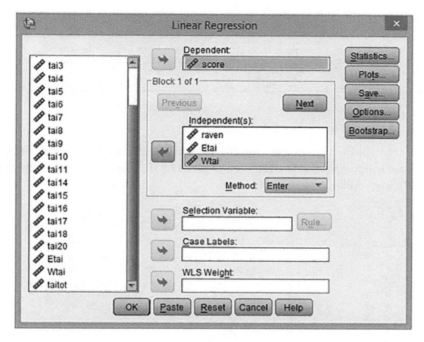

Figure 12.72

We now compare results of the analyses using strategies 2, 3, 4, and 5 above. First, we try excluding *Etai*. If we exclude one of the two highly correlated predictors, it makes most sense to exclude *Etai*. *Etai* has a weaker correlation with *score* than does *Wtai*, and reportedly is unrelated to academic performance. Using this model we find that $R = 0.335$, $R^2 = 0.112$, and $R^2_{adj} = 0.108$. The *Coefficients* table (Figure 12.73) reveals that the coefficients of *raven* and *Wtai* are significant and there is no longer any issue regarding *tolerance* or *VIF*. The model is significant, but it only accounts for 10.8% of the variance of *score*.

Coefficients[a]

Model		Unstandardized Coefficients		Standardized Coefficients	t	Sig.	95.0% Confidence Interval for B		Correlations			Collinearity Statistics	
		B	Std. Error	Beta			Lower Bound	Upper Bound	Zero-order	Partial	Part	Tolerance	VIF
1	(Constant)	.256	.207		1.234	.218	-.151	.663					
	raven	.080	.019	.184	4.318	.000	.044	.117	.225	.189	.181	.973	1.028
	Wtai	-.053	.009	-.251	-5.892	.000	-.071	-.035	-.281	-.254	-.248	.973	1.028

a. Dependent Variable: score

Figure 12.73

Our second strategy is to try combining *Etai* and *Wtai*. If we assume that *Etai* and *Wtai* both are measures of 'test anxiety', then the sum of the two scores can be used as a single variable. In the SPSS *Data Editor* this combined variable is labelled *taitot*. When *score* is regressed on *raven* and *taitot* we find $R = 0.286$, $R^2 = 0.082$, and $R^2_{adj} = 0.078$. The coefficients of *raven* and *taitot* are significant (Figure 12.74), and again there is no issue regarding *tolerance* or *VIF*. The model is significant, but its explanatory power is reduced relative to the previous model, as indicated by R and R^2.

Coefficients^a

Model		Unstandardized Coefficients		Standardized Coefficients	t	Sig.	95.0% Confidence Interval for B		Correlations			Collinearity Statistics	
		B	Std. Error	Beta			Lower Bound	Upper Bound	Zero-order	Partial	Part	Tolerance	VIF
1	(Constant)	.054	.220		.246	.806	-.378	.486					
	raven	.085	.019	.196	4.523	.000	.048	.122	.224	.198	.194	.977	1.024
	taitot	-.019	.005	-.181	-4.167	.000	-.028	-.010	-.210	-.183	-.179	.977	1.024

a. Dependent Variable: score

Figure 12.74

Third, we try stepwise regression. To run the stepwise regression we change the *Method* on the *Linear Regression* window from *Enter* to *Stepwise* (Figure 12.75). Also, in the *Statistics* window, select the *R squared change* option.

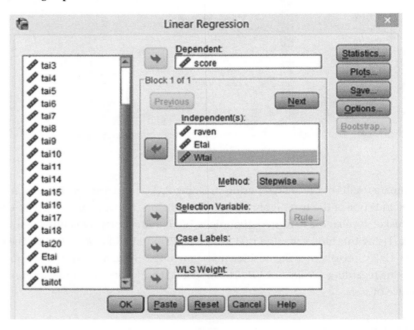

Figure 12.75

Raven, Etai, and *Wtai* are entered into the variable list as potential predictors. In the basic form of stepwise regression, the procedure first looks for the predictor that accounts for the most variance in the criterion. This will be the predictor with the strongest zero-order correlation with the criterion. Recalling the correlation matrix, that will be *Wtai*. If that proves significantly different from 0, which it does, the procedure will then explore the model with all other predictors paired with the first. In our case it will regress *finish* on *Wtai* and *raven* and then regress *finish* on *Wtai* and *Etai*. The pairing with the greatest R^2 is then selected. In our case that is the model with *finish* regressed on *Wtai* and *raven*. If the R^2 of this model is a significant improvement over the first model, which it is, the procedure is repeated with the remaining predictors until a test of improvement is found to be non-significant. In our case the final model tested includes all three predictors and is found to be a significant improvement over the model that includes only *Wtai* and *raven*.

Web Link 12.18 for a more in-depth description of the logic of the procedures associated with stepwise regression

The *Model Summary* (Figure 12.76) reports the *R*, R^2, and R^2_{adj} for three models: *Wtai* alone; *Wtai* and *raven*; and *Wtai, raven,* and *Etai*. The first column in the *Change Statistics* portion of the table (*R Square Change*) reports the additional amount of variance accounted for by each succeeding model. The first row reports the change from complete randomness: 0.078 or 7.8%. The second row reports an additional 3.3% of the variance explained, and the third row an additional 1.3%. The *F*-tests of the R^2 changes reveal that the third model, which includes all three predictors, is superior to the second model, which includes only *raven* and *Wtai*, which itself is superior to the first model, which only includes *Wtai*. Had the *F* for model 3 been non-significant, then we would have concluded that our model should include only *raven* and *Wtai*. As it is, using stepwise regression, we conclude that the best model includes all three predictors. There is a problem, however. The original tolerance issue has returned (Figure 12.77).

Model Summary

Model	R	R Square	Adjusted R Square	Std. Error of the Estimate	R Square Change	F Change	df1	df2	Sig. F Change
1	.279ª	.078	.076	.94594	.078	42.159	1	501	.000
2	.332ᵇ	.110	.107	.92999	.033	18.329	1	500	.000
3	.351ᶜ	.123	.118	.92414	.013	7.354	1	499	.007

a. Predictors: (Constant), Wtai
b. Predictors: (Constant), Wtai, raven
c. Predictors: (Constant), Wtai, raven, Etai

Figure 12.76

Coefficientsª

Model		Unstandardized Coefficients B	Std. Error	Standardized Coefficients Beta	t	Sig.	95.0% Confidence Interval for B Lower Bound	Upper Bound	Correlations Zero-order	Partial	Part	Collinearity Statistics Tolerance	VIF
1	(Constant)	.917	.141		6.523	.000	.641	1.193					
	Wtai	-.059	.009	-.279	-6.493	.000	-.077	-.041	-.279	-.279	-.279	1.000	1.000
2	(Constant)	.252	.208		1.215	.225	-.156	.661					
	Wtai	-.053	.009	-.249	-5.820	.000	-.071	-.035	-.279	-.252	-.245	.974	1.027
	raven	.080	.019	.183	4.281	.000	.043	.116	.224	.188	.181	.974	1.027
3	(Constant)	.088	.215		.411	.681	-.334	.511					
	Wtai	-.079	.013	-.370	-6.004	.000	-.104	-.053	-.279	-.260	-.252	.464	2.157
	raven	.080	.018	.184	4.327	.000	.044	.116	.224	.190	.181	.973	1.027
	Etai	.030	.011	.166	2.712	.007	.008	.051	-.126	.121	.114	.469	2.133

a. Dependent Variable: score

Figure 12.77

Our fourth and final strategy is factor analysis. This involves deriving a new variable(s) with a new corresponding score(s) for all subjects (see Chapter 13). Thus, presently we shall only examine the results after creating two new variables. These new variables (called factor scores) are labelled *emotiontai* and *worrytai*. They are listed in the variable lists and output as *REGR factor score 1 for analysis 1* and *REGR factor score 2 for analysis 1*. If you examine the correlation between these new variables, you will find them to be independent of each other: $r = 0$. This is a result of the magic mentioned above. When *score* is regressed simultaneously (*Method = Enter*) on *raven, emotiontai,* and *worrytai*, we find that $R = 0.343$, $R^2 = 0.117$, and $R^2_{adj} = 0.112$. The *Coefficients* table (Figure 12.78) reveals only *raven* and *worrytai* to be significant. The emotional component (*emotiontai*) of test anxiety is no longer significant ($p = 0.801$). Furthermore, there is no longer any issue with respect to multicollinearity: all tolerances are greater than 0.90.

Coefficients[a]

Model		Unstandardized Coefficients		Standardized Coefficients	t	Sig.	95.0% Confidence Interval for B		Correlations			Collinearity Statistics	
		B	Std. Error	Beta			Lower Bound	Upper Bound	Zero-order	Partial	Part	Tolerance	VIF
1	(Constant)	-.538	.139		-3.865	.000	-.812	-.265					
	raven	.081	.019	.185	4.354	.000	.044	.117	.224	.191	.183	.974	1.026
	REGR factor score 1 for analysis 1	-.010	.041	-.011	-.253	.801	-.092	.071	-.031	-.011	-.011	.994	1.006
	REGR factor score 2 for analysis 1	-.263	.043	-.262	-6.164	.000	-.346	-.179	-.289	-.266	-.259	.980	1.021

a. Dependent Variable: score

Figure 12.78

Contrary to the results from the stepwise regression, when factor analysis is employed to produce new variables, the emotional component of TAI is found to contribute almost nothing to the prediction of *score*. Thus, we remove it from the model and rerun the regression analysis. We find little change in the model summary: $R = 0.342$, $R^2 = 0.117$, and $R^2_{adj} = 0.114$. Furthermore, there is little change in the regression *B*s (Figure 12.79).

Coefficients[a]

Model		Unstandardized Coefficients		Standardized Coefficients	t	Sig.	95.0% Confidence Interval for B		Correlations			Collinearity Statistics	
		B	Std. Error	Beta			Lower Bound	Upper Bound	Zero-order	Partial	Part	Tolerance	VIF
1	(Constant)	-.541	.139		-3.898	.000	-.813	-.268					
	raven	.081	.018	.186	4.389	.000	.045	.117	.224	.193	.184	.980	1.021
	REGR factor score 2 for analysis 1	-.263	.043	-.262	-6.173	.000	-.346	-.179	-.289	-.266	-.259	.980	1.021

a. Dependent Variable: score

Figure 12.79

There is very little to differentiate the various approaches to the multicollinearity in terms of R, R^2, and R^2_{adj}. The exception is the strategy of additively combining *Etai* and *Wtai*, which appears the least effective. In terms of conceptual sense, because most of the previous research has found *Etai* to be unrelated to academic performance, we may choose the model based on the scores derived from factor analysis (*raven* and *worrytai*). This rationale will become clearer in the next chapter.

Return to the imputed data file you saved in Section 12.7. If you rerun the above four analyses to address the issue of collinearity you will find that there are negligible differences in the results from those reported above. For example, examine the *Model Summary* table (Figure 12.80) and *Coefficients* table (Figure 12.81) for the analysis where *score* is regressed on *raven* and the new *worrytai* score (*REGR factor score 2*) produced by factor analysis. The *Model Summary* reveals little variation in R, R^2, and R^2_{adj} across the original and five imputed versions of the data. The same can be said with respect to the *B*s reported in the *Coefficients* table. Such consistency is common when the sample size is large and the proportion of missing data is relatively small, particularly when MCAR can be assumed, as in our present example.

Earlier we discussed the issue of normality of variables and said that there was another form of normality assumed in multiple regression. Once a final model is arrived at, we need to inspect the

Model Summary

Imputation Number	Model	R	R Square	Adjusted R Square	Std. Error of the Estimate
Original data	1	.342[a]	.117	.114	.92632
1	1	.346[a]	.120	.116	.92500
2	1	.336[a]	.113	.109	.93133
3	1	.340[a]	.116	.113	.92255
4	1	.355[a]	.126	.123	.91590
5	1	.349[a]	.122	.119	.92035

a. Predictors: (Constant), REGR factor score 2 for analysis 1, raven

Figure 12.80

Coefficients[a]

Imputation Number	Model		Unstandardized Coefficients B	Std. Error	Standardized Coefficients Beta	t	Sig.	95.0% Confidence Interval for B Lower Bound	Upper Bound	Correlations Zero-order	Partial	Part	Collinearity Statistics Tolerance	VIF
Original data	1	(Constant)	-.541	.139		-3.898	.000	-.813	-.268					
		raven	.081	.018	.186	4.389	.000	.045	.117	.224	.193	.184	.980	1.021
		REGR factor score 2 for analysis 1	-.263	.043	-.262	-6.173	.000	-.346	-.179	-.289	-.268	-.259	.980	1.021
1	1	(Constant)	-.482	.135		-3.563	.000	-.747	-.216					
		raven	.073	.018	.167	4.051	.000	.037	.108	.206	.174	.166	.981	1.019
		REGR factor score 2 for analysis 1	-.276	.041	-.281	-6.808	.000	-.356	-.197	-.304	-.284	-.278	.981	1.019
2	1	(Constant)	-.472	.135		-3.493	.001	-.738	-.207					
		raven	.071	.018	.164	3.955	.000	.036	.107	.201	.170	.162	.981	1.019
		REGR factor score 2 for analysis 1	-.268	.041	-.271	-6.551	.000	-.349	-.187	-.294	-.274	-.269	.981	1.019
3	1	(Constant)	-.504	.134		-3.765	.000	-.767	-.241					
		raven	.076	.018	.176	4.261	.000	.041	.111	.214	.182	.175	.980	1.021
		REGR factor score 2 for analysis 1	-.262	.041	-.267	-6.459	.000	-.341	-.182	-.292	-.271	-.265	.980	1.021
4	1	(Constant)	-.570	.134		-4.269	.000	-.832	-.308					
		raven	.084	.018	.194	4.719	.000	.049	.119	.232	.201	.192	.980	1.020
		REGR factor score 2 for analysis 1	-.265	.040	-.271	-6.591	.000	-.344	-.186	-.299	-.276	-.268	.980	1.020
5	1	(Constant)	-.531	.133		-3.980	.000	-.792	-.269					
		raven	.079	.018	.184	4.461	.000	.044	.114	.226	.191	.182	.976	1.025
		REGR factor score 2 for analysis 1	-.264	.041	-.269	-6.519	.000	-.344	-.184	-.298	-.273	-.266	.976	1.025
Pooled	1	(Constant)	-.512	.141		-3.628	.000	-.789	-.235					
		raven	.077	.019		4.091	.000	.040	.113	.216	.184	.175		
		REGR factor score 2 for analysis 1	-.267	.041		-6.509	.000	-.347	-.187	-.297	-.276	-.269		

a. Dependent Variable: score

Figure 12.81

residuals for normality. The residuals are the differences between what is *expected* from the final model and what we *observe* (the original data). Concretely, they are the difference between the actual *scores* of the subjects and their predicted *scores* that result from the model. There are many ways to produce the residuals; we shall only describe two.

We rerun the regression using our two predictors, *raven* and *worrytai* (*REGR factor score 2* in variable list). In the *Linear Regression* window, select *Plots*. When the *Linear Regression: Plots* window opens, move *ZRESID* to the top open box in the *Scatter 1 of 1* area and move *ZPRED* to the bottom open box. Also check the *Histogram* option in the *Standardized Residuals Plots* area (Figure 12.82). Click *Continue* and run the analysis.

Scrolling down the output, we arrive at the *Charts* section. First we find a frequency histogram of the residuals (Figure 12.83). The assumption is that the residuals will be normally distributed. The smooth line is a normal curve. The bars represent the frequencies of the observations for the standardized residuals. The histogram reveals that the residuals from our model are quite normal.

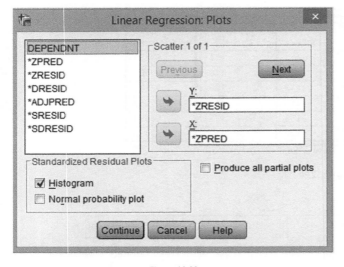

Figure 12.82

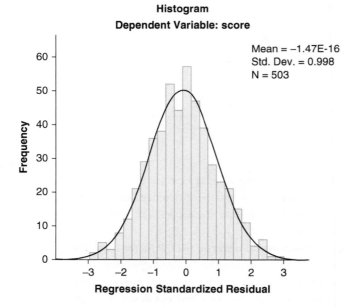

Histogram
Dependent Variable: score

Mean = −1.47E-16
Std. Dev. = 0.998
N = 503

Figure 12.83

The second chart is a scatterplot of the regression standardized residuals plotted against the regression standardized predicted values (Figure 12.84). This is the 'difference between the actual and the expected scores' (y-axis) plotted against the expected scores (x-axis) derived from our model. Ideally the plots should be symmetrically distributed above and below the zero point on the y-axis and most of the points should cluster between −1.5 and +1.5 on the y-axis. Finally, there should be no discernible pattern. It should look like a random swarm. This is a plot of error and error should always look random, regardless of the type of analysis. The data from our model are a reasonable fit with these criteria.

Figure 12.85 illustrates a typical violation of the third criterion where the points are close to zero at low levels of the predicted values (x-axis), but are spread between −3.0 and +3.0 at high levels of the predicted values. Figure 12.86 illustrates another typical violation. In this case the points form a clear inverted U or quadratic pattern. Such violations usually indicate a missing variable (third-variable problem) that interacts with one of the predictors.

Comparing standardized regression coefficients

This may be a good point to address the issue of comparing unstandardized and standardized regression coefficients (*Beta*) for the purpose of determining the relative importance of the predictors in a model. Comparing the *unstandardized coefficients* is not very useful because the coefficients are likely scored in different units of measurements. For example, if the coefficient for the height of a horse were recorded in inches rather than *hands*, the corresponding *B*s would be very different. The change in *B* does not represent a change in the variable's importance.

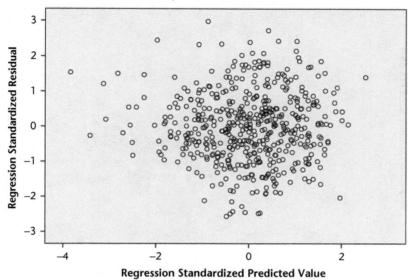

Figure 12.84

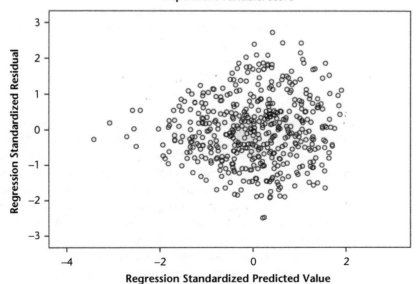

Figure 12.85

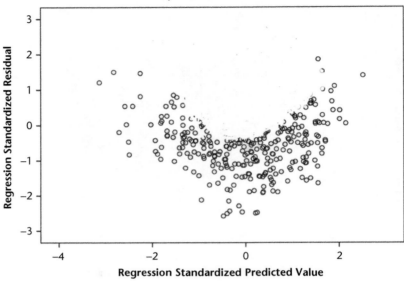

Figure 12.86

═══════════════ REVIEW QUESTION ═══════════════

If the regression coefficient related to hands was –0.21, what would be the corresponding regression coefficient if the height of the horses were measured in inches? (*Hint*: We defined *hand* earlier in this chapter.)

Web Link 12.19 for an answer to the review question.

Often researchers attempt to solve the question of relative importance by comparing the *standardized coefficients*. Standardized coefficients are created by converting all variables in a model (criterion and predictors) to z-scores. The standardized regression coefficients, then, represent the change in the criterion for a one standard deviation change in a predictor. Advocates of using standardized regression coefficients to compare coefficients argue that the coefficients are now in the same units of measurement. The problem has only been put off. Because the variables are standardized, there is no reason why a standard deviation in one predictor should be equivalent to a standard deviation in another predictor. The original range of one of the predictors may have been restricted for some reason, and this influences the resulting z-scores for the variable. Finally, when addressing the issue of importance, we must remember that some variables are more easily modified than others. For example, the amount of time spent studying is easier to modify than native language, or even test anxiety. In the end, determining the relative importance of predictors must be guided by the specific theoretical or practical question being addressed.

12 ◉ 11 INTERACTIONS

In the previous chapter we said that an interaction exists between two variables when the effect of one independent variable is contingent upon the level of another independent variable. For example, an interaction exists when someone asks us for the effect study time has on memory, and we need to tell them it depends upon the student's memorization strategy. The amount of memory improvement obtained for an hour of study time is different for different study techniques. Interactions (also referred to as moderation) are also possible in multiple regression where we have two or more measurement predictors. For example, if the effect of *worrytai* (the regression coefficient) on *score* is different for subjects with different *raven* scores, that is an interaction. If the *B*s were the same, regardless of *raven* score, then there is *no* interaction. In Chapter 11 we described three questions that pertain to interactions:

1   Is there an interaction?
2   If there is an interaction, what is its strength?
3   If there is an interaction, what is its nature?

In regression analysis, there are various approaches for answering the first question. One approach involves dichotomizing two of the predictors using median splits and then doing a 2×2 ANOVA using the criterion as the dependent variable. Thus, the test for an interaction is based on the same logic as that described in Chapter 11: $SS_{\text{interaction } AB} = SS_{\text{treatment/total}} - SS_{\text{treatment } A} - SS_{\text{treatment } B}$. Although the reasoning behind this approach is sound, by dichotomizing the predictors the power of this test can be greatly reduced. Consider what happens. All scores below the medians of the predictor variables are made identical, as are those above the median. In our case there would be only two *raven* scores and two *Wtai* scores.

Our second and preferred approach for identifying the presence of an interaction begins by creating a multiplicative term. There are arguments for and against standardizing the predictors (*z*-scores) prior to creating the multiplicative term. Because at this point we are only concerned with knowing if there is an interaction, whether we use *z*-scores or the original unstandardized scores makes no difference. The necessary *z*-scores have already been created in the data set when it was examined for univariate outliers. We are not interested in the resulting coefficients for the two original predictors. We only wish to know if the coefficient for the multiplicative terms is significant at $\alpha = 0.01$. The null hypothesis of this test is that the linear slopes (*B*s) of *score* regressed on *Zworrytai* are *random* with respect to *Zraven* scores.

· · · · ·

The null hypothesis of interaction can also be viewed as testing whether the linear slopes (regression coefficients) of *score* regressed on *Zraven* are random with respect to *Zworrytai* scores. The choice of version of the null hypothesis is of concern only under circumstances where the researcher considers one predictor variable to be influencing the criterion and the other predictor to be possibly moderating that effect. A thorough discussion of interaction effects is beyond the scope of this book, but an excellent discussion can be found in Jaccard and Turrisi (2003).

The multiplicative term can be created by selecting *Compute Variable* under *Analyze* in the SPSS *Data Editor* window. When the *Compute Variable* window opens (Figure 12.87), type a name for the new multiplicative term in the *Target Variable* area (e.g., *ravenzworrytaiz*). Highlight and move *Zscore(raven)* and *Zscore: REGR factor score 2 for analysis 1* into the *Numeric Expression* window. Separate them with a *, indicating multiplication. Unfortunately, the name SPSS gives computed variables is different from the name you provide and the name that shows up in various windows and outputs. *REGR factor score 2 for analysis 1* will show up as *Zworrytai* in the *Numeric Expression* window. Then click *OK*. The new variable should show up in the right-hand column in the data set.

Rerun the regression using *zraven*, *worrytai*, and the new variable *ravenzworrytaiz* as the predictors of *score*. The important aspect of the output is the *B* for *ravenzworrytaiz*, the *t*-value for which is –0.660 with a *p*-value of 0.510 (Figure 12.88). We cannot reject the null hypothesis. We have no evidence that there is an interaction.

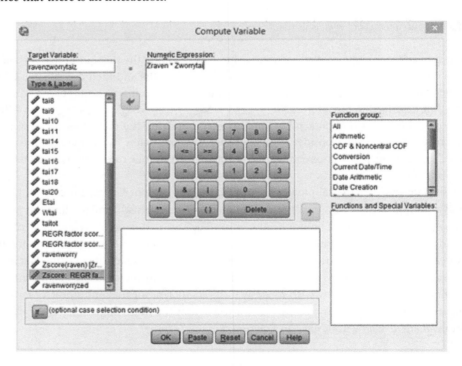

Figure 12.87

Coefficients[a]

Model		Unstandardized Coefficients		Standardized Coefficients	t	Sig.	95.0% Confidence Interval for B		Correlations			Collinearity Statistics	
		B	Std. Error	Beta			Lower Bound	Upper Bound	Zero-order	Partial	Part	Tolerance	VIF
1	(Constant)	.037	.042		.881	.379	-.045	.119					
	Zscore(raven)	.183	.042	.186	4.368	.000	.101	.265	.224	.192	.184	.979	1.021
	Zscore: REGR factor score 2 for analysis 1	-.267	.043	-.267	-6.192	.000	-.352	-.183	-.289	-.267	-.260	.951	1.051
	ravenzworrytaiz	-.026	.040	-.026	-.660	.510	-.104	.052	.017	-.030	-.028	.971	1.030

a. Dependent Variable: score

Figure 12.88

If the *B* for the multiplicative term were significant, next we would need an index of the strength of the interaction. There are several ways to express the strength of such an interaction, the most readily understood being the difference between the model that includes the interaction term and the model without the interaction term. The R^2 for the model which included the interaction term was 0.344 and the R^2 for the model without the interaction term was 0.342. The strength of the interaction would be estimated at 0.002, which is non-significant.

The above test must be qualified. It is a test for a bilinear interaction. A bilinear interaction exists when the *B* of one measurement predictor changes as a function of the scores on a second measurement predictor. In our example, the slopes of *score* regressed on *Zworrywatiz* would need either to systematically increase or decrease as a function of *Zraven* scores. As can be seen when comparing Figures 12.89–12.91, there is a slight systematic increase in the slopes when the data set is divided into low, medium, and high *raven* subjects. The systematic increase as a function of *raven* would have described the nature of the interaction, had the interaction been statistically significant.

 Web Link 12.20 for an alternative data set for exploring a significant interaction between two measurement variables.

Interaction with categorical variables

There is another common form of interaction we should introduce. Recall that *gender* and *natv_spk* were deemed irrelevant for predicting *score*. Despite the fact that there is no zero-order correlation between

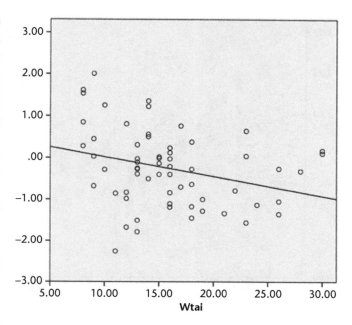

Figure 12.89   Subjects with low *raven* scores; $B = -0.047$

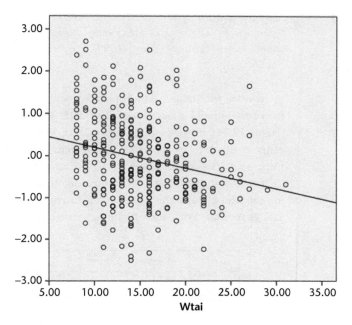

Figure 12.90   Subjects with medium *raven* scores; $B = -0.049$

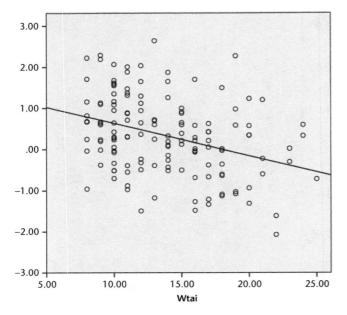

Figure 12.91 Subjects with high *raven* scores; $B = -0.078$

Variables such as *gender* and *natv_spk* are special cases of dummy variables. For an extended discussion of such variables and interpreting interactions that involve them, see Allison (1999).

either of them and *score*, it is possible that an interaction between them and *raven* or *Wtai* could be significant. This is analogous to the situation in the previous chapter where an independent variable's main effect could be non-significant, but an interaction involving that variable and another independent variable could be significant.

The procedure for testing for an interaction between a dichotomous variable such as *gender* and a measurement variable such as *Wtai* is no different than it was when two measurement variables are involved. A multiplicative term is created and then included in a regression. When examining an interaction which includes a dichotomous variable, however, other significant predictors typically are excluded from the model. This is done to isolate the interaction for purposes of interpretation. Let us first examine *score* regressed on *gender* and *Wtai* without an interaction term. The overall model is significant: $R = 0.286$, $F(2, 523) = 23.235$, $p < 0.001$. As seen in the *Coefficients* table (Figure 12.92), where the *B* of *Wtai* is significant, the *B* of *gender* is not. This is not surprising since the correlation between *gender* and *score* approached 0.

Now we will include a multiplicative term found in the data set and labelled *genderwtai*. Again, the overall model is significant: $R = 0.305$, $F(2, 522) = 17.789$, $p < 0.001$. It is the *Coefficients* table (Figure 12.93), however, that is fascinating. Researchers who use $\alpha = 0.05$ as the criterion for significance at this level of analysis would conclude that there is a significant interaction. Furthermore, using $\alpha = 0.05$ as the criterion for significance, the *B* for *gender* is also significant.

If we assume that the interaction is significant, then we need to answer the questions concerning the strength and the nature of the interaction. Both questions are answered by the *B*s of *gender* and *genderwtai*. With such dichotomous variables coded 0 and 1, in our case men and women

Coefficients[a]

Model		Unstandardized Coefficients		Standardized Coefficients	t	Sig.	95.0% Confidence Interval for B		Correlations			Collinearity Statistics	
		B	Std. Error	Beta			Lower Bound	Upper Bound	Zero-order	Partial	Part	Tolerance	VIF
1	(Constant)	.934	.142		6.576	.000	.655	1.213					
	gender	-.025	.069	-.012	-.280	.780	-.199	.150	-.057	-.012	-.012	.974	1.026
	Wtai	-.060	.009	-.284	-6.679	.000	-.077	-.042	-.285	-.280	-.260	.974	1.026

a. Dependent Variable: score

Figure 12.92

Coefficients[a]

Model		Unstandardized Coefficients		Standardized Coefficients			95.0% Confidence Interval for B		Correlations			Collinearity Statistics	
		B	Std. Error	Beta	t	Sig.	Lower Bound	Upper Bound	Zero-order	Partial	Part	Tolerance	VIF
1	(Constant)	1.449	.248		5.852	.000	.962	1.935					
	gender	-.746	.298	-.356	-2.502	.013	-1.332	-.160	-.057	-.109	-.104	.086	11.667
	Wtai	-.097	.017	-.462	-5.623	.000	-.131	-.063	-.285	-.239	-.234	.257	3.887
	genderwtai	.051	.020	.426	2.533	.012	.011	.091	-.140	.110	.106	.061	16.263

a. Dependent Variable: score

Figure 12.93

respectively, the two Bs represent the slopes for the two groups. The B for *gender* is the B for men (*gender* = 0): –0.746. The B for the multiplicative term (*genderwtai*) is the difference between the Bs for men and women. Therefore the B for women is –0.746 – (+0.051) or –0.797. The individual slopes (Bs) for men and women represent the nature of the interaction and the B of *genderwtai* an estimate of the effect size.

━━━━━ REVIEW QUESTION ━━━━━

Is there an interaction between *natv_spk* and *Wtai* ?

↖ Web Link 12.21 for an answer to the review question.

There are several circumstances that produce false interaction effects – Type I errors:

1   Unequal intervals. When ordinal data are treated as measurement data, the Bs at different levels of a third variable can appear different.
2   Unequal validity. If the validity of a variable differs for different subjects in the study, different Bs are more likely to appear due to chance alone. For example, many diagnostic instruments are more valid for the clinical population than they are for the non-clinical population. A study that involves samples from both populations needs to be sensitive to this artefact.
3   The same can be said with respect to group difference in reliability.

There are two circumstances that often lead to a failure to identify a true interaction – Type II error:

1   Multicollinearity is a common source of obscured interaction effects. The multicollinearity may not appear to be a significant problem when examining the predictors themselves, but it may be a problem for uncovering true interactions.
2   As was the case with ANOVA, in multiple regression analyses small samples frequently lack the power for correctly identifying interactions.

Questions not asked

The steps followed in a multiple regression allow the researcher to remove predictor variables that are irrelevant. This reflects the 'questions asked and answers given' aspect of multiple regression.

The answer given in some cases is that the predictor is not useful for predicting the criterion, at least with respect to the population from which the sample was drawn. Such variables have no correlation with the criterion, are not predictive of the criterion once other predictors are controlled, and do not appear to be a part of an interaction term.

But what about important relevant predictors that may have been left out of the model? The effects of missing important variables are biases in the results. Important predictors may be left out for many reasons. For example, often when the data are collected there is no intention to use them for future purposes. Such is the case with the data set we have analysed in this chapter. Or, for example, you may be attempting to predict the recidivism rate for a particular disorder, but the hospital at which you work does not keep all relevant personal information about patients. In the current case, I suspect that the amount of time students spent preparing for the examination may be an important predictor of *score*. But the information was not collected. The effect of including study time in the model might have had important consequences. Because the amount of time students spend preparing for an examination certainly is related to examination performance, study time would likely substantially increase the explanatory power of the model (R^2). Also, since study time is likely related to *Wtai* and *gender*, the relative importance of these variables may change if study time is included in the model. These issues reflect the 'questions not asked and answers not given' aspect of multiple regression.

When important predictors are not included in a model, the researcher must be aware of how this necessitates qualifying the results and conclusions. For example, without the inclusion of study time we might suggest that what is most needed is a programme to reduce students' test anxiety. With the inclusion of study time we might conclude that ways of encouraging students to study more would be more effective than attempting to reduce test anxiety. In an ideal situation, we might wish to do as much of both as is possible. But with limited resources, choices must be made.

12 ● 12 WHAT CAN GO WRONG?

Multiple regression is an important tool for researchers, particularly when the researchers' data are observational in nature. Because it is an import tool, we must understand what can go wrong and what must be considered when presenting the results and drawing conclusions:

1   Nonlinearity of relations can distort results and conclusions. Although there are no perfect linear relations, researchers hope to be able to assume linearity. Even when we can assume linearity, there is always a 'bit of a curve'. This is why it is important to examine scatterplots. Chapter 8 in Allison (1999) provides an introduction to analysing nonlinear relations.
2   Univariate and bivariate outliers can produce distorted correlations and subsequent misleading results. Scatterplots are also useful for identifying bivariate outliers. Bivariate outliers left unresolved can either exaggerate or diminish the actual relation between two variables, particularly with small sample sizes. *Scatterplots, scatterplots, scatterplots!!!*
3   Multivariate outliers are also a source of distortion, particularly with small samples. It is necessary to save Mahalanobis scores and examine them.

4   Weak reliabilities and differences among reliabilities can distort the relations among the variables and lead to misleading models. When the reliability of one predictor is substantially weaker than that of the others, that variable's correlation with the criterion and the other predictors is attenuated. This can result in an underestimate of the variable's importance or in discarding it altogether. Furthermore, when the reliabilities of the predictors vary greatly the correlation matrix is unreliable and the results are suspect. It is important for the researcher to know the reliabilities of his or her measures, as they pertain to the population from which the sample is drawn.

5   In some instances substantial multicollinearity can be tolerated (pun intended); in other instances it can be a source of extremely misleading results. It is advisable to explore several strategies for analysing the data, even when there is moderate multicollinearity. Always select collinearity diagnostics when running a multiple regression.

6   It is important to know how to qualify the results and conclusions, with respect to both variables and sample. What important variables may not have been included in the model? How might they have influenced the findings? To what population can the results be generalized? Remember, an analysis is always an analysis of both the variables and the population from which the sample was drawn.

12 ● 13 CHAPTER SUMMARY

This chapter was intended to familiarize you with the basic design, assumptions, forms of analysis, and typical problems associated with *multiple regression*. We concentrated on a set of procedures based on the intersection of (1) a question of *relations* (or associations) and (2) *measurement* data. We focused on extending the ordinary least squares regression method covered in Chapter 7. Unlike in Chapter 7, however, the designs covered in this chapter contained more than one *predictor variable*. Where in a factorial ANOVA multiple independent variables are controlled through the experimental design, when multiple regression is used to analyse observational data, control is accomplished statistically. Similarly to factorial ANOVAs, multiple regression also allows for the identification of interactions. Several strategies were described for testing for their presence.

We paid particular attention to the key assumptions and to the annoying problems that are typically encountered when the predictors are not independent of one another. In addition to the issue of normality and linearity, we devoted considerable time to addressing the problems of missing data and multicollinearity. There were four strategies described for addressing missing data: listwise deletion, pairwise deletion, imputation, and multiple imputation. The last of these was deemed the most desirable if the missing data were missing completely at random. It was also argued that when the sample size is large and the proportion of missing data is less than 5%, all strategies will produce the same general findings. We examined the various circumstances that could produce multicollinearity and its negative consequences. We discussed five approaches for reducing the multicollinearity: two approaches that involve removing a variable, combining variables, stepwise regression, and creating a new variable with factor analysis. All of the approaches have their uses and limitations. The problems related to (1) relevant variables missing from the analysis and (2) unequal reliabilities were also briefly covered.

It must be remembered that, more than any other analysis we have covered thus far, multiple regression is an iterative series of analyses involving much of what has been presented in earlier chapters.

12 ●14 RECOMMENDED READINGS

Allison, P. D. (2002). *Missing data*. Thousand Oaks, CA: Sage.

This book provides a non-technical discussion of the topic of missing data. Allison also includes useful examples of the strategies that were briefly described in our chapter.

Allison, P. D. (1999). *Multiple regression: A primer*. Thousand Oaks, CA: Pine Forge Press.

This book is an excellent companion to this chapter. It elaborates topics that were covered, extends the coverage with different examples, provides links to other material we have covered, and illustrates how the logic of multiple regression is applied in more complicated designs.

Jaccard, J., & Turrisi, R. (2003). *Interaction effects in multiple regression* (2nd ed.). London: Sage.

This book covers numerous forms of interaction which space did not allow in our chapter. Furthermore, it is an accessible introduction to two-way and three-way interactions.

Vik, P. (2014). *Regression, ANOVA, and the general linear model: A statistics primer*. London: Sage.

It is one thing to say that ANOVA is a special case of multiple regression, it is another to systematically demonstrate it. This book contains a detailed treatment of the relation between ANOVA and regression. After reading it, you may wish to do all of your analyses, regardless of design, with a regression technique.

12 ●15 CHAPTER REVIEW QUESTIONS

Multiple-choice questions

1   In a multiple regression analysis with one predictor variable R is _____.

    a   the proportion of variance in the criterion associated with the predictor

    b   the unit change in the predictor associated with each unit change in the criterion

    c   the unit change in the criterion associated with each unit change in the predictor

    d   equal to the zero-order correlation between the predictor and the criterion

    e   the square root of the *y*-intercept

2   When two predictors are substantially correlated, _____.

    a   the assumption of linearity is likely violated

    b   multicollinearity is likely to be an issue

    c   heteroscedasticity is likely to be an issue

    d   All of the above are likely to be an issue

    e   None of the above are likely to be an issue

3   A scatterplot allows the researcher to _____.

    a   look for bivariate outliers

    b   assess if the relation is linear

    c   assess the assumption of homoscedasticity

    d   All of the above are true

    e   None of the above are allowed for by a scatterplot

4 An R^2_{adj} _____.

    a   can never be greater than R^2

    b   will always be greater than R^2

    c   is always equal to r^2

    d   is always equal to r^2_{adj}

    e   is the square root of R

5 The Mahalanobis test is intended to identify _____.

    a   violations of linearity

    b   violations of normality

    c   violations of homoscedasticity

    d   univariate outliers

    e   multivariate outliers

6 The general effect of a failure to include an important variable in the analysis is _____.

    a   violations of linearity

    b   violations of normality

    c   biased results

    d   multicollinearity

    e   an overestimate of R^2

7 A tolerance of 0.2 equates to _____.

    a   An R^2 of 0.04

    b   A VIF of 5

    c   An R^2 of 0.40

    d   A VIF of 0.04

    e   None of the above

8 A VIF of 10 means _____.

    a   the standard errors for evaluating the coefficients are inflated by a factor of 3.16

    b   the standard errors for evaluating the coefficients are inflated by a factor of 10

    c   the standard errors for evaluating the coefficients are inflated by a factor of 100

    d   the t-values for evaluating the coefficients are inflated by a factor of 3.16

    e   the t-values for evaluating the coefficients are inflated by a factor of 10

9 When assessing the interaction between a dichotomous variable and a measurement variable the B (slope) for the multiplicative term represents _____.

    a   the difference between the slopes of the two dichotomous groups

    b   the slope for one of the dichotomous groups

    c   the proportion of the variance accounted for by the interaction

    d   the square root of the proportion of the variance accounted for by the interaction

    e   None of the above

10 Which of the following can produce a false interaction effect?

    a   When ordinal data are treated as measurement data

    b   If the validity of a variable differs for different subjects in the study

    c   If the validity of a variable differs for different subjects in the study

    d   All three of the above can produce a false interaction

    e   None of the above can produce a false interaction

Short-answer questions

1 If we had one criterion variable and two predictor variables, what are the differences between conducting a single multiple regression analysis and conducting two separate simple regression analyses and summing the results?

2 In terms of R^2, when would there be no difference between running the two separate regressions and a single multiple regression as described in Question 1? Why?

3 What is multicollinearity and what are the circumstances that produce it?

4 What are four possible strategies for addressing multicollinearity?

5 What are the three questions regarding possible interactions and how are they addressed?

6 What is the difference between *missing at random* (MAR) and *missing completely at random* (MCAR)?

7 What are four possible strategies for addressing missing data?

Data set questions

1 Create a data set in SPSS ($n = 10$) with a criterion and two predictors where the presence of a multivariate outlier substantially affects the results. Demonstrate the effect by removing the outlier and rerunning the regression.

2 A (fictitious) psychology researcher examined the existing literature on happiness and proposed the following model of happiness. He deemed work to be important. The more we feel productive at work, the happier we will be. He deemed pleasure to be important. Pleasure is fun and the more fun we have, the happier we will be. The literature also indicated to him that there may be an interaction between work and pleasure. Finally, he deemed a simple openness to everyday experience to be important. Being able to enjoy the moment, any moment, simply for itself, appeared to him to be crucial to real happiness. He called this the Zen factor, for lack of a better term. He tested a large number of subjects using psychometric tests of these variables. The data are listed in the file *happinessstudy.sav* on the book's web page. The predictor variables are *age*, *work*, *pleasure,* and *zenatt. Happiness* (regr. factor score) is considered the measure of overall personal happiness and is the criterion variable. What is the best model of happiness that you can derive from his data? Be sure to address the issues of missing data, tests for all types of outliers, linearity, multicollinearity, and a test for the normality of the residuals. Present a final model (with or without interaction term) along with the R^2, the adjusted R^2, and the individual regression coefficients (slopes). Also include any conclusions you wish to make. What limitations do you see with respect to your analysis and findings?

Don't forget to use the online resources! Meet your supporting stats tutor through an **introductory video**, review your maths skills with a **diagnostic pre-test**, explore statistical principles through **interactive simulations**, practice analysis techniques with **SPSS datasets**, and check your work with **answers to all in-text questions**.

https://study.sagepub.com/bors

13

Chapter contents

FACTOR ANALYSIS

KEY CONCEPTS: manifest variables, latent variables, principal axis analysis, principal component analysis, component loadings, component scores, eigenvalues, communalities, unrotated solution, rotated solution, orthogonal rotation, varimax rotation, oblique rotation.

Figure 13.1

13 1 PURPOSE

In this final chapter we will dive down Alice's rabbit hole and introduce an entirely different wonderland of statistical analysis to a world that is orthogonal to the one we have been exploring thus far. The purpose of this chapter is to familiarize you with the basic logic and techniques behind a set of techniques which are collectively referred to as *factor analysis*. We begin by describing how the research questions that require the use of factor analysis differ from most of the research questions addressed thus far in this book.

The first key to appreciating factor analysis is to understand how it is designed to reduce a larger set of *observed variables* to a smaller set of derived *latent variables* or components. Once we grasp the nature of a component, we will see how a subject's scores on a set of observed variables can be transformed into fewer scores associated with a set of derived components. We will see how a theoretical understanding of the topic being studied is crucial for making the decisions which must be made during the analysis. Finally, we will explore other uses of factor analysis as well as its common limitations.

13 2 INTRODUCTION

You may remember the name Charles Spearman from your introductory psychology course. He is largely responsible for the way researchers and the general public understand the concept of intelligence (Spearman, 1904b, 1927). Spearman began with the observation that cognitive abilities were *not random* with respect to each other; people who performed well on one task of cognitive ability tended to perform well on all other such tasks. You may have noticed that those of your peers who do well in one course tend to do well in others. It was this pattern of positive correlations among cognitive tasks which lead Spearman to postulate that intelligence is primarily determined by a single, general cognitive ability (*g*). He deemed this single, underlying ability to be the chief factor determining how an individual performed on any given cognitive task.

You also may remember the name Louis Thurstone. He agreed with Spearman concerning the existence of a pattern of positive correlations among the tests of cognitive abilities. Thurstone had a different interpretation of that pattern of correlations, however. In addition to the overall pattern of positive correlations, he saw an arrangement of distinct clusters among the tasks. Thurstone (1924, 1938) proposed that these clusters reflected *seven primary mental abilities* and in combination they were responsible for performance on the multitude of possible cognitive tasks. The ongoing debate concerning the nature of intelligence – which includes the position that intelligence is merely a statistical artefact – can be traced back to this early one-factor versus multiple-factors debate.

You may wonder why we are reviewing the origins of the debate over the nature of

> The term *factor* is used here as it was used in previous chapters. A factor is another way to refer to an *independent variable* or a *predictor variable*. Regarding intelligence, from his observational studies Spearman argued for a single important predictor variable. He went one step further and argued that the single predictor was the primary determinant of intelligence.

intelligence in a statistics book. It is because the history of the intelligence debate and the history of the development of the statistical technique called *factor analysis* are intimately intertwined. In large part, early factor-analytic techniques were developed as tools that could be used to settle the debate over the nature of intelligence. Unfortunately, although valuable in many respects, those tools have been unable to settle the matter. By the end of this chapter you should have some sense of why.

Before beginning our presentation, it must be said that factor analysis itself has been controversial. Some scientists view factor analysis, or at least some uses of it, as statistical *alchemy*. Defiantly, others assert that factor analysis can actually transmute lead into gold, metaphorically speaking. This debate is not unique to factor analysis. Both positions have always been directed at statistics in general. Recall Mark Twain's claim that there are 'lies, damned lies, and statistics'. With respect to both factor analysis and statistics in general, it is best to acknowledge that there are both appropriate *uses* and inappropriate *abuses* of all techniques. The goal is to differentiate between the two. Remember, even a mean can be meaningless.

13●3 WHAT IS FACTOR ANALYSIS?

The term *factor analysis* covers a number of related statistical techniques designed to reduce a set of *observed variables* to a smaller set of unobserved or *latent components*. Another way to describe factor analysis is to think of it as a method for displaying how a set of variables group or cluster themselves. The basis for the clustering of the observed variables is their pattern of shared variance or intercorrelations. The clusters are the basis of the new *latent components*. Researchers may find that all of the variables in the analysis share enough variance to conclude that there is only a single component, such as Spearman proposed regarding cognitive abilities.

The nature of the latent component is determined by examining the content of the observed variables that cluster together and, if there is more than one cluster, how those variables as a group differ from the variables in other clusters. Because factor analysis is based on comparing and contrasting shared and unshared variance, the variables that are included, as well as those excluded, will influence the resulting clusters, as well as the researcher's interpretation. For example, if measures of athleticism, musical talent, and social awareness are included with more typical measures of cognitive abilities, it is unlikely that a single latent component of general ability will emerge (Neisser et al., 1996). You conclude either that intelligence is more than one latent component or that athleticism, musical talent, and social awareness are not constituents of intelligence and should be excluded from the analysis. Your decision can only be made theoretically – the outcome of the factor analysis cannot decide the matter.

As stated above, there are several related techniques that are often referred to as *factor analysis*. The first distinction to be made is between exploratory factor analysis and confirmatory factor analysis. The primary aim of *exploratory* factor analysis is to discover how a set of variables cluster or fail to cluster. Even when a researcher has good reason to *expect* a particular pattern of clustering, statistically there is no formal null hypothesis (H_0) that is being tested. Until the analysis reveals otherwise, it is *assumed* that the *observed variables* are all *independent* of each other. This assumption, however, is not an H_0 which will be statistically tested. In *confirmatory* factor analysis researchers have an explicit hypothesis (H_1) concerning the pattern of clustering. The analysis allows for the testing of the researcher's predicted patterns of clustering against the *expectation* of either no pattern (H_0) or an alternative pattern (H_2). Thus, with confirmatory factor analysis we are back to examining the difference between *expected* and *observed* outcomes, and the probability associated with the *observed difference*. Paul Kline (2002) provides an excellent introduction to both exploratory and confirmatory factor analysis which goes well beyond the scope of this chapter.

Here we are concerned with a form of exploratory factor analysis, of which there are two common types: *principal axis analysis* (PAA) and *principal component analysis* (PCA). In addition to some analytic differences, the primary distinction between the two pertains to what is analysed. In a PAA, only the variance that is shared among the observed variables is analysed. The variance that is unique to each variable is excluded. In a PCA all variance (shared and unshared) related to the observed variables is analysed. Figure 13.2 is a simple illustration of the difference between PAA and PCA. The three circles represent the variance of three observed variables. The areas that overlap – shaded in blue – represent shared variance, the basis for the bivariate correlations among the three variables. The unshaded areas of the circles represent the variance unique to each variable. Both shaded and unshaded areas are analysed by PCA, but only the blue area is analysed by PAA.

Although it has been shown that PAA and PCA can on occasion produce somewhat different results, and that PCA is best used for the initial exploration of data, the results of the two analyses usually differ only in terms of details and not in terms of the number of derived components. The strength of the clustering may vary somewhat, but how the variables cluster rarely varies. The focus of this chapter will be on PCA, which was first proposed by Karl Pearson (1901b), of correlation fame, and later further developed by Harold Hotelling (1933).

PAA and PCA are used for three general purposes (Field, 2013):

1   These techniques are used to help researchers explore the structure of theoretical constructs. Intelligence and personality are areas that initially received great attention, but factor analysis is now applied to everything from happiness to racism, from athletic ability to economic performance, and many other areas of investigation.

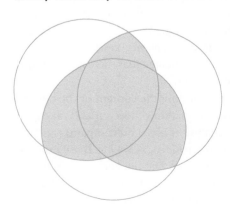

Figure 13.2

2   In several areas of psychology and the social sciences, researchers use these techniques to help in the construction of tests and questionnaires. PAA and PCA can alert researchers to the fact that a test or questionnaire measures constructs in addition to those intended (Kline, 1986). PAA and PCA also are used to examine possible cultural differences in the clustering of the test items.

3   PAA and PCA techniques are used to combine scores from several variables, creating a single new score which is used in further statistical analyses. In certain circumstances this is an effective way to resolve the problem of multicollinearity, as discussed in the previous chapter.

Before proceeding, one additional general point should be stressed. Most of the analyses we have examined in this book involved (1) an independent or predictor variable and (2) a dependent or criterion variable(s). With respect to *t*-tests, ANOVAs, all forms of regression analyses, and their nonparametric alternatives, the researcher is concerned with identifying circumstances (predictors or independent variables) that influence or are associated with a dependent or outcome variable. The simplest general model, regardless of whether the research is experimental or observational in nature, is

observed outcome = expected outcome + possible effects of predictors + error.

The logic is one of antecedents and consequences. No such distinction exists in PCA. The variables are not segregated onto one side or the other of an equals sign. The primary goal of PCA is to examine how a set of *observed* variables may segregate or group themselves. This does not preclude aspects of the analysis subsequently being used in other forms of analysis. We saw an example of this when resolving the multicollinearity problem in the previous chapter.

13●4 CORRELATION COEFFICIENTS REVISITED

We begin our presentation of PCA by returning to the concepts of correlation and shared variance. Figure 13.3 illustrates with a Venn diagram two variables that are completely uncorrelated ($r = 0$). There is no overlap in the areas of the two depicted variables. The light blue circle represents the variance associated with one variable and the dark blue circle represents the variance associated with a second variable. Figure 13.4 illustrates two perfectly correlated variables ($r = 1.0$). The medium blue circle represents the complete overlap of the two variables' variances.

When two variables are completely uncorrelated as in Figure 13.3, or are perfectly correlated as in Figure 13.4, it is relatively easy to interpret the situation. In the first case, the two variables are *random* with respect to each other. Knowing the change in one variable does nothing to help you predict the change in the other variable. The two variables are measures of *unrelated* or *independent* phenomena. In the second case, there is nothing random at all about the relation between the two variables; they are *perfectly related*. Knowing the change in one variable allows you to predict perfectly the change in the other. We think of them as two measures of a single phenomenon. In the case of Figure 13.3, there can be no common latent component. In the case of Figure 13.4, the common latent component is perfectly reflected in either of the two variables.

Figure 13.3   Figure 13.4

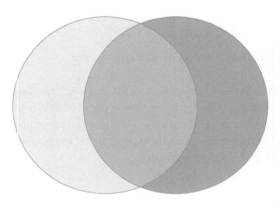

Figure 13.5

The situation changes when we look at Figure 13.5 where the light blue and medium blue areas represent the variance associated with one variable and the dark blue and medium blue areas represent the variance associated with a second variable. The medium blue area represents the overlap, the variance shared by the two variables. In this case, there is both a random and a non-random dimension to the relation between the two variables. Knowing the change in one variable *in part* allows us to predict the other. This is reflected in the non-random or medium blue portion of the figure.

We can think of these two variables as measures that partially reflect a common underlying component. Such a relation may exist between an algebra test and a calculus test, or between playing baseball and playing cricket. There may be an underlying *quantitative abilities* factor that the two tests have in common, and there may be an underlying *athletic ability* factor that the two sports have in common. There is always more than one interpretation, however. Someone may argue that the basis for the relation between the two tests is a *general intelligence* factor, for example. Or, someone may argue that the correlation reflects an *academic motivation* factor.

 Web Link 13.1 for an interactive demonstration of shared variance, scatterplot, and correlation.

This issue of interpretation exposes an important fact about PCA and factor analysis in general. PCA cannot be a substitute for theoretical appreciation and knowledge of the research area, nor is PCA a magic bullet that will resolve theoretical disputes. But as we have seen in earlier chapters, the same may be said of any form of statistical analysis.

The issues become more complex as we increase the number of variables. Figure 13.6 illustrates three interrelated variables where each shares variance with the others separately and collectively.

The light blue, cross-hatched, dotted, and solid grey areas represent the area or variance associated with the first variable. The medium blue, striped, cross-hatched and grey areas represent the second variable. The dark blue, striped, dotted and the grey areas represent the area of the third variable. Additionally:

1   The cross-hatched area represents the variance shared by only the first and second variables.
2   The striped area represents the variance shared by only the second and third variables.
3   The dotted area represents the variance shared by only the first and third variables.
4   The grey area represents the variance shared by all three variables.

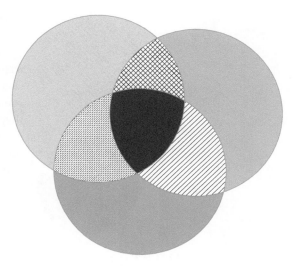

Figure 13.6

The grey area thus represents the variance associated with a latent component common to all three observed variables. Interpreting the grey area requires comparing and contrasting the shared, partially shared, and unshared sources of variance. Again, this requires both a theoretical appreciation and knowledge of the research area.

Web Link 13.2 for an interactive demonstration of the shared variances and correlations among three variables.

13 ● 5   THE CORRELATION MATRIX AND PCA

Although we input individual responses into the SPSS *Data Editor* window, the correlation matrix (sometimes called the *R*-matrix) or covariance matrix is the real data the PCA analyses. Figure 13.7 represents the correlation matrix for four variables.

The empty cells in the upper right of Figure 13.7 are simply duplicates of those in

	Var1	Var2	Var3	Var4
Var1	1.0			
Var2	0.0	1.0		
Var3	0.0	0.0	1.0	
Var4	0.0	0.0	0.0	1.0

Figure 13.7

the lower left. When we create a Venn diagram of this correlation matrix (Figure 13.8), we see four completely non-overlapping circles. We have four totally independent variables, all random with respect to the others. There is no need for PCA; we shall find four latent variables. No reduction in the number of variables is possible when there is no shared variance. This is what is *expected* when the researcher begins with the assumption that there is no common underlying component. Of course, this pattern of correlations is rarely *observed*.

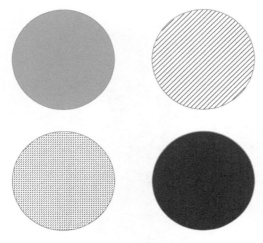

Figure 13.8

	Var1	Var2	Var3	Var4
Var1	1.0			
Var2	1.0	1.0		
Var3	1.0	1.0	1.0	
Var4	1.0	1.0	1.0	1.0

Figure 13.9

Figure 13.9 also represents the correlation matrix for four variables.

When we create a Venn diagram of this correlation matrix (Figure 13.10), we see only one circle. We have four variables that behave in concert. There might be four different tests, but they all appear to measure exactly the same phenomenon or set of phenomena. Again, there is no need for PCA, we necessarily will find only one latent variable: a one-component model. When there is absolutely no *unshared* variance, there can be only one latent variable or component. This is what is *expected* when the researcher begins with the assumption that there is a single, common underlying component. Similarly to the previous pattern, this matrix of correlations is rarely *observed*. As was the case with other forms of statistical analyses, there is always a difference between what is *expected* and what is *observed*. The problem of evaluating the difference in PCA is somewhat more difficult than the other forms of analyses we have covered.

In both of the above cases interpretation is *relatively* easy. The only question is: what do the variables measure? Although in comparison to other situations this is a relatively easy task, it can be at times quite daunting. For example, even when researchers studying intelligence agree upon a single-factor model, they often disagree on the nature of that single factor.

Figure 13.11 also represents a somewhat more complex situation. When we create a Venn diagram of the correlation matrix in Figure 13.11, we see two non-overlapping circles. The light blue circle in Figure 13.12 represents the perfect overlap of *Var1* and *Var2* from Figure 13.11. The dark blue circle in Figure 13.12 represents the perfect overlap of *Var3* and *Var4*. The non-overlap of the two circles represents the fact that *Var1* and *Var2* share no variance with *Var3* and *Var4*. We have four measures that behave like two unrelated measures. Furthermore, there is no

	Var1	Var2	Var3	Var4
Var1	1.0			
Var2	1.0	1.0		
Var3	0.0	0.0	1.0	
Var4	0.0	0.0	1.0	1.0

Figure 13.10

Figure 13.11

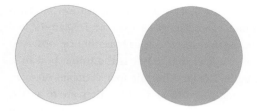

Figure 13.12

	Var1	Var2	Var3	Var4
Var1	1.0			
Var2	0.4	1.0		
Var3	0.6	0.3	1.0	
Var4	0.2	0.4	.15	1.0

Figure 13.13

unshared variance within each pair. Yet again, there is no need for PCA; we necessarily will find two latent variables: a two-component model. The only question is what each pair measures. In the real world of research we never find correlation matrices like those in Figures 13.7, 13.9, or 13.11. Figure 13.13 is more representative of what is often found.

Stare at Figure 13.13 as long as you wish, it gets no easier to make a *non-random* guess about the number of clusters into which these four variables segregate. The Venn diagram (Figure 13.14) of the overlapping areas associated with the four variables is of little help. Furthermore, in such cases we find that determining the number of clusters remains debatable, even after a PCA.

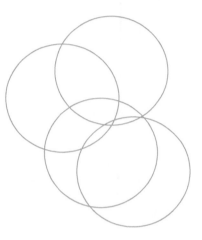

Figure 13.14

13●6   THE COMPONENT MATRIX

The mathematics of PCA which takes the data and produces new latent components is beyond the scope of this book. There are currently many books that do an excellent job of explaining the procedure; some require more mathematical sophistication than do others, however. For those with adequate mathematical skills, one place to start would be Kim and Mueller (1978). For our current purposes, let it be said that PCA is a *linear* technique for fitting an *n*-dimensional ellipsoid (a multidimensional ellipse) to the observed data, where *n* is the number of observed variables. Each axis of the ellipsoid is a principal component. The axes are derived from largest to smallest. If an axis of the ellipsoid is too short and the percentage of the total variance associated with that axis is small, then that axis (component) may be eliminated from the model and there will be one fewer retained latent component. All subsequent derived axes necessarily will be even smaller and will also be eliminated.

Although this description is incomplete, we might think of fitting the first axis (a straight line) within the ellipsoid similarly to the way we fitted a regression to a scatterplot line back in Chapter 7. The aim is to account for as much of the variance as possible. Once the first axis has been established, PCA then fits a second line that is kept orthogonal (at a right angle) to the first. Again, the line of best fit is computed. In the case of the second axis, the axis is rotated 360° in three-dimensional

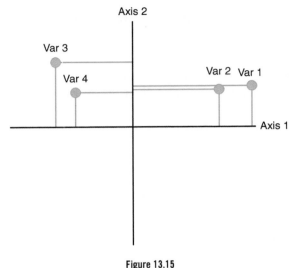

Figure 13.15

space to find the best fit. Although it is shown in two-dimensional space, Figure 13.15 depicts the fit the two axes have with respect to four hypothetical observed variables. The fact that axis 1 is the initial best fit is illustrated by the fact that the four variables on average are much closer to axis 1 than they are to axis 2. All subsequent axes will radiate from the central point called the origin.

After the second axis has been fitted, a third axis is fitted in four-dimensional space and kept orthogonal to both axis 1 and axis 2. It is difficult to visually imagine or to depict spinning the axis in the fourth dimension; it can only be understood mathematically.

If there are four observed variables there are four new latent variables. Axis 4 will be fitted in five-dimensional space. You might ask how we have reduced the number of variables, if we began with four observed variables and ended up with four latent variables. The answer goes back to our brief description of the mathematics of PCA: 'If an axis of the ellipsoid is too short and the percentage of the total variance associated with that axis is small, then that axis (component) may be eliminated from the model and there will be one fewer retained latent component.'

> There will always be as many new latent variables (components) created as there are observed variables included in the analysis. What changes is the distribution of the variance. PCA attempts to redistribute as much of the total variance in the observed variables onto as few new variables as possible. As will be discussed, only those new variables that meet a criterion selected by the researcher are retained.

> Remember that weak correlations are those that range from 0.1 to 0.3; moderate correlations range from 0.3 to 0.5; and strong correlations range from 0.6 to 1.0. The same can be said of component loadings, which are themselves correlations. For our current purposes, these three categories of correlations are all that is needed.

The four new latent components represent a redistribution of the variance associated with the four observed variables. Although four new components are created – at this point they are still simply axes – it is very likely that at least one of the axes will account for too little variance to be retained. Although it is a simplification, the process of adding or discarding new components is similar to the process of adding and retaining predictor variables during a stepwise multiple regression analysis.

The results of this stage of a PCA are presented and summarized in what is called a *component matrix* or a *factor loadings matrix*. Figure 13.16 depicts a hypothetical component matrix for eight observed variables and where three new latent variables (components) have been retained. The first column lists the variable names. The second, third, and fourth columns record the strength of the relations (component loadings) between the original observed variables and the three retained components. Although the loadings in Figure 13.16 are shown only as strong, moderate, and weak, in practice these loadings are numbers ranging from 0 to 1. Showing the component loadings as strong, moderate, and weak is done here for illustrative purposes. Component loadings are actually the correlations between the observed variables and the derived components.

Variables observed	Components			
	Component 1	**Component 2**	**Component 3**	**Communality**
Var1	Strong	Moderate	Moderate	.900
Var2	Moderate	Moderate	Weak	.800
Var3	Weak	Moderate	Weak	.710
Var4	Moderate	Weak	Moderate	.650
Var5	Moderate	Weak	Moderate	.630
Var6	Weak	Moderate	Weak	.560
Var7	Moderate	Weak	Weak	.550
Var8	Moderate	Moderate	Weak	.720
Eigenvalue	3.0	1.5	1.1	

Figure 13.16 Component matrix

Eigenvalues

How was it decided that only three of the possible eight components would be retained? The most common criterion for deciding how many components to retain was developed by Kaiser (1960). The Kaiser or K1 criterion states that for a derived component to be retained it must account for at least as much of the total variance as does the *average observed variable* in the data set: an

> Why is the eigenvalue of 1 used as the threshold? Rationally, it makes little sense to create a new latent variable that accounts for less variance than did the average observed variable. Remember, the goal is to reduce the number of variables. PCA can metaphorically be considered a semi-legal form of distilling a great amount of material down to its valuable essence.

eigenvalue of at least 1. If there are eight observed variables, on average, each variable accounts for (100% / 8) or 12.5% of the total variance. A component that accounts for 37.5% of the total variance has an eigenvalue of 37.5/12.5 = 3.0, as does our component 1 in Figure 13.16. An eigenvalue of 1.5, as we find associated with component 2 in the table, indicates that the component accounts for $12.5 \times 1.5 = 18.75\%$ of the total variance. The eigenvalue of 1.1 associated with component 3 indicates that this component accounts for 13.75% of the total variance. When we sum the percentages associated with the three components, we find 69.0% of the variance in our original data is accounted for by the three-component model.

The issue of how many components to retain is dealt with in greater detail later in the chapter. Two points should be made, however. First, there are times when components with eigenvalues less than 1 should be retained, and there are times when there are components with eigenvalues greater than 1 that should be eliminated. Second, knowledge of previous research, theoretical understanding of the area, and conceptual clarity regarding the phenomenon under investigation are all irreplaceable when it comes to deciding the number of components to retain and how those components may be interpreted.

Communalities

The fifth column in Figure 13.16 reports the *communalities* associated with each observed variable. Communalities can be considered the multiple R^2 values resulting from a multiple regression analysis (as described in Chapter 12) where each observed variable is the criterion and the retained derived components are the predictors. The value of an observed variable's communality can be interpreted as the proportion of that variable's variance accounted for by the retained components.

A communality of 1 indicates that the retained components explain all of the variance in that observed variable. A communality of 0 indicates that the retained components explain none of the variance in that observed variable. Ideally, communalities should be greater than 0.6. If a variable's communality is less than 0.6, the researcher should consider removing that variable on the grounds it may not belong with the others. In our case, the three components do a better job for some observed variables than they do for others. If we sum all of the communalities, the total communality value is 5.52. That total divided by 8 (the number of observed variables) and multiplied by 100 is 69 or 69.0%. Recall that this is the percentage of the total variance in the observed variables that was accounted for by the three derived components as calculated using their eigenvalues.

13.7 THE ROTATED COMPONENT MATRIX

When more than one component is retained, we have the option of redefining the components by redistributing the explained variance among them. Recall that initially the components are defined in a purely mathematical manner from largest to smallest. The first derived component accounts for the largest portion of the total variance, and each successive component accounts for a smaller and smaller proportion.

The result of this purely mathematical approach frequently poses serious interpretive difficulties. A simple example was illustrated back in Figure 13.15, where the initial analysis conceals two clusters. Mathematically, all four variables are associated most closely with axis 1. As can be seen in the figure, however, *Var1* and *Var2* comprise one cluster (to the right) and *Var3* and *Var4* comprise a second cluster (to the left). When there is more than one retained component, the task of interpreting the pattern of initial loadings can often feel like doing a jigsaw puzzle with ill-shaped pieces.

The logic and mathematics behind various forms of rotation are beyond the scope of this book. A good explanation can be found in Chapter 5 of Kline (2002).

When more than one component is retained, researchers often *rotate* the axes to find a more interpretable model. As long as the axes are kept orthogonal, the total variance accounted for by the model is unchanged, and only the distribution of the accounted for variance across the retained components changes. That is, any position in the rotation mathematically is as good a fit as any other position. The most common form of orthogonal rotation (varimax) aims to maximize or minimize each observed variable's loading on each component. The rotated component matrix in Figure 13.17 illustrates the change in the loadings for our hypothetical analysis in Figure 13.16. Notice that Figure 13.17 has fewer moderate loadings than does Figure 13.16. Reducing the number of moderate loadings is often the key to finding an interpretable model. After rotation the eight observed variables are more closely associated with one particular component, which allows for easier interpretation.

Variables observed	Components		
	Component 1	Component 2	Component 3
Var1	Strong	Weak	Weak
Var2	Weak	Strong	Weak
Var3	Weak	Strong	Weak
Var4	Strong	Weak	Moderate
Var5	Moderate	Weak	Strong
Var6	Weak	Strong	Weak
Var7	Strong	Weak	Weak
Var8	Moderate	Weak	Strong

Figure 13.17 Rotated component matrix

Figure 13.18 illustrates the post-rotation new relation of the four variables and two components depicted earlier in Figure 13.10. The two clusters that were initially masked in the unrotated analysis are now revealed. The four variables are seen to be associated with two different components. While *Var1* and *Var2* are closer to axis 1 than they were initially, *Var3* and *Var4* now are closer to axis 2.

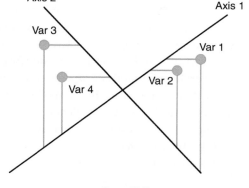

Figure 13.18

13●8 A DETAILED EXAMPLE

This example of PCA will illustrate the following points:

1   The steps involved in conducting a PCA using SPSS.
2   Some common issues and ambiguities that are often encountered.
3   The process of choosing between orthogonal and oblique rotations.

4   The use of PCA as a strategy for addressing multicollinearity encountered in a multiple regression analysis.

5   The use of external criteria as an aid when deciding on a final factor structure.

6   The effects of variable choice on the final model.

The data used in this example are drawn from the data set used in Chapter 12. The data were collected in an undergraduate introductory psychology course and reported in Bors et al. (2006). The study included an examination of the Spielberger et al.'s (1980) Test Anxiety Inventory (TAI). As you recall from Chapter 12, parts of the TAI are said to measure a *worry* component which reflects the subject's thoughts concerning the consequences of failure. Other items are said to measure an *emotionality* component which reflects autonomic nervous system's responses, such as sweaty palms. Finally, recall from Chapter 12 that only the *worry* component has been associated with academic performance.

The data file (*factoranalysistai.sav*) for this example is found on the book's web page. The data are in a rectangular file. Each row represents a subject, in this case a student. Each column represents a variable. Ideally, all students should have a value entered for all variables. The general problem with missing data was dealt with in detail in Chapter 12.

In the case of PCA, if you have hundreds of subjects and only a few (less than 2%) have missing data, the safest and easiest approach is to simply delete those subjects from the data set. If a subject is missing values for several variables, even if you have relatively few subjects, again it is safest to delete that subject. If there is a variable for which more than 10% of the subjects have missing data, it is best to delete the variable. Various approaches to *imputing* missing data and the notion of data *missing completely at random* were addressed in Chapter 12.

> TAI items 3, 4, 5, 6, 7, 14, 17, and 20 are identified as *worry* items. Items 2, 8, 9, 10, 11, 15, 16, and 18 are identified as *emotionality* items.

For PCA, SPSS offers three simple options for addressing the problem of missing data: *exclude cases listwise*, *exclude cases pairwise*, and *replace with mean*. Excluding cases (sources or subjects) *listwise* is the safest approach. Any subject who is missing any of the values to be used in the analysis is deleted. Excluding cases *pairwise* uses as much of a subject's data as possible. A subject is only excluded from those aspects of the analysis for which his or her missing data are needed. The differences found in the component loadings of these two approaches to missing data can range from negligible to considerable, but the general pattern of the loadings rarely changes. As the percentage of missing data increases, so do the chances of there being substantial differences in results. In most circumstances, the third option of replacing the missing data with the variable's mean is no longer recommended.

Correlation matrix

To begin our PCA open the data set on the book's web page.

   Web Link 13.3 for the *factoranalysisTAI.sav* data set.

When the SPSS *Data Editor* appears you will notice that the columns have the variable names you saw in Chapter 12. There are data for 603 students. Initially we are interested only in the variables that begin with the letters *tai*, of which there are 16. Four of the 20 TAI items have been removed because they are not clearly associated with either worry or emotionality.

The first step in conducting a PCA is to examine the correlations among the variables included in the study. **Under *Analyze* in the *Data Editor* window's menu bar, select *Correlate* and then *Bivariate*. When the *Bivariate Correlations* window opens, move the 16 TAI items over to the *Variables* box (Figure 13.19). Leave the *Pearson* option checked and click *OK*.**

Figure 13.20 reports the bivariate correlations among the 16 TAI items. First, notice that all of the correlations are positive and range from slightly less

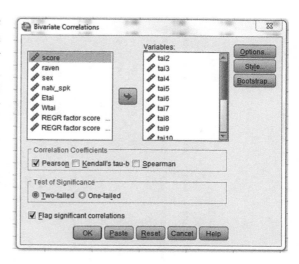

Figure 13.19

than 0.20 to slightly less than 0.60. This is similar to what Spearman found when he examined the correlations among an array of cognitive tasks. Next, notice the frustration you experience if you attempt to visually examine the correlation matrix with the aim of identifying two clusters: worry and emotionality. If there are two distinguishable sets of variables, we might *expect* to see moderate to strong correlations between the variables within each group and weak correlations between variables across the two groups. Such a pattern is not discernible.

Because of the nebulous pattern of correlations, at first glance it seems reasonable to conclude that the TAI is best understood as a scale dominated by a single latent component. Perhaps that component can be interpreted as *general test anxiety*, or perhaps it reflects a *general anxiety trait*. If we settle on a one-component model for the TAI, we will require further research to help us choose between those competing interpretations. As we will see, the notion of a two-component model of the TAI (worry and emotionality) cannot be ruled out.

After examining the correlation matrix, scroll down the *Analyze* menu to *Dimension Reduction*. **Then move over and select *Factor*. When the *Factor Analysis* window opens (Figure 13.21), move the 16 TAI items over to the *Variables* box. Next, click on the *Extraction* button. When the *Factor Analysis: Extraction* window opens (Figure 13.22), leave the *Method* on the *Principal components* setting, ensure that both the *Unrotated factor solution* and *Scree plot* options in the *Display* box are selected, ensure that *Eigenvalues greater than* is set at 1, and click *Continue*.**

When you return to the *Factor Analysis* window, click *Rotation*. When the *Factor Analysis: Rotation* window opens (Figure 13.23), select the *Varimax* option in the *Method* box. Notice that the *Rotated solution* option in the *Display* box is automatically selected. Also select *Loadings plot(s)* and then click *Continue*. If you wish to change the option regarding the handling of missing data, click *Options* in the *Factor Analysis* window. After making your selection in the *Factor Analysis: Options* window (Figure 13.24), click *Continue*. When the *Factor Analysis* window reappears, click *OK*.

Correlations

		tai2	tai3	tai4	tai5	tai6	tai7	tai8	tai9	tai10	tai11	tai14	tai15	tai16	tai17	tai18	tai 20
tai2	Pearson Correlation	1	.310**	.414**	.263**	.276**	.346**	.542**	.492**	.263**	.529**	.390**	.543**	.541**	.357**	.477**	.384**
	Sig. (2-tailed)		.000	.000	.000	.000	.000	.000	.000	.000	.000	.000	.000	.000	.000	.000	.000
	N	610	610	610	610	610	609	607	610	609	607	607	609	609	610	608	610
tai3	Pearson Correlation	.310**	1	.427**	.333**	.363**	.550**	.301**	.321**	.297**	.365**	.472**	.452**	.420**	.438**	.366**	.360**
	Sig. (2-tailed)	.000		.000	.000	.000	.000	.000	.000	.000	.000	.000	.000	.000	.000	.000	.000
	N	610	610	610	610	610	609	607	610	609	607	607	609	609	610	608	610
tai4	Pearson Correlation	.414**	.427**	1	.335**	.405**	.440**	.431**	.416**	.207**	.437**	.488**	.518**	.443**	.386**	.424**	.510**
	Sig. (2-tailed)	.000	.000		.000	.000	.000	.000	.000	.000	.000	.000	.000	.000	.000	.000	.000
	N	610	610	610	610	610	609	607	610	609	607	607	609	609	610	608	610
tai5	Pearson Correlation	.263**	.333**	.335**	1	.327**	.334**	.298**	.270**	.176**	.260**	.319**	.358**	.331**	.422**	.325**	.280**
	Sig. (2-tailed)	.000	.000	.000		.000	.000	.000	.000	.000	.000	.000	.000	.000	.000	.000	.000
	N	610	610	610	610	610	609	607	610	609	607	607	609	609	610	608	610
tai6	Pearson Correlation	.276**	.363**	.405**	.327**	1	.400**	.324**	.275**	.165**	.274**	.404**	.392**	.294**	.340**	.286**	.399**
	Sig. (2-tailed)	.000	.000	.000	.000		.000	.000	.000	.000	.000	.000	.000	.000	.000	.000	.000
	N	610	610	610	610	610	609	607	610	609	607	607	609	609	610	608	610
tai7	Pearson Correlation	.346**	.550**	.440**	.334**	.400**	1	.379**	.385**	.319**	.422**	.491**	.505**	.451**	.536**	.380**	.433**
	Sig. (2-tailed)	.000	.000	.000	.000	.000		.000	.000	.000	.000	.000	.000	.000	.000	.000	.000
	N	609	609	609	609	609	609	606	609	608	606	606	608	608	609	607	609
tai8	Pearson Correlation	.542**	.301**	.431**	.298**	.324**	.379**	1	.539**	.301**	.511**	.383**	.604**	.486**	.354**	.478**	.411**
	Sig. (2-tailed)	.000	.000	.000	.000	.000	.000		.000	.000	.000	.000	.000	.000	.000	.000	.000
	N	607	607	607	607	607	606	607	607	606	604	604	606	606	607	605	607
tai9	Pearson Correlation	.492**	.321**	.416**	.270**	.275**	.385**	.539**	1	.423**	.567**	.382**	.580**	.533**	.400**	.496**	.469**
	Sig. (2-tailed)	.000	.000	.000	.000	.000	.000	.000		.000	.000	.000	.000	.000	.000	.000	.000
	N	610	609	610	610	610	609	607	610	609	607	607	609	609	610	608	610
tai10	Pearson Correlation	.263**	.297**	.207**	.176**	.165**	.319**	.301**	.423**	1	.391**	.259**	.366**	.426**	.363**	.361**	.252**
	Sig. (2-tailed)	.000	.000	.000	.000	.000	.000	.000	.000		.000	.000	.000	.000	.000	.000	.000
	N	609	609	609	609	609	608	606	609	609	606	606	608	608	609	607	609

		tai2	tai3	tai4	tai5	tai6	tai7	tai8	tai9	tai10	tai11	tai14	tai15	tai16	tai17	tai18	tai20
tai11	Pearson Correlation	.529**	.365**	.437**	.260**	.274**	.422**	.511**	.567**	.391**	1	.450**	.601**	.578**	.399**	.555**	.468**
	Sig. (2-tailed)	.000	.000	.000	.000	.000	.000	.000	.000	.000		.000	.000	.000	.000	.000	.000
	N	607	607	607	607	607	606	604	607	606	607	604	606	606	607	605	607
tai14	Pearson Correlation	.390**	.472**	.488**	.319**	.404**	.491**	.383**	.382**	.259**	.450**	1	.557**	.429**	.438**	.417**	.456**
	Sig. (2-tailed)	.000	.000	.000	.000	.000	.000	.000	.000	.000	.000		.000	.000	.000	.000	.000
	N	607	607	607	607	607	606	604	607	606	604	607	606	606	607	605	607
tai15	Pearson Correlation	.543**	.452**	.518**	.358**	.392**	.505**	.604**	.580**	.366**	.601**	.557**	1	.629**	.478**	.552**	.523**
	Sig. (2-tailed)	.000	.000	.000	.000	.000	.000	.000	.000	.000	.000	.000		.000	.000	.000	.000
	N	609	609	609	609	609	608	606	609	609	606	606	609	608	609	607	609
tai16	Pearson Correlation	.541**	.420**	.443**	.331**	.294**	.451**	.486**	.533**	.426**	.578**	.429**	.629**	1	.485**	.500**	.462**
	Sig. (2-tailed)	.000	.000	.000	.000	.000	.000	.000	.000	.000	.000	.000	.000		.000	.000	.000
	N	609	609	609	609	609	608	606	609	608	606	606	608	609	609	607	609
tai17	Pearson Correlation	.357**	.438**	.386**	.422**	.340**	.536**	.354**	.400**	.363**	.399**	.438**	.478**	.485**	1	.438**	.448**
	Sig. (2-tailed)	.000	.000	.000	.000	.000	.000	.000	.000	.000	.000	.000	.000	.000		.000	.000
	N	610	610	610	610	610	609	607	610	609	607	607	609	609	610	608	610
tai18	Pearson Correlation	.477**	.366**	.424**	.325**	.286**	.380**	.478**	.496**	.361**	.555**	.417**	.552**	.500**	.438**	1	.425**
	Sig. (2-tailed)	.000	.000	.000	.000	.000	.000	.000	.000	.000	.000	.000	.000	.000	.000		.000
	N	608	608	608	608	608	607	605	608	607	605	605	607	607	608	608	608
tai20	Pearson Correlation	.384**	.360**	.510**	.280**	.399**	.433**	.411**	.469**	.252**	.468**	.456**	.523**	.462**	.448*	.425**	1
	Sig. (2-tailed)	.000	.000	.000	.000	.000	.000	.000	.000	.000	.000	.000	.000	.000	.000	.000	
	N	610	610	610	610	610	609	607	610	609	607	607	609	609	610	608	610

Figure 13.20

**. Correlation is significant at the 0.01 level (2-tailed).

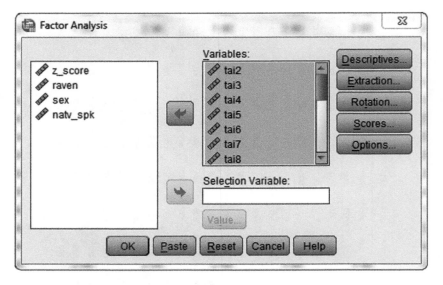

Figure 13.21

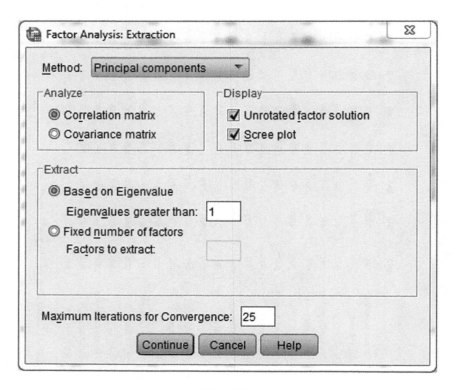

Figure 13.22

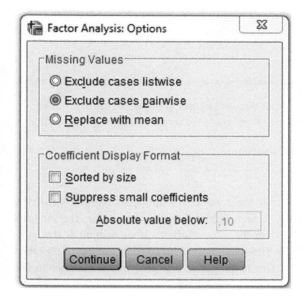

Figure 13.24

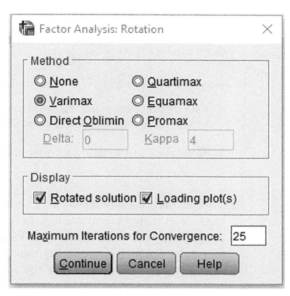

Figure 13.23

The first table that will appear in the output reports the *Communalities* (Figure 13.25). The first column lists the name of the item. In the second column, labelled *Initial*, are the communalities for the variables, if all 16 of the new components are used to predict the observed variables. By definition, if all of the new components are used to account for the variance in the observed variables, the model would be perfect every time: all variance would be accounted for. The goal, however, is to account for as much of the variance in the *observed variables* as possible with as few *new components* as possible. The third column (*Extraction*) in the table lists the communalities for the 16 observed variables using only the retained components, those with eigenvalues greater than 1.

As described earlier in this chapter, communalities can be considered to be multiple R^2 values resulting from each TAI item being regressed on the retained derived components. The value of an observed variable's communality can be interpreted as the proportion of that variable's variance explained by the components. For example, retained components explain or account for 63% of the variance in TAI item 9, with 37% left unexplained. The retained components account for only 31.9% of the variance in item 10, with 68.1% left unexplained.

Communalities

	Initial	Extraction
tai2	1.000	.550
tai3	1.000	.531
tai4	1.000	.512
tai5	1.000	.372
tai6	1.000	.489
tai7	1.000	.578
tai8	1.000	.558
tai9	1.000	.630
tai10	1.000	.319
tai11	1.000	.645
tai14	1.000	.532
tai15	1.000	.684
tai16	1.000	.615
tai17	1.000	.511
tai18	1.000	.535
tai20	1.000	.474

Extraction Method: Principal Component Analysis.

Figure 13.25

One assessment of a PCA model is obtained by examining the communalities. Ideally, the communalities should be as close to 1 as possible. If all communalities were 1, however, there would be no need for PCA.

━━━━━━━━━━ CHALLENGE QUESTION ━━━━━━━━━━

If our retained components resulted in communalities that were all near 1, why would there be no need for PCA? What would the correlation matrix look like? What would the component loadings look like?

Web Link 13.4 for an answer to the challenge question.

Remember, a communality of 1 indicates that the retained components explain all of the variance in that observed variable. In our case, as seen in the *Communalities* table, the retained components do a better job for some variables than they do for others. If we sum all of the communalities, the total communality value is 8.54. The total divided by 16 (the number of observed variables) and then multiplied by 100 is 53.34. This is the percentage of the total variance in the *observed variables* that is accounted for by two retained components.

How many components would we need to retain to have the communalities all above the threshold of 0.60? Figures 13.26–13.28 show the communalities for the 3-component,

Communalities

	Initial	Extraction
tai2	1.000	.608
tai3	1.000	.586
tai4	1.000	.593
tai5	1.000	.374
tai6	1.000	.549
tai7	1.000	.620
tai8	1.000	.618
tai9	1.000	.630
tai10	1.000	.742
tai11	1.000	.645
tai14	1.000	.538
tai15	1.000	.694
tai16	1.000	.628
tai17	1.000	.603
tai18	1.000	.536
tai20	1.000	.519

Extraction Method: Principal Component Analysis.

Figure 13.26   3-Components

Communalities

	Initial	Extraction
tai2	1.000	.617
tai3	1.000	.630
tai4	1.000	.602
tai5	1.000	.908
tai6	1.000	.549
tai7	1.000	.650
tai8	1.000	.632
tai9	1.000	.630
tai10	1.000	.745
tai11	1.000	.650
tai14	1.000	.594
tai15	1.000	.695
tai16	1.000	.629
tai17	1.000	.625
tai18	1.000	.549
tai20	1.000	.563

Extraction Method: Principal Component Analysis.

Figure 13.27   4-Components

4-component, and 5-component solutions. As you can see, even with the five-component solution, there is still one TAI item that is below the ideal cut-off of 0.60: *tai18*. The ideal communality cut-off cannot be the only, or even the primary, principle that determines the number of retained components.

Although it would be preferable to have higher values for the 16 individual communalities, there always exists a tension between the completeness of the final structure and its parsimony. There is a desire to account for as much of the variance in the observed variables as possible (completeness), yet at the same time there is a desire to keep the number of retained components as small as possible (parsimony). There is one additional dimension to this tug-of-war: comprehension. In the end, the structure needs to be comprehensible and make sense conceptually and theoretically.

Communalities

	Initial	Extraction
tai2	1.000	.675
tai3	1.000	.730
tai4	1.000	.602
tai5	1.000	.909
tai6	1.000	.736
tai7	1.000	.671
tai8	1.000	.632
tai9	1.000	.657
tai10	1.000	.849
tai11	1.000	.655
tai14	1.000	.621
tai15	1.000	.699
tai16	1.000	.638
tai17	1.000	.627
tai18	1.000	.549
tai20	1.000	.682

Extraction Method: Principal Component Analysis.

Figure 13.28   5-Components

How many components should be retained?

The next table in the output window (*Total Variance Explained*, Figure 13.29) contains the statistics for the new components. The first column lists the new components in the order in which they were derived. Because we chose the default *Eigenvalue* setting of 1, only the first two components met the Kaiser criterion of K1. Because the TAI was described as having two subtests (worry and emotionality), it is not surprising that two components emerged with eigenvalues greater than 1. As presented in the earlier brief description of component extraction, the eigenvalues become progressively smaller as subsequent components are derived. The second column in the table lists the eigenvalues that correspond to all 16 derived components. The third column translates the eigenvalue of each component into a percentage of the total variance. All of the components with eigenvalues less than 1.0 are associated with less than 6.25% of the variance.

An English logician and Franciscan friar developed the heuristic philosophical principal of parsimony. Ockham's razor, as it is called, is often interpreted as 'the simplest solution or model is the best model'. Regarding PCA, this is reflected in the desire of researchers to retain as few components as possible.

REVIEW QUESTION

Why do all of the components with eigenvalues less than 1 in the *Total Variance Explained* table have less than 6.25% of the variance associated with them?

 Web Link 13.5 as the answer to the review question.

Recall the relationship between (1) the percentage of the total variance explained, (2) the number of observed variables, and (3) the eigenvalues. With 16 observed variables, each observed variable contributes on average $100\%/16 = 6.25\%$ of the total variance. A component that explains 45.421% of the total variance then has an eigenvalue of $(45.421/6.25)$ or 7.267, as is reported for component 1 in the *Total Variance Explained* table. The fourth column accumulates the third column values from top to bottom. Thus, if we included all 16 components in our model, we would account for 100% of the total variance in the observed variables. We would have gained nothing in terms of parsimony, however. Retaining only the two components with eigenvalues greater than 1, we account for $45.521\% + 7.929\% = 53.35\%$ of the total variance. Earlier we arrived at the same percentage using the average communality to make the calculation.

Counting from the left of the figure, columns 5–7 repeat the information from columns 2–4, but only for those components with eigenvalues greater than 1. Columns 8–10 provide the same information for the next step in our analysis.

Total Variance Explained

Component	Initial Eigenvalues			Extraction Sums of Squared Loadings			Rotation Sums of Squared Loadings		
	Total	% of Variance	Cumulative %	Total	% of Variance	Cumulative %	Total	% of Variance	Cumulative %
1	7.267	45.421	45.421	7.267	45.421	45.421	4.614	28.839	28.839
2	1.269	7.929	53.350	1.269	7.929	53.350	3.922	24.511	53.350
3	.947	5.919	59.268						
4	.785	4.906	64.174						
5	.664	4.150	68.324						
6	.623	3.896	72.220						
7	.554	3.465	75.685						
8	.532	3.326	79.011						
9	.505	3.154	82.166						
10	.494	3.084	85.250						
11	.464	2.900	88.150						
12	.421	2.631	90.781						
13	.413	2.583	93.365						
14	.397	2.484	95.848						
15	.364	2.275	98.123						
16	.300	1.877	100.000						

Extraction Method: Principal Component Analysis.

Figure 13.29

Recall that random error variance is that portion of a variable's variance that is unrelated to any variable in an analysis. This variance that is unexplained is also sometimes called *noise*.

Below the *Total Variance Explained* table is the scree plot which offers a visual strategy for determining the number of components to be retained (Cattell, 1966). The word 'scree' comes from an Old Norse term for the rubble that accumulates at the base of a cliff and slowly dissipates as it moves away. Examining the scree plot for the 16 derived components (Figure 13.30), the drop of the cliff and the rubble at the bottom are clear. The pieces of rubble – components that account for little variance – are thought to represent primarily random error variance and are thus unreliable and insignificant components (Kashigan, 1986).

The problem with relying solely on the scree plot to determine the number of retained components is the difficulty of identifying where the cliff ends and the rubble begins. In the scree plot of our 16 components, where does the rubble begin? Does it begin with component 2? If so, then we would retain only one component. Remember that component 2 had an eigenvalue greater than 1, indicating it should be retained. Perhaps the rubble does not begin until component 5, where the rubble appears to flatten out. If so, then we should move to a four-component model, repeat the analysis, and rotate four components. The iterative nature of factor analysis is probably becoming clear to you.

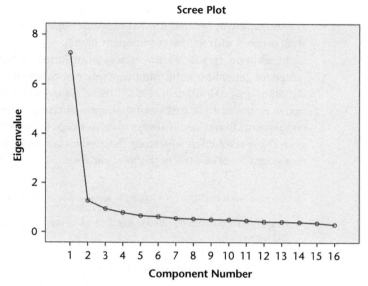

Figure 13.30

================ CHALLENGE QUESTION ================

You can return to the *Factor Analysis: Extraction* window and select the *Fixed number of factors* option and then indicate that you wish to extract 4 factors (Figure 13.31). Then rerun the PCA using a four-component model. How do these results compare to the two-component model in terms of the total variance accounted for and the component loadings?

👆 Web Link 13.6 for an answer to the challenge question.

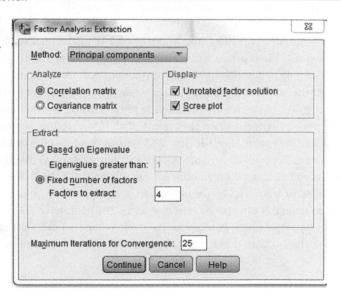

Figure 13.31

Researchers often proceed with several models until one appears to stand out as the best solution. For the moment, because the TAI literature suggests that there are two types of TAI questions, we shall proceed with the two-component model.

In addition to Kaiser's K1 strategy and Cattell's scree plot, several strategies have been suggested for determining the number of retained components. A popular approach is parallel analysis (Humphreys & Montanelli, 1975). There are dedicated online software packages that offer estimates of the complicated computations associated with this approach. The issue of how many components to retain will always involve a tug-of-war between completeness and parsimony, however. Those researchers who stress the need for completeness suggest retaining enough components to account for 80%–90% of the total variance.

▬▬▬▬▬▬▬ ▬ REVIEW QUESTION ▬ ▬▬▬▬▬▬▬▬

How many components would need to be retained to account for 80% of the variance in our 16 TAI items?

🔖 Web Link 13.7 for an answer to the review question.

Others who stress the need for parsimony argue that accounting for only 50% of the total variance is sufficient, especially if additional components make interpretation difficult. Because the literature identifies only two clusters of items (worry and emotionality), retaining more than two components in our current TAI example will complicate our interpretation and require a reconsideration of the nature of the TAI.

Comprehension must play the role of a mediator in the struggle between completeness and parsimony. We must be able to interpret the pattern of loadings on all retained components and also be able to describe how each component is different from the others. Additional completeness is of little benefit if we cannot make sense of one or more of your model's components. Parsimony for the sake of parsimony makes little sense. Even components with eigenvalues slightly less than 1 cannot be ignored when they result in an interpretable component.

The *Component Matrix* in the SPSS output window (Figure 13.32) reports the component loadings of each observed variable on the two components. As described earlier, a component loading is the correlation between an *observed* variable and a retained new component. As can be seen in the *Component Matrix*, all 16 TAI items load positively on component 1. All the loadings are also moderate to strong. It can also be seen that all 16 TAI items have their strongest loading on component 1. This pattern of loadings suggests that a one-component model may be the most appropriate, despite Spielberger's claim that the TAI has both a *worry* and an *emotionality* dimension.

Rotated model

Because we decided to retain more than one component, we have the option of redefining the components by redistributing the explained variance between the two retained components.

Remember that correlations come in three *qualitative* forms: weak, moderate, and strong.

⌕ Web Link 13.8 for an interactive demonstration of the relation between correlations and component loading. Circles (variables) are dragged into varying degrees of overlap. Data are then created to be inputted into SPSS and analysed.

⌕ Web Link 13.9 for an interactive demonstration of the relation between correlations and component loading. This is a five-variable advanced version of Link 13.8. Students are asked to produce data that will result in three different outcomes.

Component Matrix[a]

	Component	
	1	2
tai2	.672	-.313
tai3	.621	.380
tai4	.691	.186
tai5	.503	.345
tai6	.548	.434
tai7	.684	.330
tai8	.691	-.283
tai9	.714	-.347
tai10	.502	-.260
tai11	.743	-.305
tai14	.686	.247
tai15	.820	-.111
tai16	.758	-.203
tai17	.677	.230
tai18	.705	-.195
tai20	.682	.095

Extraction Method: Principal
Component Analysis.

a. 2 components extracted.

Figure 13.32

Recall how the components are defined initially. The first derived component accounts for as much of the total variance as is possible, and each successive component will account for smaller and smaller portions. This purely mathematical distribution of explained variance frequently poses serious problems for interpretation. This is particularly true when the researcher attempts to interpret components other than the first. With most of the variables loading best on the first component and relatively few variables loading highly on any other component, the task of interpreting the loadings of each item on all retained components appears hopeless. For example, looking at the loadings on the second component in our *Component Matrix*, there

How do we statistically evaluate the component loadings? When is it imperative to consider an observed variable when interpreting a component? Remember, component loadings are correlation coefficients and, as such, can be evaluated with a *t*-test. If we do so, because of our sample size (*n* = 600), we will find that virtually all of the TAI loadings would be significant. Stevens (2002) constructed a table of critical values for the component loadings. For samples sizes of 600 he recommended that a loading should be greater than 0.21 for it to be considered significant. Field (2018) recommends an absolute value of 0.4, which would mean that the component accounts for at least 16% (r^2) of the variance in the observed variable. Using Stevens' criterion, we would face the problem that a number of TAI items are significantly related to both components. Using Field's criterion, the problem is greatly reduced. As with other aspects of analysis, often there is not a simple answer to the question.

are no variables that load strongly enough to provide a basis for defining the component independently of the first component.

Of course when only one factor is retained, no such problem exists. The task is one of identifying what all of the variables in the analysis have in common. This task is not always easy, however. For example, if we accept Spearman's one-factor model of intelligence, what is that one component? Is it a general cognitive ability, is it an ability to sustain attention, or is it motivation?

Typically after retaining more than one component the researcher rotates the axes to find a 'fit' (pattern of loadings) which is more interpretable. The rotation is fixed at the origin, the point through which all axes pass. As a result of this, the total variance accounted for by the model will not change. Only the distribution, the relative amounts of

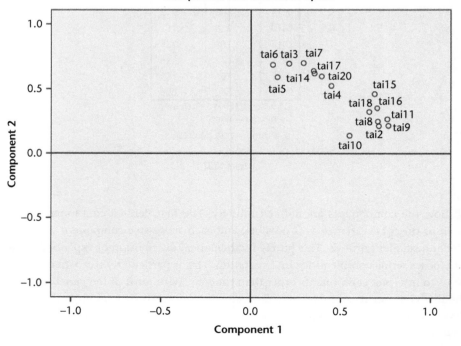

Component Plot in Rotated Space

Figure 13.33

variance associated with each axis, will change. This is true as long as the axes remain orthogonal to each other. The most common form of orthogonal rotation is *varimax*. Varimax rotation is guided by a simple principle: maximize or minimize each observed variable's loading on each component. The ultimate goal is to create a component matrix of 1s and 0s. If this goal were achievable, there would have been no need for PCA or for a rotated solution. The goal is simply the ideal for which the varimax algorithm strives. The *Component Plot in Rotated Space* in the SPSS output window (Figure 13.33) depicts our 16 TAI items in relation to the two components after rotation.

As seen in the component plot, there are two identifiable clusters, one closer to component 1 (items 3, 4, 5, 6, 7, 14, 17, and 20) and one closer to component 2 (items 2, 8, 9, 10, 11, 15, 16, and 18). These two clusters correspond perfectly to the items that comprise Spielberger's *worry* and *emotionality* dimensions. Thus the plots lends support to a two-component model. The component loadings in the *Rotated Component Matrix* found in the output window reflect this clustering. The stronger of the two loadings for each TAI item is on the same component as the other items associated with the same dimension. For example, item 2's stronger loading is on component 1, just as are those of items 8, 9, 10, 11, 15, 16, and 18. Also, in comparison to the initial loadings, notice how the items' after-rotation loadings are weakened on one component and strengthened on the other.

Rotated Component Matrix[a]

	Component	
	1	2
tai2	.710	.214
tai3	.211	.697
tai4	.392	.598
tai5	.146	.592
tai6	.121	.689
tai7	.291	.702
tai8	.704	.249
tai9	.764	.216
tai10	.547	.139
tai11	.758	.266
tai14	.348	.641
tai15	.686	.462
tai16	.701	.353
tai17	.353	.622
tai18	.656	.323
tai20	.446	.525

Extraction Method: Principal Component Analysis.
Rotation Method: Varimax

Figure 13.34

The fact that the rotated component loadings (Figure 13.34) segregate exactly as *expected* by Spielberger makes a good case for retaining a rotated two-component model.

Web Link 13.10 for an interactive demonstration of the relation between correlations and rotated component loading. This is an extension of Link 13.9. Students are asked to produce data that will result in three different sets of rotated loadings.

If you return to the *Total Variance Explained* table (Figure 13.29) and examine columns 8–10 (again counting from the left of the figure), you will see how the rotation has redistributed the variance across the two retained components, but has left the total explained variance unchanged. The eigenvalues for components 1 and 2 have changed from 7.267 and 1.269 to 4.614 and 3.922, respectively. The corresponding percentages of variance accounted for by components 1 and 2 have changed from 45.421% and 7.929% to 28.839% and 24.511%, respectively (Figure 3.35). After rotation the two components are more equal in magnitude and are now more interpretable.

To further assist us in deciding which model to choose, we turn to Spielberger's prediction concerning the predictive power of the two TAI dimensions. As we described in Chapter 12, where *worry* is said to predict academic performance (*score*), *emotionality* is said not to.

We can calculate *worry* and *emotionality* scores using the *Compute Variable* option under the *Transform* menu on the SPSS *Data Editor* page. When the *Compute Variable* window

Total Variance Explained

Component	Initial Eigenvalues			Extraction Sums of Squared Loadings			Rotation Sums of Squared Loadings		
	Total	% of Variance	Cumulative %	Total	% of Variance	Cumulative %	Total	% of Variance	Cumulative %
1	7.267	45.421	45.421	7.267	45.421	45.421	4.614	28.839	28.839
2	1.269	7.929	53.350	1.269	7.929	53.350	3.922	24.511	53.350

Figure 13.35

You may wish to return to the *Factor Analysis: Extraction* window (Figure 13.36) and again fix the number of factors at 4. After rerunning the analysis with varimax rotation, examine the new component loadings and their clustering.

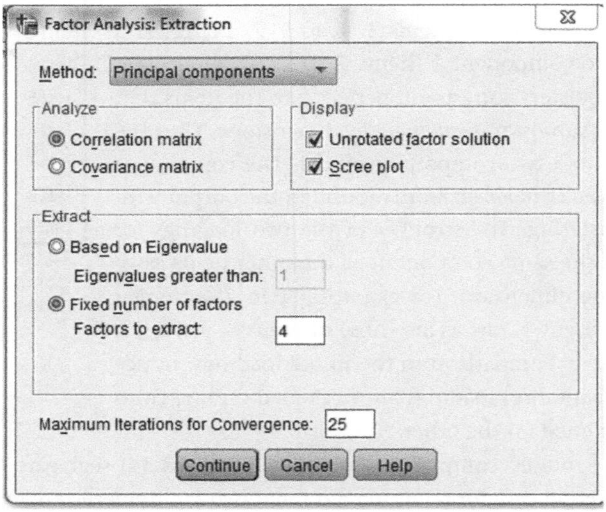

Figure 13.36

opens (Figure 13.37), we type the name of a new variable (*Wtai*) into the *Target Variable* box and sum the variables associated with worry in the *Numeric Expression* box, and then do the same for emotionality (*Etai*).

We then examine how *Wtai* and *Etai* subtotal scores correlated with student performance in an introductory psychology course (score). Under the *Analyze* menu on the *Data Editor* page select *Correlate* and click *Bivariate*. Highlight and move the variables *score, Wtai,* and *Etai* over to the *Variables* box (Figure 13.38) and click *OK*.

In the output window we find both *Wtai* and *Etai* to be negatively correlated with *score* (Figure 13.39). This means that the greater the student's *worry*, the lower his or her *score* tends to be in the introductory psychology course ($r = -0.286$). Also, the greater a student's *emotionality*, the lower his or her *score* in the course ($r = -0.123$). Both of these correlations are significant ($p < 0.01$). As we noted in Chapter 12, there is a strong correlation between worry and emotionality

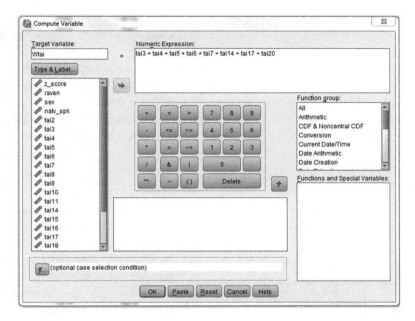

Figure 13.37

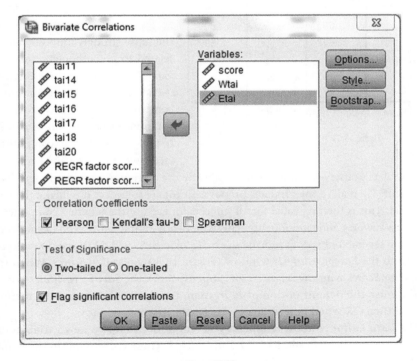

Figure 13.38

($r = 0.715$). The fact that both *Wtai* and *Etai* are correlated with *score*, along with the fact that *Wtai* and *Etai* are strongly correlated, may suggest to us that a one-component model is better than the two-component model after all.

As discussed in Chapter 12, the substantial correlation between *Wtai* and *Etai* may indicate something else, however. It may be that TAI items are neither purely worry nor purely emotionality in nature. A TAI item that appears to measure worry may also measure the student's emotionality to some degree, and vice versa. That is, although the two theoretical components are orthogonal (independent, uncorrelated) the TAI items from which they are derived need not be.

Factor scores

In Chapter 12 we used *component scores* or *factor scores* to resolve the problem of *multicollinearity* arising from the substantial correlation between two predictor variables: the worry and the emotionality TAI subtotals. Factor scores are the smaller number of new scores to which the larger number of originally observed scores have been reduced. Subjects are assigned a new score for each of the new latent components. In terms of our TAI analysis, each student will have a factor score for *worry* and a factor score for *emotionality*: 16 *observed scores* are reduced to two *factor scores*. Factor scores are based on the notion that the more strongly an observed variable is related to a component (reflected in the variable's component loading), the more it contributes to the factor score for that component. Variables that have a weaker component loading should contribute less to that factor score. To compute a subject's factor score for a given factor, the z-scores of all of the subject's observed scores are multiplied by the corresponding component loadings for that component. Then all of the products (in our case 16) are summed, producing the factor score for that subject. This is then repeated for all subjects for each of the retained components, which in our case is two: worry and emotionality. This is an overly simplified version of the procedure, of which there are several, but it does provide the basic logic. SPSS will do the computations for us.

Correlations

		score	Wtai	Etai
score	Pearson Correlation	1	-.286**	-.123**
	Sig. (2-tailed)		.000	.005
	N	531	527	527
Wtai	Pearson Correlation	-.286**	1	.715**
	Sig. (2-tailed)	.000		.000
	N	527	599	592
Etai	Pearson Correlation	-.123**	.715**	1
	Sig. (2-tailed)	.005	.000	
	N	527	592	596

**. Correlation is significant at the 0.01 level (2-tailed).

Figure 13.39

We return to the *Factor Analysis* window (Figure 13.40) and click *Scores*. When the *Factor Analysis: Factor Scores* window (Figure 13.41) opens, check the *Save as variables* box. In terms of *Method*, we use the default option of *Regression*, the most commonly used method. Click *Continue* and then *OK* when you return to the *Factor Analysis* window.

When the *Data Editor* window reappears you will notice that two new variables have been created at the end of the data set: *FAC1_1* and *FAC2_1*. These correspond to the emotionality factor scores and the worry factor scores, respectively.

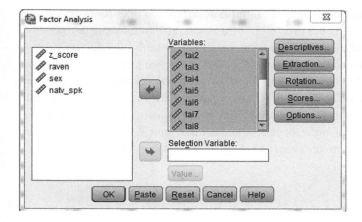

Figure 13.40

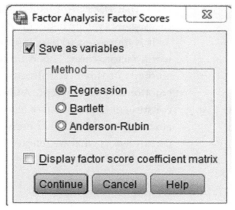

Figure 13.41

We now re-examine the correlations among *score, worry,* and *emotionality,* this time using the factor scores (Figure 13.42). First of all, notice the correlation between *REGR factor score 1* (emotionality) and *REGR factor score 2* (worry), which is –0.003. A rounding limitation is the only reason why it is not a perfect 0. This reflects the fact that

> You might ask how to determine which new SPSS factor score variable corresponds to which component, given that the names are not very informative. The emotionality items loaded more strongly on the first component in the rotated component matrix and worry items loaded more strongly on the second component.

the two components during varimax rotation are kept orthogonal, as are their corresponding factor scores. Also notice that the correlations between the two TAI dimensions and *score* are changed. The correlation between *emotionality* and *score* has been attenuated to near zero (–0.028), while the correlation between *worry* and *score* has been augmented to –0.296. This is consistent with the

Correlations

		score	REGR factor score 1 for analysis 1	REGR factor score 2 for analysis 1
score	Pearson Correlation	1	-.028	-.296**
	Sig. (2-tailed)		.527	.000
	N	531	523	523
REGR factor score 1 for analysis 1	Pearson Correlation	-.028	1	-.003
	Sig. (2-tailed)	.527		.944
	N	523	592	592
REGR factor score 2 for analysis 1	Pearson Correlation	-.296**	-.003	1
	Sig. (2-tailed)	.000	.944	
	N	523	592	592

**. Correlation is significant at the 0.01 level (2-tailed).

Figure 13.42

claim that *worry* TAI predicts academic performance, but *emotionality* TAI does not. Furthermore, this suggests we are better off retaining the two-component model, at least for some purposes.

It is important to bear in mind that all 16 TAI items contribute to both the emotionality and worry factor scores. This is understood by conceiving of all items as being composed of varying amounts of three constituents. A response to any given TAI item reflects both a worry and an emotionality constituent. Additionally, the item reflects a random error constituent. This third constituent is composed of all of the other unknown factors which influence the response and are absorbed by the 14 other derived but unretained components that were not retained. This third constituent is what we referred to as rubble (scree) when we examined the scree plot.

Oblique rotation

If we look back at the *Component Plot in Rotated Space* in the output window (Figure 13.33), it can be seen that the axes of the two components do not bisect the two clusters of TAI items. Furthermore, any rotation that keeps the two components orthogonal will not allow the axes of the components to bisect the two clusters simultaneously. The axes can be turned to have one axis bisect a cluster, but then the other axis would be further away from the second cluster. For the two axes to bisect the clusters and create what might be considered a better fit requires us to allow the axes to rotate in a non-orthogonal or *oblique* manner.

This can be done by returning to the *Factor Analysis: Rotation* window and selecting either *Direct Oblimin* or *Promax* rotation (Figure 13.43). In our example we will use *Direct Oblimin*. Then rerun the analysis.

When the output is examined, nothing has changed in the *Communalities*, *Total Variance Explained,* and *Component Matrix* tables, nor has the scree plot changed. At this point, our new analysis is simply a replication of the previous analysis. Now, however, the *Rotated Component Matrix* has been replaced by a *Pattern Matrix* (Figure 13.44) and a *Structure Matrix* (Figure 13.45). The pattern matrix contains the new component loadings associated with the new oblique axes. The row for each TAI item is the equivalent of a regression equation where the standardized observed variable is expressed as a function of the two regression coefficients (slopes). The new loadings are in effect regression coefficients. The structure matrix represents the correlations between the TAI items and the oblique components. Because the two components are correlated, the regression coefficients and correlations are not identical. For orthogonal rotations, such as varimax, where components are uncorrelated, the pattern matrix and structure matrix are identical (i.e., the rotated component matrix).

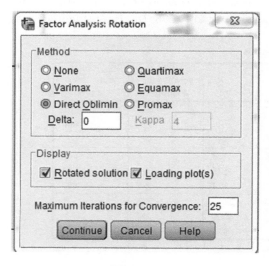

Figure 13.43

Pattern Matrix[a]		
	Component	
	1	2
tai2	.763	-.036
tai3	-.026	.744
tai4	.230	.552
tai5	-.061	.645
tai6	-.130	.770
tai7	.068	.716
tai8	.742	.008
tai9	.826	-.055
tai10	.598	-.058
tai11	.799	.007
tai14	.160	.621
tai15	.635	.269
tai16	.697	.133
tai17	.174	.596
tai18	.655	.116
tai20	.324	.442

Extraction Method: Principal
Component Analysis.
Rotation Method: Oblimin

Figure 13.44

Structure Matrix		
	Component	
	1	2
tai2	.741	.427
tai3	.426	.728
tai4	.566	.692
tai5	.331	.608
tai6	.338	.692
tai7	.504	.758
tai8	.747	.459
tai9	.792	.446
tai10	.563	.305
tai11	.803	.492
tai14	.537	.718
tai15	.799	.656
tai16	.777	.556
tai17	.536	.701
tai18	.726	.514
tai20	.593	.639

Extraction Method: Principal
Component Analysis.
Rotation Method: Oblimin

Figure 13.45

The *Component Plot in Rotated Space* (Figure 13.46) for the oblique rotation produced by SPSS requires clarification. It appears that the axes are orthogonal and the TAI items have moved. Actually, the axes have moved, not the TAI items. The axes are no longer orthogonal, even though they appear so. The plot does effectively depict, however, how the axes now bisect the two clusters of items.

The oblique component loadings found in the pattern matrix are different from those we saw in the orthogonal rotated component matrix. In general, the loadings in the pattern matrix represent a better fit than those found in the rotated component matrix. These results argue for a consideration of an oblique two-component model. Similar to *Alice in Wonderland*, we find ourselves falling further and further down the rabbit hole.

The correlations between the TAI items and the oblique components represented by the structure matrix have all increased, relative to the values in the rotated component matrix. All TAI items now correlate at least moderately with both emotionality and worry. With oblique rotation the goal is no longer to maximize or minimize the component loadings on the orthogonal components.

Finally, the *Component Correlation Matrix* (Figure 13.47) reports a strong correlation ($r = 0.608$) between the two oblique components. This correlation, along with the moderate correlations that all TAI items have with both oblique components, requires us to reconsider the one-component model. The results suggest that there is only one dominant component cutting across all TAI items

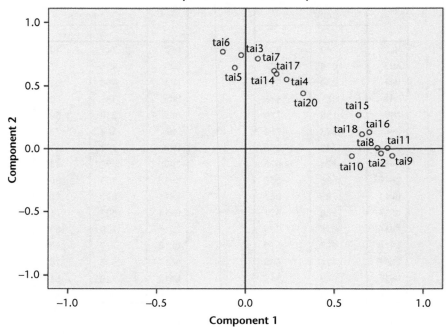

Figure 13.46

Once the correlation between two oblique components reaches 0.80 or greater, it might be argued that the two components are really one. Many psychometric tests and questionnaires have test–retest reliabilities between 0.80 and 0.90. That is, if your statistics professor administered an examination to his class today and then again next week, he would not expect to find a perfect correlation of 1 between the two sets of scores. Rather, he would expect a correlation somewhere around 0.90. Once two oblique components have a correlation similar to that of test–retest reliability, reasons other than eigenvalues are required for the retention of both components.

(i.e., test anxiety), while the clustering is relatively less important. This interpretation assumes that *worry* and *emotionality* are not independent. This idea of a relation between *worry* and *emotionality* was suggested at the outset of the analysis by the correlations among all 16 TAI items and the initial difficulty in visually discerning two clusters in that matrix.

We might next re-examine the correlations between the factor scores and the students' *scores* in the introductory psychology course. As you recall, the two factor scores resulting from the orthogonal rotation were virtually uncorrelated ($r = -0.003$). Where the emotionality factor score was uncorrelated with *score* ($r = -0.028$), the worry factor score was significantly correlated with *score* ($r = -0.296$). The factor scores derived from the oblique rotation revealed a different pattern. The emotionality and worry factor scores resulting from the oblique rotation were substantially correlated ($r = 0.608$). Furthermore, both the *emotionality* factor score ($r = -0.121$, $p < 0.01$) and the *worry* factor score ($r = -0.288$, $p < 0.01$) were significantly correlated with *score*. This new pattern of correlations reduces the differentiation between the two components and makes interpretation more problematic.

We are not short of possible interpretations. At this point, the various results support three possible models: a one-component model, an orthogonal two-component model, and an oblique two-component model. Actually, as we shall see in Section 13.11, the results also hint at a fourth possible model.

Component Correlation Matrix

Component	1	2
1	1.000	.608
2	.608	1.000

Figure 13.47

13 ● 9 CHOOSING A METHOD OF ROTATION

While both orthogonal and oblique rotations have their adherents and detractors, most researchers choose the type of rotation that best serves their purpose. As we have seen, there are valid reasons for either form of rotation. The choice of rotation is based on a number of issues. At times one issue may be paramount, at other times two or three issues may need consideration, and compromises must be made.

1   What is expected? Do you judge the underlying theoretical constructs to be independent or related? If you deem (*expect*) the components to be independent, then using an oblique rotation to gain a somewhat 'better fit' is inappropriate. What you *observe*, of course, might change your mind concerning your assumption of independence. The loadings of the rotated model may not lead to the clear segregation of the variables expected (see point 4 below). In our case of the TAI, the orthogonal two-component model resulted in a clear segregation of the items. Furthermore, and crucially, the items segregated as predicted. On the other hand, the oblique rotation resulted in the strongest set of component loadings, if we allowed the components to be related.

2   Does previous research indicate how the components may or may not be related? In the case of TAI, previous research informs us to *expect* that the worry and emotionality components behave differently with respect to academic performance. This differential performance was *observed* best with the orthogonal two-component model. The factor scores from this model maximized the difference between worry and emotionality with respect to predicting performance in introductory psychology. The factor scores derived from the oblique rotation produced little differentiation.

3   What is the purpose of the analysis? Is it an initial exploration of the data? For example, if PCA is an attempt to construct a test that contains two subtests, we may be looking to eliminate any items that do not segregate well (i.e., load moderately on both components after rotation). Or, for example, is the goal to produce appropriate factor scores that can serve other purposes? This was our aim in Chapter 12 where we used the worry and emotionality factor scores from orthogonal rotation to resolve the problem of multicollinearity.

4   The principle of a *simple structure* (Bryant & Yarnold, 1995) needs to be taken into account. A factor analysis has a simple structure to the extent that the loadings tend towards either 0 or 1. Zero should be understood as a loading of less than ±0.10. (For details concerning such a pattern of loading, see Thurstone (1947). Although Thurstone wrote this over half a century ago, it remains an important approach to PCA and its interpretation.). In our ongoing analysis, if we compare the loadings from the

rotated component matrix with loadings from the pattern matrix, we find that the oblique model better satisfies the desire for a *simple structure*.

5   Earlier in the chapter we mentioned how confirmatory factor analysis (CFA) allows us to examine statistically the difference between *expected* and *observed* outcomes. Under certain circumstances, CFA allows researchers to statistically compare different models derived from the same data. Although this is a useful procedure, like the other considerations it is not a magic bullet. The fact that one model or form of rotation produces a statistically better fit does not necessarily mean that it is the best overall model. For an introduction to conducting CFA with SPSS's Amos program, see Reinhard (2006).

13 ● 10   SAMPLE SIZE REQUIREMENTS

Much has been written about factor analysis and sample size requirements. There are rules of thumb ranging from 5 to 15 subjects per observed variable. There also have been empirical investigations into the relation between sample size and the stability of the results (Arrindell & van der Ende, 1985) indicating that there is little relation between the subjects-to-variables ratio and the stability of results. The current wisdom on the topic concurs with Tabachnick and Fidell's (2012) proposition that a sample size of 300 will ordinarily ensure the stability of the results.

In the end, what will determine the stability of the results of PCA, or, for that matter, any statistical procedure involving correlation coefficients? It is the stability of the bivariate correlation matrix. A matrix's stability is signified by the strength of correlation between (1) the bivariate correlation coefficients derived from one sample and (2) those correlations derived from another sample drawn from the same population. Figure 13.48 provides a simple hypothetical example of stability in the correlation matrix. If we enter the information into the SPSS *Data Editor*, treating *Correlation Sample 1* and *Correlation Sample 2* as variables (columns), we find that the correlation between the two sets of correlations is 0.90. This strong correlation between the pairs of bivariate correlations foretells the stability of PCA results. When the relative strengths of the correlations are stable, rarely will the pattern of component loadings change.

Figure 13.49 shows an example where the correlation matrix lacks stability. After computing a correlation between the two sets of correlation coefficients in Table 13.9, we find a weak correlation ($r = 0.38$). In such circumstances there is little likelihood of replicating the results of a PCA.

Variable Pairs	Correlation Sample 1	Correlation Sample 2
Var1/Var2	0.6	0.5
Var1/Var3	0.4	0.5
Var1/Var4	0.7	0.6
Var2/Var3	0.1	0.2
Var2/Var4	0.5	0.4
Var3/Var4	0.2	0.1

Figure 13.48

Variable Pairs	Correlation Sample 1	Correlation Sample 2
Var1/Var2	0.6	0.5
Var1/Var3	0.4	0.7
Var1/Var4	0.7	0.4
Var2/Var3	0.1	0.3
Var2/Var4	0.5	0.4
Var3/Var4	0.2	0.3

Figure 13.49

An important factor in determining the stability of the correlation matrix is the individual reliabilities of the original measures. As discussed in Chapter 7, as a variable's test–retest reliability becomes weaker, so does the possible maximum correlation with another variable. Stated otherwise, as the proportion of error variance in the measurement of a variable increases, the correlation between that variable and another variable becomes more and more random in nature, regardless of the true relation between the two variables. Therefore, in addition to a sample size of at least 300, it is imperative to ensure that the observed variables are reliable.

13 ● 11 HIERARCHICAL MULTIPLE FACTOR ANALYSIS

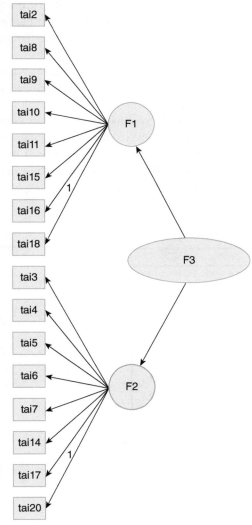

Although there is not the space for a detailed presentation of the topic, it would be negligent not to mention *hierarchical multiple factor analysis* (HMFA). In HMFA, the pattern of correlations among observed variables is organized into a hierarchical structure where clusters or components at an initial stage of analysis may be combined into even fewer components at a subsequent stage of analysis. When clusters are correlated, HMFA often provides a model that is more interpretable than competing models derived at the initial stage of analysis.

For example, perhaps the structure of the TAI is best modelled by the diagram in Figure 13.50. In the figure the individual TAI items are represented by the squares. The worry and emotionality latent components (depicted by the circles) are allowed to be correlated at the initial stage. Circle *F1* represents the emotionality component and circle *F2* represents the worry component. The second stage of the analysis is based on the correlation between the components derived at the initial stage. Subsequent to oblique rotation, if there were little or no correlation between the components, there would be no reason for further analysis. Because of the substantial correlation that existed with oblique rotation, worry and emotionality can be viewed as sub-components of a *higher-order* component which is depicted in the *F3* oval. The *F3* component might be understood as *general test anxiety*. In fact, it is such a hierarchical structure that Bors et al. (2006) concluded best fitted the TAI.

Figure 13.50

13●12 THE EFFECTS OF VARIABLE SELECTION

GIGO is an old expression that means 'garbage in, garbage out'. Stated in a more sanitized manner, the observed variables that go into PCA determine the components that come out. As was briefly discussed early in this chapter, the choice of what to include in a PCA will influence the model that emerges. First of all, 'noisy' measures will lead to results that will be difficult to replicate. Also, as you will recall, if measures of athleticism, musical talent, and social awareness are included with more typical measures of ability, it will be very difficult to interpret the results as reflecting a single component of general intelligence (Neisser et al., 1996). There are researchers, however, who consider one or more of those additional measures as reflective of intelligence.

Similarly, we might imagine constructing a set of TAI items that address the issue of self-concept. Although some of the current items may partially address self-concept, we might create six or more other items to address the issue, such as 'failing a test means that I am a failure'. It is possible that with these additional items we might discover that three correlated components underlie the TAI. Removing items from a PCA can also considerably change the results. In this section we reanalyse the TAI data using all eight of the emotionality items but only four of the worry items: *tai3*, *tai14*, *tai17*, and *tai20*.

To begin with, you may wish to rerun a correlation matrix. You will find that all of the bivariate correlations in the reduced matrix are unchanged from the counterparts in the original matrix. Individual bivariate correlations are altered. But there are changes beginning with the *Communalities* table (Figure 13.51). In comparison to those in the 16-item analysis, nearly all of the communalities have been reduced. That is, the model explains less of the variance in nearly all of the individual

Communalities

	Initial	Extraction
tai2	1.000	.489
tai3	1.000	.346
tai8	1.000	.503
tai9	1.000	.557
tai10	1.000	.287
tai11	1.000	.602
tai14	1.000	.443
tai15	1.000	.688
tai16	1.000	.611
tai17	1.000	.431
tai18	1.000	.528
tai20	1.000	.450

Extraction Method: Principal Component Analysis.

Figure 13.51

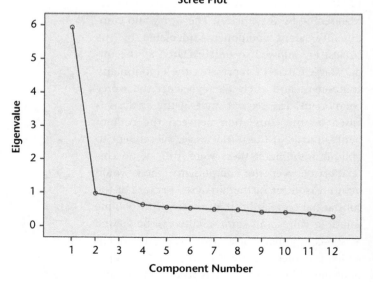

Figure 13.52

Total Variance Explained

Component	Initial Eigenvalues			Extraction Sums of Squared Loadings		
	Total	% of Variance	Cumulative %	Total	% of Variance	Cumulative %
1	5.936	49.464	49.464	5.936	49.464	49.464
2	.970	8.082	57.546			
3	.849	7.076	64.621			
4	.633	5.279	69.900			
5	.559	4.656	74.556			
6	.533	4.444	79.001			
7	.503	4.193	83.194			
8	.490	4.082	87.276			
9	.427	3.558	90.834			
10	.417	3.473	94.308			
11	.381	3.178	97.486			
12	.302	2.514	100.000			

Extraction Method: Principal Component Analysis.

Figure 13.53

observed variables. As can be seen in the scree plot (Figure 13.52) and the *Total Variance Explained* (Figure 13.53) table, the reduced communalities are the result of the fact that only one component is retained using the Kaiser K1 criterion. There is only one strong component that explains almost 50% of the variance. The scree plot also strongly suggests the retention of only one component.

Notice that in the *Component Matrix* (Figure 13.54) the unrotated component loadings also have changed relative to their loadings in the original analysis. Some of the loadings have been slightly reduced, but others have been increased. Because only one component has been retained, in the current analysis there is no rotated component matrix.

Had we conducted the original PCA on these 12 TAI items, we would have concluded that a one-factor model best fits the TAI.

Finally, it must be stressed that the results of PCA or any form of factor analysis do not reveal a hidden reality underlying the correlational pattern among a set of variables. Our descriptions of the techniques and of results may sound as if factor analysis is able to perform alchemical feats. We have already seen how the final model will be the product of (1) the researcher's purpose in performing the analysis, (2) the variables the researcher chooses to include in the analysis, and (3) the reliabilities of those variables. In addition to these, the population from which the sample of subjects was drawn is crucial. A model that may be derived from subjects representing

Component Matrix[a]

	Component
	1
tai2	.700
tai3	.588
tai8	.710
tai9	.746
tai10	.536
tai11	.776
tai14	.666
tai15	.829
tai16	.782
tai17	.657
tai18	.727
tai20	.671

Extraction Method: Principal Component Analysis.

Figure 13.54

one population may not be the model derived from subjects drawn from another population. Population does not refer simply to geographical location. Populations may be defined in many terms: age, educational background, income, gender, etc. The factor structure of TAI derived from a sample of university students may differ from the structure derived from a sample of secondary school students.

Simply put, the results of factor-analytic studies are not universal in nature, they are local descriptions. They describe patterns of correlations among a specific set of measures administered to a particular group of subjects for a certain purpose. It is when this limitation is ignored that unnecessary disagreements arise.

13●13 CHAPTER SUMMARY

Exploratory factor analysis, and PCA specifically, are methods for revealing how a set of observed variables cluster themselves. The basis for the analysis is the observed variables' pattern of intercorrelations. Thus, the selection of appropriate and reliable variables is paramount. The clusters are the basis for interpreting the new *latent components*. One way to state the purpose of factor analysis is that it is set of techniques for reducing a set of specific variables to a smaller set of more general variables.

This chapter carries on the plot we have been following throughout the book, but in some ways it is a more primitive version. PCA involves examining the difference between the *expected* and the *observed*, but there are some distinctive differences. The *expected* is not always related to the notion of chance or randomness or a definable null hypothesis. If the researcher believes that all of the observed variables are measures of a single underlying component, a matrix of strong correlations among the observed variables is to be *expected*. Furthermore, all of the observed variables are *expected* to load strongly on the first *unrotated* component. If the researcher believes that the observed variables are unrelated, then the correlations among the observed variables are expected to be weak and the variables will load on different components. Taking it one step further, if the researcher believes that there are several underlying components, as was the case in our working example, then relevant clusters of strong intercorrelations and *rotated* component loadings are expected. There will always be a difference between what is *observed* and what is *expected*. As the analysis proceeds, rather than formal statistical tests, there are rules of thumb and guidelines to be used to arrive at a final model.

First the researcher must decide on the number of components to retain, typically by using the K1 criterion or the scree plot. If more than one component is retained, the researcher must choose a form of rotation, either orthogonal or oblique. The choice of rotation is based on several possible considerations:

1   What is expected? Do you judge the underlying components to be independent or related?
2   Does previous research indicate how the components may or may not be related or may behave differentially?
3   What is the purpose of the analysis?
4   The results should tend towards a *simple structure* where the component loadings tend towards either 0 or 1.

The results of PCA are not universal in nature, but rather local descriptions. They describe relations among a specific set of variables that were administered to a sample drawn from a particular population for a certain purpose. Finally, there are no simple answers to interpreting PCA results. The researcher must use all of his or her knowledge and understanding of the phenomenon under investigation.

13 ● 14 RECOMMENDED READINGS

Horst, P. (1965). *Factor analysis of data matrices*. Ventura, CA: Holt, Rinehart and Winston.
This is one of the seminal works detailing the theory and mathematics behind factor analysis. A
    working knowledge of advanced mathematics is required. The trouble is worth the effort.
Kline, P. (2002). *An easy guide to factor analysis*. London: Routledge.
This easy-to-read book provides an excellent introduction to both exploratory and confirmatory
    factor analysis which goes beyond what could be covered here. The description of
    confirmatory factor analysis is particularly effective.
Reinhard, J. C. (2006). *Confirmatory factor analysis through the Amos program*. London: Sage.
This book offers an in-depth presentation of all aspects of confirmatory factor analysis. Reading
    Kline (2002) is a good primer for this book.

13 ● 15 CHAPTER REVIEW QUESTIONS

Multiple-choice questions

1   Ten variables are analysed with PCA. Assume that all of the bivariate correlations are 0. Theoretically, how many new components will be derived?

   a   1
   b   0
   c   5
   d   10
   e   20

2   Ten variables are analysed with PCA. Assume that all of the bivariate correlations are 1. Theoretically, how many new components will be derived?

   a   1
   b   0
   c   5
   d   10
   e   20

3   Which of the following indicate the strength of the association between the original variables and the retained derived components?

   a   Communalities
   b   Eigenvalues

    c   Scree plots

    d   Factor loadings

    e   Varimax rotation

4   _____ indicate the proportion of the variance in an original variable that is explained by the retained derived components.

    a   Communalities

    b   Eigenvalues

    c   Scree plots

    d   Factor loading

    e   Varimax rotation

5   _____ indicate the proportion of the total variance in the original variables that is accounted for by a derived component.

    a   Communalities

    b   Eigenvalues

    c   Scree plots

    d   Factor loadings

    e   Oblique rotation

6   Using the 'percentage of the total variance accounted for' as the criterion for evaluating a model derived using PCA, it might be argued that the model should account for at least _____.

    a   95% of the total variance

    b   5% of the total variance

    c   10% of the total variance

    d   50% of the total variance

    e   Percentage of the total variance accounted for is not used as a criterion for evaluating a model

7   If we sum the communalities of all of the observed variables, divide that total by the number of observed variables, and then multiply by 100, we would know _____.

    a   the percentage of the total variance in the observed variables accounted for by the model

    b   the percentage of the total variance in the observed variables unaccounted for by the model

    c   the total variance in the observed variables analysed

    d   the total variance in the observed variables analysed accounted for by the model

    e   the total variance in the observed variables analysed unaccounted for by the model

8   If there are 20 original variables entered into a PCA, a derived component that accounts for 20% of the total variance in the original variables has an eigenvalue of _____.

    a   1

    b   20

    c   2

    d   5

    e   4

9   If there are 16 original variables entered into a PCA, a derived component with an eigenvalue of 4.4 accounts for what percentage of the total variance in the original variables?

    a   16%

    b   42%

    c   4.4%

    d   70.4%

    e   27.5%

10 Assume that three derived components were retained following a PCA of 10 observed variables. Also assume that the components' eigenvalues were 5.0, 2.0, and 1.5. What is the total proportion of the variance in the observed variables accounted for by the three retained components?

a 8.5%

b 15%

c 11.76%

d 85%

e The total proportion of the variance in the observed variables accounted for by the three retained components cannot be estimated with the information provided

Short-answer questions

1 Explain the 'tug-of-war' between *parsimony* and *completeness* as it pertains to the issue of determining the number of factors to retain.

2 What is the difference between orthogonal and oblique rotation?

3 What is the driving principle of varimax rotation?

4 Why are the reliabilities of the individual observed variables of concern when conducting a PCA?

5 Discuss four factors that influence the researcher's choice of rotation and final model.

Data set question

1 A social psychologist who is interested in 'life satisfaction' devised a scale to estimate what she thought were three factors of importance: work, fun, and detachment (being unconcerned with most events). She also thought that there would be a difference between men and women on the various factors. Finally, she wanted to know if any of the three proposed factors were related to hopefulness, optimism, resilience, and mindfulness. To explore the topic and her scale she administered the scale to 277 students in her introductory sociology course. Conduct a PCA on the *lifeSatisfactionScale.sav* data set on the book's web page. Is there evidence for the three components? The work items are labelled with *workgoal*, the fun items are labelled with *fungoal*, and the detachment items are labelled with *detach*. Evaluate both individual items (communalities) and the overall model. If there are three components (orthogonal or oblique), are any of them related to hopefulness, optimism, resilience, or mindfulness? What limitations do you think she would need to consider when interpreting her findings?

Don't forget to use the online resources! Meet your supporting stats tutor through an **introductory video**, review your maths skills with a **diagnostic pre-test**, explore statistical principles through **interactive simulations**, practice analysis techniques with **SPSS datasets**, and check your work with **answers to all in-text questions**.

https://study.sagepub.com/bors

APPENDICES

APPENDIX A STANDARD NORMAL DISTRIBUTION AND PROBABILITIES (Z-SCORES)

Standard Normal Distribution and Probabilities

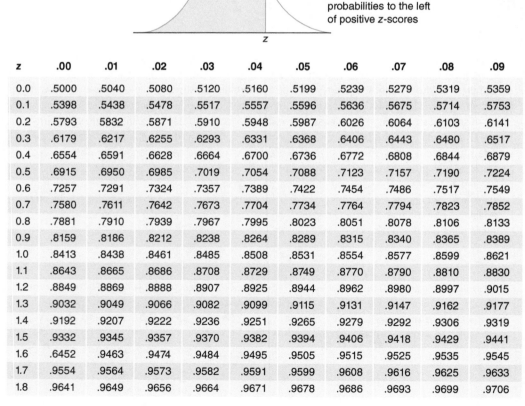

z	.00	.01	.02	.03	.04	.05	.06	.07	.08	.09
0.0	.5000	.5040	.5080	.5120	.5160	.5199	.5239	.5279	.5319	.5359
0.1	.5398	.5438	.5478	.5517	.5557	.5596	.5636	.5675	.5714	.5753
0.2	.5793	5832	.5871	.5910	.5948	.5987	.6026	.6064	.6103	.6141
0.3	.6179	.6217	.6255	.6293	.6331	.6368	.6406	.6443	.6480	.6517
0.4	.6554	.6591	.6628	.6664	.6700	.6736	.6772	.6808	.6844	.6879
0.5	.6915	.6950	.6985	.7019	.7054	.7088	.7123	.7157	.7190	.7224
0.6	.7257	.7291	.7324	.7357	.7389	.7422	.7454	.7486	.7517	.7549
0.7	.7580	.7611	.7642	.7673	.7704	.7734	.7764	.7794	.7823	.7852
0.8	.7881	.7910	.7939	.7967	.7995	.8023	.8051	.8078	.8106	.8133
0.9	.8159	.8186	.8212	.8238	.8264	.8289	.8315	.8340	.8365	.8389
1.0	.8413	.8438	.8461	.8485	.8508	.8531	.8554	.8577	.8599	.8621
1.1	.8643	.8665	.8686	.8708	.8729	.8749	.8770	.8790	.8810	.8830
1.2	.8849	.8869	.8888	.8907	.8925	.8944	.8962	.8980	.8997	.9015
1.3	.9032	.9049	.9066	.9082	.9099	.9115	.9131	.9147	.9162	.9177
1.4	.9192	.9207	.9222	.9236	.9251	.9265	.9279	.9292	.9306	.9319
1.5	.9332	.9345	.9357	.9370	.9382	.9394	.9406	.9418	.9429	.9441
1.6	.6452	.9463	.9474	.9484	.9495	.9505	.9515	.9525	.9535	.9545
1.7	.9554	.9564	.9573	.9582	.9591	.9599	.9608	.9616	.9625	.9633
1.8	.9641	.9649	.9656	.9664	.9671	.9678	.9686	.9693	.9699	.9706

(Continued)

z	.00	.01	.02	.03	.04	.05	.06	.07	.08	.09
1.9	.9713	.9719	.9726	.9732	.9738	.9744	.9750	.9756	.9761	.9767
2.0	.9772	.9778	.9783	.9788	.9793	.9798	.9803	.9808	.9812	.9817
2.1	.9821	.9826	.9830	.9834	.9838	.9842	.9846	.9850	.9854	.9857
2.2	.9861	.9864	.9868	.9781	.9875	.9878	.9881	.9884	.9887	.9890
2.3	.9893	.9896	.9898	.9901	.9904	.9906	.9909	.9911	.9913	.9916
2.4	.9918	.9920	.9922	.9925	.9927	.9929	.9931	.9932	.9934	.9936
2.5	.9938	.9940	.9941	.9943	.9945	.9946	.9948	.9949	.9951	.9952
2.6	.9953	.9955	.9956	.9957	.9959	.9960	.9961	.9962	.9963	.9964
2.7	.9965	.9966	.9967	.9968	.9969	.9970	.9971	.9972	.9973	.9974
2.8	.9974	.9975	.9976	.9977	.9977	.9978	.9979	.9979	.9980	.9981
2.9	.9981	.9982	.9982	.9983	.9984	.9984	.9985	.9985	.9986	.9986
3.0	.9987	.9987	.9987	.9988	.9988	.9989	.9989	.9989	.9990	.9990
3.1	.9990	.9991	.9991	.9991	.9992	.9992	.9992	.9992	.9993	.9993
3.2	.9993	.9993	.9994	.9994	.9994	.9994	.9994	.9995	.9995	.9995
3.3	.9995	.9995	.9995	.9996	.9996	.9996	.9996	.9996	.9996	.9997
3.4	.9997	.9997	.9997	.9997	.9997	.9997	.9997	.9997	.9997	.9998

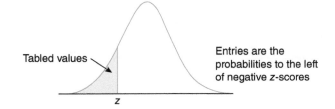

Tabled values

Entries are the probabilities to the left of negative z-scores

z

z	.00	.01	.02	.03	.04	.05	.06	.07	.08	.09
−3.4	.0003	.0003	.0003	.0003	.0003	.0003	.0003	.0003	.0003	.0002
−3.3	.0005	.0005	.0005	.0004	.0004	.0004	.0004	.0004	.0004	.0003
−3.2	.0007	.0007	.0006	.0006	.0006	.0006	.0006	.0005	.0005	.0005
−3.1	.0010	.0009	.0009	.0009	.0008	.0008	.0008	.0008	.0007	.0007
−3.0	.0013	.0013	.0013	.0012	.0012	.0011	.0011	.0011	.0010	.0010
−2.9	.0019	.0018	.0018	.0017	.0016	.0016	.0015	.0015	.0014	.0014
−2.8	.0026	.0025	.0024	.0023	.0023	.0022	.0021	.0021	.0020	.0019
−2.7	.0035	.0034	.0033	.0032	.0031	.0030	.0029	.0028	.0027	.0026
−2.6	.0047	.0045	.0044	.0043	.0041	.0040	.0039	.0038	.0037	.0036
−2.5	.0062	.0060	.0059	.0057	.0055	.0054	.0052	.0051	.0049	.0048
−2.4	.0082	.0080	.0078	.0075	.0073	.0071	.0069	.0068	.0066	.0064
−2.3	.0107	.0104	.0102	.0099	.0096	.0094	.0091	.0089	.0087	.0084
−2.2	.0139	.0136	.0132	.0129	.0125	.0122	.0119	.0116	.0113	.0110
−2.1	.0179	.0174	.0170	.0166	.0162	.0158	.0154	.0150	.0146	.0143
−2.0	.0228	.0222	.0217	.0212	.0207	.0202	.0197	.0192	.0188	.0183

(Continued)

(Continued)

z	.00	.01	.02	.03	.04	.05	.06	.07	.08	.09
−1.9	.0287	.0281	.0274	.0268	.0262	.0256	.0250	.0244	.0239	.0233
−1.8	.0359	.0351	.0344	.0336	.0329	.0322	.0314	.0307	.0301	.0294
−1.7	.0446	.0436	.0427	.0418	.0409	.0401	.0392	.0384	.0375	.0367
−1.6	.0548	.0537	.0526	.0516	.0505	.0495	.0485	.0475	.0465	.0455
−1.5	.0668	.0655	.0643	.0630	.0618	.0606	.0594	.0582	.0571	.0559
−1.4	.0808	.0793	.0778	.0764	.0749	.0735	.0721	.0708	.0694	.0681
−1.3	.0968	.0915	.0934	.0918	.0901	.0885	.0869	.0853	.0838	.0823
−1.2	.1151	.1131	.1112	.1093	.1075	.1056	.1038	.1020	.1003	.0985
−1.1	.1357	.1135	.1314	.1292	.1271	.1251	.1230	.1210	.1190	.1170
−1.0	.1587	.1562	.1539	.1515	.1492	.1469	.1446	.1423	.1401	.1379
−0.9	.1841	.1814	.1788	.1762	.1736	.1711	.1685	.1660	.1635	.1611
−0.8	.2119	.2090	.2061	.2033	.2005	.1977	.1949	.1922	.1894	.1867
−0.7	.2420	.2389	.2358	2327	.2296	.2266	.2236	.2206	.2177	.2148
−0.6	.2743	.2709	.2676	.2643	.2611	.2578	2546	.2514	.2483	.2451
−0.5	.3085	.3050	.3015	.2981	.2946	.2912	.2877	.2843	.2810	.2776
−0.4	.3446	.3409	.3372	.3336	.3300	.3264	.3228	.3192	.3156	.3121
−0.3	.3821	.3783	.3745	.3707	.3669	.3632	.3594	.3557	.3520	.3483
−0.2	.4207	.4168	.4129	.4090	.4052	.4013	.3974	.3936	.3897	.3859
−0.1	.4602	.4562	.4522	.4483	.4443	.4404	.4364	.4325	.4286	.4247
−0.0	.5000	.4960	.4920	.4880	.4840	.4801	.4761	.4721	.4681	.4641

APPENDIX B COHEN'S EFFECT SIZE AND SAMPLE SIZE TABLES

Effect Size Table (B.1)

ES indexes and their values for small, medium, and large effects

Test	ES index	Effect size		
		Small	Medium	Large
1. m_A vs. m_B for independent means	$d = \dfrac{m_A - m_B}{\sigma}$	.20	.50	.80
2. Significance of product moment r	r	.10	.30	.50
3. r_A vs. r_B for independent rs	$q = z_A - z_B$ where z = Fisher's z	.10	.30	.50
4. $P = .5$ and the sign test	$g = P - .50$	.05	.15	.25
5. P_A vs. P_B for independent proportions	$h = \phi_A - \phi_A$ where ϕ = arcsine transformation	.20	.50	.80
6. Chi-square for goodness of fit and contingency	$w = \sqrt{\sum_{i=1}^{k} \dfrac{(P_{1i} - P_{0i})^2}{P_{0i}}}$	.10	.30	.50

(Continued)

Test	ES index	Effect size		
		Small	**Medium**	**Large**
7. One-way analysis of variance	$f = \dfrac{\sigma_m}{\sigma}$	.10	.25	.40
8. Multiple and multiple partial correlation	$f^2 = \dfrac{R^2}{1-R^2}$	.02	.15	.35

Note: ES = population effect size.

Sample Size Table (B.2)

N for small, medium, and large ES at power = .80 for α = .01, .05, and .10

	α								
	.01			**.05**			**.10**		
Test	**Sm**	**Med**	**Lg**	**Sm**	**Med**	**Lg**	**Sm**	**Med**	**Lg**
1. Mean diff	586	95	38	393	64	26	310	50	20
2. Sig r	1,163	125	41	783	85	28	617	68	22
3. r dif	2,339	263	96	1,573	177	66	1,240	140	52
4. $P = .5$	1,165	127	44	783	85	30	616	67	23
5. P dif	584	93	36	392	63	25	309	49	19
6. χ^2									
1*df*	1,168	130	38	785	87	26	618	69	25
1*df*	1,388	154	56	964	107	39	771	86	31
3*df*	1,546	172	62	1,090	121	44	880	98	35
4*df*	1,675	186	67	1,194	133	48	968	108	39
5*df*	1,787	199	71	1,293	143	51	1,045	116	42
6*df*	1,887	210	75	1,362	151	54	1,113	124	45
7. ANOVA									
2*g*[a]	586	95	38	393	64	26	310	50	20
3*g*[a]	464	76	30	322	52	21	258	41	17
4*g*[a]	388	63	25	274	45	18	221	36	15
5*g*[a]	336	55	22	240	39	16	193	32	13
6*g*[a]	299	49	20	215	35	14	174	28	12
7*g*[a]	271	44	18	195	32	13	159	26	11
8. Mult R									
2*k*[b]	698	97	45	481	67	30			
3*k*[b]	780	108	50	547	76	34			
4*k*[b]	841	118	55	599	84	38			
5*k*[b]	901	126	59	645	91	42			
6*k*[b]	953	134	63	686	97	45			
7*k*[b]	998	141	66	726	102	48			
8*k*[b]	1,039	147	69	757	107	50			

Note: ES = population effect size, Sm = small, Med = medium, Lg = large, diff = difference, ANOVA = analysis of variance. Tests numbered as in Table B.1.
[a]Number of groups. [b]Number of independent variables.

APPENDIX C CRITICAL VALUES OF THE χ^2 DISTRIBUTION

Critical χ^2 Values

$\alpha =$	0.050	0.025	0.010
df			
1.	3.841	5.024	6.635
2.	5.991	7.378	9.210
3.	7.815	9.348	11.345
4.	9.488	11.143	13.277
5.	11.070	12.833	15.086
6.	12.592	14.449	16.812
7.	14.067	16.013	18.475
8.	15.507	17.535	20.090
9.	16.919	19.023	21.666
10.	18.307	20.483	23.209
20.	31.410	34.170	37.566
30.	43.773	46.979	50.892
40.	55.758	59.342	63.691
50.	67.505	71.420	76.154

APPENDIX D CRITICAL VALUES OF T FOR TWO-TAILED TESTS

Critical t-Values for Two-Tail Tests

$\alpha =$	0.100	0.050	0.025	0.010
df				
1.	6.314	12.706	31.821	63.657
2.	2.920	4.303	6.205	9.925
3.	2.353	3.182	4.177	5.841
4.	2.132	2.776	3.495	4.604
5.	2.015	2.571	3.163	4.032
6.	1.943	2.447	2.969	3.707
7.	1.895	2.365	2.841	3.499
8.	1.860	2.306	2.752	3.355
9.	1.833	2.262	2.685	3.250
10.	1.812	2.228	2.634	3.169
11.	1.796	2.201	2.593	3.106
12.	1.782	2.179	2.560	3.055
13.	1.771	2.160	2.533	3.012

(Continued)

$\alpha =$	0.100	0.050	0.025	0.010
14.	1.761	2.145	2.510	2.977
15.	1.753	2.131	2.490	2.947
16.	1.746	2.120	2.472	2.921
17.	1.740	2.110	2.460	2.898
18.	1.734	2.101	2.450	2.878
19.	1.729	2.093	2.433	2.861
20.	1.725	2.086	2.423	2.845
21.	1.721	2.080	2.414	2.831
22.	1.717	2.074	2.410	2.819
23.	1.714	2.069	2.400	2.807
24.	1.711	2.064	2.391	2.797
25.	1.708	2.060	2.385	2.787
26.	1.706	2.056	2.380	2.779
27.	1.703	2.052	2.373	2.771
28.	1.701	2.048	2.368	2.763
29.	1.699	2.045	2.364	2.756
30.	1.697	2.042	2.360	2.750
40.	1.684	2.021	2.330	2.704
50.	1.676	2.009	2.311	2.678
100.	1.660	1.984	2.276	2.626
∞	1.645	1.960	2.289	2.576

APPENDIX E CRITICAL VALUES OF F_{MAX} FOR HARTLEY'S HOMOGENEITY OF VARIANCE TEST

Critical Values of F_{max} for Hartley's Homogeneity of Variance Test

The upper value in each box is for $\alpha = 0.05$. The lower value is for $\alpha = 0.01$. The test assumes that there are equal sample sizes in each group (n). For unequal sample sizes, use the smaller of the df for the two variances being compared.

df (n–1)	Number of treatments (k)										
	2	3	4	5	6	7	8	9	10	11	12
2	39.0	87.5	142	202	266	333	403	475	550	626	714
	199	448	729	1036	1362	1705	2063	2432	2813	3204	3605
3	15.4	27.8	39.2	50.7	62.0	72.9	83.5	93.9	104	114	124
	47.5	85.0	120	151	184	216	249	281	310	337	361
4	9.6	15.5	20.6	25.2	29.5	33.6	37.5	41.1	44.6	48.0	51.4
	23.2	37.0	49.0	59	69	79	89	97	106	113	120

(Continued)

(Continued)

					Number of treatments (*k*)						
df (*n*–1)	2	3	4	5	6	7	8	9	10	11	12
5	7.2	10.8	13.7	16.3	18.7	20.8	22.9	24.7	26.5	28.2	29.9
	14.9	22.0	28.0	33	38	42	46	50	54	57	60
6	5.82	8.38	10.4	12.1	13.7	15.0	16.3	17.5	18.6	19.7	20.7
	11.1	15.5	19.1	22	25	27	30	32	34	36	37
7	0.99	6.94	8.44	9.70	10.8	11.8	12.7	13.5	14.3	15.1	15.8
	8.89	12.1	14.5	16.5	18.4	20	22	23	24	26	27
8	4.43	6.00	7.18	8.12	9.03	9.78	10.5	11.1	11.7	12.2	12.7
	7.50	9.90	11.7	13.2	14.5	15.8	16.9	17.9	18.9	19.8	21
9	4.03	5.34	6.31	7.11	7.80	8.41	8.95	9.45	9.91	10.3	10.7
	6.54	8.50	9.9	11.1	12.1	13.1	13.9	14.7	15.3	16.0	16.6
10	3.72	4.85	5.67	6.34	6.92	7.42	7.87	8.28	8.66	9.01	9.34
	5.85	7.40	8.6	9.6	10.4	11.1	11.8	12.4	12.9	13.4	13.9
12	3.28	4.16	4.75	5.30	5.72	6.09	6.42	6.72	7.00	7.25	7.43
	4.91	6.1	6.9	7.6	8.2	8.7	9.1	9.5	9.9	10.2	10.6
15	2.86	3.54	4.01	4.37	4.68	4.95	5.19	5.40	5.59	5.77	5.95
	4.07	4.9	5.5	6.0	6.4	6.7	7.1	7.3	7.5	7.8	8.0
20	2.46	2.95	3.29	3.54	3.76	3.94	4.10	4.24	4.37	4.49	4.59
	3.32	3.8	4.3	4.6	4.9	5.1	5.3	5.5	5.6	5.8	5.9
30	2.07	2.40	2.61	2.78	2.91	3.02	3.12	3.21	3.29	3.36	3.39
	2.63	3.0	3.3	3.4	3.6	3.7	3.8	3.9	4.0	4.1	4.2
60	1.67	1.85	1.96	2.04	2.11	2.17	2.22	2.26	2.30	2.33	2.36
	1.96	2.2	2.3	2.4	2.4	2.5	2.5	2.6	2.6	2.7	2.7
∞	1.00	1.00	1.00	1.00	1.00	1.00	1.00	1.00	1.00	1.00	1.00
	1.00	1.00	1.00	1.00	1.00	1.00	1.00	1.00	1.00	1.00	1.00

APPENDIX F CRITICAL VALUES OF THE MANN–WHITNEY *U*-TEST

Critical Values of the Mann-Whitney U
(Two-Tailed Testing | $\alpha = 0.05$)

									n_1						
n_2	α	3	4	5	6	7	8	9	10	11	12	13	14	15	16
3	.05	–	0	0	1	1	2	2	3	3	4	4	5	5	6
4	.05	–	0	1	2	3	4	4	5	6	7	8	9	10	11
5	.05	0	1	2	3	5	6	7	8	9	11	12	13	14	15
6	.05	1	2	3	5	6	8	10	11	13	14	16	17	19	21
7	.05	1	3	5	6	8	10	12	14	16	18	20	22	24	26
8	.05	2	4	6	8	10	13	15	17	19	22	24	26	29	31
9	.05	2	4	7	10	12	15	17	20	23	26	28	31	34	37

(Continued)

n_1

n_2	α	3	4	5	6	7	8	9	10	11	12	13	14	15	16
10	.05	3	5	8	11	14	17	20	23	26	29	33	36	39	42
11	.05	3	6	9	13	16	19	23	26	30	33	37	40	44	47
12	.05	4	7	11	14	18	22	26	29	33	37	41	45	49	53
13	.05	4	8	12	16	20	24	28	33	37	41	45	50	54	59
14	.05	5	9	13	17	22	26	31	36	40	45	50	55	59	64
15	.05	5	10	14	19	24	29	34	39	44	49	54	59	64	70
16	.05	6	11	15	21	26	31	37	42	47	53	59	64	70	75

APPENDIX G CRITICAL VALUES OF THE *F*-DISTRIBUTION

Table $F(\alpha = 0.05)$

$\alpha = .05$ Table
Critical F-Values

Degrees of Freedom Treatment

df	1	2	3	4	5	6	7	8	9	10
1	161.4	199.5	215.8	224.8	230.0	233.8	236.5	238.6	240.1	242.1
2	18.51	19.00	19.16	19.25	19.30	19.33	19.35	19.37	19.38	19.40
3	10.13	9.55	9.28	9.12	9.01	8.94	8.89	8.85	8.81	8.79
4	7.71	6.94	6.59	6.39	6.26	6.16	6.09	6.04	6.00	5.96
5	6.61	5.79	5.41	5.19	5.05	4.95	4.88	4.82	4.77	4.74
6	5.99	5.14	4.76	4.53	4.39	4.28	4.21	4.15	4.10	4.06
7	5.59	4.74	4.35	4.12	3.97	3.87	3.79	3.73	3.68	3.64
8	5.32	4.46	4.07	3.84	3.69	3.58	3.50	3.44	3.39	3.35
9	5.12	4.26	3.86	3.63	3.48	3.37	3.29	3.23	3.18	3.14
10	4.96	4.10	3.71	3.48	3.33	3.22	3.14	3.07	3.02	2.98
11	4.84	3.98	3.59	3.36	3.20	3.09	3.01	2.95	2.90	2.85
12	4.75	3.89	3.49	3.26	3.11	3.00	2.91	2.85	2.80	2.75
13	4.67	3.81	3.41	3.18	3.03	2.92	2.83	2.77	2.71	2.67
14	4.60	3.74	3.34	3.11	2.96	2.85	2.76	2.70	2.65	2.60
15	4.54	3.68	3.29	3.06	2.90	2.79	2.71	2.64	2.59	2.54
16	4.49	3.63	3.24	3.01	2.85	2.74	2.66	2.59	2.54	2.49
17	4.45	3.59	3.20	2.96	2.81	2.70	2.61	2.55	2.49	2.45
18	4.41	3.55	3.16	2.93	2.77	2.66	2.58	2.51	2.46	2.41
19	4.38	3.52	3.13	2.90	2.74	2.63	2.54	2.48	2.42	2.38
20	4.35	3.49	3.10	2.87	2.71	2.60	2.51	2.45	2.39	2.35
22	4.30	3.44	3.05	2.82	2.66	2.55	2.46	2.40	2.34	2.30
24	4.26	3.40	3.01	2.78	2.62	2.51	2.42	2.36	2.30	2.25
26	4.23	3.37	2.98	2.74	2.59	2.47	2.39	2.32	2.27	2.22

Degrees of Freedom Error

(Continued)

(Continued)

df	1	2	3	4	5	6	7	8	9	10
28	4.20	3.34	2.95	2.71	2.56	2.45	2.36	2.29	2.24	2.19
30	4.17	3.32	2.92	2.69	2.53	2.42	2.33	2.27	2.21	2.16
40	4.08	3.23	2.84	2.61	2.45	2.34	2.25	2.18	2.12	2.08
50	4.03	3.18	2.79	2.56	2.40	2.29	2.20	2.13	2.07	2.03
60	4.00	3.15	2.76	2.53	2.37	2.25	2.17	2.10	2.04	1.99

Table $F(\alpha = 0.025)$

$\alpha = .025$ Table
Critical F-Values

Degrees of Freedom Treatment

Degrees of Freedom Error

df	1	2	3	4	5	6	7	8	9	10
1	647.8	799.5	864.2	899.6	921.8	937.1	948.2	956.7	963.3	968.6
2	38.51	39.00	39.17	39.25	39.30	39.33	39.36	39.37	39.39	39.40
3	17.44	16.04	15.44	15.10	14.89	14.73	14.62	14.54	14.47	14.42
4	12.22	10.65	9.98	9.60	9.36	9.20	9.07	8.98	8.90	8.84
5	10.01	8.43	7.76	7.39	7.15	6.98	6.85	6.76	6.68	6.62
6	8.81	7.26	6.60	6.23	5.99	5.82	5.70	5.60	5.52	5.46
7	8.07	6.54	5.89	5.52	5.29	5.12	4.99	4.90	4.82	4.76
8	7.57	6.06	5.42	5.05	4.82	4.65	4.53	4.43	4.36	4.30
9	7.21	5.71	5.08	4.72	4.48	4.32	4.20	4.10	4.03	3.96
10	6.94	5.46	4.83	4.47	4.24	4.07	3.95	3.85	3.78	3.72
11	6.72	5.26	4.63	4.28	4.04	3.88	3.76	3.66	3.59	3.53
12	6.55	5.10	4.47	4.12	3.89	3.73	3.61	3.51	3.44	3.37
13	6.41	4.97	4.35	4.00	3.77	3.60	3.48	3.39	3.31	3.25
14	6.30	4.86	4.24	3.89	3.66	3.50	3.38	3.29	3.21	3.15
15	6.20	4.77	4.15	3.80	3.58	3.41	3.29	3.20	3.12	3.06
16	6.12	4.69	4.08	3.73	3.50	3.34	3.22	3.12	3.05	2.99
17	6.04	4.62	4.01	3.66	3.44	3.28	3.16	3.06	2.98	2.92
18	5.98	4.56	3.95	3.61	3.38	3.22	3.10	3.01	2.93	2.87
19	5.92	4.51	3.90	3.56	3.33	3.17	3.05	2.96	2.88	2.82
20	5.87	4.46	3.86	3.51	3.29	3.13	3.01	2.91	2.84	2.77
22	5.79	4.38	3.78	3.44	3.22	3.05	2.93	2.84	2.76	2.70
24	5.72	4.32	3.72	3.38	3.15	2.99	2.87	2.78	2.70	2.64
26	5.66	4.27	3.67	3.33	3.10	2.949	2.82	2.73	2.65	2.59
28	5.61	4.22	3.63	3.29	3.06	2.90	2.78	2.69	2.61	2.55

(Continued)

df	1	2	3	4	5	6	7	8	9	10
30	5.57	4.18	3.59	3.25	3.03	2.87	2.75	2.65	2.57	2.51
40	5.42	4.05	3.46	3.13	2.90	2.74	2.62	2.53	2.45	2.39
50	5.34	3.97	3.39	3.05	2.83	2.67	2.55	2.46	2.38	2.32
60	5.29	3.93	3.34	3.01	2.79	2.63	2.51	2.41	2.33	2.27

Table $F(\alpha = 0.01)$

$\alpha = .010$ Table
Critical F-Values

Degrees of Freedom Treatment

df	1	2	3	4	5	6	7	8	9	10
1	4048	4993	5377	5577	5668	5924	5992	6096	6132	6168
2	98.50	99.01	99.15	99.23	99.30	99.33	99.35	99.39	99.40	99.43
3	34.12	30.82	29.46	28.71	28.24	27.91	27.67	27.49	27.34	27.23
4	21.20	18.00	16.69	15.98	15.52	15.21	14.98	14.80	14.66	14.55
5	16.26	13.27	12.06	11.39	10.97	10.67	10.46	10.29	10.16	10.05
6	13.75	10.92	9.78	9.15	8.75	8.47	8.26	8.10	7.98	7.87
7	12.25	9.55	8.45	7.85	7.46	7.19	6.99	6.84	6.72	6.62
8	11.26	8.65	7.59	7.01	6.63	6.37	6.18	6.03	5.91	5.81
9	10.56	8.02	6.99	6.42	6.06	5.80	5.61	5.47	5.35	5.26
10	10.04	7.56	6.55	5.99	5.64	5.39	5.20	5.06	4.94	4.85
11	9.65	7.21	6.22	5.67	5.32	5.07	4.89	4.74	4.63	4.54
12	9.33	6.93	5.95	5.41	5.06	4.82	4.64	4.50	4.39	4.30
13	9.07	6.70	5.74	5.21	4.86	4.62	4.44	4.30	4.19	4.10
14	8.86	6.51	5.56	5.04	4.69	4.46	4.28	4.14	4.03	3.94
15	8.68	6.36	5.42	4.89	4.56	4.32	4.14	4.00	3.89	3.80
16	8.53	6.23	5.29	4.77	4.44	4.20	4.03	3.89	3.78	3.69
17	8.40	6.11	5.18	4.67	4.34	4.10	3.93	3.79	3.68	3.59
18	8.29	6.01	5.09	4.58	4.25	4.01	3.84	3.71	3.60	3.51
19	8.18	5.93	5.01	4.50	4.17	3.94	3.77	3.63	3.52	3.43
20	8.10	5.85	4.94	4.43	4.10	3.87	3.70	3.56	3.46	3.37
22	7.95	5.72	4.82	4.31	3.99	3.76	3.59	3.45	3.35	3.26
24	7.82	5.61	4.72	4.22	3.90	3.67	3.50	3.36	3.26	3.17
26	7.72	5.53	4.64	4.14	3.82	3.59	3.42	3.29	3.18	3.09
28	7.64	5.45	4.57	4.07	3.75	3.53	3.36	3.23	3.12	3.03
30	7.56	5.39	4.51	4.02	3.70	3.47	3.30	3.17	3.07	2.98
40	7.31	5.18	4.31	3.83	3.51	3.29	3.12	2.99	2.89	2.80
50	7.17	5.06	4.20	3.72	3.41	3.19	3.02	2.89	2.78	2.70
60	7.08	4.98	4.13	3.65	3.34	3.12	2.95	2.82	2.72	2.63

Degrees of Freedom Error

APPENDIX H CRITICAL VALUES OF THE STUDENTIZED RANGE STATISTIC

Studentized Range Statistic
$\alpha = .05$

k	2	3	4	5	6	7	8
df							
1	17.90	27.90	32.82	37.17	40.41	43.31	45.41
2	6.08	8.33	9.80	10.88	11.73	12.43	13.03
3	4.50	5.91	6.82	7.50	8.04	8.48	8.85
4	3.93	5.04	5.76	6.29	6.71	7.05	7.35
5	3.64	4.60	5.22	5.67	6.03	6.33	6.58
6	3.46	4.34	4.90	5.30	5.63	5.90	6.12
7	3.34	4.16	4.68	5.06	5.36	5.61	5.82
8	3.26	4.04	4.53	4.89	5.17	5.40	5.60
9	3.20	3.95	4.41	4.76	5.02	5.24	5.43
10	3.15	3.88	4.33	4.65	4.91	5.12	5.30
11	3.11	3.82	4.26	4.57	4.82	5.03	5.20
12	3.08	3.77	4.20	4.51	4.75	4.95	5.12
13	3.06	3.73	4.15	4.45	4.69	4.88	5.05
14	3.03	3.70	4.11	4.41	4.64	4.83	4.99
15	3.01	3.67	4.08	4.37	4.59	4.78	4.94
16	3.00	3.65	4.05	4.33	4.56	4.74	4.90
17	2.98	3.63	4.02	4.30	4.52	4.70	4.86
18	2.97	3.61	4.00	4.28	4.49	4.67	4.82
19	2.96	3.59	3.98	4.25	4.47	4.65	4.79
20	2.95	3.58	3.96	4.23	4.45	4.62	4.77
24	2.92	3.53	3.90	4.17	4.37	4.54	4.68
30	2.89	3.49	3.85	4.10	4.30	4.46	4.60
40	2.86	3.44	3.79	4.04	4.23	4.39	4.52
60	2.83	3.40	3.74	3.98	4.16	4.31	4.44
120	2.80	3.36	3.68	3.92	4.10	4.24	4.36
∞	2.77	3.31	3.63	3.86	4.03	4.17	4.29

THE CORE STORY TOLD THROUGH FORMULAE

An observation (score) $= y$ The sum of the observations $= \Sigma y$

$$\mu = \frac{\Sigma Y}{N} \quad \bar{Y} = \frac{\Sigma Y}{n} \quad GM = \frac{\Sigma n_j \bar{y}_j}{\Sigma n_j} = \frac{\Sigma y_{ij}}{N} \qquad GM = \Sigma \frac{\bar{y}_j}{K}$$

$$\sigma^2 = \frac{\Sigma(y - \mu)^2}{N} \quad S^2 = \frac{\Sigma(y - \bar{y})^2}{n}$$

$$\sigma = \sqrt{\frac{\Sigma(y - \mu)^2}{N}} = \sqrt{\sigma^2} \qquad S = \sqrt{\frac{\Sigma(y - \bar{y})^2}{n}} = \sqrt{S^2}$$

$$\mu_{\bar{y}} = \frac{\Sigma \bar{y}}{k} \qquad \sigma_{\bar{y}}^2 = \frac{\Sigma(\bar{y} - \mu)^2}{k} \qquad \sigma_{\bar{y}}^2 = \frac{s^2}{n}$$

$$\sigma_{\bar{y}} = \sqrt{\frac{\Sigma(\bar{y} - \mu)^2}{k}} \qquad \sigma_{\bar{y}} = \frac{s}{\sqrt{n}}$$

$$P(A) = \frac{A}{A + B} \qquad P(A \text{ or } B) = P(A) + P(B) \qquad P(A \text{ or } B) = P(A) + P(B) - P(A \text{ and } B)$$

$$P(A \text{ and } B) = P(A)P(B) \qquad P(x \text{ IF } y) = \frac{P(x)P(y \text{ IF } x)}{P(y)} \qquad z\text{-score} = \frac{y - \mu}{\sigma}$$

$$P_K^N = \frac{N!}{(N - k)!} \qquad C_k^N = \frac{N!}{k!(N - k)!} \qquad P(k) = C_k^N P^k q^{(N - k)}$$

$$q = 1 - p \qquad \text{mean (binomial)} = Np \quad \text{variance(binomial)} = Npq \quad \sqrt{Npq}$$

$$\chi^2 = \Sigma \frac{(O - E)^2}{E} \qquad \chi^2 = N\Sigma \frac{(p_{Oi} - p_{Ei})^2}{p_{Ei}} \qquad W = \Sigma \frac{(p_{Oi} - p_{Ei})^2}{p_{Ei}} \qquad G = 2\Sigma[O\ln(O/E)]$$

$$z(\text{mean}) = \frac{\bar{y} - \mu}{\sigma/\sqrt{n}} \qquad t = \frac{\bar{y} - \mu}{s/\sqrt{n}} \qquad t = \frac{(\bar{y}_1 - \bar{y}_2) - (\mu_1 - \mu_2)}{\sqrt{\dfrac{s_1^2}{n_1} + \dfrac{s_2^2}{n_2}}} = \frac{\bar{y}_1 - \bar{y}_2}{\sqrt{\dfrac{s_1^2}{n_1} + \dfrac{s_2^2}{n_2}}} \qquad t = \frac{\bar{d} - \mu}{S_d/\sqrt{n}}$$

$$F_{\max} = \frac{s_{larger}^2}{s_{smaller}^2} \qquad d = \frac{\bar{d} - \mu}{\sigma_d}$$

$$\chi^2 = \Sigma \frac{(O - E)^2}{E} \qquad \chi_{\text{Yates}}^2 = \Sigma \frac{\{(O - E) - 0.5\}^2}{E} \qquad \phi = \sqrt{\frac{\chi^2}{N}} \qquad V = \sqrt{\frac{\chi^2}{n(k - 1)}}$$

$$d = 2\sqrt{\frac{\chi^2}{N - \chi^2}} \qquad \text{likelihood ratio} = 2\Sigma\left(O\ln\frac{O}{E}\right) \qquad \lambda = \frac{E_1 - E_2}{E_1}$$

$$cov_{xy} = \frac{\Sigma(x - \bar{x})(y - \bar{y})}{n - 1} \qquad r = \frac{cov_{xy}}{S_x S_y}$$

$$r = \frac{\text{cov}_{xy}}{s_x s_y} = \frac{\frac{\sum(x-\bar{x})(y-\bar{y})}{n-1}}{\sqrt{\frac{\sum(x-\bar{x})^2}{n-1}}\sqrt{\frac{\sum(y-\bar{y})^2}{n-1}}} = \frac{\sum z_x z_y}{n-1}$$

$$t = \frac{r\sqrt{n-2}}{\sqrt{1-r^2}} \qquad r_{\text{adj}} = \sqrt{1 - \frac{(1-r^2)(n-1)}{n-k-1}} \qquad r_s = \frac{\text{cov}(rg_x rg_y)}{\sigma_{rgx}\sigma_{rgy}} \qquad d = \frac{2r}{1-r^2}$$

$$\hat{y} = Bx + a \qquad B = \frac{\frac{\sum(x-\bar{x})(y-\bar{y})}{n-1}}{\frac{\sum(x-\bar{x})^2}{n-1}} \qquad B = \frac{\text{cov}_{xy}}{s_x^2} \qquad a = \bar{y} - B\bar{x}$$

$$S_{y.x}^2 = \frac{\sum(y-\hat{y})^2}{n-2} \qquad S_{y.x} = \sqrt{\frac{\sum(y-\hat{y})^2}{n-2}} \qquad S_B = \frac{S_{y.x}}{S_x\sqrt{n-1}} \qquad t = \frac{B-0}{S_B}$$

$$\sigma^2 = \frac{\sum s_j^2}{k} \qquad \sigma_y^2 = \frac{s^2}{n} = ns_{\bar{y}}^2 \qquad s_{\bar{y}}^2 = \frac{\sum(\bar{y}-GM)^2}{k-1}$$

$$y_i = \mu + \tau_i + e_i \qquad\qquad Y_i = GM + (\bar{y}_j - GM) + (Y_i - \bar{y}_j)$$

$$SS_{\text{total}} = \sum(y - GM)^2 \qquad SS_{\text{treatment}} = \sum n(\bar{y} - GM)^2 \qquad SS_{\text{error}} = \sum\sum(y_i - \bar{y}_j)^2$$

$$\sum\sum(y - GM)^2 = n\sum(\bar{y} - GM)^2 + \sum\sum(y_i - \bar{y}_j)^2 \qquad\qquad F = \frac{MS_{\text{treatment}}}{MS_{\text{error}}}$$

$$\eta^2 = \frac{SS_{\text{total}} - SS_{\text{error}}}{SS_{\text{total}}} = \frac{SS_{\text{treatment}}}{SS_{\text{total}}} \qquad\qquad \omega^2 = \frac{SS_{\text{treatment}} - (k-1)MS_{\text{error}}}{SS_{\text{total}} + MS_{\text{error}}} \qquad f = \sqrt{\frac{\eta^2}{1-\eta^2}}$$

$$y_i = \mu + \tau_k + cov + e_i,$$

$$y_i = \mu + \tau_k + \beta_j\,(\text{block}) + \varepsilon_i$$

$$y_i = GM + (\bar{y}_j - GM) + (\bar{y}_{\beta j} - GM) + (Y_i - \bar{y}_J - \bar{y}_{\beta j} + GM)$$

$$(Y_i - GM) = (\bar{y}_j - GM) + (\bar{y}_{\beta j} - GM) + (Y_i - \bar{y}_J - \bar{y}_{\beta j} + GM)$$

$$\sum\sum(Y_i - GM)^2 = \sum\sum(\bar{y}_j - GM)^2 + \sum\sum(\bar{Y}_{\beta j} - GM)^2 + \sum\sum(Y_i - \bar{y}_J \ \bar{y}_{\beta j} + GM)^2$$

$$\sum\sum(Y_i - GM)^2 = n\sum(\bar{y}_j - GM)^2 + bn\sum(\bar{Y}_{\beta j} - GM)^2 + \sum\sum(Y_i - \bar{y}_J \ \bar{y}_{\beta j} + GM)^2$$

$$y_i = \mu + \tau_k + \varsigma_j\,(\text{subject}) + \varepsilon_i$$

$$y_i = GM + (\bar{y}_j - GM) + (\bar{y}_{\varsigma j} - GM) + (Y_i - \bar{y}_J - \bar{y}_{\varsigma j} + GM)$$

$$(y_i - GM) = (\bar{y}_j - GM) + (\bar{y}_{\varsigma j} - GM) + (Y_i - \bar{y}_J - \bar{y}_{\varsigma j} + GM)$$

$$\sum\sum(Y_i - GM)^2 = n\sum(\bar{y}_j - GM)^2 + \varsigma n(\bar{y}_{\varsigma j} - GM)^2 + \sum\sum(Y_i - \bar{y}_J - \bar{y}_{\varsigma j} + GM)^2$$

P(at least one Type I error: familywise) $= 1 - \left(1 - \mathrm{pc}\alpha\right)^c$

$$t = \frac{\bar{y}_1 - \bar{y}_2}{\sqrt{\dfrac{MS_{error}}{n_1} + \dfrac{MS_{error}}{n_2}}} \qquad SS_{contrast} = \frac{nL^2}{\Sigma c_j^2} \qquad MS_{contrast} = \frac{SS_{contrast}}{1}$$

$$q_k = \frac{\bar{y}_{largest} - \bar{y}_{smallest}}{\sqrt{MS_{error}/n}} \qquad \text{min. diff.} = \text{critical } q\text{-value} \sqrt{\frac{MS_{error}}{df}}$$

$$SS_{interaction} = SS_{treatment/total} - SS_{treatment\ A} - SS_{treatment\ B}$$

$$SS_{A\ at\ B1} = n\Sigma\left(\bar{y}_{Aj} - GM\right)^2 \qquad\qquad SS_{A\ at\ B2} = n\Sigma\left(\bar{y}_{Aj} - GM\right)^2$$

$$SS_{total} = \Sigma\Sigma\Sigma(y - GM)^2$$

$$SS_{bs} = n\Sigma\left(\bar{y} - GM\right)^2 \qquad\qquad SS_{ws} = SS_{total} - SS_{bs}$$

$$SS_{grp} = n\Sigma\left(\bar{y}_{grp} - GM\right)^2 \qquad\qquad SS_{trt} = n\Sigma\left(\bar{y}_{trt} - GM\right)^2$$

$$SS_{wrgp} = SS_{bs} - SS_{grp} \qquad\qquad SS_{int} = SS_{trt/tot} - SS_{grp} - SS_{trt}$$

$$SS_{trt \times grp/error} = SS_{ws} - SS_{trt} - SS_{int}$$

$$df_{trt/tot} = k - 1$$

$$df_{int} = df_{trt/tot} - df_{grp} - df_{trt}$$

$$df_{trt \times grp/error} = df_{ws} - df_{trt} - df_{int}$$

$$R^2 = 1 - \frac{\text{sum of the squares in the criterion about the regression line}}{\text{sum of the squares in the criterion about the mean of the criterion}}$$

$$F = \frac{R^2}{1 - R^2} \frac{N - K - 1}{K} \qquad\qquad R_{adj}^2 = 1 - \frac{\left(1 - R^2\right)(n - 1)}{n - 1 - k}$$

REFERENCES

Abdi, H., & Williams, L. J. (2010). Contrast analysis. In N. J. Salkind (Ed.), *Encyclopedia of research design* (pp. 243–251). Thousand Oaks, CA: Sage.

Abelson, R. P. (1997). On the surprising longevity of flogged horses: Why there is a case for the significance test. *Psychological Science, 8*, 12–15.

Allison, P. D. (1999). *Multiple regression: A primer*. Thousand Oaks, CA: Pine Forge Press.

Allison, P. D. (2002). *Missing data*. Thousand Oaks, CA: Sage.

Andrade, H. L. (2013). Classroom assessment in the context of learning theory and research. In J. H. McMillan (Ed.), *Research on classroom assessment*. London: Sage.

Aronson, E., Wilson, T. D., Akert, R. M., & Fehr, B. (2007). *Social psychology* (4th ed.). Toronto: Pearson Education.

Arrindell, W. A., & van der Ende, J. (1985). An empirical test of the utility of the observations-to-variables ratio in factor and components analysis. *Applied Psychological Measurement, 9*(2), 165–178.

Bausell, R. B., & Li, Y. (2002). *Power analysis for experimental research: A practical guide for the biological, medical and social sciences*. New York: Cambridge University Press.

Berk, R. A. (2004). *Regression analysis: A constructive critique*. London: Sage.

Berkovits, I., Hancock, G. R., & Nevitt, J. (2000). Bootstrap resampling approaches for repeated measures designs: Relative robustness to sphericity and normality violations. *Educational and Psychological Measurement, 60*(6), 877–892.

Bigg, N. J. (1979). The roots of combinatorics. *Historia Mathematica, 6*(2), 109–136.

Boneau, C. A. (1960). The effects of violations of assumptions underlying the t test. *Psychological Bulletin, 57*(1), 49–64.

Bonferroni, C. E. (1936). *Teoria statistica delle classi, e calcolo delle probabilità*. Florence: Seeber.

Bors, D. A., & Forrin, B. (1996). The effects of post-weaning environment, biological dam, and nursing dam on feeding neophobia, open-field activity, and learning. *Canadian Journal of Experimental Psychology, 50*, 197–204.

Bors, D. A., & Vigneau, F. (2001). Effet à long terme d'un environnement précoce enrichi sur l'activité open-field chez le rat. In A. Flieller, C. Bocéréan, J.-L. Kop, E. Thiébaut, A.-M. Toniolo, & J. Tournois (Eds.), *Questions de psychologie différentielle: Actes des XIVe Journées de Psychologie Différentielle* (pp. 333–337). Rennes: Presses Universitaires de Rennes.

Bors, D. A., Macleod, C. M., & Forrin, B. (1993). Eliminating the IQ-RT correlation by eliminating an experimental confound. *Intelligence, 17*, 475–500.

Bors, D. A., Vigneau, F., & Kronlund, A. (2006). L'anxiété face aux examens: Dimensionnalité, similitudes, et différences chez les étudiants universitaires. *Canadian Journal of Behavioural Science, 38*, 176–184.

Box, G. E. P. (1953). Non-normality and test of variance. *Biometrika, 40,* 318–335.

Bradley, J. V. (1968). *Distribution-free statistical tests.* Englewood Cliffs, NJ: Prentice Hall.

Braver, M. C., & MacKinnon, D. P. (2003). *Levine's guide to SPSS for analysis of variance* (2nd ed.). Mahwah, NJ: Erlbaum.

Bridgman, P. W. (1927). *The logic of modern physics.* New York: Macmillan.

Brown, R. G. (1997). *Advanced mathematics: Precalculus with discrete mathematics and data analysis.* Evanston, IL: McDougal Littell.

Bryant, F. B., & Yarnold, P. R. (1995). Principle-components analysis and exploratory and confirmatory factor analysis. In L. G. Grimm & P. R. Yarnold (Eds.), *Reading and understanding multivariate statistics* (pp. 99–136). Washington, DC: American Psychological Association.

Burnham, K. P., & Anderson, D. R. (2002). *Model selection and multimodel inference: A practical information-theoretic approach* (2nd ed.). New York: Springer.

Carlson, J. E., & Timm, N. H. (1974). Analysis of non-orthogonal fixed-effects designs. *Psychological Bulletin, 81*(9), 563–570.

Cassady, J. C., & Johnson, R. E. (2002). Cognitive test anxiety and academic performance. *Contemporary Educational Psychology, 27*(2), 270–295.

Cattell, R. B. (1966). The scree test for the number of factors. *Multivariate Behavioral Research, 1,* 245–276.

Cianciolo, A. T., & Sternberg, R. (2004). *Intelligence: A brief history.* Malden, MA: Blackwell.

Cohen, J. (1988). *Statistical power analysis for the behavioural sciences* (2nd ed.). Hillsdale, NJ: Erlbaum.

Cohen, J. (1990). Things I have learned (so far). *American Psychologist, 45*(12), 1304–1312.

Cohen, J. (1992). A power primer. *Psychological Bulletin, 112*(1), 155–159.

Cook, R. D., & Weisberg, S. (1982). *Residuals and influence in regression.* New York: Chapman & Hall.

Cook, T. D., & Campbell, D. T. (1979). *Quasi-experimentation: Design and analysis issues for field settings.* Chicago: Rand McNally College Publishing.

Daniel, W. W. (1990). *Applied nonparametric statistics* (2nd ed.). Boston, MA: PWK-Kent.

Dixon, W. J., & Mood, A. M. (1946). The statistical sign test. *Journal of the American Statistical Association, 41,* 557–566.

Dunn, O. J. (1961). Multiple comparisons among means. *Journal of the American Statistical Association, 56,* 52–64.

Field, A. (2018). *Discovering statistics using IBM SPSS Statistics* (5th ed.). London: Sage.

Fisher, R. A. (1922). On the interpretation of χ^2 from contingency tables and the calculation of P. *Journal of the Royal Statistical Society, 85,* 87–94.

Fisher, R. A. (1927). Studies in crop rotation. IV. The experimental determination of the value of top dressings with cereals. *Journal of Agricultural Science, 17*(4), 548–562.

Fisher, R. A. (1935). *The design of experiments.* Edinburgh: Oliver and Boyd.

Fleiss, J. L. (1969). Estimating the magnitude of experimental effects. *Psychological Bulletin, 72,* 273–276.

Fox, J. (2000). *Nonparametric simple regression.* London: Sage.

Frane, A. V. (2015). Are per-family Type I error rates relevant in social and behavioral science? *Journal of Modern Applied Statistical Methods, 14*(1), 12–23.

Freeman, L. C. (1965). *Elementary applied statistics for students in behavioral science*. New York: Wiley.

Friedman, M. (1937). The use of ranks to avoid the assumption of normality implicit in the analysis of variance. *Journal of the American Statistical Association, 32,* 675–701.

Friedman, M. (1939). A correction: The use of ranks to avoid the assumption of normality implicit in the analysis of variance. *Journal of the American Statistical Association, 34,* 109.

Gates, A. I. (1917). *Recitation as a factor in memorizing*. New York: Science Press.

Girden, E. R. (1992). *ANOVA: Repeated measures*. Newbury Park, CA: Sage.

Göktaş, A., & İşçi, Ö. (2011). A comparison of the most commonly used measures of association for doubly ordered square contingency tables via stimulation. *Metodološki zvezki, 8,* 17–37.

Goodwin, L. D., & Leech, N. L. (2006). Understanding correlation: Factors that affect the size of r. *Journal of Experimental Education, 74*(3), 251–266.

Hagen, R. L. (1997). In praise of the null hypothesis statistical test. *American Psychologist, 52*(1), 15–24.

Haitovsky, Y. (1968). Missing data in regression analysis. *Journal of the Royal Statistical Society, Series B, 30*(1), 67–82.

Hartley, H. O. (1950). The use of range in analysis of variance. *Biometrika, 37,* 271–280.

Hastings, C., Mosteller, F., Tukey, J. W., & Winsor, C. P. (1947). Low amounts for small samples: A comparative study of order statistics. *Annals of Mathematical Statistics, 18*(3), 413–416.

Hinton, P. R., Brownlow, C., McMurray, I., & Cozens, B. (2004). *SPSS explained*. Hove: Routledge.

Holm, S. (1979). A simple sequentially rejective multiple test procedure. *Scandinavian Journal of Statistics, 6,* 65–70.

Hotelling, H. (1933). Analysis of a complex of statistical variables into principal components. *Journal of Educational Psychology, 24,* 417–441 and 498–520.

Howell, D. C. (2002). *Statistical methods for psychology* (5th ed.). Pacific Grove, CA: Duxbury.

Howell, D. C. (2013). *Statistical methods for psychology* (8th ed.). Belmont, CA: Wadsworth Cengage Learning.

Hulley, S. B., Cummings, S. K., Browner, W. S., Grady, D. G., & Newman, T. G. (2007). *Designing clinical research*. Philadelphia: Lippincott, Williams & Wilkins.

Humphreys, L. G., & Montanelli, R. G. Jr. (1975). An investigation of the parallel analysis criterion for determining the number of common factors. *Multivariate Behavioral Research, 10,* 193–205.

Iversen, G. R., & Norpoth, H. (1987). *Analysis of variance*. London: Sage.

Iverson, G. J., Lee, M. D., Zhang, S., & Wagenmakers, E. J. (2009). Prep: An agony in five fits. *Journal of Mathematical Psychology, 53,* 195–202.

Jaccard, J., Becker, M. A., & Wood, G. (1984). Pairwise multiple comparison procedures: A review. *Psychological Bulletin, 96,* 589–596.

Jaccard, J., & Turrisi, R. (2003). *Interaction effects in multiple regression* (2nd ed.). London: Sage.

Jackson, S., & Brashers, D. E. (1994). *Random factors in ANOVA*. London: Sage.

Julious, S. A., & Mullee, M. A. (1994). Confounding and Simpson's paradox. *British Medical Journal, 309,* 1480–1481.

Kaiser, H. F. (1960). The application of electronic computers to factor analysis. *Educational and Psychological Measurement, 20,* 141–151.

Kashigan, S. K. (1986). *Statistical analysis*. New York: Radius Press.

Kaufman, R. L. (2013). *Heteroskedasticity in regression*. Thousand Oaks, CA: Sage.

Kendall, M. G., & Stuart, A. (1958). *The advanced theory of statistics*. New York: Hafner.

Keppel, G., & Wickens, T. D. (2004). *Design and analysis: A researcher's handbook* (4th ed.). Upper Saddle River, NJ: Prentice Hall.

Kerby, D. S. (2014). The simple difference formula: An approach to teaching a nonparametric correlation. *Comprehensive Psychology*, *3*, article 1.

Keuls, M. (1952). The use of the 'studentized range' in connection with an analysis of variance. *Euphytica*, *1*(2), 112–122.

Killeen, P. R. (2005). An alternative to null-hypothesis significance tests. *Psychological Science*, *16*(5), 345–353.

Kim, J.-O., & Mueller, C. W. (1978). *Factor analysis: Statistical methods and practical issues*. London: Sage.

Kline, P. (1986). *A handbook of test construction: Introduction to psychometric design*. London: Methuen.

Kline, P. (2002). *An easy guide to factor analysis*. London: Routledge.

Kraemer, H. C., & Thiemann, S. (1987). *How many subjects? Statistical power analysis in research*. London: Sage.

Kuhn, T. (1996). *The structure of scientific revolutions* (3rd ed.). Chicago: University of Chicago Press.

Langsrud, Ø. (2003). ANOVA for unbalanced data: Use Type II instead of Type III sums of squares. *Statistics and Computing*, *13*(2), 163–167.

Lee, H. B., Katz, G. S., & Restori, A. F. (2010). A Monte Carlo study of seven homogeneity of variance tests. *Journal of Mathematics and Statistics*, *6*(3), 359–366.

Lenth, R. V. (2001). Some practical guidelines for effective sample size determination. *American Statistician*, *55*, 187–193.

Levine, T. R., & Hullett, C.R. (2002). Eta squared, partial eta squared, and misreporting of effect size in communication research. *Human Communication Research*, 28, 612–625.

Lewis, D., & Burke, C. J. (1949). The use and misuse of the chi square test. *Psychological Bulletin*, *46*(6), 433–489.

Liddell, D. (1976). Practical tests of 2 × 2 contingency tables. *The Statistician*, *25*, 295–304.

Liebetrau, A. M. (1983). *Measures of association*. London: Sage.

Little, R. J. A. (1988). A test of missing completely at random for multivariate data with missing values. *Journal of the American Statistical Association*, *83*(404), 1198–1202.

Lord, F. M. (1967). A paradox in the interpretation of group comparisons. *Psychological Bulletin*, *68*(5), 304–305.

MacDonald, P. L., & Gardner, R. C. (2000). Type I error rate comparisons of post-hoc procedures for $I \times J$ chi-square tables. *Educational and Psychological Measurement*, *60*(5), 735–754.

MacLeod, C. M., & Kampe, K. E. (1996). Word frequency effects on recall, recognition, and word fragment completion tests. *Journal of Experimental Psychology: Learning, Memory, and Cognition*, *22*(1), 132–142.

Mahalanobis, P. C. (1936). On the generalised distance in statistics. *Proceedings of the National Institute of Sciences in India*, *2*(1), 49–55.

Mann, H. B., & Whitney, D. R. (1947). On a test of whether one of two random variables is stochastically larger than the other. *Annals of Mathematical Statistics, 18*, 50–60.

Marcus, R., Peritz, E., & Gabriel, K. R. (1976). On closed testing procedures with special reference to ordered analysis of variance. *Biometrika, 63*, 655–660.

Mauchly, J. W. (1940). Significance test of sphericity of a normal *n*-variate distribution. *Annals of Mathematical Statistics, 11*, 204–209.

McBurney, D. H., & White, T. L. (2009). *Research methods* (8th ed.). Belmont, CA: Wadsworth Learning.

McGraw, K. O., & Wong, S. P. (1992). A common language effect size statistic. *Psychological Bulletin, 111*(2), 361–365.

Mewhort, D. J. K. (2005). A comparison of the randomization test with the F-test when error is skewed. *Behavioral Research Methods, 37*, 426–435.

Miller, G. A., & Chapman, J. P. (2001). Misunderstanding analysis of covariance. *Journal of Abnormal Psychology, 110*(1), 40–48.

Morgan, G. A., Gliner, J. A., & Harmon, R. J. (2000). Quasi-experimental designs. *Journal of the American Academy of Child and Adolescent Psychiatry, 39*(6), 794–796.

Neisser, U., Boodoo, G., Bouchard, T. J. Jr., Boykin, A. W., Brody, N., Ceci, J. S., Halpern, D. F., Loehlen, J. C., Perloff, R., Sternberg, R. J., & Urbrina, S. (1996). Intelligence: Knowns and unknowns. *American Psychologist, 51*(2), 77–101.

Nestor, P. G., & Schutt, R. K. (2015). *Research methods in psychology: Investigating human behavior* (2nd ed.) Los Angeles: Sage.

Newman, D. (1939). The distribution of range in samples from a normal population, expressed in terms of an independent estimate of standard observation. *Biometrika, 31*, 20–30.

Neyman, J., & Pearson, E. S. (1933). On the problem of the most efficient tests of statistical hypotheses. *Philosophical Transactions of the Royal Society of London, Series A, 231*, 289–337.

Olton, D. S. (1979). Mazes, maps and memory. *American Psychologist, 34*(7), 583–596.

Pearson, K. (1900). On the criterion that a given system of deviations from the probable in the case of a correlated system of variables is such that it can reasonably be supposed to have arisen in random sampling. *Philosophical Magazine, 50*, 157–175.

Pearson, K. (1901a). *National life from the standpoint of science*. London: Adam & Charles Black.

Pearson, K. (1901b). On lines and planes of closest fit to systems of points in space. *Philosophical Magazine, 2*(11), 559–572.

Pitman, E. J. G. (1937). Significance tests which may be applied to samples from any populations. *Royal Statistical Society Supplement, 4*, 119–130 and 225–232.

Privitera, G. J. (2016). *Research methods for the behavioral sciences* (2nd ed.). Los Angeles: Sage.

Rasmussen, J. L. (1987). Estimating correlation coefficients: Bootstrap and parametric approaches. *Psychological Bulletin, 101*(1), 136–139.

Reinhard, J. C. (2006). *Confirmatory factor analysis through the Amos program*. London: Sage.

Reynolds, H. T. (1984). *Analysis of normal data*. London: Sage.

Roediger, H. L., & Karpicke, J. O. (2006). Test-enhanced learning: Taking memory tests improves long-term retention. *Psychological Science, 17*(3), 249–255.

Rubin, D. B. (1973). Matching to remove bias in observational studies. *Biometrics, 29*, 159–183.

Rutherford, A. (2001). *Introducing ANOVA and ANCOVA: A GLM approach*. London: Sage.

Scheiner, S. M., & Gurevitch, J. (2001). *Design and analysis of ecological experiments* (2nd ed.). Oxford: Oxford University Press.

Schmuckler, M. (2001). What is ecological validity? A dimensional analysis. *Infancy, 4*, 419–436.

Seber, G. A., & Wild, C. J. (1989). *Nonlinear regression*. New York: Wiley.

Seibenhener, M. L., & Wooten, M. C. (2015). Use of open-field maze to measure locomotor and anxiety-like behavior in mice. *Journal of Visualized Experiments, 96*, e52434.

Šidák, Z. (1967). Rectangular confidence regions for the means of multivariate normal distributions. *Journal of the American Statistical Association, 62*, 626–633.

Simonsohn, V., Nelson, L. D., & Simmons, J. P. (2014). P-curve: A key to the file drawer. *Journal of Experimental Psychology: General, 143*(2), 534–547.

Simpson, E. H. (1951). The interpretation of interaction in contingency tables. *Journal of the Royal Statistical Society, 13*, 238–241.

Smith, H. V. (1972). Effects of environmental enrichment on open-field activity and Hebb-Williams problem-solving in rats. *Journal of Comparative and Physiological Psychology, 80*, 163–168.

Sokal, R. R., & Rohlf, F. J. (2012). *Biometry: The principles and practices of statistics in biological research* (4th ed.). New York: W.H. Freeman.

Spearman, C. (1904a). The proof and measurement of association between two things. *American Journal of Psychology, 15*(1), 72–101.

Spearman, C. (1904b). General intelligence: Objectively determined and measured. *American Journal of Psychology, 15*(2), 201–292.

Spearman, C. (1927). *The abilities of man*. London: Macmillan.

Spielberger, C. D., Gonzalez, H. P., Taylor, C. J., Anton, E. D., Algaze, B., Ross, G. R., & Westbuerry, L. G. (1980). *Test anxiety inventory: Preliminary professional manual*. Palo Alto, CA: Consulting Psychologists Press.

Stevens, J. P. (2002). *Applied multivariate statistics for the social sciences* (4th ed.). Mahwah, NJ: Erlbaum.

Stevens, S. S. (1946). On the theory of scale of measurement. *Science, 103*(2684), 677–680.

Stigler, S. M. (1986). *The history of statistics: The measurement of uncertainty before 1900*. Cambridge, MA: Belknap Press of Harvard University Press.

Student (1927). Error of routine analysis. *Biometrika, 19*, 151–164.

Tabachnick, B. G., & Fidell, L. S. (1996). *Using multivariate statistics*. New York: HarperCollins College Publishers.

Tabachnick, B. G., & Fidell, L. S. (2012). *Using multivariate statistics* (6th ed.). Boston, MA: Pearson Education.

Thurstone, L. L. (1924). *The nature of intelligence*. London: Kegan Paul Trench Trubner e.

Thurstone, L. L. (1938). *Primary mental abilities*. Chicago: University of Chicago Press.

Thurstone, L. L. (1947). *Multiple factor analysis: A development and expansion of vectors of the mind*. Chicago: University of Chicago Press.

Tukey, J. W. (1949). Comparing individual means in the analysis of variance. *Biometrics, 5*, 99–114.

Tukey, J. W. (1953). The problem of multiple comparisons. In H. Brown (Ed.), *The collected works of John W. Tukey, Volume VIII: Multiple comparisons: 1948–1983* (pp. 1–300). New York: Chapman & Hall.

Tukey, J. W. (1977). *Exploratory data analysis.* Boston, MA: Addison-Wesley.

Vik, P. (2014). *Regression, ANOVA, and the general linear model: A statistical primer.* London: Sage.

von Hippel, P. T. (2007). Regression with missing Ys: An improved strategy for analyzing multiple imputed data. *Sociological Methodology, 37,* 83–117.

Wilcox, R. R. (1987). New designs in analysis of variance. *Annual Review of Psychology, 38,* 29–60.

Williams, M. N., Grajales, C. A. G., and Kurkiewicz, D. (2013). Assumptions of multiple regression: Correcting two misconceptions. *Practical Assessment, Research & Evaluation, 18*(11), 1–13.

Yates, F. (1934). Contingency tables involving small numbers and the χ^2 test. *Supplement to the Journal of the Royal Statistical Society, 1*(2), 217–235.

Yates, F. (1984). Tests of significance for 2×2 contingency tables (with discussion). *Journal of the Royal Statistical Society, Series A, 147*(3), 426–463.

Yerkes, R. M., & Dodson, J. D. (1908). The relation of strength of stimulus to rapidity of habit-formation. *Journal of Comparative Neurology and Psychology, 18*(5), 459–482.

Zhang, N., & Henderson, C. (2014). Test anxiety and academic performance in chiropractic students. *Journal of Chiropractic Education, 28*(1), 2–8.

INDEX